Otago

Otago

150 YEARS OF NEW ZEALAND'S FIRST UNIVERSITY

ALISON CLARKE

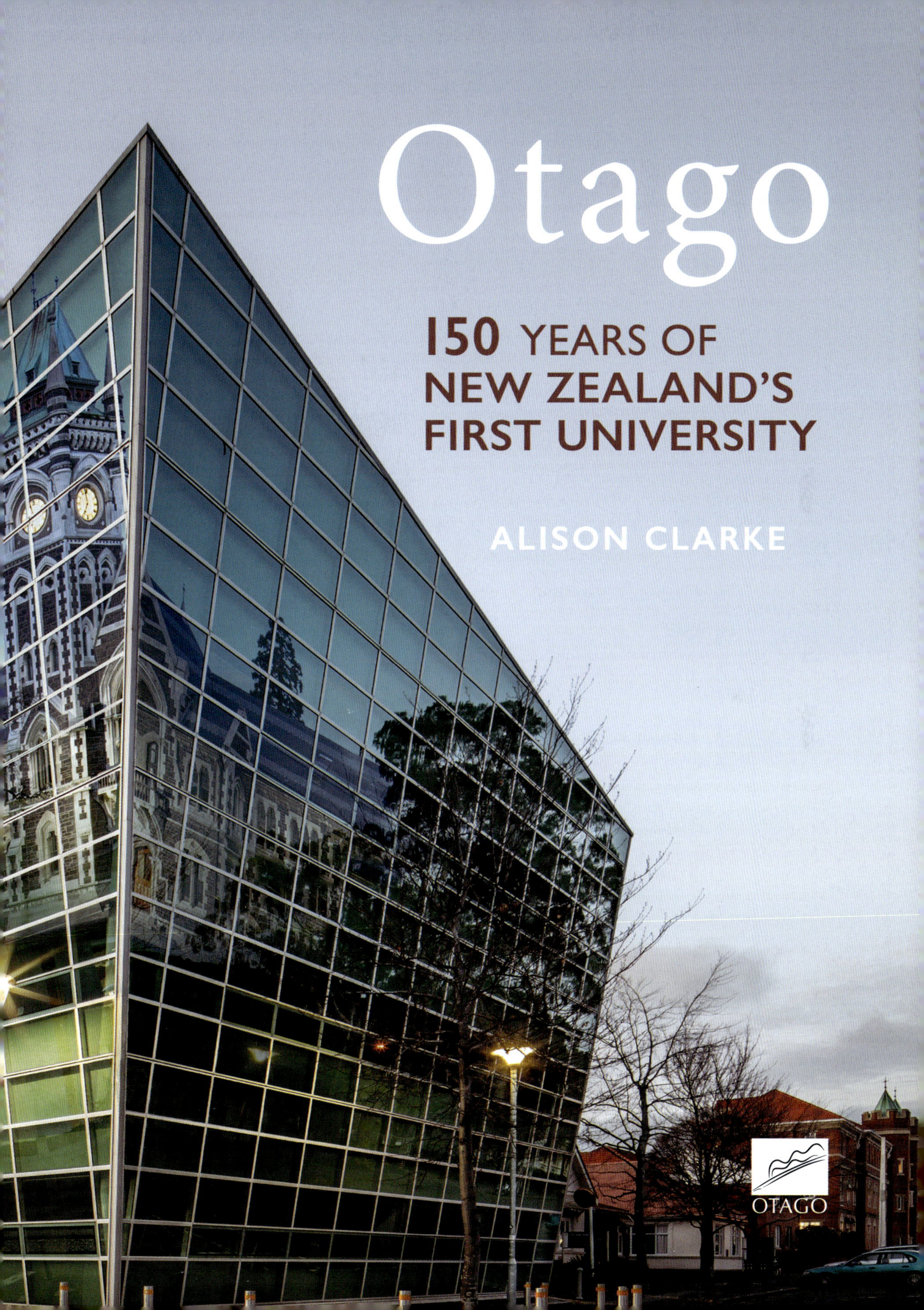

OTAGO

Published by Otago University Press
Level 1, 398 Cumberland Street
Dunedin, New Zealand
university.press@otago.ac.nz
www.otago.ac.nz/press

First published 2018

ISBN 978-1-98-853133-5

A catalogue record for this book is available from the National Library of New Zealand.

The publisher gratefully acknowledges funding assistance from the University of Otago.

Front cover photograph by Graham Warman. Digital artwork © University of Otago

Editor: Gillian Tewsley
Design/layout: Fiona Moffat
Indexer: Diane Lowther

Printed in China through Asia Pacific Offset.

Contents

Abbreviations

ACC	Accident Compensation Corporation
AIT	Auckland Institute of Technology
AOSM	Associate of the Otago School of Mines
AUS	Association of University Staff
AUT	Association of University Teachers
AUT	Auckland University of Technology
AVC	assistant vice-chancellor
AVLC	Audio Visual Learning Centre
CAL	computer-assisted learning
CAPS	consumer and applied sciences
CHE	Crown health enterprise
CIT	Central Institute of Technology
CSC	Computing Services Centre
CTA	Clinical Training Agency
CU	Christian Union
DCC	Dunedin City Council
DCE	Dunedin College of Education
DSIR	Department of Scientific and Industrial Research
DVC	deputy vice-chancellor
EEO	equal employment opportunity
EFTS	equivalent full-time student
EU	Evangelical Union
FoRST	Foundation for Research, Science and Technology
FUW	Federation of University Women
HAL	history, art and literature
HEDC	Higher Education Development Centre
HERAC	Higher Education Research and Advisory Centre
HRC	Health Research Council
HSFY	Health Sciences First Year
ISB	Information Services Building
ITS	Information Technology Services
MIHI	Māori/Indigenous Health Institute
MRC	Medical Research Council
NHNZ	Natural History New Zealand
NZIMLT	New Zealand Institute of Medical Laboratory Technology
NZSA	New Zealand Society of Accountants
ODT	*Otago Daily Times*
OHB	Otago Hospital Board
OLC	Otago Language Centre
OUCA	Otago University Childcare Association
OUDS	Otago University Dramatic Society
OUSA	Otago University Students' Association
OUTC	Otago University Tramping Club
PBRF	Performance-Based Research Fund
PGSF	Public Good Science Fund
PVC	pro-vice-chancellor
QCS	Quantitive and Computer Studies
SCM	Student Christian Movement
SIT	Southern Institute of Technology
TTC	Teachers' Training College
TEC	Tertiary Education Commission
TEU	Tertiary Education Union
TSCF	Tertiary Students' Christian Fellowship
UBS	University Bookshop
UGC	University Grants Committee
VC	vice-chancellor
VCAG	Vice-chancellor's Advisory Group
VERT	virtual environment radiation therapy training system
WEA	Workers' Educational Association

Foreword

Vice-Chancellor Harlene Hayne

The establishment of the University of Otago in June 1869 was a bold move by early Scottish settlers in Dunedin who held a deep conviction about the value of education. Those settlers knew that education was crucial to improving the lives of their children, and of their children's children. They wanted a better life, a more egalitarian life, that provided opportunity for all, and they knew that the way to achieve that goal was through education. Today, the University of Otago remains staunchly committed to this ideal and our 150th anniversary provides a unique opportunity to celebrate that commitment.

In this book, Dr Alison Clarke provides a panoramic view of the university's history. She chronicles the important role the university has played in the lives of its staff and students. Through words and photographs, we encounter the university as a place deeply committed to teaching and learning, as a tertiary institution that continues to produce research of the highest quality, as a forum for debating ideas and new ways of understanding the world, as a workplace where careers have flourished, as a built environment that has been integral to the university's mission and to the wider life of the city of Dunedin, and as a university with multiple campuses in New Zealand that now have both national and global reach. Most importantly, Dr Clarke reminds us that the University of Otago is a place where young people come to learn and to live, and to experience the joys and challenges of emerging adulthood.

In exploring these stories, Dr Clarke has documented not only the university's many milestones and successes, but also the very real challenges it has faced, and the tough times when things didn't go as planned. She also traces the interplay between the university and our wider society, highlighting how the University of Otago has both led and been caught up in cultural change.

Universities are about people, and people are the centrepiece of this book. Dr Clarke has elegantly highlighted many important individuals in the history of the University of Otago, including our first woman graduate, Caroline Freeman, and our first Māori graduate, Te Rangi Hīroa (Peter Buck). Many of our current staff and students, as well as our alumni, will see themselves and their own Otago experiences captured here. Indeed, the human heart of these stories is due in large part to many Otago people who so generously shared memories and photographs with Dr Clarke.* In addition to stories about people, there is also a chapter dedicated to the university's physical environment, illustrating the developments that have made our Dunedin campus one of the most beautiful in the world.

The University of Otago's founders showed great foresight when they established this institution. Over the past 150 years the university has earned an international reputation for excellence, and today it ranks among the top universities in the world. From just 81 students when the first classes were held in 1871, the roll now exceeds 20,000. Generations of outstanding young people have, along with our staff, energetically taken up the challenge set in 1869: *Sapere aude* – dare to be wise. They dared!

As the current Vice-Chancellor of this august institution, I want to sincerely thank Alison Clarke for this engaging history; it is beautifully written and illustrated and I hope it will be read and enjoyed by staff, students, alumni and members of our wider community. Gaining a greater understanding of our past allows us to set a bold course for the future. The founding of this university was inspired by the Scots; our next 150 years will be inspired by the people who are here now. In addition to our proud Scottish heritage, our future will reflect a greater contribution by Māori, Pasifika and Asian students, and staff of all genders. As the human face of our community continues to change, so will the nature of this university. Our 150th anniversary is a time for all of us to celebrate our illustrious history; it is also a time for us to imagine our illustrious future. Like Dunedin's early European settlers, we will warmly embrace this challenge.

Hapaitia te ara tika kia pumau ai te rangatiratanga mo nga uri whakatipu.
Foster the pathway of knowledge to strength, independence and growth for future generations.

Professor Harlene Hayne
Vice-Chancellor, University of Otago

* Over the five years that Alison Clarke was researching this book she wrote a fascinating blog, titled *University of Otago 1869–2019 – writing a history.* This is now managed by the Hocken Collections and can be found at otago150years.wordpress.com

Preface

The University of Otago has always taken pride in its status as New Zealand's first university. Starting a university in 1869 was a bold move: other regions observed Otago's action with a mixture of surprise, scepticism and envy. The venture paid off: from small beginnings, the university grew into a large institution with local, national and international significance. Two previous histories have marked the university's jubilee and centenary;[1] this book marks the 150th anniversary of its foundation.

Like any organisation the university has had its good times and its bad times. It has been at some periods and in some ways deeply conservative, and in other ways boldly entrepreneurial. Various schemes did not succeed while others flourished, subjects have come and gone and it has never been easy to fund all of its desired programmes. A good history is a critical assessment rather than a public relations exercise, but, overall, the University of Otago's achievements over 150 years are remarkable.

There have been many changes at Otago since the centenary history appeared in 1969. The student roll has quadrupled and the small branch medical faculties in Christchurch and Wellington have developed into large health science campuses. The university began a joint degree programme with the Dunedin College of Education in the 1970s, became a direct competitor with the college for teacher education programmes in the 1990s, and in 2007 the two institutions merged; among other things, that gave the university a campus in Invercargill. The remnants of the once-prominent School of Mines departed for the University of Auckland in the 1980s, and the once-prominent School of Home Science gradually devolved, leaving its legacy in programmes in human nutrition and food science. New professional programmes in the 1990s and early 2000s cemented Otago's strength in the health sciences, extending its teaching and research into medical laboratory science, nursing, dental therapy, dental hygiene, dental technology and radiation therapy.

All of those developments receive attention in this history, along with many other changes in Otago's programmes of teaching and research over the last 50 years. It also delves back into Otago's first 100 years, telling its story from the beginning and developing some themes that are not considered in Thompson and Morrell's histories. Every history reflects the era in which it is written and the perspective of the historian. For instance, the university purchased its first computer in 1966, but that received no mention in the centenary history. Technology has since revolutionised research and teaching, and it is highlighted here. Otago's staff and students are far more diverse than they once were: women students have been in the majority since 1986, and this book seeks out the stories of early women students and staff and notes the impact of this changing demography. It tells the stories of early Māori students and staff, and the university's sometimes troubled relationship with the Māori community, along with the stories of students and staff from the Pacific Islands and an increasingly large and diverse body of international students. Overall, this book pays a lot more attention to the students, who received surprisingly little coverage in the jubilee and centenary histories – though that was corrected by Sam Elworthy's history of student life, published to mark the centenary of the students' association in 1990.[2]

One reason for the general absence of women, Māori and students from the 1969 centenary history was its focus on Otago's senior staff: Morrell mentioned every professor who had ever been on the payroll and that left little room for anyone else. The rate of expansion of the university means this is no longer possible, even if it were desirable. A considerable number of senior staff – including all the vice-chancellors and registrars – are mentioned in this book, but many important people, including deans, deputy vice-chancellors and others in senior roles, have not made the cut. That doesn't mean their role in the university was minor, simply that there is not space here for everybody. Likewise, there have been so many outstanding researchers at Otago that it is impossible to include them all in a one-volume history. It would be a challenge even to include all the remarkable research under way at present: Otago is a powerhouse of discovery in many fields and this book can only touch briefly on some of the projects. The book does, however, include the stories of some less prominent staff as representatives of the wide range of people who have contributed to Otago's wellbeing. It pays attention to beginnings and often mentions the first person in any particular role; and there is a timeline of major events and milestones at the back of the book. The university's foundation and its relationship with the University of New Zealand – which it formed part of from 1874 to 1961 – are covered here, but that part of the story is kept concise to make room for more recent events. Interested readers can explore those aspects of the history of Otago and of the University of New Zealand in detail in previous books.[3]

This history is arranged thematically. The first chapter tells of the university's foundation, and how it has been administered over its first 150 years. As well as covering its governance and management, it includes the all-important issue of how Otago has been funded. That has varied considerably, from its beginning as a land grant university to one almost entirely reliant on government cash grants and then, after New Zealand's economic reforms of the 1980s and 1990s, one that needed to diversify and that relied increasingly on student fees (including those of international students), external research grants and commercialisation of intellectual property.

The next three chapters concentrate on students. Chapter 2 gives an overview of the student body: it starts with the founding students (whose identity has been little studied before) and then considers the changing student demography over time, along with the rise and fall of the student roll. Chapter 3 explores student life through the years, and Chapter 4 investigates the places where students have lived, from boarding houses to residential colleges and flats. Chapter 5 gives a general overview of Otago's staff and the organisations they have created.

Chapters 6 to 9 are the core of the book, covering the history of the university's academic departments and schools and the development of research and teaching programmes. They are arranged according to the current structure of four academic divisions: humanities, science, commerce and health sciences.

Chapter 10 moves the story beyond Dunedin: it takes a long view of the history of the Christchurch and Wellington campuses and their academic programmes, and covers the university's presence in Auckland and Invercargill. Chapter 11 concentrates on the university's key support services: its libraries, press, student health and counselling services, disability services, Māori Centre and Pacific Islands Centre. Chapter 12 focuses on teaching: changes in teaching styles, examining methods and the organisation of the academic year, distance education, and the development of research and education about tertiary teaching through the Higher Education Development Centre. It also covers the university's involvement in adult education, including the Workers' Educational Association and the Department of University Extension, and the emergence of foundation studies. Chapter 13 investigates the university's built environment, from its beginnings in the 'new post office' in Princes Street to its ever-expanding presence in North Dunedin. The final chapter considers the university's place in the world – its relationship with the city of Dunedin, its interaction with mana whenua and its importance to New Zealand and to the Pacific. It looks at Otago's cultural contribution to the world, exemplified in its arts fellowships and the collections of the Hocken Library, and some of its life-changing research discoveries.

In 1948, while he was working on the history of Victoria University of Wellington (then Victoria University College), John Beaglehole wrote to a friend that it had been 'hard work, but amusing ... it would be easier to write the history of the whole British Empire than of this place. There are too many things One Can't Say, unless one leaves immediately for foreign parts.'[4] As the author of this current history, I have no plans for travel and can only hope that those who contributed to the project find the outcome acceptable.

It has been a great privilege to work on this book and I have met many interesting and helpful people along the way. My biggest challenge has been converting a huge amount of information into a readable narrative; the book is big, but it would have run to multiple volumes if it included all the interesting tales of Otago's past that turned up in my research. I interviewed 88 people and had informal conversations and correspondence with many others. Dorothy Page generously shared the interviews she conducted with Medical School staff when she was researching her book *Anatomy of a Medical School*. Not all of those interviewed are quoted here but their input helped inform my views and I am most grateful to them.[5]

Many people shared photographs from their personal collections that have helped enliven this book. I am grateful to all those who have researched and written memoirs or histories of their part of the organisation, from published books and articles to summaries on websites and overviews in departmental review documents – they have made my job a lot easier. The staff at the Hocken, keeper of the university's archives and many other relevant collections, were enormously supportive and helpful; I especially thank Anna Petersen, Mary Lewis and Richard Munro for assistance with images and David Murray for his great architectural history knowledge. Chris Scott and Alison Breese of the Dunedin City Council Archives were very helpful, as were the staff of the Hewitson Library and Presbyterian Research Centre, Bevan James and others at Otago's Corporate Records Office, Maryanne Ashford of Property Services, David Thomson and others of the Planning and Funding Office, Sarah Gallagher, creator of the Dunedin Flat Names project, and John Broughton of the Dental and Medical schools. Many departments patiently answered my obscure questions and helped me find and identify photographs. Staff from the Christchurch and Wellington campuses and the Auckland Centre made me welcome there, and although I didn't make it to the Invercargill campus, staff there were most obliging from a distance. Current and former vice-chancellors Harlene Hayne, David Skegg and Graeme Fogelberg all gave generously of their time and I am grateful for their interest in the project.

While I was researching and writing this history I ran a blog.[6] That proved a useful testing ground for some of the material that appears in this book, and allowed me to tell interesting stories for which there wasn't sufficient room here. I am very grateful to the many people who interacted with my blog posts, corrected my bloopers, helped identify photographs and provided me with information, contacts and clues. I thank those who helped publicise the blog and the project, especially the Hocken, Department of History and Art History, Alumni Relations and Marketing and Communications. I am indebted to the people who read all or parts of the manuscript and made suggestions for improvement and to Gillian Tewsley for her expert editing. It has been a pleasure working with Rachel Scott and the great team at Otago University Press. Fiona Moffat deserves a special mention for her work on the design of this beautiful book.

For this project I reported to a committee chaired by Barbara Brookes; she and the other members of the committee were most supportive throughout. I commend their foresight in organising the writing of a history well in advance of the 150th anniversary, which meant I could work on it part-time over a long period (five years). That meant this project absorbed my attention for a long time, and I am most thankful to my family and friends for their tolerance, and for listening patiently to endless stories about the University of Otago.

Ngā mihi nui ki a koutou katoa,
Ali Clarke
Dunedin, 2018

CHAPTER ONE

Founding and administration

'A university of the highest order is urgently required in New Zealand' – this was the firm opinion of Arthur Thomson, author of the first major written history of New Zealand, published in 1859. Thomson noted that 'intelligent settlers' had seen 'their children growing up, smart in the way of making money, but in a wild state of intellectual degradation'. Their concern hastened the development of primary schools, but a gap in higher education remained.[1]

Dunedin in 1859 must have seemed an unlikely location for New Zealand's first university. Just over 2000 people lived in the town, which was the administrative centre of the 11-year-old Otago colony, established according to the theories of Edward Gibbon Wakefield by supporters of the Free Church of Scotland. The population of the entire province of Otago numbered around 9000;[2] that included local Māori, who were Ngāi Tahu and the closely related iwi Waitaha and Ngāti Māmoe – collectively known as Ngāi Tahu Whānui or, in the southern dialect, Kāi Tahu Whānui. Southern Māori had a long history of interaction with Pākehā incomers, including early sealers, whalers, traders and missionaries, and their engagement with technology, trade, Christianity and literacy shaped the history of the region in the early nineteenth century. Kāi Tahu Whānui were enthusiasts for education, and the promise of schools and hospitals contributed to their willingness to sell land for the Otago colony. The promise was broken, along with that of adequate land reserves and access to traditional food sources; the colonists largely ignored Māori rights or interests and Kāi Tahu Whānui soon found themselves on the economic and political margins of southern New Zealand. Only after generations of campaigning was Te Kerēme – the Ngāi Tahu claim, begun in the 1850s, for the government to keep its promises – taken seriously by those in authority.[3]

New Zealand changed in the 1860s. There was a large influx to the northern provinces of imperial troops arriving to fight 'rebel' Māori who were determined to retain their land. Meanwhile, goldrushes drew many people to Otago. Dunedin became the country's largest and wealthiest town; by the end of the decade it boasted around 15,000 residents.[4] There was, of course, more to founding a university than size and wealth. Historian Jim Gardner suggests the idea of a university 'must have seemed irrelevant and even retrogressive to the great mass of emigrants. If they thought about universities at all, it was probably as part of an exclusive establishment they were glad to put behind them.' To establish a colonial university was a 'formidable task' requiring 'as much political finesse as educational vision'.[5]

The Scottish colonists of Otago had a different vision of education from those in other parts of the country where English colonists dominated. Scotland made education more widely available than England, partly because of its distinct religious culture. Training clergy was one of the biggest roles of universities in Scotland, and since the Presbyterian ministry lacked the elite posts that attracted the upper classes to join the Anglican clergy, Scottish universities drew students from less rarified backgrounds. The Scots were also early to develop effective medical schools and tertiary education in sciences that fostered industry and agriculture.[6] By the nineteenth century the Scots provided a mix of liberal and professional higher education that appealed to a range of students; the image of the 'generally educated Scottish lad of parts' contended with that of 'the Oxbridge genteel amateur'.[7]

The Scottish colonists of Otago brought with them their belief that a university education should be available to any capable person who desired it, and that a local institution should be established as soon as feasible. A future college was among the inducements offered in publicity for the Otago Association's settlement scheme, and some of the money that settlers paid the association for land was set aside in a Religious and Educational Uses Trust to endow those twin pillars of civilisation: religion and education. Since the Otago provincial government took on the responsibility of providing elementary education, in 1866 the Presbyterian Church came up with a scheme for the trust's funds: two thirds became the 'ecclesiastical fund', to be used for building and maintaining churches and manses and establishing theology professors, and the remaining third was the 'educational fund', to be used to endow literary chairs in any university established in Otago. Presbyterian leaders were among the main cheerleaders for local tertiary education; only a lack of funding prevented the earlier beginnings of local theology training, together with the 'secular' education in arts that the church expected of its prospective clergy.[8]

The Presbyterian Church of Otago Lands Act of 1866, which legislated for the educational fund to provide some of the costs of a university, led to a national discussion about the need for higher education. Frank Simmons, the Oxford-educated Anglican clergyman who was rector of Otago Boys' High School, in 1867 sent a petition to parliament asking it to establish scholarships 'for the purpose of maintaining young men of this Colony at a University in the United Kingdom', that might encourage parents not to withdraw their sons from high school 'at an age when it is impossible for them to have received a liberal education'. Simmons was 'convinced that the time is not yet arrived for founding a University in this Colony', so scholarships should be for institutions in Britain. In response, the House of Representatives appointed a select committee which consulted over 40 'gentlemen'; its final question to them was: 'What is your opinion as to the propriety of establishing a New Zealand University?' There was widespread support for scholarships, but most believed a local university would be premature ('absurd', said George Macfarlan, a Cambridge graduate and the parliamentarian for Lyttelton). The select committee recommended scholarships but not, as yet, a New Zealand university. It did, however, suggest that the government 'embrace the opportunity of setting apart portions of the confiscated lands' to endow a university 'whenever the proper time may come for founding one', and it recommended that the provinces, too, set aside land for this purpose.[9] Late in 1868 the New Zealand University Endowment Act legislated accordingly, and crown land in Southland was set aside, together with land confiscated from Taranaki Māori, but 'no scholarships were ever held, and the Government's invitation to the provinces to make the statutory reserves was met by a complete and desolating lack of interest'.[10]

The select committee's recommendation was a setback to those who were keen to establish a university immediately – among them Otago's provincial superintendent James Macandrew, an entrepreneur and politician of 'visionary dreams, considerable achievement and frequent failure'.[11] With typical ebullience Macandrew had suggested to the select committee that the funds required for scholarships should instead be dedicated to funding 'a couple of chairs in a New Zealand University'. Otago would fund two or three more professors, and thus, 'instead of two scholarships, there will be placed within the reach of the whole youth of the Colony the means of acquiring an education as liberal, as advanced, and as complete as can be acquired in – for example the University of Aberdeen – which, it is admitted, has turned out as great a proportion of scholars and of able men as any similar institution in Europe'.[12] When the government decided the time was not right to found a university, Macandrew determined that the province of Otago should go it alone. It was, like many of his schemes, bold and somewhat reckless, but he had the confidence to carry it through; and when he died in 1887 the university recorded that Macandrew had 'the honour of being its chief founder'.[13]

Kāi Tahu Whānui were not fans of Macandrew, who headed a provincial government with no sympathy for Māori rights or interests; generations later, their views ensured no building would be named after the university's principal founder. Although Māori students attended the university from the late nineteenth century, another century passed before it began to take seriously its responsibilities to mana whenua and their aspirations for education, and to incorporate appropriate tikanga more fully into administration, teaching and research – a shift that is discussed in chapter 14.

From the colonists, Macandrew quickly mustered support: the Presbyterian Church declared it had sufficient endowment funds to establish the promised literary chairs immediately, a public meeting urged the provincial council to proceed, and a special committee of the provincial council recommended 'that the time has now come when the establishment of a College in this City may, with propriety, be proceeded with'. The council set aside 100,000 acres (40,468ha) of pastoral land as an endowment and passed the University of Otago Ordinance on 3 June 1869, thereby creating the new institution.[14]

GETTING UNDER WAY

At the heart of the university lay its council, which met for the first time in November 1869; Macandrew appointed its first 12 members. It was granted 'the entire management of the university', including its core function – the power to confer, after examination, degrees in arts, medicine, law and music. The council also had the power to make and alter its own statutes and regulations. Although the Presbyterian Church funded chairs, this was a secular institution. The ordinance outlawed religious tests for students or staff, thus opening the university to people of all religious persuasions (or none) at a time when there were religious barriers in most British universities (though reform was underway). Otago was required to have at least six lay people on its council; the three clergy appointed initially included the Anglican Robert Stanford alongside the town's two senior Presbyterian ministers, Donald Stuart and Thomas Burns.[15] There were limits to its secularity, however: Burns, the religious leader of the Otago colony, was elected as first chancellor; and at its first meeting the council decided that its proceedings should 'now, and for the future, be opened with prayer'.[16]

The University Council was an exclusively white, male and middle-class body, but within those limits it included a range of people – five Scots, six English and one born in India. Other inaugural councillors included runholder Charles Graham; John Richardson, a farmer and former soldier; medical men Edward Hulme and Robert Burns; magistrate Alfred Strode; supreme court judge Dudley Ward; and businessmen Edward Cargill, John Hyde Harris and William Reynolds. They were men used to running colonial organisations and several were politicians, but not all had personal experience of universities. Perhaps there were simply not sufficient graduates in Dunedin to make up the full council; maybe Macandrew, who had not attended university himself, felt the council required a mixture of academic and business experience. Thomas Burns, Robert Burns and Graham had all studied at the

University of Edinburgh, Stuart and Hulme at St Andrews, and Stanford and Ward at Oxford.[17]

The council wasted no time. At its first meeting it appointed office bearers, including the university's first administrator, honorary secretary John Hislop (also secretary of the Otago Education Board); decided on the subjects of chairs and made arrangements to advertise them; set fees and terms (the session would be six continuous months, to cater for students coming from afar); made plans for a library and equipment; and set up a subcommittee to investigate leases and finances.[18] The weight of Scottish experience on the council influenced the University of Otago's format: rather than the Oxbridge-style tutorial, its teaching was based on the Scottish-style professorial lecture. Of course, as Morrell points out, at Otago the 'tutorial system of the English universities was hardly capable of transplantation, if only for lack of tutors'.[19]

Scotland also inspired the choice of subjects. A strong emphasis on philosophy distinguished the usual Scottish curriculum (and the German one); most Scottish students followed a course divided between philosophy, classics and mathematics/physics.[20] Otago's first three professors fitted that pattern. The fourth chair, in natural science (chemistry and geology), reflected more recent developments in Scotland as well as colonial pragmatism. Macandrew was a champion of that chair, since education concerning mines and agricultural chemistry 'would be of great practical importance in this province'. The council reported it had insufficient funds to establish a fourth chair but 'a small temporary grant by the Government and the Provincial Council' would enable it, 'to the advantage and profit of the entire community'. Macandrew convinced the provincial council to come up with that grant.[21]

In an era of slow boat transport, it took time for advertisements for professors to be placed in the 'home and colonial papers', applications to arrive, the council to communicate its decisions and the professors to travel to Dunedin. National-level negotiations about the university's future caused further delays. Finally, on 21 June 1871, the *Wild Deer* sailed into Port Chalmers ex Glasgow, bearing the precious cargo of professors Duncan MacGregor, George Sale and John Shand, together with the books and scientific apparatus the council had instructed them to purchase.[22] Two weeks later, on 5 July 1871, the official opening ceremony of the University of Otago took place in its Princes Street building. The first chancellor, Thomas Burns, did not survive to witness the event; his replacement, John Richardson, led proceedings. Macandrew was absent too, confined at home after an accident. With characteristic optimism he wrote to Richardson that 'all other things being equal, the University which you are this day inaugurating is not unlikely to be the principal seat of learning in the Southern Hemisphere – at all events, there can be no harm in aiming this high'.[23]

BEYOND OTAGO – THE UNIVERSITY OF NEW ZEALAND

The University of Otago was a provincial institution when provincial government held considerable power, but that power did not extend beyond its geographical boundaries. An 1871 legal opinion from the attorney-general remarked that Otago was entitled to create a university but, without a royal charter, its degrees would be recognised only within its own territory.[24] However, as the country's sole university Otago would become – in effect, if not by law – a national institution. That sparked protests from other provinces and forced the central government into action. A royal battle ensued. At first it seemed there might be a straightforward process of converting the University of Otago into a national institution, with its own endowments supplemented by those set aside, but yet unused, by the government; Premier William Fox indicated his support for such a move. On the advice of a select committee, in 1870 the New Zealand University Act was passed. It created the University of New Zealand, whose ruling body – the senate – was empowered to negotiate with the University of Otago; if negotiations for amalgamation were completed within six months and Otago's endowments were transferred to the University of New Zealand, the new university would be located in Dunedin.[25]

Negotiations did not proceed smoothly. Otago's hopes of providing a home to the country's sole university met resistance from Cantabrians, led by Henry Tancred, an influential politician and educationist who was elected chancellor of the University of New Zealand. The Cantabrians' ideal of a university was an English one, with the University of London a particular model: the university examined students and awarded degrees but left teaching to affiliated colleges. That model had advantages in the colonial setting: it encouraged institutions throughout the country to affiliate, and gave students broad access to degrees. However, it took no interest in the quality of teaching and provided little financial support to affiliated institutions. Advocates of the examining-only university formed a majority on the senate and negotiations for amalgamation with Otago collapsed. The government was not pleased that the senate had overridden its intention that the university should be a teaching institution, but another select committee and bill led only to fiery debate and the impasse remained. By the end of 1871, notes University of New Zealand historian Hugh Parton, Otago University had professors, students and the power to award degrees that were recognised only within one province; the University of New Zealand, meanwhile, had no professors and no students, but the power to award degrees of national standing.[26]

The University of Otago and the University of New Zealand both applied for royal charters in 1872; the Queen's advisers asked which the New Zealand legislature preferred and there was further fruitless debate. Meanwhile, several high schools and theological institutions affiliated to the University of New Zealand. In 1873 the Canterbury provincial government established Canterbury College, intended as an institution within the University of New Zealand scheme. Before applying for affiliation the college approached the University of Otago to suggest they apply together under favourable terms. The stalemate was broken, the Otago and Canterbury councils came to an agreement with the University of New Zealand and, in 1874, a new Act established the University of New Zealand as a purely examining and degree-conferring institution. In affiliating with the University of New Zealand, Otago put aside the right to award degrees but retained its original name; and the affiliated colleges retained their endowments and independent administration. Otago and Canterbury insisted that New Zealand degrees should be of a standard at least as high as those of the University of Melbourne. In 1876 the University of New Zealand received a royal charter, giving its degrees standing throughout the British Empire.[27]

Otago was not entirely content with the new system, particularly the affiliation of secondary schools. In 1877 it protested about alleged proposals to the University of New Zealand Senate that the standard of examination should be lowered; that would be 'a direct breach of faith' with Otago, which had affiliated under 'express assurance that the present standard should be faithfully maintained'.[28] The proposal was foiled, but Otago remained uneasy. Macandrew, who believed Otago had 'sold her birth-right for a mess of pottage', urged councillors to apply again for a royal charter for Otago, and they did so in 1878, prompting counterpetitions from the University of New Zealand and Canterbury College. The application was declined, but it was a symptom of wider dissatisfaction with the University of New Zealand, and in 1878 the government appointed a royal commission to investigate.[29] The commission vindicated Otago's concerns. It commended the Otago and Canterbury colleges, but was highly critical of the affiliation of secondary schools and of examinations that 'resembled more an examination for matriculation than for a University degree'. There was 'a large mass of evidence' showing the need for dedicated university colleges in Auckland and Wellington as well as in Dunedin and Christchurch.[30]

The commission's report was 'moderate, wise, and far-seeing', wrote Beaglehole, but 'unfortunately it recommended the expenditure of money'.[31] New Zealand's system of provincial government had been abolished in 1876, so the cost of funding fell to the central government, which was strapped for cash. After drawn-out negotiations, Auckland University College opened for business in 1883, but Victoria University College in Wellington did not begin classes until 1899. Meanwhile, degree standards rose and schools dropped out of the university system; Nelson College was the last to go in 1887.[32] Spurred on by the irrepressible Macandrew, in 1887 Otago made one more unsuccessful application for a royal charter.[33] It then resigned itself to being part of the University of New Zealand until 1961, when that institution dissolved itself and its colleges became independent, with the power both to teach and to award degrees.

GOVERNING THE UNIVERSITY

The original University of Otago Council established the format and tone of the institution and selected most of its staff; the Presbyterian Church selected holders of the chairs it funded. The professors, too, had huge influence on the style of the fledgling university; they formed a professorial board (known as the senate from 1961), which reported to and advised the council. Many of the early staff and council members gave long service to the university: the last member of the inaugural council, Robert Burns, died in 1907, and inaugural professors Black and Shand did not retire until the 1910s. Council members were appointed for life, though some resigned as they left the district or took on other roles. The council subdivided its work from its very first meeting, when it adjourned for a couple of hours while three members prepared 'a plan of proceedings'. The meeting also resulted in two subcommittees – one to investigate leases 'and the subject of revenue generally' and the other to take charge of advertising for professors and several other matters.[34] It was an efficient system that captured the varying expertise and availability of councillors.

Appointing councillors fell to the provincial superintendent, and after the abolition of the provinces the governor of New Zealand took on the responsibility. Through the years (see Appendix 1), changes were made to the composition of the council – some initiated by the university and others by government. The changes in the first 100 years broadened representation on Otago's governing body. The 1879 Royal Commission on the University of New Zealand suggested various groups should select council members: government deserved some control, since most university funding came from public grants; professors knew best 'the inner working of the colleges'; and graduates had 'personal reasons for desiring to see its efficiency and reputation well maintained'.[35] Otago's founding ordinance provided for councillors to be elected by a senate, to be made up of the university's graduates once there were at least 30 of them. By 1890 there was just one University of Otago graduate; close to 100 graduates had completed their University of New Zealand qualifications through Otago, yet still had no say on council. After a couple of failed bills, Otago politicians steered the 1891 University of Otago Council Election Act through parliament; it legislated for a mixture of government, professorial board and graduate appointments (the graduate electors were later termed the court of convocation). New council members were elected for terms of five years rather than life, but could be re-elected.[36]

It was graduate representatives who pushed for further reform of the University Council. In 1903 graduates expressed concern that the university 'existed too much in a corner' and needed to 'interest as many within the community as possible'. In response the council asked the government to allow representatives of local merchants and the town council, but reforms weren't legislated until 1911, after further campaigning.[37] The new Act enlarged the council, reduced the government appointments and included representatives of the primary and secondary education sectors, Dunedin City Council (DCC) and the hospital board, which had an important relationship with

The University Council, photographed in 1949, took their duties seriously. On the right, nearest the camera, is chemistry professor Frederick Soper, then the Professorial Board representative. He was Otago's VC from 1953 to 1963. In the chancellor's chair is David Herron, who was minister of Knox Church.

PRIME MINISTER'S DEPARTMENT PHOTOGRAPH, BOX-184-081, S17-182B, HOCKEN COLLECTIONS.

the university via the Medical School.[38] Opening the council to broader representation led to requests from other groups, but there were no further changes for many years.[39] Meanwhile, the court of convocation made the most radical appointments. In 1933 it elected the president of the Otago University Students' Association (OUSA), Jack Butler, to council.[40] In 1938 it went even further and elected a woman, Muriel May, a teacher at Otago Girls' High School; during her time on council she became a school inspector and then principal of Southland Girls' High School. May later reflected that in 1938 women graduates were 'anxious to break into what had been from the beginning an exclusively male enclave'. She was cautious as councillor: 'It seemed then important to be accepted, to provoke no antagonism and to prepare a smooth path for dynamic successors.'[41] There were no successors for a couple of decades: May departed in 1946 and the next women on council commenced in 1965 – they were home science professor Patricia Coleman, appointed by the senate, and Elsie Edgar, a Southland teacher elected by the high schools boards.[42]

During the 1960s students pushed for further involvement in governance. They had a representative, but that person could not be a current student; a new generation felt their man on council – an OUSA president of a decade earlier – did not adequately represent their concerns over the university's disciplinary powers. It was an era of protest and students wanted their voices heard; they petitioned parliament and, in 1969, OUSA won two council representatives with no bar on undergraduates or current students. Students also gained three representatives on senate.[43] 'Student Representation has become entrenched in the structure of the University', reported OUSA president Errol Millar in 1970; 'Many problems still exist but much has been achieved.'[44] Sitting at the table of council and its committees, knowing what was happening and having a voice in governance was a great boon to students –

though other council members did not invariably support OUSA's perspective and meetings could be tense, as during the setting of fees in the 1990s or introduction of the code of conduct in the 2000s.[45]

In 1978 the council reached its peak size of 25–27; the newest representatives were from the Dunedin College of Education (DCE) and Otago Polytechnic.[46] Subsequent changes were in a different direction: reforming governments wanted to transform university councils into slimmer bodies resembling the boards of business corporations. New legislation in 1990 restricted councils to between 17 and 20 members. Some councillors lost their positions, though additional groups got a voice: the general staff, the central organisation of employers and central organisation of workers each gained a representative. Student and academic staff reps were also mandated, and the minister of education would appoint four members; the rest of the appointments were left to individual councils to determine. The Otago council decided to keep its DCC representative (in practice, the mayor) and three people elected by the court of convocation. The minister continued the convention that government appointments would include people with business experience and somebody from Southland; and he added a Ngāi Tahu voice.[47]

In 2012 the tertiary education minister, Steven Joyce, revealed he was reviewing governance. That stemmed, in part, from a University of Canterbury request for changes as it dealt with the aftermath of earthquakes, but it also fitted with the government's focus on universities as engines of economic growth; their councils were 'potentially a bit large and unwieldy', said Joyce, who wanted them 'to take a more entrepreneurial approach'.[48] His 2013 bill, which removed all mandatory representation and reduced the maximum council size to 12 (four ministerial appointees and up to eight council appointees), attracted protest from university staff and students. The Otago council opposed the changes – it believed the representative model with its broader range of members was better for the institution – but the changes were legislated in 2015.[49] This left the council to decide how to allocate its appointments. Staff and students campaigned to retain their representation; OUSA pushed to keep two student reps.[50] The council decided to retain as members one student (the OUSA president), two staff (one elected by the academic staff and one by the general staff) and the vice-chancellor (VC); the four other members would be appointed according to the skills they could bring to governance.[51]

It was difficult for a smaller council to achieve diversity – a long-standing issue for council. The 1990 Act stated it was 'desirable that the Council of an institution should reflect so far as is reasonably practicable: the ethnic and socio-economic diversity of the communities served by the institution; and the fact that approximately half the population of New Zealand is male and half the population is female'. Minister and councils were enjoined to 'have regard' to this when making appointments, and 'to ensure that the Council had a sufficient number of members with expertise in management to enable the Council properly to perform its functions'.[52] Results were mixed. The 1991 Otago council included eight women – two more than its predecessor – and the minister appointed Ngāi Tahu anthropologist Atholl Anderson; Mere Montgomery, of Māori and Tongan descent, was the first union appointment.[53]

The 2015 Act had a similar section on diversity, and insisted that at least one council member must be Māori. The minister reappointed Donna Matahaere-Atariki, who had been on the council since 2009 and was Māori, but she was one of just three women on the new council alongside VC Harlene Hayne and OUSA president Laura Harris. The Tertiary Education Union complained that, nationally, Joyce had privileged business experience and had appointed few women; but Otago was as much to blame as the minister for the lack of gender balance on its council: staff elected two men as their representatives, and the council's four unspecified seats all went to men. Chancellor John Ward commented that council would 'diversify membership over the next few years, as vacancies arise'.[54]

An increasing focus on business experience was evident in the university's chancellors, who chaired the council (see the list below). In 1982 Jim Valentine, an accountant and former Otago lecturer, took on the role. Three of his five successors were accountants and businessmen. The two exceptions were Otago's only female chancellor, Judith Medlicott, and Royden Somerville – both lawyers. Earlier generations of chancellors came from the church and the law: Burns, Stuart, Cameron, Herron, Ryburn and Jack Somerville were all Presbyterian ministers, Chapman and Williams were judges and the two Sideys – father and son – were lawyers. The only chancellors not to fit that mould were Richardson, a farmer, politician and retired soldier; Allen, a businessman and politician; and Morrell, rector of Otago Boys' High School. Royden Somerville provided a link to the university's beginnings: he is a descendant of Thomas Burns, the first chancellor.

Otago was fortunate in its chancellors, who were elected by the council from its own members. Graeme Fogelberg, who became VC in 1994 as an outsider, notes how beneficial it was having chancellors who were Otago graduates; they had a 'loyalty and commitment' to the university.[55] Andrew Cameron, an Otago student of the 1870s, became the first locally produced chancellor in 1912, and from 1955 all chancellors were local graduates. Those who had been educated elsewhere also showed enormous commitment: Morrell and Herron, for instance, 'were prepared to spend a great deal of time on University affairs' in the years before executive VCs.[56]

Chancellors of the University of Otago

1869–71	Thomas Burns
1871–76	John Richardson
1876–79	Henry Chapman
1879–94	Donald Stuart
1894–1909	Joshua Williams
1909–12	James Allen
1912–25	Andrew Cameron
1925–33	Thomas Sidey
1933–45	William Morrell
1946–55	David Herron
1955–70	Hubert Ryburn
1970–76	Thomas Sidey
1976–82	John (Jack) Somerville
1982–92	James (Jim) Valentine
1993–98	Judith Medlicott
1999–2003	Eion Edgar
2004–08	Lindsay Brown
2009–17	John Ward
2018–	Royden Somerville

POUNDS, SHILLINGS AND PENCE

'The story of the University finances is a gloomy one,' declared Thompson in his jubilee history.[57] With careful shepherding over the next century the institution built up its resources, but securing sufficient income to deliver the university's programmes was always a challenge. Otago was a land grant establishment: it started with an endowment of land that was intended to supply its basic running costs via rental income – a convenient way for a provincial government with plenty of land to fund an institution. It was a distinctly 'new world' model of funding higher education. Many European universities were founded by wealthy donors or churches and grew their endowments through further philanthropy. Others, such as Edinburgh, were established by town councils and funded by regular cash grants. The two Australasian universities that pre-dated Otago – Sydney and Melbourne – received their income from annual state grants. In the United States, meanwhile, land grants became the foundation of numerous state universities.[58]

In 1870 the Otago provincial government granted the university 100,000 acres (400 square kilometres) of land, made up of three pastoral runs: Burwood and Mararoa in the Te Anau Basin and Barewood on the Strath Taieri. The run leases became payable to the university. The church trustees paid the salary of one of the professors, but all other expenses had to be supported by the pastoral rents, supplemented by student fees. The provincial government also gifted to the university its first premises (see chapter 13). Initial expenses, including building adaptations, books and equipment and the professors' moving costs, quickly stretched the council's resources. The provincial council provided an extra cash grant to help fund the fourth chair, but by 1872 it was evident the university needed additional funding, especially if it extended into medicine and law. To keep the fledgling institution going and growing, in 1872 the provincial government presented it with a further 100,000 acres of land – the Benmore run in the Waitaki district. In 1875, after its affiliation with the University of New Zealand, Otago acquired the 10,000-acre Forest Hill run in Southland. When the New Zealand provinces were abolished in 1876 the university lost its chief financial supporter and had to compete with the institutions of other provinces for central government funding. It also acquired sole responsibility for running the Otago Museum; that came with a land grant (Lamb Hill in Strath Taieri), but it did not fully cover costs.[59]

The land grant system of funding universities failed in New Zealand. It was tried at Otago and Canterbury and in both cases the land returned insufficient income for the purpose, though it did make the institutions partially independent of government. Furthermore, while the authorities gave it no thought at the time, the university's status as a large landowner did not assist its relationship with Māori, and cemented its place as one of the agents of colonisation. As the Waitangi Tribunal reported in 1991, after the Crown's land purchases from Ngāi Tahu, it failed to keep its promises to 'provide the reserves, the food resources and the health, educational and land endowments that were needed to give Ngai Tahu a stake in the new economy' – in other words, it disregarded the iwi's rights under the Treaty of Waitangi. In addition, Ngāi Tahu and the Crown did not always agree over exactly which land was included in sales.[60] The university's Benmore run was near the settlement Te Ao Marama, established by Ngāi Tahu prophet Te Maiharoa in 1877 to assert claims to land in the area. A government 'indifferent' to Māori claims evicted Te Maiharoa and his followers in 1879 after complaints were made by local runholders, including the university's Benmore lessee Robert Campbell – one of the country's wealthiest men.[61] Ranginui Walker wrote in a 1998 Treaty of Waitangi review of the university that Ngāi Tahu had not forgotten that event and that, because of it, the university had incurred a 'moral obligation' to the iwi.[62] Of course, as discussed in chapter 13, the university's site in North Dunedin was also formerly Ngāi Tahu land.

In its early decades Otago was in a 'financial strait jacket', wrote Morrell.[63] The income from its leases was variable and when the price of wool dropped and rabbits infested the land, tenants failed and replacements had to be found at 'knock down' prices. The only direct government support came in the form of a grant to the School of Mines, plus, until 1891, a subsidy for chemicals used by the chemistry professor in his role as government analyst. Spending was always kept to a minimum, and during a tricky period at the turn of the century the staff took a pay cut and the law lecturers were laid off. Salaries were always the chief ongoing expense, but the capital costs of the expanding institution were also considerable. The council was burdened with debt when the sale of its original building in Princes Street failed to meet the cost of building its premises in North Dunedin. It tried to increase its income: the sale of timber rights and prospecting rights on its runs were lucrative for a while (there were quartz reefs on the Barewood and Lamb Hill runs), but those were short boosts. Land reclaimed in the 1890s from the Leith riverbed on the university's own site, funded by further borrowing, created building sites to lease out; these became a more enduring income source.[64]

New Zealand did not develop a tradition of large-scale philanthropy to universities, but occasionally the council benefited from gifts or legacies. Some were directed to specific causes, such as scholarships or prizes or professorial chairs, while others contributed to general running costs. In 1903, for instance, Wolf Harris of Dunedin importing firm Bing, Harris and Co. promised a gift of £2000 (around $350,000 in 2018 values) towards the endowment of a chair of physiology.[65] A year later Alexa Lothian, an early Otago colonist who farmed with her husband at Andersons Bay but later retired within cooee of the university clocktower, bequeathed the residue of her estate to the university; the interest on around £500 (around $90,000 today) gave a small but useful income stream.[66]

The generosity of both Harris and Lothian was probably sparked by the council's 1902 plea to the public to help it out of its financial difficulties. Dunedin's main newspapers, the *Otago Daily Times* (*ODT*) and *Evening Star*, took up the cause and organised citizens' funds, and the Dunedin Savings Bank contributed from its trust funds. Pleas for further government funding were less successful, but the government did subsidise some of the public donations and, over the next few years, gave several one-off grants to help the university out of debt and to fund construction projects. More importantly, in 1905 it revised its funding of all university colleges; although Otago still received no assistance for its 'general' courses, it benefited from the new 'specialisation grant', which contributed an annual sum towards the running of special schools. Thus the longstanding grant for the Mining School was boosted with further government contributions for the Medical School and, after it was established in 1907, the Dental School.[67]

The pastoral runs gradually declined as contributors to Otago's accounts. The government took responsibility for funding the new colleges in Auckland and Wellington from the late nineteenth century and, as all of the colleges expanded, state funding increased: the income from Otago and Canterbury's endowments was simply deducted from the total grant.[68] The government took over the administration of the leases in 1904 and guaranteed a minimum return to the university.[69] The runs were chosen on the basis that they would not be required for future development, but that proved not to be the case: in 1960 the Crown took over Mararoa as it wanted part of the run near Lake Te Anau for closer settlement; and soon afterwards it required part of the Benmore run for a hydroelectric power project. In compensation, the government enlarged Otago's annual grant. The independence that the land grants offered was now only illusory. When the government suggested in the 1960s that the time might be opportune for Otago to return all its endowments, however, the university demurred: 'for historical and perhaps sentimental reasons' it did 'not like to see a complete severance of all its endowed lands'.[70] The runs provided a valued link to Otago's foundation, and some are still in university ownership.

Government grants accounted for just 6 per cent of Otago's income in 1900; by 1945 they were contributing half the total income. In 1948 the University of New Zealand Senate established a University Grants Committee (UGC), which advocated successfully for more support for the expanding university sector; by 1960 government grants accounted for 90 per cent of Otago's income. The UGC calculated each institution's quinquennial (five-yearly) grant according to the anticipated student roll and the projected expenses of the special schools, and there were separate grants for large capital projects.

In 1961 the University of New Zealand, which had gradually devolved more responsibility to its colleges, came to an end; Otago regained its independence and the other colleges became full universities. However, government still wanted to control the tertiary sector, and a new UGC took on some of the former roles of the University of New Zealand, including the approval of courses and the coordination of capital and general funding allocations. Separate funding for special schools ended; the UGC provided quinquennial grants to each university as a block sum, allowing more flexibility (and frustrating the special schools, which became more subject to central control by the university). Government spending on the university sector was large but the system nevertheless 'remained a relatively inexpensive one'; other countries spent considerably more per student on universities. Otago remained, as ever, on a tight budget.[71]

For a university that was heavily dependent on government grants, the 1970s and 1980s were financially challenging. There were adjustments to allocations during five-year periods to compensate for wage increases, but none for other expenses.

In an era of surging oil prices, high inflation and fluctuating exchange rates, that was a problem.[72] In 1979 Otago pursued 'a rigorous policy of cutting expenditure … with particular emphasis on reduction of energy use'.[73] In 1982 it resorted to a 'complete shut-down of heating during the summer, along with a year-round programme of conservation'. Overall, the university 'trod a narrow path between economising and maintaining standards'. Its problems were aggravated by a drop in the roll in 1981 and 1982: jumps in travel and accommodation costs, compounded by changes to student grants, were especially hard on Otago, which attracted many of its students from the North Island. Income from student fees dropped and residential colleges fell on hard times; a couple of them closed (see chapter 4). The university embarked on its first big marketing campaign: its 30-minute documentary *Learning is a Way of Life* appeared on television and in schools.[74]

Salaries were the greatest cost and Otago could not afford sufficient staff to maintain its desired staff–student ratios when the roll surged again: government grants rose, but did not keep pace with the roll. In 1986 the UGC calculated that, nationally, the funding per student had declined by more than 25 per cent since 1975. 'If efficiency is defined as the production of required outputs at the lowest possible level or resource input,' it noted, 'the New Zealand university system has become increasingly efficient, to an extent which can have few parallels elsewhere.' This was a dig at a government seemingly intent on turning state services into efficient businesses.[75]

A series of reports into tertiary education recommended major changes. The most extreme suggestions did not eventuate, and Otago VC Robin Irvine expressed relief that the Education Amendment Act of 1990 'gratifyingly, appeared in a very much modified form from the original draconian Bill', largely thanks to the advocacy of the Vice-Chancellors' Committee.[76] Nevertheless, the fourth Labour government's reforms revolutionised the sector with the twin goals of advancing 'both excellence and equity', according to the minister, Phil Goff. Universities were already growing beyond population trends – government wanted to continue their shift from institutions for the elite to places of mass participation, educating New Zealanders for employment in a changing economy. That was to be achieved in a cost-effective way by making universities more market-driven and efficient as they competed with one another and with other tertiary institutions. The UGC disappeared, leaving each university to negotiate independently with the Ministry of Education. The bulk funding system was based entirely on student numbers. The state continued as principal funder but expected universities to 'enhance government funding through the provision of saleable services' – including the education of full fee-paying international students – and it demanded a larger contribution to fees from New Zealand students.[77]

Student fees were always part of student life, although from 1962 to 1989 most were funded by the government through bursaries. In 1900 Otago received about a quarter of its income from fees. That crept up to over a third by 1945, then plummeted to just 3 per cent of income in 1989.[78] In 1990 the government set university tuition fees at $1250, four times their previous level. In subsequent years fee setting was left to individual university councils. To pay for the continuing growth in tertiary participation, the National government progressively reduced its contribution for each student, and councils had to increase fees to maintain their programmes. At the same time the government reduced student allowances. The students protested: Otago proctor Ron Chambers recalled it as 'a time of confrontation and sometimes violent passions'. In 1993, as the council met to set student fees, representatives of student protestors joined them as observers while others surrounded the council chamber; some confronted chancellor Judith Medlicott and another councillor after they left the meeting. At the meeting the following month a large group of students, denied entry to the building, protested loudly outside; things turned violent when riot police cleared the way for council members to leave.[79] 'I was sitting on the front steps of registry,' Kyle Matthews later recalled, 'and next thing I knew a police officer was updating my phrenology profile with his baton.'[80] Irvine commented: 'the Government has very clearly set students against the University over the tuition fees issue.'[81]

Fogelberg, Irvine's successor, expressed similar frustration after protests in 1996. Students occupied the registry for a couple of days in 1995, and in 1996 there was another occupation, this time for a week. The council was 'between the proverbial rock and the hard place', said Fogelberg, and really on the same side as students; reduced funding from a government with a 'misguided belief' that universities had far more potential to increase efficiency left those universities with no choice but to increase fees.[82]

Council and students were certainly united in opposition to a funding cut for Otago's most expensive course, dentistry. Unlike the Medical School, which provided clinical tuition mainly within publicly funded health services, the Dental School had to run its own clinics to teach students. That difference eluded the minister of education, Lockwood Smith, who decided dental education should be funded at the same rate as medical education, and cut the Dental School grant from $40,334 to $25,001 per student per year. The 1994 announcement shocked the Dental School and the university, which had not been consulted, and there was an outcry. The university committed to leaving fees unchanged for existing students, but had to raise them for new dental students: they soared from $7600 to $23,000 per year. There was another round of protests in 1999 when the government was forced to release a previously suppressed 1997 Ministry of Education report that advised that dental education was seriously underfunded – advice the government had ignored. In 2000, under the Labour-led government, funding for dental education was restored to something like its former level and student fees dropped. However, a generation of students were left with big debts; they headed to higher-paying jobs overseas and gaps started appearing in the dental workforce. The university tried unsuccessfully to negotiate reimbursement for the years of underfunding. Fogelberg was determined to have the injustice put right, and in 2001 Otago resorted to the unusual move of suing the government. High Court Justice Lowell Goddard ruled the funding cuts were 'unlawful' and 'irrational', prompting the government to settle with Otago for $15 million (including interest and legal costs). First call on the payout went to the student loans of the 460 graduates who had joined the university in the legal case; and nearly $5 million went to the Dental School to compensate for the money that ought to have been spent on equipment and improvements during the years of underfunding.[83]

Fees protests eventually died down as students became resigned to the system; Matthews comments that the campaign 'was only really lost when first year students could no longer remember a time when education, along with many other things, was paid for by taxes rather than users.'[84] The government made life easier for students but more difficult for the university when it imposed a freeze on fees in return for a little more funding in 2001 and it subsequently set annual maximum fee movements. By then student fees accounted for almost a quarter of the university's income. Government grants were still the largest source of funds, although they had dropped to 42 per cent of the total.[85]

BECOMING COMMERCIAL

Other income sources such as external research grants and consulting fees became more important – just as the government intended. Otago staff had always provided advice to the general public, business and other institutions as a service to the community. In 1970 the university started to formalise advisory services: it appointed a consultant, Alan Fricker, based initially in the Mineral Technology Department, to manage calls from industry for technical aid from the Science Faculty.[86] The Technical Advisory and Consultancy Service, as it became known, helped people to tap the available expertise and charged for services at professional rates.[87] In 1972 the university established a Business Development Centre; the centre received funding from government as part of its regional development policy, but recovered most of its costs from consultancy and research fees.[88] Otago gradually became more entrepreneurial. In 1983 the Technical Advisory and Consulting Service morphed into the Advisory and Consulting Service – run through the University Extension Department – which helped develop and market products and services. In 1984 Otago became the first New Zealand university to set up a holding company for commercial ventures: Univord (University of Otago Research and Development). By 1986 it was working on joint ventures for a dental instrument (Unident), teleconference control box (Unitel), archiving software (Univault), an alarm unit for the Cot Death Society and microbiological controls for pasture pests (Univord Microbials). The Advisory and Consulting Service also brought in growing income from consultancy services, much of it from overseas, and set up a Food Product Development Unit with the government Department of Scientific and Industrial Research (DSIR).[89] A year later the University Council established a Commercial Activities Board (named, predictably enough, Unicom). Headed by businessman Colin Wise, the board oversaw a Research and Development Office, directed by 'retired' microbiology professor Margaret Loutit.[90] Univord Energy Ltd, founded in 1988, was one of Otago's foremost commercial enterprises: it used the expertise in the Physics Department to advise clients on energy efficiency.[91]

By the early 1990s Otago's commercial activities, restructured as the Consulting Group under a director of commercial development, John Scandrett, were bringing in around $1 million a year.[92] In the changed funding climate, however, still more was needed. In 2000 Otago received $36 million from commercial and consulting activity; as financial controller John Patrick reported, this 'clearly demonstrates the growing success of the University at forming business relationships'.[93] The Centre for Innovation, built in collaboration with the DCC to promote innovation and business development in Dunedin, opened in 2001.[94] Designed as 'a unique, upmarket "shop front"' to demonstrate that Otago had 'an innovative focus for its research', the centre was a venue where researchers could collaborate with business.[95] Otago Innovation Ltd, established in 2002, became the university's vehicle for the commercialisation of intellectual property.[96]

When it emerged that one of the greatest business development opportunities lay in biotechnology – and what start-up biotech companies needed most was high-level physical containment laboratories – part of the building was converted into lab space. By 2006 the centre housed a range of biotech and information technology companies, some owned by the university and some private, but all with close ties to the university. It also provided a home for the Research and Enterprise Office, which assisted Otago staff with funding applications and with taking their research into commercial applications.[97] In 2007 Otago Innovation instigated an annual proof of concept competition; the winners received $50,000 to help develop their project, and Otago Innovation offered support to other promising candidates as well.[98] In 2015 Otago Innovation chief executive Pete Hodgson acknowledged that teaching and research were the 'core roles of a university', but at times, the commercialisation of intellectual property 'is the right thing to do'. There was a high attrition rate among the many projects that emerged from the life sciences, but there were 'some extraordinary technologies' under development.[99] Commercial ventures had evolved to become an integral part of university life, accounting for over 10 per cent of Otago's total revenue.

FUNDING FOR RESEARCH

From the beginning, academics at the University of Otago contributed to the advance of human knowledge through research as well as teaching. Research was limited in the early years by high teaching loads – although not all research required costly equipment or materials or travel, it did require staff time. Additional research funding helped employ more staff and slowly transformed Otago into an institution that fulfilled the ideal of research-led teaching. The national Medical Research Council (MRC), established in 1937 to manage new government research funding, was particularly important to Otago. It funded numerous staff, equipment and projects, and located some of its own research units at the university.[100] Although New Zealand's per capita spending on research in all fields was still low, obtaining support for good projects from the MRC was relatively easy until the 1980s, when a burgeoning of medical academics meant more competition for funds.[101] In 1990 the Health Research Council (HRC) replaced the MRC: it supported research in a wider range of health professions and targeted more funding into public health research. Biomedical researchers needed to look further afield for funding.[102]

Health research attracted public support, and over the decades the Medical School built up trust funds from donations and bequests both large and small. Some public goodwill came via charities like the British Empire Cancer Campaign (later the Cancer Society), which funded research at Otago from the 1920s, or the National Heart Foundation, a source of research funding since the 1960s.[103] Other public support was harnessed through the Medical Research Foundations in Canterbury and Wellington (both established 1960) and Otago (1967), which funded projects in their respective regions; they followed the model of an Auckland foundation, established in the 1950s 'to wrest some research funding away from Dunedin to Auckland'.[104] New Zealanders' fondness for gambling helped research through state lottery funds. A notable example at Otago was the £45,000 (equivalent to $1.8 million in 2018 values) obtained in the 1960s by Betty Batham, director of the Portobello Marine Station, for a research vessel; a government awash with funds from the popular Golden Kiwi lottery was looking for a major scientific project to fund.[105] Large contributions came from time to time from businesses and overseas organisations such as the international Wellcome Trust, built on a pharmaceutical fortune, which funded a building for medical research at Otago in the 1960s – the Wellcome Institute.[106]

The creation of the HRC was part of a shakeup of state research funding by the reforming governments of the 1990s. In 1990 the Foundation for Research, Science and Technology (FoRST) became the government vehicle for purchasing, through its Public Good Science Fund (PGSF), science and technology 'outputs'. Initially, university staff could apply to the fund only through cooperative projects with non-university agencies, but in 1992 universities became independently eligible for PGSF funding – though they had to pay a large fee to join the PGSF. Meanwhile, the former UGC-funded research and scholarship funds were abolished. 'Uncertainties remain about adequate support for research,' Irvine noted warily in 1992; the VC was concerned about the 'new competitive, rather than collaborative, environment within the whole tertiary and scientific field'.[107] He was more upbeat the following year when Otago researchers secured more than $1.7 million from the PGSF, although there was 'still a distressing shortfall in research funding available'.[108] Likewise, Fogelberg was encouraged by Otago's success in the first Marsden Fund allocation in 1995; the fund directed further government money into 'blue skies' research rather than the applied focus of the PGSF.[109] Success in the competition for funds became part of promoting Otago: 'we attracted more contestable research funding than any other New Zealand university', the 1999 annual report boasted.[110]

Not all government funding came through FoRST – for example, in 1997 Otago's Education Assessment Research Unit earned a contract of nearly $10 million from the Ministry of Education to continue its annual monitoring of student achievement in primary and intermediate schools.[111] Meanwhile the university was still attracting funding from nongovernmental sources: a large award from the US-based Howard Hughes Medical Institute to biochemist Warren Tate in 1992 confirmed that Otago had 'research workers of the highest rank'.[112]

FUNDING UNIVERSITIES IN THE TWENTY-FIRST CENTURY

Under the National-led governments of the 1990s, tertiary policy centred on 'unbridled competition and decentralisation': the government provided funding via simple block grants and left it to the market to control efficient delivery. The Labour-led governments of the 2000s, concerned about quality and direction, asserted closer control: the Tertiary Education Commission (TEC), established in 2002, took over funding from the Ministry of Education and monitored targets set under each institution's charter and 'profiles' (later replaced with 'investment plans').[113] The Performance-Based Research Fund (PBRF) removed a large sum from the tertiary bulk grant and allocated it according to each institution's success in research – measured by the number of research degrees awarded, the amount of income attracted for research, and 'quality evaluation', a peer-reviewed assessment of individual researchers.[114]

Otago's fourth-place ranking in the first PBRF round in 2003 came as 'an awful shock' to the university, David Skegg recalls; it had 'started to believe its own hype' and become complacent. Lifting morale and encouraging research became one of Skegg's goals as VC; he achieved this when Otago came top in the 2006 assessment.[115] From a financial perspective, PBRF was 'a godsend' from the start, recalls John Patrick, then financial controller: as a large, research-intensive university Otago gained more from the addition of PBRF than it lost from the reduction of the bulk grant. In 2009 its PBRF income reached over $50 million – 9 per cent of total revenue; with another $86 million from external research funds, a quarter of the university's operating money came directly through research; and Otago's research capability also contributed to its commercial income of $65 million. Some research income came via new government programmes designed to encourage collaborative research in strategic fields, such as the Centres of Research Excellence the government established from 2002 onwards and, from 2014, large sums targeted to various 'national science challenges'. Otago was selected to lead some challenges, and it participated in others. Research income was critical to the university: when the roll dropped in the 2010s, with a consequent drop in income from roll-related bulk funding and fees, research income helped minimise cuts in staff.[116]

The university survived numerous financial challenges – from government reforms to the global financial crisis – remarkably well. That required much work and planning. In the late twentieth century marketing became critical: Otago sought the best students and the best staff. After it gained independent control of funding for capital development in the 1990s, Otago invested heavily in constructing buildings and refurbishing older ones. Ensuring the quality of infrastructure was an important strategic goal: the university spent millions on earthquake strengthening, fire safety systems and, in cooperation with the regional council, flood-control works for the Leith.[117]

The Leading Thinkers scheme of the 2000s demonstrated the rewards that came from investing in people. After the government agreed to match funds raised for a University of Auckland Business School building, sparked by a donation from entrepreneur Owen Glenn (a piece of 'shameful pork barrel politics', according to Skegg), it extended its 'partnerships for excellence' scheme to other universities. The scheme was intended for buildings, but in 2003 Otago convinced a sceptical government that human capital was worth funding as well. Otago already had an 'advancement' programme to attract philanthropy from university stakeholders, notably alumni. Functions for graduates around the world increased around the time of the university's 125th anniversary celebrations in 1994; the dynamic Gill Parata was the first head of the Alumni Office.

Otago alumnus Brian Merrilees alerted the university to a successful fundraising campaign at the University of Toronto. That inspired Otago's own fundraising drive to enhance its intellectual capacity through 'knowledge leaders'. The project was led by Clive Matthewson, a former cabinet minister who became director of development. Funds had already been raised for some projects at Otago before the government came on board, and

Directors of the Edgar Diabetes and Obesity Research Centre with benefactor Eion Edgar in 2014. This centre was the first project funded under the Leading Thinkers scheme after a 2003 donation from Edgar, who was Otago's chancellor from 1999 to 2003. From left: Rachael Taylor, Jim Mann, Eion Edgar, Kirsten Coppell.
SHARRON BENNETT PHOTOGRAPH, EDGAR DIABETES AND OBESITY RESEARCH CENTRE COLLECTION.

eventually 27 projects were funded through the official Leading Thinkers scheme. It took a gift of at least $1 million, matched by the government, to establish a permanent professorial chair, and most of the projects enabled the university to establish a professor or a research centre.[118]

Perhaps the most fitting donor to the Leading Thinkers scheme was the education trust of the Presbyterian Church of Otago and Southland, which had funded one of Otago's first three professors. By 1940 the trust was funding the bulk of the salaries of four professors; in 1943 that funding was allocated to three professors, and the university took over the other chair. The church selected the holders of the posts it funded, which was anathema to those who treasured the university's secular status, among them powerful people on the University of New Zealand Senate. In 1945 that body ruled it would no longer approve any appointment 'that does not lie wholly in the hands of the University'; the 75-year arrangement ended and government took over the funding of the positions.

Ironically, in that same year the University of New Zealand approved a theology degree after decades of lobbying. The Presbyterian education trust allocated some of its freed funds to the Presbyterian Theological Hall, which provided many of the honorary staff at Otago's Theology Faculty, established in 1946; and in the 1960s it funded the first religious studies lecturer. The trust later diversified to support a wider range of educational and community projects, but it still aided the university, notably by providing finance for chaplains, a Bioethics Centre and a lecturer in pastoral theology – all fitting reminders of the founders of the Otago colony and their commitment to higher education.[119]

RUNNING THE UNIVERSITY

For the first seven decades Otago's administration lay in the hands of the council and professorial board. The council's first two secretaries were honorary appointments – John Hislop, secretary of the Otago Education Board, followed by Alexander Livingston, the former provincial auditor; but in 1873 the council appointed a full-time secretary who took on the title of registrar.[120] The role was a broad one, since the only other general staff member was the janitor: as keeper of the records and secretary to council, the registrar dealt with the correspondence, accounts, student enrolments, minutes and many other things needed for the smooth running of the university – including sole responsibility for the library. The library – and student access to it – suffered as the registrar became busy with other tasks; the first dedicated librarian was appointed in 1913.[121] Gradually others joined the administrative staff, from clerks and secretaries to accountants and assistant registrars; they took over some of the tasks, but they were additional responsibilities in the registrar's growing empire.

Council secretaries and registrars of the University of Otago

1869–71	John Hislop (honorary)
1871–73	Alexander Livingston (honorary)
1873–74	Henry Clapcott
1874–90	William Mansford
1890–03	Augustus Hamilton
1903–05	James Garrow
1905–11	William Mason
1911–48	Herbert Chapman
1948–75	Jock Hayward
1975–95	Douglas Girvan
1995–98	Keith Houghton
1998–2002	Tim Gray
2002–18	Jan Flood
2018–	Chris Stoddart

Otago's registrars brought different qualifications to the role. Cambridge-educated Clapcott was a former runholder and provincial treasurer; Mansford was a surveyor who became one of the first storekeepers at Gabriels Gully during the goldrush, and a prosperous merchant at Port Chalmers.[122] Hamilton published nearly 30 scientific papers during his 14 years as Otago registrar, as well as a work on Māori art; he left to become director of the Colonial Museum. He was an impressive scholar but not the best of Otago's registrars: according to one contemporary he had no head for business.[123] Garrow was a local graduate who had worked as a teacher, sharebroker and secretary of the Otago Employers' Association. He completed his law qualifications while working as registrar, departed to go into legal practice, then returned as Otago's first full-time law lecturer.[124] Mason, educated at University College, Dublin, 'occupied several responsible positions in Dunedin' before he became registrar.[125] Chapman was the longest-serving registrar: originally from Canterbury, he completed his BA at Otago while teaching at Otago Boys' High School; he administered the university with great competence through the depression and two world wars, and participated in major changes.[126]

In 1913, with the roll at over 500 students, the council organised the university into six faculties: arts/science, dentistry, home science, law/commerce, medicine and mines. It hoped this move would 'facilitate the administrative work and stimulate interest in the academic functions of the University'.[127] Each faculty had a dean in charge, and at regular meetings the academic staff debated the issues of the day and made recommendations on developments. This system eased the burden on the chair of the professorial board – a key person who was the academic head of the university and worked with the chancellor and registrar on its overall management (the role rotated around the senior staff). Other faculties emerged in subsequent decades. In 1920 law and commerce split into two separate faculties. In the 1940s, in addition to the Theology Faculty, Otago acquired a new programme in physical education, though it did not earn faculty status until 1981.[128] The Arts and Science Faculty struggled to get through the agenda at its 'somewhat protracted' meetings and, in 1944, it split into two separate faculties.[129]

THE VICE-CHANCELLOR EMERGES

A staffing crisis during World War II forced a rethink of the university's management. When the chancellor fell seriously ill, his deputy – the vice-chancellor – had limited ability to take over because he was a busy parish minister. Meanwhile, some of the registry staff were away on war service, and this pushed the registrar to the limit. The chair of the professorial board, Robert Bell, crammed his maths teaching into the morning and spent the rest of the day on administration.[130] The university was 'rather like an over-grown child at present', wrote economics lecturer Geoffry Billing to the former professor of economics, Allan Fisher, in 1946. 'We very sadly need a full-time academic head.'[131] The council had decided in 1944 that the time had come to appoint one, but it had to wait for the war to end and the government to provide funding. The new VC would chair the professorial board and report to the council; and the old role of vice-chancellor, as deputy to the chancellor, acquired the title of 'pro-chancellor'.[132]

Vice-chancellors of the University of Otago

1948–53	Robert Aitken
1953–63	Frederick Soper
1964–66	Arthur Beacham
1967–73	Robin Williams
1973–93	Robin Irvine
1994–2004	Graeme Fogelberg
2004–11	David Skegg
2011–	Harlene Hayne

Robert Aitken, Otago's first VC (1948–53).
JOHN MCINDOE LTD RECORDS, MS-3247/584, S11-532E, HOCKEN COLLECTIONS.

Otago persuaded one of its own star graduates, Robert Aitken, back to New Zealand to become first VC in 1948. Aitken was born in Wyndham, the son of a Presbyterian minister; he graduated top of his medical class in 1923 and headed to Oxford on a Rhodes Scholarship. After completing a doctorate in respiratory physiology he practised medicine and taught at Hammersmith, a postgraduate medical school in London, for some years before he became professor of medicine at Aberdeen in 1939.[133] As VC at Otago Aitken furthered his reputation as a good administrator, already established at Aberdeen, and earned support from those who had been sceptical about the position; when he left in 1953 the student publication *Otago University Review* commented, 'He has shown us that vice-chancellors are, if not an essential thing, at least a very good one',[134] and the Arts Faculty noted that he 'fully appreciated the central position of an Arts Faculty in a University and his keen analytical mind quickly gave him a grasp of Arts Faculty affairs'.[135] Ironically it was probably the Medical Faculty that least appreciated Aitken – though the medical academics were initially enthusiastic about his appointment, they did not appreciate his progressive views on medical education or his abolition of their special sub-committee of the University Council.[136] Aitken was recruited back to Britain to become VC at Birmingham in 1953. Wise, fiercely intelligent and thoughtful of others – though somewhat austere – he had set a high standard for his successors.[137]

To replace Aitken the council looked closer to home: it appointed Frederick Soper, professor and head of chemistry since 1936. Soper was a Welshman who served in World War I and lectured at Bangor before migrating to New Zealand. He became known for his research into wool and took a leadership role in New Zealand's scientific work during World War II. He later wrote that the main features of his 10 years as VC were 'the beginning of the upwards surge in student numbers', and the planning and completion of several university buildings. He was on good terms with the students: 'student unrest and claims for a greater say in the running of the University had not yet crossed the seas, although political interest was alert and lively', he recalled. He had morning tea every week with some of the OUSA executive and entertained them at the VC's official residence, the Lodge, a couple of times a year. When he retired in 1963 he was delighted to be made a life member of OUSA.[138]

The next VC was another Welshman. Arthur Beacham, the son of a coalminer, was an economist with research interests in mining and monopolies. He visited Otago on sabbatical from Aberystwyth in 1956 and liked the place enough to return as VC in 1963. He stayed only three years in the job, but they were crucial ones. Otago was adjusting to its independence after the demise of

Arthur Beacham (right), VC from 1964 to 1966, with PVC and physics professor Robert Nimmo (left) and registrar Jock Hayward (centre).

UNIVERSITY OF OTAGO REGISTRY RECORDS, MS-3201/007, S17-611D, HOCKEN COLLECTIONS.

Robin Williams (right) with long-serving registrar Jock Hayward soon after Williams became VC in 1967.

UNIVERSITY OF OTAGO REGISTRY RECORDS, MS-3201/009, S15-592A, HOCKEN COLLECTIONS.

the University of New Zealand. The special schools resented having to compete with other parts of the university under the altered funding regime, and Beacham was unpopular with the medical and mining schools. He was 'fearless and very astute' and something of 'a terrier', recalls Tim Gray, who was in the early stages of a long career in the registry. Beacham was a fierce advocate for Otago and, at one stage, had a falling out with Prime Minister Keith Holyoake over inadequate funding of universities. According to Morrell, the fiery VC had 'an alert, analytical mind, a persuasive tongue and great energy and drive'.[139]

The challenges of growth and tight funding persisted under Beacham's successor, Robert (known as Robin) Williams, recruited in 1967 from the State Services Commission. He grew up in a Christchurch vicarage and studied maths and physics at Canterbury before taking up radar development work with the DSIR in 1941. He was seconded from that role to work on the US-led Manhattan Project, which developed the first atomic bomb. After the war he studied at Cambridge then returned to the DSIR in Wellington and subsequently worked for the commission. At Otago, Williams oversaw the reforms that led to the renaissance of the Medical School. He was a far-sighted leader with a lifelong concern for ethics and social justice – although his term as VC coincided with the first stirrings of student unrest, with protests over mixed flatting and student disciplinary regulations. One legacy of Williams' time was a group of outstanding senior staff. The DSIR had a policy of appointing bright young people and he carried that tradition to Otago, where he oversaw the recruitment of several very young professors. Some, like George Petersen in biochemistry and Alan Musgrave in philosophy, went on to have long and outstanding careers at the university. Williams left Otago to become VC of Australian National University in Canberra in 1973; he returned to New Zealand as chair of the State Services Commission in 1975.[140]

After two VCs who came from outside the university, in 1973 Otago appointed an insider, Robin Irvine, who had demonstrated his administrative skills as clinical dean of the Medical School, helping develop the clinical schools in Christchurch and Wellington. An Otago graduate, he worked in Auckland and London before he returned to the Medical School as a researcher and clinical teacher specialising in kidney disease and hypertension. The challenges of an expanding institution accelerated during Irvine's 21 years in the role: when he started Otago had just over 6000 students and when he retired there were over 14,000. In addition to the administrative difficulties that brought, Irvine faced the complications of the neoliberal government reforms of the 1980s and 1990s. Like Otago's other medical VCs, he consciously took a wider view of the Medical School's role within the institution – an attitude that was not always popular with the school. Irvine's appetite for hard work became legendary, as did his immaculately tidy office.[141]

RESTRUCTURING

Irvine implemented a revised structure at Otago in 1989. The nine faculties were reorganised into four academic divisions of roughly equal size: commerce; health sciences (dentistry and medicine); humanities (arts and music, law, theology) and sciences (consumer and applied sciences, physical education, science). Two further divisions encompassed the rest of the university: the Academic Services Division (library, computing services, university press, University Extension, Higher Education Development Centre); and the Administrative and Student Services Division (a wide range of services from finance and staffing to works and accommodation). The goal was to 'decentralise and streamline decision making'; the university had grown too large to be tightly managed centrally by the chancellor, VC and registrar. The restructure also reflected government reforms that were about to be implemented in the Public Finance Act, with additional expectations of publicly funded institutions. Irvine reported that Otago's revised organisation should 'encourage greater accountability'. Each division had its own board and an academic head – the assistant vice-chancellor (AVC), retitled pro-vice-chancellor (PVC) in 2005 – except the Administrative and Student Services Division, which was headed by the registrar.[142]

The restructuring was controversial; some senior academics looked with nostalgia on the era of faculties, when they felt they had more say in university affairs. However, academic departments gained more control. In 1991 John Patrick, an Otago accounting graduate with extensive private-sector experience, became financial controller – a new role to oversee the remodelled financial system. Resources were allocated to each division, which then allocated them to individual departments. Preparing budgets was a challenge for heads of department; until then finances were controlled centrally and departments had just a 'chalk budget' for minor expenses. They acquired the freedom to choose how their money was spent and to invest in further programmes. The divisional level acted as a buffer; if a department got into trouble – as they did from time to time through unwise decisions or swings in student subject preferences – the rest of the division would subsidise it (albeit not happily). Otago was an early adopter of the devolved system of 'responsibility centre management'. It was effective and, unlike some other universities, Otago never ran into deficit, though it went close occasionally.[143]

As government restructuring of education persisted through the 1990s it was perhaps appropriate that the next VC, Graeme Fogelberg, had an academic background in business – a rarity in New Zealand university leadership at the time. Fogelberg graduated in accountancy at Victoria University of Wellington and lectured there before doing an MBA and PhD at the University of Western Ontario. He returned to Victoria as professor of business administration and was deputy VC there before he took on the role at Otago in 1994. His ambitious strategic vision for Otago fitted the competitive era. Under his watch Otago attracted further international students and developed its alumni relations as part of the search for additional sources of funding; it marketed itself aggressively and developed a base in Auckland. Fogelberg was uncompromising and not everybody liked his managerial approach. Small departments came under threat in the funding environment of the time. The closure of the small Russian programme was particularly unpopular with staff and students; however, with the VC's advocacy the popular Spanish programme got underway. Fogelberg retired in 2004, leaving behind a university with more students and a more diverse funding model than he had inherited.[144]

Fogelberg continued the management restructuring commenced under Irvine. Otago developed a more corporate look. The structure brought together a senior management team, the Vice-chancellor's Advisory Group (VCAG). In addition to the AVCs and registrar, the group included a director of external relations (responsible for liaison, alumni, public relations and corporate and government relations) and director of information services (responsible for computing services and the library). The chief financial officer (previously the financial controller) was included, to ensure 'the financial impact of all decisions upon the University is always evaluated'. What raised eyebrows the most was Fogelberg's creation of two full-time deputy vice-chancellor (DVC) roles.[145] The PVC had served as deputy to the VC since the 1960s, and the role of a second PVC for academic affairs was created in 1992. The role could be demanding and, in 1986 and 1987, PVC Richard Mulgan acted as VC for a year while Irvine took leave. However, those roles were part-time, carried out by professors with other responsibilities.[146] The DVCs had more time to devote to managing Otago's academic and research priorities, freeing the VC to concentrate on strategic tasks. In 1995 two Australians commenced as the DVCs; perhaps coincidentally, Australian universities had provided inspiration for the management structure.[147] Ian Smith, the DVC Research and International, came from senior roles in the university and private sectors, while Phil Meade, the DVC Academic, hailed from Griffith University in Brisbane, where he had developed quality audit programmes. At Otago, his experience was invaluable as the university introduced its own academic review system and dealt with various audits – essential in achieving good rankings as the concept of 'measuring' universities emerged. Meanwhile, Smith proved energetic and entrepreneurial in developing international relationships and enterprise.[148]

The retirement of registrar Douglas Girvan in 1995 marked the end of an era at Otago. Girvan and his predecessor, Jock Hayward, were effective and long-serving registrars. Hayward was a local who studied commerce at Otago, starting out in registry as an accountant before taking on the top job in 1948. The genial Hayward was known for his diplomacy and sympathy for others as well as his efficiency. Girvan was a Scottish lawyer who arrived at Otago in 1975 with experience in administration in several Scottish and English universities. Like Hayward he contributed to the wider community as well as the university and was known for 'his shrewd appraisal of people and events'.[149] The university had grown so large that the registrar could no longer efficiently oversee such a range of services; in subsequent years various functions were carved off as independent services with their own directors. There was a reshuffle in the wake of registrar Keith Houghton's dismissal in 1998 – Houghton was good at the job but had personal financial difficulties and resorted to using his university credit card to cover his debts; he was convicted of theft as a servant. Assistant registrar Tim Gray stepped up to the senior role until he retired in 2002, when Jan Flood became registrar. Formerly a physical education teacher, Flood moved into university administration for a change of scene and quickly proved her worth. She worked initially in the Law Faculty and then as the VC's executive assistant. The role of registrar was more circumscribed than in earlier decades but still important: she spent about half her time as council secretary and the rest with a variety of matters and, in particular, the increasingly demanding legal compliance issues.[150]

David Skegg was the third VC to have a medical degree from Otago and the second

The three most recent VCs in 2015: Graeme Fogelberg (1994–2004), Harlene Hayne (2011–) and David Skegg (2004–11).
MARY FOGELBERG PHOTOGRAPH, GRAEME FOGELBERG COLLECTION.

former Rhodes Scholar. He was the popular and long-serving head of Dunedin's Department of Preventive and Social Medicine when he was appointed Fogelberg's successor in 2004. Skegg brought a focus on academic excellence to the role: he carried on with his own research into cervical and breast cancer during his time as VC and encouraged others in the senior leadership team to continue their research too. He was delighted with Otago's success with the Marsden Fund and PBRF, and with the development of chairs and research centres through the Leading Thinkers scheme, set up during Fogelberg's time. Skegg made various changes to VCAG and administration, including the appointment of Otago's first chief operating officer: the highly competent finance officer John Patrick took on the role in 2005.[151] Another Skegg innovation was the PVC International – a role created in 2006. The DVC Research and International was increasingly occupied with PBRF; the new position provided a senior person to focus on Otago's international links and international students.[152] After many years of rapid growth, student numbers began to settle – though the postgraduate contingent rose, as did the Māori and Pacific Island roll. Strengthening staff collegiality was one of Skegg's priorities – he was himself an Olympic-class networker – and there was a lift in morale under his leadership. Dealing with the 'high-spirited behaviour' of students was a challenge – in particular the notorious Undie 500. Skegg led the introduction of the controversial student code of conduct in 2007, along with the Campus Watch system. In 2011 he retired from a successful seven-year term to focus again on his research.[153]

Harlene Hayne, who became VC in 2011, is another distinguished researcher: she came to the role after a couple of years as Otago's DVC Research and Development. After a PhD at Rutgers and three years as postdoctoral fellow at Princeton, Hayne became a lecturer in Otago's Psychology Department in 1992, and professor from 2002. Along with heading one of Otago's largest departments she served on numerous committees and as chair of the board of UniCol. As VC, Hayne quickly earned a good reputation with Otago students: she demonstrated a concern for student wellbeing that stemmed in part from her psychology background. She appeared regularly in a hands-on role at student events. Like Skegg, Hayne prioritised Otago's academic success. In 2015 she introduced a convocation ceremony to formally mark the beginning of the academic

Harlene Hayne with Red Frog volunteers at the Hyde Street party, 2012. Volunteering became popular with Otago students in the 2010s, inspired by the efforts of the Student Volunteer Army in Canterbury after the earthquakes.
OUSA COLLECTION

year and to remind students celebrating orientation of the main purpose of the university. Like Skegg, she is still an active researcher and – a first for New Zealand VCs – she secured a 2015 Marsden grant for a project on interviewing children in a forensic context.[154]

Like her predecessors, Hayne introduced changes to the university's structure. She upgraded the senior international role further in 2015: she appointed anatomy professor and PVC International Helen Nicholson as a third DVC, with responsibility for external engagement. The new External Engagement Division encompassed marketing and communications, international matters, development and alumni relations.[155]

Bigger reorganisation was to come. Hayne's predecessors had faced the challenges of a university experiencing rapid growth in the roll. She faced a different sort of challenge, dealing with an organisation with reduced revenue because of reduced student numbers, alongside a programme of big, expensive building developments necessitated partly by concerns about the safety of some of the university's older buildings. Several academic departments lost staff because of the reduced income. Financial stringency prompted a comprehensive review of Otago's support services, which had developed in a somewhat ad hoc manner and varied in different parts of the organisation. The review, launched in 2015, investigated 'all operational and administrative processes undertaken by general staff', with an eye for improving efficiency and ensuring 'uniformly excellent support services'. Hayne announced in 2017 that Otago would implement a 'shared services' administrative model. General staff might remain embedded in individual departments and sections but they would be centrally managed. In addition there were extensive changes to central administration, including the introduction of an all-purpose 'AskOtago' contact centre. With these changes came the loss of 160 full-time equivalent jobs.[156]

On his retirement in 2004, DVC Ian Smith commented that Otago was 'by its very nature quite a conservative university. And I admit I came head to head with great resistance to any change.'[157] That conservatism could be a strength as well as a weakness. Patrick notes that dramatic change does not work well in universities – they are institutions built on people, and morale is critical. Otago did not experience revolutions, but it underwent ongoing evolutionary change, overseen by a highly capable group of executives and chancellors.[158]

CHAPTER TWO

The students

When classes commenced at the University of Otago in July 1871, the first student to sign on was lawyer Robert Stout, admitted to the bar just a few days previously. Though nobody knew it at the time, Otago's first student was an omen of a good future: Stout became premier of New Zealand and later chief justice; he was also principal founder of Victoria University of Wellington.[1] Otago attracted 81 students to its first session. Few student records survive for the early years, but 20 of the 1871 intake successfully passed their exams;[2] the other 61 presumably failed their exams or abandoned their studies – 'not a few dropped attendance, finding the task of preparation too burdensome', noted council member Donald Stuart.[3] Many, like Stout, were full-time workers and part-time students; half were 'solely engaged as students' and half were 'engaged in some pursuit'.[4] Some were ill prepared for university study and not all had the privilege of a high-school education. When the *Evening Star* in 1878 referred to maths and physics professor John Shand as 'the lucky tenant of one of the University sinecures', former student Gustav Hirsch rushed to his defence, noting Shand's heavy workload and his teaching success: 'One of his first students was taken from an elementary school at a very small place up-country, and had just managed to pick up a little mathematical knowledge from

Founding student Robert Stout, photographed in 1875 by the NZ Photographic Co., Dunedin. Stout's political career began in 1872 when he was elected to the Otago Provincial Council, but he still found time to serve as the university's first law lecturer from 1873 until 1875 when he was elected to parliament, spelling the end of his academic career. His influence on New Zealand universities was immense. As well as serving on the Otago and Victoria university councils, he was on the senate of the University of New Zealand for 46 years, and was its chancellor from 1903 to 1923.

BOX-030-001, S10-021A, HOCKEN COLLECTIONS.

Peter Seton Hay became well known for the railway viaducts he designed, but also for his 'prodigious mental calculations' and his ability to solve 'abstruse mathematical problems in his leisure hours'. He was a founding student at Otago.

P2010-011/1-024, ALBUM 605, HAY FAMILY PORTRAITS, S16-683A, HOCKEN COLLECTIONS.

Charles Connor's photograph sat alongside that of Peter Hay in the Hay family album – they both lived in the Clutha district. Perhaps these photos date from the time they began at university, when Peter was about 18 and Charles just 15. Connor was a Presbyterian minister's son, and he later became a minister.

P2010-011/1-025, ALBUM 605, HAY FAMILY PORTRAITS, S16-683B, HOCKEN COLLECTIONS.

the mathematical volume of the "Circle of the Sciences". Under Professor Shand's guidance this student a few years afterwards graduated a first-class, with honours in mathematics, and is now an MA.'[5] That student was Peter Hay, raised on a farm at Kaihiku in the Clutha district; he became a noted engineer.[6]

Hay was one of the few early students to complete a degree – most students attended classes for a year or two but did not graduate. The first degree awarded by Otago was a Bachelor of Arts to Alexander Watt Williamson in 1874. Otago then lost the right to award degrees: only the University of New Zealand could do so until 1961. Williamson was a young schoolteacher in the Whanganui district who came to Dunedin to attend the University of Otago.[7] Otago had a national catchment from the beginning: seven of the class of 1871 came 'from other provinces' and 13 hailed from 'country districts of Otago'.[8] Thomas Hutchison was another student from Whanganui, just 16 years old. He was destined for a career in the law and as a magistrate – lawyers and future lawyers were quite a feature among the foundation students.[9] Sitting alongside Stout in mental science lectures was William Downie Stewart, the lawyer who had trained him; and another of Stewart's law pupils, his future legal partner John Edward Denniston, was studying Latin.[10] For several other foundation students the university was a step to a career in the church. David Borrie of West Taieri, Charles Connor of Popotunoa, John Ferguson of Tokomairiro and John Steven of Kaitangata all studied at Otago before undertaking theological training to become Presbyterian ministers. Ferguson and Steven were already 'pupil teachers', learning teaching on the job – a common route to 'improvement' for those who did well at school.[11] Thomas Cuddie was intent on a career in the ministry but he died (probably of tuberculosis) just a couple of months after classes began.[12]

Ferdinand Faithfull Begg – Ferdie to his family – was one of several businessmen among the founding students. The son of prominent Edinburgh cleric James Begg, he joined his brother in Dunedin in 1863 where he worked in a bank and at a large land agency. He performed well in the advanced mathematics class at university in 1871. In 1872 he returned to Scotland where he became a prominent stockbroker; he chaired the Edinburgh Stock Exchange and, later, the London Chamber of Commerce, and he was a member of parliament. Another of Begg's claims to fame is that he was 'the first to ride a bicycle on the streets of Dunedin': in 1871 he imported a 'boneshaker' complete with wooden wheels, brass pedals and iron tyres, backbone and handles. This photograph dates from the 1880s.

ALBUM 398, P.17, CARGILL FAMILY PORTRAITS, S16-683C, HOCKEN COLLECTIONS.

These were just the sort of people the university's founders had in mind – they helped boost the ranks of well-educated teachers, lawyers and ministers, meaning the country was less dependent on imported professionals. Most might be described as middle class, but some were of humbler origins. Cuddie, for instance, was the son of labouring parents with a small, struggling farm on Saddle Hill; he was born aboard the *Philip Laing*, which brought some of the earliest colonial settlers to Otago in 1848. It would have been impossible for this pious but poor family to fund an education further away without substantial help.[13]

There is evidence of a 'brain drain' among the first students – some of the brightest were attracted to further study and other opportunities in Europe, and not all returned. Hay's professors were keen to send him to Cambridge but he did not go, as he had 'other than mathematical plans in which Cupid played a part'.[14] Connor and Ferguson, who both won scholarships, later travelled 'Home' for further study in Scotland, but eventually returned.[15] For others of that migrant generation the ties to Otago and New Zealand were weaker. Cecil Yates Biss studied Latin and Greek at Otago in 1871 then headed to Cambridge, where he completed the Natural Sciences Tripos with first-class honours in 1875. He later qualified in medicine and became a respected physician, researcher and lecturer in England – though his career was cut short by illness. Biss, a leading member of the Plymouth Brethren, was 'rather given to admonishing his patients in regard to excesses and irregularities in living, in addition to ministering to their immediate ailments'.[16]

ADMITTING WOMEN STUDENTS

No women featured among the original students, but this did not last long. In August 1871, in response to a petition from 149 women, the University Council agreed to admit women to all courses.[17] That was welcome news to Learmonth Dalrymple, advocate for educational opportunities for New Zealand women and girls. Dalrymple arrived in Otago with her family in 1853, carrying 'an abiding resentment against the conventional and limited education for Scottish girls which she had suffered in the 1830s and 1840s'.[18] In quiet but determined fashion she led a long campaign for the provincial government to establish Otago Girls' High School, the first public high school for girls in the southern hemisphere. After the school opened in 1871, she and her supporters turned their attention to the fledgling university. They had

Mary Montgomery began studying at the University of Otago in 1877. In 1887 she left to become headmistress of New Plymouth Girls' High School. She continued her teaching career in other North Island schools after her marriage to Charles Baker-Gabb, and later completed her BA through Victoria.
NEW PLYMOUTH GIRLS' HIGH SCHOOL COLLECTION.

Caroline Freeman, Otago's first woman graduate, demonstrated more determination than most: for several years she walked 11 kilometres home to Green Island after a full day's work followed by lectures. She later moved to Dunedin city and continued her university study while teaching at Otago Girls' High School. This photograph was taken in 1885 by Steffano Webb.
P2017-009, S17-028A, HOCKEN COLLECTIONS.

good support on the council, especially from John Richardson, the chancellor.[19] The council was not willing, however, to go as far as offering degrees to women; as Richardson explained, they would instead be admitted 'to competition for Certificates which will be equivalent to degrees'.[20] That corresponded with restrictions in the few other universities in the British Empire that admitted women: the most notorious examples were Oxford, which did not grant degrees to women until 1920, and Cambridge, which followed suit in 1948.[21] In practice, Otago's ban on degrees for women had no impact as, by the time the first woman qualified, all degrees were awarded through the University of New Zealand, which had no such ban; historian Jim Gardner notes that an institution desperate for enrolments could not afford to 'turn away degree students in skirts'. Kate Edger of Auckland became New Zealand's first woman graduate in 1877.[22]

Although no women enrolled at Otago in 1871, at least four, and possibly several more, applied for admission in 1872.[23] Anna Barton, who completed part of the chemistry course in 1872, was among them, and her mother, Jane Crichton Barton, probably attended as well; Williamson recalled attending classics lectures with the Bartons, and both women featured among the successful chemistry students of 1873.[24] Jane, the daughter of a Scottish clergyman, was married to Dunedin lawyer and later judge George Barton. Their son Edward attended Otago at the same time as Anna; he became a leading engineer in Australia, but Anna's later life remains obscure.[25] Another likely brother and sister among the early students were John and Miss M. Langmuir; she was probably Margaret, the daughter of Caversham market gardener John Langmuir (senior). Both Langmuirs passed the chemistry exams in 1873, and a Langmuir (unspecified) passed in English and senior Latin in 1872.[26]

Like their male counterparts, most of the early women students at Otago did not complete degrees. The first to do so, Caroline Freeman, appeared in the exam lists in 1875, when she topped the class in psychology and logic and passed junior German. She did not graduate BA until 1885, as she still worked full-time, teaching during the day and attending university in the evening. Freeman had no higher schooling; she followed the same path as many early students who became pupil teachers when they finished primary school. After graduating she established private schools for girls in Dunedin and Christchurch.[27]

Although it had taken over a decade for Otago to produce its first woman graduate, others quickly followed and by 1900 there were 58. Many went on to teaching careers and became role models for future generations of women.[28]

CONTROLLING ENTRY AND EXPANDING NUMBERS

Otago did not restrict entry in its first year: 'any one can attend any classes he pleases' was the council secretary's response to an 1871 enquiry.[29] That reflected the Scottish attitude to education, which encouraged all who were interested to improve themselves. Standards were a concern, though, and from 1872 the professors set a matriculation exam that prospective students needed to pass to be eligible for a degree. Those who failed or did not sit matriculation were still welcome to enrol; since only seven people matriculated in 1872, other students were critical to the university's survival.[30] Non-matriculated students 'will be admitted to the classes on paying fees, but on the understanding that the instruction is adapted to the regular students', the secretary explained to a parent in 1872.[31] Some of the earliest students were very young, and in 1873, in response to a request from the professors, the council set an age limit of 15 years (lifted to 16 in 1895).[32] The academic readiness of students improved over time – helped, no doubt, by the increasing availability of secondary education. In 1884 students who had matriculated outnumbered the non-matriculated for the first time, and by 1900, 217 of the 257 students had matriculated.[33]

Competitive scholarships encouraged the brightest minds into university study. In 1871 Richardson, the chancellor, converted a scholarship he had donated for Otago Boys' High School into one for high-school boys going on to university; and in the 1880s the scholarship was opened up to women too. Otago's first year of classes coincided with the centenary of the birth of popular Scottish writer Walter Scott: the public raised funds for a Walter Scott Scholarship and, in 1875, George Montgomery was the first winner. In 1872 Dalrymple and her friends raised funds for a Women's Scholarship; it was offered for the first time, in 1892, to Jessie Polson – first dux of Waitaki Girls' High School.[34] Otago students also competed for the University of New Zealand's junior and senior scholarships; and some received support from their local communities. In 1879, for instance, Tokomairiro High School provided scholarships to three of its pupil teachers who were heading to Dunedin for further teacher training; two of them – Mary Maxwell Brown and Sarah Dawson – matriculated and attended the university alongside their teaching programme.[35]

The roll of 257 did not seem as tiny in 1900 as it does now. Classes were at their lowest ebb in 1874 with just 50 students; the opening flurry of people trying out the institution was over. Otago took comfort from knowing it had more students in its first decade than the universities of Sydney and Melbourne at similar stages.[36] The council pressed on boldly, starting other courses – and, although from the beginning students came from beyond Otago to study arts and sciences, it was the specialist courses that turned Otago into a truly national university.

MĀORI STUDENTS

The Medical School produced Otago's first Māori graduates. In 1899 Peter Buck, also known as Te Rangi Hīroa, and Tūtere Wī Repa arrived at Otago, the first of a succession of pupils from Te

Te Rangi Hīroa (Peter Buck), Otago's first Māori graduate.
GEORGE RAMSDEN PHOTOGRAPH, 1/2-037931-F, ALEXANDER TURNBULL LIBRARY.

Aute College, the Hawke's Bay Anglican boarding school for Māori boys. Buck, of Ngāti Mutunga and Irish descent, completed his MB ChB in 1904 and then an MD in 1910. He worked as a medical officer to Māori and became a key member of the Young Maori Party – a driving force behind the Māori renaissance of the early twentieth century. He spent five years in parliament; later he became a distinguished anthropologist and served as director of the Bishop Museum in Hawai`i. Wī Repa (Te Whānau ā Apanui and Ngāti Porou) graduated in 1908, spent a year working at Dunedin Hospital then headed back north to a long career in medicine in Gisborne, Te Karaka and Te Araroa.[37]

Local Māori may well have felt ambivalent about the university because of the part it played in the wider colonisation project. Despite the cultural and educational barriers, however, some southern Māori engaged with the university in the early twentieth century. The third Māori medical graduate, Edward (Ned) Ellison, was another Te Aute old boy but had spent some of his childhood at Ōtākou and had Ngāi Tahu as well as Te Āti Awa whakapapa. Ellison obtained a MB ChB in 1919 and later returned for postgraduate studies in tropical medicine. He had a long career in public health, mostly in the Pacific Islands.[38] His father-in-law, Teone Taiaroa (also known as John or Jack), possibly attended university classes much earlier, in the early 1880s. He was a grandson of leading Ngāi Tahu warrior chief Te Mātenga Taiaroa and son of Hōri Kerei Taiaroa, long-serving MP for Southern Māori. After an education at Otago Boys' High School, Jack Taiaroa trained as a lawyer in the office of Robert Stout. An obituary notes that he 'distinguished himself at the University of Otago', but there are no surviving enrolment records for that period and he did not graduate.[39]

The local iwi provided hospitality and support to Māori students from beyond Dunedin, some of whom married into well-known Ngāi Tahu families. For instance, Leonard Broughton (Ngāti Kahungunu), who graduated in medicine in 1944, married Margaret Evans, whose mother Ani Parata Evans was the daughter of Tame Parata of Puketeraki, MP for Southern Māori. Broughton was one of several Māori medical students from the north who boarded at Te Maraenui, Ani Parata Evans' Dunedin home, in the 1930s. The Broughtons' son John graduated in dentistry and became a pioneer in teaching Māori health at the university.[40] Later Ngāi Tahu leaders who welcomed students and helped them retain their sense of māoritanga while far from home included Magda Wallscott, Edna Wesley, the Paratas, Ellisons and Pickerings, and the Ōtepoti branch of the Maori Women's Welfare League regularly put on dinners for students.[41]

Medicine wasn't the only drawcard for Māori students: Emere Kaa (Ngāti Porou), a qualified nurse, spent a year at the Home Science School in 1935.[42] A 1967 study by Māori student liaison officer John Harré identified 59 people of Māori descent who first enrolled at Otago between 1955 and 1964 and who studied for more than a year. The largest group studied physical education (16), 13 studied medicine, five were in dentistry, three each in home science, commerce and law, one in engineering and the other 15 students were in arts and science.[43]

BECOMING INTERNATIONAL

The special schools also drew international students to Otago. Jione (Tom) Dovi, who came from a chiefly Fijian family, commenced at Otago in 1929 and graduated in medicine in 1935. Other Fijians of noble descent soon followed him to Otago, among them Immanuel Vosailagi, who graduated in dentistry in 1944 and – perhaps the most famous – Kamisese Mara, who commenced his medical studies at Otago around 1943 but continued his education (in history) at Oxford. Mara served as prime minister of Fiji from 1970 to 1992 and as president until 2000. Mutyala Satyanand was an early Indo-Fijian student who graduated in medicine in 1940 and afterwards settled in New Zealand (his son Anand, who spent a year at Otago himself, was governor-general of New Zealand from 2006 to 2011).[44] Cook Islander Thomas Davis graduated in medicine in 1945 and had a career in public health and research physiology before becoming prime minister of the Cook Islands from 1978 to 1987.[45] Sione Tapa was the first Tongan to earn a medical degree in 1953; he was a long-serving minister of health and took Tonga into the World Health Organization; he presided over the 1977 World Health Assembly, which famously set the goal of 'health for all by the year 2000'.[46]

Later Pacific students were a mixture of the privately funded and those sponsored by their governments or through aid programmes, including the Colombo Plan (discussed below). In 1965 Otago had 27 international students from the Pacific and by 1979 there were 59, hailing from the Cook Islands, Fiji, New Guinea, Niue, Samoa, Tonga and Tuvalu. Otago also hosted students from Solomon Islands, the Marshall

Jione (Tom) Dovi was probably Otago's first Pacific Island student. After graduating he practised medicine in New Zealand and served with the New Zealand Expeditionary Force in the Solomon Islands before settling back in Fiji. He is pictured centre front with Otago's team for the 1930 New Zealand University Tournament. On the far right of the second to back row is another accomplished athlete, future Olympic champion runner Jack Lovelock.

ZENITH STUDIO PHOTOGRAPH, P.S.DeQ. CABOT PAPERS, MS-2734/003, S17-564, HOCKEN COLLECTIONS.

The Knox farce was a regular feature of capping concerts for many years. The cast of the 1946 farce 'Cameo and Mabelette' included Kamisese Mara, future prime minister of Fiji (standing at centre). Mara's towering stature and sporting brilliance helped make him one of the best-known students of his generation.

MICHAEL SHACKLETON COLLECTION

Islands, Nauru, the New Hebrides (Vanuatu), Papua and Tokelau in the 1960s and 1970s.[47] As Pacific migration rose from the 1960s onwards, a generation of Pacific Island students who grew up in New Zealand joined those coming direct from the islands for their education. By the mid-1980s around 2 per cent of Otago students identified their ethnicity as Pacific Islander, and a growing proportion of these were New Zealand-born or resident. Thirty years later, Pacific Islanders made up nearly 4 per cent of the roll.[48]

Clarence Piliso arrived in 1931 and was a contemporary of Dovi's at the Medical School and Knox College. He was sponsored by the New Zealand Student Christian Movement (SCM), which decided to support a black South African medical student after hearing of a shortage of Indigenous doctors in that country, where a 'colour bar' kept them out of universities. Piliso spent three years at Otago, but he was unhappy in New Zealand and in 1934 he headed to Glasgow to complete his medical training with ongoing support from the SCM. He became a general practitioner in Birmingham, England, where he campaigned against racism and presided over the Afro-Caribbean Organisation.[49]

It was a while before other African students arrived at Otago. The Commonwealth Education Scheme offered opportunities for high-performing students to complete postgraduate study abroad: in 1960 and 1961 six Otago students headed to Britain and Canada on scholarships, and Otago welcomed postgraduate students from Singapore, India, Uganda and Canada.[50] New Zealand joined the Special Commonwealth Africa Assistance Programme in 1961 and the first Otago students

Above left: Otago's first Chinese graduate, Kathleen Pih (Pih Zhen-Wah) was born in 1902 in Antung, China, and came to New Zealand in 1908 with her foster mother Margaret Reid, a Dunedinite who had been working with the China Inland Mission. Pih enrolled at Otago in 1921, graduated in medicine in 1929 and returned to China as a missionary for some years. She later completed specialist training in ophthalmology in London and married anatomy professor Francis Chang of Shanghai. They worked in China, Singapore and Hong Kong before retiring to New Zealand in 1969. PHOTOGRAPHED BY J.J. WEBSTER, DUNEDIN, C.1930. P-A154.19-59, PRESBYTERIAN RESEARCH CENTRE.

Above right: New Zealand Chinese students Peter Chin and Jocelyn Wong (centre front) at the St Margaret's College ball, early 1960s. PETER CHIN COLLECTION

arrived that year: Benedict Mba and Moses Olayinka qualified in history and education before returning to Nigeria to teach.[51] By 1965 there were 28 African students from seven different countries on campus. Patrick Cole – another history student from Nigeria – was vice-president of OUSA in 1964 and Ebraima Manneh was president in 1971; Manneh was an arts student 'with fairly radical views' who later became a senior public servant and ambassador to the United States for his home country, The Gambia.[52] The number of African students declined through the 1970s, but a surge of African migration to New Zealand from the late twentieth century added many more Africa-born students to the roll – most of them white South Africans.

In the second half of the twentieth century the largest group of international students at Otago came from Asia. In the 1950s Pākehā New Zealanders who, for generations, had looked 'home' to Britain, became more conscious that they were part of the Asia–Pacific region, and the arrival of Asian and Pacific students on New Zealand university campuses contributed to that perspective.[53] Of course New Zealand already had its own Asian communities, and the first ethnically Chinese students at Otago were New Zealand residents. Otago's first Chinese graduate was Kathleen Pih (later Chang), who studied medicine in the 1920s.[54] Hers was an unusual case: for many decades immigration policy prevented Chinese women and children from settling in New Zealand. Restrictions were eased during World War II and the Chinese community grew.[55] Otago's second Chinese student, who arrived before the war, opened opportunities for others. Roy Ting Shang Law commenced his medical course in 1937 and, after graduating, established a successful general practice in Wellington. When Chinese New Zealanders saw how acceptable a Chinese doctor was to wider society, they encouraged their children to study medicine. James Ng, who came

Tng Sai Tin (left), Lim Hwee Kheng and Lee Seok Cheng, Colombo Plan students from Singapore, received home science diplomas in 1970. They are pictured with Patricia Coleman, home science dean, outside Studholme.

FACULTY OF CONSUMER AND APPLIED SCIENCES RECORDS, 97-081/008, S17-610F, HOCKEN COLLECTIONS.

from Ashburton to study medicine in 1954, was 'at the tail end of the first wave' of New Zealand Chinese university students. His parents were initially reluctant about tertiary study – they thought business offered better opportunities – but Law's success changed their minds. Douglas Ngan Kee of Whanganui became the first Chinese dental graduate in 1950. The health sciences continued to attract Chinese students, as did mining and home science; a smaller group, mostly southerners, studied arts and law.[56] Statistics on ethnicity are first available from 1986 when there were 274 New Zealand-born or resident Asians on the Otago roll; together with 164 Asian international students they made up nearly 6 per cent of the student body.[57]

The Colombo Plan, a 1950 agreement between various Commonwealth countries to promote economic and social development in Asia and the Pacific, brought the first large wave of around 3500 international students to New Zealand from the 1950s to the 1970s. Otago's first Colombo Plan students arrived in the early 1950s, and numbers gradually increased.[58] In 1965 more than half of Otago's 160 international students came from Asia, many of them on the Colombo scheme.[59] Most lived in residential colleges for at least part of their course, so the government funded an extension to Arana Hall; its Colombo Wing opened in 1968. However, the government wanted international students integrated into the community; they were spread around all the residential colleges, and enjoyed the hospitality of New Zealand host families during the holidays. Arriving in Dunedin, with its temperate climate, could be a shock for students from other countries, and in the 1950s many New Zealanders were unaccustomed to the presence of 'foreigners' and tended to treat anybody who spoke another language with suspicion. Fortunately, there were others who welcomed the visitors, and the students certainly appreciated the opportunity to learn about Kiwi culture.[60]

Competition for Colombo Plan scholarships was fierce, and it brought some especially bright minds to Otago. Mazlan Othman, who arrived in the early 1970s as an undergraduate science student, became the first woman to complete a PhD in physics at Otago. She threw herself into student life, enjoyed all the capping events, attended protest rallies, played in a band, worked in a restaurant, visited the mountains and enjoyed long discussions at the pub with other students. Othman returned to Malaysia to teach and later became director of the United Nations Office for Outer Space Affairs.[61] Soedjati Djiwandono, who studied education, politics and languages at Otago before completing postgraduate studies in London, became a distinguished political scientist in Indonesia.[62] The connections made through the Colombo Plan had a long impact on the university – the goodwill built up during that period encouraged further generations of international students to enrol at Otago. Malaysians were the largest group of Otago Colombo Plan students, and they were still conspicuous on the later international student roll. Indeed, Otago's links with Malaysia extended back to before the Colombo Plan: John Mackie, professor of surveying, wrote that the close relationship 'must have sprung originally from the comparatively large number of graduates of the School of Mines who worked in the mining industry there from around the 1920s'.[63] Sulaiman bin Haji Daud, who graduated in dental studies at Otago in 1962 and went on to become a leading Malaysian politician in various portfolios including education and health, was a great advocate for Otago.[64]

THE RISE OF WOMEN

In 1986 a milestone occurred at Otago: women students outnumbered men for the first time. The shift in the gender balance started in the 1970s, in the midst of second-wave feminism. As greater employment opportunities opened to women and paid work became, for many, a lasting commitment rather than a brief experience ended by marriage or childbearing, more turned to university study. Some were interested in professions that were traditionally dominated by men, such as accountancy and medicine. The proportion of women students varied enormously in different parts of the university. David Thomson, a history student in 1986 and now director of the Planning and Funding Office, recalls being one of just two men in a pioneering class on women's history, 'within a faculty where men had been in the minority for years'.[65] Indeed, in 1986 women made up 69 per cent of arts students, 56 per cent of physical education students – and 100 per cent of students in the Home Science Faculty, which attracted only the occasional male student. Men still narrowly outnumbered women in law (47 per cent female) and medicine (44 per cent), though not for long. The gap was wider in the other faculties: 38 per cent of science students, 37 per cent of commerce and dentistry students and 34 per cent of theology students were women that year. Some of the faculties with lower proportions of women had, in fact, experienced the biggest change: 10 years earlier, just 18 per cent of commerce students were female.[66]

Even within the faculties there were big – and persistent – gender differences. Although women outnumbered men as science students from the late 1990s, there was a distinction between the physical sciences (more popular with men) and the biological sciences (more popular with women). This stemmed from the subject choices made at high school, which then affected options for tertiary studies. Among Otago students who completed undergraduate science degrees in 2015, fewer than a third majoring in physics, applied geology, information science, computer science, chemistry, geology and maths were female, whereas women were in the majority in all the biological science majors and, especially, in consumer food science, human nutrition, food science and reproduction, genetics and development.[67] As Thomson notes, Otago's strength in the biological and health sciences attracts many women students, while the absence of an engineering school means that people drawn to that male-dominated profession may opt to go elsewhere to study the physical sciences.[68] In fact, in 2015 all New Zealand universities except Lincoln had more female than male students, but only Auckland University of Technology had a higher proportion of women than Otago.[69]

The increase in women students created some tension. Elworthy, in his history of OUSA, described the division of campus into 'two cultures'

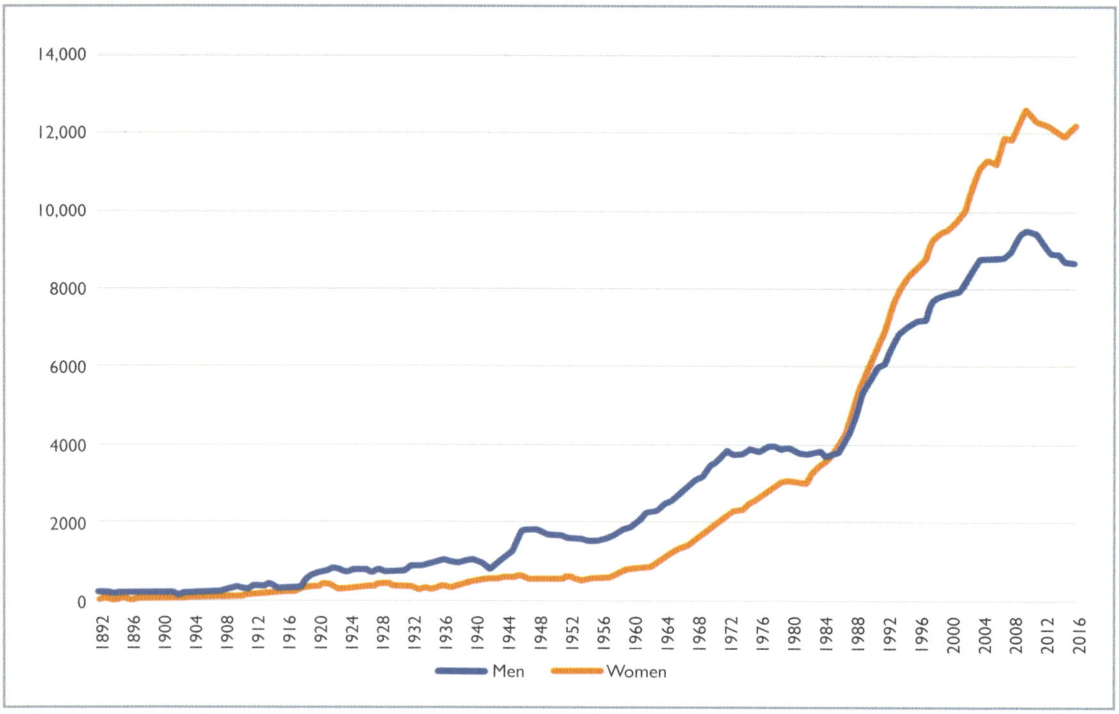

University of Otago enrolments by gender, 1892–2016.

SOURCE: UNIVERSITY OF OTAGO ANNUAL REPORTS, SUPPLEMENTED BY UNIVERSITY OF OTAGO STUDENT STATISTICS. COURTESY OF UNIVERSITY OF OTAGO PLANNING AND FUNDING OFFICE.

in the early 1980s: the 'traditional' student culture of 'Capping, drinking and initiations' and a more radical opposing culture. 'The division was almost even and the battles were epic.' Many women 'who would not necessarily have identified themselves as feminists' entered male strongholds such as the Medical School and all-male residential colleges; that 'sharpened more general anxieties over gender roles and injected a peculiar intensity of feeling into the battles over the [Springbok rugby] tour, Capping and the women's room.'[70]

LATER INTERNATIONAL STUDENTS

The Colombo Plan was not purely altruistic: it formed part of a cold war-era strategy to stem the spread of communism in Asia. It did focus, however, on improving the fortunes of less developed countries. Private overseas students sat alongside their Colombo Plan compatriots; they paid the same fees as New Zealanders and were thus subsidised, but many people viewed that as another contribution to development in the Asia–Pacific region. Some stayed on in New Zealand as well-qualified migrants.[71]

As the communist 'threat' declined, New Zealand's foreign policy shifted. The commitment to the Colombo Plan was wound back, but a steady rise in international students continued. Questions arose about subsidising the education of wealthy international students. Government and the universities set quotas as resources became stretched: Otago did so in 1971 when overseas students exceeded 8 per cent of the total roll. There was pressure from other countries to raise quotas, and they did increase – but so did fees for international students. In 1979 the government announced a $1500 fee for private international students (those from the Pacific were exempt).[72] Otago VC Robin Irvine expressed concern: in the previous year, 208 of the university's 289

Top source countries of Otago international students

YEAR (total internat'l students)	1965 (162)	1975 (379)	1985 (240)	1995 (908)	2005 (2720)	2015 (2592)
1	Malaya	Malaysia	Malaysia	Malaysia	China	US
2	Fiji	Fiji	Fiji	US	US	China
3	Sabah	Australia	Samoa	Fiji	Malaysia	Malaysia
4	Thailand	Samoa	US	Germany	Germany	India
5	Australia	Canada (5=)	Singapore	Hong Kong	Hong Kong	Britain
6	Hong Kong (6=)	Thailand (5=)	Indonesia (6=)	Singapore	Canada	Germany
7	Sarawak (6=)	Hong Kong	Tonga (6=)	Japan	Korea	Iran
8	Singapore (6=)	Singapore (8=)	India	Samoa (8=)	Japan	Brunei
9	Uganda	Britain (8=)	Hong Kong (9=)	Thailand (8=)	Singapore	Canada
10	Nigeria	US (8=)	Niue (9=)	Tonga (8=)	Thailand	Saudi Arabia

SOURCE: OVERSEAS STUDENTS BY COUNTRY OF ORIGIN, UNIVERSITY GRANTS COMMITTEE RECORDS, R12485704, ARCHIVES NEW ZEALAND, WELLINGTON (1965–1975 FIGURES); UNIVERSITY OF OTAGO ENROLMENT STATISTICS, 1985, COURTESY OF UNIVERSITY OF OTAGO PLANNING AND FUNDING OFFICE; UNIVERSITY OF OTAGO ANNUAL REPORTS, 1995–2015.

overseas students were private; only 53 of those came from the Pacific and many others were 'in the senior student or postgraduate segment from which we derive considerable benefit, especially in the research field'.[73] International enrolments declined, but from 1982, despite the fees, they recovered slightly before taking off spectacularly in the 1990s.[74] The government removed subsidies for international students and tertiary education was reconceptualised as an export that brought economic benefits to the country, in line with the neoliberal reforms of the era.[75] In 1988 the UGC noted that several universities had 'accepted with enthusiasm' the 'opportunity presented by a full fee foreign student market'. Concerns that that might disadvantage New Zealand students were countered by the argument that the additional income could be used for facilities that would benefit all.[76] International students became more important in the efforts of universities to balance their books.

Through the 1980s and 1990s Otago sought exchange agreements with overseas institutions and, by 2000, it had arrangements with 53 individual universities, including 11 added that year, ranging from Finland and Scotland to Japan and China. In 2000, 59 Otago students headed away on exchange and 62 overseas students spent time at Otago. The exchange figures were dwarfed by others – the 1116 international students that year made up 6.5 per cent of Otago's total roll.[77] The goal set in the 1990s of recruiting international students as 10 per cent of the student body was reached in 2003; as the international contingent kept rising the council set a policy that limited international students to 12 per cent of the roll.[78] Tertiary education minister Steven Joyce later criticised the cap as 'very low', but it meant Otago was less affected than other New Zealand universities during a widespread drop in international enrolments in the mid-2000s. As the government continued to push internationalisation as a source of funding, Otago lifted its cap and, by 2015, was aiming to recruit 15 per cent of its roll from overseas.[79]

The international student market was susceptible to changing political and economic conditions in the countries involved, and Otago faced mounting competition from other tertiary institutions around the world. Malaysian enrolments dropped in the wake of the Asian financial crisis of 1997, when their government axed tax concessions for overseas study. At their high point, in 1996, there were 771 Malaysian students at Otago, accounting for 67 per cent of international students; they hit a low of 118, just 6 per cent of the total, in 2003. They subsequently recovered, but meanwhile Otago was increasingly recruiting students from China, with a leap from single figures in 1999 to a peak of 700 – a quarter of the international roll – in 2005. Other students came from a diverse range of countries, including in Europe, Asia and the Pacific, as always, and an expanding group from South America and the Middle East.[80]

Overall, the largest group of international students on campus after 2000 came from the United States. Enrolments escalated after 1992 when Otago joined the Study Abroad programme run by Butler University – a small liberal arts college in Indianapolis that acted as agent for dozens of other US tertiary institutions. Otago joined at the suggestion of the president of the Institute of Study Abroad, 1960s Otago geography graduate Geoffrey Bannister. By 1999 Otago was hosting around 110 students on the Butler programme and around 120 independent students from the United States. Overseas student adviser Laurel Gilks noted that the Americans were 'bright' students, 'very outspoken, articulate and confident, so it's beneficial for our students to rub shoulders with them'.[81] Harlene Hayne met with former Otago students on a 2016 trip to the United States; she noted that they were 'thrilled by our great outdoors' and that 'the opportunity to learn more about Māori culture left a lasting impression on them'. Studying at Otago was no sinecure, though. Hayne reported that US students found the academic standards higher than they were accustomed to and the expectation that they should 'take responsibility for their own learning' was 'initially a bit daunting' to many. Still, they encouraged her to 'jealously guard our standards in the wake of an increasingly customer-focused approach to university education'.[82]

Hayne's visit was one of many overseas visits made by Otago leaders as the university developed and nurtured relationships with institutions and governments and its own alumni around the world in order to advance research links as well as student recruitment. It also rolled out the red carpet for visiting dignitaries. The International Office emerged in the 1990s: it was responsible for the pastoral care of international students, and it took over the administrative burden of admissions, liaison, student recruitment and the organisation of exchanges.[83]

COSTS AND OPPORTUNITIES

Increasing access to education was one of the main contributors to growth at Otago. Working-class families were always underrepresented on its student roll, especially in the early decades. In the 1800s and early 1900s few New Zealanders attended high school, let alone university; once they reached the age of 13 most children had to work and contribute to the family economy. From 1903 children who passed the proficiency exam were entitled to two years of free secondary education, with additional 'free' years for those who passed further exams, but high school was still for only a minority. The ambitious might attend night classes after work to further their education. The gaps in education levels narrowed in the 1930s when the government abolished 'proficiency' and opened free secondary schooling to all children who completed primary school; and when the official school-leaving age was raised to 15 in 1944, secondary education became the norm and more young people had the opportunity to study for matriculation – renamed university entrance.[84]

Although there were fewer educational and cultural barriers to higher education, there were still financial barriers. Fees varied greatly through the years. The foundation students at Otago paid fees of £3 3s for each subject plus a £1 entrance fee – a total of around £10 9s ($1500 in 2018 values) for three subjects.[85] By 1920 tuition fees had not altered, though examination fees payable to the University of New Zealand cost an extra guinea per subject and, from 1890, there was an additional fee for OUSA membership. Taking inflation into account, even with these additions the real cost of a full-time arts course had dropped by almost half.

Specialist degrees cost more. The 1920 university calendar advised that the total of all fees for a five-year medical degree came to £177 9s ($16,300 in 2018 values), provided it was completed in the minimum time. At the same time a four-year dentistry degree would set a student back £120 15s ($11,000) and a four-year home science degree cost just under half that. Fees rose and fell in real terms over the next few decades; in 1968 they reached their highest level to date. The 1970s and 1980s were decades of high inflation, but tuition fees rose very little, meaning a marked decline in real costs; by 1989 compulsory annual fees for an arts degree were at their lowest ever level.[86] In 1990 tuition fees quadrupled overnight due to government reforms; 'user pays' was the mantra of the age. The next government steadily reduced the level of funding per student, leaving universities no choice but to increase their fees. By 2000 tuition costs to students had doubled again, and they have continued to rise steadily since. One rationale behind the reduction in government funding per student was to offer more places to students, and to make tertiary education more widely available: that was achieved, but at a cost to students.[87] In 1993 retiring VC Robin Irvine noted that fees were 'now a fact of academic life but there is no doubt that they deter some, possibly many, able people from furthering their education'.[88]

On the other side of the ledger was government support for students, which varied greatly through the decades. In 1970 Lindsay Wright, an Otago philosophy graduate and research officer for the New Zealand University Students' Association, commented that 'our university students tend to be drawn from the more privileged section of New Zealand society'. In 1969 the fathers of nearly half the students worked in professional, administrative, executive, or managerial occupations; only 17 per cent of fathers were in a manual occupation. The level of financial assistance offered to students placed 'often insuperable barriers in front of the talented sons and daughters of our less affluent members of society', said Wright.[89] Government financial support was already higher than it had been. There were always scholarships for the most gifted students, but life was harder for the average student. In 1907 the government introduced

Brothers Ian (left) and Alan Chirnside, from a large working-class family, started working at the Dental School as technicians in their early teens. The brothers, pictured here around 1924, decided to become dentists, but as they had no secondary schooling they first had to study for matriculation at night classes; after years of hard work Alan graduated in dentistry in 1938 and Ian in 1940. Ian later taught at the Dental School and retired in the 1970s; he had evolved from junior lackey to associate professor, complete with doctorate. ANNABEL RAYNER COLLECTION.

FEES
MUST
GO!
EXTREME

bursaries that paid tuition for those who obtained credit in its scholarship exam, but the scholarships were still awarded only to the few with the highest exam marks. Over the next 50 years government provisions evolved and by 1959 – the year of the Parry Report, produced by a committee appointed by the minister of education to make recommendations on the future of university education in New Zealand – there was an array of schemes that offered financial assistance to about 60 per cent of New Zealand students. The level of support was low, however; many received only the cost of all or part of tuition fees, with no living allowance. Meanwhile, generous grants to cover tuition and living costs were paid to those on a teacher studentship – a scheme that bonded the recipients to government teaching service. The report stated that 'more generous general bursaries are required in order to induce more young people to forgo immediate earning power and undertake full-time university study'. Dropout rates were high, exacerbated by the numerous part-timers, who accounted for just under half of all New Zealand university students.[90] Thanks to its special schools, where full-time study was mandatory, Otago had fewer part-timers than other universities, but there were still plenty; in its early decades the university was sometimes known as 'the night school on the Leith'.[91]

From 1962 a more generous University Bursaries scheme paid the tuition fees of most students admitted to university. In addition, full-time students with Higher Leaving Certificate (awarded on the completion of a fourth year of high school), and those who did not have the certificate but who passed a first-year course received a bursary. With the addition of holiday earnings most students could survive on the bursary. This meant full-time study became more accessible – especially for men; women were paid about half the amount that men were paid for holiday work. By 1969, 81 per cent of Otago students were full-timers – and they stayed at over 75 per cent until the late 1980s. The 1962 bursary scheme carried on with minor modifications until 1989, although payments did not keep pace with inflation and holiday work was not always readily available.[92] Economic reform ended the bursary scheme: from 1989 students received a less generous student allowance that was means-tested according to parental income.

In 1992 the government set up the student loan scheme, which enabled students who were liable for rapidly mounting tuition fees to borrow from the government to fund their study. The scheme charged students interest on their loans after they ended their studies; from 2006 the loans were made interest-free for those who stayed in New Zealand. Over time, students complained about the inadequacy of the student allowance; they were forced to borrow to cover living costs as well as fees, and many accumulated large debts. Part-time study became more prevalent: the proportion of full-time students at Otago dropped through the 1990s and reached a low point of just under 69 per cent in 2002.[93]

Opposite: An Otago student protest against rising fees, 28 September 1993. OUSA campaigned vigorously against the rising cost of education, as did students all over the country, to little effect.
OUSA RECORDS, AG-540/011, S15-500A, HOCKEN COLLECTIONS.

THE TWENTY-FIRST-CENTURY OTAGO STUDENT

Students of the twenty-first century were far more diverse than their predecessors. Although many of the early students were born overseas, part of a migrant generation, most came from somewhere in the British Empire and almost all were white. By contrast, the cohort this century includes students from all over the world and of many ethnicities. Māori and Pacific Island students are still underrepresented when compared with the overall population, but their numbers are rising rapidly; indeed, students at Otago from 2013 to 2015 were more likely to be Māori than were their University of Auckland counterparts (even though the much larger Auckland roll had a higher Māori head count).[94] By 2000, Otago had over 1000 students who identified as Māori, representing 6.2 per cent of the roll, and that rose to 8.9 per cent in 2016 thanks to higher Māori engagement with tertiary education and Otago's recruitment and support of Māori. Meanwhile, the percentage of students at Otago who identified as Pacific Islanders doubled, from 2.1 per cent in 2000 to 4.2 per cent in 2016; that, too, was the result of more active engagement with Pacific communities and targeted recruitment and support. Asians – who, like Pacific Islanders, were a mix of local and international students – accounted for 19.2 per cent of the roll in 2016, and 3.4 per cent of students identified as Middle Eastern, Latin American or African.[95]

Other standout differences from earlier periods were the high proportion of women among Otago students and, most marked of all, the size of the student body, which swelled from 50 students in 1874 to a high of 22,139 in 2010. With every decade, the roll increased – though at varying rates. The growth rate was greatest in the 1910s when the size of the student body more than doubled, largely because of opportunities for higher education offered to World War I returned servicemen. Growth flattened in the 1920s, the decade of least expansion. It was particularly high in the 1960s, when the roll doubled again as the first of the baby-boomer generation reached their late teens, and enhanced government support made university study more affordable. In both the 1980s and the 2000s the roll grew by over 4000, but the biggest growth was in the 1990s when it jumped by almost 6000.[96]

Otago faced an unfamiliar scenario when, starting in 2011, the roll declined for five successive years; the decades of sustained growth had ended. The lower roll resulted partly from demography, as cohorts of school leavers in New Zealand diminished. The increase in availability of employment played a part, too, as did variations in international enrolments. A policy of attracting students from a wide range of countries reduced the risk of sudden drops due to changes in one part of the world, but the international market could be fickle.

In the end, a major factor in changes in the roll was Otago's choice to focus on quality rather than quantity: it did not want to grow ever larger, but it did want to be the best. David Skegg noted in 2005 that a small decline in the roll that year would 'provide an opportunity for consolidation: while we are keen to maintain the quality and diversity of our student population, the rapid growth during the 1980s and 1990s posed significant challenges'. In order to recruit 'students of the highest calibre' the university added more postgraduate scholarships and launched undergrad scholarships for '30 promising Māori and Pacific Islands secondary school students' and 'the dux of every New Zealand secondary school'.[97] Ninety school duxes, including one from Niue, took up the scholarship in 2006. That same year Skegg announced another incentive: the Leaders of Tomorrow scholarship for 50 students 'who have shown leadership potential at school or through their contributions to the wider community'.[98]

When enrolments surged again at the end of the decade the council decided that in 2011 it would limit entry to all undergraduate programmes, not just the long-restricted professional courses. It was the only way, Hayne said, to face 'the dual challenge of a burgeoning student roll and constrained government funding, together with our own strategic commitment to recruiting a higher proportion of "top calibre" students'.[99] In 2014 the New Zealand Qualifications Authority raised the standard of university entrance in response to concerns about high dropout and failure rates among students who were ill equipped for university study – and that further reduced the pool of potential students.[100] Otago was 'holding firm' on the more stringent standard, Hayne noted, when enrolment figures were announced in 2015.[101] Of course, it was not the only university trying to recruit the best students. In 2015, for instance, Canterbury attracted attention when it offered top

Māori health science students at a tutorial in the Māori Centre, 2000.
MĀORI CENTRE TE HUKA MĀTAURAKA COLLECTION.

Auckland students free ski trips, rugby tickets and accommodation scholarships.[102] In an environment of 'intense competition', that same year Otago announced additional first-year scholarships and boosted the funding for existing ones.[103] 'We do not want financial hardship to be a barrier to young people with potential and are committed to providing opportunities for high achievers,' Hayne wrote.[104]

Those changes meant the average student of the twenty-first century had higher credentials than those of earlier generations.[105] Returning students had higher standards to reach, too: through the years the university had added more support for strugglers, but it also developed a lower tolerance for failure and, in 2009, it put in place a tougher academic progress policy.[106] Students in the new millennium were more likely to be postgraduates: in 2007 the university held a gala ball at Larnach Castle to celebrate the milestone of enrolling over 1000 PhD students in one year.[107] Students of a century earlier could not have imagined such an event – the University of New Zealand introduced the PhD degree in 1922, but it ran into problems thanks to a requirement for full-time study and was soon abolished; just nine people graduated, including three from Otago. After World War II, as the country came to value the research work of universities, the PhD was reintroduced – this time to stay. It took a while for the prejudice against 'colonial' degrees to die down, but eventually the best scholars no longer felt compelled to travel overseas for doctoral work, and candidates came from other countries to study at Otago; by 2008 around a third of PhD students were international.[108]

Studying in the relaxed atmosphere of the Pacific Islands Centre, 2011.

GRAHAM WARMAN PHOTOGRAPH, UNIVERSITY OF OTAGO MARKETING AND COMMUNICATIONS COLLECTION.

After the devolution of the scholarships that had been run nationally by the UGC, Otago committed heavily to providing postgraduate financial support: in 1995 it granted 97 scholarships to PhD candidates and 89 to masters students, more than any other New Zealand university.[109] This was part of a policy to increase the proportion of postgrads on the roll; they accounted for 15 per cent of Otago students that year.[110] In 1996 Paul Theivananthampillai became the 1000th person to graduate with a PhD from Otago. Like many others he was already a staff member there: he completed his study while lecturing in the Accountancy Department.[111] The next 1000 Otago PhD graduates took just nine years to produce. A reduction in the number of years of government financial support to students made scholarships critical. The additional scholarships that Otago provided attracted high-performing students and, by 2015, one in five people on its roll were postgraduates.[112]

CHAPTER THREE

Student life

A light-hearted 1993 article in *More* magazine compared New Zealand's seven universities and found that the best thing about Otago was its campus life (the worst thing was 'the cold'). Otago was ranked as one of the friendlier universities and, while a 'good night out' at all seven institutions involved drinking, Otago had the benefit of great music: 'expect to be run down by marauding students, high on Speights and the latest alternative band'.[1] For some, Otago's extracurricular activities were as big an attraction as its academic standing.

A CORPORATE LIFE?

Sam Elworthy notes that it took time for students at New Zealand's first university to establish a common culture, or '*esprit de corps*', as they called it. They were inspired by student traditions overseas and wanted to establish a firm identity in the face of some local scepticism about higher education.[2] Foundation student Alexander Williamson recalled: 'there was very little corporate life in the Varsity in those days. We seemed to see very little of one another outside class hours'. Work and study left little time for a social life, and 'the professors were quick to let anyone see that they would stand no idling'. The only 'social' activities, wrote Williamson, were 'Professor Black's geological tramps, when we explored various places of geological interest in the neighborhood of Dunedin'.[3] The foundation students also played team sports; they organised football and cricket matches in their first year. During the 1880s graduation, popularly known as capping, became a festive and rowdy occasion and a focus for public display of student 'culture'. The first official student group was the Debating Society, established in 1878. It met once a fortnight for formal debates and informal discussions, and that soon became an important social gathering.[4] Older students who were concerned about the 'larrikin' element at Debating Society meetings, which featured noisy choruses and crude humour, decided to form a responsible association to run student activities and represent their interests with the staff and university authorities: in May 1890 they established the Otago University Students Association.[5]

A PLACE FOR WOMEN

In its early years OUSA was 'rather staid', says Elworthy, and its respectability won it the favour of university authorities. It negotiated various benefits for students, sponsored clubs and societies, and organised social events. One of its first actions was to get better spaces where students could relax. They previously had one dingy, cold room, but with a levy on students and support from the council, OUSA refurbished it as the men's common room and acquired a women's common room as well. For years nobody blinked at such gender separation. In contrast, when a women's room was set up in 1983 it was criticised in a backlash against feminism. First-wave feminism caused ructions a century earlier: men didn't like it when women hissed and played castanets during their speeches in a debate on women's franchise in 1907 – though women speakers often attracted catcalling.[6] Debating remained one of the most active clubs on campus. Pearl Jennings, who signed up as a student in 1904, recalled it as 'a flourishing activity that enticed the unwary to enter its portals; for not every student could afford the time outside study-time to indulge in argumentation. However, the announcement of a popular Debate assured the promoters of a "full house".'[7]

The OUSA executive included representatives of various faculties (medicine, mining, arts, and so on), but women had a separate student faculty of their own. Initially the women's representatives on OUSA were male. From 1894 they could elect female representatives but they did not do so until 1902, when Elsie Roberts and Florence Bressey became the first female members of the OUSA executive.[8] By the 1910s the women's faculty was 'a strong and well organized body possessing considerable influence in student affairs', Agnes Blackie recalled. In their own common room, Blackie noted, women entertained 'any interesting women who visited Dunedin. Several times a year a most popular women students get-together called a Kahanga provided a hilarious evening when we enjoyed the now seemingly lost art of just having fun.' Women 'had a wide range of friends in all faculties and a vigorous and enjoyable life of their own, independent of male co-operation.'[9] Despite those advantages, in 1920 the women students dissolved their faculty and became members of their respective faculty associations; there was some resistance to this from male medical and dental students who did not want women joining their rowdy organisations. The restructured OUSA executive included men and women vice-presidents elected by general ballot; the latter were popularly known as 'lady vice'.[10] In 2006 OUSA, which bestowed life membership on its former presidents, extended the privilege to Nola Holmes (née Ross) as a representative of 'all of the women who served OUSA on the executive and in assisting roles since our beginnings whose contributions, before the 1980s, were largely unacknowledged'.[11] Ross, the lady vice-president in 1947, was remembered for holding the association together when the president resigned.[12]

BUILDING A UNION

OUSA's first campaign was to improve student facilities but they soon became inadequate. 'Certainly nothing is more urgently required by us at the present time than a suitable building for the use of students,' wrote Thomas Gilray, chair of the Professorial Board, in 1908.[13] The University Council had no funds to spare. Students raised money at carnivals and Gilray harnessed community support. The 'ladies of Dunedin' raised a large sum at a 1909 bazaar; it was then time, said Gilray, 'for the men of the community to do something'. Local worthies donated generous sums, led off by the chancellor, James Allen – an influential parliamentarian who persuaded the prime minister, Southlander Joseph Ward, to commit the government to a generous subsidy, contributing £2 for every £1 raised.[14] One celebrity donor was Antarctic explorer Ernest Shackleton, who donated the proceeds of a public lecture to the student building fund.[15] Finally, in 1914 the governor of New Zealand, Lord Liverpool, opened Otago's first Student Union and wished students 'the best of luck, frivolity and joy'. Dunedin's mayor, former student William Downie Stewart, was reported as saying that men and women students would be able to have afternoon tea 'in company … an undreamt of luxury in his day'. The

The building contained an assembly hall (named Allen Hall in recognition of the chancellor's contribution to the project and the university), executive room, men's and women's common rooms, dressing rooms, bathrooms, a 'buffet' (canteen) and 'other accessories of an up-to-date building'. It became a venue for occasions both formal and informal, for meetings, dances and all sorts of 'frivolity and joy'.[16]

There were around 600 students at Otago when the Student Union opened, but as numbers crept up it became crowded; by the 1940s students were squashed in shoulder to shoulder at dances, and it was difficult to fit everybody in when there was a large meeting. After another long period of planning and fundraising, a University Union, jointly run by OUSA and the university, opened in 1960. It expanded along with the roll: it acquired another storey in 1969 and, in 1986, an extension towards Cumberland Street replaced the 'crumbling North House'.[17]

OUSA obtained further facilities for sports and other services. The Clubs and Societies Centre, opened in 1980, was a million-dollar investment; and OUSA acquired the University Book Shop (UBS) 'in what is possibly the greatest corporate takeover ever', suggests Kyle Matthews. UBS was founded in 1945 by the Presbyterian Bookroom and a group of university people convened by chaplain Harold Turner. It was sold to John Griffin in 1956 and then to Whitcombe and Tombs in 1962. In 1975 OUSA sought to purchase a half-share of UBS but was turned down; it threatened to start its own competing bookstore with volunteer labour. Whitcombe and Tombs gave in and OUSA became half-owner without paying any money upfront; its profits went towards the purchase price, which it paid off within a few years. OUSA later bought out the company's share and became full owner.[18] It was an uncharacteristically bold move by OUSA; most of its assets were acquired through membership fees and building levies – a source that disappeared when membership of OUSA became voluntary in 2011.

FOOD, GLORIOUS FOOD

The Union provided cheap meals for students. Neil Howard, a 1950s student, recalled that after English tutorials 'we continued them in the OUSA canteen over the archway presided over by the very efficient and friendly Mrs Harrison. We argued on before the roaring coke stoves with a sixpenny cup of coffee.'[19] When the University Union opened in 1960 it had just one food supply – the cafeteria, which offered 'an attractive, reasonably-priced three-course lunch' as well as morning and afternoon tea.[20] As the building expanded other options were added, including three meals a day in the main cafeteria, a coffee bar in the basement and the Terrace Dining Room on the top floor. The treats on offer in 1976 included curried lamb, sausages and chips or the more extravagant steak. For the adventurous there were chicken chow mein or Hungarian goulash, and the hard-up could choose a filled roll or a pie in a bag.[21] A major facelift in 1995 turned the old cafeteria into a food court featuring the Wok Factory, Lunch Pail, Burger Inc. and the Coffee Mill.[22] There are now various options with cafés in modern buildings such as the Link, the St David Building, the University Plaza and the Hunter Centre.

Of course, there were iconic student food haunts beyond the Union cafeteria. Sylvia Norie, who lived at residential college Studholme in the 1920s, recalled 'a little tuck shop' in Union Street, 'owned by a dear old body called Mrs Gollan. She made delectable custard tarts and fly cemeteries and we were very good customers … We often went down to fill in the cracks after a balanced dinner. Consequently we all put on weight despite getting up at 6am to practise for the basketball and hockey teams.'[23] The 'fresher five' – the five pounds (later five kilograms) acquired by new students – has a long history. There were small shops on nearly every corner until the university expanded into the blocks of housing adjoining its original buildings.[24] Many of the eating places recommended by the 1975 student handbook have gone: the Sirocco in Lower Dowling Street was

The Tui Café in Albany Street, popularly known as Joe Tui's, was 'famed in campus lore and legend – but no reported deaths!', according to the 1975 student handbook. Opened in 1970, it was a student staple for takeaways until 2005. It had a successor further down Albany Street in the Flying Squid, where queues formed to buy chips. Photographed in 1973.

CITY ENGINEER'S ALBUM - CUMBERLAND/CASTLE STREET DEVIATION, DUNEDIN CITY COUNCIL ARCHIVES.

'one of the City's better coffee shops', Big Daddy's in the Octagon was 'Great for a hot pie at 6am' and the Kandel-Light Coffee Lounge at St Clair was 'a great place for evening coffee'. Other 1970s haunts – Potpourri, the Best Café and the Savoy – survived.[25] Another notable survivor is Governor's Café, established in 1977 by Paul Gourlie to help fund his way through university. Gourlie, who dressed in a tail suit and a cape and was known as the Governor, served as OUSA president in 1979 and 1980.[26]

RELIGIOUS GROUPS

Besides OUSA, the largest student society for many years was the Christian Union (CU). It was inspired by the World Student Christian Federation, started in Sweden in 1895; a tour by its secretary John Mott 'created great enthusiasm' and the Otago branch, set up in 1896, was one of several in New Zealand. The union's lofty goal was 'world evangelisation'; it aimed to prepare students 'as future Christian leaders and missionaries'.[27] The CU, which became the Student Christian Movement (SCM), was 'a very active body' in the 1910s. It held weekly meetings and retreats at East Taieri a couple of times a year, and many members attended the national summer conference. About 200 people belonged to the SCM bible study circles, which met weekly. Monthly social evenings with music, games and competitions were important occasions for students who held religious scruples against dancing.[28] Some outsiders mocked the CU 'as a front for "smooging"', and later generations joked that SCM stood for 'students contemplating marriage' and that TSCF (Tertiary Students' Christian Fellowship) stood for 'the search for a Christian fiancé'.[29] TSCF – originally the Evangelical Union (EU) – developed out of the Inter-Varsity Fellowship, a British organisation. Its travelling secretary Howard Guinness visited New Zealand in 1930; his visit inspired conservatives at Otago and other universities to break away from SCM and form their own groups. Some 'disaffected evangelicals', unhappy at the growing liberalism of the SCM, had already set up a small group that became the basis of Otago's EU.[30]

The SCM and EU were rivals, but both were Protestant groups. Catholics had their own organisation, the Catholic Students' Club (later known as the Catholic Students' Society or CathSoc), established late in 1921 as 'the first of its kind in New Zealand'. Its main objectives were 'the fostering generally of a Catholic spirit and the promotion of the social life among the members'. Like its Protestant counterparts, it ran social gatherings, evenings with discussion and speakers (often but not always Catholic clergy) and religious worship.[31] It was another place where students might find romance: author Dan Davin and Winnie Gonley met at a Catholic students' social in 1931. Their friend Teddy McCullough, a medical student, recalled such occasions: 'Admission strictly Ticket only. Price a florin to include Homemade scones, jam and cakes. Speights beer from the keg at 3d a glass extra.'[32]

Student involvement in religious groups slowly declined, although religious diversity increased with the boom in international students from the 1950s: many students from overseas were Christian, but others were Muslim, Hindu and other faiths. It wasn't always easy for them to practise their religion in Dunedin. By 1995 there were about 100 Muslim students on campus; they formed an association and met for prayer as well as sports tournaments, Islam Awareness Week, day trips and annual camps.[33] The first mosque in southern New Zealand, Masjid Al-Huda, opened in 2000 in Clyde Street, a handy location for students, who made up a big part of Dunedin's Muslim community.[34] Other groups emerged in the 1970s as young New Zealanders became interested in Eastern religions: for instance, the Ananda Marga Yoga Club taught 'meditation, yoga, yoga philosophy, health practices etc.', and the Students' International Meditation Society offered 'the Transcendental Meditation Programme founded by his Holiness Moharishi Mohesh Yogi'.[35] By the 2010s Otago students could join Baha'i, Jewish or Sikh clubs, a Shamanic Circle or the Society of Atheists, Rationalists and Skeptics. In addition to old favourites like CathSoc and SCM, there was an array of Christian groups to cover every shade of theology. Alongside that diversity sat the Otago Students Interfaith Group, with a mission 'to promote peace and understanding between all faiths/spiritual groups by encouraging respect and dialogue'.[36]

A SPORTING UNIVERSITY

Sport played a big part in Otago student life. The first serious sporting fixture involved rugby, though it was a different game from the one played today. In September 1871 Otago's 81 students mustered a team of 22 for a game of football against Otago Boys' High School; the game extended over several hours and two Saturdays and was a draw, with each side scoring one goal. George Sale, the classics professor and an old boy of Rugby School in England, played alongside the students, and in 1872 he became inaugural president of the Dunedin Football Club, the first in town. By the early 1880s there were several clubs in the district, and the university formed its own club in 1884. Other clubs were unhappy at losing some of their best players and refused to play 'Varsity' teams for several years. In 1886 the Varsity team played a match against a university team from Canterbury and finally, in 1887, regular matches against other local senior teams commenced.[37]

The first cricket match involving a university team took place in October 1871 against the Citizens Cricket Club. Cricket historian George Griffiths described that match as 'archetypal': it 'began disgracefully late, two selected players failed to turn up, and University were resoundingly beaten'. Still, it was impressive 'that cricket had been played at all'. Enthusiasts formed a University of Otago Cricket Club in 1876 but it lasted only three seasons; a second attempt survived from 1895 to 1900. The university scratched together teams for matches against other institutions, then in the 1930s it again formed a club that played regularly in the local competition.[38]

Tennis was another favourite: it needed few people, and men and women could play together. In 1884 students petitioned the University Council for a tennis court and it duly obliged; the students formed a tennis club and within a couple of years raised funds for a second court. It was a competitive as well as a social pursuit, with matches against other clubs and, starting in 1887, an annual match against Canterbury College.[39] Otago women students were early

The Otago University Cycling Club, c. 1897. The club was established in 1896 in response to a growing interest in the bicycle as transport. Cycling technology was making big advances, but it would be many years before bikes acquired gears, which may explain why the first road race followed an 18-mile (29km) route around the Taieri Plains. The club held '7 successful runs' in its first year.

MOLLER BROTHERS PHOTOGRAPH, BOX-168-001, S13-245, HOCKEN COLLECTIONS.

adopters of the new sport of basketball (known as netball from 1970); some found it preferable 'to the more strenuous game of hockey', and it was 'a better game for girls of average strength who have not much opportunity of exercising during the week'.[40] University teams first appeared in reports of local matches in 1915, the year that the Otago Basket Ball Association, New Zealand's first, was established.[41]

One of the most enduringly popular clubs on campus, the Otago University Tramping Club (OUTC), started in 1927. The 1930 report noted that students could 'appreciate the joy of a brisk tramp, with its accompaniments of wood-fires and billy-teas'. Among the 'scenic resorts' explored by university trampers that year were Harbour Cone, the Spit, Red Hut, Mt Charles, Tomahawk Creek and Chain Hills Tarn.[42] The club had a few prejudices to overcome, as a 1947 report reveals:

> *We are convinced that the only thing which keeps our membership below the 100-mark is the popular illusion that a tramper is one who steams round the landscape at a steady 20 miles per hour, bowed to earth by a Bergan of the size and shape of a young bungalow … We prefer to stroll gently along with fitting dignity, stopping for the regulation ten minutes in every half-hour. Of course we have a large number of young 'keen types' in our membership, but many of us are completely decrepit.*[43]

The rowing club was founded in 1929 – later than some other university sports clubs, but it was destined to flourish. Initially members used the facilities of the Otago Rowing Club and, later, the North End Rowing Club, but by the late 1930s the club had its own boats and dozens of members. The 1950–51 men's eight crew included, from left: P.G.R. Dawe, P.J. Molloy, L.W. Edwards, T.C. Svensen, E.W. Abrahams, R.H. Boswell, D.M. King, J.S. Maclaurin and T.M. Sherman (cox).

UNIVERSITY OF OTAGO MEDICAL SCHOOL ALUMNUS ASSOCIATION RECORDS, MS-1537/524, S17-610A, HOCKEN COLLECTIONS.

A mixed game of hockey in 1949, during the weekly break: Wednesday afternoons were free of classes and set aside for sports. Men's and women's hockey clubs started in 1905: 'the hockeyites are enthusiastic and promise great things', wrote the women's correspondent for the *Review*.

PRIME MINISTER'S DEPARTMENT PHOTOGRAPH, BOX-184-081, S17-182C, HOCKEN COLLECTIONS.

Arthur Porritt, a medical student in the early 1920s, recalled that 'statutory work accomplished, we indulged to the maximum extent possible in sport, and nearly as much in social activities ... "Billy" Fea and Mackereth – two "All Blacks" – were our heroes – and we rejoiced in winning the Inter 'Varsity Tournament.'[44] Porritt, later governor-general of New Zealand, was a pretty good athlete himself – he won bronze in the 100m at the 1924 Olympics in Paris.[45]

Team games were most popular with students, but athletics took off after the Easter Tournament commenced in 1902. Teams from Otago had previously competed against Canterbury students in rugby, tennis and debating; in 1902 Canterbury organised the Easter Tournament, with teams from Victoria and Auckland as well as Otago. It was 'a great success in every way', noted the *Otago University Review*: 'The competition was keen and the performances good from an athletic point of view, whilst from a social point there is nothing that can foster the feeling of friendship and good-comradeship between the colleges more than an annual tournament of this description.'[46] It was an important event in student politics; as Elworthy notes, the tournament tradition 'began to tie the

The Otago University Tramping Club introduced many people to the joys of tramping and the beauty of the natural world around Dunedin and further afield – a positive experience for most, apart from the occasional tragic accident. This group was photographed in 1946.

OTAGO UNIVERSITY TRAMPING CLUB RECORDS, 96-063/036, S15-592B, HOCKEN COLLECTIONS.

New Zealand student bodies together'.[47]

Soon after the 1902 tournament the long-jump champion, Peter Buck, presided at the inaugural meeting of the Otago University Amateur Athletic Club. Otago had to affiliate to the New Zealand Amateur Athletic Association before it could host future Easter Tournaments, but pride was at stake, too: if Otago wanted to beat its main foe, Canterbury, it needed to select and train its best athletes. The club ran annual inter-faculty events that served as trials for the Otago tournament team.[48] In 1923 the Athletic Club acquired an 'offspring', the University Harrier Club, which held Saturday afternoon long-distance runs.[49] The Harrier Club reported in 1930 that its 'finest individual performance' came from one J. Lovelock, 'the best distance runner whom Otago University has yet produced'.[50] Jack Lovelock was a medical student in 1929 and 1930 and headed to Oxford on a Rhodes Scholarship in 1931; he was destined to become 'one of the most celebrated of all Olympic champions' when he won gold in the 1500m at the 1936 Berlin Olympics.[51]

As the university expanded and diversified, students indulged in a wide variety of sports, as can be seen from a list of clubs affiliated to OUSA in 1991: archery, association football, women's soccer, men's hockey, women's hockey, judo, tae kwon do, aikido, chi kune jow do, swords (fencing), badminton, basketball, golf, Fiji cricket/soccer, harriers and athletics, diving, fullbore rifle, smallbore rifle, netball, rugby league and orienteering. The tramping, rowing, rugby and cricket clubs were still active, though they apparently failed to affiliate to OUSA that year.[52] Additions to the list 25 years later, in 2016, included Australian rules football, canoeing, capoeira (a martial art), cycling, figure skating, futsal, handball, three variations of karate, kayaking, kiteboarding, lacrosse, longboarding, rugby sevens, snow sports, squash, surfing, table tennis, touch rugby, ultimate frisbee, water polo and yachting.[53]

Some elite athletes were drawn to Otago's School of Physical Education – for several decades the country's only tertiary sports science centre. Many of its alumni became household names, such as netballers Adine Wilson and Anna Rowberry, rugby players Anton Oliver, Josh Kronfeld and Jamie Joseph and cyclist Greg Henderson. One phys ed student, Farah Palmer, first took rugby seriously after arriving in the south; she went on to captain the Black Ferns to three world cup wins – and to complete a PhD.[54] Sports stars studied in other disciplines as well. In 1998 Otago claimed a 'captaincy treble': Palmer was captain of the national women's rugby team; Taine Randell, a 1997 law and commerce graduate, was captain of the men's rugby team; and Belinda Colling, a 1998 psychology graduate, was captain of the national netball team.[55] The university and OUSA supported elite sportspeople: they awarded 'blues' in recognition of outstanding achievements in sports, and subsidised sports clubs. One of OUSA's largest investments was the Aquatic Centre, opened in 2002 to house the rowing club, which lost its old premises and boats in a suspicious fire in 1999. With the assistance of grants from the Lotteries Commission and Community Trust of Otago, the club and OUSA raised over $1 million to build the centre, complete with club room, boat storage, and an indoor rowing tank used to improve technique.[56]

Unipol Recreation Centre, 2008.
OUSA COLLECTION.

OUSA also developed facilities for those who just wanted to keep fit and have fun. The Clubs and Societies Building opened in 1980 and was soon hosting aerobics classes and weight training. It quickly proved inadequate for the growing student roll, so OUSA agreed to a scheme proposed by the Otago Polytechnic Students Association. The two associations and the university converted a former stationery factory in Anzac Avenue into the Unipol Recreation Centre, which opened in 1990.[57] The university developed a Recreation Services department in 1984 with the aim of supporting healthy recreational activities for students. It built up a store of equipment for hire, ranging from surfboards and skis to tramping and camping gear, and organised courses and trips; it held the contract to run Unipol.[58] In 2012 Unipol moved to a larger space in the University Plaza building, attracting a jump in patronage. Soon afterwards OUSA sold its share of Unipol to the university: it was unwilling to commit more funds and was confident the university had student needs at heart. Student president Logan Edgar cited an example where Unipol refused a gym booking to the All Blacks 'when it would have limited the space of students attempting to work out'. OUSA put the proceeds towards an upgrade of the Clubs and Societies Building, completed in 2014.[59]

Otago students were keen spectators as well as players: cheering on the local team on the terraces of Carisbrook or, later, in 'the zoo' at Forsyth Barr

Stadium was an iconic part of student culture. That presumably contributed to the university's 2014 decision to sponsor the local Super Rugby team, the Highlanders. The decision raised eyebrows and attracted some opposition, notably from the Tertiary Education Union, which was unhappy with the extent of spending on marketing by universities.[60] Fortunately the university's sponsorship of the Highlanders coincided with a marked improvement in their results, and when they won the championship in 2015 with 'University of Otago' emblazoned on their shirts it was a proud moment for their sponsors.

CAPPING

For generations of Otago students the events surrounding graduation, known as capping, were the major student festival. With one exception – Otago's first graduate, Alexander Williamson – until 1961 all Otago degree students graduated from the University of New Zealand, but it held capping ceremonies in each of its constituent colleges. Dunedin's first graduation ceremony took place in 1879 in the library; George Montgomery and Alfred Barclay received their BA diplomas before 'a very large' audience.[61] It was a dignified event. During the 1880s, however, students used the graduation ceremony to 'show their wit and at the same time air their grievances before the public and the University authorities'. They donned costumes, played trumpets and shook rattles, sang 'improvised lyrics to well known tunes' and alternately cheered and heckled the speakers. The University of New Zealand authorities soon tired of that behaviour, which was replicated in Canterbury and Auckland; from 1894 to 1898 they banned public graduation ceremonies. At Otago students carried on holding concerts and social celebrations for local graduates, and when the public graduation ceremony returned in 1899, students continued their own separate event; 'the grave and the gay parts did not blend, so that their separation is a decided benefit to both', said the *Review*.[62] The essential features of the 'grave' part – Otago's formal graduation ceremony – had by the 1920s settled into a format that endured, with various minor changes and one particularly notable one: from 1995 there was a Māori element, with a welcoming kōrero from the Māori orator on behalf of Kāi Tahu Whānui.[63]

Meanwhile, in addition to the 'capping carnival' (later known as the capping show), students began two events in 1899: the capping ball and the capping procession ('procesh'). The procession –

Cross-dressing, blackface and other carnivalesque behaviour at capping in 1920. The young man in the gymslip in the centre is future history professor Willie Morrell. From left: F.H. McDowall, G.A. Naylor, J.S. Adam, W.P. Morrell, L.S. Rogers, A.G. Crust.
JUDITH NATHAN COLLECTION.

The 1936 capping ball, complete with staff chaperones on the stage.
M.B. TAYLOR PHOTOGRAPH, P2000-029-001, S13-217H, HOCKEN COLLECTIONS.

featuring satire, cross-dressing and crazy musicians – started with a group of students driving through Dunedin in a horsedrawn vehicle playing 'mixed instruments'. It gradually evolved into an event with multiple floats, watched by large crowds; participants begged donations from spectators for their chosen charities. It flourished through to the 1970s, but by the late 1980s students were starting to lose interest and public tolerance declined due to the 'excessive' behaviour of some participants.[64] After a recess through the 1990s, the procession with floats was reinstated by OUSA in 2000, but it did not survive as the big event that students and public had once enjoyed.[65] More successful was the academic procession of graduates – revived by OUSA in 1998 following an example set by pharmacy graduates a few years earlier: the public and supporters cheered graduates as they marched

'Paddy's Band of Angels', featuring the notoriously balding cabinet minister Paddy Webb, perform for a large crowd at the 1946 capping procession. Groups from faculties and residential colleges put considerable effort into creating their floats, which often reflected current events and political controversies; later they were more centred on student life.
ARTHUR CAMPBELL PHOTOGRAPH, ARTHUR CAMPBELL COLLECTION.

The 1962 Sextette (as the Sextet was then spelled) in traditional clown costume. Back from left: Doug Cox, Alastair Stokes, Terry Wilson, Peter Chin. Front: Roger McElroy, Gus Ferguson (pianist/guitarist), Ian Robertson. The group once had a piano accompanist and sang in unison, but singing in harmony became a feature in the 1970s.

DE CLIFFORD PHOTOGRAPH, PETER CHIN COLLECTION.

in their finery along George Street, led by a piper, university bigwigs and an OUSA banner, to the formal capping ceremony in the Town Hall.[66]

The capping concert, an immediate hit with students and the public, offered amusing commentary on university life as well as on the rest of Dunedin and the wider world. Profits from the show helped fund OUSA activities. Comic skits with music and dance were its standbys. Participants eased performance anxiety with alcohol and the consequences could be amusing or unfortunate. George Petersen recalled one early 1950s production involving

> *a special effect with a twist. A flying fox had been designed to enable a witch to float gracefully above the actors' heads. On the night, however, a rather intoxicated witch shot straight across the stage, caught some scenery on her broomstick and proceeded to hurtle back again, scenery and all. There was a moment of agonised silence, before the audience exploded into laughter.*[67]

That act was part of the Knox farce – one of several residential college performances that came and went through the years. The most famous was the Selwyn Ballet, which started in 1928 as a spoof of popular musicals but settled into a well-rehearsed classical ballet act performed by men in tutus.[68] One reason for the emergence of cross-dressing in the capping show and procession was that women were banned from performing. After women campaigned to change this, in 1938 the OUSA student council decided they could take part, as they did on other campuses. At first nothing changed, and then the war intervened and capping was suspended. When the concert returned in 1945 women were still absent, but in 1947, after a petition and an enormous battle, they finally took to the stage, 'promoted from make-up to "acting"'.[69]

In the 2010s, with gender politics more complex and gender identities more fluid, some students have expressed concern about cross-dressing traditions like the Selwyn Ballet, but it remains a popular feature of the show.[70] Another carnivalesque tradition – blackface, the make-up used by non-black performers to play caricatured black people – was once popular at capping but has now disappeared because of the racist stereotypes it portrayed. It featured in the beginnings of the

Above left: The Sexytet performs at the 2014 capping show. The Sextet was an all-male affair, though there was a one-off all-female vocal group at the 1966 capping show. In 2001 a female a cappella group, the Sexytet, debuted and became a regular feature: they wore '1950s housewife' costumes and performed witty, smutty songs in beautiful harmonies, in the Sextet tradition.
DANIEL CHEW PHOTOGRAPH, OUSA COLLECTION.

Above right: Pirates versus ninjas at the 2006 capping show.
ROB MCCANN PHOTOGRAPH, OUSA COLLECTION.

most successful capping show act, the Sextet. One of the Sextet's best-known old boys, conductor and composer Tecwyn Evans, traced the group's origins to the appearance of 'Coon's Quartette' at the 1903 capping concert; a review of the 1905 show noted that 'a coon tableau and a cake walk by a quartet of coloured gentlemen went well'. Various four- or five-man combinations followed, and the first six-man singing group appeared in 1912. By 1919 the Sextette (as it was spelled until the mid-1960s) was a regular feature of the capping concert, famous for its cheeky words sung in angelic voices.[71] The lyrics varied 'from the traditional to the topical and from the harmless to the emphatically unsuitable', according to a 1991 article.[72] The innuendo became more explicit, and in 2010 Rape Crisis criticised the Sextet for trivialising rape and sexual abuse in some lyrics.[73] The quality of performances varied from year to year, but its singers included future opera stars Roger Wilson, Martin Snell, Simon O'Neill and Jonathan Lemalu.[74]

In the early 1980s, capping was central in the cultural wars on campus, with proponents of 'traditional' masculine-dominated activities on one side, and 'radicals' concerned about gender and race politics on the other. Phyllis Comerford, the 1983 president, viewed capping as 'a tradition for the pissheads at the expense of all other students' and was determined to change it. To try and control drunken behaviour on stage, the OUSA executive passed control of the show's budget from the capping controllers to the producer and director.[75] In 1984 two professionals – writer Roger Hall and director Lisa Warrington – were brought in to 'save' the show and under their guidance the capping show became 'focused, short and funny' and more family-friendly. But as capping show historian David Large notes, it was difficult for 'other writers following in Hall's (rather large) footprints' to maintain the standard, and in the 1990s it became a 'bland, unfocused event' and lost money. In 1996 a turnaround of the struggling

A piper leads the official party in to Otago's first Malaysian graduation ceremony, held on 26 April 1997 at the Shangri-La Hotel in Kuala Lumpur. Several subsequent graduation ceremonies were held in Malaysia, including at Kuching.
UNIVERSITY OF OTAGO INTERNATIONAL OFFICE RECORDS, MS-3522/002, S13-561A, HOCKEN COLLECTIONS.

show began. After a century in city theatres, it moved back on campus and focused more on student audiences. The quality improved after the director was authorised 'to cast only actors that could, in fact, act', overturning a policy of participation by anyone who was interested.[76]

Another capping tradition, the capping book or magazine, did not survive. Started in 1926, it featured a list of the graduates, the programme of the capping show, cartoons, comic verse and satirical articles. Students sold copies to the public as a charity fundraiser: it was popular, with a print run in the tens of thousands in the 1960s. The mag was witty, but misogynistic; it became ever more crude and a target of feminist critique as women became a larger force on campus. The 1981 mag, *Thrust*, with a cover illustration of a phallic clocktower rocket between a woman's legs, provoked outrage; and there was a similar outcry from traditionalists when the OUSA executive censored the 1983 mag. By the late 1980s, students were still selling 'around 5000 copies of the Capping magazine each year but, deprived by the censors of the racist and sexist material which it had come to rely on for its humour, the book does not have a lot left to say'. It fizzled out after that, and the last issue appeared in 1997.[77]

THE DECLINE OF CAPPING

The decline of the capping carnival was not only due to cultural shifts. Once internal assessment counted for final course grades, fewer students were keen to participate in extracurricular activities mid-year; 2016 capping show producer Jerome Cousins commented that the workload for performers was 'like taking another university paper'.[78] Perhaps the biggest factor in the slow decline of capping was, however, the multiplication of graduation ceremonies. In 1951 Otago added to its traditional May graduation a second ceremony in December for medical and dental graduates. In 1990 a second May ceremony was introduced, since the 2000 or so May graduates, along with supporters, could not squeeze into Dunedin's biggest venue, the Town Hall. Other changes followed: in 1993 the university added another ceremony in July (August in subsequent years) and, in 1995, a second December graduation that was not restricted to health science students. By 2012 Otago had 14 graduation ceremonies: five in May, one in August and eight in December. Two of the December ceremonies were for the Southland campus's teaching graduates – one in Invercargill and another at Te Rau Aroha Marae in Bluff, for graduates in bilingual education.[79]

Music during orientation week in 1974.
BOX 239-002, S13-217A, HOCKEN COLLECTIONS.

The impact of the explosion of graduations on student traditions is exemplified by the capping ball. This was a longstanding event: Pearl Jennings recalled that the party after the formal capping ceremony 'continued with dancing till the early hours of the morning' in the early 1900s.[80] Stephen Hall-Jones was capping controller in 1986 and was then appointed as the first full-time social activities officer. In the 1980s the capping ball was 'enormous' and a good money-spinner for OUSA, he says, but the break-up of graduation into numerous ceremonies made it difficult to organise, with no one date suitable, so it was scrapped.[81]

ORIENTATION

As capping became less of an annual party, orientation took over as the main student festival. It was late getting started. John Murdoch, a shy young Southlander, arrived at Otago in 1907 and found the 'only organised attempt to make new students feel welcome came through the Christian Union'.[82] By the 1920s OUSA was running a 'freshers' welcome' in Allen Hall: 'We were all very shy but we danced, talked and had supper and met students of the opposite sex equally shy', Sylvia Norie recalled.[83] Student clubs held social events to welcome students. There were lots of 'hops' – dances with live bands – at Allen Hall at the beginning of the year, recalls Nancy Carr (née Deal), who arrived from Wellington to study home science in 1955. The 1957 freshers' handbook advertised a dance every weekend at Allen Hall in March, organised by the tennis, swimming, yacht and athletic clubs. There was also an SCM freshers' welcome, an informal OUSA weekend 'congress' at Trotters Gorge (north of Dunedin) and a weekend of inter-faculty sports at Logan Park.

Many students made enduring friendships with people they met at an orientation function, and some led to a lasting romance. At the first dance she attended at Otago in the 1950s, Nancy Deal met Melville Carr, a chemistry student from Central Otago; they are still together over 60 years later.[84] Mary Scanlon, a medical student from Wellington, met her future husband at an orientation dance in the early 1980s. It wasn't a promising start – Bill English, a first-year arts and commerce student from rural Southland, was shy and 'socially unaccomplished', and he was on crutches after breaking his foot in a Selwyn initiation ceremony – but they became firm friends and later married.[85]

Residential colleges and some faculty associations had their own orientation activities. Most were harmless fun, but some involved humiliating initiation rites for freshers that were

Opposite: Orientation 1990 featured an impressive line-up of performers. The poster was the work of Robert Scott, member of acclaimed bands The Clean and The Bats. OUSA COLLECTION.

supposed to foster belonging and group loyalty. The 'traditions' at the men's colleges and the phys ed school were notorious. Attempts by university and college authorities to rein in the worst excesses met with resistance from students, despite the psychological and physical harm they caused. Some traditions survived, somewhat modified, into the twenty-first century – including the well-known Selwyn run through the Water of Leith, complete with 'stolen' Knox bath, that has been held since 1935 (it was a collision with that bath that broke English's foot).[86]

By the 1960s OUSA was running an official 'orientation week'. Activities in 1964 included an official welcome from the VC, student forums, lectures and suppers, club displays to recruit members, a production by the dramatic society, a couple of hops in the Union hall and a special freshers' hop in the Town Hall.[87] Films became a popular attraction: 1966 students could enjoy 'two colour cinemascope features'.[88] During the 1970s music became more of a feature. There had always been dance bands at hops; now rock bands joined the mix and Otago became part of a touring circuit of national and international acts, organised by the New Zealand Students' Arts Council.[89] By the mid-1980s orientation was almost a music festival: the 1984 programme included five evening and three lunchtime concerts, plus an 'end of summer musical afternoon' on Sunday afternoon. There were other events – market days, debates, performance poetry, movies, a barn dance, beer and wine tasting, clubs and societies day – but music was the star. Dunedin developed a thriving alternative

Above: Macklemore concert at the stadium, Orientation 2013. Below: Freshers on the toga parade, 2006. OUSA COLLECTION.

GROUNDSWELL STUDENT INSURANCE
GROUNDSWELL STUDENT INSURANCE
GROUNDSWELL STUDENT INSURANCE
MUTANT HILLBILLY
ORIENTATION 1990
WE WANT YOU
THE CLEAN
STRAITJACKET FITS
HEADLESS CHICKENS
BAILTER SPACE
THE JEAN PAUL SARTRE EXPERIENCE
UPPER HUTT POSSE
STEPHEN
THE BIG MUFFIN SERIOUS BAND
PLAGAL GRIND
3D'S
SAM HUNT
GARRY McCORMICK
THE DIANNE SWANN BIG BAND
VERLAINES
THE BATS
SNAPPER
DEATH RAY CAFE
SISTERMATIC
WHEN THE CATS BEEN SPAYED
TORQUEMADAS
WEETBIX BOYS
LUCKY TICKET NUMBER
WINS $1250 IN ONE DOLLAR NOTES
TO PAY THE NEW TUITION CHARGES
PROTEST FEES TODAY!
ONE WINNER IS NOT ENOUGH !!!
CONTACT O.U.S.A (777 961) FOR DETAILS
WINNER WILL BE ANNOUNCED 2ND ISSUE OF CRITIC
TICKETS $40 RAD ONE DISCOUNT
NO DOOR SALES AT ALL - STUDENT ID'S ESSENTIAL
Winston Darling travel ltd
University Book Shop
Bank of New Zealand
SPEIGHT'S
SAMMY'S NIGHT CLUB THE ONLY ALTERNATIVE

Dignitaries at the first convocation ceremony, held in the Forsyth Barr Stadium in 2015 and presided over by the chancellor and academic staff in their robes. From left: John Ward (chancellor), John Key (prime minister), Michael Woodhouse (MP), Harlene Hayne (VC), Edward Ellison (Ngāi Tahu kaumātua). Guest speakers in subsequent years have included the deputy prime minister, the governor-general and the prime minister.
SHARRON BENNETT PHOTOGRAPH, UNIVERSITY OF OTAGO MARKETING AND COMMUNICATIONS COLLECTION.

music culture and orientation was an opportunity for bands to recruit fans.[90]

Bands that struggled to get airplay on commercial stations reached an audience through Otago student radio, which started as a short-term orientation broadcast in 1975, and returned each year. Other New Zealand universities had permanent student stations. Finally, in 1984, Otago's Radio One began – Dunedin's first FM station. In addition to featuring alternative music and student and community groups, it provided employment for some musicians: early staff included members of Netherworld Dancing Toys, Sneaky Feelings and Look Blue Go Purple.[91]

One orientation activity dreamed up by Hall-Jones became a popular tradition. There had been a social event just for freshers at orientation for years, but in 1991 he added a new element: the toga.[92] The toga party became an annual event, and returning students developed their own tradition of throwing eggs and flour at groups of freshers heading to the party. In 2001 Rob McCann, the next social activities manager, added another event for freshers: the 'first-day parade' along George Street. 'In the past,' noted the orientation programme, 'student parades have been exclusively reserved for graduation ceremonies … But now first years get to do it before they've even got around to attending lectures, let along thinking about graduating … remember to wear your toga for the Toga Party later in the evening!'[93] Within a few years the 'toga parade' became troublesome and in 2009 it 'descended into disorder', as the *ODT* reported; it left the main street 'littered with eggs, rubbish and glass, car and shop windows smashed and participants injured'. In the aftermath, several students were suspended.[94] The toga parade came to an end, but the toga party in the Union hall continued; it later shifted to the stadium and is still a highlight of orientation for freshers.[95]

Orientation was a student festival run by OUSA, but in the 2010s it took a different direction when VC Hayne added another event: the convocation ceremony. In 2012 she began hosting a 'welcome' for first-year students, incorporating formal greetings from local iwi, the mayor, OUSA president and VC, and in 2015 it became a formal ceremony, as 'used in other great universities around the world to set the tone for university study'.[96] The formal convocation proceedings were followed by a variety show with 'an exciting range of acts, iconic to this university'; it featured the Sextet and the Sexytet, along with other student and graduate performers.[97]

CULTURAL LIFE

University clubs came and went, but there was always something to satisfy students' cultural yearnings. In 1946, for instance, the *Review* noted that the Photographic Society had come to a halt but the Literary Society had staged a comeback; the debating societies were 'moderately active'. A Chess Club was waiting for chess sets to arrive – the game had 'a large following' in the Medical School. A Musical Union was formed to give a 'long-needed union between the various musical groups', with regular 'gramophone recitals' and chamber music recitals in Allen Hall. A piano recital by Lili Kraus, a Jewish Hungarian recently released from a Japanese concentration camp, was a highlight of the year, and the Dramatic Society and Dramatic Club both staged productions.[98]

Drama was one of the earliest clubs. In 1889 – 'less than a decade after the foundation of the Oxford OUDS', as its historian Alister McDonald points out – the women students' Haringa Club presented an elaborate charade in the library, and a year later students performed extracts from *She Stoops to Conquer* to raise money for the football club's trip to Christchurch. That was a great success, prompting a drama critic to suggest forming a university club 'for the study of classical comedies, with a view to their representation in public'. The Dramatic Club had its formal beginning in 1891 with a full production of *She Stoops*, though it was only 'with great difficulty, and by dint of sheer importunity' that its founders, Charles Mouat and James Montgomery, managed to convince enough students and graduates to fill the cast. With just a couple of hundred students on the roll, any major production was remarkable; and the 1892 production of *The Rivals* even travelled with the football and tennis teams to the tournament with Canterbury College. After its 1893 production, *The School for Scandal*, the club disappeared for several decades; any dramatic tendencies were redirected to capping show skits and the occasional play reading.[99]

The Otago University Dramatic Society (OUDS) re-emerged out of the literary society in the 1930s, and by the 1940s was putting on a full-length play and several one-act dramas each year. In 1944 it performed its first recorded première, a one-act play by promising young New Zealand playwright Bruce Mason, whose fiancée, medical student Diana Shaw, was president of the club. Some productions involved classics, others were experimental.[100] A 1963 satirical revue, *Yes or No as the Mood Takes Us: The revue with the knife in it*, poked fun at bourgeois society. Targets included royalty, the clergy, politicians, radio, television and the press; the knife, reported the *ODT*, was 'wielded with varying degrees of deadliness'. Writer Bill Manhire attended the revue as a high-school student and was impressed; he was disappointed later, when he arrived at university, to discover the campus was not filled with witty people as he had hoped.[101] Some plays were directed by students; others had professionals at the helm, including the university drama tutors or others brought in on contract with subsidies from the university. Plans to build a 'Little Theatre' got quite advanced in the 1960s, but fell through in the 1970s because of insufficient funds and the unwillingness of property owners on the desired sites to sell up; OUSA directed its building funds to the Clubs and Societies Building instead. OUDS flourished through the 1970s and 1980s, but put on its last production in 1994; it 'fell victim to Rogernomics', McDonald wrote; rising student fees made it 'harder to justify a time-consuming hobby like amateur campus theatre'. It was not the end of drama on campus: theatre studies developed into a full academic programme and students 'with a theatrical bent' could participate in productions 'with the prospect of academic credits later'.[102]

MĀORI CLUB

Other cultural activities reflected the growing diversity of students. The Māori Club started in 1960, 'although there were relatively few Māori students, or perhaps because there were so few,' founding secretary Mason Durie recalled. Law student Te Pakaka Tawhai was the first president.

Top: Freddy Rewa (left) and Allan Ngaparu and Maarire Goodall (right) tend a Māori Club hāngī in 1974. The social element was just as important to the club as its cultural activities: 'we had good parties', says John Broughton, who arrived at Otago as a dental student in 1974.

MERE MONTGOMERY COLLECTION.

Bottom: Otago University Māori Club and visitors from Canterbury at Ōtākou marae in 1974. Standing in front (left to right) are Roslyn Quick, Talei Pickering, Mere Meanata, Sally Plunket and Brenda Burton. At the back are Ellen Robertson (partially obscured), unidentified Christchurch visitor, Jackie Haimoana, Wilson Whare Isaac, Mori Ellison, Laura Van Peer (behind Mere), Virginia Callahan and Simon Wenley (behind Virginia). From 1974 the club held an annual hui at the marae on Te Rā Nui o te Reo Māori (Māori Language Day).

MERE MONTGOMERY COLLECTION.

There were perhaps 30 Māori studying at Otago, and not all participated – but for those who did the Māori Club became an important network.[103] Kapa haka was one of the club's strengths right from the start, and medical student Bruce Gregory was one of the first haka leaders. Club members performed at various functions, including the capping show. By the mid-1970s the Māori Club was one of the largest on campus with about 80 members. Only 15 or so of those were Māori; it welcomed any interested student and its members included Pākehā, Pacific Islanders and Asian international students. The club built relationships with Māori beyond the university, too, especially through Ōtākou marae and later the urban marae, Araiteuru, which some students helped to build. Links with students beyond Otago came through the national Māori University Students Association. Members travelled to – and occasionally hosted – national hui where they met future Māori leaders and gained inspiration from past graduates.[104]

The Māori Club had a political side. Members campaigned for an undergraduate Māori course at Otago, and participated in Te Rā Nui o te Reo Māori, Māori Language Day, which commenced in 1973. Some members were dedicated activists. Mere Meanata (later Montgomery), whose whakapapa was Māori and Tongan, was involved in the Polynesian Panthers in Auckland and established a Dunedin branch when she came to Otago in 1973. The Panthers ran a homework centre for children from low-income families of all ethnic backgrounds, organised legal advice and visited prisoners. A few other Māori Club members joined her in the Panthers' social justice activities. Politics could be divisive and by the 1990s the club had split into two groups, one with a focus on kapa haka and the other with more political goals – and some people belonged to both groups.[105] Te Roopū Māori developed as a parallel students' association for Māori, aiming to advance Māori 'through the halls of academia in every area'; it liaised with the broader Māori community, represented members' interests in the university and provided for their cultural and social needs.[106]

GOING INTERNATIONAL

The International Club was one of the most active groups at Otago in the 1950s and 1960s. As the international student contingent rose, Arana residents Vallabh Patel and David Gray saw a place for an organisation 'to promote friendship and mutual understanding between students from other countries and New Zealand students'. A group met informally in 1950 and set up the club in 1951, with Patel as president. It quickly attracted support from international students, with a slower uptake of New Zealanders. In its first year it held several social evenings as well as evenings hosted by various 'national groups' – Indian, Malay, Chinese, American – who 'entertained with national dances, songs, or other aspects of their native culture'. Staff provided support, in particular chemistry lecturer Tsu Sheng Ma and his wife Gioh-Fang Ma, who no doubt contributed to the 'outstanding' Chinese evening that members enjoyed 'not only for the variety of the programme and the effort put into it, but also for the Chinese food that was served with it'.[107] By 1960 the club was an important support group for international students; it held weekly suppers, as well as hops, tours of Dunedin and camps in rural Otago, and it introduced locals to the 'exotic glamour and strangeness' of other cultures through its annual concerts.[108]

Physics lecturer Agnes Blackie was an early supporter of the International Club; after years as a patron she was 'proud to have friends of many races scattered widely over the globe' and hoped that 'the problems caused by the tendency to hive off into racial groups will be satisfactorily solved and students of different races will continue to make lasting friendships'.[109] The International Club ended in the 1970s: the growing roll meant students could 'hive off' into a variety of national and ethnic associations: by 1975 there were Polynesian and Chinese clubs on campus and by 1980 there were Fiji, Malaysian and Samoan associations. These groups were open to all but their primary purpose was to provide support and social activities for their 'own' students, and links to their ethnic communities beyond the university.[110]

Students from the Sri Lankan Association serving food at the OUSA International Food Festival in 're-orientation' week, July 2013.

DANIEL CHEW PHOTOGRAPH, OUSA COLLECTION

NEW VENTURES

The growth of different ethnic associations reflected, in part, the failure of 'traditional' Otago student culture to adjust to the changing makeup of the student body. In the 1970s, writes Elworthy, Malaysian students 'challenged the dominant student culture mostly by avoiding it'; likewise, Māori students 'tended to develop their own social life through Te Roopū and other groups'.[111] Hall-Jones recalls that few international students attended the events he organised as OUSA social activities manager in the 1980s and 1990s; he was 'catering for the mainstream'. A more diverse crowd attended student market days, and eventually the international rep on OUSA started organising international events; the international food festival was a popular fundraiser for the clubs involved.[112]

The social activities manager, who replaced the former orientation and capping controllers, coordinated other events through the year; Hall-Jones tried several ideas. Regular quiz nights had about 50 teams competing in their heyday, and the 'winter slam' – a wrestling competition where students choreographed their own moves – went well for three years. The winter games, complete with porridge wrestling, haggis hurling and the inimitable Waitati Militia (an eccentric 'army' fond of mock battles), were another shortlived innovation. The most successful new event of the 1990s was the Mothra competition, inspired by Hall-Jones watching the Ken Russell movie *Gothic* and thinking that students could make better 'bad' movies. Named after the 1961 Japanese horror movie *Mothra*, the competition required students to make a 15-minute movie on equipment provided by OUSA. *Formyka, the Samurai Coffee Table*, won the best video gong at the inaugural 1990 contest, which attracted eight entries. Mothra grew bigger – there were 70 entries in 1998 – and progressed from analogue to digital equipment, but retained its 'disrespectful student essence'. It fizzled out in the 2010s as costs rose and it had to compete with the popular 48Hours national film contest, but for a couple of decades it was the cause of much creativity and hilarity, and even inspired a few participants to enter careers in the film industry.[113]

OUSA: THE POLITICAL AND THE PROFESSIONAL

The appointment of a social activities manager signalled the emerging professionalisation of OUSA. It employed a secretary from the 1940s and attracted capable and long-serving people to the role: Helen Harris, Bridget (Biddy) Rennie and Donna Jones became legends on campus. They loved working with students, had their interests at heart and acquired great institutional knowledge, though OUSA executives 'didn't care about the past and wanted to do things their way', Rennie says. There was 'a lot of work and hardly anybody to help' when Rennie became secretary in 1976, but slowly more office, reception and finance staff appeared. Harry Evison joined the team in 1976 as the first full-time activities officer. Jones, who took over when Rennie retired in the 1990s, comments that OUSA became 'more corporate'. As the organisation and its financial and regulatory responsibilities grew, the elected reps – who once did most of the tasks themselves – employed professionals to implement their decisions; a general manager oversaw administrators, welfare staff, media people, recreation staff and an events team. Being on the executive was still a big responsibility. OUSA paid its president and finance rep an honorarium from 1970 and eventually all exec members received payment in recognition of the time and expense involved in their commitment.[114]

The role of OUSA president, as chair of the association and public spokesperson for the students, carried particular responsibility. In some years there was stiff competition for the position, and winning the election required charm, ambition and political nous. William Edward Spencer, a 26-year-old postgrad science student, became the first president in 1890. Spencer, who became a teacher and later a senior civil servant and editor of the *School Journal*, was an 'able and energetic' president who got things off to a good start.[115] Other 'able and energetic' people followed him in the role, with few rogues among them (one from the 1990s could be detected approaching by the scent of marijuana, and the rest of the executive largely ignored his decrees). The role was a mostly male Pākehā preserve until the 1980s, with the notable exception of Peter Buck in 1903. Other trailblazers in the role were Ebraima Manneh, the first international student in 1971, and Phyllis Comerford, the first woman in 1983; both led OUSA during turbulent years.[116]

Buck, Manneh and Comerford were all politicians at heart, but many OUSA presidents and executives were not. Although students had a reputation for radicalism, there were few passionate campaigners among them; most were apathetic about politics. Historian Sharon Dooley notes that 'OUSA, a fairly apolitical body, spent the depression years discussing problems such as the purchase of crockery for the Union cafeteria, the design for the new official blazer and university jumper'.[117] Meanwhile, the hardships they witnessed inspired some students to take an interest in politics; among them were future history professor Angus Ross and Alexander Maclure, a Canadian who arrived at the School of Mines in 1931 and was the outstanding political activist of his generation. A committed member of the Communist Party, Maclure drove the formation of the first formal left-wing groups on campus. The Public Questions Union, first affiliated to OUSA in 1932, organised regular discussions and mock parliaments; it also served as a 'front' for the Independent Radical Club, 'an influential cell' of more radical students, with about 30 members by 1935.[118] In 1937 Maclure headed to the Spanish Civil War; later that year he was 'killed in action defending, with his comrades in the International Brigade, freedom and world peace against the Fascist invaders', as the *Workers Weekly* reported.[119] Many Otago students and graduates served in the two world wars and some lost their lives, but Maclure's commitment to a

Grant Robertson, one of the most politically astute OUSA presidents, led some of the campaigns over education funding in the 1990s. He became a senior cabinet minister in the Labour-led government of 2017.

OUSA RECORDS, MS-4225/288, S17-611F, HOCKEN COLLECTIONS.

'foreign' cause was unusual; he was 'an outsider, laughed at by the majority of students', writes Elworthy.

Later generations had different battles to fight. In the 1960s and 1970s a few more students became activitists and campaigned against alleged spy bases, environmentally destructive power schemes, sporting contact with South Africa, and the Vietnam War. Feminism, gay liberation and the rights of Māori were major causes from the 1970s onwards; and debates over the 1981 Springbok tour split the campus – as they did New Zealand society in general. By the late 1980s much of the turmoil had died down and political activity among students was 'largely confined to some tiny Labour and National clubs'; but it returned in 1989 when half the student body joined a protest against rising student fees. Education itself was the primary topic of protest in the 1990s, as students who were paying large sums to attend university campaigned for more government funding.[120]

DISCIPLINE

There was one thing guaranteed to fire up any generation of students: the university expanding its disciplinary powers. There were always a few students who behaved badly. The Professorial Board occasionally imposed fines or excluded students for short periods; students could appeal to the council and more serious cases were referred there. In 1916, after disagreements over the length of exclusion for Sylvester Geerin, a science student with a poor academic record and a history of disrupting classes (setting off detonators in physics was the last straw), the council established a Board of Discipline and Appeal Committee.[121] In the late 1920s and 1930s 'a sort of unholy alliance between the bohemian types and the drinking boys' challenged respectability on campus. In 1931, after lots of drunkenness at a dance in Allen Hall, the Board of Discipline fined some students and expelled a medical student who insulted a lecturer at the same event. When *Critic*, the student newspaper, dared to criticise punishment it thought excessive, its editors were threatened with disciplinary action and were forced to apologise. In 1932, when the council banned the capping procession and ball on the grounds of drunkenness the previous year, another *Critic* editor, Joe Small, published articles that were highly critical of the council and staff. The council responded by excluding Small for a year and setting up a Board of Control, with council, staff and student representatives, to oversee the running of student facilities Allen Hall and Logan Park; it could refer miscreants to the Board of Discipline, where students no longer had any right of appeal. It was like a military court, the *ODT* reported.[122]

In 1947 the University Council famously forced OUSA president John Child to resign and apologise, under threat of expulsion, after a controversial freshers welcome speech he made that 'ridiculed … morals, religion, rugby and the auspicious role of the University'.[123] It was a hint of things to come. In the 1960s Otago students were swept up in the international mood of youth rebellion among the baby-boomer generation. Only a minority indulged in countercultural lifestyles and activism, but many resented university interference in the personal lives of students – as demonstrated in the mixed flatting protest of 1967 (see chapter 4). Protest flared again in 1971 when the council reviewed its discipline regulations: students wanted them limited to activities that disrupted the academic function of the university, rather than the existing broader powers to prohibit conduct that 'tends to bring discredit on the University', no matter where it occurred. After failing to convince the council to limit its controls, a crowd of students, led by OUSA president Manneh, staged a registry sit-in. VC Robin Williams, faced with 2300 protestors – over a third of the student roll – 'agreed grudgingly' to their demands and the council compromised by setting regulations that confined charges of misconduct to academic matters and damage to university property. A new Board of Discipline was made up of three students, three council representatives and an independent chair.[124]

Students won their freedom fight in 1971, but lost those freedoms in 2007. Most behaved well most of the time, but it took only a small proportion of 20,000 students to create a lot of trouble. The national media took great interest in any problems, and Otago's reputation was at stake. Students had been setting fire to the occasional couch for some time but, by the early 2000s, couch-burning had become a frequent occurrence. Some of the residential streets close to campus developed a reputation as party zones, and traditions like the Hyde Street keg party and the Undie 500 (a Canterbury engineering student event, involving a drive/pub crawl from Christchurch to Dunedin) led to serious drunkenness and disorder, including bottle throwing and fires; in some years there were multiple arrests.[125] The University Council appointed a high-level working party on student behaviour and in 2007 a new code of conduct came into effect, giving the university power to discipline students for off-campus actions; its aim, stated VC David Skegg, was to 'ensure that all students enjoy a safe environment, and that the

The annual Hyde Street party in 2012. It began in the 1990s as a keg-drinking race between flats on Hyde Street, a popular student residential area right next to campus. It grew into a large, chaotic event and in 2013 OUSA stepped in to assist with ticketing and safety.
OUSA COLLECTION.

exceptional relationship between this University and its local community is not impaired'.[126] OUSA staunchly opposed the code; 'there was pretty open warfare for a couple of years', recalls Skegg. In 2009 OUSA took the university to court when a student was suspended for a semester after throwing rubbish at a car and breaking its windows during the unruly toga parade. The judge upheld the university's right to discipline students for off-campus conduct. Initial plans by OUSA to appeal the finding were dropped in 2010, and in a 2011 referendum students voted to adopt a 'neutral' stance on the matter, meaning they could again be represented on the Disciplinary Appeals Board (OUSA had been excluded because of a conflict of interest when it opposed the conduct code).[127]

Over the years the university took different measures to curb bad behaviour and promote student safety. It appointed a part-time 'special university officer' in 1957 after concerns about student conduct at hops; in 1969 it became a full-time post, renamed proctor. The proctor monitored university functions where alcohol was served and dealt with theft and damage to university property. By the early 2000s, as Ron Chambers explained, the proctor's main role was 'to act as guardian and protector of students and, if required, to deal with matters concerned with order and good behaviour (or should that be bad behaviour?)'. Chambers, a well known figure as proctor in the 1980s and 1990s, used his charisma and wit to develop a good relationship with students; his background in the Royal Ulster Constabulary in Belfast ensured their respect.[128] His role was complemented by the 'campus cop' – an official police appointment established in 1997, following precedents at Waikato and Massey.[129]

In 2007, as the new code of conduct came into force, the university appointed a deputy proctor and created Campus Watch. This was a service unique to Otago, devised by director of student services David Richardson and proctor Simon Thompson, inspired partly by similar systems in Cardiff and Colchester. A team of 40 people, selected for their maturity and ability to engage with young people, became a pastoral and security force among students. They walked the campus and surrounding area in shifts, 24 hours a day, looking for potential problems and providing friendly advice; a safety patrol vehicle kept an eye out for isolated or heavily intoxicated people and transported them home (or to hospital). OUSA was wary of Campus Watch, but it became popular with most students.[130] A 2012 study by Kimberly Cousins found it had a positive effect, 'reducing hazardous drinking, some alcohol-related harms, crime rates, and nuisance fires. The programme's flexibility and its balance between

Campus Watch team members talking with student flatters, 2011.

ALEX LOVELL-SMITH PHOTOGRAPH, UNIVERSITY OF OTAGO MARKETING AND COMMUNICATIONS COLLECTION.

enforcement and pastoral care were important to the programme's success.'[131]

Under the leadership of VCs with expertise in epidemiology and psychology, Otago targeted the root cause of much student ill-discipline: alcohol. The Sale of Liquor Act of 1989 and amendments extended pub opening hours, and alcohol became available in supermarkets; both off-licence and on-licence premises proliferated. In 1999 the legal age for purchasing alcohol dropped from 20 to 18 years, and incoming students were often already practised binge drinkers.[132] Research showed a relationship between the density of alcohol outlets and student harm, prompting a campaign by the university for fewer licensed premises in the student quarter.[133] The Captain Cook Tavern ('the Cook') and the Bowling Green Hotel ('the Bowler'), which both dated from the 1870s, along with the Gardens Tavern ('the Gardies'), established in the 1960s, were popular student hangouts that fell foul of the university's approach. It objected to the extension of the Gardies' hours of trade and the renewal of liquor licences for the Bowler and the Cook. The Cook was notorious for its all-day 'Cookathon' drinking sessions, while the Bowler ran 'objectionable' promotions, such as a 2007 competition to win a petrol-soaked couch and matches. As Richardson later commented, 'all 3 businesses seemed unable to operate commercially as when forced to comply with the requirements of the Act and the conditions imposed on them by the Court, all 3 ceased trading shortly afterwards'. In 2009 the university purchased the Bowler and converted it into academic office space; a year later it bought the Gardies, which became the Marsh Study Centre, easing congestion in the crowded library. The Cook closed in 2013, but reopened in 2016 as 'a gastro-themed pub for more than just students'.[134]

The university also tackled alcohol promotion. At Skegg's urging, in 2009 the council banned 'alcohol advertising and sponsorship from all campuses and at University-organised events wherever they are held'. That left OUSA looking for a new sponsor for its orientation events, which had been supported by Speight's brewery for several years.[135] Some staff, as well as students, disliked the university's attitude to alcohol, but as an institution famous for its health sciences, producing evidence about alcohol-related harm while seeing the effects on its students – from health problems and unwanted pregnancies to injuries and troubles with the law – Otago had strong incentives to act.

GOING VOLUNTARY

By the 1920s all students were required to belong to OUSA unless they could convince it they had good cause for exemption and would not use any of its services. In the late twentieth century, however, the rise of neoliberal ideology made unions unfashionable. In the 1990s a series of private members' bills mandating voluntary membership of students' associations failed to make it through parliament, but a 1998 Act enabled associations to become voluntary through a referendum. Students at Auckland and Waikato universities chose voluntarism, with mixed results. At Waikato it 'completely devastated our services, student culture, and ability to support students', the union reported; it had to rebuild its assets after students voted to return to universal membership in 2001. In Auckland, after a similar drop in revenue, the association made membership free and the university raised its student levies and contracted the association to provide services.[136]

At Otago, both the University Council and OUSA campaigned against voluntary membership, but had to institute it after the Education (Freedom of Association) Amendment Act of 2011. Hayne and OUSA president Logan Edgar negotiated a 'service level agreement'. As Hayne explained, the university wanted 'to maintain the high quality of student support that is offered at Otago', and as the new Act 'effectively eliminated OUSA's primary source of revenue', the university had contracted OUSA 'to provide the high quality services that they have provided in the past'.[137] As *Critic* pointed out, under the agreement 'OUSA will get basically the same amount of money as last year, except this time OUSA has zero fees – the Uni collects the money from students and passes it on to OUSA, thus nimbly sidestepping the VSM legislation'.[138] OUSA considered all students to be members unless they opted out, which annoyed students on the right of politics since it went against the spirit of the legislation; Edgar claimed this was not illegal as they weren't paying any direct fees.[139]

Life carried on: OUSA still provided students with entertainment, recreation services, publications and radio; it remained a voice for students on the University Council and elsewhere. Hayne claimed in 2015 that voluntary membership had increased student influence in university operations: 'Student representation is firmly embedded in all of our processes. Rather than yelling from the sidelines, students now have a seat at the table.' Others, notably activists of the 1990s, felt the contract had a chilling effect on student political advocacy; younger student politicians suggested the decline in visible protests was due to generational change, and debate and advocacy had shifted online.[140] One thing was clear: the relationship between OUSA and the university was strong and neither could manage without the other.

STUDENT JOURNALISM

Critic endured as a source of news, entertainment, media experience and the occasional controversy under the changed funding regime. It wasn't the first Otago student rag: that honour went to the *Otago University Review*, first published in 1888. There were just 184 students, most of them 'lukewarm' about the idea, but a group of enthusiasts led by Robert McNab (a future parliamentarian) and William Sim (a future judge) got the project going. The *Review* came out several times a year, with readers paying a subscription. In 1891 OUSA took over its management.[141] During World War I it became a twice-yearly publication, and by the 1920s problems meeting production costs and attracting contributions had made it 'the despair of its editors'. OUSA came to the rescue by putting up student subs so it could publish a newspaper, *Te Korero*; the *Review* became an annual publication, freed to concentrate on literary items. It later appeared under various titles, the most recent being *Scribbler*.[142] *Te Korero* survived only a few years; by 1924 it had diminished from 20 pages to four. In 1925 medical student Francis Bennett, editor of the *Review*, recommended a student newspaper to replace *Te Korero*, 'a dismal rag which [Dan Aitken] and I usually filled up with imaginative froth a few hours before it went to press'.[143] OUSA agreed and *Critic* was born.

Editor Archibald Campbell explained in the first issue that *Critic* would include plenty of news, but would also provide a place where 'criticism may be brought into the open'.[144] Its quality and style varied through the years, but *Critic* always included a lively mixture of campus news, humour and commentary. Sometimes it pushed the boundaries. In 2013 the New Zealand Press Council noted that student magazines 'are a particular genre, with a long history of provocation and even offensiveness. They are also usually noted for their edgy and ironic tone'.[145] On that occasion the Press Council dismissed a complaint against *Critic*, but it wasn't always so. In 2010 it upheld a complaint about a *Critic* article on some well-known Dunedin 'vagrants' with mental health problems.[146] The tone of an article led *Critic* into trouble in 2005, too, when a piece intended to highlight date rape was banned by the censor, though by then several months had passed since publication.[147]

It was politics that caused trouble on an earlier occasion. In 1952 the *ODT*, which printed *Critic* under contract to OUSA, refused to print a front-page article titled 'U.S. Germ Warfare in Korea?' because it objected to its 'Communist point of view', though the *ODT* later agreed to publish it in the next edition accompanied by an article 'giving the opposing point of view'. Paul Oestreicher, who was *Critic* editor that year and later became an Anglican priest known for his work for peace, recalls that 'liberality was in 1952 not in tune with the national (nationalistic) mood. McCarthyism was not just an American aberration.'[148] The relationship with the *ODT* remained interesting, as editor Holly Walker wrote on *Critic*'s 80th anniversary in 2005: 'As far as I can tell, *Critic* has always been, and will always be, dominated by sex, funny stories about freshers, stupid letters to the editor, apathy about student elections, and antagonism for the *ODT*. Long may it continue.'[149] Walker, later an MP, was one of several *Critic* staff who became public figures; for Geoffrey Cox, Jim Mora and Chris Trotter it was the start of a media career.[150]

Not everyone liked *Critic* and it had occasional shortlived challengers: the appropriately named *Challenge* in 1927, and *Critique* in 1979.[151] A longer-lasting maverick publication was *Falus*, which appeared sporadically in the 1960s. John Robson's flat was involved in its production; they would 'sit around a battered typewriter sniffing correcting fluid and crank out very badly set-out Gestetner sheets which were then run off by a sympathiser in one of the University's departments'. The flatmates would 'churn out lengthy doggerel in rhyming couplets about the Vietnam war and other matters of moment. Bad (and sexually explicit) language abounded: that being the progressive thing to do in those days.'[152] It was the language – especially sweary by 1960s standards – rather than the radical politics that caused the most fuss. Many students were offended, and OUSA executive member Lorraine Isaacs set fire to a copy for dramatic effect at a student forum; that created minor panic after the rubbish bin she threw it into caught alight. OUSA condemned *Falus* and reprimanded two of its producers, David Moore and Lloyd Chapman, but it kept publishing and got a scoop with the tale of a student in trouble with the university over mixed flatting. That developed into a large protest and *Falus* achieved its greatest coup – as first publisher of James K. Baxter's 'A small ode on mixed flatting'.[153]

There were other student publications, too. The CU first produced a student handbook with useful information in the early 1900s, and OUSA later took over responsibility for this. By the 1980s the annual guide incorporated an 'anti-calendar' with frank advice on most first-year university courses. Another frank OUSA publication was its 1970s *Sexuality* advice book, which other New Zealand university student associations also distributed or used as a model. Students in some faculties launched their own magazines: medical students produced the *Medical Digest*, *Borborygmi*, *Enema* and the *New Zealand Medical Student Journal*; law students had *Estoppel*; dental students put out *Dentago* and science students had the *Science Record*. A range of other productions, some only shortlived, emerged from various student groups, and no residential college could stand proud without its own annual magazine.[154]

Overall, there was plenty of opportunity for Otago students to get their original work into print, be it sexist cartoons in the capping mag or serious poetry in the *Review*. Many well-known writers, from Janet Frame to Fleur Adcock, contributed to the *Review*, either in their student days or while on the Burns Fellowship.[155] A few wrote novels featuring the university: C.R. Allen's *A Poor Scholar* (1936), Dan Davin's *Not Here, Not Now* (1970) and Fiona Farrell's *Book Book* (2004) all included vivid portrayals of Otago student life. Merton Hodge's play *The Wind and the Rain* was popular on the London stage in the 1930s and was later made into two films; the tale of a group of medical students sharing lodgings was set in Edinburgh but was said to be 'moulded on personalities he met while at Otago University' as a medical student.[156] For later generations the best known portrayal

Designers and writers earned their stripes on student publications. *Critic* became a sophisticated production and won various plaudits for its design. When this June 2012 cover for an issue with a mental health theme featured on design industry blog Coverjunkie, it caught the eye of the staff of *Newsweek*. The *Critic* team of Sam Clark, Joe Stockman and Sam Stuchbury adapted their design for the cover of the US giant that boasted a readership of 14 million. CRITIC COLLECTION.

of life at Otago was the film *Scarfies* (1999) by Robert Sarkies and Duncan Sarkies, based on the adventures of students living in a dilapidated Brown Street house. It wouldn't please a health and housing expert, but it was an affectionate study of Otago students – or scarfies, as they had been called for decades.[157]

CHAPTER FOUR

A place to live: Lodgings, colleges and flats

In 1871 William Hutchison, editor of the *Wanganui Chronicle*, wrote to the University of Otago requesting information. Among other things, he asked: 'Will any arrangement be made touching the lodging of students – that is, any sort of supervision or recommendation as to the character and position of those with whom students may live?'[1] Council secretary John Hislop sent a reassuring reply: 'The Rev D.M. Stuart, Vice-Chancellor, and all the university authorities will be glad to do all they can for the proper supervision of youths from a distance. We shall do all in our powers to secure suitable persons with whom students may live. In all probability arrangements may be made hereafter for students lodging in the University building under proper supervision.'[2] Hutchison evidently accepted this reassurance, as his 16-year-old son Thomas became one of Otago's foundation students.

The university hoped to provide accommodation, but it was decades coming. Late in 1873 the University Council and provincial superintendent James Macandrew agreed that 'the want of boarding accommodation and supervision prevented parents and guardians in other Provinces from sending students to Dunedin to attend the University'. The council had its eye on the Otago Boys' High School rectory, but Macandrew explained that the education board had other plans for that; he suggested the council might 'anticipate its revenue to the extent of £5000 or £6000 in order to provide a suitable boarding establishment'.[3] That, together with plans to expand classes, sparked the scheme to move the university to purpose-built premises at a new location. The council hoped to include accommodation for 40 students but, when money ran short, classrooms and laboratories took priority. The plans for student accommodation were reduced to 20 places, then quietly dropped altogether.[4]

LODGINGS AND LANDLADIES

In 1872 council secretary Alexander Livingston explained to concerned parent Benjamin Wells of Taranaki that a student from out of town 'should call at the college upon landing and any luggage he may have would be taken charge of and information would be given to him of persons willing to take boarders'; in other words, the university was acting as an accommodation bureau. Livingstone also mentioned another approach: 'Cases more than one occurred last winter of 3 or 4 students renting a house, supplying themselves with a few needful things, and doing the cooking in turn'[5] – although flatting, as it became known, was not common until later, it was there from the beginning. Private board was the usual choice for students from beyond Dunedin for decades; even after residential colleges opened it appealed as a cheaper option. That would have pleased those who disapproved of 'the old monkish idea' of university residences, such as Robert Gillies, who wrote to the *ODT* in 1877 expressing concern that the university contemplated the 'clubbing of numbers of young men together without the salt of family influence surrounding them'.[6] Such attitudes reflected a Scottish and Presbyterian suspicion of residential colleges. In contrast with the old English universities, based on such institutions, Otago resembled the universities of Scotland where students lived independently.[7]

The landlady was a big influence on student life in the first 100 years at Otago: some were eccentric or irritating; others were loved. 'Your typical landlady can be classified under two headings – a) Avaricious. b) Maternal,' wrote a student in the 1940s.[8] Some families had spare rooms they rented out to provide a student with a 'home away from home', but many landladies were widows or single women who offered several rooms to lodgers as their only source of income. Amelia Muir, who had been offering 'superior board and residence for families and gentlemen' in View Street since 1862, wrote to the university in 1871 to call attention to her establishment's availability for 'Professors, students, or other gentlemen connected with the university'.[9] Whether anybody took up the offer is unknown. Alexander Williamson, an early student, paid Mr Frazer 23/6 a week (around $170 today) for lodgings, and student Thomas Cuddie was boarding with Mrs Brebner in London Street when he died in 1871.[10]

Street directories in the 1880s listed several boarding houses close to the university buildings. From the mid-1870s, Caledon House offered accommodation in Albany Street: it provided 'every convenience', including harmonium and bath.[11] Later advertisements promoted Caledon's convenience for students.[12] Standards varied. In 1890 Charles Hector and Bartholomew Wilford boarded with Mrs Taylor. In the manner of concerned parents of any generation, Hector's father was unhappy to discover him 'hard at work in a cold room – no fire', when he visited from Wellington. Wilford became ill with rheumatic fever shortly afterwards and Hector was sent by his father to other lodgings. When Wilford developed possible symptoms of typhoid, Hector senior wrote to his wife: 'I have told Charlie that he must not go back to Mrs Taylor's again. The back premises are not what they should be' (a discreet reference to the toilet arrangements). Wilford died soon afterwards of acute rheumatic disease.[13]

In 1932 the council established a Board of Control with council, staff and student reps; though the board was primarily set up to deal with disciplinary issues, it was concerned with student wellbeing and had a lodgings subcommittee. It listed approved lodgings and matched students with rooms. Agnes Blackie, who was chair of the subcommittee for some years, recalled the procedure: 'In early December the chairman visited the approved lodgings to find out about probable vacancies. The landladies would almost unanimously declare that nothing on earth would induce them to take students again. A second visit in January would find them cheered up again and willing to re-enter the fray.' Blackie developed 'a kindly feeling for the landladies; many of them were battle-scarred veterans who had conducted lodgings for many years, terribly over-worked, but very proud of their past students and what they had done in life'. After Blackie's stint, the administration of the lodgings committee was taken over by a part-time lodgings registrar, and evolved into the Student Accommodation Office.[14]

Maurice Matich boarded with two others at the Wright family home in Queen Street in the 1940s. The Wrights were 'strong Irish Catholics' and 'fanatical Labour supporters'; Matich got the digs through his Dargaville parish priest. It was 'the coldest place in Dunedin', but Mrs Wright looked after them well. 'She was an adequate cook', recalled Matich, but 'I still cannot forgive her for boiling lamb chops that her brother brought down from his sheep holding in Central Otago'.[15] Some lodgers enjoyed 'all the comforts of home', but many experienced frustrations with 'petty restrictions and nagging concerning the use of various facilities'.[16] In the 1960s Chris Heath boarded with 'gentle dear people' in St Kilda but found it 'stultifying'. He was allowed a bath once a week, in cold water. After being served a poached egg for breakfast every day, he avoided them ever after.[17] Regular cooked meals were convenient for students, although the quality varied. Poor living conditions were the payback for cheap board, which made a university education more affordable to the less well-off; and the working-class origins of most landladies kept students from privileged backgrounds in touch with the concerns of working people as they dined at their table each day.

THE FIRST RESIDENTIAL COLLEGE: SELWYN

Since the university failed to build student accommodation, the churches established Otago's first residential colleges. Their aim was to provide oversight and pastoral care to students, and some colleges also had connections to theological training. Selwyn College was the brainchild of Samuel Nevill, first bishop of the Anglican Diocese of Dunedin. The southern church was small and short of funds, but Nevill was determined to set up local theological training and embarked on a fundraising campaign for a college in 1872. In the same year, two students started out as candidates for the Anglican ministry, living in Nevill's own home, and others followed. Nevill faced considerable apathy and opposition from other Anglicans, but his college fund slowly grew and, in 1886, he announced: 'I have taken another step forward in this matter by the purchase of a house, very conveniently situated in relation to the university, which I should wish future students to attend if possible.' That house was home to the theology tutor for the next few years, before it became the warden's residence.[18]

Building started in 1891 and in 1893 Selwyn College, named after New Zealand's first Anglican bishop, opened. It was a 'mixed' college, open to men studying at the university alongside trainee priests; the foundation residents included five candidates for holy orders and one medical student. Selwyn struggled in its first few decades from lack of funds. By 1909 there were 25 residents and, with no shortage of applications, the warden was anxious to expand. In 1911 Selwyn Collegiate School – a private school for boys, which had been taken over by the Anglican Church and installed

The first Selwyn College building, photographed in the early 1900s. On the left is the Selwyn Collegiate School building, erected in 1907.

SELWYN COLLEGE RECORDS, 84-086/062, S16-503A, HOCKEN COLLECTIONS.

A Selwyn College bedroom/study, from an album by photographer C.M. Collins. It probably dates from around 1930, when another storey and a new wing were added. The new wing included a dining hall funded as a memorial by the family of the Massey brothers, killed in World War I.

SELWYN COLLEGE RECORDS, 84-086/062, S16-503B, HOCKEN COLLECTIONS.

in the Selwyn College grounds – closed and the school building became part of the college. Some residents had rooms in a neighbouring house purchased by Alice Woodthorpe, the warden's wife, and later the board of governors, which took over management of Selwyn from the St Paul's Cathedral Chapter in 1914, purchased other neighbouring houses. Resident numbers dropped during World War I and the college closed for a year in 1918. In 1919 L.G. ('Algy') Whitehead began a 31-year stint as Selwyn warden, during which time he earned widespread respect and affection. He set about renovating the rundown buildings and, aided by politician James Allen, raised enough money to build another wing and add a third storey to the original building. Later, in the 1950s and 1960s, further buildings and extensions meant the college could accommodate over 90 students.[19]

Early Selwyn residents soon developed communal traditions. Theology students were quickly outnumbered by others – particularly medical students, many of whom lived in the college for five years or more. Nevertheless, religion was an integral part of Selwyn. Until the mid-1980s all the wardens were Anglican clergy; they led services at the adjacent All Saints Church, which students were expected to attend. Whitehead started holding regular high teas around 1920: a wine connoisseur, he noted that the events started as 'a soft drink affair, then … ascended to wine, but later degenerated to beer'.[20] One of Selwyn's best known former residents, Arthur Porritt, later recalled that life in Selwyn in the early 1920s was

> *cosmopolitan to a degree, very free and easy (in contrast to Knox!) and though we were relatively few in numbers we could produce a team in almost any sport. Despite our 'Boys about Town' reputation we were 100% loyal to our 'Headmaster' – the Rev Algy Whitehead (and his two spinster sisters who cared for our material and domestic welfare) and tried to ensure that our not infrequent pranks brought no odium on him.*[21]

Above: The first stage of Knox College under construction, c. 1908.

UNIVERSAL POST CARD CO., G. CAMPBELL SERIES. BOX-308-006, S16-548B, HOCKEN COLLECTIONS.

Below: An aerial view of Knox College in 2008. The Somerville Court flats are to the left of the main building, and the Presbyterian theological hall (now the Knox Centre for Ministry and Leadership) and library are at the rear.

GRAHAM WARMAN PHOTOGRAPH, UNIVERSITY OF OTAGO MARKETING AND COMMUNICATIONS COLLECTION.

PRESBYTERIAN COLLEGES – KNOX AND ST MARGARET'S

In 1909 Selwyn acquired a rival for sports contests and other bragging rights: Knox College. Like Selwyn, Knox had its origins in the needs of theological students but also welcomed others. The campaign for a Presbyterian college was started in 1902 by minister Andrew Cameron, an early Otago graduate who was on the University Council (and later chancellor) and convened the church's committee on theological training. Presbyterians trained their own ministers locally from the 1870s with classes in theology professor William Salmond's home in Leith Street, but that became cramped. The campaign for a college kicked off with a donation from one of New Zealand's wealthiest men, John Ross, of importing and manufacturing firm Ross and Glendining. Other donations trickled in and in 1908 the foundation stone of an imposing building was laid in Opoho. The first residents of Knox – which was named after John Knox, founder of the Presbyterian Church of Scotland – were 19 students of the

St Margaret's College residents and staff in 1924.
ST MARGARET'S COLLEGE RECORDS, AG-157-N2, S10-532A, HOCKEN COLLECTIONS.

Theological Hall (also located at the new college) and 21 university students. Knox expanded to house 94 residents by 1914.[22]

Knox, which was Otago's largest college for several decades, played a big role in university life. Its masters were well-known figures; several were members of the University Council and two – Hubert Ryburn and Jack Somerville – served as chancellor. The first residents established an ethos that encouraged academic achievement but also nurtured social, sporting and cultural life. They downed their books for 'supper parties' each evening, where men of different backgrounds and interests discussed life, the universe and everything. As befitted Presbyterian culture of that time, alcohol was banned, but Knox did allow 'lady visitors', albeit at heavily restricted times; women were completely banned at Selwyn. Although students gravitated to residences that matched their own religious background, the church colleges were not exclusive – they admitted residents of any denomination (or none). Through the decades life at Knox changed markedly, but it clung to some practices, such as formal dress for dinner, that gave it a reputation for cherishing 'tradition'.[23]

All students living at Knox and Selwyn were men, but women needed accommodation too. In 1909 Presbyterians who were interested in establishing a women's college formed the Women Students' Hostel Committee. After various political complications they secured the lease of the building vacated by the Theological Hall when Knox opened. It was rundown but the site, right next to the university, was ideal. After hurried repairs, early in 1911 the first residents moved into St Margaret's College, named after a devout medieval queen of Scotland. By the end of that year the college had 15 residents, including 12 training college and three university students. It was a small beginning, but the college council had big plans. After a major fundraising effort, in 1914 construction began on a brick building, and by the end of 1917 it was complete, with room for 70 residents.

Life in St Margaret's was strictly controlled, but the women established a happy community at a time when not all parts of the university welcomed them. Almost a third of Otago students were women in the 1910s, even more in the war years and, as St Margaret's historian Susannah Grant points out, the college 'stood on the hill as a visible symbol of women's increasing participation in higher education'. It was a focal point and meeting place for all women students.[24]

The original Studholme House (later known as Lower Studholme), on the corner of Leith and Union streets, 1919.

C.A. ARMSTRONG PHOTOGRAPH, UNIVERSITY OF OTAGO JUBILEE ALBUM, P2008-011/022A, S13-292B, HOCKEN COLLECTIONS.

A COLLEGE FOR HOME SCIENTISTS: STUDHOLME

The university established its own first residential college in the 1910s for women studying home science. The college served a dual purpose: it provided accommodation for home science students and gave them experience in the field while they studied institutional administration. The university purchased two joined houses on the corner of Leith and Union streets (where UniCol stands today) and converted them into a hostel that opened in 1915. The hostel was named after John Studholme, the philanthropist who helped establish the chair in home science at Otago. Winifred Boys-Smith, the home science professor, no longer had to teach the practical aspects of the course – especially laundry work – in her own home.[25]

Until the 1960s all Studholme residents were home science students, and all home science students from out of town lived at Studholme. The original premises soon became too small so the university bought more houses. The most important of these was a large house at 127 Clyde Street – still in use as the west wing of Studholme – that opened in 1930 as 'Upper Studholme', and the original premises became 'Lower Studholme'. By the 1950s, home science students were spread between Upper and Lower Studholme, St Helens (the former maternity hospital), St Anne's (a former private hospital in Leith Street, next to Lower Studholme) and various smaller houses.

Upper Studholme House in 1949.

PRIME MINISTER'S DEPARTMENT PHOTOGRAPH, BOX-184-091, HOCKEN COLLECTIONS.

Lower Studholme became decrepit but was deemed uneconomic to repair. Sadie Andrews was one of several 1951 students who had a lucky escape; after they had departed at the end of the year, the roof collapsed on their beds. With that the Lower Studholme bedrooms were abandoned, but the kitchen and dining room were still used for some years.[26]

Although conditions were far from luxurious at Studholme – or perhaps because of that – it developed a strong community spirit. Nancy Carr was at St Anne's in the mid-1950s, when residents were only allowed to heat water for baths once a week to save on electricity; they sneaked in extra baths by lighting fires in a copper in an outhouse and bathing two at a time in the laundry tubs with somebody standing guard at the door.[27] In 1961, after decades of planning and fundraising, a new block opened in the grounds of Upper Studholme. It spelled the end of Studholme's days as a residence purely for home science students, as there was now room for other women students too.[28]

AD HOC DEVELOPMENTS: ARANA AND CARRINGTON

After opening Studholme in 1915 the university waited over 50 years to establish another residential college. Meanwhile, religious organisations opened establishments to cater for the expanding roll. In 1940 Harold Turner, assistant minister at Knox Church, came up with a scheme for a small hostel in the former Presbyterian Women's Training Institute in Cumberland Street (later the site of part of the University Union). He formed a committee with other enthusiasts, among them George Carrington (secretary of the Otago Education Board) and businessmen Cecil Wardell and Gifford Laurenson; Turner later described them as 'a private voluntary group on a religious but interdenominational basis'. In 1941 Stuart House opened to 29 men, some of them in an 'annexe' at the former teachers' college building across the road. In 1942, with many men heading off for military service but an influx of women students instead, the council decided to change Stuart House to a women's residence. Some men had already been offered places so the council found them bedrooms in private homes nearby; they became 'associate members' of Stuart House, which they attended for meals and social activities. The makeshift arrangement was popular with residents, and Turner, the warden, was pleased that the house was 'much quieter and more orderly than it was last year'.[29]

Demand for student accommodation increased, and the Stuart House Council looked for suitable buildings to convert. Turner later commented that its next venture 'had a very ad hoc pragmatic origin when the [Stuart House] Council needed a property for its plans for a permanent hall, but had no money, and the University had some money but no plans for a hall'.[30] In 1942 James Allen died and his Clyde Street residence, a large 1880s brick home known as Arana (Māori for Allen), came on the market. The house had already proved its worth for student accommodation: in the 1920s, while Allen was in London as New Zealand High Commissioner, the Home Science School used Arana for a year as overflow for Studholme.[31] The Stuart House Council convinced the university to purchase the property and the council leased it back from the university as a student residence. A couple of years later the university cancelled the lease and appointed the council to manage the hall on its behalf.[32]

Upper Stuart House, as it was known until it became Arana Hall at the end of 1944, opened in 1943. There was room for 20 students but a total of 40 came to the main residence for their meals; the council rented an additional house and found bedrooms for others in nearby homes. Turner, warden for the first eight years, came up with

Arana Hall residents up to mischief outside Marama Hall, probably as part of their initiation. There is 'a scallywaggery that goes back to the first students', says long-serving warden Jamie Gilbertson. They were 'very robust young men with a wicked sense of humour and a large appetite for playing pranks and jokes on the long-suffering staff'.

ARTHUR CAMPBELL PHOTOGRAPH, ARTHUR CAMPBELL COLLECTION

The Arana Hall lounge, photographed in 1964, had all the mod cons, including television and radiogram.

HURST AND PALMER PHOTOGRAPH, DALZIEL ARCHITECTS RECORDS, MS-2756/025, S17-619A, HOCKEN COLLECTIONS.

A resident's room, typical of those in purpose-built colleges of the era, in the new wing of Arana in 1964.

HURST AND PALMER PHOTOGRAPH, DALZIEL ARCHITECTS RECORDS, MS-2931/078, S17-619B, HOCKEN COLLECTIONS.

'ingenious ideas' for accommodating more. The garage was lined and divided into bedrooms, an army hut was installed on the lawn and, in 1944, a fibrolite and pinex building to house 21 students appeared on the tennis court. Quite a few residents still slept in nearby houses leased or bought by the council; a group had their bedrooms in the top storey of the old Union Street home purchased by the university in 1945 that was also home to the Geography Department. Saturday morning geography labs were held to the accompaniment of the 'Mellor House boys' singing in the shower, and fuses blew as residents plugged toasters into light sockets. The Geography Department later expanded upstairs, and the last Arana 'boys' lived at Mellor House in the late 1950s. Financial stringency and postwar building delays meant some of Turner's schemes didn't come to fruition – a steel Nissen hut became the new dining room, rather than a more substantial extension – but by the time he departed at the end of 1951 Arana was 'a thriving hall with more than 80 residents'.[33]

Arana had a reputation as a 'wild place' in its early years, 1950s resident Melville Carr recalls; it was less 'sophisticated' than Selwyn or Knox. Many early residents were returned servicemen who chafed at restrictions designed for school leavers; compulsory attendance at chapel services became one point of dispute. Still, the food was good, Carr remembers, and they could try interesting dishes sent to Malay students by their families. Otago's first Colombo Plan students lived at Arana, and the government funded a new wing, opened

Building a float for the 1946 capping procession, in front of the first house purchased for Carrington. The man with saw in hand is Murray Menzies, who became a surgeon. CARRINGTON COLLEGE COLLECTION.

A happy group at Carrington in the late 1940s. Residents were a mixture of teachers' college and university students and – more radically – men and women.
ROBIN COOK ALBUM, CARRINGTON ALUMNI ASSOCIATION, COURTESY OF BILL DAWSON.

in 1964, to compensate Otago for the increased demand the Colombo Plan placed on its residential colleges. Another wing was completed at Arana in 1968, meaning there was space for 140 residents.[34]

The Stuart House Council's ventures did not end with Arana. In late 1944 a property on Heriot Row came on the market and Carrington bought it on spec, having heard a rumour the government was planning to provide money for teachers' college student accommodation. Fortunately the rumour was true; the Education Board funded the building, leaving its management in the hands of the renamed Stuart Residence Halls Council. A group of women university and teachers' college students moved into Carrington Hall in 1945. Accommodation for male students was in short supply as the war wound down so, not long after, the council offered rooms to men in one of two neighbouring houses purchased for Carrington. The generous grounds of the old houses provided room for yet more accommodation and in 1947 a new wing was built, named Stuart House, and army huts provided further temporary space. That year Carrington housed 105 students and the original Stuart House in Cumberland Street became flats.[35]

Accommodating women and men in the same residential college was a pragmatic response to needs and opportunities rather than a deliberate scheme, but since it worked it carried on. For several years Carrington was Australasia's only 'co-residential' student hall of residence. The liberals of the 1940s weren't completely liberal, though: there were strict rules about men and women mixing at Carrington. They socialised freely in communal spaces but had segregated bedroom wings and were permitted to visit one another's quarters only on Sunday afternoons. Women – but not men – were locked in from 10pm. Until 1976 all of the wardens were clergymen, some more conservative than others; legend has it that one warden and his wife listened in at the men's doors to ensure any women had left before curfew. In 1973 conversion into mixed dormitories commenced, though men and women had separate floors for many years.[36]

Turner wrote in the 1950s about the advantages of mixed residences where students socialised in a 'natural and happy' way and formed 'decent and sensible friendships'; it made 'the men less crude, and the girls less giggly'. Co-residence could be 'too distracting for some students', though, said Turner, and some people thought it was 'good for men to spend some years in a thoroughly masculine environment; presumably the parallel position is true of women'.[37] Arana remained such a 'thoroughly masculine' residence until the late 1970s.

Dominican Hall. The house was originally built in the 1880s for Robert Gillies, a businessman and amateur astronomer, who included an observatory in the roof and named it Transit House in honour of the Transit of Venus. An OUSA listing of student residences for 1967 noted that at Dominican Hall 'most necessary facilities are present although there is generally a theme of austerity'. Any austerity must have contrasted with the surviving 'opulent elegant detail' of the building, from embossed plaster ceilings to Minton floor tiles and ornate door handles.

F15/5/1, DOMINICAN SISTERS ARCHIVES.

THE CATHOLICS – DOMINICAN AND AQUINAS

Like the other churches, Catholics wanted to provide for their young people coming from around the country to Dunedin. In 1945 the Dominican Sisters, a teaching order at the forefront of Catholic education in Otago since they arrived in 1871, purchased a grand stone home in spacious grounds in Park Street. In 1946 the building became Dominican Hall, a residential college for 20 women students.[38] One of them, Shona Scannell, later recalled that they formed a 'lovely family … We went to the pictures together and had social sports groups. I thought it was wonderful.'[39] In 1948 the sisters added another storey; with that and other alterations plus the purchase of a neighbouring property in 1953, Dominican Hall expanded to house 48.[40] Some women had single rooms but, as in most residential colleges of the day, others shared. Residents of the 'dormitory' reported on their exploits in the 1960 Dominican Hall magazine. 'Life with seven in a room can be rather hectic,' Maureen Donnelly noted, but 'a great sense of comradeship has grown.' They took part in all the social and sporting activities on offer, and 'If there is any trouble we are all in it together, be it smoking in unlawful places, creeping in rather late, or just not sweeping the floor. We have formed a Rock'n Roll Recorder Group and at one stage our singing was of such quality it was mistaken for the radio.'[41]

Students singing compline led by Father Ambrose Loughnan OP, Dominican Hall, in 1956. Religion was an important feature of Dominican life. The students were cared for by a small group of sisters and a resident chaplain; they hosted visits from the bishop and meetings of the Catholic Students' Club, held retreats and had their own branch of the Children of Mary sodality.

F15/8/2, DOMINICAN SISTERS ARCHIVES.

An early view of Aquinas Hall. It was the first major project of renowned Dunedin architect Ted McCoy, who later designed several prominent buildings on the University of Otago campus.
AQUINAS COLLEGE COLLECTION.

The 1966 residents of Second Floor North pose for the Aquinas magazine *Veritas*
AQUINAS COLLEGE COLLECTION

This still left a gap in accommodation for Catholic men. In 1948 Dunedin bishop James Whyte wrote to the Dominican Order in Australia to ask if they might do something about 'the crying need in Dunedin of a hostel for the Catholic students who come here to the Medical School'.[42] Dominican priests Leo McArdle and Denis Crowley arrived in Dunedin in 1949 to take over Sacred Heart Parish in North East Valley and establish a college. They raised funds through public subscriptions, a bank loan and a government subsidy, and building commenced in 1951 on land donated by the Dominican Sisters, adjacent to their Santa Sabina Convent. In 1954 the first residents moved into Aquinas Hall, named in honour of medieval theologian St Thomas Aquinas, the most famed of Dominican friars. The 72 pioneering residents included many medical and dental students and a variety of others, including physical education and teachers' college students; about two thirds were Catholic. Fathers Bernard Curran and Ambrose Loughnan and Brothers Martin Keogh and Peter O'Hearn joined McArdle to form the college's first Dominican community. In keeping with the scholarly goals of the college and of the Dominican order, the residents had a library and tutorial rooms as well as their common rooms and chapel. They had views over the city and directly across North East Valley to Knox; Knox and Aquinas residents sometimes howled at one another across the valley, and they were rivals in student hijinks.[43]

The two Catholic halls often combined for social activities. In 1957 Dominican Hall reported that 'Aquinas arrived in initiation garb to entertain us, and stayed to douse each girl in the goldfish pond, an act which proved fatal for the goldfish'. Aquinas noted that 'higher circles greeted this display of mixed bathing with displeasure'.[44] Kevin Toomey, a resident in the 1970s who became a priest and university chaplain, commented in 2011 on the survival of the 'Aquinas spirit': 'Its relative smallness and distance from the centre of things give it a robust community life.'[45] In 1967 Aquinas, with room for 90 men, was not much smaller than Selwyn (96) or Arana (104); Knox (150) was considerably larger. However, the other colleges later expanded much more than Aquinas.[46]

Getting to campus from Aquinas could be tricky: foundation resident James Ng recalled 'the winter morning bike rides down the steep, treacherously ice-covered access road, hurtling out of control towards the hairpin corner at the foot of the hill. The morning bravado was followed by more exertion as we strode back for lunch, leaving our bikes halfway up the hill.' Tragically, in 1994 a resident was killed when her brakes failed going down the hill.[47]

THE METHODISTS DO THEIR BIT

Not to be outdone by the Anglicans, Presbyterians and Catholics, in 1958 the Methodists joined the student accommodation business. Like several other institutions, Wesley Hall started with the purchase of a private residence. The Park Street home had room for 14 students – all men – and a resident matron, with the Methodist Central Mission's superintendent acting as non-resident warden. The bedrooms were small and 'no studies are provided', reported the OUSA in 1967, 'but there is a common room with piano and table tennis table'.[48] The crowded conditions did not deter some residents. At the end of 1961 matron Elsie Maclean reported: 'we seem to have some bright lads at present and the majority are anxious to return again next year ... Several will be spending their fourth year here'.[49] Their behaviour was generally 'quite good till about midnight when apparently they become restive and noisy but as this seems to be the usual procedure in the student world, we patiently wait till the spasm subsides'.[50] As a small institution Wesley Hall struggled for recognition by other colleges, though the residents organised events such as a 'very enjoyable' hockey match and lunch with the women of Dominican Hall in 1964. The 1963 and 1964 presidents noted the perils of having too many residents from one district – in this case Gore – which 'tends to create a rather narrow range of acquaintances'. It could 'cause a certain amount of friction and suspicion ie "Who told my parents that I took so and so out last week?"', Kenneth Thomson reported.[51]

Unlike several other residences with small beginnings, Wesley Hall did not grow larger, though that was the original plan. Methodist superintendent David Gordon explained in 1970 that the Central Mission planned extensions for years but, on consultation with Otago VC Arthur Beacham, concluded that 'with the rising running costs for a hostel, we should build nothing smaller than a 100 bed hostel'. As time passed and the 'optimum size' enlarged, the project grew 'entirely beyond the resources of the Central Mission'. The government offered subsidies to organisations building student accommodation, and that helped with the initial set-up of Wesley Hall – but the cost of a new building was high and the church had other priorities for social service funding. Wesley had run at a loss throughout its 12 years,

The large Park Street home that became Wesley Hall was originally built in 1918 for lawyer Herbert Adams, and was later run as a guesthouse.
JOHN MCINDOE LTD RECORDS, MS-3247/584, S17-564B, HOCKEN COLLECTIONS.

and the Methodists 'decided reluctantly' to close it at the end of 1970. The building that had housed lively young men as a student residence was purchased by the Department of Health to become 'a Hostel for the Rehabilitation of Alcoholics'.[52]

THE RISE OF THE STUDENT FLAT

During the 1960s flatting took over from colleges and private board as the favourite living arrangement for Otago students. Colleges and private board couldn't keep up with the rising roll; but the change also reflected the mood of the times. Flats might be just as cold, dark and noisy as a boarding house but they offered more freedom, which became a priority for young people. The accommodation officer noted in his 1965 report a 'diminishing number of old fashioned landladies'. That year 12 per cent of Otago students lived in private board, down from 17 per cent in 1955; by 1975 this had plummeted to 3 per cent. Larger government student allowances and good holiday earnings in a period of prosperity meant students had more financial independence from their parents, so flatting became an option for locals as well as students from elsewhere. In 1955 around 28 per cent of Otago students lived with their parents; there was a small decline to 24 per cent in 1965 and a large drop to 14 per cent in 1975.[53]

Although there were a few Otago students who shared a flat with others right from the beginning, it was not common practice for the first few decades. 'The Bach' was one flat that emerged as a stringency measure during the depression of the 1930s. It was set up by a group of Presbyterian divinity students led by Lex Miller, a pacifist and social justice campaigner who became Stanford University's first professor of religion. They were joined by other students until there were about 10 men squeezed in, three to a bedroom. The Bach offered cheap living – half the cost of a residential college – and independence from conservative institutional leaders. It was a supportive community with religion as a common thread, even if beliefs varied; one year the presidents of competing student societies the EU and SCM roomed together. Ian Dixon remembered his year at the Bach as 'a very happy one. We were warm and comfortable and had plenty to eat … Life was

'The Bach' started in a house in Dalmore, with '98 steps to climb', but later moved to 208 Leith Street. It had a nameplate and residents had a calling card complete with a crest and a Greek motto that translated to 'Because of poverty'. These residents, c.1938, were future ministers and doctors, a vet and a teacher. From left: George Falloon, Dave Martin, Jim Anderson, John Mandeno, Alf Shaw and Charlie McArthur or Bryan Pinder.

GEORGE FALLOON COLLECTION, P-A336_2-009, PRESBYTERIAN RESEARCH CENTRE.

Michael Shackleton, Bernard Bowden and Gavin Andrews at their 'digs' at Surrey Street, St Clair, in 1952. 'The floor sloped up from the front door and down to the back door but it was comfortable enough – it even had a garden where we grew some vegetables,' Shackleton recalled.

MICHAEL SHACKLETON COLLECTION.

light hearted but study time was disciplined. It was a good life.' Accounts – including one at the nearby corner store – were strictly kept: John Gardiner commented that 'a common commodity was a weekly 7lb [3kg] tin of syrup which was the staple bread spread. Jam was luxury.' The Bach ended in 1941 when it became mandatory for all divinity students to live at Knox. Former 'Bachites' retained fond memories of the flat, and several said they could not have afforded to complete their degrees or ministry training without it.[54]

The number of flats increased gradually through the 1940s and 1950s, and by 1955 there were 272 Otago students – 13 per cent of the total roll – living in 'rooms and flats'.[55] A few premises were notorious, including the Shambles on the corner of St David and Great King streets. It was home to a succession of mining students, among others, and well known for its parties. The flatmates were keen homebrewers – Melville Carr recalls visiting one of his chemistry student friends there in the 1950s to check out the latest brew (which was awful). There was hardly any furniture; to keep warm they put the end of a piece of four by two in the fire and pushed it in further as it burned away.[56]

The Shambles was the sort of place that concerned university authorities. In its 1959 submission to the Committee of Enquiry on New Zealand Universities, Otago urged the government to fund more residential colleges so students would not be 'obliged to live in rooms and flats [and] undertake housekeeping for themselves. This mode of life is not invariably unsatisfactory, but for the young student, away from home for the first time, with little contact with wise and mature minds, it lacks much that a University education should provide, quite apart from the obvious inherent dangers.' Flats often meant 'sub-standard conditions', the commission noted.[57]

The expansion of colleges failed to keep up with the roll, even if students had all wanted to live there. By 1965 a quarter of Otago students lived in flats, and by 1975 it was 42 per cent.[58] Most were close to the university, and the area became dominated by students: as Elworthy puts it, 'an almost self-contained community in North Dunedin' developed 'its own independent youth culture in the 1960s'.[59]

MIXED FLATTING

Janet Mitchell followed the pattern common to many students of the early 1960s and later. After a couple of years in college she went flatting with friends she met there. She spent a year in a 'rumpty' old house with an outdoor toilet, opposite the nurses' home, then lived with four other women in the old Methodist manse in Dundas Street.[60]

Most flats at that time were all male or all female, and when mixed flatting emerged in the late 1960s there was a huge stoush. It is famous in Otago's history, in part because James K. Baxter, then Burns Fellow at Otago, wrote a catchy poem about it, 'A small ode on mixed flatting'.[61] The drama began in June 1967 when Robin Williams, the new VC, told a senior psychology student to move out of the flat he was sharing with three young women or face disciplinary action. There were perhaps a dozen mixed student flats already, but authorities were either unaware or had turned a blind eye. In this case the accommodation officer, Laurie Hogg, asked the VC to make a ruling. With a squeeze on accommodation, Hogg couldn't find a place in a male flat for the student concerned, who then found his own place in the women's flat. According to 1966 amendments to disciplinary regulations the accommodation officer could approve and inspect student accommodation. The intention was to ensure 'that students are not victimised by high rents or substandard conditions' – there was no explicit rule concerning mixed flatting.[62]

Decades later Williams commented that the attitude he and the council took 'was totally unnecessary and superfluous'. Vetoing students from substandard flats 'marginally was in the university's authority', but preventing mixed flatting wasn't.[63] Still, there was pressure from a community suspicious of students and their morals in an era of sexual liberation. William Morrell reflected a common view in his 1969 history of the university: 'Some students challenged the right of the University to regulate student life outside the classroom, a view not easily justified when the University, as a recipient of public money, has surely a duty to see that standards respected by the public are observed by its members'.[64] It was 'a student revolt against paternalism' suggests David Wilson; most 1960s students were not interested in living in mixed flats themselves, but wanted the freedom to choose their own way of life. Many were incensed about the VC's actions because the flat concerned was an 'innocent' one with no sexual relationship involved, and operating with the consent of all of the flatmates' parents and the landlord.[65] Around 1000 students – about a quarter of the roll – attended a protest, and more than 100 stayed for the entire 'sleep-in'. Protest leader Paul Alexander, an anthropology student known as an 'activist and stirrer', said that students 'may have to lick the taxpayers' boots, but we don't have to praise the flavour'. It was the first major protest in Otago's history, at a time of rising student activism around the Western world.[66]

The student whose plight sparked the protest moved out of his mixed flat on legal advice and attempts by students to have the disciplinary regulations reviewed failed, though the council agreed to accept written submissions. As Elworthy notes, 'students were beaten by the approaching exams and their basic lack of power'. The disciplinary regulations prompted further protests later (see chapter 3). While the council stood by its right to inspect where students lived until 1975, Otago never again disciplined students for mixed flatting; in that sense, students won the battle.[67] Mixed flatting became increasingly popular – and accepted by the public.

NAMING FLATS

'The Bach' of the 1930s had a nameplate: it was an early example of the 'named' flat.[68] Sarah Gallagher, who has recorded that cultural phenomenon through the Dunedin Flat Names Project, comments that although it was not peculiar to Dunedin it was more common there than elsewhere in New Zealand. Some names reflected the standard of the accommodation or the lifestyle of the residents, others the history of the building; some were crude and others esoteric. Some names persisted for decades, while others came and went – for instance, a house in Dundas Street, once known as the Greasy Beaver Lodge, became the Embassy, complete with Samoan flag, and then reverted to the Greasy Beaver.[69]

One student flat inspired a 1985 hit song for the band Sneaky Feelings. Huband House was an all-male flat in Hope Street, attached to St Matthew's Anglican Church; the women in the all-female Christian flat down the road named it 'Husband House', and Matthew Bannister, who once had a girlfriend in the Hope Street flat, referred to it in the lyrics of 'Husband House'.[70] Another famous Otago flat had musical connections but no name. In 2006 a group of friends from UniCol moved into 660 Castle Street and became known as 'the boys from 660'. When the band they formed made its first recording they selected Six60 as a name. The band went on to great success; when it performed at 2014 Orientation it attracted the biggest crowd in O-week history. The band returned to play impromptu outdoor concerts in its old student neighbourhood from time to time. One of these concerts had dramatic consequences: in 2016 a flat balcony that was overcrowded with concertgoers collapsed, injuring 18 people. Later that year the 660 Castle Street flat was badly damaged in a fire, and one resident was injured when he jumped to safety from a second-storey window.[71]

Those incidents highlighted the perils of living in some flats. Over the decades rundown dives became fewer as landlords improved properties or demolished and replaced them with warmer and healthier homes. However, living in a dingy flat survived as a rite of passage for those who preferred a shabby place in the heart of the student quarter to a superior building with similar rent but a longer walk to campus. Some people blamed greedy landlords for the state of housing; others blamed careless students. Politicians (both local and national, for the problems were not confined to North Dunedin) campaigned for a 'rental warrant of fitness' and mandatory insulation for rental housing.[72]

OUSA highlighted housing problems and, in 2007, introduced awards that showcased 'the nicer side of flatting' and rewarded good landlords and tenants – though some students took pride in the notoriety of winning the 'worst flat' category.[73] The worst flat of 2012 – the Shit Show Chateau in London Street – was ripe for transformation. A group of students from environmental group Generation Zero rented it for 2013, hoping to turn it into a healthy home as an inspiration to others. The task proved monumental and they shifted focus to 'empowering students to get their landlords to make the changes'. In 2014 the group started the Rate My Flat scheme that allowed 'students to review local flats from the tenants' perspective'. An earlier rating scheme introduced by the DCC and university accommodation office in 2010 led to improvements, but bad landlords had no incentive to obtain a rating.[74]

Pink Flat The Door, named in 1988 by a group of students including broadcaster Wallace Chapman, was a 'freedom flat' inspired by B.F. Skinner's philosophy of a free society. The door design referred to Pink Floyd's classic album *The Wall*. It was photographed by Sarah Gallagher in 2004, soon after it had been given a fresh coat of paint. SARAH GALLAGHER COLLECTION.

The DSIR (Department of Student Inebriation Research) in Union Street won a prize in a 1990s radio station 'Name your flat' competition. Some of the flatmates later worked for the other DSIR (Department of Scientific and Industrial Research). Photographed by Sarah Gallagher in 2000. SARAH GALLAGHER COLLECTION.

THE CENTENARY PROJECT: UNIVERSITY COLLEGE

Although flatting mushroomed in the 1960s, roll growth meant demand for residential college places also rose. Otago's centenary project in 1969 was the largest university residential college in Australasia: University College, generally known as UniCol. 'Our tradition dictates that we should celebrate our centenary by strengthening the communal and broader cultural aspects of university life,' VC Beacham stated at the launch of a fundraising campaign for the college in 1964. Donations from the DCC and Otago Savings Bank and, later, a substantial gift from old investment firm the National Mortgage and Agency Company, made building possible.[75] The original plan for 300 residents was enlarged to 324 to make the most of the government two-for-one subsidy on money raised; the extra rooms, which residents dubbed 'gimp rooms', were squeezed into the basement and spaces originally allocated to kitchenettes. A 1972 report noted the challenges and successes

Above: The front of University College in its early days: the cantilevered entry was quite a feature until additions built it out. The John Middleditch sculpture was a centenary gift to the university from the Association of Staff Wives. S15-008A, HOCKEN COLLECTIONS.

Left: A view across campus from one of the communal balconies at UniCol, 2013. UNIVERSITY OF OTAGO MARKETING AND COMMUNICATIONS COLLECTION.

of UniCol's first four years. Despite doomsayers, it was popular with students. It achieved full occupancy and better than average academic pass rates, but construction had been expensive and there were large debts. The 'architecture tends to control social patterns', noted the report. 'At meal times each lift delivers to the ground floor about ten or a dozen people largely from the same floor. These people join the lunch time queue in the dining room together and tend to sit at the same table.' By default, the 'floor' – mostly 18 people – became the main social unit of UniCol.[76]

Though it was a mixed-gender college, UniCol developed a 'blokey' culture. The separation of the sexes within the college didn't help: women had the north tower and men the south tower and visiting was strictly regulated. A campaign for integration of the towers emerged early, sparked by a speech from visiting broadcaster Brian Edwards in 1971. Despite overwhelming support from residents, though, the master and council resisted requests for mixing the towers for many years, in part out of concern that women needed protection from the robust behaviour of the UniCol men. When integration was implemented in 1989 after a trial the previous year, it had a positive effect on college life: among other changes, there was less noise and less damage. A few floors were kept single-sex for those who preferred that option.[77]

Integration didn't entirely end the rowdy behaviour, of course – though the skyrocket wars between the college and flats on Clyde Street disappeared; they had been a feature of Guy Fawkes season in the mid-1970s and again in the mid-1980s.[78] UniCol was still known as a 'party' college in the 1990s. Reforms around the turn of the century, led by a new full-time master with a larger staff, enhanced pastoral care, raised behavioural expectations and modified the worst excesses.[79] The facilities were smartened up with renovations and in 2004 the dining hall was extended and two four-storey wings were added. The roll increased by over 100 that year.[80] UniCol provided a home for a considerable proportion of Otago students: it was an inspired choice as a centenary project for the university.

PRESBYTERIAN EXPANSION

A year after the university launched its fundraising appeal for UniCol the Presbyterian Church started an appeal for another women's college. Its existing colleges, Knox and St Margaret's, had grown through the decades and had added wings in the 1960s but there was still demand for more beds. The new college would cater for women studying for a vocation in the church. Women who were training as Presbyterian deaconesses lived together as a small community but, by the 1960s, their leaders felt they would benefit from living alongside other students, as men training for the ministry at Knox did. In 1963 the church approved the scheme for a residence in the Knox grounds. In 1964 the Presbyterian Church approved the ordination of women as clergy – but nobody yet considered the possibility they might live alongside male theology students in the same college.[81]

Construction started in 1969 after considerable delays as the government deferred its contribution because of financial difficulties, and imposed tighter controls on the building industry.[82] In 1971 the first intake of 140 women moved in; three were students for the Presbyterian ministry and the rest were attending university or teachers' college. Salmond Hall was named for a prominent Presbyterian family, in particular Mary Salmond, former principal of the Deaconess College, and

Above: Salmond College in 2009.

LIGHTHAUS PHOTOGRAPH, UNIVERSITY OF OTAGO MARKETING AND COMMUNICATIONS COLLECTION.

Left: The newly built Salmond Hall, c. 1971.

SALMOND ANDERSON ARCHITECTS RECORDS, MS-3821/2000, S16-548A, HOCKEN COLLECTIONS.

her brother James Salmond, a minister and a leader in Christian education. The first warden, Keren Fulton, combined experience and good Presbyterian credentials; she had run the YWCA hostel Kinnaird House.[83] Though Salmond shared a few facilities such as tennis courts with Knox, and the two colleges held a few combined social events, they maintained distinct identities and cultures. Once Salmond was operational the council that ran both Knox and Salmond turned its attention to the needs of another growing group of students for the ministry: those who were married, often with children. In 1976 it opened a complex of flats in the Knox grounds, some designed for families and others for groups of single students. When demand for the flats later declined they were absorbed into Knox College.[84]

UPS AND DOWNS AND GOING CO-ED

With the opening of UniCol and Salmond and expansion of existing institutions, the number of Otago students living in a college rose from 876 in 1965 to 1508 in 1975 – though with the larger roll there was little change in the proportion of students in college.[85] In the late 1970s and early 1980s colleges encountered problems with overcapacity: the university roll flattened and even dropped for a couple of years; changes to the bursary system discouraged students from leaving home; a large portion of medical students headed to Christchurch or Wellington after their third year; and students in general were staying in colleges for a shorter time.

Colleges that took both men and women had more flexibility when applications were low; as Taryn Tait points out, 'in the end it was financial pressure and a need for numbers, not simply evolving social ideas' that prompted gender integration at Otago's residential colleges.[86] When there was a surfeit of applicants to all-male colleges in 1974, VC Robin Irvine arranged a meeting with college wardens, most of whom agreed that 'a greater degree of elasticity was desirable'. To deal with the immediate crisis Studholme accepted 12 men into what had been a female stronghold for nearly 60 years.[87] All went smoothly and residents appreciated the 'increased sporting prowess' in inter-college events, 'along with a relaxation in the regulations about male visitors'. Studholme continued as a mixed residence. For the first few years men had their own floor, but by 1983 there was a mixed floor and by 1992 one wing was completely integrated.[88]

'It appears that Studholme may be a trendsetter,' said the university staff newsletter. Indeed, other colleges soon followed suit.[89] Late in 1974, with too many applicants for the male-only Knox and too few for the female-only Salmond, the Knox and Salmond council reluctantly decided to offer 21 Salmond places to men.[90] That 'worked out very well indeed,' the council reported at the end of 1976; so well that it 'continued the policy with an additional eight men into 1976'. It reassured Presbyterians, though, that 'Salmond remains essentially a women's hall of residence'.[91] By 1979 the council was reporting that Salmond 'continues to flourish with its mixture of male and female residents'. It touted the benefits: 'Some schools, particularly in Southland, have developed a tradition of going there, and there are many families where all the children have been in Salmond (that is one of the advantages of its co-residential nature)'.[92]

An oversupply of accommodation for women proved fatal to the smallest women's residence. At the end of 1978 the Dominican Sisters announced they were closing Dominican Hall. At its peak it accommodated 50 residents, but by 1978 it had just 28, though '40 can be taken comfortably'. The decline was due to 'the growth in larger, more modern hostels', said Sister Bernadette. As a small institution it could not afford to carry many vacancies in a period of rising expenses; and the demand for improvements to meet DCC fire safety regulations was the final straw.[93] Aquinas accepted women from 1979, but the end was nigh for that college too. In mid-1980 there were 100 vacancies across all Otago's residential colleges, with little prospect of rising demand. Aquinas, the smallest surviving institution at 75 beds, could least afford the financial blow; it closed at the end of that year and the Dominicans sold the building to the Elim Church.[94]

The other colleges struggled on with fewer residents. At Knox the shared rooms that had once housed about a third of the college became large single rooms, and other colleges made similar changes.[95] Arana converted its 'out houses' into independent flats, reducing its college capacity from 167 in 1981 to 85 in 1982; being smaller offered benefits 'in terms of cohesion and a sense of community'.[96] It improved its resilience by housing women as well as men from 1978, though that was not the sole purpose of the change: it hoped the presence of women residents would calm the behaviour of the men. Like UniCol, Arana was involved in the skyrocket battles that plagued Clyde Street in the 1970s; the constant damage from that and other vandalism meant no insurance company would provide it with more than basic fire cover.[97]

Although the switch to a mixed residence went smoothly at Studholme, Salmond, Aquinas and Arana, the other single-sex colleges resisted the change. Residents and, especially, former residents were concerned at the prospect of losing college 'traditions' which, in the case of Knox and Selwyn, were aggressively masculine. Eventually they had little choice but to become co-residential; they had numerous empty rooms and faced closure, while mixed colleges were attracting more applicants. In 1981 the first six men were admitted to the 'virgin's vault' of St Margaret's; others moved into the Clyde Wing, which had now become self-catering accommodation for senior students and staff. St Margaret's warden Roy Miller reported that the first male residents were 'a pleasant bunch' who were integrated into college life 'with no problems whatever', and the intake of men increased over subsequent years.[98] Knox College master Peter Marshall reported that the 37 women admitted in 1983 'were a sensible lot and didn't try and throw their weight around' and noted with delight the improvement in 'community spirit, tolerance, and friendliness'. Dianna Howell, one of the brave 37, recalled that, in general, the women 'did not experience any aggravation by the returning men of the College' who, despite their resistance to the change, had been well prepared for it.[99]

It was a different story at the oldest college, Selwyn. In 1983 returning residents arrived to find women admitted, something they strongly opposed. The men maintained their resistance and subjected the warden and his family to 'boorish and tasteless' harassment. In 1988 the student president was still complaining: an increase in women, who then numbered 38, had 'signified the beginning of the end of the Selwyn of old'. His prediction that Selwyn was 'heading in the direction of just another hostel with equal proportions of male/female students' proved correct.[100] The Selwyn response was a backlash to wider changes; it became one of the last bastions of reactionary misogyny on a campus divided between 'traditional' and 'radical' cultures. However, with many students now staying in college just one year there was a rapid turnover at Selwyn. Attitudes shifted as the years passed and in 1993 Selwyn residents elected their first woman president.[101]

THE 1980s AND 1990s – EXPLOSIVE GROWTH AND NEW COLLEGES

After the difficult years of the early 1980s Otago's residential colleges experienced a dramatic turnaround as the university roll burgeoned. Marshall reported that in 1981 he received just 41 applications for residence at Knox, but in 1989 there were 367: 'In those days I worried how I was going to fill the college and keep it operating. Now I worry about where I am going to put all the people who deserve a place in college.'[102] The university was concerned, too, as potential students who could not find a place in a college went to other universities or abandoned the idea of tertiary study. The situation was aggravated by the demolition of old student flats in leaner years. There were 300 people on the accommodation waiting list in 1984. The existing colleges scrambled to create more places – they reversed earlier changes and incorporated buildings that had been leased out as flats back into the main colleges – but Otago needed far more.

The registrar, Douglas Girvan, orchestrated plans for Otago to establish several colleges at short notice.[103] In January 1984 he negotiated the lease of several unused floors of the Wakari Hospital nurses' home from the Otago Hospital Board (OHB).[104] That enabled the university to guarantee a place to a further 100 students in a residence that was christened Helensburgh House after the surrounding suburb. 'The experiment proved very worthwhile', the relieved accommodation officer Shirley Omer-Cooper noted. 'Without this bold decision these students would probably have been lost to the University and Dunedin.'[105] Girvan asked student health nurse Glenys Low to become warden. It was 'baptism by fire', with less than three weeks to prepare for the first residents. Many were sceptical that an institution filled with people who had not been accepted by other colleges would survive even six months, but Low was up to the challenge. She called them 'my bunch of rejects', and took heed of the 'best advice' of another warden, to 'have Nelson's blind eye: what you don't see you don't have to do anything about'.[106] Proctor Ron Chambers wrote about Low (later Roome) as one of the 'characters' among the wardens, who were people with 'about the toughest job imaginable': she 'ruled her charges with a perfect blend of strict discipline and affection'.[107]

Critic worried that Helensburgh House gave students 'a bleak introduction to life in Dunedin'.[108] The big problem was its distance from campus, several kilometres up and down hills. Fees were kept lower to compensate for transport costs, though residents often hitched a ride from friendly locals and a few cycled (including one who got a speeding ticket going down Balmacewen Road). The food at the residence travelled quite a way, too: meals were cooked in the University Union and transported to Wakari in insulated containers. The food was 'not good', Roome admits, though it improved over time. 'The thought of pickled pork still turns my stomach all these years later,' a former resident recalls. Helensburgh had its advantages – the rooms were large, the grounds attractive and residents became a close community – but the distance factor kept it well down the list of popular residences.[109]

In 1984 Omer-Cooper reported that demographic statistics showed the high rate of enrolment was unlikely to persist for more than five or six years; it would be unwise to invest a lot of capital in further colleges. Instead the university invested in building flats, and it took over the lease on the whole of Helensburgh House. Within a few years it became evident that these predictions were wrong: a larger proportion of school leavers went on to university, and Otago's roll doubled between 1983 and 1993. The accommodation office was besieged by frustrated parents, teachers and potential students.[110] With several hundred about to be turned away for 1988, Girvan again looked for buildings that could be converted to student accommodation at short notice. A disused building at Wakari Hospital became an annexe of Helensburgh, lifting its total capacity to over 200. Girvan convinced the Elim Church to sell the former Aquinas Hall to the university and two weeks later, as Dalmore House, it opened its doors to 73 students.[111] That took a lot of hard work, led by its warden Reywa Clough. The facilities were rundown, with holes in the walls, temperamental boilers and leaks; 'one memorable morning at breakfast, the ceiling fell down on us in slow motion', Clough recalled – but the first residents were 'a wonderful group' who handled such trials with good humour.[112]

Dalmore was slowly upgraded and at the end of the year the university leased the neighbouring former Santa Sabina Convent, which became home to a further 20 or so residents. The addition of two more floors in 1990 took Dalmore's capacity to nearly 140, and other additions in the 1990s lifted it to around 160. One welcome change around the turn of the century was the development of the kitchens, meaning meals no longer had to be brought in. The institution lost its religious associations when the university bought it; the chapel was converted into a gym. However, in 1996 the warden, Ashley Day, who thought Dalmore House sounded like a halfway house, campaigned for a name change and it became Aquinas again. Like Helensburgh, it was seldom the first choice of potential residents, who were put off by its distance from campus. Also like Helensburgh, students quickly became fond of Aquinas; they were more likely to stay home and socialise together than in some other colleges. They made the most of their grounds, too; a surprised warden once discovered a 'pig farm established in the tree line' – after shooting a wild pig, a resident discovered her piglets, felt sorry for them and had brought them home.[113]

In 1988 the OHB decided to demolish the oldest wing of its Cumberland Street nurses' home and use the space as a carpark rather than spend the millions required to upgrade it. The university was still desperate for accommodation and convinced the board to lease it the building for five years; it undertook to pay for the upgrade of the 1916 building to current fire and seismic standards.[114] Cumberland House opened in February 1989 with 145 residents. Warden Joy Bennett reported that it 'started its year under extreme difficulties with building work incomplete, no kitchenette facilities and rooms requiring some or all furniture'. During the year snow brought down guttering and fascia boards, necessitating urgent repairs, and residents sometimes ended up with cold showers as the old waterheating system struggled to cope with demand. Despite the challenges, student morale was high; the Cumberland student council was 'extremely enthusiastic which led to a very successful social calendar for Cumberland House', Bennett noted.[115] Cumberland was well down the popularity list at first but as it was refurbished its reputation improved.

The college extended into the other wings of the nurses' home and the university later purchased the building from the health board.[116] A dining room and kitchen refurbishment in 2000 and 2001 was a great improvement – meals had previously been prepared offsite and residents recalled food

Helensburgh House residents, known as Burgers, formed a strong community: 'We made our own fun' and 'became a very tight-knit group'; parties in the basement were a feature. Warden Glenys Roome discovered some old nurses' caps in a cupboard and those, paired with lab coats, became their uniform at events like the intercollege swimming sports.

GLENYS ROOME PHOTOGRAPH, GLENYS ROOME COLLECTION.

Sports were an important part of life at Cumberland College. Like all colleges, it developed its own traditions: these 2014 residents were taking part in Colour Wars Day, held on the old tennis courts and lawn.

CUMBERLAND COLLEGE COLLECTION.

'floating in unknown liquid that arrived from the union kitchen' and 'the mass exodus of students from the entire building on fish pie night'.[117] The historic building brought problems, though. It was strengthened just before the college opened in 1989, but a careful review of university buildings in the wake of the Canterbury earthquakes of 2010 and 2011 revealed it to be the most vulnerable major building on campus. It was first priority for further strengthening, carried out over the summer before 2012 residents moved in.[118] The old building gave Cumberland character and in 2011 its dining room was transformed into 'Hogwarts' to celebrate the opening of the final *Harry Potter* film.[119] The college boasted its own ghost, though not everybody welcomed it: the university chaplain and a kaumātua were called on to calm residents after sightings of the 'Grey Lady' in 2012.[120]

Helensburgh House ended its life as a student residence at the end of 1991. It would have carried on but the health board was closing Cherry Farm, its main mental health facility, and shifting some of its facilities to Wakari Hospital; it needed Helensburgh's building back. Fortunately for Otago the board had other accommodation available: the incorporation of the remaining wing of the Dunedin nurses' home into Cumberland was a direct swap for Helensburgh.[121] The health board had other space on offer, too, after it moved maternity services into the main Dunedin Hospital ward block. The former Queen Mary Maternity Hospital had been on the market for over a year when the university bought it in July 1991 and converted it into a 150-bed student residence. Hayward Hall – named after former registrar Jock Hayward and his sister Vera Hayward, both former members of the hospital board – opened in 1992. Roome moved from Helensburgh to Hayward and served as its warden for the first seven years. Hayward lacked the bucolic charms of Helensburgh – there was very little outdoor space – but it was in a convenient lcation close to campus, and that gave it instant popularity. It had a very efficient heating system and large bedrooms that made it the envy of every other residence, says Roome. Hayward provided a home for many of the Muslim medical students who came to Otago from various countries in the 1990s; it had a diverse group of residents and developed a good reputation for accommodating students with disabilities. When Jacob Phillips appeared on television at the start of a race at the Rio Paralympics in 2016 he made the Hayward 'H' sign, to the delight of his fellow residents.[122]

BRANCHING OUT – TOROA, UNIVERSITY FLATS AND CITY COLLEGE

Bill Dawson became first director of accommodation services in 1993; it was a strategic role and all the heads of the university-owned residential colleges reported to him. The days when full-time academics or general staff served as heads of colleges in their spare time ended: they became full-time positions as Otago sought to improve its accommodation, both physically and pastorally. Despite the development of Helensburgh, Dalmore, Cumberland and Hayward, capacity was still a challenge as Otago expanded rapidly in the 1990s. Adding rooms to existing colleges was cheaper than building new institutions so, with funding tight, a constant programme of smaller projects helped house more students, albeit not as fast as they were pouring in.[123]

One project developed existing resources to cater for international students, who sometimes had trouble adjusting to life in college. 'They are very polite but for some the change of diet is traumatic,' Dawson noted in 1995.[124] Toroa International House – named for the albatross, a wandering bird that made its home on the Otago Peninsula – opened that year in university-owned flats in Queen Street. The university purchased another house to serve as headquarters, appointed live-in staff – and a different sort of accommodation was underway. The residents were supported and supervised but did their own cooking and other chores and lived in groups of mixed nationalities. In 2003 Gretchen Kivell, the

Toroa College residents, 2010.
LIGHTHAUS PHOTOGRAPH, UNIVERSITY OF OTAGO MARKETING AND COMMUNICATIONS COLLECTION.

warden, explained that the rationale was 'to give students the opportunity to cook familiar foods for themselves. Up to 42 countries have been represented at Toroa and no chef could provide traditional meals 21 times a week for people from so many nations.' Residents enjoyed meeting students from other countries along with the few New Zealanders who lived there.[125]

Toroa started with just over 100 residents. As neighbouring properties were acquired it quickly grew to 131. In 2000 a family home was redeveloped into an administrative and community space named Manawa, although it was too small to host all of the community at once. Gradually the New Zealand contingent at Toroa became larger to help meet demand from domestic students, and the name changed from Toroa International House to Toroa College in 2009 to reflect its move 'closer in ethos towards the other residential colleges' – although it still accommodated more international students than others.[126] Later residents did not prepare their own meals: lunches and dinners were served down the road at the University Union. A project completed in 2014 added another 20 bedrooms, a large communal space and a rooftop terrace. With a capacity of 152 Toroa was still one of the smaller Otago colleges and marketed that as an advantage: 'everyone gets the chance to know everyone else, so studying and socialising with good mates is what makes life at Toroa very comfortable.' Its 'suites' offered 'the freedom of independence and a little taste of life after College.'[127]

When Toroa shifted its focus from international students, the university's other flats took up the slack. Otago first built flats in the 1980s when many old houses occupied by students were demolished and private building projects did not make up the difference. In 1984 the university embarked on a scheme to build flats to house up to 300 students by 1990. It started with 11 units in Clyde Street and seven in Queen Street (which later became Toroa), followed by a larger development in 'Block N' (bounded by Cumberland, Great King, St David and Union streets).[128] These could accommodate a variety of users, including those with particular requirements such as students with impairments. They were especially useful with the rise in single-semester exchange students: private landlords in Dunedin required students to pay a 52-week lease, so the university used its own flats to guarantee accommodation for exchange students, placing them with New Zealand student 'hosts'. It later added other community support because some cultures – for example, students from North America – were not accustomed to flatting and could find 'the New Zealand culture overwhelming'.[129] Some of the Cumberland Street flats became part of Cumberland College in 2005; as Cumberland Court they offered a 'sheltered, apprentice flatting experience' to around 100 students.[130] By 2009 the University Flats service was accommodating 234 people in flats it owned, and 221 more in flats it leased. In 2015 it acquired yet more space when it took over Cumberland Court from Cumberland College.[131] A glowing review in 2016, when University Flats managed over 700 beds, noted its critical role in enhancing the experience of international students.[132]

Between 1993 and 1998 the university spent $9.5 million upgrading its existing accommodation and increasing student places by another 300.[133] Building a residential college from scratch was a luxury, beyond the means of each of Dunedin's tertiary institutions. The DCC wanted to attract more students to the city and knew accommodation was critical; in 1998 it entered a joint venture with the university, polytechnic and college of education to build City College. The DCC put up $2.5 million of the total cost of $8 million; the rest was divided among the three tertiary institutions. The Dunedin City Tertiary Accommodation Trust, established in 1999, oversaw the project. Mason and Wales designed the 'attractive yet functional' Cumberland Street building so it could operate as a full residential college or, if required later, independent apartments. A college with residents attending different institutions faced challenges because of their different schedules, but they were mixed through the apartment blocks and many set up flats together after a year at City College. 'From governance to student socialising, City College is a melting pot,' long-serving head of college Joy Crawford reported in 2009. By then the college had expanded, with another apartment block built and neighbouring houses purchased.[134] In 2018 Otago Polytechnic opened its own large student accommodation village, meaning it no longer required places at City College. The university bought out the polytech's share and took full management of the college, and renamed it Caroline Freeman College in honour of Otago's first woman graduate.[135]

BACK TO THE FUTURE – ABBEY AND TE RANGI HIROA COLLEGES

After the successful City College venture and the addition of more rooms to existing colleges, Otago returned to the method that had worked well in the 1980s and 1990s: adapting existing buildings to create additional colleges. Abbey College was New Zealand's first fully catered residence open only to postgrads. It was a big investment for Otago, which paid around $8 million for the property and more than $2 million altering it.[136] The 1979 Abbey motel complex was built in the then-popular 'hacienda style' by Pat and Margaret O'Connor; its past life gave it benefits not found in the average residential college, including a swimming pool, sauna and spa.[137] It opened as a college in 2008 with 72 rooms, with accommodation for singles and couples, and more flexible admission dates than the colleges primarily set up for young undergraduates.[138] Kivell, previously at Toroa, was the inaugural head. She soon found postgrads were 'very different from dealing with undergrads … they had all lived independently and knew what they wanted'. They 'worked harder, were more exacting of themselves and others, and more

A resident's room in Te Rangi Hīroa College, 2014.
GRAHAM WARMAN PHOTOGRAPH, UNIVERSITY OF OTAGO MARKETING AND COMMUNICATIONS COLLECTION.

focused', and appreciated the opportunity to live in a supportive collegial space without the distraction of sometimes rowdy first-year students.[139] The Abbey College experiment paid off: it helped attract senior students and visiting scholars to Otago, the majority of them from overseas, and earned praise for its 'stimulating academic environment and outstanding pastoral support'. The purchase of a neighbouring house for the head of college in 2014 took Abbey's capacity to around 80 residents, and this made it a little more cost-effective.[140]

Otago's latest residential facility sprang from a failed private venture. In 2005 LivingSpace Properties Ltd, a company owned by Christchurch property developer David Henderson, converted the former 1950s Glendermid tannery building in Castle Street into a 128-suite complex with the addition of two more storeys and another section at the back. The aim was to attract the 'top end' of the student accommodation market, but parents didn't want to send their offspring to a place that was not affiliated to the university and that lacked the pastoral care and tutorial support of the colleges. LivingSpace became a private hotel. Henderson turned down an offer by the university to purchase it. In 2010 Henderson went bankrupt after he overstretched on numerous projects and businesses, and in 2013 Otago purchased the building for $6.75 million – considerably less than it had offered a few years earlier.[141]

The new college was named in honour of Otago's first Māori graduate, Te Rangi Hīroa (Peter Buck).[142] Local Māori had a long connection with Te Rangi Hīroa's iwi, forged through the support Ngāi Tahu gave to Ngāti Mutunga who were among those imprisoned in Dunedin in the 1880s for their involvement in the passive resistance movement at Parihaka. Ōtākou kaumātua Edward Ellison made the initial request to use Te

Rangi Hīroa's name to his iwi and whānau and, together with the university's director of Māori development, Tuari Potiki, led a formal delegation to discuss the project at Urenui pā. The whānau was delighted about the project; they donated a carving and other taonga to adorn the college foyer, and the university commissioned a tukutuku panel. Otago's Te Tumu donated panels celebrating the life and achievements of Te Rangi Hīroa that were formerly part of an Otago Museum display, as encouragement to residents using the college study centre. At the formal opening in 2014 leading Māori academic Mason Durie, who studied medicine at Otago and had been inspired by Te Rangi Hīroa, said that the challenge for the college would be 'to create … a fitting environment for the name it carries … it's an honour on the one hand but it's a challenge to live up to the name. The students will carry that responsibility.'[143] Founding head Ashley Day, former head of Carrington, UniCol and Aquinas who was enticed out of retirement to set up the college, was committed to that kaupapa; he wanted the college to 'reflect the values of Te Rangi Hīroa: respect and love for people and love of learning'. Although it was not explicitly marketed to Māori, the name and the environment attracted Māori students. There was just a month to advertise before college applications closed for 2014 and, despite the higher charges, which reflected superior rooms (with ensuite), 92 people selected Te Rangi Hīroa as their first choice, including 25 Māori.[144] It was an auspicious start.

Otago now had 15 residential colleges – 10 fully owned by the university and another five affiliated to it (see Appendix 2). It had come a long way from the days of private lodgings and suspicion of 'the old monkish idea' of residential communities. By the 2010s over 3000 Otago students lived in residential colleges; in a well-established pattern, most undergraduates from out of town lived in a college for a year before going flatting. The colleges offered far more than bed and board – they supported young people through the transition to student life and gave them a ready-made community and opportunities to participate in social, sporting and cultural events. They also provided mentors and other pastoral and academic support. Concerns that first-year students living at home, boarding or flatting were missing out on such benefits prompted Otago to introduce a Locals programme in 2011; it started with social, sporting and academic events during orientation and expanded into a year-round support system. Stephen Scott, a zoologist who was the Science Division's associate dean Māori and a driving force behind the initiative, became the university's inaugural director of first-year experience in 2016, overseeing the Locals programme and other schemes to enhance students' transition to university.[145]

Otago's large financial commitment to colleges from the late 1990s indicates their importance in attracting students. While some universities contracted out their residential services, Otago increased its involvement. In 1995 it took over running Arana and Carrington from the Stuart Residence Halls Council, and in 2006 it purchased the buildings. With the proceeds the council made generous gifts back to the university; among other things it endowed a chair in science communication and in Scottish studies, carried on supporting facilities at Carrington and Arana and, in 2016, donated a Paul Dibble sculpture to mark the council's 75th anniversary.[146] In 2006 VC Skegg noted that Otago had 'a residential learning environment that is unparalleled in this part of the world'. That year the remaining 'halls' became 'colleges', reflecting 'more accurately the role that the colleges play in providing academic and pastoral support, as well as accommodation for students'.[147] With many student flats and colleges close to the university, North Dunedin gradually evolved into a distinct student quarter, integral to the development of the famed student lifestyle that drew students to Otago.

CHAPTER FIVE

The staff

The University of Otago began with a staff of three professors, a janitor and an honorary secretary; a century later it had around 2000 on the payroll and was one of Dunedin's largest employers.[1] A university is all about people. It could not exist without the intellectual power of its academics, and the academic staff could not carry out their teaching and research without the support of others, once known as the 'non-academic' staff – now the general or support staff. This chapter considers overall staffing trends and organisations.

AN INTERNATIONAL TEAM

People came from all over the world to work at Otago. The earliest professors were from Scotland and England, and those two countries long dominated the lists – which was unsurprising as they were the countries of origin for most New Zealand colonists and the model for the university. Few of the early academics hailed from another source of New Zealand migrants, Ireland. Lindo Ferguson (English-born but raised and educated in Ireland) was a notable exception; he joined the lecturing staff in 1886 and later became dean of medicine.[2] Other early staff came from continental Europe, among them the early French and German lecturers and the first mining professor, George Ulrich, who came from Germany via Australia.[3]

As the university developed, it employed its own graduates as academics. When professors needed assistants they often turned to their best students: one of the foundation students, Peter Hay, was soon assisting his former chemistry professor, James Black, in his analytical laboratory work.[4] Other graduates were employed as assistant lecturers, and professionals working in Dunedin – some of them educated at Otago – lectured part-time in fields such as law and economics. During the 1890s several men who had completed their degrees at Otago joined the lecturing staff: Alex Purdie and John Don in geology, John Findlay in economics, William Stout and William Milne in law and George Howell in German.[5]

Otago liked its senior staff to hold qualifications from distinguished old world universities. Generations of the brightest New Zealand graduates headed overseas for further study and, although many never returned, some leapt at the opportunity to apply for vacant chairs – for example John Inglis and Francis Dunlop, appointed to the chairs of chemistry and philosophy at Otago in 1911 and 1913.[6] Occasionally, when there was an especially able local without overseas qualifications or experience, Otago appointed them as professor. First in

Some of the university staff and council members in 1902. Back row, from left: Frederick Gibbons (maths professor), Patrick Marshall (geology lecturer), George Thompson (French lecturer), Daniel Stewart (council), John Scott (anatomy professor), Thomas Gilray (English professor), Andrew Cameron (council), George Sale (classics professor), William Mawson, Daniel Waters (metallurgy lecturer), Augustus Hamilton (registrar). Front row: William Salmond (philosophy professor), David White (council), John Shand (physics professor), Edward Cargill (council), James Black (chemistry professor), William Benham (biology professor), James Park (mining professor). White joined the staff as education lecturer in 1904, and in 1909 he became Otago's first locally educated professor.

BOX-240-003, S15-381l, HOCKEN COLLECTIONS.

that category was David White, who became Otago's first education professor in 1909; he had been lecturing in education since 1904 and was principal of the Dunedin Training College.[7] Talented local graduate and lawyer Harry Bedford, who lectured in economics from 1906 and also in history from 1910, was promoted to Otago's first professor of those subjects in 1915 and the following year George Thompson, a local graduate who had been a popular French lecturer since 1902, became first professor of modern languages. Both had migrated to New Zealand as children, from England and Ireland respectively.[8] Dunedin-born and educated Thomas Adams became Latin lecturer in 1908 when foundation classics professor George Sale retired, and Adams was promoted to the long-vacant classics chair in 1917.[9] It is likely that war conditions influenced the university's choice of locals for those last three chairs: as men were redirected to military service, transport became difficult and immigration almost ground to a halt, the university had little hope of recruiting academic staff from overseas. When Bedford died unexpectedly in 1918 the university appointed an acting professor. After the war it looked again to Britain for its senior academics; in 1920 Scotsmen John Elder and William Pringle were appointed as professors of history and economics respectively.[10]

WOMEN ON STAFF

War conditions affected less senior appointments, too. With so many men leaving for military service, the university resorted to employing

Among those enjoying the Latin picnic at Whare Flat in 1920 were two of Otago's early women academics, sisters Phyllis Calvert (née Turnbull) (seated third from left) and Isabel Turnbull (seated far right). Thomas Adams, the classics professor, is standing on the left.
EMILY TURNBULL PHOTOGRAPH, ANDREW CALVERT COLLECTION.

women. Isabel Turnbull became assistant lecturer in Latin in 1915, Gladys Cameron in bacteriology and public health in 1917, Winifred Farnie in biology in 1917, Emily Siedeberg in dental anaesthetics in 1917 and Phyllis Turnbull in French in 1918. Others appointed soon after the war included Agnes Blackie in physics (1919), Bertha Clement in English (1919), Vida Barron in French (1920), Winifred Betts in botany (1920), Marion Fyfe in zoology (1921), Susannah Sinclair in pathology (1923), Muriel Bell in physiology (1923), Malvena Oldham in dentistry (1924) and Christina Bell in maths (1925). All were outstanding local graduates. Some did not remain long – they departed for other work or left paid employment when they married – but others, notably Isabel Turnbull, Blackie, Barron, Fyfe and Muriel Bell, had long academic careers at Otago.[11] In a period when 'departments' were tiny, often only two staff, they carried considerable responsibility. Cameron held bacteriology and public health together in 1920 and 1921 as the professor, Sydney Champtaloup, succumbed to tuberculosis.[12] Betts was Otago's first botany lecturer: the status of women academics was revealed when botany later dated its beginning as an independent department from 1924, when her male successor commenced.

Of course, the best-known women academics at Otago dated from before World War I; they belonged to the school created just for women: home science. Englishwomen Winifred Boys-Smith and Helen Rawson were the foundation staff of the school, whose courses commenced in 1911. Both completed the natural science tripos at Cambridge but were denied degrees because they were women. Home science segregated women to some extent, but it offered them opportunities in academia: for decades the school employed the country's only women professors and deans, together with numerous other women lecturers. Boys-Smith was New Zealand's first female professor and Rawson succeeded her in the home science chair.[13] Until the 1990s home science was a bastion of women's leadership as women professors emerged in other disciplines. Then, between microbiology professor Margaret Loutit's retirement and the arrival of religious studies professor Elizabeth Isichei, Otago had a 'barren patch' of 18 months with no women professors because consumer and applied sciences – as home science became – appointed men as dean and professors.[14]

As a minority on the academic staff, women supported one another. The Otago University Women's Association was established in 1914 'to act as a band of union among the women graduates of Otago University; to further the education of women in various branches of knowledge by the discussion of literary, social, and political subjects and current matters of importance; and to discuss matters of importance to women, with the object of improving their status'.[15] The committee was made up of several staff members with Flora Allan, an 1880s graduate and principal of Otago Girls' High School, as president. There were regular meetings and an annual social reunion.[16] In the 1920s the association morphed into a branch of the Federation of University Women (FUW), a 'world-wide league of women with University training'. In 1920 home science professor Helen Rawson returned from a trip to Britain and America a disciple for the FUW, and soon there were branches in all New Zealand university centres. In addition to its collegial and advocacy role, the FUW built up a fellowship fund to support women going overseas to do research. In 1933 the Otago branch started a useful means of fundraising: hiring out academic regalia for graduations.[17]

The FUW, renamed the Federation of Graduate Women in 2000, then Graduate Women New Zealand in 2016, was 'very good at bringing women academics from different departments together,' recalls Ann Wylie, a 1940s graduate who returned as botany lecturer in 1961. It was good to have the support of other women, Wylie says. She didn't experience outright prejudice, but 'it was a case of you behaving as an honorary man, rather than the men adapting themselves to you. It was a one-way process, but that was the way it was then, if you wanted to get on.'[18] Women staff supported women students, too, especially in courses where they were outnumbered. Lynley Hood, who completed first-year physics in 1961, was invited with all the other women students in her class to Sunday afternoon tea in Blackie's home.[19]

BECOMING MORE DIVERSE

It was a woman who broke one barrier at Otago: in 1921 Ann Gilchrist Strong became its first American professor. Many people of British background at the time viewed American degrees with suspicion, but the United States' superiority in the field of home science was clear. Strong, who was subsequently dean of Otago's Home Science School for many years, recruited other lecturers from the United States, and many of the best local graduates travelled there for postgraduate training. Home science flourished at Otago under Strong's leadership and she was the driving force behind it developing its community outreach through an extension service.[20] She made an impression on New Zealanders: at a 1923 Catholic women's conference in Christchurch, one speaker reported that Studholme House was 'in the charge of Professor Strong, an American woman of culture and refined tastes' and 'a very good example of the success of modern American training in the art of Homemaking'.[21] The Catholic women may have felt less warmly towards Strong had they known she was divorced, but she kept that quiet in New Zealand, passing herself off as a widow.[22]

The prejudice against US degrees slowly declined. Ralph Souter, a talented Otago graduate, completed a doctorate at Columbia in New York and returned to Dunedin as economics professor in 1936.[23] Gradually, more staff arrived with degrees from beyond Otago's traditional choices of Britain, Germany, Australia and New Zealand. Tsu Sheng Ma arrived at Otago in 1949 with a PhD from Chicago; he had returned to China for several years after studying in the United States, but fled because of the revolution.

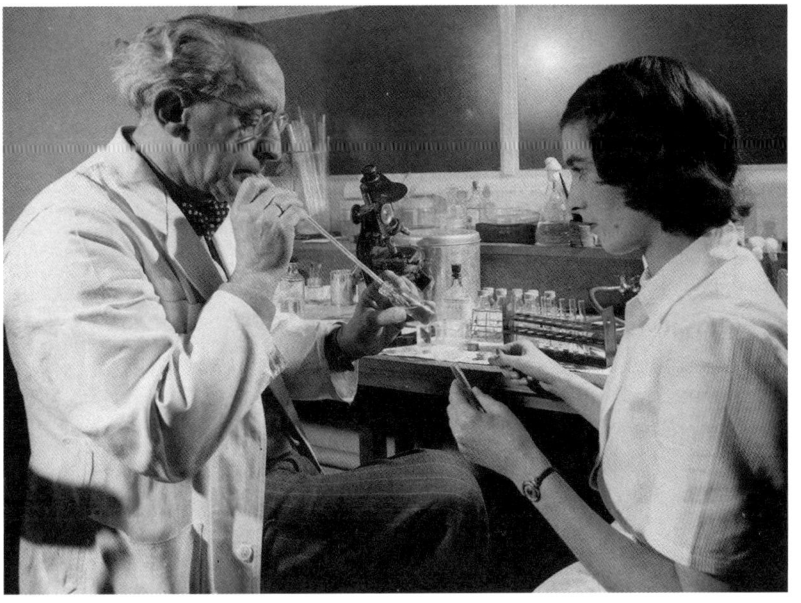

Leopold (Poldi) Kirschner, who joined the Otago staff in 1948, was one of several Jewish émigré academics. Originally from Austria, Kirschner worked on leptospirosis in Indonesia but was interned there during the war. He continued his work on leptospirosis at Otago in the MRC's Microbiology Research Unit. This photograph was probably taken in 1949, long before mouth pipetting went out of fashion.
DEPARTMENT OF PHYSIOLOGY RECORDS, MS-4333/009, S16-521C, HOCKEN COLLECTIONS.

The Otago Chemistry Department was looking for a microanalytical chemist and recruited Ma to help develop its laboratory; he stayed for a couple of years before going on to a distinguished academic career in New York.[24] Another graduate of Tsinghua University in Beijing joined the Otago staff in 1949: Fwu Tarng Dun, who completed his doctorate at Jena, Germany, became a physiology lecturer that same year; like his compatriot he left Otago for the United States in 1951.[25]

China was not the only country experiencing turmoil in the mid-twentieth century; Otago benefited from the talents of academics who fled Europe for the haven of New Zealand, many for the rest of their lives. Notable among them were several Jews who escaped Nazi persecution. Walter Griesbach arrived from Hamburg in 1939; his wife, Olga Hallenstein, had family in Dunedin. The Society for the Protection of Science and Learning, an organisation that sought work for German scientists driven from their posts, approached the university at a time when the Medical School was building its research capacity, and the Carnegie Corporation funded Griesbach's travel and two years of his salary. He stayed on in the MRC's Thyroid Research Unit until his retirement in 1958. He and others like him who were forced to leave Europe contributed enormously to Otago's research, and their training in academic traditions that differed from those of their Dunedin colleagues was valuable. Griesbach worked with local chemistry and medical graduate Dick Purves. Another member of the thyroid research group, Duncan Adams, described this collaboration as 'a marriage of the systematic morphological type of study of the old Austro-German school with the functional physiological approach characteristic of Anglo-Saxon investigators'; it was highly productive in researching pituitary cells and hormones.[26]

Others from the European diaspora had more complicated journeys to Otago. Biochemists Franz and Marianne Bielschowsky fled fascist regimes twice, first in their native Germany and then in Spain. In 1948 they moved from England to Otago, where Franz was director of the Cancer Research Laboratory; he had a productive research career at Otago until his sudden death in 1965. Marianne, who worked alongside him, carried on her research until her death in 1977. She was renowned for the development of special strains of mice that were in demand from medical researchers around the world; she was known to transport them internationally in her handbag.[27] Not all of the Jewish émigrés were in the Medical School: classicist Felix Grayeff left Germany for Australia in 1938 and came to Otago the following year, where he revived the teaching of German language and literature. He stayed until 1952, and later settled in England.[28] Otago was a safe destination but not everyone found it easy to adjust to life here. Those who came from the old cities of Europe found New Zealand a cultural wasteland and some experienced anti-Semitism.[29]

By 1990 the academic staff were from a more diverse background, especially in fast-expanding areas such as commerce. There was a small but growing group of Māori academics in addition to those who taught Māori studies: Les Williams (physical education), Eru Pomare (medicine, Wellington) and Atholl Anderson (anthropology) were all appointed in the 1970s, John Broughton and Papaarangi Reid were appointed to the Medical School in Dunedin and Wellington respectively in the 1980s, and Russell Bishop joined the Department of Education in 1990.[30] One of the earliest Māori academics – possibly the first, besides those who tutored adult education courses in te reo Māori in the 1950s – was Otago medical graduate Maarire Goodall. He was appointed to the Hugh Adam Cancer Research Unit in 1961 then spent a few years researching in Chicago before returning to Otago, where he eventually became director of the unit. Goodall was of Ngāi Tahu descent and was heavily involved in iwi activities; after retiring from medical research in 1985 he worked for the Waitangi Tribunal.[31] In addition to the permanent staff there were Māori guest lecturers who supported the undergraduate curriculum at the Medical School, including Bruce Gregory, Colin Mantell, Mason Durie and Manuka Henare, and Piri Sciascia at the physical education school.[32]

Māori were still underrepresented on the staff in the 1990s, though: when Ranginui Walker conducted a Treaty of Waitangi review of the university in 1998 he noted there were 15 Māori on the academic staff (just over one per cent of the total). As Walker pointed out, the 'pool of qualified Maori to teach in universities is extremely limited' and Otago needed to nurture those it had; already Anderson and Bishop had been enticed away.[33] As the pool of Māori graduates got larger and Otago took active steps to recruit and retain them, representation improved. By the 2010s there were around 70 academic staff who identified as Māori. They established a formal organisation, the Māori Academic Staff Caucus (later Te Poutama Māori) in 2008, with Jacinta Ruru (law) and Janine Kapa-Blair (Office of Māori Development) as leaders.[34]

Te Poutama Māori quickly became a 'well-oiled machine': it held workshops and conferences to support and promote Māori academic staff achievement, and it served as an inspiration to Pacific Island staff at Otago, who established their own academic staff caucus in 2016. VC Harlene Hayne stated at the launch that 'although our Pacific academic staff numbers are currently small, our aim is to grow more of our own in the future'. The Pacific caucus is chaired by law professor Rex Tauati Ahdar, who has been on the Otago staff since 1985, and includes academics from anatomy, physiology, preventive and social medicine, politics and public health (Wellington), as well as from Te Tumu, the School of Māori, Pacific and Indigenous Studies.[35]

STAFF WIVES

Like all migrants, academics who came to Dunedin from elsewhere faced the challenge of adjusting to a different society and culture. The collegiality of their workmates helped and, in the earlier years when academics were often married men whose wives were not in paid employment, the wives supported one another. Eileen Soper, wife of head of chemistry Frederick Soper, recalled that she and other wives 'kept in touch with the families of their husbands' staffs'. Eileen Soper completed a BA at Otago in the 1920s and worked as a journalist for the *ODT* and *Otago Witness*; she carried on writing after her marriage, and participated in many social and cultural activities. She was first president of the Staff Wives Association, established in 1948.[36] In 1954 when Frederick became VC they moved into University Lodge, the elegant St Leonards home gifted to the university by Annie Stevenson in 1950. (Stevenson, whose father Isaac had built a successful mechanical engineering business, also made large donations to Studholme and the Home Science School, of which she was a foundation student.)[37] Frederick Soper wrote that the lodge filled an important gap as there was 'a lack of facilities for entertaining in the University itself' – the Sopers and their successors used it to host visitors to the university and it was a good venue for social occasions for staff, council members and other influential Dunedin people.[38]

The Staff Wives Association set out 'to promote friendship between members and to entertain visitors and new arrivals'; it later added the lofty goal of extending 'the cultural and social influence of the University'. Members 'cherished the wives of newcomers, introducing them to academic neighbours and helping them to solve the problems of baby-sitting and lack of domestic help,' Eileen Soper recalled. Membership was confined to the wives of professors, lecturers and administrative staff, who had some status in society; they held dances and sherry parties and tennis mornings at the lodge, and there were clubs for music, art, bridge, chess and handicrafts, as well as a gourmet club. They raised funds for university projects, arranged flowers and refreshments for university functions and provided practical support to newcomers, lending them 'cots, prams, pots and pans'. As women's roles changed, the association still offered friendship and support. It became the Staff Families Association in 1987 and opened to a broader membership, and while it is not the key organisation it was earlier, it still flourishes.[39]

WORKING WIVES AND MOTHERS

For early women academics, marriage generally spelled the end of their university career. A notable example was Helen Rawson, who resigned as home science dean after she married geology professor Noel Benson in 1923.[40] A few married women maintained their academic careers, but it wasn't easy. Molly Marples, an English zoologist who came to Otago in 1937 when her husband Brian Marples was appointed zoology professor, could not get a job herself so she studied medicine instead. In 1946 she joined the staff of the Bacteriology and Public Health Department. Margaret Loutit, later a member of the Microbiology Department (which split from Public Health), comments that 'some of the more established wives didn't like these upstarts'; Marples got 'little reminders: "your husband has a button missing from his coat, maybe you would be better at home"'. Loutit, who came from Australia to Otago in 1956 when her husband John Loutit was appointed lecturer in the Microbiology Department, faced additional challenges and criticism as a working mother of young children. Already armed with an MSc, she obtained part-time work as a botany demonstrator and then microbiology lecturer while working on a PhD. Paying for private childcare was expensive, but her hard work was rewarded with the completion of her PhD in 1966, and in the following year she became a full-time academic.[41]

Improving the provision of childcare helped the next generation of academic women. Several younger staff wives instigated the university's first crèche, designed to provide part-time childcare for students – who generally had to abandon their studies if they gave birth. Since the university was unwilling to provide childcare, the founders set it up as a community venture; the vicar of All Saints Anglican Church offered the use of the old

The university crèche in its original premises in the old All Saints Church Hall, with voluntary helpers at the back.
OTAGO UNIVERSITY CHILDCARE ASSOCIATION COLLECTION.

church hall.[42] They invited women students to a meeting late in 1968 and 'it was evident from the animated discussion that a nursery would fulfil a need'.[43] The University Nursery Association – later renamed the Childcare Association (OUCA) – was a parent cooperative. Jean Dodd, whose husband Jack was professor of physics at Otago, was the first president; she had previously set up a playcentre in Leith Valley. The crèche opened in 1969 with kindergarten teacher Barbara Horn and Karitane nurse Ann Leary as its first supervisors. Parents provided assistance according to a roster.[44]

Access to an affordable and convenient crèche, along with the availability of the pill and other forms of contraception, made a big difference to women. Rosemarie Smith, a student at the time, says: 'gaining control over fertility and creating childcare revolutionised women's access to education – and also to employment in the university'. Smith graduated in 1971 'with a BA and a baby thanks to that crèche' and then worked on the general staff for a couple of years.[45]

There was some resistance to the crèche. Most people in a position of authority in the university (generally men) saw no need for it, and there was opposition from some women who were uneasy about working mothers. There was, however, a demand for childcare and OUCA grew quickly, from 39 paying members in 1969 to 83 in 1971. That year it moved into the Cumberland Suite of the University Union (an old house) and, in 1973, into a house at 525 Great King Street that was provided by the university as temporary accommodation, since it intended to demolish the building to make way for a carpark. Instead it became a long-term home for OUCA, which expanded into two adjoining houses in the 1980s.[46]

Using childcare became less controversial as more women joined the workforce. OUCA helped overcome resistance in its early years by insisting it was a part-time service, but from 1980 it offered full daycare. Increasingly staff used the service too, although students had priority. In 1994 there were 138 families with children in university childcare; 71 were staff and 55 were students. The crèche remained affiliated to, rather than owned by the university, although the university provided the buildings, and grants from the university and OUSA covered a small portion of its expenses.[47] OUCA attracted highly capable people to its management committee. Among the parents who served were some who subsequently held senior posts in the university, including Hayne; she was succeeded as president by historian Barbara Brookes, who suggests it 'was perhaps the most important committee in the university in terms

Te Pā opened in 2014. Built behind the façades of several villas in Castle Street, across from Selwyn College, it incorporated premises for the Otago University Childcare Association, including a bilingual centre, Te Pārekereke o te Kī. OUCA now had five centres – one of them at the College of Education – and was licensed to care for 170 children.

GRAHAM WARMAN PHOTOGRAPH, UNIVERSITY OF OTAGO MARKETING AND COMMUNICATIONS COLLECTION

of the connections we made'. Through the OUCA, Brookes, her husband Paul Roth (an academic in the Law Faculty and long-serving OUCA honorary solicitor) and their children all made 'deep friendships that nourish us today'.[48]

EMPLOYMENT EQUITY

From the 1970s more flexible working arrangements, including part-time work, helped women continue their careers. Jocelyn Harris and her husband and young children returned to Otago in 1971 after postgraduate study and work in England and the United States. 'Wonderful Alan Horsman [the English professor] actually made me a half-time job,' Harris recalls, 'and he made sure I got promoted and had leave and things as though I was full-time.' Horsman was more enlightened than most heads of department when it came to women's issues: his wife Dorothea Horsman was a feminist and was later president of the National Council of Women.[49] Harris and other women academics with children, such as Anne Smith in education, 'pioneered the business of half-time which made a huge difference to me' says archaeologist Helen Leach; 'I wouldn't have ended up with my career if I hadn't been able to take a half-time post and then return to full-time.' Half-time work was no sinecure, Leach recalls. She worked in the morning, then rushed home to breastfeed and care for her baby: 'it was hard work and I slipped behind in research because I was still doing basically the same number of lectures'.[50]

Those departments with a positive attitude to women academics with children attracted and retained future leaders: Loutit, Brookes, Harris, Smith and Leach all became professors. In the early 1990s when psychology head Geoffrey White offered positions to a couple of hotshot US researchers, Hayne and husband Mike Colombo, he did not realise they were about to have their first child. When they told him, 'he didn't miss a beat'; he warmly congratulated them and informed them there were others in the department with small children. It was 'not the reaction I expected,' Hayne recalls. They intended their Otago 'adventure' as 'a bit of an academic OE' and planned to stay only three years; instead they remained on, both became professors and Hayne became VC. One reason they stayed was that they 'could balance being parents of a small child and having ambitious careers' at Otago, 'made possible by a supportive departmental atmosphere plus world-class childcare right on the doorstep of campus'.[51]

Even with such women, there was a shortage of women in senior positions at Otago – and at most of the other universities. Women mentored and supported one another and in 1983, at the suggestion of Brookes and Pamela Tate, they formed the Staff Women's Caucus – open to both general and academic staff. The caucus held lunchtime gatherings with speakers on a range of issues of interest to women.[52] 'We hoped it would both provide a social focus (at a time when men hung out in the staff club billiard room which was decidedly unwelcoming to women) and an advocacy role,' says Brookes.[53] Members expressed their concerns about the status of women at the university. In response, in 1987 Otago adopted a policy of equal employment opportunity (EEO) and in 1988 appointed a fixed-term EEO officer to review employment in the university.[54] Jennifer Child's report revealed that 'only 3 of the 101 Professors currently employed are women' and there were 'few women in top level positions, by salary, in the general staff establishment'. Some departments had no women staff – even in the Arts Faculty, where there was 'a common perception that women are well represented'. In fact, although 66 per cent of arts students were women they made up just 18 per cent of the faculty's academic staff. One barrier to change was a shortage of women with PhDs; although women accounted for more than half the student roll, only a third of doctoral students were women. EEO was not solely about gender: Child reported there were 'no statistics available on the ethnic breakdown or cultural identity of University staff, but it is clear that Maori representation is low'. There were no statistics either on people with disabilities.[55]

Child's report prompted some immediate changes – such as the removal of the age barrier on postgraduate scholarships, which reduced access for women who took time out to have children. Having an EEO policy was mandated in the 1988 Universities Amendment Act and, a year later, the State Sector Amendment Act. Otago promoted itself as an EEO employer, appointed an EEO committee, and in 1990 Kris Smith became full-time EEO coordinator.[56] In 1991 the University Council approved an EEO management plan and in 1992 it adopted an affirmative action policy. That year Otago ran EEO training programmes, developed Treaty of Waitangi education and introduced a new parental policy. EEO observers reviewed promotion procedures, and there was an emphasis put on support for Māori and people with disabilities.[57]

Through the 1990s the university made further efforts to reduce employment barriers. It introduced a 'women in leadership' programme 'with the dual aims of enhancing the leadership potential of women in the University and increasing the participation of women in decision-making processes', and it set up a mentoring programme for women on the general staff.[58] Staff training and development officer Penny Love was 'brilliant at getting courses running for women to help them develop,' Harris recalls, although 'men complained they didn't have similar'. Many university men supported women in their aspirations but there were still numerous barriers to be overcome. 'When Kris Smith did a sexist language pamphlet perfectly intelligent people raised their eyebrows,' says Harris. 'Nobody would say something openly offensive now [2013],' but discrimination is 'still there deep

Some of the Pacific Academic Caucus at its launch in 2016. Front (from left): Daryl Schwenke, Rex Tauati Ahdar, Faumuina Fa`afetai Sopoaga. Back: Michelle Schaaf, Ramona Tiatia, Nanai Anae Iati Iati, Alumita Durutalo, Latika Samalia.
SHARRON BENNETT PHOTOGRAPH, PACIFIC DEVELOPMENT OFFICE COLLECTION.

down'. Reducing institutional discrimination was more straightforward than reducing the sexism and racism that pervaded society – much of it unconscious. One example was the university printery where, in the 1980s, 'sexy' posters printed by the staff covered the walls, making it an uncomfortable environment for women to enter.[59]

The university was painfully slow to improve leadership diversity. By 2000 there were still just seven women among Otago's 103 professors (measured in full-time equivalents), and none of the general staff at senior management level were women.[60] In 2008 Margaret Baird, associate professor in microbiology and immunology, convened a workshop to encourage women postgraduates in the sciences and health sciences into academic careers. Although 65 per cent of postgraduates in those fields were women, female applicants for academic jobs were nowhere near that percentage. Concern about 'balancing a competitive academic workload with having a family' was still a disincentive. The speakers at the workshop included two senior women who had combined motherhood and an academic career – Hayne as DVC and Helen Nicholson as dean of medical sciences. 'You don't need to be a superwoman,' said Nicholson, 'but you do have to be passionate, and you have to want to do it.'[61]

THE GENERAL STAFF

In 1993 the Association of University Staff (AUS) – the union for general and academic staff – published a national survey which showed that for women on the general staff, 'gender discrimination was felt to be secondary to that based on status.'[62] It was a persistent problem. Andrew McNaughton, manager of the Anatomy Department's Confocal Microscopy Centre, wrote in 2005 that the 'image of the Alpha academic supported by the Betas and Gammas, who dealt to his every whim, is how the general public perceives university life. Not surprisingly, some within the institutions see it that way too.' McNaughton noted that the term 'general' staff 'is misleading as often many staff are highly trained in their own right ... Modern universities are too big and too complex for academics alone. Like it or not, the expertise of the general staff is vital, both within their job descriptions and beyond.'[63]

By the 1980s Otago employed around 1000 general staff in a wide range of roles: lab technicians, librarians, architects and engineers, cleaners, computer experts, secretaries, personnel staff, accountants, printers, cooks, nurses and doctors, gardeners, administrators of various types and many others.[64] It started, though, with just one man: janitor Alexander Purdie. Like many staff who followed, Purdie brought various useful skills to the university. He was a wire worker by trade but a naturalist by inclination, and he took an interest in the flora and fauna of New Zealand after he migrated here from Scotland in 1860. He worked with the New Zealand Exhibition of 1865, caring for the natural science exhibits that became the nucleus of the Otago Museum. When the collection was moved from storage to the 'new post office' building Purdie went with it as caretaker and curator, and when the university started in the same building in 1871 it employed him as janitor. When the museum and the university moved into separate premises in the late 1870s he took up residence in the janitor's house in Leith Street and became full-time university caretaker. The role was a broad one at a time when the university was small. Purdie may have been self-taught but he was respected by academic scientists; he was a founding member of the Otago Institute and the Dunedin Field Naturalists' Club, and the Dunedin Horticultural Society praised him for his fern collection. His son Alex, who had the advantage of a university education, lectured briefly at Otago then became director of the Bendigo and Adelaide Schools of Mines in Australia. When Purdie resigned in 1893 because of failing health, a grateful University Council voted to pay him a year's salary.[65]

By then Otago had a registrar and several 'attendants' on its payroll.[66] For most of the university's history academics outnumbered general staff but the gap slowly closed and, in 2002, general staff became the majority for the first time.[67] Some of the growth in general staff came through the addition of services that nobody imagined in the early decades – from Disability Support and Campus Watch to the numerous information technology staff. Meanwhile, some once important roles like telephonist and typist declined or disappeared altogether.

William Henry Harris, known affectionately to students as 'Prof Harris', was janitor from 1893 to 1923; he quickly learned the names of all new students and told them tales of their parents' activities on campus. He enjoyed recounting anecdotes of his adventures at sea, and sometimes wrote them down for publication in newspapers or in the *Review*. The university has employed many interesting and charismatic people over the decades, but in his day Harris stood out as 'a rare personality, as outstanding in his way as any professor'; he earned an obituary as long as that of the classics professor in the *Review*.

OTAGO UNIVERSITY REVIEW, SEPTEMBER 1923, S17-613A, HOCKEN COLLECTIONS.

Marinus Koreman, one of many skilled technicians at Otago – seen here with lathe and drill press in the Wellcome Institute workshop. Through the window can be seen the old Knox Sunday School building, which accommodated various Medical School researchers until it was replaced with living quarters for resident doctors (later converted into the Hunter Centre).
PAULINE FRASER COLLECTION.

The experience of one secretary illustrates the changes to that role. Shirley Kelly worked in the Geology Department as its only administrative staff member from 1965 to 1969. The main tools of her trade were a 'plod, plod, plod' typewriter and a messy Gestetner duplicating machine. After a break she returned to the university as VC's secretary in 1972. By the time she left in 1980 Kelly was using a state-of-the-art sensitive-touch electric typewriter and photocopying had replaced the Gestetner – though nobody could understand the badly translated photocopier manual. After a year overseas Kelly returned to Otago, where the Accounting and Finance Department needed somebody to type theses. To her surprise the department was using computer word processing; an expensive typewriter identical to the one she used as VC's secretary a year earlier sat in the corner – 'they used it for typing envelopes'.[68] As computers became common, staff and students did their own typing and secretaries became personal assistants and departmental administrators.

Like the academic staff, the general staff became more diverse over time. Women made up a large part of the workforce from early on and, at the time of the first survey in the 1988 EEO report, 58 per cent of general staff were women. They were not spread evenly around the various occupational groups, though – there was just one woman among the trades staff and no men among the secretaries; clerks and librarians were mostly women and computing staff were mostly men. There were more men in senior positions, too.[69] The general workforce became more feminised after that EEO report and, by 2000, women made up 67 per cent (by EFTS) of the total; this dropped slightly to 65 per cent by 2015.[70]

One marked change in the twenty-first century was the increase in Māori and Pacific Island staff. In 1998 Ranginui Walker identified only 15 Māori on a general staff of around 1500, but in 2015 they accounted for 5.6 per cent of those general staff who disclosed their ethnicity, with a further 1.6 per cent identifying as Pacific Islanders.[71] Some were employed at the Māori Centre, Pacific Islands Centre and Office of Māori Development. Others were in a range of positions including leadership roles, such as Sagato (Ziggy) Lesa, head of Studholme College from 2002, and Kim Ma`ia`i, director of Student Health from 2004 to 2018.[72]

UNIONS

In 1974 general staff members formed an Otago branch of the Association of University Non-academic Staff of New Zealand; the association clarified that this was 'not a union but a domestic, non-militant organisation interested in the welfare and cohesion of non-academic staff members'.[73]

University staff had mixed feelings about unions but found them useful in advocating for their interests with the university and its main funder, the government. Historian Nicholas Tarling noted that academics 'had reservations about the whole concept of an association' since 'their focus on scholarship and research emphasised the individualism of academics and their belief that a single voice should not be silenced by the many'. Nevertheless, the academics were the first university staff to form an association – the national University Teachers' Association in the 1920s. It faded out a few years later with the formation of local lecturers' associations.[74] Agnes Blackie recalled the beginnings of the Otago Lecturers' Association, set up in 1930 because a growing contingent of lecturers who had worked overseas 'wanted a more active part in university affairs and a better means of settling grievances than just an appeal to the head of their department'. It was a lively group that aimed to support members and improve staff relations with students, as well as make suggestions on university policy; the Professorial Board and University Council consulted it regularly. The 'vigorous, well-supported, highly respected Association' was supplanted in the 1940s by the Association of University Teachers (AUT), which included both lecturers and professors.[75]

Technicians formed an association at Otago in the 1960s and in 1973 it became part of a national University Technicians Union – though they were 'reluctant unionists', as historian Peter Franks put it. University library staff formed an association in the late 1970s too. These and the Association of Non-academic Staff developed in that decade as a defence against other unions. Technicians were wary of powerful organisations such as the engineers, carpenters and electrical workers unions that sought to sign up university staff; since 'flexibility and multi-skilling were, and are, essential features of the jobs of most university technicians', they didn't want to get caught in demarcation disputes between craft-based unions.[76] AUT supported the 1970s unions and in the late 1980s and early 1990s they amalgamated to form AUS. That was a response to the legislative and employment climate, which made unions less powerful; amalgamation helped them survive.[77] Some Otago employees belonged to other unions such as the Public Service Association, but AUS was the largest on campus and took on most of the work of bargaining for pay and conditions, to the advantage of both members and non-members. In 2009 AUS merged with the Association of Staff in Tertiary Education, which included staff beyond the universities, to form the Tertiary Education Union. This latest amalgamation reflected the need to attract more members to survive in a society where union membership was no longer the norm.[78]

AUS brought the academic and general staff together – as did some other groups on campus, in particular the Staff Women's Caucus. All staff were welcome to socialise in the Staff Club, too. In 2005, with multiplying teaching and research prizes for academic staff, Otago realised that general staff also deserved recognition. It introduced an annual award for exceptional performance by general staff that, like the teaching awards, carried a monetary prize to be used for professional development. The inaugural award was shared by two technicians, Louise Kewene from the Music Department and Murray McKenzie from zoology. Kewene, an audio engineer and computer whizz as well as a musician and composer, took care of the department's studios and music gear. McKenzie, an electrical engineer who had worked for the university since 1970, was the senior technician who coordinated the zoology general staff and helped project manage the construction of the Benham Building.[79] Both had been nominated by the academic staff they worked alongside. It was, after all, a close relationship; academic and general staff both needed each other – and without the diverse physical and intellectual skills of its people the university could not exist.

CHAPTER SIX

The humanities

The humanities have been at the heart of the university since its beginning. Two of its first four professors were in the arts: Duncan MacGregor (mental and moral philosophy) and George Sale (classics and English) represented the traditions of Scotland and England that moulded the fledgling university's ideals and practice. Sale was a product of the English establishment, though he had colonial experience.[1] MacGregor epitomised the intelligent Scot of humble background who had benefited from an egalitarian education system; he held degrees in philosophy and medicine from Aberdeen and Edinburgh.[2]

George Sale, the foundation classics professor, was imposing both physically and intellectually. Educated at Rugby and Cambridge, he brought to Otago his experience as a Canterbury sheep-station manager, gold miner, first editor of the *Press*, treasurer of Canterbury Province and commissioner on the West Coast goldfields.
PA1-Q-197-11-2, ROLLESTON ALBUM 2, ALEXANDER TURNBULL LIBRARY.

THE FIRST CLASSES – CLASSICS, ENGLISH AND PHILOSOPHY

On 10 July 1871, at Otago's first inaugural lecture, Sale admitted that Latin and Greek were of little practical use to the colonial worker; nevertheless, the classics were at the heart of a liberal education, 'which here ought to be open to all'.[3] Other university authorities agreed, and Latin (or Greek, from 1903) was made a requisite for a New Zealand arts degree until 1917, when other languages could be substituted.[4] Students respected Sale, although they feared his scathing criticism; he found colonial students very different from those at Cambridge. John O'Shea, a student in the 1890s, arrived at university 'a bit rough in Latin'. Others were worse: they 'virtually started Latin at the University. They used to annoy the professor to frenzy.'[5] Sale, in his first year, taught Plato's *Apology* to a Greek class of 19 and Cicero's Second Philippic to a Latin class of 33. He also taught English to 22 students – something he was less familiar with, but in a small institution the staff had broad portfolios.[6] Sale remarked that neither Cambridge nor Oxford had a professor of English so he looked to the Scottish universities for inspiration; he concluded that their teaching encouraged 'that very vice which it should be the especial object of a University to eradicate – shallowness and superficiality. He was therefore compelled to strike out a line for himself.' English students in 1871 started the session with Chaucer, plunging straight into Middle English.[7] When the class progressed to 'the more modern language' of Shakespeare's sonnets after its 'thorough and profitable perusal of the *Canterbury Tales*', this warranted a report in the *ODT* – perhaps the reporter was a student.[8]

MacGregor had a broad remit, too. Mental and moral philosophy, often called mental science in Otago's early decades, embraced philosophy, psychology and political economy (economics).[9] In his inaugural lecture he stated that 'the subjects included in mental science were most difficult': this was discouraging but, nevertheless, 19 of Otago's 81 founding students attended his classes.[10] He was an excellent lecturer and did not shy away from controversy, and his radical social Darwinist views caused problems with the Presbyterian Synod, which funded his chair. That probably contributed to his decision to leave when another opportunity arose and, in 1886, he became national inspector of lunatic asylums, hospitals and charitable institutions.[11]

INTO NEW TERRITORY – LAW AND MODERN LANGUAGES

Otago's Law School opened just two years after the first university classes, but for decades it was a precarious, part-time enterprise. The first law lecturer was Robert Stout, who had been the university's first student. In 1873 he gave lectures in common law to a class of 18, the largest number for many years to come. Stout resigned in 1875 when he was elected to parliament, and a series of local practitioners became part-time law lecturers, teaching specialist papers for LLB – a degree awarded by the University of New Zealand from 1877. Classes stayed tiny because qualification as a solicitor or barrister required apprenticeship with a trained lawyer and passing exams conducted by the judiciary; university classes were supplementary. Most law students worked in law firms; they attended classes after-hours in the lecturers' chambers or at the Supreme Court building, and studied in the Otago District Law Society library.[12]

Otago was the first university in Australasia to admit a woman law student – Ethel Benjamin, who enrolled in 1893 and graduated in 1897. That same year she was admitted as barrister and solicitor, to the consternation of the Otago District Law Society. Despite a lack of support from her male colleagues, Benjamin established a successful law practice and became the first woman to appear as counsel in any case in the British Empire. After she moved to England with her husband in 1910 she was unable to practise law (women were not permitted to do so there until 1919), but her business experience was put to good use in merchant banking. Her remarkable achievements were not forgotten: in 1997 the Otago Women Lawyers' Society and the New Zealand Law Foundation established the prestigious Ethel Benjamin Commemorative Address to 'honour and preserve' her 'pioneering spirit' and to encourage future generations of women to study law.[13]

Otago's next expansion was into modern languages in 1875: Arthur Buechler taught German and Edmond de Montalk lectured in French and

Italian.[14] Italian classes did not survive past that first year, when just one student enrolled; it was difficult attracting students to a language that was not taught in New Zealand schools. De Montalk was the Paris-born son of a Polish nobleman who died in the Mexican War of Independence, and Edmond had fought in the 1859 campaign for Italian independence.[15] He was the first of several people with an adventurous past to teach languages at Otago. The German class, after an opening flurry, dropped to single digits for over a decade, and the French class did not reach double digits until 1885.[16] This was to be expected, given the university's total roll was yet to reach 150, but language lecturers were not paid a salary; they depended on class fees to make a decent living, and most taught high-school classes as well.[17] Not all Otago students appreciated the benefits of native-speaking language teachers. John Callan, who studied French under Jean Aristide Dallas, lecturer from 1879 to 1901, recalled that students 'found his foreign ways amusing, and sometimes made them the subject of unseemly mirth'; they complained, 'somewhat unjustly', that his English was not good enough to teach French to 'English' students.[18]

Enrolments stayed low, but Otago added more academics with further funding from the Presbyterian Synod. In 1881 Cambridge graduate John Mainwaring Brown was appointed to the inaugural chair of English, constitutional history and political economy, and took over Sale's English and MacGregor's economics classes. Brown stated in his opening address in 1882 that his 'first duty [was] with the teaching of English.'[19] Constitutional history was part of the law course and attracted few students, but English enrolments, which had languished to just three students in 1880 under Sale, jumped into double figures with the popular new professor.

Brown's career ended sadly when he disappeared during a tramping expedition in Fiordland at the end of 1888.[20] The University Council, after consulting with the synod, split the chair and advertised for a professor of English and separate lecturers for constitutional history and political economy.[21] Thomas Gilray arrived in 1890 as Otago's first dedicated professor of English. A period of stability followed: Gilray and his successor, Herbert Ramsay – both Scots – held the English chair for three decades each.

Until 1945 the synod retained the power to select professors for the chairs it endowed. It had entrusted the selection of the first philosophy professor, MacGregor, to experts in Scotland, and as his replacement in 1886 it appointed one of its own. William Salmond had been theology professor and a charismatic lecturer at the Theological Hall for 10 years. Like MacGregor, he got into trouble with the synod – his liberal theology, evident in a controversial 1888 pamphlet that questioned the doctrine of eternal punishment, offended religious conservatives and the Dunedin Presbytery found him guilty of heresy – but that did not affect his university appointment, which he held until his retirement in 1913.[22]

INTO ANOTHER CENTURY

In 1901, faced with a financial crisis, the university sacrificed its small Law School. In 1905 the District Law Society convinced it to begin legal classes again, with the lecturers funded solely from student fees, and three years later James Garrow was appointed as the first full-time law lecturer. Unfortunately for Otago, Garrow left after three years to become foundation law professor in Wellington. After a two-year interval the university reverted to appointing part-time lecturers, this time heavily subsidised by the District Law Society. In 1913 when the Faculty of Law was created it boasted 47 students, probably all part-time. Numbers fluctuated over the next 40 years, to as high as 91 in 1928 and just eight students in 1942.[23]

The humanities ventured into another professional field, too – education. The Otago Education Board began an apprentice-style system, training its own 'pupil teachers' on the job, in the 1860s. In 1876 it opened New Zealand's first teachers' training college (TTC), based at the

Normal School in Moray Place. It encouraged its students to attend university, and TTC students and already-qualified teachers made up a large proportion of the total university roll – 68 of a total of 167 students in 1887, for example.[24] Gilray commented that the TTC students' academic work was 'very creditable', but that they experienced more illness than other students.[25] A report from women students in 1898 suggested why: 'to combine a University with a Normal School or pupil teacher's course, as half our number do … is simple madness. Those who attempt it will, sooner or later, have to pay for it.'[26]

In 1901 a council committee investigated potential course developments at the university. Growth in enrolments had faltered, especially in the arts, with 'a disappointing absence of that steady increase in the attendance at the University which we might well expect in a young and prosperous community'. A drop in TTC students at the university was especially concerning: their TTC course had been shortened and additional practical and technical subjects replaced university options. The committee recommended that the university introduce a course in 'the history, science, and art of teaching' and that the TTC encourage its students to take the course, together with English and mental science, at university.[27] In 1904, after years of refusals, the University of New Zealand approved education as a BA subject.[28] Under a new national training system, prospective teachers studied 'non-special subjects' at university in each of the four main centres while going through their practical training at the TTC and associated schools. The TTC principal served as university education lecturer: in 1904 David White delivered Otago's first course in the principles and history of education to six students.[29] The course became one of the university's most popular, and by 1909 Otago was urging the government to fund larger classrooms to accommodate the growth in student numbers, 'owing to the closer attachment with the Training College'. That year White became Otago's first professor of education.[30]

At the request of the Presbyterian Church, Hebrew was added to Otago's humanities syllabus in 1901. Theology was controversial as a university subject, but the council and churches had a cordial relationship and the Hebrew classes were evidence of that. Michael Watt, one of Otago's pioneer Presbyterian ministers and a professor at the Theological Hall, known for 'his fine Highland courtesy and his thorough scholarship', was appointed lecturer in Hebrew late in 1901. His appointment incurred no cost to the university, and classes took place at the Theological Hall. This arrangement meant theology students could credit their language studies towards a BA, and other students could also study Hebrew there, though it never attracted large numbers.[31]

WAR AND RECOVERY

Enrolments were still not growing as rapidly as some would like. In 1912 the Department of Education toughened its matriculation exams and this led to a decrease in arts and science students.[32] Soon afterwards World War I brought a bigger challenge: students in law and arts rushed to enlist, and unlike others, they could not use their studies to justify an exemption once conscription began in 1916. Male enrolments in arts and law dropped by a quarter in 1915 and continued a slow decline through the war.[33]

Of course, enrolments weren't the only measure of the university's development. Before entry standards were raised, universities were 'forced to cover much of the ground which was rightly the province of the secondary school', the minister of education said in a report; the 'standard of work taught' at the universities could now be 'considerably raised'.[34] As student numbers declined, teaching in the humanities improved and the departments prepared for an anticipated postwar influx. Harry Bedford and George Thompson were appointed to new chairs in economics/history and modern languages during the war, and Thomas Dagger Adams was promoted to the chair of classics, which had been vacant since Sale's retirement in 1908; the financially straitened university, obliged to pay Sale a pension, had replaced him for nine years with two lecturers.[35] The humanities acquired its first woman academic, Isabel Turnbull, in 1915. Her job title of 'assistant lecturer' was a misnomer: Adams departed on military service in 1917, leaving all of the Latin teaching in the capable hands of Turnbull for 1918 and 1919, and other assistants took over Greek classes.[36]

Otago's already struggling German programme was one casualty of the war. In 1899 Gilray, chair of the Professorial Board, reported that it had suffered because 'the teaching of German is almost entirely abandoned in Otago schools'; he hoped it might be revived, for 'every Student knows that it is impossible to get to the bottom of almost any subject without a knowledge of German'.[37] Part-time lecturer Frank Campbell's enthusiasm kept the German class going, but early in 1915 he resigned as he had no students; German may have been the language of much scholarly publishing, but students in the grip of patriotic fervour were unwilling to learn it. The University Council regretted 'the removal, even for a time, of so important a study as that of German from the subjects of instruction within the University'.[38] Classes commenced again in 1918, but not because of demand from arts students; the classes catered to science students who had to demonstrate reading capacity in a foreign language to complete their degree. Thompson added German teaching to his schedule and Phyllis Turnbull became assistant lecturer in French in 1918.[39]

Bedford's promotion was a sign of the rising importance of history and economics. Initially appointed as economics lecturer in 1907, from 1914 he also taught 'English history'. That marked the beginning of history as a subject in its own right at Otago – the existing constitutional history course was designed for lawyers. From 1916 Bedford added to his schedule two lectures a week on 'Modern History, as prescribed for Commerce students'. He was an inspiring teacher – but he too was destined for an early death; he drowned while on holiday at the beach in 1918. The council appointed Anglican archdeacon and retired Selwyn warden Robert Woodthorpe as acting professor. But it felt the time had come to separate the expanding disciplines of economics and history, and in 1920 John Elder of Aberdeen was appointed to a chair in history, endowed by the Presbyterian Church, and William Pringle as economics professor.[40] A 'conservative and hard working Presbyterian', the notoriously dour Elder was also innovative: he published extensively on New Zealand history at a time when 'it was highly unusual for colonial professors to publish anything'. He expanded the curriculum to include more coverage of this country and other colonies among the broad history courses on offer. He valued archival research and required it of history MA students – using the resources of the Hocken Library.[41]

EXPANDING THE ARTS

There was a brief postwar surge in arts students as men began or returned to their studies. Two additional subjects – both introduced thanks to philanthropists – gave them more options. In 1918 Otago became the first university in Australasia to employ an anthropologist after a 'generous citizen' – later identified as the merchant and collector Willi Fels – gifted £200 per year for five years to subsidise a lecturer in ethnology, who would also serve as assistant curator at the Otago Museum.[42] The post went to Henry Skinner, a fossicker from childhood who had completed a zoology degree at Otago. After serving at Gallipoli he was invalided out of the army; he studied anthropology at Cambridge and explored Māori and Moriori material culture in British museums.[43] Skinner started an extension course in 1919 and, from 1920, anthropology was made available to undergraduates.[44] He was a dedicated researcher. In 1930, for instance, he and assistant David Teviotdale got a grant to investigate 'line fishing of the Otago Maoris', including a survey of sites along the north shore of Foveaux Strait and a 10-day excavation at Little Papanui on the Otago Peninsula. In collaboration with Bishop Museum in Honolulu, Skinner worked on ground stone-cutting implements of Polynesia and made a research trip to Tahiti.[45] One Skinner project proved of special value to Ngāi Tahu Whānui: in 1920 he supervised Herries Beattie, an experienced journalist and oral historian, in a compilation of ethnological notes that became a key study of southern Māori lifeways.[46] Education was becoming more research-focused, too; in the 1930s postgraduate students examined the relationship between intelligence and scholastic achievement in a project directed by education professor Richard Lawson for the Carnegie Educational Research Council.[47] In 1939 Lawson established a Child Guidance Clinic, which provided experience for education students and 'dealt successfully with "problem" cases'.[48]

Otago was not a pioneer in music studies – they had been taught at Auckland from 1888 and Canterbury from 1891 – but in 1925 it was the recipient of a bequest from Dunedin seed merchant John Blair for the appointment of a music lecturer. It did not have to look far to find a qualified candidate: Victor Galway, the University of Melbourne's first doctoral graduate in music, was organist at First Church, conductor of the Dunedin Choral Society and its orchestra, a private music teacher and lecturer for the Workers' Educational Association.[49] Music classes were small at first, with 12 students in the first year. Early courses included harmony, counterpoint, musical appreciation and history and, for advanced students, composition and orchestration. Performance did not become part of the curriculum until much later, although staff and students enhanced Dunedin's cultural life through musical activities outside class.[50] Galway, who was promoted to professor in 1939, was a good teacher, as 1940s student Honor McKellar recalls; he gave a thorough technical training and she could 'write a fugue backwards'. His musical tastes were conservative: he famously described nineteenth-century opera as 'the lowest form of art'.[51]

The foundation disciplines branched out after the war, too. From 1923 students could study Greek history, art and literature (known as Greek HAL) – the first move from classical languages into a broader classical studies curriculum.[52] 'The classes were small, the lecturer sympathetic and the students a bit more interesting,' recalls 1920s student Elizabeth Mason (who didn't think much of her French course).[53] The collection of classical antiquities at the Otago Museum – ranked 'third in the empire outside Great Britain' by an expert in 1949 – provided source material.[54] The mental and moral philosophy department consisted solely of the professor until 1925, when an assistant was appointed who was shared with economics. Six years later Henry Ferguson, a Scot, became lecturer in experimental psychology. 'This University has been lagging behind in regard to Experimental Psychology but the new appointment should rectify that,' noted Robert Jack, the dean of arts and sciences.[55] Psychology developed as a subject and by the late 1940s the department was listed in the calendar as 'philosophy and psychology', with six academic staff.

DEPRESSION AND MORE WAR

At the beginning of the 1930s economic depression, the Faculty of Arts and Science roll increased: 'The difficulty of finding suitable appointments has no doubt induced many young men and women to carry on with Higher Education instead of merely marking time,' the dean, George Thompson, wrote in 1932.[56] As the depression worsened the roll dropped, largely because of changes at the TTC. The teacher training course was shortened because of a teacher shortage in World War I, then from 1922 the TTC took over the 'general education' aspects of teacher training, including English – previously a university subject. That reduced the number of teacher trainees at the university, but they were still a good proportion of part-time undergrads. In 1933, with many teachers unemployed, a financial crisis and a strategy to centralise teacher education, the government forced Dunedin's TTC to downsize and many students transferred to Christchurch. In 1934 and 1935 all New Zealand TTCs closed. A few more students

Latin picnic at Whare Flat, 1932. Dan Davin is on the far right, with Christopher Johnson on his right and Angus Ross seated in front of him. Other students include Frank Hall (back left), Winnie McQuilkan (centre front) and Ida Lawson (in dark jacket behind her). The Classics staff, Thomas Adams and Isabel Turnbull, are at front left.

1/2-166716-F, ALEXANDER TURNBULL LIBRARY

enrolled at Otago in 1934 after the Christchurch TTC had gone, but it was not until the Dunedin TTC reopened in 1936 that there was a healthy revival in arts student numbers.[57] The Law Faculty experienced a steady decline through the depression; it dropped from 91 students in 1928 to 32 in 1938.

The next major challenge was World War II. As with World War I, the humanities fared worst with the loss of students to the forces; the Law School almost came to a halt with just eight students and only half the usual courses offered.[58] Staff headed off to war too: perhaps best known of these was history lecturer Angus Ross, who earned several military honours and wrote a history of his battalion. After the war he studied at Cambridge before returning to Otago; his career included 11 years in the chair of history.[59] In contrast with the previous war, the German programme actually grew during World War II. The lecturer, Felix Grayeff, was a classicist by training; he was one of several German Jewish émigrés who arrived at Otago in the 1930s and 1940s (see chapter 5). During the mid-1930s Otago offered German only to Stage 1, but with Grayeff's appointment in 1939 it returned to full degree status. A preliminary course enabled students with no prior knowledge of German to embark on Stage 1, and the German science reading class continued.[60]

THE DELAYED BIRTH OF THEOLOGY

Theology was an important subject in the universities of Europe and America, but it took nearly seven decades to be introduced at Otago, even though the university was in a colony of Presbyterians who expected their clergy to complete undergraduate and postgrad education. New Zealand was 'the only country of any importance in the British Empire that did not provide for degrees in theology,' a 1930 University of New Zealand committee reported. Religion had influence at Otago: the Presbyterian Synod funded some of its professors; clergy served as chancellor; and Christian groups were among its first and largest student societies. Religion was, however, a subject of much debate in a country with no state religion and citizens of varied beliefs or none; the prospect of teaching theology raised the question, 'whose theology?' At the University of New Zealand Senate, proponents of university theology met resistance from those who believed religion had no place in public education. There were other hurdles, including governments that were reluctant to court controversy and some churches (notably the Catholic hierarchy) that were anxious about bias.[61]

Various churches, meanwhile, established their own Dunedin theological colleges. Samuel Nevill began educating Anglican ordinands in his home soon after he arrived as Anglican bishop in the early 1870s, and he established Selwyn as a theological college in 1893. It was conveniently close to the university, which many of its students attended. The Presbyterian Theological Hall held classes in the professor's home in Leith Street from the mid-1870s, and at Knox College from 1909; many future Presbyterian clergy completed a degree at Otago before their specialist postgraduate training at the hall. The Catholic Church opened a national seminary, Holy Cross, at Mosgiel in 1900, and the Churches of Christ set up their New Zealand college in Dunedin in 1927.[62] After decades of lobbying, in 1945 a postgraduate degree in theology, the Bachelor of Divinity, won University of New Zealand approval. The academic staff of the Presbyterian, Anglican and Churches of Christ colleges became honorary staff of the university in a Faculty of Theology. Their respective churches kept paying their salaries and classes took place in the colleges; 12 students enrolled for the degree in its first year, 1946. The faculty also offered extramural programmes to students around New Zealand.[63]

THE POSTWAR INFLUX

Rehabilitation Department funding to employ tutors for the many returned servicepeople helped university staff cope with an influx of students following World War II.[64] Geography was a new addition popular with students. In 1945 the government had added more emphasis on social studies in the secondary school curriculum, and the demand for teachers had grown with a change in the school leaving age to 15 from 1944 and a policy to reduce class sizes. Principals had been campaigning for a full degree in geography for years. Students who had enjoyed it at school wanted more, and for some New Zealanders overseas war service – or simply following the events of the conflict – had prompted a passion for geography. The Geography Department at Otago commenced when Cambridge graduate Ben Garnier arrived late in 1945 as first lecturer; from 1946 students could take a BA major in geography. Richard Greenwood, who arrived in 1948 as a second geography lecturer, recalled that the students 'were a stimulating mixture of school leavers and returned servicemen'. He taught on the regional geography of Europe and Asia, and Garnier concentrated on physical geography, including his specialty field of climatology. Students interpreted maps and carried out urban and rural surveys; the Taieri and Karitane were popular fieldwork locations.[65]

Political science got off the ground as a subject after the war, too, promoted by history professor William Morrell.[66] Lecturer Ted Olssen, an Adelaide graduate, commenced classes in 1948 and students emerging from the war and its clash of ideologies demonstrated an appetite for the subject. The most popular course introduced 'democratic political institutions, with special reference to Britain, the Dominions, the USA and France' and 'non-democratic institutions, with special reference to Nazism, Fascism, and Communism'; another explored the history of political theory. Stage 3 papers on European liberalism, twentieth-century totalitarian states and international relations began in 1949.[67] Olssen

Geography students on a Stage 3 field trip outside the Vulcan Hotel, St Bathans, Central Otago in about 1953. Head of department Ron Lister is front row, third from left, just in front of the woman in a pale beret. Students attended residential field camps in locations around southern New Zealand; the camps contributed to the friendly atmosphere that made the department popular with students. PATRICIA GRAHAM COLLECTION.

The English Department staff outside their premises in Cameron House, a grand two-storey family home on Leith Street (later knocked down to make way for UniCol), in 1961. Until tutorials were introduced, the department fitted into a small room in the Clocktower Building. From left: Keith Maslen, Lenore Harty, Gregor Cameron, Alan Horsman, Margaret Dalziel and Bob Robertson.
DEPARTMENT OF ENGLISH AND LINGUISTICS COLLECTION.

was joined by other politics lecturers, including Keith Jackson and Austin Mitchell, who famously dubbed New Zealand 'the half-gallon quarter-acre pavlova paradise' and later became a British MP.[68] Politics stayed within the History Department until 1967.

In 1948 arts dean Geoffry Billing commented that 'greatly enlarged staff with diverse interests has provided not only an opportunity for more effective coverage of teaching duties but a great stimulus in discussion and exchange of experience'.[69] However, after the brief flurry of the 1940s, no further subjects were introduced for 13 years. In 1961 Ross, then dean, expressed concern that 'stability may breed stagnation'; improved salaries after the Parry Report meant Otago lost fewer staff to better-funded universities overseas.[70] There was, of course, some staff turnover, and nowhere did that inspire more change than in English. English professor Herbert Ramsay boasted in a 1950 valedictory speech to the University Council that he had never asked them for more staff: he and long-serving lecturer Gregor Cameron did all the teaching, with one additional junior lecturer from the late 1940s, and they retained their committment to the Scottish lecture-only system. Ramsay was 'one of the university's best lecturers' and students delighted in his thoughts on Shakespeare, but the courses were conservative, covering a traditional British canon and plenty of Old English and Middle English. John Greig, a Scot who taught in England, the United States and South Africa, introduced radical changes as professor from 1952 to 1956. No fan of the conventional lecture, he introduced group tutorials; as a consequence, the number of academic staff in the department jumped from three to seven, plus part-time tutors. Greig modernised the curriculum, adding works by twentieth-century authors (Sean O'Casey, T.S. Eliot, Virginia Woolf) and New Zealand poetry and short stories.[71]

The inclusion of New Zealand literature in universities was controversial. As Otago lecturer Robert Robertson explained, it was generally taught as 'a dutiful recognition' that first-year students should be aware of New Zealand poetry. There was an element of colonial cringe, but teaching local literature was hard work for staff, who had only 'partial bibliographies, few collected works, no collected letters, not a standard biography, incomplete histories only and a scattered body of occasional criticism of varying merit'.[72] Alan Horsman, a New Zealander who had studied and taught in England, arrived as Otago's English professor in 1957. He recalls it as a significant year, with the publication of Janet Frame's *Owls Do Cry* and Ian Cross's *The God Boy*, novels that stood comparison with the best English writing; and there was already poetry 'of top quality'. He was reluctant, though, to introduce a paper devoted to New Zealand literature.[73] Lawrence Jones, an American who arrived as lecturer in 1964, found Otago students responded more enthusiastically to Janet Frame than to Thomas Hardy, and his research interests shifted to New Zealand literature. In 1977, in response to student demand, an honours paper fully devoted to New Zealand work was introduced; other undergrad courses followed and research expanded.[74]

EXPANDING IN THE 1960s AND 1970s

In 1960 the number of arts students surpassed the previous high point of the 1946 postwar influx, and it doubled again by 1970 as the baby-boom generation reached university age. That strained resources but justified further expansion.[75] Rapid growth had already changed the Law School: in 1959, more than 80 years after its first law lectures, Otago appointed Frank Guest as the first full-time law professor; he was dean in a faculty of 14 staff and 99 students. Classes became too large for the court building and in 1966 law moved to the main campus. The decades of the part-time 'night school' ended as most law students became full-time – they participated fully in student life, in contrast to previous generations, who were geographically, socially and intellectually isolated from the university.[76]

Russian, the first new arts subject for many years, was introduced in response to interest in the Soviet Union sparked by the Cold War, along with increased scientific publications in Russian.[77] In 1960 the Department of Modern Languages started Russian tutorials and, in 1961, a degree programme. The department divided in three in 1969: existing professor Eric Herd became head of the Department of German Language and Literature, and Ray Stone was promoted to a chair in French and headed that department. The Department of Russian Language and Literature did not have a professor: Herd served as 'administrative head of department' until the mid-1970s, when Peter Stupples became 'lecturer in charge'.[78] In an institution with plenty of eccentrics the Russian Department was renowned for its eccentricity and exoticism; many regarded it fondly for that reason alone. The first lecturer, Maximilian Edwards, loved music and kept a grand piano in his office. Nicholas Zissermann was a Russian–Austrian émigré who escaped the revolution and lived in China and Australia before winding up at Otago in 1961; his dog accompanied him to classes. Peter Soskice was an Oxford graduate, the son of an exiled Russian revolutionary journalist father and a relation of several pre-Raphaelite artists; he acted at the Globe Theatre and worked with Charles Brasch to translate modern Russian poetry. Jim Harvie was less exotic – he hailed from Nightcaps – but he was 'not a straight-forward person either'. All had a passion for Russian literature, while Englishman Stupples arrived in 1973 with expertise in the spoken language and Russian art; he learned Russian through the military and worked in intelligence in Berlin, then taught at the University of York. He made several long trips to Soviet Russia.[79]

Religion courses expanded in the 1960s to cater for lay people as well as ordination candidates. In 1966, in a joint venture of the faculties of Theology and Arts, the university appointed its first lecturer in religion, Albert Moore (previous theology appointments had been made by the churches). Moore taught phenomenology of religion, later known as religious studies, to undergraduates from 1967. The course covered Western and Eastern religions; it was popular and became a BA major in 1976.[80] Meanwhile, in 1972 the Faculty of Theology introduced the Bachelor of Theology, Australasia's first undergraduate theology degree. It catered for lay students as well as those aiming to enter the ministry, and many students included theology papers in a BA. Ecumenical cooperation developed in the wake of Vatican II; in 1970 Ian Sanders, the rector of Holy Cross College, became the first Catholic on the faculty staff and theology classes took place at Holy Cross and Knox.[81]

During the 1960s some subjects that had been in the shadow of others became flourishing independent departments, although not every field that wanted a professor got one. The Arts Faculty 'very fully and responsibly' debated its recommendations for professors, noted Ross in 1961; 'some felt that a department should be fully developed before it should be given a Chair, others that it is best to get a Professor who can plan the development of his department'. It was agreed to try both methods. The departure of Betty Bernardelli, senior psychology lecturer in the Department of Philosophy and Psychology, prompted reorganisation of that department.[82] Otago staff carried out considerable research in psychology and there was more student interest in it, but it was only taught at first-year level.[83] Victoria, Canterbury and Auckland universities all separated their philosophy and psychology departments in the 1950s; Otago fell behind. Bernardelli arrived at Otago in 1948 ex-Oxford, Cambridge and the Royal Navy; she found that psychology had been stifled in the department – something she attributed to the Oxford background of its recently departed head, David Raphael (there was little support for psychology at Oxford).[84] Daniel Taylor, philosophy professor from 1960, was a supporter and under his leadership the disciplines finally separated. In 1964 Stephen Griew arrived from Bristol to become Otago's first psychology professor, and from 1965 Otago offered full degree programmes in psychology. The new department quickly outgrew its former stablemate in philosophy; it moved from the Arts Faculty to its more natural home in the Faculty of Science (see chapter 7 for its subsequent history).[85]

Anthropology, like psychology, had been long taught at Otago, but 'it was felt that the needle had stuck in the Stage I groove for long enough', the 1961 Arts Faculty report noted. Skinner retired in 1952; remembered for his inspirational teaching and hair-raising driving to digs, he almost single-handedly kept an interest in anthropology alive in the south. Every year he introduced another 15 or 20 students to the discipline, but he made no attempt to extend the course; as curator at Otago Museum, and its director from 1937, he had plenty else to do.[86] There was a hiatus after Skinner left; visiting

Anthropologists outside Ōtākou marae in 1970. Left to right: Kevin Jones (postgraduate student), Foss Leach (assistant lecturer), Edmund Leach (visitor to the department, a distinguished anthropologist from Cambridge University), Sally Mirams (student).
HELEN LEACH PHOTOGRAPH, HELEN LEACH COLLECTION.

lecturers offered the course some years before Peter Gathercole, another Cambridge graduate, became the anthropology lecturer in 1958 and revived the Stage 1 course. Gathercole campaigned for a full degree programme and in 1962 his position, previously shared with the museum, became full-time. John Harré and Les Groube joined him in 1963 and the department began in earnest; students could major in anthropology for the first time.[87] Helen Leach (then Keedwell) was one of the first anthropology majors; they were a motivated group, she recalls, and persuaded the department to develop postgraduate courses promptly so they could continue their studies at Otago rather than Auckland, which had offered anthropology from the 1950s. Leach completed the Otago department's first MA in 1968 and taught there for many years; she became famous for her food research – especially her assertion that New Zealand, rather than Australia, was the first to create the pavlova. Several other postgrads of the 1960s and 1970s had distinguished anthropology careers; those who taught at Otago included Foss Leach, Ian Frazer and Atholl Anderson.[88]

There was no difficulty attracting students: the challenge was to keep staff–student ratios respectable. Charles Higham, yet another Cambridge graduate, arrived as anthropology lecturer in 1967 and became the first professor in 1968. He was destined for a long career at Otago and became a world-leading authority on the archaeology of Southeast Asia.[89] By 1970 anthropology was burgeoning, with students at all levels. 'Explosive' growth carried on through the 1970s as interest in the social sciences skyrocketed; by 1975 there were over 500 first-year students and eventually the class had to be divided as it couldn't fit into the largest lecture theatre on campus.[90] The archaeologists carried out important research on various sites of early Māori settlement, notably at Shag River Mouth where, in the 1980s, Anderson and Ian Smith led 'a well planned assault on a badly fossicked site'. Supplemented by radiocarbon dating, this work advanced knowledge of southern Māori settlement and material culture.[91]

Anthropology got its professor four years after the department began, but geography had to wait 20 years for its chair: it took time to gain credibility, perhaps because it crossed the boundaries between art and science. It started as an arts subject but became a BSc major as well from 1950; some scientists regarded it as a 'soft' option and the department did not gain admission to the Faculty of Science until 1963. Thereafter

In 1982 the language lab was updated to allow interactive group teaching; lecturers could use reel or cassette tapes, records, radio and slides. New formats were added and by 1990, when the laboratory became the Language Learning Centre and this photograph was taken, computer-aided learning had been added to the mix.
UNIVERSITY OF OTAGO PHOTOGRAPHIC UNIT RECORDS, MS-4185/030, S15-500C, HOCKEN COLLECTIONS.

it belonged to both faculties, although its direct oversight and funding stayed with arts. Ron Lister, who replaced Garnier as senior lecturer in 1952, was appointed to the new chair of geography in 1965. Lister was an outstanding teacher who did much to promote the study of geography; the department's happiness was demonstrated in enrolments – it was one of Otago's most popular majors.[92]

Politics was another subject granted a chair and full departmental status in the 1960s. Otago recruited as professor a young American who was teaching politics at Canterbury. Jim Flynn arrived in 1967 and quickly proved a dynamic force in the humanities and wider university; his research and publications – particularly those on intelligence – were internationally renowned. Flynn and the existing and new lecturers developed a curriculum where students could specialise in political philosophy or international relations; the departments around New Zealand made a strategic decision to build up different specialties. The arrival of staff with expertise in New Zealand politics (Antony Wood) and quantitative methods (Chris Rudd) built up research capability in New Zealand political behaviour. The department became 'the best in Australasia', according to Flynn. The 1968 annual report noted frequent media appearances by Flynn and Stuart Greif; and Otago politics staff maintained a strong presence as political commentators. The Politics Department attracted few postgrads in its early years, but it prided itself on a strong honours programme.[93]

NEW TECHNOLOGY AND A NEW BALANCE

A state-of-the-art language laboratory opened in the Arts Building in 1969: students listened and recorded onto reel-to-reel tapes to improve their listening and speaking skills. New formats were gradually added and a major 1994 redevelopment put Otago 'at the forefront of language teaching technology': students could develop their language skills using interactive multimedia computer facilities. None of the technologies were cheap: the redevelopment cost close to $1 million.[94] Besides the power of technology, the language labs demonstrated more emphasis on spoken as well as written fluency in language learning. The language departments appointed native-speaking tutors, generally young people who visited Otago from Europe for a year or two; from 1976 to 1984 the Russian tutors came from the Pushkin Institute, an official Soviet cultural organisation.[95] Still, language departments struggled to attract students. This was partly the fault of the Arts Faculty: it had once argued that 'reasonable competence in a foreign language' was 'a fundamental part of the education of an Arts graduate', but in 1970 it abolished its compulsory language requirement.[96] Given a freer choice of subjects, most students opted for the social sciences. In 1976 the dean, philosopher Bob Durrant, updated the council on the 'imbalanced' state of the Arts Faculty. The 'more traditional Arts departments' had been 'losing ground to the social sciences' for some time

One way of gaining competence in languages was through drama; it also provided fun for both staff and students. The 1971 French Department production of 'Le Malade Imaginaire' at Allen Hall featured, from left: Cilla McQueen, Malcolm Glenny, Ray Stone (French professor) and Jack Thompson. ROGER COLLINS COLLECTION.

and the process had 'recently accelerated,' he said. 'Enrolments in French and German fell sharply in 1975, while Stage 1 Anthropology soared to almost embarrassing heights'. Greater freedom in other faculties contributed to the imbalance: from 1973 medical intermediate students could include arts subjects in their course and they, too, flocked to anthropology.[97]

Classics, which battled to recruit students as the subject declined in schools, countered the liberal arts trend by introducing classical studies, which offered 'a classical education without tears'.[98] Championed by classics professor Richard Mulgan and his successor John Barsby, who described it as 'a blend of the old-fashioned and the new-fangled', the course included various aspects of the Roman and Greek classical worlds, studied in English – building on the old Greek HAL course. Otago first offered classical studies at Stage 2 in 1968 and it became a BA major in 1974. Few students majored in classical studies, but many took a paper or two; the range of papers, from literature and thought to art and architecture, ensured wide appeal.[99] Classics changed its language papers, too. Greek did not assume any prior knowledge, but Latin did. In 1978 only two students enrolled in Latin I, and one of them didn't complete; in response the department converted Latin I into a class for beginners and enrolments soared to over 50.[100]

Classics had, as Durrant noted, 'a whole civilisation at their disposal, and have been able to court popularity while still providing courses of high academic standard'; he was sceptical of radical changes around what might prove 'quite transitory changes in fashion' in other subjects.[101] The forces of conservatism were strong at Otago, but other arts departments were stepping warily into fresh fields. English, in addition to taking New Zealand literature seriously, offered its first paper in American literature in 1967. In history, the focus moved beyond traditional imperial history towards 'imperialism from the perspective of the colonised'. John Omer-Cooper, a specialist in African history, took up the newly established second chair in history in 1973 and a revamped curriculum enabled history majors to focus on

New Zealand, Australia, the Pacific or Asia in addition to Europe.[102] Erik Olssen and Dorothy Page, both appointed in 1969, became pioneers of social history and women's history respectively, and W.H. ('Hew') McLeod, appointed in 1971, gained international renown as a scholar of Sikh history.[103] The education and economics departments established second chairs in the 1970s, too, and English in 1966. The foundation English chair became the Donald Collie Chair in honour of a pioneer Southland farmer whose son made a bequest; lecturer Margaret Dalziel – a future dean and PVC – was promoted to second professor.[104]

Geography instigated interdisciplinary ventures in the 1970s. There was mounting concern about the environment and students lobbied for a course in environmental studies. Lister directed a first-year half-unit, 'Man and the environment', in 1975 that involved botany, geology, history, law, microbiology, physics, psychology, nutrition and zoology as well as geography. The popular course was renamed 'Environment and society' in 1990, and other papers were added in the twenty-first century. For the scientifically minded, geography later developed a course in environmental management for the Bachelor of Applied Science.[105] And Lister, notorious for his involvement in a 'bewildering network of local, regional and national organisations', developed professional planning courses at Otago; it was a response to rising interest in southern regional development and the frustration of geography and surveying graduates who had to go to Auckland for professional qualifications in planning. Lister recruited Ali Memon, a Kenyan planning lecturer, to the Geography Department in 1977, and in 1978 the university put a proposal to the UGC for a course in regional and resource planning. It began as a postgraduate diploma in 1980, and was upgraded to a master's degree in 1984. The regional focus was timely as government policy shifted in that direction; graduates were in demand. Memon directed the course until 1999 – he was based in geography but drew on the resources of economics, law, management, politics and surveying, and took pride in the course's interdisciplinary nature.[106]

Evidence of an accommodation squeeze. At the beginning of 1992, faced with a double booking, linguistics lecturer Graham McGregor conducted a first-year English class on the lawn in front of the clocktower.
OTAGO DAILY TIMES PHOTOGRAPH, DEPARTMENT OF ENGLISH AND LINGUISTICS COLLECTION.

The Arts Faculty ventured into other applied fields in the 1970s. John Lehrberger became faculty lecturer in linguistics in 1971 and pioneered Stage 1 papers in descriptive and historical linguistics. Donn Bayard, lecturer in the Anthropology Department from 1970 to 2002, also had expertise in linguistics, and he researched and taught at various times in linguistics alongside his work in Southeast Asian archaeology.[107] Lehrberger left in 1975, and it wasn't until 1979 that a new lecturer, Ray Harlow, offered the faculty linguistics course again. Despite his other responsibilities teaching Māori (discussed below), in 1985 Harlow added Stage 2 linguistics to the schedule.[108] The English curriculum always concentrated on literature, though from 1980 it offered an introductory English language paper and it gradually added further language-focused papers. In 1990 the linguistics programme, by then led by lecturer Graham McGregor, moved into the English Department; other staff joined him and from 1994 students could major in linguistics. In the

John Drummond, Blair Professor of Music and opera expert, poses with electric guitar in 1999 to publicise Otago's new contemporary music degree.
OTAGO DAILY TIMES PHOTOGRAPH, JOHN DRUMMOND COLLECTION.

late 1990s, as interest in language acquisition and language teaching rose, the programme moved into more applied fields and offered a Graduate Diploma in Second Language Teaching.[109]

By 1944 the Arts Faculty was making plans for a 'dramatic art' course, comprising 'drama as a literary form' alongside training in speech, acting, production and stage management; a year later a university group presented plays at the British Drama League Festival under the leadership of Ailsa Stephens, an Otago home science graduate of the 1920s who was active in Dunedin theatre.[110] In the early 1950s John Trevor was 'lecturer and adviser in drama' within the English Department; there was no specialist course, but Trevor brought his experience from the English stage and as a wartime entertainer of troops to university dramatic productions.[111] He wasn't replaced, though University Extension drama tutor Rodney Kennedy helped with university dramatic performances alongside his community work.[112] In 1972, thanks to a bequest from William and Fanny Evans, directed to 'music, drama, the Hocken Library and visitors to the university', Otago appointed David Carnegie as drama lecturer and a credited course for undergraduates kicked off.[113] Carnegie persuaded the university to upgrade Allen Hall into 'a flexible teaching space and theatre studio'. Jane Oakshott, who replaced Carnegie in 1977, started a lunchtime theatre programme featuring drama students that became a popular feature of campus life. Meanwhile playwright Roger Hall, Burns Fellow in 1977 and 1978, stayed on in the English Department to teach a playwriting course; he helped keep theatre going between Oakshott's departure and the arrival of Lisa Warrington in 1981. The drama programme flourished under Warrington's leadership. She added a directing course in 1990 and theatre studies, as it was renamed, expanded into a major in 1994.[114]

The Music Department also expanded because of the Evans legacy. In 1964 the professor, Peter Platt, reported that 'all other New Zealand universities have now included practical training in their courses'; Otago was falling behind.[115] The department added 'performance and repertoire' for students with proven musical skill and, in 1967, Platt boasted that Otago could now 'offer excellent instruction to many different sorts of musicians: composers, scholars and executants'. There were already seven performance students, with practical tuition supplied by 'three excellent local teachers'.[116] The bequest enabled Otago to appoint Honor McKellar (voice) and Maurice Till (piano) as William Evans Executant Senior Lecturers in 1971; they gave recitals and demonstration lectures in addition to performance teaching. Otago was fortunate in its first executant lecturers: both were acclaimed performers with international experience and, like their successors, they attracted good musicians and tutored them expertly.[117] One of the greatest musicians to emerge from the university was an early performance student: the department reported in 1973 that 'Mr Michael Houstoun, a senior student was awarded third place in the Van Cliburn International Piano Contest held in Fort Worth, Texas, USA.'[118]

THE BACHELOR OF EDUCATION

The Education Department thrived. Some students, like future academic Bruce McMillan, were recruited into the discipline because it offered a path for the study of human behaviour before psychology became a major.[119] From 1957 TTC students could credit Education I to professional studies and enrolments jumped. There was another sharp surge after 1966, when the TTC primary course increased from two years to three, giving teaching students more time and opportunity for university study.[120] By the 1970s experts had been recommending closer involvement of the universities in New Zealand teacher education for a century, with limited effect. The 1962 Currie Report, arising from a royal commission on education, proposed that teacher training transfer to universities, working with affiliated TTCs. The recommendation was not followed, but it prompted further discussion. In 1970, at the request of the minister of education, a joint working party of the Dunedin TTC and University of Otago entered discussions on closer cooperation.[121] In 1972 the Arts Faculty voted down a proposal that professional TTC courses be recognised as BA units, 'chiefly on the grounds that professional studies, of whatever kind, are not an appropriate part of an Arts degree', but it recommended that the senate consider a Bachelor of Education (BEd) degree.[122] A Joint Board of Studies was set up and in 1976 the four-year BEd commenced. Designed as a professional course for primary school teachers, it included university, TTC and jointly taught papers. Despite considerable goodwill there was mutual suspicion between the staff of the two institutions over teaching methods and standards. Flynn recalls that the degree attracted more lively debate than any other issue in the Arts Faculty; he chaired a 1979 senate committee which investigated its standard, allaying concerns it was a 'soft' option.[123] It was popular with prospective teachers as it gave more employment opportunities; in 1977, 95 per cent of the TTC intake enrolled in the four-year degree rather than a three-year diploma. From 1984 students in the early childhood education course, which evolved out of a Kindergarten Association course transferred to the TTC in 1975, could also complete a BEd.[124]

Otago's Education Department did not stop at the BEd. From 1978 it offered a Postgraduate Diploma in Educational Psychology, including supervised practice in an approved agency; a Master of Education degree was designed to facilitate the educational psychology course and 'provide a future framework for graduate training in a variety of professional areas'.[125] As schools acquired computers the Education Department, an early adopter of technology, gave instruction on its three Apple II microcomputers, plus another on loan from the government, to current and prospective teachers in PILOT, a language designed for writing computer-based lessons; and it offered a paper on 'Computer applications in education' from 1983.[126] In 1987 it set up the Otago Computer Education Resources Centre 'to provide support and to meet the needs of the computer education community in this region'; its inaugural 'hands-on week' that introduced educators to computers in classrooms attracted over 100 teachers in 1988.[127] Postgrad study expanded during the 1980s and the department developed several research specialties, notably educational psychology, reading recovery and special education – a key field as schools introduced mainstreaming of students with impairments.[128]

DEVELOPING MĀORI PROGRAMMES

The Education Department was an early adopter of bicultural awareness – by Otago standards, at least. The TTC introduced compulsory courses in Māoritanga in the 1970s. The university didn't add specialist papers on Māori and education until

1991, though material appeared earlier within other papers. The TTC had its own struggles adapting to calls for a Māori perspective, but cooperation between the two institutions was important. In 1990 one of the TTC staff, Huata Holmes, became the Education Department's first pou here tangata and provided Māori support and a link with mana whenua.[129]

There was another important step for Māori at Otago in 1990: the establishment of a Māori Studies Department. Otago was late to do so, partly because of the low Māori population in the south, but also because of the university's conservative wariness of the academic credentials of Māori studies. Otago did, however, offer classes in te reo Māori much earlier: in 1957 the Adult Education Department held an introductory class in Māori. The tutor was Harold Tarewai Wesley of Ōtākou, said to be the last native speaker of the local dialect, and the 12-class course was 'well attended by members of the local Maori community' with 51 enrolments.[130] Evening classes in te reo Māori carried on with a succession of tutors and, as the Māori renaissance gathered momentum, demand increased. Classes took place around the region; Level 2 and 3 options were added and, from 1971, Otago offered an extension certificate – a formal qualification after three years of classes (considered equivalent to Stage 1).[131]

In 1971 the university began plans for an undergraduate course in te reo. An Arts Faculty committee examined the case for establishing courses in Māori and concluded it was 'both an opportunity and a responsibility for all New Zealand universities'; there was 'genuine and wide interest'.[132] Plans were shelved until the next government five-yearly block grant, but in 1975 the university advertised a lectureship in Māori. The faculty committee recommended it as 'essential' that the first person appointed was 'of very high academic quality and that the appointment be made at the level of senior lecturer at least'.[133] This requirement for high-level academic qualifications had unfortunate consequences: in June 1975 the Academic Staffing Committee decided neither of the two applicants was suitable. Conscious that Māori language teachers were rare and in hot demand, the committee took an alternative approach. Ray Harlow was an able linguist with a PhD teaching in Germany; he planned to study Polynesian languages and literature at the University of Munich. Otago offered him a postdoctoral fellowship to study for a year in Germany, followed by a year at Auckland, studying Māori with Bruce Biggs. After that, they expected to offer him a position lecturing in Māori.[134]

News that Otago's first Māori lecturer was to be a Pākehā with, as yet, little knowledge of te reo caused an outcry. The Māori Club criticised the two-year delay and the appointment of a person without standing in the Māori community; letters appeared in the press around the country and over 1000 people signed a petition protesting the delay. Otago received a delegation from the Maori Graduates Association, a high-powered group who made it clear that Māori had taken offence at the university's actions; the language could not be so readily separated from Māoritanga. In a concession to Māori concerns the university brought forward its original intention to appoint a second lecturer; this time it hoped to attract 'a suitably qualified native-speaker of Maori'.[135] Harlow, meanwhile, completed his fellowship and returned to Otago in 1977; he was appointed lecturer in linguistics and Māori and started teaching linguistics. The university's efforts to recruit another lecturer failed: in 1979 the arts dean reported that the position had been offered to three people over the past four years but all had declined.[136] The faculty decided it could delay no longer and introduced a half-unit in Māori language, taught by Harlow, in 1981 – 'an interim measure pending the introduction of a full unit in Maori when a native-speaking lecturer can be appointed'.[137]

After a 10-year search the university found its first Māori lecturer in te reo in Godfrey Pohatu, who arrived in 1986. He was an experienced teacher, active in Māori cultural groups and partway through a Master of Education degree at Canterbury; he later completed a PhD at Otago. There were big expectations of Pohatu, who was fortunate to have the support of his wife

Māori Studies staff in 1991. Standing (from left): Mark Laws, Maureen Bruce, Godfrey Pohatu, Meredith ?, Michael Reilly, Mereana Smith. Seated: Lorraine Johnson, Toroa Pohatu. They are photographed at the Mataatua wharenui at Otago Museum, which was often used for Māori Studies events before it was returned to Ngāti Awa in Whakatane in 1996.

UNIVERSITY OF OTAGO PHOTOGRAPHIC UNIT RECORDS, MS-4185/016, S14-561A, HOCKEN COLLECTIONS.

Toroa Pohatu; she joined him as lecturer in the programme in 1988, when there were 212 first-year students.[138] A paper introducing cultural concepts, mythology, arts and crafts was added to the language paper in 1987; it quickly became one of the largest on campus as students sought a basic understanding of the Māori world.[139] Te Kapa Haka o Te Whare Wānanga o Ōtākou, a cultural group tutored by Godfrey and Toroa Pohatu, got going in 1987.[140] Stage 2 papers started in 1989 and from 1990 students could major in Māori studies; the programme earned full status as a department that year. Godfrey Pohatu was active in initiatives for the betterment of Māori at Otago; he was a powerful and respected figure and some students and staff found him intimidating.[141] Assertiveness was essential in dealing with university authorities: a 1995 review reported that securing sufficient resources to deal with the explosive growth in enrolments depended on the 'political skill and vigilance of the Head of Department'.[142]

The review led to big changes. In 1996 Tania Ka`ai arrived as Otago's inaugural professor of Māori studies. To a department that was overwhelmed with teaching responsibilities she brought a focus on research. Recruiting staff with suitable academic credentials was still difficult, but Ka`ai employed promising young Māori scholars, so the department could grow its own. Staff completed qualifications in second language teaching and by 2002 Otago had 'the country's best programme in te reo'.[143] In 1998, at the suggestion of Wharehuia Milroy of the University of Waikato, Māori Studies adopted the name Te Tumu, a term found in various Pacific languages but especially relevant in the Māori phrase 'te tumu herenga waka', the mooring post for tying up canoes.[144] A 2002 review noted Te Tumu's growth and 'a dynamic striving for recognition and excellence which deserves nurturing and admiration'.[145] Problems with leadership developed and Ka`ai left amid controversy in 2007 for a position at Auckland University of Technology.[146] Despite the turmoil, Te Tumu's academic reputation developed. Longstanding links with Pacific institutions, set up by Pohatu and developed under Ka`ai, who was of Māori and Hawaiian descent, evolved into a programme in Pacific Islands studies. Undergraduate papers commenced in 2001 and from 2002 students could add to the core papers taught at Te Tumu a selection from other disciplines to complete a major in Pacific Studies. A Master of Indigenous Studies programme began in 2003; enrolments were low at first, but shot up when it was offered as a distance-learning programme from 2006.

From 2012 students could major in Indigenous Development/He Kura Matanui for a BA – an interdisciplinary course with papers in Māori and Pacific Islands studies supplemented by other offerings from the humanities. The Bachelor of Māori Traditional Arts course, introduced in 2006, was less successful. It offered two majors – whakairo (carving) or raranga and whatu (plaiting and weaving) – but was prohibitively expensive to provide and there were few enrolments; the programme quietly closed after a couple of years.[147]

RESTRUCTURING AND LANGUAGES

In 1989 the faculties of arts and music, law and theology became the Humanities Division under Otago's revised structure. One of the biggest arts departments, economics, moved to the Commerce Division – a blow when enrolments were all-important in competing for funding. However, humanities had more students than the other divisions: it competed with science as the largest division through the 1990s, and for 10 years from 2001 it was the biggest until health sciences took top spot from 2012. The devolution of budgeting and staff appointments allowed a faster response to changing enrolments, although funding lagged behind student growth.[148]

As Māori courses flourished, the more established language programmes struggled. Teaching languages required intensive staff time and expensive equipment; achieving economies of scale was difficult when students hesitated to enrol because of the time commitment required in learning a language. The UGC had recognised that language teaching was more expensive than other arts subjects but the bulk-funding system introduced in the 1990s meant the end of that differential government funding; Alistair Fox commented to a review that 'No language taught properly to an internationally acceptable standard at University level is likely to pay its own way in the current environment.'[149] Nevertheless, Otago ventured into further language programmes. In 1991 VC Robin Irvine set up a working party which reported that Asian studies was critical to the future of university and nation. Otago offered Asia-related papers in anthropology, economics, history, politics and religious studies, but no Asian languages. All other New Zealand universities except Lincoln had popular Asian language programmes; Otago 'would find itself at a steadily worsening competitive disadvantage if corrective measures are not taken urgently'.[150] Undergraduate courses in Mandarin and Japanese commenced in 1993; the Taiwan-based Chiang Ching-kuo Foundation helped fund the Mandarin programme.[151]

The Humanities Division created a School of Languages late in 1993 in an attempt to enhance cooperation between programmes, and Fox was seconded from the English Department as head.[152] It included the departments of French, German, Russian and Māori studies, together with the Chinese, Japanese and linguistics programmes. The fit with Māori was awkward: it had far more students and strategic importance as the Indigenous language and culture. When the Humanities Division restructured into five schools in 1998, Māori Studies became an independent school and the other languages became part of the larger School of Languages, Literature and Performing Arts – alongside the schools of Law, Liberal Arts and Social Sciences. The aim was to devolve administration and 'foster co-operation across departments through a better system of representation and participation'.[153] Though devolution had its advantages, the system of schools created another, unwelcome layer of bureaucracy. In 2006 VC David Skegg abolished the system: Law and Māori Studies retained the 'school' title – and their deans – but other disciplines returned to their departmental status.[154] That ran counter to an international trend for universities to merge departments into larger entities; at Otago, individual disciplines retained strong identities.

Some disciplines were too small to exist as departments – and Russian was one programme that did not survive incorporation into the School of Languages. A series of reports in the mid-1990s on the funding of small departments, the future of

The German play was a popular annual event from 1954 onwards. The 2002 production was Max Frisch's *Don Juan, oder Die Liebe zur Geometrie*, featuring Harley McCabe (centre) as Don Juan.
ALYTH GRANT PHOTOGRAPH, ALYTH GRANT COLLECTION.

language study and the future of the Humanities Division culminated in a 1997 report, approved by senate, that recommended the Russian Department close. The report found 'considerable support in principle' for continuing Russian, but enrolments were 'well below the level required to justify its retention as a major subject'; it had just 30 equivalent full-time students at all levels and its funding met only half the budget. The French and German departments did survive, but needed more students to secure their future; German lost its honours programme.[155] The closure of Russian created protest: VC Graeme Fogelberg received letters from all over the world. He is still unrepentant: 'the university's long-term interests couldn't sustain it', he says, and the cost to other departments of $14,000 to subsidise each student of Russian was hard to justify when Russian did not seem to be 'a major language of the future'.[156] Victoria closed its Russian programme soon afterwards, and Auckland downsized its programme from a full major – distant reverberations from the collapse of the Soviet Union. Although many Russian students were more interested in culture than politics, the language 'came in because of politics and went out because of politics', Stupples suggests.[157]

Fogelberg was not opposed to languages as such: he promoted the introduction of Spanish at Otago in 2001. Geopolitics was again at play: a 1996 review of languages at Otago noted that Spanish was 'important as a Pacific Rim language. South and Central America are likely to become of greater significance to the future of New Zealand, both commercially and culturally, in the coming decade.' Short courses in Spanish were popular at Otago Polytechnic and Auckland had a successful Spanish programme. The Academic Development Fund set up by Fogelberg funded the first three years of Spanish. It was popular and, by 2003, it was second only to Māori in language enrolments.[158] The success of Spanish prompted Otago into another venture: in 2003 it became the only New Zealand university to offer Portuguese, a strategic move to strengthen Latin American and European offerings at the university and to enhance exchange programmes with two Brazilian universities. The Camões Institute helped fund a lecturer. By 2008 there were about 20 students taking first-year papers in Portuguese and 10 in second year, plus a cultural paper at Summer School; but enrolments became unsustainable and it was dropped in 2014.[159]

In 2003 the Division of Humanities created a Department of Languages and Cultures, encompassing all of its European and Asian language programmes. After more than a decade of uncertainty, there was now a period of stability. The chairs of French and German had been vacant since the retirement of Stone and Herd in 1985. Tim Mehigan, a specialist in German, arrived from Melbourne in 2003 to become the professor of languages, and a commitment to employ at least three permanent academics for each of the core languages – Chinese, French, German, Japanese and Spanish – added five new staff in 2005. Language research was not traditionally a strength at Otago, though some individuals had produced important publications. The department worked to improve its research profile in the performance-based funding environment. Honours programmes were reinstated, and a requirement for students to complete one semester of their fourth year at an overseas partner university meant minimal extra resourcing was required, although funding the languages remained a challenge.[160] The closure of the language labs, once central to language learning but a huge drain on the budget, assisted finances; they became obsolete with access to online resources.

RESTRUCTURING THEOLOGY AND RELIGION

Theology was popular and in 1985, with limited space at Knox and Holy Cross, first-year classes moved on campus. The university provided support to the church colleges, but theology staff were still paid by the churches. In 1991, when the government started funding according to enrolments, the university commenced paying theology staff salaries and enlarged its contribution to college teaching expenses; the university, Presbyterian Church and Catholic bishops signed a formal agreement about the teaching of university theology qualifications in 1992.[161] That was a milestone year for the phenomenology of religion programme, too: it was renamed religious studies, gained full departmental status and acquired its first professor in Elizabeth Isichei, a scholar of African religion who was appointed to a personal chair (that is, a professorship awarded to her personally, rather than a permanent one for the department).[162] 'The study of the religious systems of the world has its own intrinsic attraction', Isichei said in a 1994 report on increasing student numbers; she also noted that 'Dunedin people are sometimes confused by the relationship between the Department of Religious Studies and the Faculty of Theology'.[163]

Problems developed, after decades of goodwill between the university and the churches. The Presbyterian college was 'swamped in factionalism and partisan politicking',[164] and the Catholics wouldn't let their students attend the classes of certain lecturers – including one who left Holy Cross and the priesthood when he married but kept teaching at the university. More importantly, the university had no control over appointments; some staff were not active researchers and the theology curriculum catered primarily for ministry students, although they were a minority. In 1997 the university withdrew from its agreement with the churches and took full control of theology, which became part of a combined department with religious studies. Some of the Holy Cross and Knox staff were appointed to the department, and Gerald Pillay, who had come from South Africa to be foundation professor of theology, was one of several new staff. The university's actions created a crisis for the church colleges. Rather than setting up courses in opposition, the Presbyterians restructured their ordination training and the Catholics moved theirs to Auckland.[165] The Department of Theology and Religious Studies (renamed Theology and Religion in 2009) had awkward origins, but it flourished. It attracted numerous postgrads, and its distance-learning undergraduate programmes were still popular. New subjects emerged: Sanskrit – 'an essential building-block to reading sacred texts' for those who wished to advance in Hinduism or

Buddhism – was first offered in 2010, and from 2011 students could major or minor in Islamic studies, which included papers in politics and history as well as religion. It incorporated Arabic language, first taught at Otago as a Summer School paper in 2005 after requests from students.[166]

'NEW BLOOD' AND WOMEN'S STUDIES

In 1988 the Academic Staffing Committee, concerned at the lack of turnover and the imbalance of gender and ethnicity among senior academics, decided to fund three 'new blood' lecturers, inspired by an Oxbridge model.[167] After a campaign and investigations the three posts went to artificial intelligence, Māori health and women's studies. All were interdisciplinary, especially women's studies, with a working party that attracted support from staff in 16 humanities, science and health science departments. Their proposal pointed out that Otago would soon be the only New Zealand university without a women's studies programme and risked losing students, including to a new Massey extramural course.[168]

In 1989 Anna Smith became Otago's first women's studies lecturer. In 1990 she established a Stage 2 paper in feminist theory, and she coordinated an interdisciplinary programme, starting with papers from classics, education, English, French, history and religious studies. Feminist theory attracted good enrolments; there was a clear demand for women's studies and it became a BA major in 1994. Staff turnover was rapid in the early years: women's studies seemed precarious as a subject, and large responsibilities were placed on junior staff. Eventually things settled down and a 2006 review commended Annabel Cooper, Chris Brickell and Rebecca Stringer, all long-serving, as 'a talented core of gender studies educators who should be cultivated and retained as some of the nation's best'. Support from other departments helped it flourish, though boundary negotiation was needed: women's studies had arisen because older disciplines failed to represent women and sometimes, when it introduced successful papers, the original discipline might decide to integrate that material into its own courses.[169]

Anna Smith, a doctoral student in English at Canterbury and critical editor of *Landfall*, was Otago's first lecturer in women's studies.

DEPARTMENT OF ENGLISH AND LINGUISTICS COLLECTION.

Women's studies programmes elsewhere declined or disappeared but Otago's kept strong.[170] As the subject faded worldwide the study of gender grew, which suited Otago's culturally focused programme. There was a tentative name change from 'women's studies' to 'gender and women's studies' in 1998, then to 'gender studies' in 2007. The original feminist theory paper was still at the core, but a wider range of subjects joined it. The study of masculinities broadened its appeal, and in 2000 the programme introduced a paper on bodies and sexuality as a strategic move to attract more first-year students; it brought people into the discipline who might not have otherwise considered it – an important first step for a programme that enjoyed 'superb levels of student satisfaction'. Studying sexuality was a particular drawcard for US exchange students who had no such offerings in their home institutions. The addition of an honours programme in 2007 provided a clear pathway to higher study, though there were still not many postgraduates.[171]

The programme had many administrative changes. It started with a base in the English Department, simply because Smith, the first lecturer, was from that discipline.[172] When the Humanities Division was organised into schools in 1999, Gender and Women's Studies became an independent unit within the School of Liberal Arts, and from 2001 it was part of the Anthropology Department.[173] In 2011 Gender Studies became part of the Department of Sociology, Gender and Social Work, which brought together three programmes that were not considered independently viable.[174]

GETTING SOCIAL

Social work has a complicated history at Otago. The professionalisation of social work was controversial because of its roots in the community sector; many social workers had no formal qualification.[175] In 1959, in conjunction with the recently established Otago Association of Social Workers and a similar Southland association, Otago's Adult Education Department ran well-attended short courses for people who were already working in social services. Staff from Victoria University, which had introduced social work in 1950, led those first southern courses. The University Extension Department at Otago continued holding seminars for social workers through the 1960s.[176] By the 1970s doctors were concerned about a 'deplorable lack' of trained medical social workers. Cyril Dixon, professor of preventive and social medicine, proposed a one-year diploma course at Otago. It did not eventuate because the New Zealand Association of Social Workers gave no support, believing it would be 'inadequate, unrecognised and unsupervised'. The concentration on 'medical' social work was a problem for the association, which considered a broader professional education was needed; presumably social workers did not want their training controlled by the powerful medical profession. The association lent support to courses elsewhere: an undergraduate degree at Massey and postgraduate courses at Canterbury and Auckland all started in the mid-1970s.[177]

Otago decided to carry on with social work education through its extension service. In 1974 it set up a two-year part-time course for a Certificate in Theory and Practice of Social Work, and two years later Patrick Shannon took on the role of lecturer in social and community studies.[178] The course was not a 'professional' qualification and received no accreditation from the New Zealand Social Work Training Council, but it was, nevertheless, valued in social work education and provided a base for further study. It was popular and enrolments had to be limited.[179]

Meanwhile, there were related developments in home science. Although that faculty focused on applied science, it included some social material. In 1977 the long-standing paper in 'home management' became 'management for family living' and, in 1981, 'family studies'; those courses included 'the interrelationship of the family and the community' and 'community health and welfare'.[180] In 1987 David Buisson, the dean of Consumer and Applied Sciences (CAPS), created a Community and Family Studies Development Unit to give 'impetus for developments in the social science and social policy areas'. Advanced courses in community and family studies replaced the old one-level course.[181] There were obvious synchronicities between the unit and University Extension's Community Studies Centre, and late in 1988 they merged, bringing the popular Certificate in Social Work into CAPS.[182] In the 1990 CAPS restructure (see chapter 7) the Community Studies Unit and its social work programme became part of a Department of Consumer Sciences. Students could major in community and family studies and there were additional options in social work. The certificate course evolved into a Diploma in Social and Community Work, and in 1994 a Postgraduate Diploma in Social Services was added.[183]

In a controversial move, in 2001 Community and Family Studies became a full department within the Humanities Division. That had

Social work students Anita Oliver (seated at table) and Trudi Myers (standing) work through a scenario in their practice suite, 2010.

CLAIRE PERRY PHOTOGRAPH, DEPARTMENT OF SOCIOLOGY, GENDER AND SOCIAL WORK COLLECTION.

advantages: it already had strong links with Māori studies, anthropology and education. However, like all professional programmes, social work was not cheap to run; it struggled to meet its budget with lower humanities funding.[184] The department flourished in other ways: in 2003 its social work programmes were the first to be approved under the Aotearoa New Zealand Association of Social Workers' new certification process. 'We got incredibly good ratings and there was nothing that had to be improved,' boasted Raylee Kane, director of professional programmes.[185] A university review the same year commended the department's 'dedicated, enthusiastic and hard working' staff, good relationships with Ngāi Tahu and community groups, and its reputation with the social work profession. It was a 'university leader in Treaty and related issues'. But in the changing university environment, the department's strong focus on practice, sometimes at the cost of research, emerged as an issue.[186] Adjustments took time, but a change in name in 2005 to the Department of Social Work and Community Development better reflected its work, and in 2007 Amanda Barusch became Otago's first professor of social work.[187]

The introduction of social worker registration in 2003 forced curriculum changes: registration was voluntary, but qualifications needed to fit its framework; new legislation for compulsory registration is before parliament in 2018. In 2007 Otago started a four-year Bachelor of Social and Community Work (from 2011 the Bachelor of Social Work) to meet the minimum requirements of a bachelor's degree, and the undergraduate diploma was phased out. Registration requirements killed the popular Postgraduate Diploma in Social and Community Work. The department simplified its postgraduate social work offerings in 2013: it introduced a Master of Social Work to replace several other qualifications, incorporating distance-taught papers and a thesis.[188]

In other universities social work developed alongside the related theoretical discipline of sociology. Sociology had been offered at Victoria and Canterbury from the 1950s and, from 1971, at Waikato, Auckland and Massey, but Otago was a latecomer to the subject.[189] Its absence at Otago was partly pragmatic. The university expanded in the 1960s but couldn't offer every subject; in that cooperative era there was, it seems, a gentlemen's agreement that Otago would teach anthropology and Canterbury sociology. However, there was also resistance to a discipline that some viewed as intellectually shallow. Many influential Otago staff came from Oxbridge universities, where sociology had a long struggle for acceptance; and some staff had experienced student riots in

Europe in the 1960s and attributed them partly to the rise of sociology. A group of Otago staff with sociological interests met regularly in the 1980s, but their advocacy for its introduction was to no avail. The group's existence demonstrated that sociology already had a presence at Otago; staff held sociology qualifications and there was a long history of sociology research in home science, education, preventive medicine, physical education, anthropology, management and other disciplines. In the late 1990s, when Canterbury introduced an anthropology programme, the barrier of the 'gentlemen's agreement' fell over; and by then sociology could not be dismissed as a radical outlier. The Department of Anthropology provided an initial departmental base for the programme.[190]

In 2002 Otago offered its first explicit sociology paper and from 2003 sociology was available as a minor. Lesley Procter and Hugh Campbell – a sociologist employed in the Anthropology Department since 1994 – taught the first papers. From 2005 when Martin Tolich joined them as head of the programme, students could major in sociology. Enrolments were impressive from the start. The programme diversified as more staff were appointed, and Campbell became its first professor in 2011.[191] From 2015 students could take a minor in criminology, a subject that had emerged as 'one of the most popular subjects in the humanities and social sciences'; that coincided with huge interest in crime in popular culture, from Nordic noir to US television drama. There were already thriving programmes in criminology at other New Zealand universities and Otago was a late starter. It was an interdisciplinary project but was hosted by Sociology, Gender and Social Work, with a compulsory first-year paper in sociology.[192]

MANOEUVRES IN EDUCATION

Among all the changes in the humanities at Otago over recent decades, none has been bigger than in teacher education. In the 1980s there was an oversupply of teachers in New Zealand as school rolls declined: fewer people trained as teachers, the North Shore TTC closed, others downsized and the Dunedin TTC came close to closure. By the 1990s teachers were in short supply as school rolls burgeoned. In response a neoliberal government opened the teacher education 'market' to other providers and promoted shorter courses. The Auckland College of Education launched a three-year BEd and in 1997 the Ministry of Education agreed to pay its graduates at the same rate as those from four-year degrees. Much of the incentive for a longer course was lost and, in a highly competitive tertiary environment, other providers had to match Auckland with three-year degrees.[193] Negotiations between the University of Otago and the TTC, by then the Dunedin College of Education (DCE), over the future of their joint BEd were tense and they couldn't reach an agreement. The university, which could ill afford to lose students, introduced an independent three-year Bachelor of Teaching in 1998. That was a major blow to the DCE; its historian David Keen noted in 2001 that it was 'stunned' and felt 'its very existence threatened'. The DCE council declined the university's suggestion that they merge, as had already happened in several other cities. In 1999, having gained the authority to award degrees, the DCE began its own three-year BEd and the two institutions became direct competitors.[194]

In 2000 Otago's School of Education, as its former Department of Education became, launched a two-year graduate degree in secondary teaching. Other New Zealand universities offered one-year secondary teaching diplomas, but Otago's was the first degree, a point of difference in a crowded market.[195] A 2004 review noted that both primary and secondary programmes were 'becoming highly regarded as innovative and of high quality by the teaching profession'. Developing courses in teacher preparation placed high demands on staff and, though they performed creditably in PBRF in the traditionally strong field of education studies, teacher education research was lagging. There was a larger problem: the demand for teacher education was insufficient to support two competing institutions.[196] 'It is a shame,' Keen wrote in 2001, 'that both institutions were sucked into a market vortex that wrecked their long-standing collaborative relationship.'[197] Inevitably, they entered merger discussions in 2005. The two organisations reached an agreement late that year, gained government approval in 2006 and, in January 2007, the University of Otago College of Education was born.[198] The DCE was the last of the traditional teacher colleges to merge with its nearest university, bringing with it the pride associated with New Zealand's first teacher training institution. The university gained another library and a suite of buildings in Dunedin, plus an Invercargill campus (discussed in chapter 10).

Many adjustments were required in joining two longlived institutions: it helped that the dean, Helen May, had relevant experience with mergers in Hamilton and Wellington.[199] The college offered all the qualifications of its predecessors but envisaged 'harmonisation and rationalisation ... in the near future'. From 2008 it replaced existing undergraduate programmes with Bachelor of Teaching and Bachelor of Education Studies degrees, each endorsed in early childhood education, primary education or primary bilingual education; and education carried on as a BA subject as well.[200] The university allowed additional staffing during the initial adjustment period, but there were job losses at the beginning and after duplicate programmes were phased out, and unfortunately they were not the last.[201] Teacher supply and demand was variable, sometimes dramatically so: the Canterbury earthquakes closed many schools in 2011 and there was an oversupply of teachers in southern New Zealand.[202] By 2014, College of Education enrolments had dropped by a third since the merger (a decline not peculiar to Otago) and further downsizing was inevitable. In 2015, when 15 full-time equivalent positions were lost, Humanities PVC Brian Moloughney explained that the redundancies were much regretted but that the university 'had subsidised the college by $13 million to date, and without change, the projected subsidy for this year was anticipated to be more than $1.6 million'. The two least popular courses – the four-year Bachelor of Education Studies and a one-year graduate diploma – were dropped; Invercargill had already lost its secondary teaching course at the end of 2012.[203]

There were positives alongside the negatives. while undergraduate numbers declined, postgraduate enrolments rose and a degree in Master of Teaching and Learning had a good start in 2014. It was New Zealand's first (jointly with Waikato) master's-level qualification for initial teacher education, and its first graduates were in demand.[204] The college maintained its research through all the changes, and it ranked first in New Zealand for education research at the 2006 and 2012 PBRF rounds.[205] It had three main research centres: the Education Assessment Research Unit (with a longstanding contract with the Ministry of Education to run the National Education Monitoring Project), the Centre for Distance Education and Learning Technologies, and the Centre for Educational Leadership and Administration.[206]

HUMANITIES FOR A NEW MILLENNIUM

As the new millennium dawned Otago ventured into two subjects that were characteristic of the twenty-first century: communication studies and visual culture. The humanities had to 'continuously renovate and develop themselves,' AVC Alistair Fox noted in 1998; 'New subject fields are emerging; new modes of communication have arisen; new social and political circumstances have eventuated that need to be analysed and understood'.[207] The study of the visual was not unknown on campus: unlike some universities, Otago had no fine arts course (the Dunedin School of Art belonged to Otago Polytechnic), but several staff had a scholarly interest in art. Classics had included art history in the Greek HAL syllabus from the 1920s, and art featured in language, philosophy and religious studies papers. In 1978 Roger Collins of French began a specialist half-unit in modern French art, and Peter Stupples offered a Russian visual arts course from 1979.[208] Other suggestions were met with resistance: in 1979 the Arts Faculty rejected the idea of a course in art history, 'largely on the grounds that the proposed course was insufficiently integrated, though some also objected to staff teaching subjects different from those they had been appointed to teach'. The faculty later approved a half-unit in New Zealand art history but it was deferred by senate, wary of adding subjects in a period of declining rolls.[209] A proposal in the late 1980s reported the 'speedy growth' of art history in schools; degree programmes at Canterbury and Auckland were having to limit entry.[210] Papers in art history and theory were added from 1990 and it became a BA major, with postgrad courses added later. The programme was taught by Stupples and Collins, together with Peter Leech, who transferred from the University Extension department. Specialist staff joined the programme as it developed, but it was always too small to qualify for full departmental status; after some years as an independent programme it joined the History Department in 2001.[211]

Another visual discipline, film studies, dated from Patrick Fuery's appointment as an English lecturer in 1990. Along with teaching critical theory he introduced a 200-level paper on film in 1991.[212] The course was popular and, in 1996, his successors Thierry Jutel and Rochelle Simmons added more papers. These were coded as film studies rather than English, reflecting the distinctiveness of the discipline; most enrolments came from theatre studies, design or art history majors.[213] Writer Lisa Scott recalled Jutel's 'incredibly kinetic, almost surrealist Film and Media lectures … The idea of applying Marxist or Lacanian mirror theory to movie-watching blew my mind.'[214] The evolution from 'film studies' to 'film and media studies' reflected coverage of a broadening range of technologies.[215] Film studies was available as a BA major from 2000, as were the two other subjects introduced that year: communication studies and visual culture. The communication discipline was aimed at those 'who wish to build a fundamental knowledge of communication process and practices';[216] it later defined itself as an interdisciplinary programme studying 'the processes and effects of interpersonal and mass communication' in all sorts of formats, including 'aural, verbal and visual messages'. Communication was a subject designed to research the consequences of the information age. The initial push came from the English Department, but the working party that developed the major represented various disciplines within the humanities, science and commerce. Visual culture was a related discipline that sought 'to understand visual artefacts (such as documentary photographs, diagnostic imaging, fashion and cityscapes)' and the way people interpret them.[217]

Tony Schirato, who helped found communication studies at Central Queensland University and oversaw its massive growth there, was appointed foundation professor at Otago in 2000; and from 2001, Communication studies – incorporating film and media studies, visual culture and linguistics – became an independent department.[218] Linguistics found it an awkward fit and moved back to the English Department two years later. Communication studies – from 2007 more accurately titled the Department of Media, Film and Communication – attracted students, but its first 10 years were difficult and it had a succession of heads of department. The appointment of long-serving lecturer Vijay Devadas as head in 2011 heralded an era of stability and department morale improved. Media, film and communication had to prove its worth to other disciplines and, at the same time, forge a clear identity in a competitive field with no national consensus on curriculum. Many Australasian programmes had a professional focus but Otago started with an unapologetic 'almost exclusive emphasis on scholarly research', which nonetheless gave graduates a basis for future professional training 'in a variety of arenas'.[219] Later it compromised to meet student demand for practical papers alongside theoretical ones: it added a course in writing for the media in 2013.[220]

LEADING THINKERS

The Leading Thinkers scheme in the 2000s sparked other humanities specialties. Tony Binns, appointed in 2004 as inaugural Ron Lister Professor of Geography, established development studies at Otago; his research centred on community-based development in sub-Saharan Africa and the Pacific. A trust set up to recognise Lister as Otago's first geography professor funded the Ron Lister Fellowship, which brought visiting scholars in development studies to Otago; and interdisciplinary postgrad qualifications in development studies were offered from 2009.[221] The Philosophy Department received a boost with the arrival of Peter Anstey to an endowed Chair in Early Modern Philosophy in 2006. The 'friends of the department' who funded it were revealed, after their deaths, to be Annette and Kurt Baier. Annette Baier was an Otago philosophy graduate with a distinguished academic career in the United States alongside her husband, an equally distinguished Austrian philosopher. The Baiers retired to New Zealand in 1995 and took part in the academic and social life of the Otago department.[222]

In 2006 the Alexander McMillan Trust, which managed a bequest from businessman and property developer McMillan to the people of Otago, funded a Chair in Childhood Studies and secured the Children's Issues Centre. The centre had opened in 1995 to provide authoritative information and education on children's issues, with five years of funding from a trust established for that purpose.[223] Anne Smith, an early childhood specialist from Otago's Education Department, was first director, and her successors, Gordon Harold and Nicola Taylor, had a background in psychology and social work/law respectively.[224] The centre was dynamic and productive: it held the first of a series of national and international conferences in its first year and, in 1997, launched the journal *Childrenz Issues*. Staff completed influential research on policy issues, including the physical punishment of children, and the role of children in decisionmaking after their parents separated. They developed distance teaching postgraduate programmes to meet 'the different needs of professionals working in areas relating to children's rights and welfare, such as health, psychology, counselling and family support'.[225] The centre had numerous shifts of governance, and in 2012 it became part of the Department of Sociology, Gender and Social Work.[226]

Two Leading Thinkers chairs expanded the humanities into the Celtic world. In 2006 Peter Kuch was appointed as Eamon Cleary Professor of Irish Studies and in 2009 Liam McIlvanney became Stuart Professor of Scottish Studies. They were appointed co-directors of an interdisciplinary Centre for Irish and Scottish Studies, and Angela McCarthy joined them as professor of Scottish and Irish history in 2008.[227] Kuch and McIlvanney were literary scholars – and McIlvanney had a sideline as a crime writer. They provided intellectual stimulation to an English Department that was already a mix of the old and the new: along with esteemed scholars of historic writers, it employed academics with interests in digital literature, postcolonial literature and the avant-garde, among other fields. Its writing programme – a 'sizeable operation' – was introduced after other departments expressed concern over students' communication skills. In 1993 English introduced a paper on 'the fundamentals of effective speaking and writing'; it was designed for students of health science, where it was compulsory until 2006, but other departments recommended or required it at various times, and students in general found it useful. It morphed into 'English for university purposes'. Later the department expanded beyond the remedial or introductory, with courses in advanced writing, writing for the professions and a creative writing paper in poetry. Meanwhile, Middle English, Old English and Old Norse were still spake here. Rick McGregor, a 1992 Auckland PhD graduate, came to Otago to research the use of Icelandic sagas by modern Swedish writer Per Olof Sundman because Old Norse was still on offer in the south: conservatism had advantages.[228] Eventually the older languages disappeared, and from 2019, after Greg Waite's retirement, English at Otago will begin with Middle English – where it began in 1871.

The thriving Law School also benefited from the Leading Thinkers scheme. After it moved to the main campus in 1966 law expanded rapidly: enrolments exceeded 200 in 1967 and 500 in 1975. With the assistance of local practitioners, law students established a legal referral service in 1972; this provided experience for them and a useful service for other students. It was absorbed into the Dunedin Community Law Centre in 1980, which gave wider community access to the supervised skills of volunteer law students.[229] Numbers kept mushrooming. All who passed first-year legal systems could enter second year, and in 1983 dean Richard Sutton observed that pass rates had gone up: 'today's first year law student is much more likely to be putting a great deal of effort into the subject'.[230] Entry restrictions became essential: Otago was already straining at the seams, and with other universities restricting admissions it did not want an additional influx of the least able candidates. From 1987 only the top 160 applicants were admitted to Otago's second year; this increased to 200 as additional staff were funded.[231] More options were added to the LLB and in 1988 the professional programme – compulsory for admission as a barrister and solicitor after completing a degree – became an intensive 13-week course rather than a part-time fifth-year course.[232]

After Ethel Benjamin's 1897 graduation there were hardly any female law students for decades. Future high court judge and governor-general Silvia Cartwright studied at Otago in the 1960s, with 'only a handful [of women] in the law faculty, often not together in one lecture … I was often lonely and found it difficult to achieve reasonable results, given that I worked largely on my own', she recalled.[233] By 1998 women were 62 per cent of Otago law students – 'the most dramatic change within the Faculty over the past 20 years or so', according to John Smillie.[234] The Law School attracted a growing cohort of Māori and Pacific Island students, too. The syllabus reflected the challenge to longstanding white male dominance in the law profession. After the Waitangi Tribunal was established in 1975 there was demand for legal expertise in things Māori; Otago offered a paper in Māori land law from 1988 and another on the Treaty of Waitangi from 1993. In response to student demand, a paper on gender and the law was introduced in 1995, and by the early 2000s there was a paper on the law and Indigenous people.[235]

The faculty took pride in the achievements of its students, who won numerous prizes and awards, including a remarkable 10 Rhodes scholarships between 1992 and 2013. It celebrated the career successes of its graduates, such as Wilson Isaac, appointed chair of the Waitangi Tribunal in 2009: Te Ihaka, a programme established by Māori law academic Jacinta Ruru in 2015 to support the success of Māori law students, was named in Isaac's honour.[236] The undergraduate programme thrived, but it was difficult to attract law postgrads; the profession lacked a strong tradition of postgraduate study. There were several degrees available, including a Master in Bioethics and Health Law, offered jointly with the Division of Health Sciences from 1995. 'As in many law schools, the shift to doctoral instruction has come late to the University of Otago,' a 2013 review noted, though numbers had increased in recent years. There was a strong research culture among staff, though, and some of their work appeared in the internationally respected *Otago Law Review*, first published in 1965.[237]

Law research was boosted with two Leading Thinkers research centres. The New Zealand Law Foundation, which already funded the interdisciplinary Human Genome Project led by Otago law dean Mark Henaghan, endowed a chair and research centre in emerging technologies in 2007. The centre built on the genome project to guide research into emerging and future technologies that were likely to raise issues of concern to society.[238] Colin Gavaghan, a medical law and ethics scholar, arrived from Glasgow to lead the centre in 2009. Its early research encompassed the regulation of nanotechnologies, genetics and neuroscience, and it established

Students working in the Law Library in 1979, before it moved into the Hocken (now Richardson) Building.
UNIVERSITY LIBRARY RECORDS, 96-111/018, S17-610I, HOCKEN COLLECTIONS.

undergraduate papers on law and emerging technologies.[239] In the same year Kim Economides, an expert on access to justice, arrived to take up a chair and direct the Legal Issues Centre. His successor, Bridgette Toy-Cronin, was an enthusiast for civil justice reform: for her PhD at Otago she had 'developed the skills of a social scientist to find out how the civil legal system was actually working for litigants who acted on their own behalf in court'. The centre was endowed by philanthropists Grant and Marilyn Nelson through the GAMA Foundation, inspired by their frustration with a drawn-out legal case. It aims to act as a 'critic and conscience' of the legal profession and provide insights to 'reorient the legal system so that it works better for people'.[240]

Leading Thinkers also endowed a centre for the Theology and Religion Department: the Centre for Theology and Public Issues and its associated Howard Paterson Chair were funded by the Paterson Charitable Trust (associated with the Dunedin businessman and entrepreneur Paterson, who had studied phenomenology of religion at Otago and who died an untimely death in 2003), the Presbyterian Synod, and business couple Ian and Annette Tulloch of Gore. The centre promoted 'informed theological and ethical analysis of the challenges facing contemporary New Zealand society'.[241] Andrew Bradstock, professor and director from 2008 to 2013, established a busy programme of public events: a 2014 departmental review noted the positive impact of his 'proactive outreach', with 'links extended beyond the traditional networks of the Department both within the University and across the wide range of topics and issues addressed by the CTPI'.[242]

The last humanities Leading Thinkers project was outside any existing department. The National Centre for Peace and Conflict Studies and its associated chair were endowed by a trust established for that purpose by New Zealanders with an interest in peace; they worked with the Hokotehi Moriori Trust, inspired by the peace covenant of Moriori ancestors. Kevin Clements, a New Zealander who established a similar centre in Australia, arrived at Otago in 2009 as first professor and director. Just five years later a review noted the centre was 'an outstanding success for the University and for its founding benefactors'; it had six academic staff and 24 PhD students from 19 countries. Its interdisciplinary scholars researched widely in fields such as development and peacebuilding, peace education, mediation and problem solving, nonviolent social movements and Indigenous conflict transformation. It developed a strong record of public engagement, including events beyond its Dunedin base.[243]

UPS AND DOWNS

The Leading Thinkers initiatives brought inspirational scholars to Otago, adding to the university's existing research strength in the humanities. Many of the humanities departments were ranked top in New Zealand, and in 2016–17 Otago was ranked among the top 100 universities in the world for archaeology, anthropology, development studies, education, English language and literature, geography, history, law and performing arts.[244] The Royal Society of New Zealand's Humanities Aronui Medal, awarded 'for research or innovative work of outstanding merit in the Humanities', has to date been dominated by influential Otago scholars: Jim Flynn of politics, Alan Musgrave of philosophy, former Otago anthropologist Atholl Anderson and historian Tony Ballantyne were among the first six recipients. Ballantyne, honoured 'for reshaping the scholarly interpretation of British imperial history', was 'probably the country's most original historian' according to former New Zealand Chief Historian Jock Phillips in 2014; he was among a group of 'outstanding historians of New Zealand' who combined to make Dunedin 'the powerhouse of academic history' in this country.[245] The respect in which Otago's archaeologists were held led to an invitation to work with Rangitāne iwi on an archaeological survey of Wairau Bar, New Zealand's oldest known settlement site. This was carried out in 2008 and 2009 during preparation for the return of kōiwi (bones); they had been removed to Canterbury Museum in earlier digs, resulting in a long dispute between the museum and Rangitāne and a halt for several decades to research on the bar. The new project was interdisciplinary and involved, alongside iwi, Otago teams led by archaeologist Richard Walter and biological anthropologists Hallie Buckley, who examined the precious bones prior to their reinterment, and Lisa Matisoo-Smith, who used DNA sequencing to map the Wairau people's relationships with one another and with their Pacific ancestors.[246]

Despite such important achievements, not all was rosy in the humanities: after peaking at 5971 in 2010, the number of equivalent full-time students in the division declined – to 4807 by 2016.[247] After years of government promotion of science, technology, engineering and maths (STEM) subjects, students faced with rising expenses became wary of the arts and many preferred vocational qualifications: Otago's excellent scholars and programmes could not overcome a worldwide trend that was afflicting arts subjects.[248] In 2016 several departments were downsized. 'This was not a decision taken lightly,' reported VC Harlene Hayne, 'but the level of cross-subsidisation of Humanities from other areas of the University was simply not sustainable.'[249] Staff went from anthropology, history, languages and music; the English and Linguistics Department escaped redundancies only by instigating a cooperative scheme of rostered unpaid leave.[250] The division was down but not out: all programmes and majors continued, and the campaign against the cuts revealed how deeply many people valued the humanities.

CHAPTER SEVEN

The sciences

If the humanities were the heart of the University of Otago, the sciences were its engine. Two of the first four professors were scientists and science subjects were always considered essential, studied for their own sake and as a launch pad for professional degrees.

THE FOUNDATIONS OF SCIENCE

The first science classes at Otago were in that most fundamental subject, mathematics. Its 'language was written in the laws that govern the universe. Every science must be expressed in mathematical language,' John Shand, professor of mathematics and natural philosophy, stated at his inaugural lecture in 1871.[1] The university authorities agreed: mathematics, along with Latin, was a compulsory subject for the BA – a generalist degree encompassing arts and sciences. When the Bachelor of Science (BSc) became available in 1885, maths was compulsory for both degrees, and it remained so for the BA until 1912 and the BSc until 1919.[2]

Shand, a Morayshire farm steward's son, was capable in many fields but excelled at mathematics. After studying at Aberdeen he taught in Scottish academies and the military mathematics department of the Royal Academy in Gosport, England. He was 37 years old when he started out with a class of 31 students at Otago in 1871; failing eyesight finally forced his retirement in 1913.[3] Students liked Shand. He was a 'born teacher', Thomas Pearce recalled: 'who will ever forget his blackboard performances, his cancellations and eliminations and reductions from complexity to simplicity'.[4] Like all the foundation professors, Shand had varied teaching responsibilities. He concentrated on maths initially but, from 1873, included natural philosophy in senior classes.[5] 'Natural philosophy' was 'the study of natural bodies and the phenomena connected with them' – a term later overtaken by 'physics'.[6] Shand ran physics classes for mining students in 1881, but it wasn't until 1884 that mathematics and physics were fully separated. The teaching burden on Shand became heavier as the new BSc required a practical course in physics. The council appointed an assistant in maths, then the Presbyterian Synod agreed to fund another chair. Shand continued with natural philosophy while Frederick Gibbons, a Cambridge graduate who took over the maths classes in 1886, became the professor of mathematics late that year.[7]

James Gow Black was Otago's other early scientist. He came from a Perthshire croft and started teaching at 14 years; he completed three degrees at Edinburgh, including a doctorate – a rare qualification at the time.[8] Black arrived as

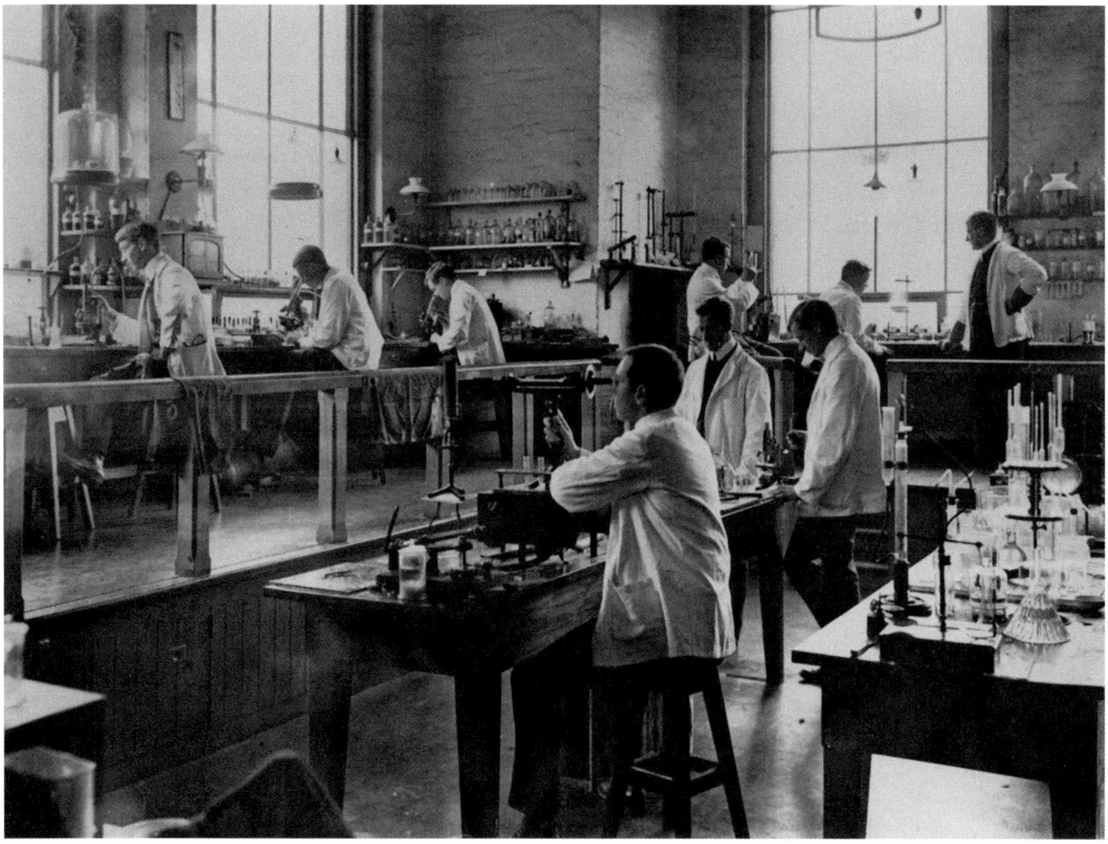

In the chemistry lab, around 1909.
UNIVERSITY OF OTAGO MEDICAL SCHOOL ALUMNUS ASSOCIATION RECORDS, MS-1537/309, S17-610J, HOCKEN COLLECTIONS.

professor of natural science in time for the 1872 session; his class of 33 students explored chemistry for half the session and geology and mineralogy for the rest.[9] The public and the provincial council welcomed this pragmatic chair: 'In every newly-settled country, man's chief employment is to vanquish physical difficulties, and in order to do this profitably, he should know exactly the nature of the substances with which he has to deal,' the *Evening Star* commented in an editorial.[10] At his inaugural lecture Black noted that chemistry and geology advanced the work of the miner and farmer, alongside other educational advantages; and his major publications – *Chemistry for the Gold Fields* (1885) and *Lectures on Agricultural Chemistry* (1895) – reflected that focus.[11] Black's classes were exciting; Violet Greig remembered 'the thud of the rock sulphur on that table as the doctor held it high and threw it noisily down to impress upon his students that it was one form of sulphur'. Black and his lab assistant 'Wullie' Goodlet toured the goldfields and gave many popular lectures. He was less popular with speculators after his optimism about the tinfields of Stewart Island proved unfounded. He moved to Stewart Island after he retired in 1911.[12]

In 1873 Frederick Hutton, just appointed as provincial geologist, became lecturer in natural sciences, and this allowed Black to concentrate on chemistry. Hutton's brief was to teach geology and zoology and to act as director of the Otago Museum. The museum started with a collection illustrating Otago's geology and natural history, created for the 1865 New Zealand Exhibition by geologist James Hector. In 1877, after the abolition of provincial government, the university assumed sole responsibility for the museum, which provided essential teaching materials. Academic staff directed it until 1955, when a trust board was set up and took over responsibility.[13] Hutton began teaching geology classes in 1874, but a plan to introduce zoology in 1875 didn't eventuate. In 1877 Otago offered a general course, 'Principles of biology', as well as papers in zoology and botany. The course attracted just one enrolment: William Will – one of Otago's first medical students – who selected botany. A year later five students enrolled for zoology and none for botany.[14] Hutton was promoted to a new chair in natural science in 1877, meaning Black's chair was limited to chemistry. Otago was anxious to secure Hutton's 'valuable services'; enrolments were low but natural history was 'essential to a full course of medical education'.[15] The appointment created controversy. The synod was ready to fund another chair but some conservatives were concerned about Hutton's evolutionary views; as they delayed proceedings, the university promoted Hutton and the synod eventually funded an English chair instead. Hutton did not stay long: he departed in 1880 to become biology professor at Canterbury.[16] The council quickly filled his place with Thomas Jeffrey Parker, 'a small, shy, rather dapper man' who had been demonstrator for famous evolutionist Thomas Huxley. Parker was both kind and witty; he was an 'authoritative and entertaining' lecturer to students and public audiences. Like many Otago colleagues he regretted the isolation from the intellectual centres of Europe, but New Zealand held advantages for biologists: Parker published on the distinctive endemic fauna that had previously been little studied by Western science.[17]

One other science dated back to the university's beginnings: psychology, which was yoked with philosophy until the 1960s (see chapter 6).

THE SCHOOL OF MINES

The university was set up less than 10 years after the region's first goldrush; the easily won gold was gone, but science and technology might extract more.[18] Macandrew recommended 'a school of Mines and of Agricultural Chemistry' to the University Council's first meeting.[19] Black's 1872 classes in geology and mineralogy were a first step; he installed a furnace for assays and the provincial government provided 'a compact little quartz battery of two stampers'.[20] In 1875 it promised funding and the professors planned a mining course, but when provincial government was abolished Otago had to seek national funding.[21] Parliament voted in 1876 to establish a School of Mines and, to save money, decided to incorporate it within an existing institution.[22] Canterbury's governors were busy with their School of Agriculture, but a small government subsidy allowed some mining exhibits there; a decade later it developed an engineering department.[23] Otago, with plans already developed for mining, seized the opportunity and obtained funding for five years.

Otago headhunted George Ulrich as professor of mineralogy and metallurgy and director of the School of Mines, and he started classes in 1879. Ulrich, a Prussian with German academic credentials and varied Australian experience, was well suited to lead a scientific approach to mining. He pointed out in a public lecture that miners who lacked knowledge wasted time and money on ill-advised ventures, failed to use improved machinery and overlooked valuable minerals. It wasn't just about economics, though: 'scores of human lives are sacrificed, and more are in danger, through want of precaution and prudence, mostly arising from ignorance of important principles of mining'. Fresh in the minds of Ulrich's audience was the 'dreadful calamity' at the Kaitangata coal mine the previous year, when 34 men lost their lives in an explosion.[24] The School of Mines developed its own qualification, Associate of the Otago School of Mines (AOSM); students specialised in mining, metallurgy or geology. The school also offered certificates in mine and land surveying, and in metallurgical chemistry and assaying.[25] During the 1880s the government developed an extensive network of schools of mines that offered practical training, but only the

Otago school had the kudos of attachment to a university.[26]

In its early years the school struggled as straitened finances and low enrolments prevented it employing more staff. When the five-year subsidy ended there was a delay before the government was persuaded to continue funding; then things looked up. In 1887 lecturers in applied mechanics, surveying and geology joined the staff, and later that year Donald Henderson, Adolph Hamann and Thomas Butement were awarded the first AOSM diplomas. A couple of years later student numbers sneaked into double figures and, with the 1891 arrival of a lecturer in metallurgy, staffing was 'complete'. The appointment of Richard Seddon as minister of mines in 1892 was a setback: Seddon believed the Otago school was elitist and insisted it lower its assay fees and 'meet the requirements of all classes of students'. Evening classes, intended to improve access, did not attract more students, however.[27]

Ulrich had to defend the public cost of a school whose graduates mostly headed overseas. Professional schools, he noted, were established 'to afford parents opportunity to have their sons trained in professions promising them a satisfactory status and income in after-life. If their own country offers openings in this respect, no doubt the young men remain. But if it does not, they are obliged, and prepared, to try their fortune in other countries.' Some students obtained vacation employment in mining companies, but others struggled to complete the year of practical experience the AOSM required in New Zealand. The government refused to allow graduates who held the Otago qualifications any reduction in the experience required for a statutory mine manager certificate, and this contributed to the attraction of work overseas. Mining was a global industry, and the export of Otago graduates persisted; 'by the intelligent discharge of their duties', they 'spread the fame of the Otago University far and wide'.[28] A dredging boom late in the century bolstered mining and persuaded the government to continue funding mining education. The School of Mines was never completely confident of its survival, but it entered the new century in good heart – apart from its grief at the 1900 death of Ulrich, a man regarded with fondness by colleagues, students and miners alike.[29]

INTO A NEW CENTURY

By the turn of the century the sciences were well established at Otago, though enrolments were still small. William Benham, an English zoologist who specialised in annelid worms, became biology professor in 1898 after Parker's death, and James Park, a Scottish geologist who had directed the Thames School of Mines, became director of the Otago School of Mines in 1901.[30] The part-time mining lecturers departed and Patrick Marshall became full-time geology lecturer, the first step towards geology's independence from the School of Mines.[31]

The university was still impoverished. At graduation in 1900 Benham spoke of the university's 'requirements in the way of more class room accommodation, additions to the library, and a replenishing of the apparatus and appliances needed for a proper practical pursuit of science'.[32] A public appeal in 1902 raised funds to pay off Otago's overdraft and support the School of Mines, which was again under threat of closure or (Seddon's preference) a transfer north. A windfall came from Dunedin watchmaker and property investor Arthur Beverly, who bequeathed his scientific instruments and the bulk of his estate to the university, directed to 'the teaching of mathematical, mechanical, and physical sciences and subjects akin thereto'. It was used for scholarships and a demonstrator in physics, 'the first adequately paid assistant any professor had ever had'.[33] In 1913, in a plea for more government funding, the chancellor noted that some science professors were 'miserably paid and overworked'; he recommended improved salaries and a 'trained assistant' each for biology and maths.[34] Otago employed several lab assistants, but help with teaching was still a luxury. War exacerbated matters: for instance Oswald Napier, appointed assistant lecturer in chemistry in 1914, was serving with the Royal Flying Corps by 1917.[35] In 1918 a council committee noted that a lack of assistants in science 'was chiefly due to the fact that suitable men were not available'.[36] The war prompted Otago to appoint women academics such as zoology honours graduate Winifred Farnie, who became assistant lecturer in biology in 1917.[37]

New professors added youthful liveliness to the sciences but included some tempestuous individuals. Welshman David Richards, maths professor from 1907, had good academic credentials from Cambridge but proved unpopular: he insisted on open windows, even when snow was drifting in on students; ordered people he didn't like out of his classroom; and had to move often between boarding houses because of his antisocial habits such as playing the piano during the night.[38] After 10 years the council lost patience with him and advised him to retire gracefully before he was dismissed; he departed at the end of 1917.[39] Meanwhile, Park and Marshall (promoted to a new chair in geology in 1908) had a bitter dispute – conducted in public lectures and in the press as well as in scientific publications – over glaciation in New Zealand. Park believed the South Island had been covered by an ice sheet extending from Antarctica; Marshall disagreed.[40] Posterity has shown Park to be incorrect, but he oozed confidence (and was 'redolent with the odour of good cigars with perhaps a whiff of "Highland dew"'). Marshall refused to back down; his 1916 resignation probably resulted from the acrimonious relationship as much as from the better salary offered by Wanganui Collegiate.[41]

Noel 'Bennie' Benson in characteristic pose, pointing out a feature of geological interest during a field trip in 1924. Benson was a very good geologist but famously absent-minded. DEPARTMENT OF GEOLOGY RECORDS, MS-3195/132, S16-591B, HOCKEN COLLECTIONS.

BECOMING INDEPENDENT: GEOLOGY AND BOTANY

Marshall offered a course in geology for arts and science students from 1904, alongside geology for mining qualifications. Among these new students were Allan Thomson and Robert Farquharson, New Zealand's first (1904) and third (1906) Rhodes scholars, who continued their geology education at Oxford.[42] Noel Benson succeeded Marshall as professor in 1917: he was a Quaker and a pacifist, so less inclined to disputes. Geology expanded and in 1927 moved into its own space: this is often seen as the birth of the independent Geology Department, though it was still under the purview of the School of Mines.[43]

Botany usually marks its beginnings as a department from 1924 when John Holloway became botany lecturer, but he wasn't the first. The biology professors were zoologists and as enrolments grew they found it irksome having to teach two subjects, 'which in England, even in fourth-rate educational institutions, have for many years been entrusted to two distinct individuals'.[44] In 1918 Benham suggested it was time for Otago to appoint a botany lecturer. The council procrastinated and there were no botany classes in 1919, but after more pressure from Benham it selected Winifred Betts as its first botany lecturer – all the applicants were women.[45] Otago had 'set the example to the other University Colleges

Winifred Betts (later Aitken), Otago's first specialist botany lecturer.

BROMA STUDIO (NELSON) PHOTOGRAPH, 'PROFESSOR'S PROGRESS' ALBUM, BOTANY DEPARTMENT RECORDS, MS-4387/224, S14-586A, HOCKEN COLLECTIONS.

by appointing a lecturer in botany', the relieved professor wrote.[46]

Betts was just 25 when she started in her role in 1920. Botanist Leonard Cockayne described her as 'the most brilliant woman scientist in New Zealand'.[47] Late that year she married another talented Otago graduate, Alexander Aitken. In an era when most women left paid employment on marriage she stayed on as botany lecturer, but in 1923 the Aitkens moved to Scotland to further Alexander's academic career in mathematics.[48] John Holloway, who replaced Winnie Aitken, was a man of parallel careers as scientist and Anglican priest; he wore his clerical collar during lectures and often preached at the cathedral. He was the entire department in his early years at Otago; one room in the museum basement served as classroom, laboratory and office, with garden outside. There Holloway researched ferns and other primitive plants, earning the international reputation that made him a Fellow of the Royal Society (London) in 1937.[49]

SCIENCE FOR WOMEN

The national School of Home Science came to Otago because Canterbury lacked enthusiasm for a scheme proposed by a local benefactor. It was an inauspicious time for new ventures: both institutions had committed to other projects – in Otago's case, the Dental School and a proposed veterinary school. And more importantly, many professors and council members, all male, had no sympathy for the concept: 'Domestic science should be taught in its proper place – the Technical School,' Shand said.[50] The initiative started with runholder John Studholme, a son of early Canterbury colonists, who was educated at Oxford and had travelled widely; he was impressed by home science education in North America.[51] He offered Canterbury a grant of £200 per year for three years towards the salary of a home economics professor. In 1907 the governors appointed Ann Gilchrist, a Columbia graduate teaching at the University of Tennessee, but she withdrew because of her impending marriage; the Canterbury governors, concerned at the expense, 'received the news with broad smiles and some sighs of relief'.[52]

In 1909, once it was clear no course would eventuate at Canterbury, Studholme entered negotiations with Otago and its council agreed to the scheme by the narrowest of margins.[53] Two of its principal supporters – lecturers Frederic Truby King (mental diseases) and Ferdinand Batchelor (midwifery and diseases of women) – demonstrated the scheme's conservative motives. Both disapproved of higher education for women; they believed that 'cram' (intensive study) damaged women's reproductive abilities – this was a concern in an era of declining birth rates.[54] But education pertaining to the home was another matter: 'After reaching the age of puberty the education of girls should be chiefly directed to domestic management, domestic economy, physiology, and hygiene,' stated Batchelor.[55] Home science would improve the nation by applying modern science to the household. Jenny Collins suggests it was also a response to the growing number of women students: those with scientific leanings could be diverted into a separate sphere, reducing the competition to men.[56]

Whatever the motives behind its establishment, in practice the Home Science School offered opportunities for women. For decades it employed New Zealand's only women professors.[57] The founding professor was Winifred Boys-Smith, whom Studholme recommended after an extensive search, and she selected Helen Rawson as lecturer; both women were Cambridge-educated.[58] Boys-Smith was 'English to the backbone', Agnes Blackie recalled, and 'had a clear idea of the respect due to her position'; she was 'a well-known figure as, clad in an ankle-length, black, caped waterproof coat and a broad-brimmed hat held securely in place with an enveloping motor-veil, she cycled from place to place round the university'.[59] Setting up the school was an enormous task, a later dean said: 'on the one hand the standards of University scientific education must be maintained, and on the other every experienced homemaker expected a highly skilled technician to emerge'.[60] The University of New Zealand approved home science as a subject for BSc, and Otago created its own shorter diploma. Classes started in 1911. Founding student Annie Stevenson recalled: 'We had no confidence, nobody seemed to want us, and we were looked upon as something encroaching upon the men's rights'.[61] In 1912 the 'technical' subjects of theoretical and practical cookery, laundry-work, housewifery, needlework and dressmaking commenced.[62]

Home science took over the miners' 'tin shed'. It was a 'deplorable building' according to early student Jane Rudall; during Rawson's 'practical chem' course, students 'suffered from the depredation of mice on specimens of food which we were saving for later weighings'.[63] Fortunately cookery courses took place in the well-appointed North Dunedin Technical School kitchen.[64] For the first few years students carried out practical 'housewifery' and laundry tasks in the professor's own home at Woodhaugh, but from 1915 Studholme House served as a residence for students as well as a practice venue for household and institutional management.[65] Early graduates obtained good jobs, and a 1917 government regulation requiring all girls in state secondary schools to study domestic science assured plenty of teaching work.[66] An academic building, opened in 1920, provided visible evidence of the success of Home Science. By then it had 70 students – and from the 1920s until the end of World War II they outnumbered Otago's other science students.[67]

Rawson replaced Boys-Smith as professor and dean in 1920; and in 1921 an additional professor of domestic arts, Ann Gilchrist Strong, joined her. Strong was the home scientist whose Canterbury appointment had fallen through; she later divorced her husband and continued her academic career. In 1923 Rawson's academic career ended when she married the geology professor, and Strong replaced her as dean. Many lecturers came and went; it was hard to maintain staff 'due to the frequent leaves of absence, temporary substitutes and marriages of our teachers', Strong explained.[68] Strong 'had a very forceful and attractive personality', a 1920s student wrote. 'One couldn't help listening to every word of her lectures.' Her fox terrier Binkie, dressed in a bright scarlet coat in winter, was a striking sight sitting alongside the professor in her prized Model A Ford.[69]

Home science expanded into other subjects and extended its diploma to three years and its degree course to four. From 1926 the BSc major became a Bachelor of Home Science (BHSc) and postgrad courses began. The first master's graduate, nutrition researcher Neige Todhunter, went on to a stellar career in the United States.[70]

Studholme wanted the school to reach out to 'teachers and other women who are not regular University students'; he was inspired by Strong's rural extension programme in the United States.[71] Strong was determined to develop a similar scheme at Otago. After a successful series of 'lecture demonstrations' for 'business girls', there were requests for lectures for homemakers, which went ahead in 1922. After attempts to coordinate work with existing organisations failed, Strong set up the Home Economics Association, 'open to all women in the city'; it attracted audiences of

A home science laundry class in the yard behind Studholme in the 1910s. Jane Rudall recalled: 'Any girls who knew the young men at Knox College borrowed their underwear for washing woollens. Our irons were small flat irons heated on a special stove. We had the most distressing times ironing starched petticoats and men's white shirts stiffened with cold starch. What would we have given for an electric iron or in the kitchen for an electric stove?'

FACULTY OF CONSUMER AND APPLIED SCIENCES RECORDS, 97-081/002, S17-610D, HOCKEN COLLECTIONS.

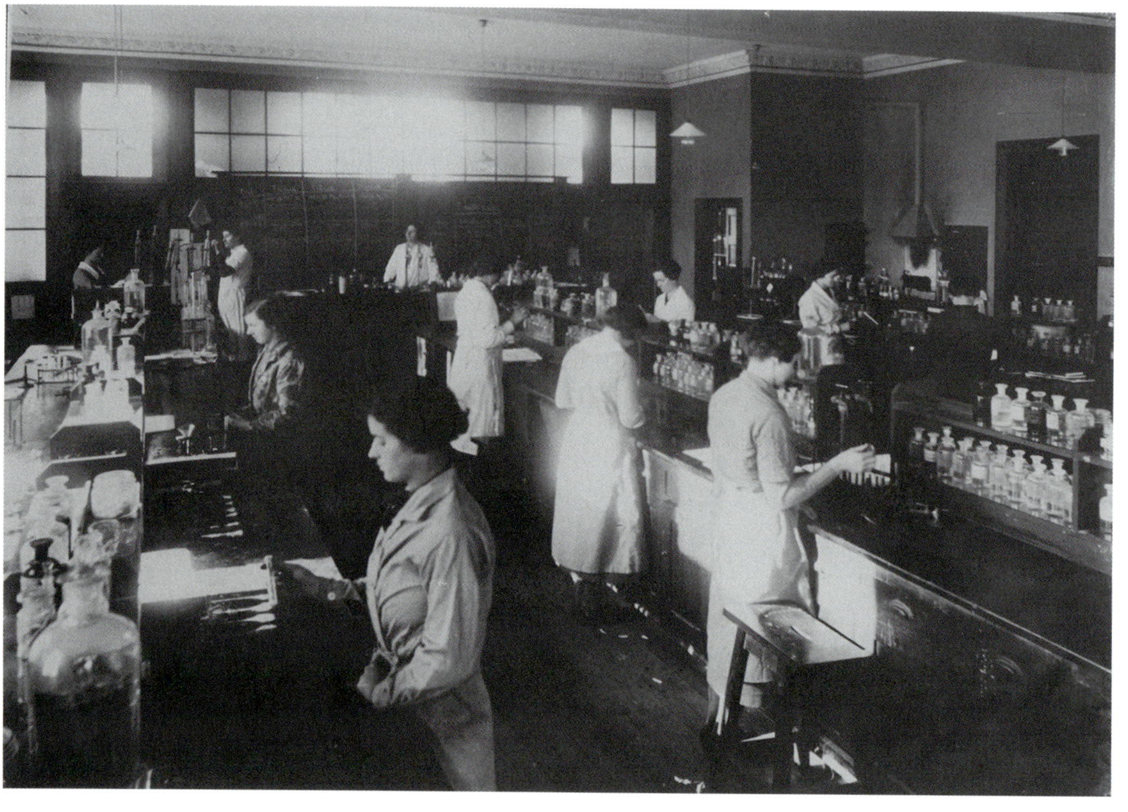

Helen Thomson (centre back) teaching a laboratory class on the chemistry of the household at the School of Home Science in 1936. Thomson was one of numerous women who made an academic career in science through the school. After completing undergraduate and master's degrees there, she was appointed lecturer in 1931 and remained on staff for 30 years, taking leave for overseas research. She graduated with a PhD in textile chemistry from Leeds University in 1947.

FACULTY OF CONSUMER AND APPLIED SCIENCE RECORDS, 97-081/004, S16-521A, HOCKEN COLLECTIONS.

Members of the Home Science Extension staff pose with the tools of their trade outside the Home Science School in the mid-1930s. The school's first staff were Otago home science graduates: Muriel Allan (née Gifford), Violet Macmillan and Isobel Crowe. Ann Strong, the home science professor who started the extension service, is on the right in a large hat.

FACULTY OF CONSUMER AND APPLIED SCIENCES RECORDS, MS-1517/064, S15-621E, HOCKEN COLLECTIONS.

around 200 to lectures and demonstrations. She also travelled beyond Dunedin 'urging women to organize for the study of Home Science'. She worked with the Women's Division of the Farmers' Union, helping them form branches, but funding was always a barrier. With Studholme's assistance, in 1929 Strong secured a five-year grant from the Carnegie Corporation that allowed the university to establish a 'home science extension bureau'.[72]

The extension service was an immediate hit; in 1930 it reached around 2000 women ('excluding wireless hearers'). Its box scheme provided groups with a box full of materials, written and practical, on a particular topic, and one of the extension staff visited occasionally. The service also offered a short course at the Home Science School during Winter Show week, 'when a number of country people visit Dunedin', and Muriel Allan participated in the Department of Agriculture's farm school, which travelled the region. Her lecture, 'Two New Zealand bugbears: dental caries and goitre', with 'a demonstration on salad making and the use of vegetables', attracted women and men. When time allowed the team wrote articles for newspapers, later recycled as their popular printed bulletins. They used technology to extend their reach: each week Isobel Crowe gave a talk on 4YA in Dunedin, rebroadcast the following day from Auckland, Wellington and Christchurch; the broadcasts attracted 'letters by the hundred'.[73]

Extension work carried on under various organisational structures. In 1934 the Carnegie Corporation gave Home Science Extension another five-year grant, but required it to work with Canterbury's rural travelling library; the two organisations operated as the Association for Country Education around most of the South Island with two itinerant home science tutors, plus one in Gore and another in Alexandra. From 1940, when Carnegie funding ran out, the extension service received government funding, but finance remained tight. In 1948 it became part of the Adult Education Department (see chapter 12). Other regions employed home science tutors, but Otago maintained a national service of broadcasts and publications; for many it was the public face of the university. From making preserves and food safety to stain removal, people learned useful skills for living through Home Science Extension. Some of the material catered to aspirational middle-class women, such as the 'extension lectures in the History of Art and in the History of Furniture for groups of Dunedin ladies' mentioned in Strong's 1937 history of the school, but she also noted activities that revealed social concerns, including cookery and sewing classes for unemployed girls and assistance provided at children's health camps.[74] A trial of home science education for Māori communities did not survive. Emere Kaa (Ngāti Porou) qualified as a nurse at Dunedin Hospital; she received a year of Carnegie-funded home science education in 1935 before heading to Northland, where she toured native schools as a health and home science educator. Kaa's work as 'Maori Apostle of Home Science to carry the principles of modern housekeeping to her Race' appeared to be successful, but health and education authorities lost faith in the scheme and decided to leave health education to district nurses and home science education to schools; Kaa became district nurse at Kaikohe.[75]

FROM ONE WAR TO ANOTHER

Science staff and students were caught up in the imperial fervour of World War I and many headed to battle; metallurgy professor Daniel Waters served in the New Zealand Tunnelling Company, including a short period as commander.[76] Mining student numbers plummeted: 'The men to take up mining engineering as a profession are just the men to answer the call of the Empire,' James Park wrote.[77] The other science departments fared a little better than the all-male mining school, though they lost students and staff too. Supplying men to the forces wasn't the university's only war service. In 1915 the minister of munitions requested 'the cooperation of the Council and members of the Staff in the manufacture of certain munitions of war'. The staff agreed to assist with equipment or scientific advice, but the authorities decided it was impractical to manufacture shells in New Zealand.[78] The Chemistry Department helped with other supplies. Cedric Hicks, who was working as a chemistry demonstrator to fund his medical studies, was manpowered to manufacture chloramine-T under the supervision of John Inglis, the chemistry professor; it was needed for the treatment of meningitis, which had broken out in military camps.[79] Park, who had been rejected for active service at the age of 57, trained volunteers in explosives, surveying and military engineering.[80]

Student enrolments burgeoned after the war. In the larger departments professors had one or two assistant lecturers, together with the occasional demonstrator and lab technician. Stan Hughes began a career of over 50 years as a technician in the Physics Department in the early 1920s; eventually he was one of a staff of five, led by Robert Jack. Assistant lecturer Blackie recalled the professor as 'a bundle of nervous energy' whose workload 'curtailed his hours for sleep. He gave at least seventeen lectures a week, never giving a lecture without preparing it the night before; demonstrated eight hours weekly in the first year laboratory; spent a great deal of time helping students in the advanced laboratories; and then there was all the rest he had to do.'[81] Jack's voice – very high-pitched, with a nervous cough – made him the butt of student laughter and he was not an adept technician – he had 'more scars on him from screwdriver slippage than any other professor', recalled Hughes. Despite these drawbacks, Jack and his departmental staff, notably technician and radio hobbyist Jack Sutherland, put his theories into practice and built a transmitter, and the professor broadcast New Zealand's first radio programme in 1921.[82]

Inglis in chemistry was another busy head of department. An obituary noted he was an active researcher in previous English positions, but at Otago he faced 'the disability which is unfortunately common in the smaller universities of the Dominions, namely, that the head of a scientific department has to deal with a large and varied amount of teaching and administrative work with such inadequate assistance and facilities that the conditions for research work are most discouraging'.[83] Inglis nurtured others' work, though, and by the 1930s chemistry was one of the most active departments in carrying out research.

The commitment to science with pragmatic applications endured: lecturer Charles Carter and a series of senior students and assistants investigated the chemical composition of New Zealand natural products; in 1931, for instance, they examined the oils of the muttonbird, pōhutukawa, rimu and tōtara, among other species; other projects involved milk proteins and the effects of lime on soil.[84] Frederick Soper, who succeeded Inglis in the chemistry chair in 1936, carried on the pragmatic focus with leading research on wool.[85]

Meanwhile, the departments of geology, zoology and botany were conducting impressive research. All were led by men with what was then considered the highest honour in science: Fellow of the Royal Society (London). Zoologist Benham was elected a fellow in 1907, botanist Holloway in 1937 and geologist Benson in 1941. Elizabeth Mason, who went on to a career in zoology at Cambridge, described Benham as 'a charming, humane man and a great zoologist … He was a wonderful lecturer and blackboard artist. He could draw any developmental process in stages, working along his 30-foot blackboard … His embryology lectures were a dream.'[86] Benham's successor, Brian Marples, pursued a range of research: he was well known for his work with fossil penguins and whales.[87] When he arrived he joined two other academic staff in zoology: lecturer Marion Fyfe and assistant lecturer Beryl Brewin. They were among several women academics appointed between the wars (see chapter 5), though the university was happier to employ women than to promote them. By the time Fyfe retired in 1957 and Brewin in 1963, both were senior lecturers and Fyfe, described as 'the backbone' of the Zoology Department, had acted as its head on some occasions; and other long-serving women, such as Blackie in physics, had similar careers.[88]

Having women on staff helped when war broke out again in 1939, since young men were prone to depart. For instance, in 1941 the Physics Department reported that 'the War has resulted in much more work and less assistance'; they could not find a substitute for junior lab assistant William Sutherland, who was called up for military service.[89] Enrolments in science and home science rose steadily through the war, and a surge in medical students meant a heavy workload in intermediate classes; the School of Mines had a small drop in enrolments. Otago scientists lent their expertise to the war effort, in cooperation with government scientists and other universities. The Physics Department worked on infrared sensors for the detection of shipping and on accurate lighting control.[90] Soper chaired the chemical section of the national Defence Science Committee, which worked on products that were in short supply, including munitions and items that were normally imported. Otago staff worked on an antidote for war gases, chemicals required for naval sonar and smoke bombs, and testing New Zealand ergot – a drug that was essential to obstetrics. Stanley Slater of the Chemistry Department produced morphine using opium confiscated by the police under drug legislation.[91] The Home Science School trained local women in cooking for large groups so they would be prepared in case of emergencies in hospitals; and its clothing and textile experts advised on the manufacture of garments for soldiers.[92] By 1945 the psychological clinic was assisting returned servicemen with a range of problems.[93]

SCIENCE TAKES OFF

Science enrolments soared after the war, except in the Home Science School; this reflected the different impact of war on women. The home science roll reached 200 in the final years of the war, then dropped and did not reach that mark again until the mid-1960s. Women who may have enrolled were, it seems, instead engaged with their own families as the nation settled down to domesticity and a baby boom. Returned servicemen kept other departments busy: in 1945 for the first time the Physics Department had to repeat lectures as the class couldn't fit into the lecture room; there were extra military-funded tutorials for the benefit of returned servicemen and women.[94] Science enrolments did not increase as rapidly as those in health sciences – and that concerned scientists. 'This country and the Empire needs more scientists,' the science dean, mathematician Robert Bell, wrote in his 1946 report; 'it is hoped that as the present rush into professions dies down, there will be a rapid growth in the numbers taking pure science'.[95] By 1950 the need for school science teachers was a concern; a sharp rise in demand was anticipated in the late 1950s, when the first baby boomers started high school.[96] Scientists were needed inside the universities too; New Zealand universities had proved the value of their research through the war and its expansion 'was necessary … to achieve a proper balance,' Soper recalled.[97]

The reintroduction of the PhD degree in New Zealand in 1946 boosted research. The first Otago student to graduate with a PhD under its brief earlier appearance was Rudolf Penseler in 1927, with a thesis entitled 'Experiments on the synthesis of apofenchocamphoric acid'.[98] Otago's first postwar PhD graduate was another chemist, Richard (Dick) Batt, in 1948; he became a noted alcohol researcher at Massey; and the next PhD graduate, Batt's flatmate Arthur Campbell, made his chemistry career at Otago. By the end of the 1950s another 12 PhD graduates had been added to Otago's credit, most in chemistry, biochemistry and microbiology, and one in botany; and after that they proliferated.[99] The biochemistry and microbiology PhDs resulted from a new opportunity for Otago scientists: in the 1940s and 1950s they gained access to courses in the 'medical' sciences of physiology, biochemistry and microbiology – previously restricted to students who were completing a degree in home science or health science.

PHYSICAL EDUCATION

Otago students had another new choice in the School of Physical Education. In the early twentieth century educational authorities promoted physical training in schools to prepare children as good citizens, and health authorities such as Charles Hercus, dean of the Medical School, promoted its health benefits. Qualified teachers were needed. In the late 1930s Otago sought approval from the University of New Zealand for a physical education degree, but the war held matters up. Auckland, too, liked the idea of beginning a diploma in physical education. Matters became urgent in 1946 with a revised secondary-school curriculum that made phys ed compulsory for all pupils. Earlier plans for a degree were put aside and Otago designed its own three-year diploma.[100]

Otago was fortunate to recruit Cambridge graduate Philip Smithells, previously superintendent of physical education for New Zealand's Education Department, as first director of its School of Physical Education. Two other staff, Peter Robertson and Emmy Bellwood, joined him in 1947 and the first class of 30 physical education students arrived in 1948. Some of their courses were taken in other departments – chemistry, physics, anatomy, physiology, education and food values (in home science) – and the school taught various theoretical and practical subjects: physical education, pedagogy, gymnastics, games, athletics, aquatics, recreation, dance and health education.[101] In the first 20 years 400 people gained a diploma. Of these, 90 per cent started their professional lives as secondary teachers, encouraged by the generous government support for teacher trainees. Others found work in child welfare institutions and mental hospitals, and many women graduates who married contributed to their local communities with 'corrective work, work with older women and in modern dance', Smithells reported. Some of the early graduates went on to further education, mostly in the United States and Canada. Though at first there were no postgraduate courses at Otago, some staff and students conducted research, assisted by 'a well equipped exercise physiology laboratory, a partially equipped biomechanics laboratory, and a library in which both the book and serial collection is superior to any in the Southern Hemisphere'. By 1967 a clinic had treated about 500 children with special needs relating to 'skill, courage, tenseness, motor control or perception', providing experience for students and service to the community.[102]

Philip Smithells (commonly known by his initials, PAS) teaching in the School of Physical Education. He was director from its foundation in 1948 until 1974.

P.A. SMITHELLS PAPERS, MS-1001/217, S14-562A, HOCKEN COLLECTIONS.

THE 1960s AND 1970s BOOM

As the first of the baby boomers reached university age in the 1960s enrolments surged, nowhere more than in the Science Faculty, where numbers swelled from 11 per cent of the Otago roll in 1960 to 27 per cent in 1970. It was an era of developments, from plate tectonics to big bang proofs, from computer technology to the first moon landing and the birth of environmentalism with the Gaia hypothesis and the publication of Rachel Carson's *Silent Spring*. Science was popular and exciting and people wanted to learn more.

The life sciences expanded. The Botany Department obtained a professor in 1952; the lack of one had been a sore point for years. Legend has it that Geoff Baylis, who succeeded Holloway as 'lecturer in charge' in 1945, engaged in 'guerrilla war with the administration … to upgrade both his own and the department's status'; his threat to resign if the department had to teach at honours level without a professor paid off.[103] Baylis, an Aucklander who completed postgraduate studies in London, arrived at Otago fresh from war service, as one student recalled: 'He had not been released from the navy so came to classes looking very resplendent in a Lieutenant's uniform. I remember him all in white, with braided epaulettes one day on the mudflats at Portobello showing us the different sea weeds.'[104] By the 1960s botany had six academic staff, including two returned local graduates destined for long careers. Alan Mark returned in 1960 with a PhD from Duke University, North Carolina; his first five years as lecturer were funded by the Hellaby Indigenous Grasslands Trust. An expert on upland tussock grasslands, Mark became well known for his work in ecology and conservation.[105]

The return of Ann Wylie in 1961 after 14 years of study and work in England signalled further expansion: she took up a new post in cytology and genetics. Wylie was based in botany but most zoology majors also came her way. When Russell Poulter, an expert in fungal genetics, was appointed to the Biochemistry Department in 1972, he and Wylie began a second-year interdepartmental course in genetics. It was, recalls Wylie, 'great fun to teach' as the students were 'the best of the crop in the Science Faculty'.[106] In 1978 immunology became a subject

Alan Mark and Kath Dickinson of the Botany Department doing fieldwork at West Dome in 1996.
BOTANY DEPARTMENT COLLECTION.

for postgraduate diploma, open to those who had majored in any of the life sciences. Like genetics it crossed disciplinary boundaries, but it kept its base in the Microbiology Department (later named the Microbiology and Immunology Department).[107] The biggest interdisciplinary endeavour of the era, however, was a first-year biology course, which replaced zoology intermediate in 1972. It was designed 'to integrate the biological teaching' and 'make use of the unique facilities that Otago possesses amongst New Zealand universities,' as science dean Ted Corbett explained. The emphasis was on 'basic biological principles with appropriate illustrations from the animal, plant and microbial kingdoms'; lecturers came from various departments.[108] Biochemistry, microbiology and physiology were on the rise; chemistry was still Otago's favourite science major, but biochemistry and microbiology weren't far behind.[109] Those subjects, previously commenced at second year, contributed to the new biology course; like the zoology course it replaced, it was an intermediate for health sciences and home science as well as general degrees. Botany retained its own intermediate course.[110]

MARINE SCIENCE BEGINNINGS

Marine science was another expanding field that crossed disciplinary boundaries. The early zoologists took some interest in marine species, as did Roy Freeman, who replaced the long-serving Marples as zoology professor in 1967, and Geoff Satchell, appointed to a second chair in zoology in 1971.[111] Otago's location close to the coastal continental shelf and deep-sea environments was ideal for research: an 'enormous range of organisms, communities and habitats … are accessible within the daily range of a relatively modest and inexpensive research vessel,' wrote John Jillett in 1974. 'This capacity cannot be matched anywhere in Europe or North America … We also have on our doorstep the biological communities and hydrological regime of the subantarctic region which would be difficult to study in detail from nearly anywhere else in the world.'[112]

In 1887 Parker recommended that the government establish 'a marine laboratory, presided over by a competent naturalist who had been trained for this particular work, and furnished with aquaria and breeding grounds, a small steamer for dredging, trawling, etc' to develop New Zealand fisheries. Fortunately for Otago, his suggestion that Wellington was a good location did not bear fruit.[113] After more advocacy, led by Dunedin naturalist and high-school teacher George Thomson, New Zealand got its first marine science facility, the Portobello Fish Hatchery and Biological Station, in 1904. Funds came from the Otago Institute and various acclimatisation societies, with a government subsidy; the Marine Department provided ongoing funding. Introducing seafood species was the first priority; as director Betty Batham later wrote, 'in a young country, the utilitarian tends to be financially supported when fundamental work is not'. Attempts at acclimatisation were not very successful, but the station's second purpose, as a base for scientific research, grew in importance, and many Otago staff and postgrads used it.[114]

During the 1930s depression the government cut funding and by the late 1940s the station was 'in a sad state of disrepair'. With some persuasion

View looking over Portobello Marine Laboratory in 1967. The two-storey building in the centre is the aquarium and research station (now demolished), opened in 1962 as a replacement for the original 1904 fish hatchery building. On the right is Quarantine Island/Kamau Taurua, and in the distance is the southern end of Portobello.
PORTOBELLO MARINE LABORATORY COLLECTION.

from John Eccles, the physiology professor, the university agreed to take over the station from 1951. Batham, a 1940s Otago graduate who completed a doctorate at Cambridge, returned to Otago in 1950 to become director. The marine laboratory site was 'a delightful one, eminently suited for marine biological work', but access was tricky. Wylie recalls working there with other postgrad students in the 1940s. They took a train to Port Chalmers, then a ferry across the harbour; once they were late back because the ferry ran aground at low tide. After ferry access wound down in the early 1950s, most users rowed across from Port Chalmers. Maintaining and improving facilities was costly; during the 1950s the station acquired the *Penguin*, but the 16-foot former lifeboat had limited capability.[115] The entrepreneurial Batham got a substantial lotteries grant in 1963 to design and build a marine research vessel and staff it for five years; and she applied to the Nuffield Foundation, which funded

The 15-metre RV *Munida* entered service in 1966. With its wide range of oceanographic equipment, it was a boon to research. Pictured aboard in the late 1960s are, from left: Les Tubman (crew, technician), Bill Tubman (skipper), Stan Deans (crew, cook), Betty Batham (marine biologist and director of the Portobello Marine Laboratory). Legend has it that Batham noticed an article in the *ODT* about lottery funds and within a week had put together a grant application, had it signed by the acting VC (allegedly he didn't read it) and sent it off. University authorities were surprised to learn they had been awarded a very substantial lotteries grant (£45,000, equivalent to close to $2 million in today's money) to design and build a marine research vessel and staff it for five years.
FROM AN ALBUM COMPILED BY BILL TUBMAN, DEPARTMENT OF MARINE SCIENCE RECORDS, MS-3302/357, 514-512A, HOCKEN COLLECTIONS.

a three-year postdoctoral fellowship in marine biology. That fellowship was awarded to John Jillett, who had recently completed his doctorate at Auckland; he succeeded Batham as director in 1974.[116] Two years later he reported that 11 Otago departments had 'programmes of teaching and research which relied on the Laboratory': it received requests from around the world and thousands of people visited the aquarium.[117]

THE PHYSICAL SCIENCES

Physics lagged behind other sciences in postgraduate enrolments, but PhD and staff research flourished from the late 1960s. Otago specialised in the upper atmosphere and solid state physics.[118] Dick Dowden, a specialist in radio propagation and emission in the earth's magnetosphere, was appointed to a second physics chair established in 1966 and additional staff were employed, though Dowden reported in 1972 that with 'very high teaching commitments during the day ... much of the research activity by staff took place at night'.[119] Some students still headed overseas for further study. Two who returned in the early 1970s after completing doctorates at Oxford were Don Warrington and Gerry Carrington, both of whom were destined for long careers at Otago. Carrington developed research into heatpumps and energy conservation and Warrington worked in one of the department's longstanding fields of expertise, the interaction between lights and atoms; the lights evolved from resonance lamps to lasers, then solid-state lasers.[120]

Enrolments dropped when physics was removed as a mandatory medical intermediate subject in 1973.[121] The department rejigged courses over the decades to cater for students with differing maths backgrounds. In 1977 it developed a first-year alternative aimed at life-science students: 'Topics of more interest to the physical scientist are simplified in content or omitted. Others such as examples of the mechanics of body movement, colour, the eye and ear, flow of fluids, osmosis, behaviour of gases, and bio-electricity, are expanded or introduced in a manner appropriate to the interests of the life scientist.'[122] The venture was 'entirely successful as evidenced by an improved pass rate and renewed student interest in introductory physics'.[123]

Geology had a growth spurt in the 1960s: students flocked to the subject as Australia offered graduates high-paying jobs in the mining industry, which was experiencing one of its periodic booms. The academic staff expanded from four in 1960 to nine in 1975.[124] At the helm was Doug Coombs, an Otago graduate who completed his PhD at Cambridge and succeeded Noel Odell as professor in 1956. Students were fascinated by Odell, 'an impressive looking man with the added mystique of having been the last man to see alive the legendary Irving and Mallory near the pinnacle of Everest in 1924,' Neil Howard recalled.[125] The interest heightened when Hillary and Tensing reached the top of Everest in 1953; Odell's next geology lecture was a detailed account of 'how Everest was conquered'. Odell was 'curiously uninterested in geology, except as a means of getting on expeditions', though students enjoyed his lectures for their illustrations of those expeditions.[126] By contrast, Coombs had a passion and flair for geology; he was a 'world leader' in several fields, including mineralogy, basalt, 'the "invention" of the zeolite mineral facies concept and the ophiolite belt. He has at least one fossil named after him and a range of hills in Victoria Land, Antarctica.'[127]

Geology as a subject was experiencing dramatic change. Geologists once regarded planet earth as relatively static and a theory of continental drift proposed in the 1910s was not widely accepted. In the 1960s plate tectonics provided an explanation for continental drift and for most modern geological structures. Like all innovative theories it had opponents, but it was quickly adopted by some New Zealand scientists, particularly at Otago. Richard Norris arrived in 1970 from Oxford and taught the new theories. This country was, he recalled, 'ripe for applying some of these concepts': he and Alan Cooper worked on the Alpine Fault.[128] In 1979 Coombs reported the department was involved in studies of 'the natural laboratory existing in New Zealand, where the dynamic

Students working in an optics lab in the Department of Physics, sometime between 1978 and 1985.
BOX-239-003, S13-217B, HOCKEN COLLECTIONS.

processes of the earth can be studied in action'. A recent local event – the Abbotsford landslide, which destroyed dozens of homes in the Dunedin suburb – had highlighted the need for geologists to vet the sites of intended land developments. New Zealand was 'a land of geological hazards – earthquakes, volcanic eruptions and landslides'; there would be 'no shortage of work for geologists in the future,' Coombs said.[129] He was right: ongoing events, from volcanic eruptions at Ruapehu to earthquakes in Canterbury, combined with booms in mining and gas exploration and concern about climate change, have created ongoing interest in geology.[130]

Chemistry was still one of the biggest departments; by 1975 it had 22 academics, including three professors.[131] The essential oils of natural products were, as ever, one of the main research fields, and PhD student Denis Lauren identified an extract from rimu with a very unusual carbon skeleton, named laurenene in his honour.[132] The department's microanalytical lab provided an essential service to researchers throughout New Zealand, conducting painstaking analysis of tiny samples. Soper, when he arrived at Otago in the 1930s, recognised that microanalysis was essential to further research; lecturer Charles Carter set it up and in 1949 Tsu Sheng Ma was recruited to develop it further, with Arthur Campbell as understudy. After Ma left, Campbell directed the lab until his retirement in 1989, when it was renamed in his honour.[133] Applied or 'industrial' chemistry, which fitted the aspirations of the university's founders, continued until it wound down in the 1990s. Otago researchers explored the chemistry of carbohydrates, pulp and paper, and plasma, and Melville Carr worked on geothermal reactions, clays, and the manufacture of liquid fuels from coal. Expansion meant the department could develop research in inorganic chemistry; future professor Brian Robinson arrived in 1967, followed by other staff who were interested in the chemistry of metals.[134]

Maths underwent the greatest evolution within the sciences in the 1960s and 70s, as it gave rise to computer science. Statistics emerged too – it had been around at Otago but in a limited way: from 1920 there was a three-month class in 'practical study of geographical and economic statistics' designed for BCom, and from 1938 a course for 'students of Economics, Education, or other subjects, whose work entails the discussion of statistical data'.[135] Local graduate Harold Silverstone did his PhD at Edinburgh with former Otago student Alexander Aitken as his supervisor; they collaborated in some pioneering statistics work. Silverstone returned to the Otago Maths Department as lecturer in 1946 and set up a Certificate in Introductory Statistics, and in the 1950s more advanced papers were introduced.[136] But the subject had an image problem, as Otago's first statistics professor, Geoffrey Jowett, noted in 1964: students were put off by 'its popular associations with thick dusty books full of closely printed tables of dull figures'. There was 'an acute world shortage of statisticians', Jowett said, with 'a good quota of jobs and potential jobs' in New Zealand.[137] Statistics wasn't an easy option – majors had to study advanced pure maths as well – and senior classes remained small.[138] One early graduate, Len Cook, who became the government statistician in New Zealand and later in Britain, recalled that Jowett was 'a lively teacher who was "very experimental" and "quite unusual" in his approach, highlighting the power of statistics in experimental applications'.[139]

The Maths Department fielded many requests for assistance from biological departments (the Medical School had its own specialist statisticians) and in 1971 it established a full-time consultancy service, the Biometrics Unit.[140] George Seber was the first biometrician; when he left the unit lapsed for a year but it was revived in 1974 under the direction of the professor of statistics, Stephen Mandel. It provided advice to arts and science departments and eventually morphed into the Centre for Applications of Statistics and Mathematics.[141]

Applied mathematics, which was taught at Otago from its earliest days, got its own chair in the 1960s. Robert Gabriel, who succeeded Bell as maths professor in 1948, believed pure mathematics was too dominant in New Zealand and he developed the applied side at Otago.[142] Bill Davidson, a Scotsman who gained an appreciation for the applications of maths while 'swinging compasses' with the RAF's Pathfinders during World War II, became Otago's first professor of applied mathematics in 1966. He contributed to resolving the 'cosmological problem' – the search for a model of the physical universe that solved Einstein's equations – and he worked on Newtonian cosmology.[143] Meanwhile Desmond Sawyer, known for 'his keen geometric insight, which none can challenge', came and went as professor of pure mathematics. He was appointed to the sole maths chair in 1956, to the frustration of his colleague Harold Silverstone, who believed he didn't get the chair on political grounds; he and his father Mark Silverstone were well-known labour activists. Membership of the Communist Party would not have endeared Harold to the university leaders, but he probably missed out simply because Sawyer had a stronger CV. Silverstone departed for Queensland in 1959, where he became a highly regarded medical statistician.[144]

In 1967 Simon Bernau, who became professor when Sawyer departed to be foundation professor at the University of Waikato, commented that 'a common attitude to mathematical research in New Zealand has been a strange mixture of resignation and apathy. For too long University Mathematics Departments have watched their best graduates leave the country immediately after graduating, often never to return.' It was a problem not peculiar to maths, though it was more acute there. The New Zealand Mathematical Colloquium agreed 'to work actively to encourage mathematics graduates to remain in New Zealand for their advanced degrees', and circulated lists of topics that could be supervised.[145] Such promotional activities bore fruit: in 1974 the Otago Maths Department awarded its first PhDs to Bramley Evans and Natalia Zotov, who investigated topics in cosmology.[146]

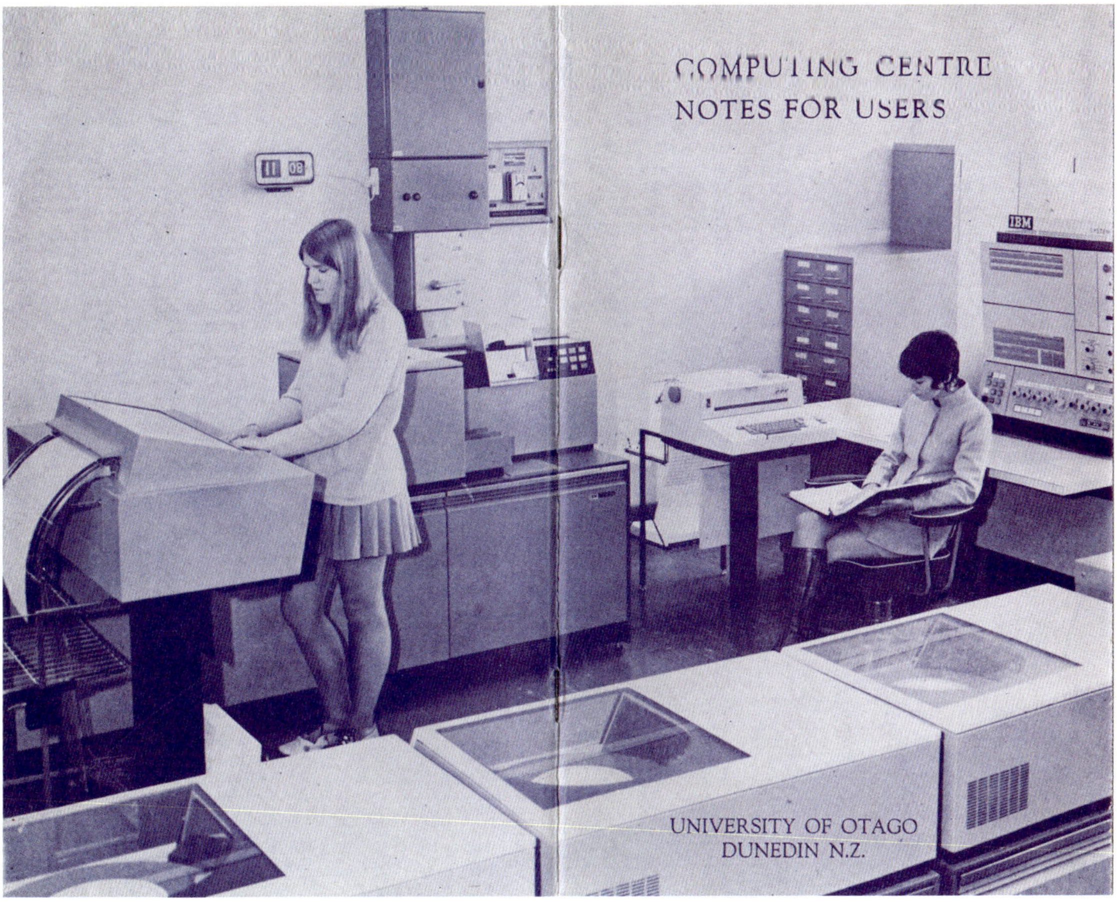

The Computing Centre's first machine, reproduced from its 1971 'Notes for users'. Otago's tardiness enabled it to invest in a 'third generation' machine that used 'micro-miniature circuits': these were faster and more reliable than the previous transistors, which were themselves a big improvement on the original valve machines. By 1971 the Otago machine had been expanded to include '32K bytes of storage, a 400 cards-per-minute card-reader, a 240 lines-per minute lineprinter and two disk drives. The computer is available for use by any University department and as one of the disk drives may be used for replaceable disk packs, large amounts of information can be stored.'
INFORMATION TECHNOLOGY SERVICES RECORDS, MS-4396/010, S13-359A, HOCKEN COLLECTIONS.

THE BIRTH OF COMPUTER SCIENCE

Otago increasingly trained its own PhD graduates, but it still benefited from the experience of returning New Zealanders who had completed their postgrad study elsewhere, none more than Brian Cox. Cox was a gifted mathematician who started his Otago studies in the 1950s and, in 1961, headed to Cambridge for a PhD. When he needed to solve equations with 128 variables his supervisor directed him to the mathematical laboratory. There Cox met computing pioneer Maurice Wilke and the electronic delay storage automatic calculator (EDSAC), an early computer; he was given books to read and a few directions and managed to program the machine to solve his equations. Thus came an introduction to computing he described as 'serendipitous'.[147] In 1963 Cox returned to

Otago as a lecturer in the Maths Department and, when he had a tricky calculation, he headed to the University of Canterbury's computer, installed in 1962. Auckland acquired a computer in 1963 and Victoria shared one with the DSIR.[148] Otago wanted to 'keep up with the Joneses … to be without a computer would affect the recruitment of staff, and the research carried out by staff and students'.[149] Otago decided in 1964 to invest in a computer, Cox recalled, and 'was looking for somebody to look after it. They searched overseas without luck, and finally looked around and said: "Well, look, you used one." I thought, that sounds interesting. I was appointed to be in charge of the Computing Centre, supervised its installation in May 1966 and remained with computers from that time onwards.'[150]

The IBM 360/30 was expensive, physically large, slow and had very little digital storage (16KB), but it was a state-of-the-art device. Cox ran it according to the model that had impressed him at Cambridge. He taught programming to anyone who was interested – dozens learned FORTRAN in preparation for the arrival of the computer – and made the computer available 24 hours a day; postgraduate students often arrived with sleeping bags for overnight stints.[151] It quickly became a mixed academic and administrative tool. Registry already used technology: it had a Burroughs bookkeeping machine for the payroll and a leased semi-programmable machine for enrolment data, student records and bursary cheques. Those functions were gradually transferred to the IBM, along with laborious tasks like figuring out the exam timetable, previously completed by two people shuffling pieces of graph paper around the floor for three weeks. The mixed use of the computer had disadvantages: if a backlog developed due to a breakdown, the payroll took precedence over a research project.[152]

The Commerce Faculty realised its students would benefit from understanding the latest technology; it was first to incorporate computing into its undergraduate courses. In the Science Faculty, programming first appeared in advanced applied mathematics course prescriptions in 1966. From those beginnings, Otago experienced the parallel development of computing within science and commerce. The divisions cooperated, with combined first-year courses later, but each field developed its own specialty: commerce focused on computer applications in business; science on the technical and scientific elements of computing.[153] The first specialist computer science course was offered in 1969 and a year later computing moved from the Mathematics Department. A computer committee was set up with responsibility for the Computing Centre. There were more postgraduate than undergraduate students at first, but in 1979 computer science became an undergraduate major.[154] In 1980 Cox reported that the 14-year-old Computing Centre had expanded to take up two-thirds of the Interim Science Building; it had a larger computer plus 'several mini-computers, and a series of terminals'; and 1200 people used the terminals each week for a range of administrative tasks, research and teaching. Planning for 'maximum efficient usage' and choosing appropriate equipment was challenging.[155] A VAX computer went live the following year.[156] In 1983 the burgeoning computing enterprise was divided: the Department of Computer Science was created and the Computing Centre continued as a service centre. Cox was promoted to a personal chair in 1978; he became head of the department, and Geoff Wyvill, John McDonald and Bruce Stephens joined him on the academic staff.[157]

THE PSYCHOLOGY EXPLOSION

Another new department had a pre-history of nearly a century as part of mental science. In 1964, after years of campaigning, psychology gained its own department and professor; it shifted to the Science Faculty and offered a full degree programme from 1965, starting with 'a synoptic introduction to the experimental study of behaviour' for first years.[158] Otago was a laggard – Victoria, Canterbury and Auckland all separated their philosophy and psychology departments in the 1950s – but inaugural professor

Stephen Griew expressed 'very great pride and satisfaction' at the state of psychology at Otago when he departed in 1967. It had 'by far the best experimental psychology department New Zealand has so far achieved'; the others would 'not easily displace ours from its pre-eminent position as the only department in the country seriously and successfully professing a modern variety of experimental psychology'.[159]

Psychology appealed to students; it overtook chemistry as the most popular science major at graduation in 1978.[160] Changes to medical intermediate in 1973 boosted first-year classes: students had more options and some chose psychology.[161] The department attracted good postgraduate students from the start. Its first PhD graduate, in 1968, was Michael Davison, who came from Bristol to study with Griew and went on to a distinguished career at Auckland.[162] Geoffrey White was another early PhD graduate, one of the department's founding first-year class in 1965. After a few years at Victoria he returned to Otago and became professor in 1988.[162] From 1975 a select group trained as clinical psychologists through an intensive postgraduate diploma course. The need for supervised clinical placements kept numbers small, though a community counselling centre, opened in 1979, provided further clinical training opportunities.[164]

The department played 'a useful part through applied research within the New Zealand community', reported head Peter McKellar in 1973.[165] In 1974 it set up research labs to study interpersonal skills, and Gay Maxwell, who realised 'that people in the community might obtain benefit from learning basic skills in developing and maintaining friendships', set up a social skills training programme. With funding from the Mental Health Foundation, it became the Social Skills Research Unit in 1979.[166] Other projects attracted public interest, notably Richard Kammann and David Marks' research on parapsychology. Several self-proclaimed psychics earned fame in the 1970s, and international stars the Amazing Kreskin and Uri Geller visited New Zealand. Marks and Kammann, prompted by their students' suggestion that the psychics' feats were genuine, investigated claims of extrasensory perception or psychokinesis. Their 1980 book *The Psychology of the Psychic* concluded that for each 'dazzling claim … a simple, natural explanation was far more credible than a supernatural or paranormal one'.[167] Marks co-founded New Zealand Skeptics in 1986.[168]

MINING AND METALLURGY

As other sciences expanded, mining and metallurgy struck trouble. The Otago School of Mines was never large, but that did not seem a problem when other departments were also small, and it provided the only New Zealand university education and research in an important industry. The boom and bust nature of that industry always presented challenges. Arthur 'Poobah' Andrew led the school through the 1930s as students struggled to find work locally and looked to the goldmines and tinfields of Southeast Asia; during the war many Otago mining graduates were caught up in battle there, or as prisoners of the Japanese.[169] The war had awful consequences for three Thai students who could not proceed to the Royal School of Mines in London – an accustomed destination for Thai students – so enrolled at Otago in 1940 instead. The school reported in 1942 that their studies had been 'interrupted': they were interned as enemy aliens, as Thailand had joined the Axis cause. All three died in an accident during their forced repatriation the following year.[170]

The dynamic Gordon Williams, who became School of Mines director in 1945, had an ambitious goal to develop a faculty of technology, incorporating schools of mining, metallurgy, surveying and economic geology.[171] In 1948 he reformed the metallurgy courses, whose scope had 'remained virtually unchanged since the School was founded'; the focus shifted to secondary metallurgy with courses that equipped graduates to work in expanding industrial enterprises such as foundries, engineering shops and fabricators. Williams revamped the drawing courses, and the applied mechanics and steam and heat engines papers morphed into engineering; he noted there was no intention to compete with the 'purely engineering' courses at Auckland and Canterbury, simply 'to give mining and metallurgical students a more adequate background in engineering'.[172]

In 1949 Ivon Graham became Otago's first professor of coal mining, and State Coal Mines established bursaries and postgraduate scholarships in an attempt to entice more students to that specialty: the closure of New Zealand's last underground goldmines in 1952 highlighted the wisdom of diversification. Demand for assaying and other consultancy services fluctuated wildly and outside the Geology Department little fundamental research was undertaken at the School of Mines before Graham's arrival. In 1951 James Stott was seconded from DSIR to assist with coal research, and the school welcomed its first full-year research student. A senior lecturer in coal mining was added in 1952, and in 1955 a building for the Coal Research Institute became the first extension to the School of Mines facilities in over 40 years. The institute was not destined for a long life, however; interest in coal declined as gas, diesel transport and electricity took over. When Graham retired in 1958 the chair of coal mining ended, though Stott continued the coal research for a while longer.[173]

There were abundant metal mines beyond these shores, and local and international students were interested in them. In 1960 the school celebrated the 'rather special part' it played in 'fostering' the Colombo Plan, with 11 current students (from Malaya, Thailand, Indonesia and Burma) and five graduates who were 'highly valued' in their home countries.[174] Among New Zealanders, public interest in mining waxed and waned, depending on the latest discoveries. In 1955 Williams commented that it was 'a sign of the times that the importance of radiometric work is superseding that of gold assaying in the correspondence that reaches us'; he gave lectures on radioactive minerals and their detection to large audiences around the country. The school's devices for measuring radioactivity were 'in keen demand' and had been used 'as far south as the Auckland Islands'.[175] Late that year, with New Zealand's first discovery of uranium, the school was 'besieged with inquiries for the loan or purchase of Geiger counters and all the available simple instruments made by our Senior Technician, Mr Wylie, were soon whisked away into the field by enthusiastic prospectors'. Further investigations revealed the Buller discovery was not a payable prospect, but still there were 'a few persons who are keenly interested in the search for uranium in New Zealand'.[176]

The Faculty of Technology, as the School of Mines was renamed in 1959, entered the 1960s with confidence, despite warnings in the Parry Report that it was 'carrying on under difficulties. It is doing some much needed training in metallurgy but we feel that consideration should be given to concentrating education for engineering technologies for the South Island at the University of Canterbury.'[177] The roll peaked at 82 students and in 1961 the university reported that 'with the discovery of natural gas in New Zealand, the promise of a large aluminium smelting plant, the possibilities of an iron and steel industry, and a carbide industry with other secondary metal developments, the future of the metallurgical side of the faculty appears assured'.[178] That assurance proved false: just four years later New Zealand's only university-level metallurgy course ended. The UGC, in light of the Parry Report, was not about to increase technology funding at Otago; in any case, from 1965 the special schools lost their dedicated funding and had to compete with other expanding faculties for the university's block grant. Apparently oblivious to that, in 1963 Williams applied for a big increase in staff, buildings and expensive metallurgy equipment, prompting VC Arthur Beacham to appoint a committee to review the Technology Faculty. The resulting cutbacks were a shock to Williams, who anticipated demand for more graduates at the Bluff aluminium smelter and New Zealand Steel, but the committee couldn't justify the funding.[179]

The changes were drastic. Surveying, taught to mining students for many decades, became

The School of Mines furnace room in 1949.

PRIME MINISTER'S DEPARTMENT PHOTOGRAPH, BOX-184-095, S17-183A, HOCKEN COLLECTIONS.

an independent department in 1963, and two years later the metallurgy courses ended; mining survived in a Department of Mineral Technology within the Faculty of Science.[180] The university created a personal chair in economic geology for Williams, but he spent the next five years working for the United Nations in Iran and returned only to retire.[181] The Department of Mineral Technology spent its early years 'preoccupied' with developing its 'remnants of disciplines' into 'an effective entity', head Douglas Buchanan reported in 1970.[182] It developed a programme that was relevant to an 'increasingly complex and scientific' industry: mineral technology courses covered 'basic mining and mineral processing material supported by mathematical and computer work, fluids, strengths, technical drawing, management and finance', and students studied other sciences

Kiwi and Thai mineral technology students at a freshers' welcome in 1964. From left: Sunan Boonmeeprasert, Ray Soper, Viroon Petpaisit, unknown, Riew Kongsangchai and Paichit Pathnopas.

DEPARTMENT OF MINERAL TECHNOLOGY ALBUM, MS-3843/005, S13-561B, HOCKEN COLLECTIONS.

too, notably geology.[183] Michael Buckenham, who succeeded Buchanan as head of department in 1977, noted many years later that the department's degrees 'were all highly regarded by industry and the University and gained professional recognition'. The basic undergraduate qualification changed in format through the years from the original AOSM, later converted to a postgraduate qualification, to a Bachelor of Engineering, then Bachelor of Science and finally Bachelor of Mineral Technology. Otago was 'ahead of the times' in marketing its mining courses as technology, Buckenham said; 'programmes of this type and name are now prominent in many of our universities'.[184]

Student numbers remained small. By 1980 there were 12 to 15 graduates each year, but for two years there was a worrying trend of no students from Asia enrolling; this coincided with the introduction of a fee for international students. On a brighter note, after more than 100 years of resolute masculinity the department had its first woman graduate, Tan Kim Lean, in 1979; another female student was completing second year, and others had shown interest in entering the course. But a cloud hung over the department: Buckenham was concerned about 'various and periodic enquiries into the "future of Mineral Technology"'.[185]

In 1979 the UGC announced a review of 'selected university activities in the light of likely academic developments and community needs in the 1980s', and one of the specified topics of enquiry was engineering.[186] The resulting 1982 report endorsed the need for mineral technology but harked back to the 1959 Parry report in regretting the Otago department's lack of any 'interaction with engineering departments' and the 'resources and facilities those could provide'. It noted that 'New Zealand is pinning many of its energy hopes on coal fields in the Waikato and Southland' and that the challenges those fields represented, particularly the 'deep seams' of the Waikato, would make 'the engineering component of mineral technology … of greater importance'.[187] The UGC set up another review on engineering education with a focus on the future of Otago's Department of Mineral Technology.[188]

In 1984, in response to that review and advice from overseas experts and the Ministry of Energy, the UGC decided to 'upgrade' the mineral technology course and shift it to the University of Auckland Engineering Faculty, which was keen to take it over. There was a public outcry: the School of Mines was a longstanding source of international kudos for the south. Other departments, notably geology, which got almost a third of its enrolments from mineral technology students, were concerned about flow-on effects. A campaign against the transfer, led by OUSA president Liam Kennedy, failed to shift the government's decision.[189] The Otago administration, while it was keen to retain mineral technology, was partly responsible for its loss – mining had never been a priority and always ran on a shoestring budget. 'We have always been a Cinderella department,' Buckenham said; Otago had missed 'a development opportunity' to invest in mineral technology as 'a nucleus for the development of earth resources'. Some of the staff felt that mineral technology would be better funded at Auckland.[190]

Early in 1987 the six academic staff and one of the technicians relocated to Auckland and became the Department of Mining Engineering, with Buckenham as head, and students who were partway through their degrees transferred to Auckland. Critics of the transfer ultimately proved correct: Auckland failed to attract more students to mining than Otago. Higher living costs over a longer engineering course were a disincentive, and anti-mining protests in the nearby Coromandel region proved 'damaging'. A promised chair and building never eventuated and staff who left weren't replaced. In 1995 the department was merged with civil engineering, and mining engineering was absorbed into a resource engineering degree. Buckenham was disappointed: 'No readily identifiable mining presence now remains at Auckland,' he said; 'mining is now lost as a professional discipline in this country.'[191] It was a sad end for the once proud Otago School of Mines.

A NATIONAL SURVEYING SCHOOL

Meanwhile, surveying was flourishing. Otago had long offered a Certificate in Mine and Land Surveying, but that concentrated on mining.[192] New Zealand land surveyors developed their own professional qualification with an apprentice-style 'cadetship' followed by rigorous exams. In 1947 John (JB or Jack) Mackie, who had recently returned to Dunedin after years as a mine engineer and then as a prisoner of war of the Japanese in Malaya, became the School of Mines surveying lecturer.[193] Mackie was energetic and agile; he was a born leader who was popular at social events and field camps for his 'inexhaustible fund of stories, anecdotes and the greatest repertoire of limericks of any man that I have ever known', one student recalled.[194] He was keen to extend the surveying programme. Some at the university thought a technical institute was a better fit for surveying but Mackie persuaded them that surveying needed to become research-orientated; he recalled 'haranguing' members of the Professorial Board who 'didn't know what surveyors did'. Dunedin's surveying community initially 'stood aloof' because Mackie wasn't a registered surveyor, so he devoted seven summer 'vacations' to completing the fieldwork required for registration.[195] He convinced surveyors that 'drastic changes were necessary if the profession were not to degenerate to technician status'. The University of New Zealand approved a three-year diploma in surveying in 1958; Auckland made 'strenuous, if belated efforts to acquire it', but Otago won the day. The Minister of Lands approved the changes that made a university course the only means of entry to the surveying profession after 1962.[196]

As the first prospective students completed their intermediate year, the Surveying Department appointed Cecil 'Chook' Fowler, recently retired as Dunedin's chief surveyor, and Ted Matthews joined the staff early in 1963.[197] The three staff started with just two students for the surveying diploma in 1963; VC Frederick Soper 'nearly had kittens' when he learned the class size, Mackie recalled, but by 1968 the department was filling its intake of 30 students.[198] One of the pioneers, Warren Garlick, remembered that his 'heart sank' when he discovered there was 'only one other to share the lectures with. This was a great change from the atmosphere of Auckland University where in the mathematics class there were over 200 students in one class. My fears were short-lived and moments after meeting Bhuwan Dutt, the other student, we were friends and fellow conspirators against our lecturers.'[199] The course started with a field camp that introduced 'practical exercises, both in the field and office environments'; and students completed major field exercises at the end of their course. The university acquired the Taieri Field Station, originally built for preliminary air-force training in World War II; it was in a good flat location for levelling exercises and urban traverses, and exercises on the Department of Agriculture's hilly Invermay research farm provided 'very realistic farm conditions with plenty of barbed wire and electric fences; shelter belts; sheep and cattle … and frequent movement of vehicles and machinery'. The field camps promoted departmental camaraderie, helped along with 'evening excursions into one or other of Mosgiel's watering holes'.[200]

When the first woman student, Joanne Waugh, arrived in 1972, surveying 'was put into a flurry of panic and had nowhere to put her during her first field camp and so she boarded with a nearby family'; by the time of her second field camp separate accommodation for women had been added. Waugh became New Zealand's first female registered surveyor.[201] The department was still predominantly male, however: it attracted just eight women students in the 1970s, and in 1996 it reported that the annual intake of women 'rarely exceeded 12% of the total'. Māori students were also rare, perhaps because of the troubled relationship between surveying and the loss of Māori land.[202]

From 1968 students could opt for a degree course with additional maths requirements, but it became 'abundantly clear' that the two years following the intermediate were 'not enough time for the department to equip students with

26

the necessary basic knowledge' required for the profession. A four-year Bachelor of Surveying replaced the older diploma and degree from 1976.[203] Many surveyors who had trained under the cadet system had their doubts about degrees, but were won over as graduates proved they were better equipped than earlier surveyors. The Surveying Institute gave 'tremendous support' to the department, says Basil Jones; for instance by supplying a grant for the school's first computer lab.[204] Mackie was promoted to a personal chair in 1969, and when he retired in 1975 surveying was granted a permanent chair.[205] Staff were becoming better qualified. The university wanted staff with a PhD, but in the beginning 'there was nobody available with any kind of degree' and it appointed registered surveyors who 'already had the equivalent of a good bachelor's degree' as academics.[206] The department later favoured overseas graduates but, as its programme matured, it produced its own pool of potential academics. Jones, former head of surveying at the University of Natal, succeeded Mackie; he was followed in the chair by local graduate John Hannah.[207]

In 1994 surveying courses were offered at first-year level for the first time; students completed introductory surveying papers along with other science courses before acceptance into the second-year professional courses. A few electives were added, but the surveying degree was still closely prescribed.[208] Repackaging existing papers with those from other departments provided further options: from the early 1980s BSc students could major in measurement science or in land planning and development, and computerisation prompted a major in land and spatial information systems, introduced in 1991. Ten years later surveying combined with the Information Science Department to offer a major in geographic information systems for the new Bachelor of Applied Science.[209] The surveying degree remained popular, especially with students from a rural background who sought an indoor/outdoor career; graduates had no trouble finding work and by 2005 the intake had risen to 60. Staff expanded in number and in expertise. The arrival of Christina Hulbe as dean in 2013 signalled the broadening research interests of the Surveying School; Hulbe, a US glaciologist, worked with colleagues from surveying and other disciplines on measuring the Antarctic ice shelf and the ocean beneath.[210]

Opposite: Lecturer Allan Blaikie with surveying students Alex Grigg (left) and Jeff Reid (right), 1984.

UNIVERSITY OF OTAGO PHOTOGRAPHIC UNIT RECORDS, MS-4386/085, S17-612C, HOCKEN COLLECTIONS.

FROM HOME TO CONSUMER SCIENCE

Otago's other main applied science – home science – continued to attract students from throughout New Zealand as well as Colombo Plan students from Asia. After a postwar dip, enrolments passed 300 in the late 1970s.[211] The courses were closely prescribed and prepared students for the school's two most popular graduate careers – teaching and dietetics. Many of the graduates went on to do registered dietetics training (run by the hospital boards) or to the secondary teaching course at Auckland Teachers' College. The 'science' specialisation included chemistry to Stage 3; not many students selected the other option of advanced physics. There was plenty of applied chemistry relating to the household and foods; and there were mandatory courses on clothing, design, anatomy, physiology, 'bacteriology, sanitary science and hygiene', home management and child development. A short course on mothercraft had students bathing babies at the local Karitane Hospital, an institution specialising in the care of young babies. Top of the list came nutrition, which everybody studied in their final year regardless of specialisation. Overall, it was a demanding course with lots of laboratory work. As Raechel Laing, a 1960s student and a future academic comments, 'a lot of it was fantastic but some of it was nonsense'; she didn't see the need to learn how to wash a sock and so skipped laundry classes.[212]

There was more flexibility from 1971, when BHSc students could select from several subjects for advanced study.[213] In the same year the school

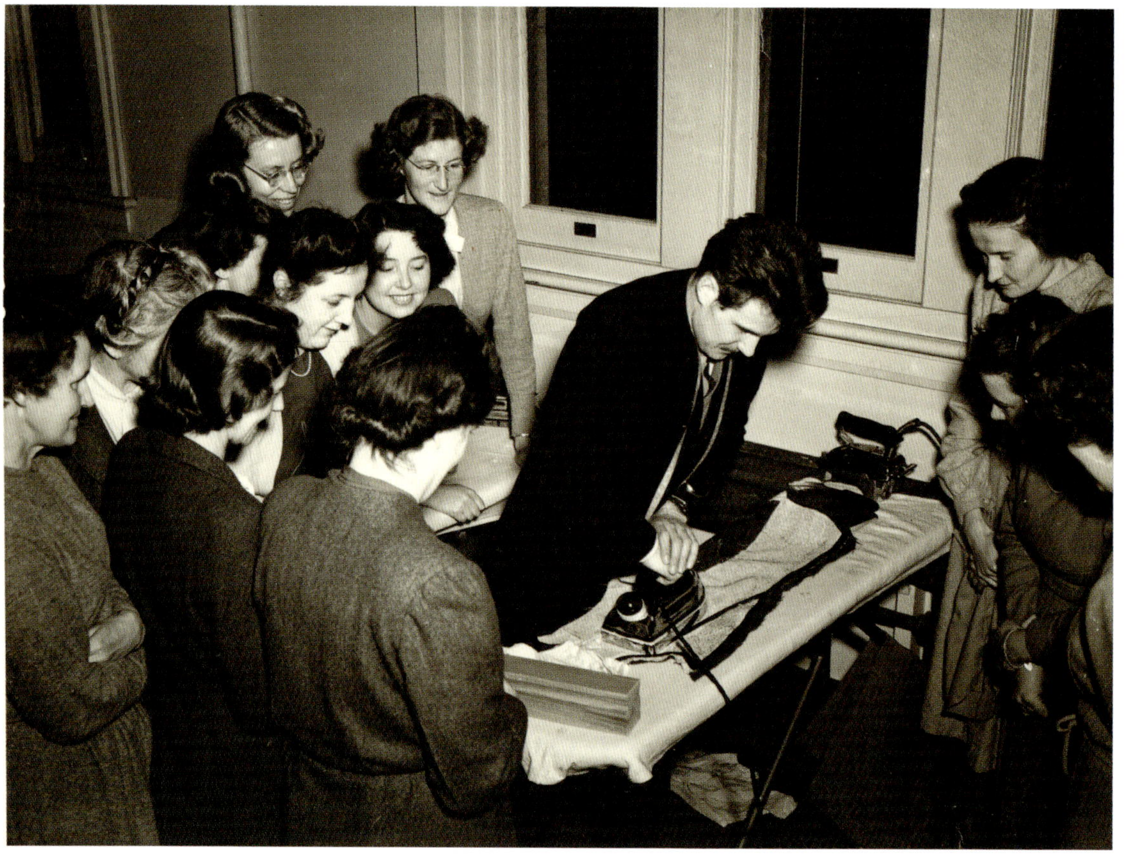

René Thevenot, lecturer in dress design, with clothing students in 1949. The Home Science School was very much a female domain, though there were a few male lecturers, in particular in design. When a male student enrolled in 1976, adapting the compulsory clothing assignments to suit a man proved a challenge. Some on campus joked that the school's primary purpose was to train good wives for professional men, especially doctors, but most of the home science women needed to earn a living and had professional ambitions.

ASSOCIATION OF HOME SCIENCE ALUMNAE RECORDS, MS-1516/076, S13-578A, HOCKEN COLLECTIONS.

offered a BSc (Hons) in human nutrition, planned for a decade but delayed by lack of funding. The degree meant students could specialise in nutrition without taking other home science subjects. It was a strategic move to extend research, and it attracted male as well as female students – whereas few men braved the home science qualifications.[214] Nutrition research had a long history at Otago, initially at the Medical School. Frederic Truby King was interested in the role of diet in mental health, and this evolved into his famous work on infant nutrition.[215] John Malcolm, physiology professor from 1905, researched the nutritional values of New Zealand foods, especially local fish. His introduction of vitamin assays led to practical advice on diets that benefited animals as well as humans: the diet he devised ensured the survival of the dogs on Richard Byrd's 1928 Antarctic expedition.[216] One of Malcolm's students, Muriel Bell, became a well-known nutritionist and long-serving member of the Physiology Department. Her 'forte was applied research into subjects of practical everyday importance', and the Department of Health employed her part-time for many years. She provided advice on war and postwar food rationing, and published a recipe for rosehip syrup to provide youngsters in the 1940s (and beyond) with adequate vitamin C.[217] From

1911 the School of Home Science provided an additional home for nutrition research; it was the most popular topic for home science theses.[218] One early master's graduate, the school's future dean Elizabeth Gregory, completed further postgraduate study in London before returning to Otago in 1932; like Bell, Gregory was frequently consulted on public health nutritional issues.[219] Marion Robinson was another student who returned, in 1958, after further study in England. The Home Science School set up a Metabolic Research Unit where Robinson launched studies in metabolic balance and set up a trace element laboratory; she earned world renown for her work on selenium.[220] Robinson was promoted to a personal chair in 1980. By then there was an established chair in human nutrition that John Birkbeck took up as foundation professor in 1975. Unlike his predecessors on the home science staff, Birkbeck was a medic; his appointment signalled a shifting focus to nutrition as a health science rather than a home science. Birkbeck held 'that nutrition should be an integral part of the training of all those engaged in the health professions'.[221]

Princess Anne (left) talks to home science students during the 1970 royal visit: (from left) Janice Subritzky (at the back), Barbara McLeod, Margaret Tompkins and Lynette Guy.

FACULTY OF CONSUMER AND APPLIED SCIENCES RECORDS, 97-081/008, S17-610E, HOCKEN COLLECTIONS.

Foods – later known as food science – had a shift in focus, too. As the role of women in society changed, students were looking beyond the traditional home science careers. Opportunities were opening up to work with food industry boards and manufacturers of food products and kitchen appliances. Courses changed accordingly, with more emphasis on consumers and industry.[222] Similar changes were taking place in clothing and textiles. Avice Bowbyes, who headed the Clothing Department from 1928 to 1961, had a passion for high-end fashion. Her successors, though, shifted the emphasis to more functional aspects of clothing and industrial aspects of textiles. Other tertiary institutions introduced fashion courses, but Otago's emphasis on the science of textiles gave it a point of difference.[223] Home science made big contributions to the university's paid consultancy services to industry, 'particularly in the applied areas of foods/food science, clothing and textile science', dean Patricia Coleman noted in 1986.[224] The establishment of specialist commercial units – the Clothing and Textile Centre, the Food Market Research Unit and the Food Product Development Unit – helped meet that demand. Projects ranged from testing a new chocolate drink to measuring New Zealand firefighters so the fit of their uniforms could be improved.[225]

The appointment of David Buisson as home science dean in 1986 attracted media attention, as the role had been the domain of women since 1911. Buisson commented that 'he wanted to get rid of the idea that home science is an area solely for women'. He had qualifications in chemistry and management and came from the DSIR, where he had coordinated fish research and acted as liaison with the fishing industry. His particular interest was consumers and food products, and he took up the new chair in food science alongside the deanship.[226] One of his priorities was a name change for the faculty and its degrees: in 1987 'home science' became 'consumer and applied sciences' (CAPS) – a name that 'reflects more aptly what is taught in the Faculty, and should remove the negative perceptions the old name had', according to Buisson. For a long time the faculty had looked beyond the home, and Coleman had proposed in the early 1970s that 'community science' might be a more relevant name.[227] The arrival of Jim Mann to the chair of human nutrition in 1988 prompted the first breakaway from the old home science alliance. Mann had a joint appointment in human nutrition and medicine; he was an endocrinologist who specialised in diabetes and obesity. Like Birkbeck before him, he saw nutrition as a health science and found it an awkward fit with the increasingly consumer-orientated focus of CAPS. Nutrition became an independent department within the Faculty of Science, though students could still include it in consumer and applied science degrees.[228]

Meanwhile, CAPS expanded its social science offerings, which was something 'long sought', as Coleman noted on her retirement; Otago students who went to North America for postgraduate study were at a disadvantage because of their weakness in that area.[229] Tony Worsley took charge of a Community and Family Studies Development Unit, designed to expand family studies beyond the one course already on offer and to further develop 'social science and social policy areas'; it later merged with the social work programme and moved to the Humanities Division in 2001.[230] The other CAPS subjects – clothing, textile science, food science, design – were destined for ongoing restructuring; in 1987 Buisson created a Department of Food Science and the other three subjects were grouped together.

PHYSICAL EDUCATION UPGRADES

Physical education, regarded with disdain by some academics, built up its credentials through the 1970s and 1980s. Smithells was promoted to a personal chair in 1969 and his successor, Peter McIntosh, had a personal chair on appointment. In 1976 the subject came of age with a permanent professorship.[231] Plans for a degree course were advanced when Smithells left in 1974, and the first students undertook the four-year Bachelor of Physical Education in 1975. McIntosh found the school in 'thriving' condition when he arrived; he paid tribute to Smithells' 'unremitting work' in creating a school that was 'highly regarded not only in New Zealand but in many other countries throughout the world'.[232] There was a 'seemingly insatiable demand' for people with phys ed qualifications, and only a lack of space and teaching capacity – in other words, funding – prevented the school from expanding more rapidly.[233] By 1975 the student intake had risen to 100. The degree was at first limited to 15 students, but from 1980 entrants could select freely between the degree or diploma and most chose the degree; the diploma was phased out from 1984. Hundreds of aspiring students were turned away; physical education was 'the most preferred of this university's degrees' noted the dean in 1988. The school acquired faculty status in 1981.[234]

Under McIntosh's guidance, the programme expanded further into the social sciences: students could take half-units in the sociology and psychology of sport and physical education. McIntosh was a popular director but he stayed just three and a half years; his wife did not like Dunedin and they returned to Britain.[235] It was a couple of years before the chair could be filled again but, in the meantime, the school did not stand still, with Bruce Ross as interim director. In 1979 the first students entered a Master of Physical Education programme, and in 1981 the first student enrolled for a PhD; instead of sending postgrads to North America, New Zealand could qualify its own academics.[236] David Russell, who arrived as professor in 1981, made it immediately clear that 'research is to assume high priority in the School'.[237] Research was hampered by poor facilities, however: 'How much longer will the University tolerate the appalling conditions under which the staff and students of this important and unique special school most operate?' Russell asked in 1982, echoing longstanding complaints.[238]

Physical education students in the 1970s.
SCHOOL OF PHYSICAL EDUCATION, SPORT AND EXERCISE SCIENCES COLLECTION

The injection of more government funding enabled more buildings and equipment, with good results. Russell reported in 1987 that Otago's biomechanical facilities were now 'world class' and had helped attract 'five outstanding overseas scholars in biomechanics' to collaborate on research projects; several had joint appointments with the Physiology Department.[239] Students using Smithells Gym still had to cross a busy highway to the changing room, but facilities were improving.[240]

From 1983 physical education students could major in either kinesiology or sport and leisure studies; in the first year of the programme three-quarters chose the social science option.[241] Some students believed the course was becoming too academic and many struggled with biology intermediate; they questioned the faculty's emphasis on research.[242] However, research was essential in furthering the discipline and it expanded, though practical aspects of the course stayed. Smithells had been interested in any human movement that could assist development, and he made dance, gymnastics and aquatics compulsory for all students. Rex Thomson, a 1960s student who returned as sociology lecturer in 1976, recalls finding dance 'a revelation' and aquatics 'a nightmare'; he appreciated the introduction to gymnastics. Those activities remained compulsory (though aquatics eventually became a remedial course, for those who didn't meet a required standard of swimming). Students enjoyed a practical outdoor education camp that was originally held at Trotter's Gorge, north of Dunedin, and later at Paradise at the head of Lake Wakatipu.[243]

Another of Smithells' interests was Māori culture. 'We have always tried to include some Maori activities in our course,' he wrote in 1973 – and that year they expanded with the availability of

Piri Sciascia as lecturer on Māoritanga.[244] By Otago standards, physical education was an early adopter of teaching on things Māori, and its courses attracted Māori. The first Māori student to qualify, Les Williams, went on to do a PhD at Berkeley before returning to Otago in 1971. His teaching and research on motor learning and control earned him a personal chair in 1984, and he was later dean for nine years.[245] In the twenty-first century the school created a specialist Māori academic position and Māori phys ed students formed their own student association.[246] Brendan Hokowhitu (later dean of the School of Māori and Pacific Development at Waikato) completed his PhD in physical education and Māori studies jointly.[247] Interdisciplinary research developed and a growing contingent took an extra year or two and completed a double degree in science, commerce or arts. Teaching remained a popular graduate destination but options diversified; current dean Doug Booth notes that once 'everybody was going to be an All Black psychologist … then everybody was going to be a sports marketer'.[248] Distance-taught undergraduate certificates and diplomas in sport studies and fitness management were introduced in 1990 and around 120 students enrolled, and later in the 1990s postgrad diplomas in physical education, dance and outdoor education were added to the curriculum.[249]

From 1998 undergraduate students had a choice of four majors: exercise and sport science; sport and leisure studies; exercise prescription and management (later renamed physical activity and health); and professional studies (including teacher education, outdoor education and dance education). The broad base of the degree meant all graduates still had a good general background, a point of difference for Otago as courses proliferated elsewhere. Once only Lincoln's parks and recreation course provided competition for New Zealand's national Physical Education School. With the deregulation of education in the late 1990s, other institutions established sports science or sports studies courses and recruitment became a bigger issue.[250] A belated name change to the School of Physical Education, Sport and Exercise Sciences in 2013 aimed to correct a common misunderstanding that Otago's course was aimed only at teachers.[251] Otago had a superior programme – it was delighted to be ranked seventh in the world for sport and sport-related disciplines in the 2017 QS world rankings – but that did not shield it from downsizing after several years of financial struggle resulting from declining enrolments.[252]

RESTRUCTURING GALORE

In 1989, when the university split into four academic divisions, the Division of Science was created from the Faculties of Science, Physical Education and CAPS. Physical education retained its integrity as a school with its own dean, and another professional programme, surveying, was upgraded from a department to a school in 2001.[253] The fate of CAPS was more complex. In 1990 Buisson, the dean, decamped to become head of the Department of Marketing (and later Commerce AVC); it had been a whirlwind few years under his leadership. The independent Department of Human Nutrition thrived, but the other former home science subjects were small in the context of the growing university, and this prompted a series of restructurings to retain viability. There was no replacement dean; longstanding staff member Nancy Carr became head of the remaining subjects in a Consumer Studies Department.[254] Textile scientist Laing comments that the alliance between the fields, previously integrated around the concept of humans and the way they lived, became awkward as each subject responded to expanding knowledge in a different way.[255] A 1990 review identified a lack of integration between disciplines; previously home science 'retained a strong identity with the vocational training of dietitians, and teachers of home economics', but the programme now lacked 'a defined professional orientation'. With rising costs, students hesitated to commit to a four-year degree that was 'not sufficiently broad' for a 'non-professional degree'.[256]

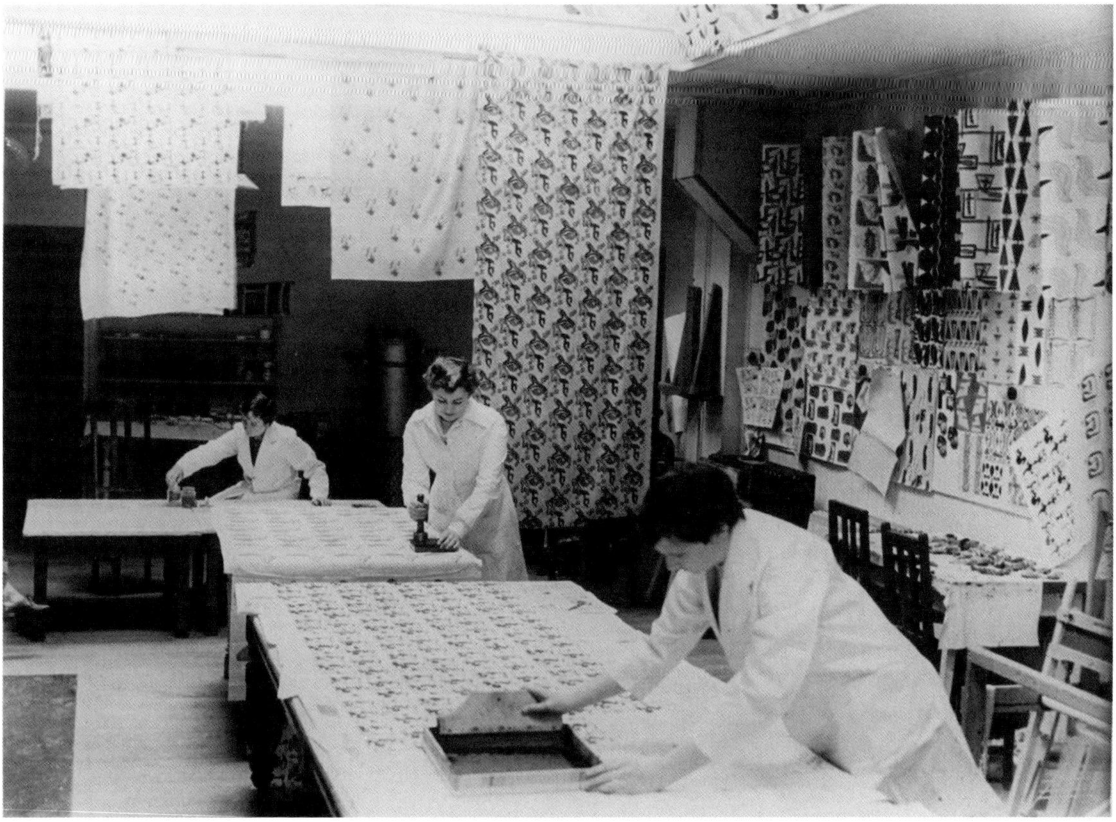

Home science design class in 1957.
FACULTY OF CONSUMER AND APPLIED SCIENCES RECORDS, 97-081/006, S17-611J, HOCKEN COLLECTIONS.

From 1993 the BCApSc became a three-year degree with a choice of six majors: clothing; community and family studies; design studies; food science; human nutrition; and textile science. Students who wished to major in community and family studies or design studies could also do so via a BA, and the other subjects were available as BSc majors.[257] It was a new status for design studies, though it had deep roots in home science: clothing and foods courses incorporated dress and kitchen design, and during the 1920s house planning and home furnishing entered the syllabus.[258] In 1948 John Murphy, with qualifications in fine arts and design from London, became Otago's first specialist design academic.[259] Design carried on as a minor subject and during the 1980s evolved from its concentration on the home to a broader purview.[260] In 1994 Nick Laird, who had been lecturing in design at Otago for 10 years, was excited by the possibilities. Enrolments were rising and graduates were 'securing good positions', and there was growing recognition at Otago and beyond of design 'as an intellectual process of enquiry and not just an extension of a trade or set of techniques'.[261]

There was more restructuring. In 2001 the community and family studies programme shifted to the Humanities Division, design studies became an independent department, and the rest became the Department of Food Science, Clothing and Textile Sciences. The Design Department had teething problems, with several changes of head before the arrival of Thomas Bley as professor in 2004. A 2005 review was impressed with the 'palpable' energy Bley had already brought; the department lacked the resources to offer 'immersion programmes in the doing of design', but 'project' papers gave students an appreciation of design practice. The syllabus lay 'somewhat between an academic study of design and a practical grounding in the doing of it'. In a crowded tertiary market, with thriving practical design programmes at Otago Polytechnic, the university had to take a more theoretical approach.[262] The two institutions cooperated in planning a design research centre to house their programmes, together with product design facilities available to industries, but the scheme collapsed in 2009 when the incoming government withdrew the funding promised by its predecessor.[263]

The collapse was badly timed: administrators were taking a serious look at departments that required subsidies, and design was one of them.[264] In 2010 design studies joined clothing and textile sciences in a Department of Applied Sciences and lost its status as an undergraduate major. News of the restructuring attracted protest, not least from Bley, who immediately resigned.[265] The downsized programme still offered a major in design for technology and postgrad options, but enrolments more than halved between 2011 and 2015, and long-term problems with research continued. The staff were talented and demonstrated quality design practice, but they weren't making a sufficient contribution to new knowledge within the discipline. A common interest in materials provided a link with clothing and textiles, but it was an awkward marriage and a 2014 review concluded it was 'an interesting initiative that has not worked'.[266] The design programme faced intense competition from other institutions; though Otago graduates performed well, it was difficult for the university to justify a programme that could not support itself and that was readily available elsewhere. In 2015 Otago announced that it would end its design courses once existing students had completed their studies.[267]

There were fewer students in clothing and textiles than in design, partly as there were no first-year papers; clothing and textiles held on for a little longer only because of its unique course offerings and research productivity.[268] The programme collaborated with industry and brought numerous contracts into its specialist Clothing and Textiles Centre. It also collaborated with other Otago departments: for instance, Laing worked with academics in physical education, preventive and social medicine and statistics, on projects concerning the effect of clothing and materials on human performance and health. Laing was an international expert in textile science and Otago awarded her a personal chair in 2004.[269] In 2016 the programme became part of a Centre for Materials Science and Technology, incorporating staff who specialised in 'fibres, textiles, biomaterials, and modelling'.[270] However, late the following year the university announced the closure of that centre: it was 'not economically viable and had not attracted enough students'.[271]

Food science, which became an independent department again in 2011, also had an enduring record of successful research. The discipline lost its professor when Buisson transferred to marketing in 1990, but in 1995 biochemical engineer Jean-Pierre ('JP') Dufour arrived from Belgium to take up a food science chair. His particular expertise was in brewing and he was in demand as a consultant to brewers. Dufour developed the programme's expertise in flavour science and ran popular intensive courses before his sudden death in 2007.[272] Other food science staff and postgraduates came from overseas, like Dufour; in 2008, for instance, staff were recruited from Malaysia, Egypt and Italy. They were from a range of disciplines, too: Phil Bremer, who succeeded Dufour as head, was an Otago-trained microbiologist. Staff with home science backgrounds became thin on the ground.[273] Food science and technology was a competitive field, offered at several New Zealand universities. Otago made a point of difference by concentrating on the fundamental sciences, with a particular strength in sensory and flavour science and research into waste and sustainability. It continued its earlier interest in consumer food science, and the Product Development Research Centre thrived.[274]

TRAINING DIETITIANS

Food science had the advantage of being compulsory for the popular nutrition major. The already lively Human Nutrition Department was boosted when it became national provider for dietetics training in the 1990s. The profession arose from concerns about hospital catering.[275] In the 1920s and 30s home science professor Ann Strong did her best to establish it in New Zealand, encouraging graduates to complete dietetics training in Australia, Britain and North America, but not all hospitals were convinced of the benefits of employing dietitians or willing to pay for them.[276] In 1940 the Health Department launched plans to register dietitians and train them in New Zealand; in consultation with the Home Science School it devised a hospital-based diploma course for people already qualified in home science or nursing. In 1951 home science dean Elizabeth Gregory noted 'a general improvement in the standard of hospital feeding' with 52 dietitians practising in this country. Their role was broader than elsewhere: 'As New Zealand has no training facilities for institutional cooks the dietitian must be able to teach and train the cooks and other staff.'[277]

By the 1990s the training of other health professions had shifted to the tertiary education sector, but the dietetics course was still run within the health sector; although New Zealand-trained dietitians had a good reputation and the Dietitians' Board was forward-thinking in developing 'competency-based' education, the profession needed to reform its training to align with current health and education policy. In 1991 the Dietitians' Board asked universities to submit proposals for dietetics education. Otago's proposal won and from 1993 the Human Nutrition Department offered a 15-month Postgraduate Diploma in Dietetics, with papers taught by distance education and clinical training in hospitals in the main centres.[278] The location of a professional course responsible to a professional body in a research-focused science department brought challenges, though there were synergies between the dietetics and human nutrition programmes. A 2010 review of dietetics identified the need for a stronger research base. In response to requests from the profession, a Master of Dietetics degree, specialising in either diabetes or gerontology nutrition, was introduced in 2009, but it failed to attract sufficient enrolments. In 2013 a restructured Master of Dietetics degree became the entry-level qualification: prospective dietitians completed a year of theoretical and clinical work in Dunedin, followed by a year of research and professional practice in another centre. The programme enhanced departmental research, but Otago lost its privileged position as sole provider of New Zealand's dietetics training; Auckland and Massey also offered masters programmes leading to registration as a dietitian.[279]

Meanwhile, scientific research in the Human Nutrition Department flourished. Mann added projects on macronutrients and their role in heart disease, diabetes and cancer: overnutrition had replaced undernutrition as a serious public health issue and Otago researchers worked increasingly in that area.[280] Micronutrients were not forgotten, though: Christine Thomson earned international recognition for her work on selenium and iodine, and in 1995 the department recruited Rosalind Gibson, acclaimed for her work on deficiencies – especially zinc – in low-income countries.[281] Staff were big players internationally – both Mann and Murray Skeaff served on the World Health Organization (WHO) Nutrition Advisory Group – and in 2004 Otago became a World Health Organization Collaborating Centre in Nutrition, joining an elite group with 16 other centres.[282] Human nutrition was one of several departments that contributed to the Edgar National Centre for Diabetes and Obesity Research, set up in 2003 with a vision of 'reducing the global burden of diabetes and obesity through research and dissemination of knowledge' (see chapter 10).[283] With nutrition

Home Science Extension reached out to thousands of New Zealanders beyond the university. These women are at the Countrywomen's School 'Towards 2000' in 1970.

EVENING STAR PHOTOGRAPH, FACULTY OF CONSUMER AND APPLIED SCIENCES RECORDS, 97-081/009, S17-610C, HOCKEN COLLECTIONS.

emerging in other New Zealand universities the department could not be complacent, but it had a proud record and was still the largest nutrition programme in Australasia.[284]

One group observed the development of human nutrition at Otago with mixed feelings: graduates of the Home Science School. 'I was very unpopular around the end of the 1980s,' says Mann; 'there was a strong feeling that removing nutrition from its home base was a major contributing factor to what was seen as the demise of home science.'[285] The end of a course that brought diverse subjects together under the concept of 'home' was inevitable with changing gender and career expectations. But the separating out of nutrition – which was increasingly identified as a health science – was a key moment: 'That's when in essence the School of Home Science disappeared,' says Carr.[286] Another key moment was in 1994 when Sadie Andrews, last remaining staff member of home science extension, retired. Andrews had joined a team of four based within University Extension in the late 1960s but was attached to the Home Science School from 1985, where she managed the information service: she answered letters and phone calls from all over New Zealand, updated the quantity recipe cards that were popular with institutions, conducted the annual food price survey (first carried out in the early 1970s) and produced radio programmes and publications. There was great demand for *Low Cost Healthy Meals*, put together with the community dietitian Moira Styles in response to benefit cuts. By the time Andrews retired, technology was changing the way the public gathered information – 'I think the talkback shows had taken it over in some ways,' she says – and the internet took off soon afterwards. But for over 60 years, before talkback radio and Google, the Home Science School had been a veritable treasure trove of information on many aspects of home life and had provided an important community service.[287] Home science left a legacy in Otago's human nutrition and food science programmes, but the last vestiges of it disappeared in 2012, one year after the centenary, when the university stopped accepting enrolments into its consumer and applied science degrees.[288] It was a quiet end for a concept that had been in decline for years but that had once drawn women from all over the country.

APPLYING AND COMMUNICATING SCIENCE

Although CAPS had died, the concept of 'applied science' flourished at Otago. In 2001 a four-year Bachelor of Applied Science (BAppSc) began, designed to link 'science, technology, innovation and entrepreneurship'.[289] It was a response to government and business calls for 'science and technology graduates who can relate to business and engage with it', as physicist Gerry Carrington, the programme's first director, explained.[290] It built on two interdisciplinary programmes started a couple of years earlier with 'industry needs in mind': energy management and environmental science.[291] Each BAppSc major was led by one or two existing departments, but a mandatory minor in a second subject – which might come from science, humanities or commerce – made it strongly interdisciplinary. All students took commerce papers such as courses in entrepreneurship and in managing innovation/growth; and the Business School contributed BAppSc majors in software engineering, spatial information and telecommunications through its Information Science Department, in collaboration with Computer Science.[292] Several science departments developed vocationally oriented courses. Other early BAppSc majors were applied geology, computational modelling, design for technology, electronics, geographic information systems, process technology and molecular biotechnology, and later additions included aquaculture and fisheries, food innovation, sport and exercise nutrition, clothing and textile sciences, consumer food science, forensic analytical science and sports technology.[293]

The degree was a success; scholarships funded by business attracted some outstanding students and the addition of work experience enhanced interaction with industry.[294] Not every major survived: process technology was an early casualty in 2005, electronics was dropped in 2011 and design technology met its demise along with Otago's other design programmes from 2016. From 2011 the BAppSc became a three-year degree and the compulsory commerce component was removed; and other postgrad options became available. A 2014 review concluded that Otago had 'the broadest and most developed Applied Science Programme in New Zealand'; it helped 'broaden the base of economic activity' in this country by educating people for 'highly skilled occupations', where they produced valuable ideas and products.[295]

Another twenty-first-century venture was science communication which, like applied science, produced people who went on to create innovative and high-end products. The subject arose in the Zoology Department, which already had an applied qualification in its Diploma in Wildlife Management, established in 1965. Designed for zoology graduates or people already working in the field, the wildlife diploma included options in wildlife administration, game management, bird conservation, noxious animal control and freshwater fisheries management. It did not attract large enrolments but it offered good job prospects; many alumni went on to work for the Department of Conservation. The course evolved and from 2000 students could progress to an MSc in wildlife management.[296]

Science communication was the brainchild of David Wharton, an Otago zoologist who was interested in organisms that were under extreme environmental stress, especially in Antarctica.[297] Wharton recommended that the university collaborate with Dunedin company Natural History New Zealand (NHNZ) on a course for filmmakers. For Michael Stedman, the CEO who developed the former Dunedin branch of Television New Zealand into a global documentary firm, it was about succession planning: 'I remember looking around this place and thinking, "Oooh, there are a lot of old farts ..." And then you do start to ask yourself where the new filmmakers are coming from.' Stedman had little respect for the media courses run by technical institutes; NHNZ needed 'people who were specialists in science and natural history', who also had skills in storytelling and the technical side of filmmaking.[298] Zoology academic Lloyd Spencer Davis was first director of the course, which was jointly taught with NHNZ. Like Wharton, Davis had research interests in the Antarctic, in his case in penguins; and he was an experienced filmmaker and had won awards for scriptwriting.[299]

The Postgraduate Diploma in Natural History Filmmaking and Communication began in 2001. It was the first tertiary natural history filmmaking course in the world and it immediately attracted international interest.[300] Davis was keen to expand the programme, and that became possible after the Stuart Residence Halls Council helped fund a chair in science communication under the Leading Thinkers scheme. In 2007 the chair was awarded to Davis and he was given a brief to develop a Centre for Science Communication. The university chipped in and appointed a second professor, Jean Fleming, a biologist with a passion for good communication. The centre was officially launched in 2008, as a Master of Science Communication commenced.[301] 'Somewhat remarkably,' Davis noted, 'the Centre is the first institution devoted to science communication in New Zealand – and one of only a few in the world to tackle the area of popularising science in such a comprehensive manner.' Students specialised in filmmaking, writing, or popularising science; the latter incorporated online digital media and exhibition design, taught in association with Otago Museum.[302] The programme attracted high-achieving students and by 2014 the first PhD students were making good progress.[303] The early entry into an emerging field brought 'considerable credit both to the Department of Zoology, of which it is a part, and to the University of Otago', a 2012 review found. Graduates won numerous awards and went on to successful careers, some of them at NHNZ, making it a

Anthony Robins teaching in the robotics lab in 2012 with Otago student Louis Lepper (left) and Philip Anderson of Kings' High School (right). They are training for the Robocup soccer event. The Computer Science Department, like several other departments, had an active outreach to secondary schools, helping to recruit the next generation of students. Robins was a leading researcher in computer science education.

TUSHAR ROBINS PHOTOGRAPH, ANTHONY ROBINS COLLECTION.

successful collaboration. The centre engaged well with the public, and its ScienceTeller Festival, a gala showing of students' natural history films, is a popular Dunedin event.[304]

INTERDISCIPLINARY PROJECTS

Increasingly, funders favoured collaboration between disciplines: the applied sciences were not the only interdisciplinary ventures in science at Otago. The Psychology Department initiated discussions for a programme in neuroscience that was offered for BSc (Hons) from 1988 and was later developed into a full undergraduate and postgraduate subject. It aimed 'to produce graduates with a broad knowledge of all aspects of the structure and function of the nervous system and of its contribution to behaviour and mental functions'. Neuroscience drew together existing papers and a few additions, using Otago expertise from anatomy, biochemistry, computer science, pharmacology, physiology, psychology and zoology.[305] Cognitive science started a couple of years later as an MSc major; it was a purely postgraduate programme. Led by psychologist Geoffrey White, it incorporated anatomy, anthropology, computer science, information science and philosophy. Cognitive science was popular overseas, but Otago's was the first programme in New Zealand to focus on an emerging field concerned with 'how biological and electronic systems represent and use knowledge'. One contributor was Anthony Robins, appointed jointly by psychology and computer science as 'new blood' lecturer in artificial intelligence.[306]

When freshwater ecologist Colin Townsend became head of the Zoology Department in 1989 he noted that there was a lot of study and research in the field of ecology at the university, prompted by New Zealand's unusual wildlife, and by the importance of the natural environment to tourism. There was expertise in this area in the botany, zoology, marine science, geology, geography, statistics and biochemistry departments, but there was not much interaction between them. Townsend advocated for an ecology major, which was offered from 1991. A 'research theme' in ecology, biodiversity and conservation promoted further collaboration.[307] Genetics, which had been available through interdisciplinary undergraduate papers since 1972, achieved full status as a major in 2000, demonstrating 'that Otago is somewhere that concentrates on Genetics and has a special competence in it', according to long-time lecturer Russell Poulter. Botany, microbiology, pathology, paediatrics and zoology all contributed. Microbiologist Clive Ronson was appointed to a chair in genetics in 2003, and from 2008 the programme worked with anatomy on a Bachelor of Biomedical Sciences major in reproduction, genetics and development.[308]

MARINE SCIENCE EMERGES

Many interdisciplinary programmes had a biological angle: 'The amount of biology that goes on in Otago is just astounding,' suggests Townsend. There was a worldwide trend for universities to bring biological disciplines together in larger units for economy of scale, but at Otago that would have created an unwieldy entity. There were discussions about mergers but none eventuated: Otago was unique in New Zealand in retaining independent departments of botany and zoology as well as microbiology, biochemistry, pharmacology, anatomy and physiology.[309] Otago bucked the trend further in creating a Department of Marine Science. In 1982 the Portobello Marine Laboratory, led by John Jillett, launched one of the university's first interdisciplinary degrees, an MSc in marine science that incorporated physical oceanography, marine chemistry and geology, and marine biology. The university anticipated growth in marine science as fisheries resource management became imperative. In 1986 it established an Aquaculture Research Centre and in 1989 Philip Mladenov, whose expertise extended from invertebrate biology to aquaculture practice, arrived from Canada to become Otago's first marine science professor.[310] In 1992 marine science was promoted to a full department, bringing together the marine lab, aquarium and postgraduate programme, with a base on the main campus.[311]

With no undergraduate course, marine science was an unusual department. It ventured into the undergraduate world in 1999 through an alliance with the Geology Department, which had lost enrolments after the departure of mineral technology. The first-year paper 'Earth and ocean science' was a hit and many students advanced in geology or marine science studies. Marine science gradually added more papers and, from 2007, contributed an aquaculture and fisheries major for BAppSc.[312] A BSc major took longer: from 2014 Otago students could select oceanography, which focused on the physical sciences; those interested in marine biology were advised to major in ecology, zoology or botany, with a minor in marine science.[313] Marine science incorporated the physical sciences, and in 1996, under the leadership of chemistry professor Keith Hunter (later AVC Sciences), Otago set up a Research Centre for Oceanography in collaboration with the National Institute of Water and Atmospheric Research (NIWA); and in 2011 the centre won the Prime Minister's Science Prize.[314] The centre benefited from the acquisition in 2006 of the *Polaris II*, funded through the Leading Thinkers initiative and gifts from philanthropic trusts. The former fishing vessel was transformed into a fully fitted lab, suited for research trips as far as the subantarctic islands.[315]

THE MODERN PHYSICAL SCIENCES

The physical sciences were still at the core of many science degrees. Enrolments relied partly on the provision of 'service' courses, and when other departments altered prerequisites it could have a big impact on student numbers. When the health sciences dropped a biostatistics paper in 2004, for example, the Maths and Statistics Department lost a quarter of its first-year enrolments and two vacant positions were not filled.[316] The Physics Department, which for years had been concerned about the threat to drop physics as a requirement for health sciences, instead ended up teaching a new biological physics paper for first-year health science students from 2007. That paper accounted for around 60 per cent of physics enrolments and required big resources; it was rated 'excellent' in a 2009 review of the department.[317] The funding environment worked well for most physical sciences: 'our long tradition of research culture has allowed a painless adaption to the incentives of PBRF', the Physics Department claimed.[318] Maths and statistics faced a bigger challenge: Peter Fenton, head at the time, says the department had a longstanding and 'monolithic' culture that prioritised teaching and service, and many staff were not active researchers. The first PBRF results prompted a special review that led to a reduction in papers taught – this freed time for research, and some staff departed. The culture changed as 'hotshots' with a passion for research joined the staff and drew others to work with them. Teaching was not forgotten, but fitted better with the 'research-led teaching' model.[319]

The Physics Department's long interest in the interactions between light and atoms evolved in the 1990s with the search for the Bose Einstein condensate. Andrew Wilson, Rob Ballagh and Crispin Gardiner established a group in ultracold atoms at Otago – one of the first in the world to produce the new state of matter. Success attracted other researchers and funding, including a large FoRST grant after the Jack Dodd Centre for Quantum Technology was set up in 2006. That collaboration with the University of Auckland became the larger multi-institutional Dodd-Walls Centre for Photonic and Quantum Technologies in 2014; it was the first of the government's Centres of Research Excellence to be hosted by Otago.[320]

Geology, previously at the mercy of 'hand to mouth' research funding, seemed suddenly 'flush with funds' after two large grants from the Public Good Science Fund in the 1990s, said Norris.[321] That allowed the purchase of sophisticated equipment such as a supercooled magnetometer, the first of its type in the southern hemisphere, installed in 2003: the paleomagnetic research facility headed by Gary Wilson used it to measure fossil magnetism in rocks and sediments and analyse historic environmental changes.[322] Rick Sibson, who joined the Geology Department in 1990, was a Fellow of the Royal Society of London and one of the most accomplished scientists to work at Otago; he 'revolutionised structural geology by illustrating that fault rocks contain an integrated record of earthquakes'.[323] A generous gift by a retired staff member who wished to remain anonymous, along with other donations, enabled a chair in earthquake science to be established. Mark Stirling took up the chair in 2016 and headed a multidisciplinary collaboration in earthquake science – a field New Zealanders had become all too aware of.[324] Geology researchers were among those who used the plasma-source mass spectrometers at the Centre for Trace Element Analysis, established by the Chemistry Department in 2007 with a Leading Thinkers grant from the Otago Community Trust.[325] Chemistry was, as ever, one of Otago's largest departments in student numbers and in research.[326]

SCIENCES OF COMPUTING AND THE BRAIN

Otago's founders might not be surprised if they could see the flourishing biological and physical sciences as the institution approached its 150th year, but the emergence of a fresh discipline based on technology might be a shock. Otago's two computing departments – computer science and the Commerce Division's information science – regularly had to justify an idiosyncratic split that had started in Otago's early years of computing. A review of the Computer Science Department in 2010 noted that the arrangement had been 'clarified, is now well understood, and serves as a basis for a collegial relationship'.[327] By the 1990s computing was pervasive: all academics needed to learn about it. From 1996 the computing departments offered a combined first-year paper designed for all disciplines, which immediately became the most popular course on campus.[328] By the late 1990s, student numbers in computer science had tripled; they then declined before stabilising, in line with a worldwide trend. Retaining postgraduates was challenging with the counter-attraction of a lucrative job market, but the quality and quantity of research students slowly grew.[329] Research in the 1990s centred on artificial intelligence, computer graphics and databases. The arrival of Mike Atkinson as professor in 2000 prompted a theory group that studied 'foundational questions into what can or cannot be computed and what resources a computation needs', and a research group on information retrieval was added later.[330]

The potential for consultancy and product development was huge. From 1970 onwards the department had the responsibility of verifying the results of the draws conducted by 'Elsie', the Bonus Bonds computer. In the early 1990s it worked on projects for wool manufacturers.[331] When work on a three-year contract with Alliance Textiles ended in 1995, the programmers concerned became an applied research unit known as Black Albatross, which was attached to the university for 10 years before it was sold.[332] Meanwhile, an entire industry arose from animated graphics software that Geoff Wyvill had designed in the 1980s. The graphics research group 'bubble[d] with creativity' and 'mild eccentricity'. It worked on graphics for Television New Zealand, such as the titles for *University Challenge*, and in 1989 it entered into a collaboration with Ian Taylor, an Otago law graduate and television presenter who had just established a production company for corporate videos and regional television advertisements. In 1992 Taylormade bought out the university's share in the venture and established Animation Research Ltd, which became famous for its 3D sports graphics; it also worked on innovative projects in air traffic control and for Māori businesses. Computer science at Otago retained its links with the company through Wyvill, who was still a director, and many of its staff came from the department.[333]

The thriving state of psychology would surprise the founders less, since it was part of the original discipline of mental and moral philosophy. The modern department became Otago's poster child for research success. Graham Goddard, an experimental psychologist known for the discovery of kindling – an important model in the study of epilepsy – arrived from Canada 'like a whirlwind' as head of department in 1981. He developed the department's strength in neuroscience and interactions with the medical sciences, and brought its research culture to life before his death in a tramping accident in 1987.[334] The research momentum carried on under his successor, Geoffrey White. The department targeted enthusiastic researchers when making appointments, and set ambitious goals.[335] The university administration took note of psychology's external grants, numerous publications and high rankings, and used its leaders to spread that research culture to other departments. White became DVC (Research) in 2004, and another leader from the department, Harlene Hayne, succeeded him as DVC in 2009.[336] Postgrads made 'an enormously important contribution to the research life at Otago, both in terms of their energy and bright ideas,' White noted on his appointment as DVC; they were the 'secret weapon' in a burgeoning Psychology Department with poor staff–student ratios.[337]

The early development of computer-based labs was key to the smooth running of the department. It created its own local area network (LAN) – its premises, scattered around old houses and prefabs, lacked sufficient links to Otago's VAX computer – and wrote software and manuals for a first-year lab course used from 1986. The lecturer trained postgrads to conduct the labs and, because only one demonstrator was needed per class, it could cope with the big demand for enrolments. The first-year course was designed as 'a showcase for the discipline of psychology': it featured lectures from the department's top academics alongside the experimental labs.[338] Psychology got a glowing report at its 2011 review: it had 'rightly earned its reputation as a high performance department, particularly in research, where it has been both a New Zealand and University leader.' Just as importantly, it was 'a good place to work; they respect each other and support each other.'[339] It was the perfect environment for producing senior administrators for the university.

CHAPTER EIGHT

Commerce

Commerce has the most recent origins of Otago's academic divisions. In a 1988 history Tom Cowan wrote of its struggle for recognition: the development of commerce subjects required 'both academic justifications and a battle for resources'. Later commerce 'served a useful role within the University as a financial "milking cow"', Cowan said, though he conceded that universities realised it was 'in their best long-term interests to foster a well-managed and profitable business sector in New Zealand'.[1] Students certainly valued commerce qualifications: the growth of the business disciplines was one of the biggest changes to the university in the twentieth century.

ECONOMICS AT THE BEGINNING

Economics, which was later absorbed into the Commerce Division, dated from Otago's foundation, when it was known as political economy: in a place where theories of colonisation had been implemented and a goldrush had recently occurred, people were especially conscious of economic theory. Conrad Blyth, a distinguished Otago economics graduate, notes that in the nineteenth century economics was an 'intellectual' discipline and was considered 'part of a general education'.[2] In Otago's early years it came under the umbrella of mental and moral philosophy, whose first professor, Duncan MacGregor, offered a course combining ethics and economics to senior students. By the late 1870s political economy was a stand-alone course.[3] In 1881 the new professor of English, John Mainwaring Brown, took over political economy; he taught a course covering the nature and history of economic science; the production of wealth; the distribution of wealth; attempts to improve the present system of distribution; the exchange of wealth; and the economic functions of governments.[4] Various lecturers taught economics after Mainwaring Brown's death in 1888, but gaps between appointments meant it wasn't always available. From 1895 to 1906 Frederick Gibbons, mathematics professor at Otago since 1886, also served as economics lecturer. Gibbons was renowned for his wizardry with figures and, though some students found him an uninspiring lecturer, others reported he was able 'to make even "the dismal science" entertaining and attractive'.[5]

EXPANDING INTO COMMERCE

In 1907 Otago appointed one of its star graduates, Harry Bedford, as political economy lecturer; he later added history and law to his portfolio, and was promoted to a chair of economics and history in 1915. Some New Zealand business leaders wanted university education in commerce – inspired by the founding of a Faculty of Commerce at Birmingham University in 1901, the first such venture in the British Empire.[6] Leading Dunedin accountant Peter Barr later noted that some older universities had declared that 'business is none of our business', but 'happily in New Zealand we are free from the prejudice that would separate the business man from the University'.[7] Auckland and Canterbury wanted commerce schools and in 1904 the University of New Zealand approved a Bachelor of Commerce (BCom), based on the Birmingham syllabus. It required economics, accounting, a language (French or German), maths (or another of the physical sciences), history, geography, commercial law and statistical methods, along with two more specialised subjects from a list that included actuarial mathematics, industrial law, economic history or currency and banking.[8] Since Otago did not teach all those subjects the BCom was not initially available in the south, but economics courses here were adjusted to fit its requirements. The 'mini-revolution' of the BCom 'launched economics as a major academic subject in the University of New Zealand', according to Blyth.[9]

Accountants instigated commerce education at Otago. In the 1890s New Zealand accountants established two associations, which joined to form the New Zealand Society of Accountants (NZSA) in 1908. The NZSA was required by legislation 'to control and regulate the practice of accountancy in New Zealand'; and it managed entry to the profession with exams. In 1911 the enterprising NZSA negotiated with the University of New Zealand for the university to run its entry exams, and the university amended the BCom syllabus to meet the NZSA qualifying requirements.[10] The NZSA offered a five-year subsidy to each of the university colleges and this, supplemented with a matching government subsidy plus student fees, enabled Otago to offer commerce.[11] In 1912 young Dunedin accountant George Reid, recently graduated BCom with honours through Victoria, became Otago's first part-time accounting lecturer, and economics lecturer Bedford added the required business law classes. The classes met a need, and 46 students enrolled in the first year.[12] In 1915 NZSA president James Brown expressed pleasure that accountants were now 'hall-marked with the stamp of the University'; the connection 'at once placed Accountancy in the category of the learned professions'.[13]

THE ACCOUNTANTS' NIGHT SCHOOL

Aspiring accountants did not have to complete a degree, or even attend university; many prepared for exams through institutions like Banks' Commercial College in Wellington, which advertised 'postal tuition'.[14] The Otago courses were attractive, though, because their students excelled in external exams.[15] In 1913 Barr, the NZSA president, expressed hope that 'the connection between the commercial student and the University should become still more real'; a student would be 'made more fit for success in his chosen vocation, through the culture and breadth of outlook, added to the special knowledge acquired during a University course'.[16] However, most commerce students were content with just the courses required for NZSA entry; by 1920 only five Otago students had graduated BCom. The first, in 1915, was Owen Wilkinson, who immediately signed on with the Field Artillery and headed to Gallipoli; he later presided over the Canterbury Chamber of Commerce.[17] The war led to a big drop in commerce enrolments, then a jump in 1919 as a wave of returned servicemen attended classes.

The story was different for women. Otago's first woman commerce student enrolled in 1914 and by 1917 there were 13. Reid reported that 'during the latter part of the war period, exceptional opportunities opened up for women in the more advanced branches of commercial work', with a 'large number of women seeking to

The Otago University Commerce Faculty Association in 1922.
PATERSON AND LANG RECORDS, 83-070 BOX 3, S16-571A, HOCKEN COLLECTIONS.

qualify themselves by attendance at the classes in commerce'. In 1920 female enrolments fell; 'evidently the reinstatement of returned soldiers in commercial occupations has made commercial training less attractive to women,' Reid noted. The faculty wanted to attract women, and emphasised in the 1920 calendar that classes were 'open to persons of *both sexes*, without restriction as to age or occupation'. That had little effect: by the time World War II broke out there were nine women studying alongside 118 men. Once again there was a drop in enrolments in commerce during the war, followed by a postwar surge.[18]

For the first five decades commerce classes were held outside business hours to suit both students and lecturers, who were practising accountants and lawyers. Cowan, a student of the 1930s and lecturer from the 1940s, noted they 'shivered through law lectures in the early mornings and … at the end of the day returned to their desks in the Lower Oliver classroom to study accounting'.[19] The part-timer 'dissipates his energy for eight hours a day in an office' and 'approaches his study with a weary mind', an anonymous commerce student noted in the 1946 *Review*; students had to develop an 'orderly and efficient' attitude – advantageous in the commercial world – and had 'little time for the frivolities and interests so precious to the average student'.[20] The part-time lecturers dedicated many years of service to the university. James ('JM') Paterson, who took over the commercial law lecturing from Bedford in 1918, was one example of this. He lectured 'six days a week at 7.45 a.m.; he always walked down from his home in Tennyson Street, and was known to be late only once'. After the lecture Paterson walked home for breakfast, then proceeded to his day job as leading partner in an established Dunedin law firm.[21] The early lecturers were not, of course, without flaws. Alfred ('Freddie') Thomas, manager of the Dunedin Savings Bank and Otago accounting lecturer from 1932, resigned suddenly in 1947.[22] A 1969 history of the faculty reported that Thomas was disabled from World War I service and therefore 'took a direct and personal interest in the rehabilitation of returned men after 1945; his enthusiasm for this work led him into conflict with various authorities'.[23] A less sanitised source reveals he was accused of embezzling bank funds, something not desirable in a man who was educating accountants.[24]

BEYOND ACCOUNTING

Accounting dominated commerce at Otago, though early on there were attempts to broaden the programme. In 1920 Reid, the dean, suggested that 'an extension of the scope of the Faculty' was necessary: the 'recent formation of guilds by those engaged in Banking, in Shipping, and in Insurance, each with "Education" as a strong plank in its platform shows clearly the growing demand for more specialised training'. The University of New Zealand approved a Diploma in Banking in response to a suggestion from the Bank Officers' Guild, and there were a few Otago candidates.[25] The BCom regulations were amended in 1927 to allow students to specialise in accountancy, banking, or industry and trade (though nobody offered the industry and trade papers, so it's unlikely anyone took that specialisation).[26] In the 1940s the University of New Zealand turned down a request from the NZSA to introduce a Bachelor of Accounting degree. It agreed to further BCom amendments, but not to a name change that would reduce its capacity to cater for other professions.[27] Accounting's close relation, auditing, was part of the accountancy major. Reid taught auditing alongside bookkeeping until 1932, when it got its first specialist lecturer, Lewis McIver, who was simultaneously head of the King Edward Technical College commercial department – a competing institution. Scott Gilkison, who was known for classes that were 'lively and full of interesting examples from his work days in the profession' and his 'uncanny knack … of asking a question of someone who was just about to drop off to sleep', succeeded McIver in 1954.[28]

While a series of part-timers taught commerce subjects, economics had a dedicated professor from 1919. After Bedford died in 1918 the University Council made short-term arrangements 'until more settled times are reached'. The retired Selwyn warden Robert Woodthorpe, a scholar of economics and philosophy, became lecturer, but the council decided economics and history warranted more attention. They gave Woodthorpe the status of acting professor of economics in 1919 and appointed professors in both disciplines in 1920.[29] Scotsman William Pringle became Otago's economics professor, but did not last long; he departed on compassionate leave in 1922 to be with his sick son in Britain, and did not return. He resigned his position but later withdrew that resignation; but the council, which discovered he had stood for parliament in Britain while on leave, decided not to take him back.[30] The trusty Woodthorpe, who had been relieving, held a fixed-term appointment as economics professor until 1924, when he was replaced by Allan Fisher, a New Zealand-born and Australian-raised graduate of the London School of Economics, just 29 years old.[31]

The economics professor had a large brief: Fisher noted 'the arduous and widely varied work which we had to attempt to cover in providing teaching in all the options required for the examinations of the University of New Zealand' in a testimonial for Geoffry Billing, who assisted him as lecturer from 1930. 'The pressure of ordinary work in Dunedin is usually such as seriously to limit the opportunities for independent research,' wrote Fisher.[32] Nevertheless, by Otago standards, the economists were impressive in research, publication and public engagement. From 1919 until 1946 the economics professors all served as directors of the Workers' Educational Association (see chapter 12).[33] In the early 1930s Fisher and Billing both won prestigious Rockefeller Fellowships to study abroad, and Fisher also took a year's leave to act as economic adviser to the Bank of New South Wales. The two men forged a 'strong collegial atmosphere' with their students, Colin Simkins recalled (Simkins was a star graduate who became professor at Auckland and then at Sydney University).[34] One of New Zealand's earliest PhDs was earned in the Economics Department at Otago by Walter Boraman in 1929; he researched the history of public finance in New Zealand.[35] It was more common, however, to head overseas for further study. Ralph Souter – 'surely the only distinguished pure theorist [in economics] New Zealand has produced', according to Blyth – completed an MA in philosophy and another in economics at Otago before heading to Columbia University in 1928.

The 1933 Commerce Faculty ball, held in the Dunedin Town Hall Concert Chamber. Though early commerce students had little contact with students from other faculties, their own association organised social events, including an annual dinner and ball and rugby matches against the law faculty; debating flourished in the 1920s and by the 1930s there was an annual post-exam fancy-dress party at the Gardens tea kiosk.
BOX 237-005, S16-548C, HOCKEN COLLECTIONS.

After studying and lecturing there he returned to Otago in 1936 as economics professor.[36]

In 1940 Souter's chair became the Donald Reid chair to mark a legacy from that southern businessman.[37] Souter died young in 1946, just as the department was dealing with the postwar influx of students. His successor, Billing, revealed in a letter to Fisher the straitened circumstances the department had been under. Billing was delighted they were moving to one of the professorial houses, where he and lecturer Harro Bernardelli had 'rooms to ourselves and the 2 Assts share one … We have a telephone & for next year £20 for Deptl library, £100 special equipment grant for filing cabinets, typewriter, etc & the "Economist" to be sent out by air mail. I can hardly believe that the spirit of progress can really have achieved so much.'[38]

Like accounting, economics was a male domain, with the occasional exception. In the wake of Souter's death, 'we have a part time girl doing the Economic History', Billing noted; and Valerie Seymour (later Muir), who won the Macandrew Scholarship in economics for 1946, was assistant lecturer from 1947 to 1950.[39]

THE FULL-TIME COMMERCE REVOLUTION

In 1952 Billing, previously dean of the Arts Faculty, became dean of the Commerce Faculty. Economics had long participated in both faculties, though it was administered through Arts. Billing wanted a combined faculty of economics and commerce but didn't find support for the idea; Cowan wrote much later that 'there was some fear of dominance by Economics, as indeed happened in some universities overseas.'[40] Economics had a professor and other full-time staff, plus BA students, while accounting and commercial law had no full-time staff and scarcely any full-time or degree students. Change was in the wind, though

Billing did not witness it: the 'wise and tolerant' professor died suddenly in 1959. Cowan, who with Jim Valentine was mainstay of the accounting staff after Thomas's downfall in the 1940s, became the dean of the Commerce Faculty.[41] More importantly, he became commerce's first full-time staff member and was promoted to a chair of accountancy in 1961. Support for the change was not unanimous: 'accounting cannot be taught adequately, effectively and with confidence unless it is also practised', according to a faculty committee that included Cowan in 1957. Still, 'a part-time teacher could do little more than teach; he lacked time for research, reading and thinking,' as a Sheffield academic told Billing when he investigated commerce degrees overseas.[42] Cowan became head of the new Department of Accountancy, comprising all of the faculty minus economics (in 1970 it was renamed the Department of Business Studies, also known as the School of Business).[43] He set up in an office 'right under the clock tower, then in a shaky condition. Perhaps there was some hope that an Act of God might crush the Commerce intruder and his fledgling Department, and, with him, the threatening aspirations of his Faculty.'[44]

In 1962 commerce classes shifted to daytime, part of a strategy to recruit full-time and degree students; it was a response to the 1960 Parry Report, which criticised the high attrition rates associated with part-time study, especially in commerce faculties.[45] With evenings free from lectures, the faculty added evening tutorials and course standards rose. Firms hesitated to employ part-time students as they needed to be released during business hours; full-time study became more attractive.[46] Accountants had mixed feelings about the changes, but the NZSA reviewed its entry standards; from 1988 accountants had to complete a degree or diploma prior to professional exams.[47] Like the university as a whole, the commerce faculty expanded rapidly in the 1960s: the roll more than doubled from 238 to 580 and full-timers rose from eight to 66 per cent of the total. By 1970 there were also 92 external students, mostly in Invercargill (see chapter 10).[48] Growth encouraged the faculty to offer more subjects; it was a virtuous circle, since more subjects attracted more students. From 1961 Otago had freedom to structure its own degrees (though approval of a central curriculum committee was still required); that aided the expansion.

DEVELOPING NEW SUBJECTS

The first addition to the curriculum was management, advocated by Billing and Cowan since the 1950s. The BCom provided 'inadequate preparation for enterprise leadership', wrote Cowan; 'high standards of management' were important for individual businesses and the wider economy. Billing convinced the University Council in 1959 that management could 'be made a suitable university discipline'; even Cambridge had recently approved a course. While Cowan lobbied for a lecturer, requests came from other departments for a course to prepare their graduates for management responsibilities. In 1962 he taught what was, 'so far as I am aware ... the first course in Management offered at a New Zealand university'.[49] Sixteen mining students completed a unit in 'industrial management', while 45 from medicine, home science, technology and commerce attended 'administration', 'for the benefit particularly of final-year students and graduates who will be undertaking administrative tasks'.[50]

With the arrival of Adolf Diegel as Otago's first management lecturer late in 1962 the subject gathered momentum. He started with two papers on 'the theory and practice of organisation' and 'the function and use of quantitative techniques to aid in management decisions'. Student enrolments 'exceeded our expectations' and advanced studies in human organisation, production management, marketing management and business policy were added.[51] Diegel, a German who completed postgraduate qualifications in Oregon, was a contrast to his conservative commerce colleagues. Cowan recorded his difficulty in 'associating the man with the long and bushy black beard with the fresh-faced young man in the photograph which accompanied his application'. Diegel and his family eschewed suburbia for an isolated small holding on Mt Cargill and Cowan evidently found his lifestyle a challenge, though he credited him as an 'intelligent and stimulating' teacher. Diegel departed Otago in 1968.[52] Finding staff was challenging: 'We in New Zealand have not been preparing graduates for full-time teaching in Commerce, and it will take some years to remedy this deficiency', said the dean in 1962.[53] The recruiting problem persisted for decades as Otago competed with 'a keen world demand for university teachers' and 'profitable career opportunities in business'.[54] The 1974 OUSA handbook was blunt about the Commerce Faculty: 'Teaching standards are not always good, since the business world, that big fat sugar-daddy, tends to lure away the good people.'[55]

The next commerce subject to be introduced was marketing, initially within management. Wilfred White was recruited as marketing lecturer; when his arrival was delayed Cowan taught the advertised 1966 course 'with the aid of brief topic outlines and references set out in aerogrammes by Mr White'. It was, Cowan believed, 'the first set of lectures in Marketing Management at a New Zealand university'.[56] Though it was initially taught as an advanced subject, marketing attracted many students and quickly expanded. In 1975 it emerged from management's oversight to become a BCom major. The first marketing professor, Guenther Mueller-Heumann, arrived in 1976 to discover that 'rather entrepreneurial' Otago staff had 'experimented with the course structure and contents', making it 'trendy and attractive for the politically aware student of the day' but moving it from its business roots. He took it in a more professional direction.[57] Marketing could not, however, escape student interest in its social aspects. Rob Lawson, who began a long career in the department in 1987, notes that marketing is a synthetic discipline, bringing together aspects of economics, psychology and sociology in particular; it attracted students from the humanities and sciences, who were not so interested in business. For some, such as physical education students who wanted to run the Rugby Union, marketing was a strategic addition to improve their career prospects. With its wide appeal, it become one of Otago's largest departments.[58]

Another BCom major added in 1975 was computer systems. In 1966, when the university installed an IBM 360/30 computer, the Commerce Faculty was anxious to 'include more work for our students in this relatively new but very important field' and immediately developed demonstration programmes for management and accounting students.[59] In 1970 it offered its first specialist computing paper as part of 'Analytical methods 2'.[60] Brian Cox, director of the Computer Centre, taught this in addition to computer science classes for the Science Faculty. Commerce's first dedicated computing lecturer, Alan Thomas, took up his post in 1972, and by 1974 there were a dozen students in 'Computer systems 3'. Accounting students were 'quick to see the advantage of a "double major" in both fields', wrote Cowan.[61]

Like marketing, management was a synthetic discipline that attracted a range of students, and its staff had varied backgrounds. The University Council approved a chair in management in 1969 and, as anticipated, it proved difficult to fill.[62] Phillip Rossell commenced as professor late in 1971; he was an industrial and economic historian who had acquired management expertise through training and 'manpower' organisation in a large British enterprise.[63] Management briefly had two professors: in 1970 Otago had also appointed Frank Pao-Shan Lu to 'a Personal Chair in Quantitative aspects of Management, in recognition not only of his own abilities but also of the importance of this field of study'.[64] Lu was a Chinese engineer who taught at Canterbury, which recruited him back after a couple of years. Kerr Inkson, a Scotsman appointed as lecturer in 1970, brought expertise in occupational psychology. He later taught for many years at Auckland, but he returned to Otago

Alan MacGregor teaching an honours accounting class, around 1985.
DEPARTMENT OF ACCOUNTANCY AND FINANCE COLLECTION.

as management professor in 2005. Alan Geare – another future management professor – arrived in 1972 as an expert in industrial relations; he was an Otago economics graduate who taught at Victoria.[65] The management academics recruited in the early 1970s were 'a quite strong and varied teaching team'.[66] There were few doctorates among commerce staff, but as it became clear that such qualifications improved opportunities, they enrolled in higher degrees.[67] Inkson was awarded Otago's first PhD in management in 1980, and the first PhD in accounting went to longtime staff member Boris Popoff in 1978. Hank Wolfe earned the first computer studies PhD in 1990, 21 years into his Otago career. And when marketing awarded its first four PhDs in 1994, three went to existing lecturers: Park Beede, John Cossens and Brendan Gray.[68]

Accounting, where it all started, remained popular. Although it was still professionally oriented, it developed courses for commerce students who were not planning to progress in accounting. 'Analysis of accounting data' was introduced in 1961, and 'Financing of business operations' in 1964; in 1968 they were combined as 'Financial management'. Finance became part of the first-year accounting course for the first time in 1975 and, that year, the department changed its name to Accounting and Finance. Accounting staff, like others in commerce, had difficulty keeping up with a rapidly expanding student roll. This was aggravated by the professor's long-standing service as dean; Cowan filled that role from 1960 to 1975. A second chair in accounting and finance was approved in 1978, but was not filled until Kenneth Moores arrived from Australia in 1984. Meanwhile Cowan retired in 1981, and Lyall McLean, who had been lecturing at Otago for 10 years, succeeded him in the original accounting chair; he took over leadership of a department that became the university's largest in 1982.[69]

SPLITTING DEPARTMENTS

Rossell was strongly business orientated and he set up a Business Development Centre in 1972, shortly after he arrived. The centre received funding from a government keen to advance regional development.[70] It soon had half a dozen staff, and in 1975 Rossell reported it had assisted over 100 firms, undertaken 'a massive Regional Resources Survey for South Canterbury' and expanded into Christchurch in association with Lu and the University of Canterbury, all 'without financial cost to the University'.[71] A cutback in government funding from 1976 led to temporary downsizing, but there was still a steady demand for the service. It later expanded into the small-business sector, but reported to University Extension rather than to the Commerce Faculty.[72] There was a serious personality clash between Rossell and Cowan, and in 1972 the VC asked Hugh Parton, recently retired as PVC and chemistry professor, to look into the matter. When Parton's mediation efforts failed the council formed a committee to look more broadly at the organisation of the Business School. In 1973 the Department of Business Studies was split into three: the Department of Accounting and Finance, headed by Cowan; the Department of Management, headed by Rossell; and the

VC Robin Irvine (right) and his wife Elizabeth (Bunty) Irvine, a physiology lecturer, talk with accounting and finance honours students Graeme Tapp and Bronwyn Donaldson at a Commerce Division function in the mid-1980s.
DEPARTMENT OF ACCOUNTANCY AND FINANCE COLLECTION.

Department of Marketing, Quantitative Methods and Computer Systems (MQCS).[73] Commerce was not the only field where personal animosities or ambitions prompted restructuring, but it happened more there, perhaps reflecting the cut-throat business world some staff came from. In 1978 MQCS split into the Marketing Department and the Quantitative and Computer Studies (QCS) Department. And in 1991, the finance staff from the Accounting and Finance Department and the quantitative staff from Quantitative and Computer Studies got together to form the Department of Finance and Quantitative Studies.[74]

Those rearrangements were enabled by the growth of the Commerce Faculty: it accelerated in the 1980s and outpaced other faculties. When the university was restructured into divisions in 1989 the Commerce Division, which included economics, accounted for 23 per cent of the Otago roll. It reached its highest point – 23.5 per cent of Otago students – in 1990, before growth in other divisions outdid it; the commerce roll peaked at 3712 full-time equivalent students in 2004 then started a slow decline.[75] There were several reasons for the growth of commerce in the 1980s: more emphasis on business as neoliberal politics gained sway; a disproportionate growth in salaries for business professionals; and – perhaps least recognised as a cause – second-wave feminism. There were no formal barriers to women's entry into accounting, but there were plenty of informal ones. In 1971 three per cent of NZSA members were women.[76] When most commerce students were aspiring accountants, that affected the gender balance: only 5 per cent of Otago's 1970 commerce enrolments were women. But an 'important trend', as Cowan described it, was about to begin. By 1977 – the year when the Human Rights Act outlawed discrimination on the basis of gender – a quarter of first-year commerce students were female; and by 1986 women made up 39 per cent of all commerce students.[77] Some women were attracted to the additional subjects offered, but accounting also drew them: by the 1990s half of those joining the accounting profession in New Zealand were women.[78] The cultural shift in women's employment choices had a direct effect on the growth of the Commerce Faculty.

Hank Wolfe, a computer expert and escapee from the rat-race of corporate Washington DC, arrived in the QCS Department in 1979; he is pictured here with the Commerce Faculty's first computer, a Digital Equipment Corporation PDP 11/34, acquired that same year. Wolfe recalls teaching students COBOL and FORTRAN, and large classes lined up to process their 'mark sense' cards (filled out with pencil, the next step up from the original punch card system).

ANDREW BOND PHOTOGRAPH, HANK WOLFE COLLECTION.

INFORMATION SCIENCE

Until the late 1970s, commerce students and staff took their punchcards to the university's central computer and returned with data printouts, but in 1979 the faculty took delivery of its own machine. It was its 'most important piece of equipment' to date declared the dean, Roger Johnson; it 'allowed senior students first hand experience in the management and operation of a computer of a size typical in New Zealand business organisations'.[79] QCS lecturers Drew Bond and Gan Tzu Jong adapted or wrote the necessary software, and soon 300 Stage 1 accounting students were completing 'simple accounting functions' on the computer, and senior QCS students were developing programs.[80] Numbers rose in the first-year course on 'the commercial use of computers', but in 1984 there were 'at least 3 positions available for each student graduated'. The department was concerned at 'the relatively low number of students attracted to Information Systems'. Some students didn't continue in the subject 'due to frustration with computer facilities' – so upgrading was a priority.[81] QCS acquired its first personal computer in 1980, a Southwest Technical Products Motorola 6809; it set it up as a word processor, and soon added other PCs. The Accounting Department, meanwhile, purchased a couple of Apple IIe computers in 1983 for its senior students' financial modelling projects. The faculty started its first computer lab with 30 IBM machines the following year, and soon every staff member had their own networked machine and students had multiple computer labs.[82]

In 1987 Philip Sallis arrived from Sydney as Otago's first professor of information systems and Ivan Jackson, who had led the department from 1978, took up a chair at Victoria.[83] Sallis applauded Otago's 'enlightened approach, where the science of computing and its application to commerce are seen as discrete disciplines'.[84] Not everybody shared that view, and Otago's organisation of computing education was unusual. The two departments had to justify their distinctiveness, especially as they both had 'science' in their names. When quantitative analysis split from the QCS Department in 1991, the computer studies contingent chose information 'science' rather than 'systems' or 'studies' as its name, so that it qualified for more funding.[85]

The evolution of technology led information science through many changes. In 1989, working together with surveying, geography and computer science, it established a Spatial Research Information Centre and recruited George Benwell (future PVC of the Commerce Division) to lead it. Database technology, software engineering and management information systems all developed further through the 1980s and 90s. In the early twenty-first century the department contributed to spatial information and software engineering BAppSc majors, and offered a Diploma in Health Informatics in conjunction with the Wellington campus.[86] New programmes helped stem a drop in enrolments that was part of a worldwide trend from the late 1990s. The dot-com bubble reduced confidence and, as technology became integrated into everyday life, many students felt

Information science honours student Akbar Ghobakhlou tutoring first-year students in a Commerce Building computer laboratory in 1997.

COMMERCE DIVISION RECORDS, MS-4183/055, S17-611H, HOCKEN COLLECTIONS.

their knowledge of it was sufficient. For those who completed degrees in computing and information technology there was abundant and lucrative employment, but the days of expanding enrolments were gone.[87]

EDUCATING EXECUTIVES

In the 1950s Billing identified a need for advanced education for business executives, and in 1959 the council approved in principle an Otago Business Diploma alongside the discipline of management. As Cowan wrote, in 'the very conservative University of Otago', obtaining such approval 'was no small achievement'.[88] With Billing's untimely death, and insufficient support from the business community, the idea was put on hold.[89] In 1963, after he had visited business schools in the United States, Cowan developed an ambitious plan: Otago could 'introduce what was recognised as the most useful and prestigious graduate programme in business studies – a New Zealand version of the MBA'.[90] The Master of Business Administration, first awarded at Harvard in 1910, spread rapidly in the United States after World War II, and other countries were adopting it.[91] Cowan suspected New Zealanders would not commit to 'an untried two-year programme', so he devised a course compressed into 48 weeks over one calendar year. After 'some interesting debate', the senate approved it in 1969 and it went to the UGC for approval. There it hit a hurdle: the curriculum committee wasn't happy with a master's degree taught in one year to people who did not hold a relevant undergraduate degree. It was willing to approve the course as a diploma, however. After rejigging the course to fit into a normal academic year, the Commerce Faculty offered the Postgraduate Diploma in Business in 1972.[92] What was, essentially, an abbreviated MBA included courses in the various commerce disciplines, 'case studies and seminars of increasing breadth and complexity' and a report on 'an approved investigation'.[93] Cowan and Rossell did not abandon the MBA dream. When Ron Moore, an Englishman with extensive business as well as academic experience, arrived as management lecturer in 1974, he was asked to revise the original proposal. In 1975 the council approved Moore's model of a 50-week MBA, divided into 10-week modules, together with an associated Diploma in Personnel Management. The UGC curriculum committee was still reluctant – other universities were not convinced there was sufficient demand for such a qualification – but eventually it gave approval.[94]

In 1977 Otago taught the first MBA class in New Zealand, and in 1978 the faculty celebrated with its first six graduates. They came from diverse backgrounds and included one woman, Shu Moo Yoong, from the Ministry of Finance in Singapore. They received 'particularly good' employment offers, 'confirming a justification of such a career-oriented course'.[95] Entry was stringent and competition for places escalated as word spread of the enhanced career prospects an MBA provided. The course was demanding and the dropout rate of the first intake was high. In 1980 the *National Business Review* called it a 'masochistic course for making master managers': students worked 14–18 hours a day, seven days a week, for 18 months. The 'generally spartan conditions' did not deter students, although the staff newsletter suggested that 'top executives from New Zealand companies' were surprised when they took part and discovered the MBA was 'taught in a converted house, with a blackboard and some rolls of newsprint as the most evident teaching aids'. The programme's success was due to 'the quality of the teaching and the ability of the handpicked students'.[96] Moore – who succeeded Rossell as management professor in 1985 – directed the course in 1977, but David Wright, who taught a similar programme in South Africa, took over late in the year. Wright, who 'combined business ability with academic brilliance', was soon full-time as director. The MBA 'made extra demands on already pressed teachers right across the Faculty', but they enjoyed teaching an energetic group with business experience. Classes were 'a lot more interactive', recalls Wolfe.[97]

When David Wright died in tragic circumstances in 1983 he left a flourishing, highly reputed course. With 49 students it was the largest postgraduate programme at Otago that year.[98] Others picked up from Wright, though the environment became more competitive. Auckland commenced an MBA in 1983 and Victoria and Canterbury quickly followed. Otago had the early advantage – it had 'established itself as "the real New Zealand MBA" and [was] the measuring rod for others', the dean noted in 1984 – but promotion of the course became more important.[99] Otago worked hard to ensure its MBA course maintained a good reputation: it brought in experts from around the country and overseas as guest lecturers.[100]

Geoffrey Lorigan was a particularly entrepreneurial director. In 1997 when Auckland withdrew from its MBA programme shortly before an intake was to begin, he led a bold move to meet the demand from Auckland executives. He developed an 'executive MBA', which taught the same material part-time through short block courses in Auckland. It was designed for 'mature achievers with impressive track records who work in demanding jobs' and who were unable to commit to a full-time course in Dunedin.[101] The Auckland course produced 102 graduates. It ended in 2004 when the resignation of its senior staff coincided with insufficient good-quality applicants for entry.[102] Lorigan also modified the Dunedin MBA course to make it more accessible to busy executives through an option of 10-week modules, taken annually over four years.[103]

Flexibility helped in a competitive market: by 2009 New Zealand had 11 institutions offering MBAs.[104] 'Choosing a Kiwi MBA is like selecting your favourite ice cream flavour: they're all good,' *NZ Business* magazine reported in 2012.[105] Otago enrolments declined but the university was committed to the course; every self-respecting Business School offered this prestigious qualification. The MBA was never a money-spinner – student fees were high but so were costs, with intensive teaching from high-level staff and visitors – and other commerce departments subsidised it.[106] In 2015 Otago offered New Zealand's first online MBA. By contrast with the increasingly prevalent massive open online course (MOOC), this was a small private online course (SPOC), a format that was emerging in business schools. The course involved 'a very high level of engagement among the students and the teaching team,' said director Ian Lafferty. The content was unchanged from the tried and tested MBA, and with advanced technology students could view live lectures and share 'interactive discussions and break-out sessions in the same fashion as their on-campus counterparts'.[107] The online option attracted two intakes in its first year and garnered positive feedback from students; in 2017 a British magazine ranked it the fourth-best online MBA in the world.[108]

CATERING TO TOURISM

The MBA was the 'capstone' of Otago's Advanced Business Programme, but not its only venture. It offered various short courses, certificates and diplomas, along with customised courses to organisations, though its programmes were expensive to run and, as McLean suggested, it was 'very hard to measure the benefit'.[109] For several years the Advanced Business Programme hosted another emerging field: tourism. In 1986 George Doxey visited Otago from Toronto to advise on tourism courses. Tourism was growing rapidly in New Zealand but this was not matched by solid research. Doxey suggested setting up a research centre to coordinate research and training. Otago Polytechnic already offered a one-year course in tourist studies; Doxey recommended postgrad programmes at the university.[110]

After further consultation with the industry, the Centre for Tourism commenced in 1989 as an initiative of the departments of geography and marketing which, along with the School of Physical Education, already taught on tourism in some of their undergraduate papers. Twelve students enrolled for New Zealand's first postgrad course fully devoted to tourism, for which they completed four papers and a short dissertation.[111] After five years the director, geographer Geoff Kearsley, reported high demand for the 30 places available and noted that other postgrad students, especially in planning, often took a tourism paper or two. Nearly 100 dissertations and theses had been completed: visitor satisfaction, environmental protection and wilderness management were the most popular research fields.[112] Kearsley, initially half-time in the role, became full-time director of the Centre for Tourism in 1993, and its administration moved from the Department of Geography to the Advanced Business Programme.[113] Research was boosted in 1995 when Kearsley and Lawson (from the Marketing Department) received a $900,000 PGSF grant for a project on sustainable tourism. Kearsley was promoted to a personal chair in tourism studies the following year.[114]

The centre offered its first undergraduate paper, 'Principles of tourism', in 1994; it attracted numerous enrolments and other papers were soon added.[115] In 1996 Kearsley commented that tourism needed to develop 'as an academic subject in its own right'; it would 'eventually stand alongside history, geography and other social sciences'.[116] Not everybody agreed. Students would enrol in an undergraduate degree in tourism, but many academics were wary of its disciplinary credentials. After failing to get approval for a BCom major, the centre had its own degree, a Bachelor of Tourism, approved in 1999. That was a first step. In 2001 tourism became a full department within the Division of Commerce and in 2007 it won its BCom major, putting an end to the Bachelor of Tourism.[117]

As the industry expanded, so did courses: Waikato, Victoria, Lincoln, Auckland University of Technology and various technical institutes offered undergraduate tourism degrees.[118] Competition was intense but Otago maintained a strong department, though smaller than the others within commerce. Postgraduate students were a source of pride: 'the Department's PhD programme is one of the strongest of its kind internationally', claimed a 2011 report; there were over 20 students each year. Attracting quality PhD applicants became more competitive, and in 2012 the department restructured its Master of Tourism degree, introduced in 1996, from thesis to coursework, to attract more students and prepare them for PhD study.[119]

Michael Cooper, professor of economics from 1976 to 1994, gives a lecture. Cooper, whose field of expertise was health economics, became chair of the Otago Area Health Board; it was a high-profile position during a period of health system restructuring. He also held various senior roles at the university and was first AVC of the Academic Services Division.

BOX-237-001, S13-2171, HOCKEN COLLECTIONS.

ECONOMICS JOINS IN

When the university was restructured into four academic divisions of roughly equal size in 1989, the Economics Department had to decide whether to stay with the humanities or commit fully to commerce. By then about three-quarters of economics majors were completing commerce rather than arts degrees, but the decision was not straightforward according to John Howells, a long-serving economics academic. The head, Michael Cooper, preferred to stay with the humanities and an initial vote favoured that; when, after a protest, the vote was limited to academic staff, the commerce option won.[120] That was a boon to commerce, as economics strengthened its academic status; some of its other disciplines were new and lacked a strong research tradition. Economics was still offered for either an arts or a commerce degree. From 2002 it was added to the BSc schedule as part of a major in economics and statistics, and from 2012 as a major on its own: it was one of the university's most versatile disciplines.[121]

When departmental secretary Maud Boock retired in 1991, she observed that 'she could never really understand economists, any six of whom would have six different ways of restoring a country's economic health'.[122] Several Otago economists were well-known public figures. One who preferred to keep out of the limelight was Heather Simpson, a local graduate who lectured in economics from 1976 to 1987: she became a powerful figure as chief of staff and adviser to Prime Minister Helen Clark, and was dubbed 'H2' by insiders.[123] Economics didn't have to be serious. In 1990 Howells, whose specialty was industrial relations, and Cypriot-born Erkin Bairam, whose interests included 'the theoretical specification and estimation of aggregate production functions and the testing of Thirlwall's law of economic growth', paired up for a research project on the success of various strategies in cricket; it attracted public interest in the application of economic theory.[124] Bairam also worked on a contentious issue: the research rankings of economics departments. His method calculated that Otago was the country's highest ranked department from 1988 to 1995; his own productivity in publications contributed to that achievement.[125] The department's long tradition of research productivity helped it in the funding environment of the twenty-first century.[126]

The Economics Department went through a difficult period from 2008 after a research fellow brutally murdered his former girlfriend, who had just completed an honours degree in economics. The trial and subsequent appeal dragged out over several years. The event was shocking and distressing for all concerned, including their colleagues in the department. Some staff left, and researchers abandoned projects they had worked on with the murderer.[127] This was not the only notorious crime involving Otago staff in the new millennium: in 2001 the former head of the Psychological Medicine Department at the Dunedin School of Medicine was convicted of murdering his wife by poisoning her – another event that led to 'an understandable destabilising of staff morale'.[128]

THE RESEARCH ENVIRONMENT AND NEW VENTURES

The research focus of the twenty-first century was challenging for the Otago Business School. There were excellent researchers but not enough of them, and Otago departments were outperformed by other universities.[129] Research had always counted in staff promotion and the prestige of a department; once it affected a substantial part of funding as well, priorities changed. The departments of accountancy and business law and finance and quantitative analysis faced the most difficulty, and the rest of the Commerce Division had to bail them out. The Finance Department paid salary supplements to recruit and retain PhD-qualified staff in the face of competition from high salaries in the business sector, and that, combined with low PBRF funding, strained its budget.[130] Meanwhile the Accountancy Department struggled to balance its professional responsibility to train accountants with 'wider academic goals', particularly research.[131] After successive reviews the university intervened and created a combined Department of Accountancy and Finance in 2011. It was the end of the road for some staff; the 'research-inactive' departed and were replaced by people with a strong research record.[132]

Although parts of the Business School struggled to adapt to the university's – and the government's – priorities for research-led teaching, it was never short of ideas. In addition to the online MBA it ventured into the emerging academic field of entrepreneurship. The Marketing Department offered a fourth-year course in small business and entrepreneurship in 1992 and the Finance Department added a paper in entrepreneurial finance in 1995. From 2001, other papers that incorporated business innovation and entrepreneurship were added to meet the needs of the BAppSc. In 2004 Otago launched a Master of Entrepreneurship, developed within the Marketing Department and directed by John Bell, director of the Advanced Business Programme. Students completed a year of papers plus a report on a 'real-life' business incubation project. The course was taught through short, intensive on-campus sessions that gave flexibility to students not resident in Dunedin.[133]

In 2007 Brendan Gray of marketing became Otago's first professor of entrepreneurship. The DCC helped establish the chair through the Leading Thinkers scheme; it wanted to encourage enterprise in the city, as well as support the university. Gray set up a Centre for Entrepreneurship, which worked closely with the DCC's economic development team. He became director of the Master of Entrepreneurship programme and encouraged development of the subject at undergraduate level; from 2011 students could include a minor in entrepreneurship in a BCom.[134] The master's programme was a hit: in

2013 it won a US award for 'outstanding emerging entrepreneurship programme abroad'. A review that year commended its 'excellent mix of theory and practice': its teachers included 'entrepreneurs with real-world experience who bring to life academic theories with real-world case studies'.[135] Perhaps the best accolades, Gray noted in 2016, were the enterprises developed by its graduates, from 'Medikidz providing medical information to children in hospital, to global internet gaming phenomenon Runaway Play, to the very successful crowd funder PledgeMe, and for the events company Highly Flammable, to mention just a few'.[136]

Another field that emerged in the 1990s and came to fruition in the 2000s was international business. Commerce AVC McLean remarked in 1998 that 'the increasing globalisation of business and economies requires graduates with a strong international perspective'. A review had revealed 'a considerable level of international content in Otago Commerce courses', but more was needed 'to remain internationally competitive and to meet competition from other New Zealand universities, particularly Auckland and Waikato'.[137] The division built on existing papers to create a BCom major in international business, first offered in 2000. It had a point of difference from degrees in the north: a compulsory language component. It involved all departments of the Business School as well as the language programmes, which welcomed the additional enrolments. Conveniently, it did not require additional academic staff other than the director: it made good use of existing resources.[138] Many students spent a semester studying at one of Otago's partner institutions overseas, enhancing the international focus of their degree.[139]

THE CORE OF BUSINESS

Otago's commerce programmes would today be unrecognisable to Owen Wilkinson, its first BCom graduate. That degree remained the foundation, but was no longer confined to accounting, commercial law and economics. The increasing range of options led to concerns about students graduating without studying the basics of all aspects of business, but a suggestion made in the 1980s to make certain 'core' papers compulsory was contentious because of the impact that would have on departmental enrolments. The requirements of international accreditation agencies eventually forced the implementation of a core programme, and from 2005 all Otago BCom degrees included specified papers in accounting, economics and business statistics. In 2008 papers in marketing, management, information science and business and society were added to the core – the final step in obtaining accreditation with the Association to Advance Collegiate Schools of Business. With that added to accreditation from the Partnership in International Management and the European Quality Improvement System, obtained in 2003 and 2004 respectively, the Otago Business School had truly come of age.[140]

Opposite: Graduation celebrations in the Commerce Building atrium, May 1997.

COMMERCE DIVISION RECORDS, MS-4183/055, S17-611I, HOCKEN COLLECTIONS.

CHAPTER NINE

Health sciences

Otago is renowned for its teaching and research in the health sciences. Its courses for health professionals have drawn students from around the country, making it a truly national university. The flourishing of those courses was not a foregone conclusion, however. They started with few resources and generally just a handful of students, demonstrating the boldness – or recklessness – of the programmes' founders. The oldest programme, the Medical School, boasts several published histories, and recent histories have marked milestones in the physiotherapy and pharmacy schools. But there are several other programmes whose history is less well known.

FOUNDING A MEDICAL SCHOOL

A medical school was a bold venture in a colonial town with a brand new university and a small hospital for the poor and needy – but bold ventures were the hallmark of its chief advocate, James Macandrew.[1] As soon as university classes began in 1871 he initiated a campaign to persuade the colonial secretary to allocate a Southland land reserve, already set aside to raise income for university purposes, to help Otago endow its fifth professorial chair. The chair could be in medicine or anatomy, which 'would permit of the establishment of a medical school in connexion with the Dunedin Hospital'.[2] The benefits of that endowment wouldn't be secured for several years and financial resources were scant, but in 1872 an Otago Provincial Council committee investigated establishing law and medical classes. Most of those consulted believed plans for a medical school were 'premature' or 'injudicious'; despite that, the committee was enthusiastic and won the support of Otago's chemistry and philosophy professors. People with big ambitions for the province of Otago believed – wrongly in the case of law, but prophetically for medicine – that 'for many years to come' New Zealand would be too small to sustain more than one law school or medical school. By getting in first, Otago would have 'the means of securing from other parts of the colony a large number of students'.[3]

The University Council wrote to the University of Melbourne, which had set up its Medical School in 1863, for advice. Perhaps it was just as well the reply took months to come as the Melbourne school, at the time, had few students and an uncooperative local hospital; it was not an encouraging example.[4] In the meantime, after further urging from Macandrew, late in 1873 the University Council voted to go ahead, and asked the province's agent in Britain to 'take steps for the

Otago's first medical professor, Millen Coughtrey. The Lancashire-born and Edinburgh-educated Coughtrey had taught in both Edinburgh and Liverpool medical schools but, as he explained in a job enquiry letter, 'ill-health and impatient ambition' brought him to New Zealand in 1873.

W.J. BURTON PHOTOGRAPH, P1997-032/10-042, S15-347A, HOCKEN COLLECTIONS.

selection of a duly qualified Professor of Anatomy and Physiology'; it hoped to commence medical classes in 1875.[5] In 1874 Otago appointed Millen Coughtrey, recently arrived in New Zealand, as founding medical professor.[6] The council sent him back to Britain to purchase books and materials for the school and to negotiate with British medical authorities for recognition of Otago's course. That recognition was critical. Otago was to start with a two-year course in medicine, which needed approval from the medical schools where students would complete their training. Once a full local course was offered, its graduates would need to have an internationally recognised qualification – without it, students with ambition and the means would most likely study elsewhere.[7]

In 1876 the council reported that it was experiencing more difficulty than it had anticipated in establishing a medical school. Enquiries to medical schools in Scotland, Ireland and England, and to the colleges of surgeons, physicians and apothecaries who controlled entry to those specialties, led to 'vague and unsatisfactory' replies. Most were unwilling to approve a course that was not yet underway. The news was not all bad: the General Medical Council and others approved the preliminary exam in general education that Otago devised after it discovered that British authorities believed the New Zealand matriculation standards were too low for prospective medical students. Glasgow and Edinburgh medical schools – arguably the best in the world at the time – were willing to accept students from Otago's two-year course provided they had pre-approved each individual teacher of that course. Edinburgh also insisted on a royal charter for the university, which the University of New Zealand obtained in 1876. According to Coughtrey's recommendations and the requirements of the Scottish universities, Dunedin Hospital agreed to admit students and lecturers for clinical teaching, divide its medical and surgical patients, and adapt its dispensing facilities.[8]

On 31 May 1875 at the gathering 'to cut the first sod of medical education in this Colony', Coughtrey gave an inaugural lecture that ranged widely in its discussion of 'the position of modern medicine; of the steps to be taken in producing thoroughly equipped and trained practitioners of medicine; and of other questions' concerning the enterprise.[9] Otago's annual report records that four students enrolled in anatomy that year but gave no further details of the students or the course.[10] In 1876, with the medical preliminary examination in place and the Anatomy Act – permitting the legal dissection of human bodies – passed into law, Coughtrey could make a more serious attempt at teaching prospective doctors.

It was not a promising beginning. Just two students – Saul Solomon and Charles Low – passed the preliminary exam and Solomon switched to law soon afterwards, leaving Coughtrey with an anatomy class of one.[11] Low, who hailed from Arrowtown, headed to Edinburgh the next year, qualified in medicine there with 'first-class honours in all his subjects' and returned to practise in Invercargill and Huntly. It perhaps helped Otago's cause at Edinburgh that this early product of the colonial medical venture did so well there.[12] For the energetic anatomy professor, the administrative hold-ups and low enrolments were frustrating and when he got into a disagreement with the university over his right to practise medicine privately – it was forbidden in his contract – he resigned. Coughtrey stayed on in Dunedin as a respected physician and opened a private hospital at St Clair in the 1890s.[13]

To a medical school that, as historian Dorothy Page writes, consisted of 'one professor, one student, one classroom and one cadaver', the loss of that professor could have been fatal.[14] But the University Council, urged on by Macandrew, stuck with its expansion plans and wasted no time appointing Edinburgh anatomy demonstrator John Halliday Scott, selected from a large pool of applicants, as the next professor.[15] Like Coughtrey, Scott was still in his twenties; he arrived in 1877 and ran the Medical School until his death in 1914. His students admired him, though he was 'scathing … on slackers and nitwits, and most of us writhed at times under his sarcastic criticism', recalled Louis Barnett, an early student who became a teaching colleague. Scott was 'without parade or fuss'; he worked hard and did what he could to save costs – useful attributes in an institution with a tight budget. His conservatism – both administrative and academic – became more evident over the years.[16]

In 1878 classes resumed: five young men studied anatomy and physiology with Scott, and chemistry, zoology and botany with chemistry and biology professors Black and Hutton. Their clinical training consisted of lectures and bedside teaching by the honorary staff of Dunedin Hospital; the university gave William Brown, who had studied alongside Scott at Edinburgh, a special appointment as lecturer in surgery.[17] As Otago students proceeded to Edinburgh to complete the final two years of their four-year medical training, the university advanced its plans for a full course. Scott ensured it would not involve the university in 'excessive expenditure' by committing to continue teaching both anatomy and physiology himself, and he suggested that other lecturers could be appointed from among local practitioners. In 1883 the University of New Zealand Senate officially recognised Otago as a full medical school; and from 1885 New Zealanders could complete their full medical training in this country.[18]

The Medical School recruited capable staff to join Scott and Brown and teach the expanded course. Several had already settled in New Zealand, among them the 'abrasive' lecturer of midwifery and diseases of women, Ferdinand Batchelor, materia medica (pharmacology) lecturer John Macdonald, pathology lecturer William Roberts and ophthalmology lecturer Lindo Ferguson. From further afield came Daniel Colquhoun, Scottish-born and London-educated lecturer in medicine, and Frank Ogston arrived from Aberdeen in 1886 to become lecturer in medical jurisprudence and public health as well as holding a post as public health officer for the DCC. The dual post was necessary to attract a suitable expert in the emerging field of public health; all the new posts were part-time and the lecturers continued their clinical practice. In 1889 two more local experts joined the staff: Frederic Truby King in mental diseases and Isaiah de Zouche in the diseases of children. Otago then boasted quality lecturers in all medical specialties of the day, and many stayed on for long teaching careers.[19]

Ledingham Christie was the first person to complete his full medical course at Otago: he was capped as the University of New Zealand's first Bachelor of Medicine in October 1887. In 1890 he was awarded an MD for his research into the toxicity of the tutu plant. Christie then trained as a surgeon in England and earned acclaim for his work helping the poor in Bristol. He later worked in Sarawak and Singapore. This photograph was taken during World War I when he served in the British Army as a surgeon.

MEDICAL LIBRARY HISTORICAL COLLECTION, MS-1643/011, S14-650A, HOCKEN COLLECTIONS.

Attracting students and providing them with adequate clinical education was less simple. For decades, many who could afford it headed overseas for their final years of medical training: the 'reputation, glamour and opportunities' of Edinburgh had a strong pull.[20] Otago's medical classes were small; despite that, sourcing clinical experience for students was difficult. New Zealand hospitals were yet to become centres of technology, open to all; they were the last resort of the ailing poor, and admission was severely means tested. Most people paid to receive private healthcare, including surgery, at home. The public were wary of medical students. In his address at the 1887 graduation of New Zealand's first home-grown Bachelor of Medicine, Coughtrey assured them that the 'presence of medical students in the hospital does not necessarily involve that the patients should be tortured, that the unfortunate sufferers should be percussed out of one disease into another'. On the contrary, students were a 'wholesome check' on senior staff, who did not want to perform badly under their gaze; under careful supervision they contributed to 'the early recovery of every ailing inmate'.[21]

There were problems with Dunedin Hospital, but complaints from the honorary medical staff had little effect until 1890 when Batchelor, supported by Colquhoun, withdrew his patients from the hospital in protest at the conditions there. A subsequent royal commission of inquiry condemned the hospital and this resulted in improvements to buildings and equipment and the employment of trained nurses.[22] Patient and medical student numbers, which had dropped substantially following the commission's revelations, expanded again once improvements had been made. In 1891 the Medical School formed an official faculty of all hospital and university staff who lectured to medical students, and Scott was appointed dean. In 1901 he was proud to report that Otago had 73 medical students enrolled; there was a total of 321 students, past and present, and '105 medical practitioners in this country who have received their education, either completely or partially, at this school'.[23]

Among the graduates were six women. Since women couldn't finish their studies at the University of Edinburgh, which didn't admit women to its medical school until the 1910s, Otago Medical School didn't admit them either in its early years.[24] From 1885, with the full course available locally, women became eligible for entry to the Otago school. Emily Siedeberg was the first to enrol in 1891, and Margaret Cruickshank joined her the following year. Page notes that in the early years women students experienced 'support, jocular condescension and downright boorishness' from their teachers. They also faced harassment from fellow students, including having lumps of flesh thrown at them in the dissection room. Despite all this, the early women graduates became respected practitioners, and this encouraged other women to enter the field. Siedeberg, who was first to graduate in 1896, completed postgraduate training in Europe before returning to Dunedin, where she maintained a private practice and ran the St Helens obstetrical hospital. Her various professional appointments included one at her alma mater, though not at the Medical School: she was the Otago Dental School anaesthetist and anaesthetics lecturer to dental students from 1917.[25] By the turn of the century the Medical School had attracted Māori students, too; it was a diverse place for its time. There were problems, but the school entered the twentieth century with confidence. Its very existence was a triumph, achieved against the advice of many and under severe budgetary constraints.

THE DENTAL SCHOOL

Otago's second health professional course greatly improved dentistry in New Zealand. Dentistry was once all about pulling teeth and was practised by many a blacksmith. But from the late 1870s advancing technology such as the foot-pedal drill and improved filling materials made conservative dentistry – which repaired and conserved the tooth rather than removing it – more achievable and it became a job that required more skill.[26] In the wake of similar legislation in Britain, the Dentists Act of 1880 made it illegal to practise dentistry in New Zealand without registration, which was placed in the hands of the University of New Zealand. New practitioners had to serve a three-year apprenticeship and pass exams, managed by a Board of Examiners that anatomy professor Scott chaired for some years.[27] The change was controversial; as historian Tom Brooking writes, dentistry 'evolved in New Zealand in an untidy fashion advancing in fits and starts, frequently encountering major setbacks'.[28] An 1891 Act removed control of registration from the university and set up four examining boards in the main centres, though only the Dunedin and Wellington boards were functional. After campaigns by leading dentists and Dunedin parliamentarian Thomas Sidey, who was on the University Council, a 1904 Act was passed that required prospective dentists to complete a degree or certificate as prescribed by the University of New Zealand Senate. There was never really any doubt that the Dental School would be established at Otago, where the Medical School already provided the necessary tuition in anatomy, physiology, chemistry and pharmacology – though apparently Richard Seddon, by now the premier, approved Dunedin only after he was convinced it had 'a good climate for students to study'.[29]

There was a flurry of activity to produce university-trained dentists before the grandparenting provisions in the Act, allowing existing practitioners to register, ran out in 1910. Hopes that the local hospital board would provide the dental hospital necessary for student training were dashed: the hospital trustees would not allocate funds and the university had to set up its own hospital. The New Zealand Dental Association raised £1000 to supplement the £1500 of promised government funding so the university could construct a building in time for opening in 1907.[30] Staff were needed too: the university appointed local dentist Owen Davies as acting

The Dental School laboratory, about 1907.
DENTAL SCHOOL RECORDS, AG-508/083/028, S17-611B, HOCKEN COLLECTIONS.

director – he had been in the first graduating class of Melbourne's dental college – and it appointed 'seven honorary dental surgeons, who will attend in turn for two hours every morning at the Dental Hospital'.[31] Percy Pickerill was just 28 when he arrived in Dunedin to become the Dental School's inaugural director; and he was given professorial status soon after he arrived. He had degrees in dentistry and medicine and had previously lectured at the University of Birmingham. Pickerill was a keen researcher who published important work on dental caries while he was at Otago. He worked to advance the profession; he played an active part in the Dental Association and edited its journal.[32] Soon after his arrival the council empowered Pickerill to appoint a 'suitable person to do mechanical work until his place would be supplied by the students'.[33] Since New Zealand had no training for dental mechanics, he recruited N.P. Hawkins from Birmingham. Hawkins commenced early in 1909 and fulfilled his duties 'with complete satisfaction', but he returned to England a couple of years later because he was 'not permitted to advance himself at all' – perhaps he had not got along with Pickerill, who was not the easiest of men. The council resolved to appoint its next dental mechanic from 'the Dominion if possible'.[34]

The Dental School was an instant hit with the Dunedin public; within nine months of opening it had conducted 1480 'operations of all kinds' on 438 patients and Pickerill was pleased that 'by far the greater number of these has been in connection with the filling and saving of teeth'.[35] He was not impressed with New Zealanders' teeth – he noted on his arrival that 'nine out of ten' people he met in the street 'appeared to have most glaring dental defects, and sometimes as glaringly remedied'.[36]

There was 'considerably more poverty amongst some of the patients' than Pickerill anticipated; and their inability to afford much in the way of fees was an early warning that dental services would not be a money-spinner for the university. The hospital board provided some funding through the years in recognition of the fact that the school provided a service to the poor and to inmates of institutions, but it was never enough to cover costs.[37]

In the first year three young men enrolled for the Bachelor of Dental Surgery (BDS) and seven dentists who were already registered came for 'a course of practical training in operative dentistry'. These 'postgraduate' courses kept the school going in its early years.[38] The school celebrated with its first three graduates – William Seed, Albert Hansen and Charles Hercus – in 1911. Pickerill declared that the course they completed was 'quite equal to that of any other dental school or University department elsewhere, and is considerably wider in its scope and capable of showing far better results than a great many others', but that 'the number of students has not been what it should have been'.[39] Over the next few years Otago turned out only a couple of dental graduates a year whereas, between 1907 and 1916, 'some 250 students have qualified without coming to the school'.[40] Amendments to the Dentists Act had extended the grace period for the old apprenticeship system and opened other back doors into dentistry for those who believed the degree course was too long and difficult. Eventually Pickerill and the Dental Association conceded they would have to allow a lower-level certificate qualification for entry to the profession; this was already permitted in the New Zealand University Senate regulations, but the certificate was so similar to the degree that nobody enrolled. In 1917 the senate approved regulations for a new, shorter certificate of proficiency in dentistry.[41]

Late in 1916 Pickerill headed to England with the New Zealand Dental Corps and served as a pioneering maxillofacial surgeon in military hospitals, treating people with injuries to the face and jaw.[42] When he returned to the Dental School in 1920 he found it flourishing under the care of the acting dean, Davies; the certificate course and bursaries for dental students had encouraged enrolments, and there were 42 new students in 1919 and 1920.[43] A system of bursaries for dental students had been established in 1918 with donations from Sidey and the Dental Association, subsidised by the government, and the government had added more bursaries in 1919 – binding recipients to several years of state service.[44] 'The fact that the State is now educating its own students has immensely strengthened the position of good dentistry and the Dental School,' Davies noted.[45] Young dental students regarded the 'somewhat austere' Pickerill, now famous for his war surgery, 'with a little awe', 1920s student Roy Hanan recalled. The dean advised them in their first lecture to 'fill the minute and fill the tooth'.[46]

Dentistry standards were still under threat: in 1921 Pickerill expressed concern at two measures that 'lessen the field for our prospective graduates': 'the training of dental nurses to take the place of qualified dentists in operating on children in the State Dental Service' and 're-opening a back door … to allow a number of dental mechanics to become registered dentists'.[47] However, students were still flocking to the Dental School – about half for degrees and half for certificates; both courses took four years but the certificate science courses were less advanced.[48] The expanding student body included the first women. Women had been practising dentistry in New Zealand for decades, but none enrolled in the Dental School in its first few years. In 1922 Miranda Whiteside became the first woman to complete the Otago certificate, and Malvena Oldham was the first woman to graduate BDS the following year. After a year in practice Oldham returned to demonstrate part-time in the Dental School, and became its first woman teacher of dentistry (though Siedeberg had been teaching anaesthetics for some years).[49]

By 1923 there were over 100 students in a building designed for 26, and a flood the following year washed away some of the building extensions (see chapter 13). The school lobbied for another building, but meanwhile there were threats to relocate the school to Auckland, or to establish a second school there. Otago retained the support of the Dental Association and won the day. It made sense for it to remain alongside New Zealand's only medical school, and Thomas Hunter, the government's director of dental hygiene, repeated the old argument that 'living conditions are cheaper in Dunedin and the climate is more suitable for work'. In 1926 staff and students moved into a spacious new building (now the Marples Building; the original Dental School is now the Staff Club). When he departed in 1927 to continue a career in plastic surgery, Pickerill left behind a Dental School with a secure future.[50]

INTRODUCING MASSAGE THERAPY

In 1913 the university ventured into another emerging health profession: physiotherapy. It developed in the early 1900s by combining three distinct areas of therapy: massage, physical agents (especially electricity, light and water) and medical gymnastics. A variety of practitioners offered those treatments, to the dismay of doctors – partly because the treatments were popular and because they competed with conventional medical practice, and partly because some practitioners were 'quacks' who were making an income from dubious treatments. Doctors slowly gained an appreciation for some of the therapies, particularly therapeutic massage, which became available in larger hospitals in the 1890s and 1900s. Some New Zealand massage therapists trained overseas; the Australasian Massage Association, established in 1906 by the amalgamation of associations in Victoria and New South Wales, promoted the introduction of diploma courses at Australian universities. A few individuals offered private courses in New Zealand, but none survived long.

The Medical Association wanted to improve – and perhaps control – standards, and it asked the University of New Zealand to approve a massage course. Early in 1913 the senate informed Otago that 'owing to the importance of massage in the treatment of certain diseases', it approved the university 'granting certificates for proficiency in massage'. The Medical School designed a syllabus based closely on the Australian model. Meanwhile, in 1912 Auckland Hospital set up a course based on the British model, whereby nurses had their training extended for a year to include massage. That programme continued until 1922, and nurses at Dunedin Hospital also received training in massage, though it was not recognised with any certificate. The Department of Health started planning a register of massage therapists.[51]

The Otago course began in the middle of 1913. The 18-month programme included six months of anatomy, physiology and massage followed by a year of public hospital instruction, supplemented by lectures on theoretical and practical medical electricity, applied massage and medical gymnastics. Lizzie Armstrong, already a masseuse at Dunedin Hospital, was Otago's first massage instructor; she had extensive experience in Sydney and had travelled to England to observe treatments and training there. Hospital radiologist Percy Cameron was appointed to teach medical electricity; William Newlands as anatomy lecturer; and home science professor Winifred Boys-Smith agreed to teach physiology in a combined massage and home science class. The Medical School professors oversaw the anatomy and physiology training. Stuart Moore was later appointed as lecturer in applied massage and medical gymnastics.[52]

Eight students signed up for the university's first massage course, but hurried planning (or lack of it) led to difficulties. An extra physiology tutor had to be appointed since the home science students had already completed half the course; and Armstrong ended up in a prolonged dispute with hospital masseur Edwin Booth, who resented her appointment as instructor. The original plan for students to complete their hospital training at various centres did not eventuate and, after considerable negotiation, they were allocated between the three Dunedin Hospital massage therapists. By then two students had dropped out of the course and just one person enrolled for the second intake, which commenced in May 1914. In August 1914 Armstrong resigned to return to

The women who, in 1914, successfully completed the School of Massage's first course were (from left): Elizabeth Washer, Frances Skevington, Edith Thomson, Ellen Smith and Flora Gray. Thomson and Gray served as masseuses with the New Zealand Army Nursing Service during World War I.

NEW ZEALAND SOCIETY OF PHYSIOTHERAPISTS OTAGO BRANCH RECORDS, 88-086, S16-503D, HOCKEN COLLECTIONS.

Sydney; soon afterwards she headed to London, where she offered her skills to the Red Cross for war work. Final exams were brought forward so she could assist with them before her departure, but the students were left to muddle along without the full period of practical training. The legislation for registration of masseurs was held up by the war; it had already been delayed because of opposition to a clause that required masseurs to undertake all treatment under the authority of a medical practitioner. Since the government did not yet have the authority to examine or certify masseurs, the university awarded its own certificate of proficiency to the five women who successfully passed their exams in 1914.[53]

In 1915, apparently to the relief of the university, the Otago Hospital Board took over administration of the School of Massage – a role it maintained until 1976. The university, which would take charge of physiotherapist training again later, retained a hand in their education through those 60 years, as it still provided the anatomy and physiology courses. The war, while it delayed the registration process, highlighted the usefulness of physiotherapy in treating injuries. So did the polio epidemic of 1915–16; masseurs had seen an outbreak of it in Dunedin in 1914. The status of the profession was further enhanced when the Masseurs Registration Act was finally passed in 1920.[54]

FAILED VENTURES

Not all Otago's ventures into professional education were successful. In 1904 the University Council entered negotiations with the government for a four-year course in veterinary science. Animal health was critical to New Zealand's economy, but the country was dependent on overseas-trained veterinarians. Like dentistry, the course could take advantage of existing staff for initial anatomy and physiology education, with a couple of additional specialist professors and assistants.[55] In early 1907 the council reported 'every prospect of the school being opened and carried on with success', but when it offered a veterinary course that year, no students applied.

Had any done so, the profession would have developed differently in this country, alongside dentistry, which commenced its course with just a handful of students in the same year.

Otago decided to try again with a shorter Certificate in Animal Hygiene, hoping a less demanding course would be more attractive, but it struck hurdles. Unlike a full degree, the animal hygiene course required specialist teaching from the beginning. In 1909 the government voted £3000 to build a veterinary school, and Otago started looking for a site near campus that was capable of housing stock 'under the same conditions as they would be on an ordinary farm', as experts recommended. It finally found somewhere on the Taieri in 1914 and submitted it for government approval, since additional funding was needed, but the outbreak of war put all plans on hold as the government now had other spending priorities.[56] New Zealanders training as vets had to travel to Australia or further afield for the next few decades. In the 1950s the government revived plans for vet education, but Otago's submission lost to an alternative proposal from Massey Agricultural College, which set up the country's first veterinary course in 1962. At least one University Council member believed it was a politically motivated decision: Massey was located in a marginal seat.[57]

Another course that raised false hopes at Otago in the early twentieth century – this time after it had attracted students – was nursing. Nurse training began with ad hoc programmes in various hospitals; nurses learned on the job and provided the bulk of the hospital workforce as they did so. From 1901, nurses who passed a state examination after completing the required years of training received their registration and standards slowly improved, but there was no higher education for nurse tutors.[58] In 1922, in response to concerns about nursing education and advocacy from the Nurses' Association, the University Council set in motion a five-year nursing diploma. In consultation with the home science and medical schools it approved a curriculum of two years of university courses, two years of 'ward work and general hospital training' and a final year of specialised nursing education; the scheme used existing courses and did not require additional teaching staff until its fifth year. The Department of Health suggested the fifth year of the Otago diploma could also serve as an advanced course for qualified nurses, and it offered to send two senior nurses overseas to prepare as lecturers for the programme.

In 1925 Janet Moore headed to London and Mary Lambie to Toronto, and the fifth year was scheduled to commence in 1926. Meanwhile several women started the first years of the programme through the Home Science School. The scheme fell apart because of misunderstandings between the University Council and the Health Department. Neither had explicitly stated who was to pay the salaries of the specialist nursing lecturers: the council assumed the Health Department's involvement meant it would pay, and the department assumed the university would pay its own staff. Those council members who had supported the project on the basis that it would cost the university nothing stubbornly refused to commit any funding, even after the Nurses' Association offered a contribution. The Health Department was equally stubborn – and a programme that could have changed the course of New Zealand nursing education collapsed over the cost of two salaries.[59]

Moore and Lambie approached Victoria University, where they got a sympathetic response. A diploma for already-registered nurses commenced in 1928 at Wellington Hospital, jointly supervised by Victoria, the Health Department and the Hospital Boards Association. For 50 years the School of Advanced Nursing Studies, as it became known, provided New Zealand's only advanced nursing education. The first two students in Otago's collapsed programme, who had already completed the first four years, proceeded to the new Wellington course. One of them, Winifred Fraser, applied to Otago for a Diploma of Nursing, and became the one and only person awarded that qualification. Most of the other women who were partway through their course switched to home science.[60] Otago kept out of nursing education for many years – it did not venture again into the education of the largest of the health professions until late in the century (see chapter 10).

THE GROWING MEDICAL SCHOOL

As other courses came and went, the Medical School slowly expanded. The arrival of a second professor in 1905 marked a big advance: John Malcolm of Edinburgh took up the physiology chair, leaving Scott to concentrate on anatomy. This was made possible by a generous gift from Wolf Harris and more secure government funding – the Medical School acquired a dedicated annual government grant, which it took pride in as recognition of its 'national' status.[61] Though funding improved, it remained tight. Soon after his arrival Malcolm wrote to his family: 'They are the most poverty-stricken set of University people possible to imagine'; he himself forked out for some of the supplies he needed. In 1910 he recruited Harry Manson, a technician he had worked with in Edinburgh, and Manson's ingenuity and technical skill helped the department make the most of its operating budget.[62] The physiology and anatomy departments – if a team consisting of one professor and a technician can be called a department – extended their responsibilities and taught dental, home science and massage students, as well as future doctors. This was confirmation of the breadth of application of those subjects, which slowly transformed into sciences studied for their own sake, not only as necessary steps in a medical degree.

Growing enrolments meant more responsibilities for other Medical School staff. Part-timers like King and Ferguson, who had offered their services free for years, were given a salary, and others got a raise.[63] In 1909, 'partly owing to the importance of the subjects lectured on and partly to the length of service of several of the lecturers', the University Council made several of the staff professors: Barnett became professor of surgery, Batchelor professor of midwifery and gynaecology, Colquhoun professor of the practice of medicine, Ferguson professor of ophthalmology, Ogston professor of medical jurisprudence and public health and Roberts professor of pathology.[64] Cynics might note it was a good way to raise status at no extra expense, for all those professors remained part-time and the promotion brought them 'no increase in salary, staff or accommodation'.[65] As enrolments kept climbing and the curriculum expanded, staff numbers finally rose.

A subject that was destined to become one of Otago's largest, microbiology (then known as bacteriology), began in the 1890s. It was an emerging field that revolutionised human health. Historian Roy Porter wrote that 'in the twenty-one golden years between 1879 and 1900 the micro-organisms responsible for major diseases were being discovered at the phenomenal rate of one a year'. Scientists developed vaccinations and, later, effective drug treatments.[66] Otago struggled to keep up. Roberts, the pathology lecturer, gave short courses on practical bacteriology to medical students from 1891, but he was a surgeon with no advanced training in pathology, let alone bacteriology.[67] Ogston, the public health lecturer, was little help – his main enthusiasm was for medical jurisprudence and his public health course concentrated on environmental health. Its content, faithfully delivered over 23 years, did not change, notes historian Warwick Brunton; his 'inertia' contributed to a period of stagnation, and the dean admitted in 1898 that the Medical School was 'old-fashioned and out of date'.[68] It was the energetic obstetrician Batchelor who urged the faculty to make changes after observing applied bacteriology at work during a visit to London. In 1910 Otago appointed Sydney Champtaloup as lecturer in bacteriology and public health, leaving a relieved Roberts and Ogston to concentrate on pathology and medical jurisprudence respectively; both of those fields were absorbed into a pathology chair, taken up by Murray Drennan in 1917.[69]

Champtaloup, promoted to professor in 1911, was 'a very fortunate appointment', Dudley Carmalt Jones wrote in his 'annals' of the medical school; he was 'a most vigorous and progressive person' and 'introduced an element of enterprise' that had been missing from the Medical School since Batchelor resigned a couple of years earlier. Champtaloup was a New Zealander who had qualified in Edinburgh; he ran the hospital and community bacteriology service and served as district health officer alongside his teaching duties. He introduced the Diploma in Public Health (DPH), provided expert advice during disease outbreaks, reorganised the laboratories (located in less than ideal conditions in an old hospital ward), and was the driving force behind a new building (see chapter 13). He was a popular teacher who inspired others to specialise in microbiology and public health. A couple of the early DPH students, John Bowie and Doris Jolly (later Gordon), assisted him in labs and lectures. But the hard-worked Champtaloup was not immune to the great microbiological scourges of the day: he recovered from influenza during the pandemic of 1918 but died of tuberculosis in 1921. One of his former students, Otago dental and medical graduate Charles Hercus, succeeded him as professor.[70]

Another of the medical sciences, pharmacology, had early origins but expanded in the twentieth century. Toxicology had been around at the university since before the Medical School opened: in 1875 the university lab analysed medicines, as well as food and bodily fluids from suspected poisoning cases.[71] Otago's first lecturer in materia medica, John Macdonald, taught according to 'Edinburgh tradition', with long lists of drug preparations to memorise.[72] In addition to theory, prospective doctors learned from the hospital dispenser the practical skills of pharmacy, making pills, ointments and potions.[73] The early pharmacology lecturers focused on teaching rather than research, but there were interesting studies elsewhere in the university. Soon after his arrival in 1905 Malcolm commenced work on tutin, the deadly toxin of the common tutu plant, along with research assistant and hospital physician Frank Fitchett. Fitchett, a local who returned to Dunedin after completing his medical training in Edinburgh, became pharmacology lecturer in 1910; he kept students alert through 8am lectures with entertaining anecdotes from his medical practice. In 1920, when Colquhoun, the part-time medicine professor, retired and another bequest wasn't quite sufficient to appoint a full-time one, the Medical School instead created two part-time chairs, and Fitchett became professor of clinical medicine and therapeutics. The other chair, in systematic medicine, went to Carmalt Jones, a recruit from England.[74] In the 1920s Fitchett visited England and Scotland to check out pharmacology programmes; Otago needed to meet the changing requirements of the General Medical Council. Otago dropped practice in hospital dispensing, which was 'condemned' as unnecessary by the council, and replaced it with a practical class in the writing and analysing of prescriptions and observation of the effects of drugs.[75]

That was just one change in the ever-evolving clinical training of medical students. In the 1890s students started their experience at the end of their first year with a summer term of 'preliminary hospital instruction, outpatient surgery and bandaging'. During second and third years they attended the surgical and medical wards, and the fourth year included 'midwifery practice' as well as the outpatients department and specialty wards. The fifth and final year required attendance at 'all departments' of the hospital (the course was soon extended from the original four years to five).[76] Most women gave birth at home, so organising obstetrics experience was challenging. Students attended births at the Benevolent Institution's ward for the destitute, and in the 1880s Batchelor set up a homebirth scheme that provided a few more opportunities to gain experience. The government opened a St Helens Hospital in Dunedin in 1905 but it was designed to train midwives, and medical students were banned. Two years later Batchelor established the 12-bed Batchelor Hospital in Forth Street. Eventually student midwives and doctors competed for births at both hospitals. As hospital births became more common, the Medical School pushed for the construction of a large maternity hospital in Dunedin. There were 'tangled negotiations' with the Hospital Board and Health

Department and initial plans were downsized because of the economic depression, but finally, in 1937, the Queen Mary Maternity Hospital opened, complete with living facilities for students doing their obstetrics training.[77]

Unlike some parts of the university, the Medical School grew during World War I. War restrictions ended the practice of completing medical training overseas. As the war dragged on, with a shortage of both military and civilian doctors, the government wanted Otago to produce more medics. Students in their senior years were exempted from military conscription and final exams were brought forward. The end of the war brought an influx of returned servicepeople; the Medical School roll swelled from just under 100 in 1910 to over 300 in 1919. It became a greater force within the university and Ferguson, the dean from 1914 to 1936, was a powerful figure in Otago and beyond.[78] From 1923, in a coordinated move with the three Australian schools, the medical curriculum was extended to six years. In a pattern that lasted for many decades, students spent their first year in a general science course, their second and third years on the medical sciences and the fourth to sixth years on clinical subjects. The extra year strained clinical placements at Dunedin Hospital, which was already stretched by the mounting roll. The solution was to send students beyond Dunedin for their final year, which was fully clinical: by 1927 Otago students were placed in Christchurch, Wellington and Auckland hospitals. That scheme created the infrastructure that evolved into the Christchurch and Wellington Schools of Medicine and the University of Auckland Medical School.[79]

In Dunedin, departments expanded to cater for more students, though staff workloads were still high. Pathology, for instance, had a professor, Eric D'Ath – an Otago graduate who returned in 1929 after teaching in Sydney – and a 'medical assistant' to do all the teaching; they acquired two student demonstrators from 1934. The pathologists also had big clinical responsibilities. Fortunately, the Health Department and Hospital Board contributed some funding, which helped pay for laboratory assistants, a mortuary attendant and a science graduate. Nesta Woods, who completed an MSc at Otago, did the Pathology Department's 'first chemical examination of the blood using the newly developed Folin and Wu technique' in 1922; she then ran the chemical pathology service for 36 years and trained technicians from around the country.[80]

D'Ath valued Woods' contribution, but not all medical academics welcomed science graduates. Fred Fastier, appointed as a chemist in the Department of Medicine in 1940, recalls receiving 'a very mixed reception at the Medical School. People like the professor of anatomy worked on the basis that anybody who wasn't there as a medical student was an intruder.'[81] Appointing scientists was important in developing research, a key goal for Hercus after he became dean in 1937. Norman Edson, who returned to Otago from Cambridge in 1940, recalled that Otago had 'a very good reputation as a centre for training general practitioners' but 'had failed to establish a reputation in research commensurable with its size as an undergraduate teaching institution'. Research was happening, but 'failed to attract attention because it was not very original or not very significant'. Notable exceptions included work on goitre, sparked by Hercus's observations of that endemic disease as a School Medical Service doctor; and a study of the neuroanatomy of the tuatara, carried out by Derek Denny-Brown, John Cairney and Archibald Durward in the Anatomy Department, which had a dynamic professor in Percy Gowland.[82]

Research accelerated with the arrival of a new professor of medicine. When Carmalt Jones and Fitchett both retired in 1939 the faculty decided to replace them with a full-timer, 'free from the calls of private practice' and able to devote his time to teaching, research and administration. Otago had the good fortune to recruit Horace Smirk, the Manchester-educated pharmacology professor at Cairo. Smirk had already carried out important work on hypertension, which he continued in Dunedin. He started with a boosted staff of lecturers and researchers and within a few years had added to his team.[83]

Horace Smirk (right) making a point to colleagues, possibly during an overseas trip. Smirk had 'tremendous vitality', recalls Fred Fastier. His colleagues wondered if this had something to do with the enormous quantities of tea he consumed: was his 'curiously strong brew' converted into something special 'by a process apparently acquired in the land of Egypt'?
PAULINE FRASER COLLECTION.

Above right: John Eccles operating, assisted by technician Molly Bradley, in 1951. The professor was 'almost a caricature of the mad scientist amongst his oscilloscopes, wires and animals', says David Cole, future dean of the Auckland Medical School, who completed a BMedSci degree with Eccles in 1945; another student recalled the day that Eccles 'arrived in great excitement, having, he said, a testable hypothesis about inhibition which had come to him, like Archimedes, in the bath that morning. He retired to his wire cage for 24 hours or more, being fed sandwiches through the door.'
PHYSIOLOGY DEPARTMENT COLLECTION.

In 1944 John Eccles arrived as physiology professor, bringing impressive credentials as a neurophysiology researcher in Oxford and Sydney, though his research 'virtually came to an end' during his first year at Otago since he had to reacquaint himself with the whole of physiology in order to teach medical students.[84] Edson was promoted to associate professor of biochemistry in 1944; it was a rapidly growing field, and in 1949 it split from physiology to become an independent department with Edson as inaugural professor. The two fields continued to work closely together.[85]

In 1951, working with physicist Jack Coombs and physiology lecturer Laurie Brock, Eccles made an important scientific breakthrough, a step in the work that won him a Nobel Prize in 1963. They inserted a tiny electrode, less than a micrometre wide, into a single nerve cell in the spinal cord of an anaesthetised cat and measured its action potentials – the first time that had been achieved in a mammal. The experiment proved that synaptic action was chemically mediated. At the end of 1951 Eccles departed to become physiology professor at the John Curtin School of Medical Research in Canberra, where he could research without the teaching load he found a burden at Otago. Coombs and technician Arthur Chapman followed Eccles to Australia, as did some of the specialised equipment, but neurophysiology experiments carried on at Otago under the next professor, Archie McIntyre, an Australian colleague recruited by Eccles to the department in 1949.[86]

The internationally important work of Hercus, Smirk, Eccles and others altered the focus at the Medical School as staff and students concentrated

Staff of the Physiology Department in 1951. Front row (from left): Laurie Brock, Ken Bradley, John Eccles, Eric Hook, Charlie Morris, Wilfrid Rall. Middle row: Arthur Chapman, Jack Coombs, Yap Tien Beng, Molly Bradley, Graham Jeffries, Pearl Cousins (née Harvey). Back row: Arnold Annand, Ron Stevenson, Dan Whyte (student). Eccles' experiments required intricate electronic equipment; he brought technician Chapman with him. Annand, whose electrical expertise was honed during service in the air force, joined the Physiology Department as a technician in 1948, beginning a career of almost 40 years building and maintaining equipment for the university's health science departments. In 1950 Eccles asked Coombs, a 'shy genius' lecturing in the Physics Department, for assistance; Coombs designed 'the best general research instruments for electrophysiology in the world', said Eccles. BOX-011-001, S17-125C, HOCKEN COLLECTIONS.

more on research. Wilfrid Rall came from the United States to study with Eccles and was one of the first students to complete a PhD within the Medical School. Others who completed PhDs at around the same time in the school included microbiologist Margaret di Menna, who in 1954 became Otago's first woman PhD graduate with her thesis on the yeasts of the human body.[87]

Some medical students took an extra year and completed a Bachelor of Medical Science, which involved a supervised research project in one of the medical sciences – Edson had been first to complete the new qualification in 1927. It was 'an outstanding success'; it introduced some of the best students to research and produced a 'steady stream' of graduates who entered clinical, teaching and research careers.[88] But in order to grow research staff, the medical science departments needed to train scientists as well as doctors. At the urging of chemistry professor Frederick Soper, physiology, biochemistry and bacteriology were added to the BSc curriculum in the 1930s, though initially that 'proved abortive in practice'.

With the support of their science colleagues, Edson and Eccles offered undergraduate science classes in biochemistry in 1945, physiology in 1946 and microbiology in 1949 to complete the 'tripod of experimental sciences', as Edson commented, giving Otago 'a strong position in the biological sciences'. Anatomy was still more closely aligned

A Stage 1 class in the biochemistry lab, Lindo Ferguson Building, about 1950.
UNIVERSITY OF OTAGO MEDICAL SCHOOL ALUMNUS ASSOCIATION RECORDS, MS-1537/441, S17-638A, HOCKEN COLLECTIONS.

with medicine, and was not taught to science students until 1978, but the other subjects had obvious relevance beyond the medical world.[89] Microbiology 'has application not only in medicine but in those industries of food and agriculture which are of such importance to this country,' Soper noted.[90] There were exciting prospects for students interested in rapidly developing fields such as genetics, but the new majors weren't easy options; for instance, biochemistry majors had to major in chemistry as well. George Petersen and Mervyn Smith, who studied biochemistry in the 1950s, were the only Stage 3 student in their respective year. Edson was 'a very good biochemist', recalls Petersen (who was himself a very good biochemist). Petersen and Smith both proceeded to postgraduate study at Oxford and other positions before returning to long careers in the Otago department.[91]

Molly Marples taught the science students microbiology; she joined the Department of Bacteriology and Public Health in 1946 and when it split in 1950 became a founding member of the Department of Bacteriology (renamed the Department of Microbiology in 1954 to better reflect the breadth of the subject). John Miles, an expert in the epidemiology of viral diseases, arrived in 1955 as professor for the department. Hercus led the remainder of the old department, which became the Department of Hygiene and Preventive Medicine (later Preventive and Social Medicine). It had a heavy teaching load and ran the therapeutic and student health clinics, which provided a public service as well as practice for medical students. Staff researched goitre, hydatids and infectious diseases in the Pacific. Research dissertations in preventive medicine, which had been required of fifth-year medical students since the 1920s, produced a large body of work. However, when Cyril Dixon replaced Hercus as professor in 1959 he was not impressed with the number of staff or their research productivity, though the department had already started to grow – like microbiology, it was destined to become one of the university's largest.[92]

GROWING DENTISTS AND DOCTORS

The Medical School did not lose sight of its core business, the production of doctors; by the late 1930s it had over 400 students. The Dental School had over 120 students; combined, they made up around 40 per cent of the university roll. Bevan Dodds succeeded Pickerill as dean of dentistry in 1927 and Otago took pride in having a 'distinguished graduate' of its own in charge of the Dental School; and local graduate Hercus was appointed medical dean in 1937.[93] Students found Dodds approachable – his lectures and demonstrations were 'lucid and instructive', and they appreciated his 'strong leaning towards the practical aspects of dentistry'.[94] During the depression years some prospective patients could not afford 'even our small fees', Dodds reported. The Hospital Board later funded it to treat the unemployed of Dunedin, though there were insufficient staff or time to 'do more than a limited amount'. The dean commented in 1935 that dental disease 'can be classed among the most urgent problems of our time', yet the Dental School had just one small lab set aside for research, with no funding to run it. There was a small drop in enrolments during World War II and graduates could not keep up with 'ordinary demand' for dentists, let alone the extra work of military services; there was already a shortage of dentists in rural districts and small towns.[95]

Despite the challenges, the Dental School made important advances. Orthodontics emerged

The Dental School operative clinic in 1939.

DENTAL SCHOOL RECORDS, AG-508/083/021, S17-611A, HOCKEN COLLECTIONS.

with a course run by Reid Burt, appointed as an associate professor along with Dodds and George Parkinson in 1926.[96] The school persuaded more of its students to enrol for a degree, and the certificate course – always an irritation to dental academics – was abolished from 1943. The degree course, which was already adapted to fit the expanded technical experience requirements of the General Medical Council (which registered dentists in England), was strengthened. From 1945 dental students completed the same intermediate year as medical students, followed by four professional years.[97]

There was a surge in students enrolling at the Medical School during World War II. At the same time, staff left on war service and became hard to replace, and war conditions delayed building plans designed to ease overcrowding. With about a third of New Zealand's medical profession serving overseas there was big demand for doctors. The government wanted the Medical School to shorten its course, but because a shorter degree would not be recognised in other countries, it refused.[98] Instead Otago reduced its output: it limited entry to the second-year medical class for the first time in 1941, initially to 100 students. Two years later, after considerable government pressure, the intake increased to 120 'as a War emergency'. In return, the government agreed to 'give every assistance' to boost staff and accommodation, and the construction of the South Block (Hercus Building) began in 1944. The strain prompted calls for a second medical school: if Otago could not produce all the doctors New Zealand needed, Aucklanders were willing to help. Hercus argued that a second school would be a public expense when the first wasn't adequately staffed or equipped, but the requests for an Auckland school persisted.[99]

Before 1941, anybody who could pay the fees, pass the exams and complete the course could qualify as a doctor; a person of reasonable intelligence could succeed, though many students repeated years. From 1941 some places were reserved for graduates and for students who were repeating second year, but entry for most came through obtaining the best exam marks in the intermediate course – and competition was tough.[100] There was a flow-on effect to the Dental School as some people who were denied entry to medicine turned to dentistry instead. Applications to the Dental School were already high with an influx of returned servicepeople and it had insufficient resources for more students; in 1947 it, too, limited second-year entry.[101] The new dental dean, self-described 'brash Australian' John Walsh, was a force to be reckoned with; Brooking notes that 'he immediately turned his national stereotype to advantage by making as much noise as possible'.[102] But even the assertive Walsh could not quickly attract government and university investment in the building he deemed necessary in his initial 1946 report, along with additional staff and equipment plus more investment in research and postgraduate education; it took 15 years before the larger premises were open for business.[103] An acute shortage of dentists continued and from 1963, two years after the building opened, the dental intake rose from 50 to 60.[104]

Competitive entry raised the standard of students, but there were side effects. Young Pākehā men, many of them sons of doctors or other professionals, had always dominated the ranks of medical students, and many did not like it when others, especially women, gained entry ahead of them. There was much angst from the medical profession, university and public over Jewish refugee doctors. To obtain New Zealand registration, those with 'foreign' qualifications (essentially any that weren't British, no matter how reputable the institution) had to complete a year at the Otago Medical School, and this was extended to three years from 1936. The idea that 'foreigners' were at the school when New Zealanders were turned away prompted anger. In 1940 a move within the Medical Faculty to ban refugee doctors was lost by only one vote. Eventually, in 1943, the government ruled it would admit no more refugee doctors during the war.[105] Paul Oestreicher, an experienced German paediatrician, described his three years requalifying in another language at Otago as 'my mental concentration camp', though his son recalls that 'most of the professors could

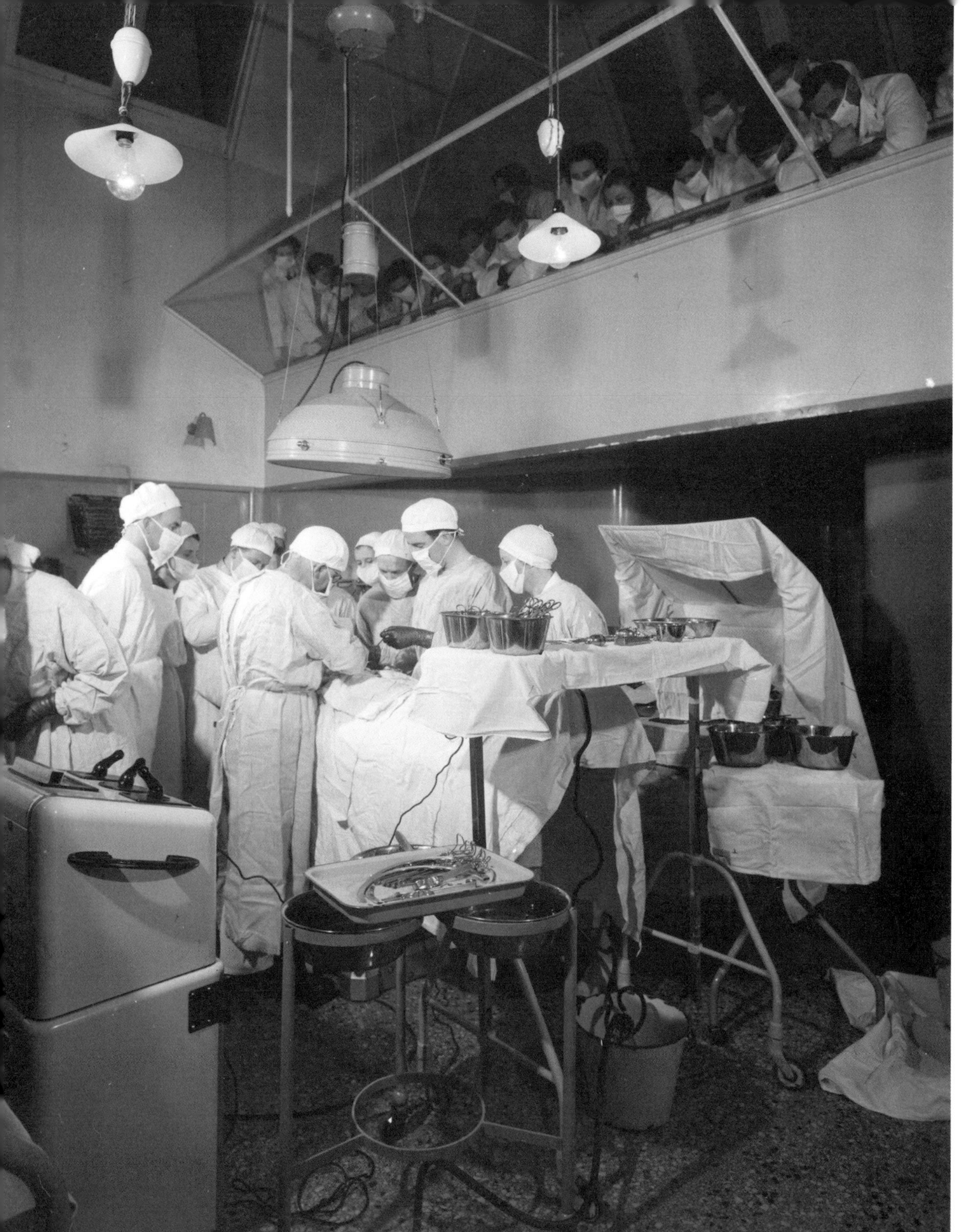

Clinical education at Dunedin Hospital in 1949: medical students look on from the gallery as surgeon and lecturer James Jenkins operates. PRIME MINISTER'S DEPARTMENT PHOTOGRAPH, BOX-184-066, S17-182E, HOCKEN COLLECTIONS.

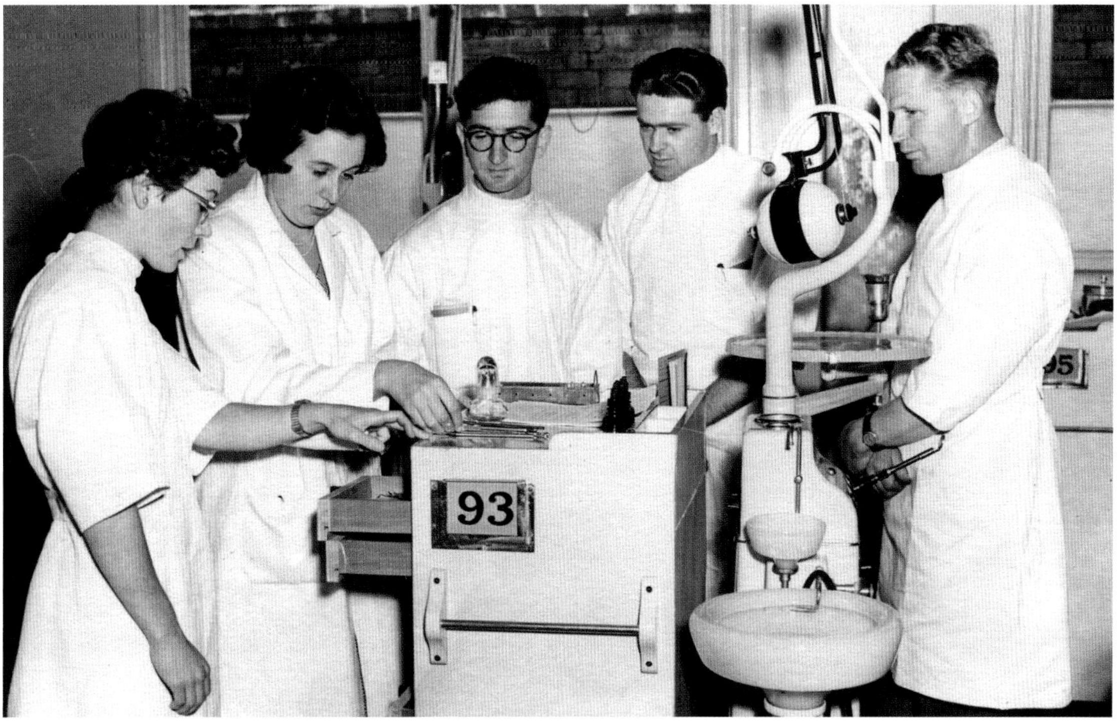

Elaine Donaldson (second from left) teaching fourth-year dental students Lorna Patrick, Maurice Potter, George Ryan and Snow Renolds in 1952. 'We were a rare breed', recalls Donaldson of women dentists. She was 'treated with respect' at the Dental School, though she was barred from the final year dinner. Donaldson – 'Mrs Head and Neck New Zealand' as she describes herself – returned to teaching in 1974, joining the Anatomy Department. *EVENING STAR* PHOTOGRAPH, ELAINE DONALDSON COLLECTION.

not have been more helpful' to the refugees – the family 'were never short of friends. Even so, anti-semitism was very common and taken for granted.'[106] Susi Williams, the daughter of refugee doctors Georg and Ruth Lemchen, notes that, with time, the public developed a 'positive attitude' to the refugee doctors, whom they discovered to be 'well qualified and charming and sophisticated', though there were still problems with the Medical Association and Returned Servicemen's Association.[107]

There was still only a handful of women in both the Medical and the Dental School. This was partly because many girls' schools did not teach physics, and this disadvantaged some young women once entry became competitive. Hercus and Bell's 1964 history of the Medical School reveals the paternalistic attitudes of the day: 'Women are natural, instinctive doctors with a strong bias to the simpler remedies; not for them complex carbon ring derivatives.' By then several women had won the Travelling Scholarship, awarded to the top graduate each year, but that failed to shift some deep-seated prejudices.[108] Women were even rarer in the Dental School. A 1980 study by Angela Pack revealed how few women registered as dentists after studying at Otago, until a jump in the 1970s; there were only six in the 1960s. Women academics were scarce at the Dental School, too; it wasn't until 2012 that 1970s graduate Bernadette Drummond 'broke the glass ceiling' to become the first woman professor.[109]

A trickle of Māori medical students followed the turn-of-the-century pioneers. Rina Moore (née Ropiha) was the first Māori woman to graduate in medicine, in 1948.[110] Walker Morete (Ngāti Porou) was the first Māori dental student, qualifying in 1928; he spent his working life as a dental officer in the public service.[111] Few Māori followed in Morete's footsteps over the next few decades. Frederick Te Tiwha Bennett studied dentistry after distinguished service with the Maori Battalion in World War II. Bennett's brother Henry had recently graduated in medicine and went on to a career in psychiatry; they were from a large Te Arawa whānau, sons of the Anglican Bishop of Aotearoa.[112] When John Broughton started the dental course in 1974 he was the only Māori in his year, and it was 12 years before there was another.[113]

ENTER PHARMACY

In the 1960s Otago ventured into educating pharmacists. The profession of pharmacy was undergoing rapid change and its education needed upgrading to keep pace. From the 1940s there was more demand for drugs, driven by new medicines and the government's recent introduction of a pharmaceutical benefit.[114] By the 1960s pharmacy demanded 'a much more intimate knowledge of pharmacology and pharmaceutical chemistry to cope with the rapid advances in drug sciences'.[115] Pharmacy had a long history of government regulation. Registration was introduced in 1881: pharmacists were required to complete an apprenticeship and to sit exams. Over the years private providers developed courses to help candidates prepare for exams, and technical institutes offered evening classes. In 1944 the Pharmacy Board took over the Wellington-based College of Pharmacy and from that year all pharmacy apprentices had to attend short courses. But the board had higher aspirations: it wanted all pharmacy training to be university-based, as it was in many other countries. A 1946 proposal from the college principal Sidney Wright gained widespread support. It proposed two years at university – one an intermediate year and the other a specialist course at Otago (the logical location, since it already taught some of the required subjects), with practical training to follow. A government advisory board approved the plan, the minister of education accepted the report and Otago expressed its willingness to participate once accommodation and finance were available.[116]

Momentum was lost with a change of government. After various reports and delays, in 1956 officials instead approved a two-tier system of pharmacy education. The majority of pharmacists would spend two full-time years at a technical institute, followed by an apprenticeship. The University of New Zealand Senate conceded that pharmacy was a suitable subject for university study, but believed that only a few people who were destined for specialist positions as researchers, lecturers, hospital pharmacists or manufacturing pharmacists needed a university qualification. The advice of the government's director of education, Clarence Beeby (the son of a Yorkshire pharmacist) was pivotal: he was an advocate of technical education and was planning a national Central Institute of Technology (CIT). The pharmacy diploma course commenced at CIT in 1960 – initially in Petone, then in Upper Hutt from 1972.[117]

Otago offered a four-year Bachelor of Pharmacy degree, with the intake initially limited to five students a year. It included several subjects that were already available – biology, physics, chemistry, physiology, biochemistry, microbiology and pharmacology – and introduced courses in pharmaceutics, pharmaceutical chemistry and pharmaceutical analysis. Pharmacy academics were scarce and both the university and CIT had problems recruiting staff. Eventually Otago asked Fred Fastier, associate professor of pharmacology, to head the course. Fastier was 'astonished' at the request: 'I was not a pharmacist and knew little about pharmacy as a profession.' He was also wary of taking responsibility 'for what was likely to be a conspicuous failure', but as 'a born optimist' he agreed. At Fastier's suggestion pharmacology, previously part of the Department of Medicine, and pharmacy combined to form a new department, thus pooling the resources of two related subjects with few staff. Two respected local pharmacists – analytical and consulting

Making up supplies of the new wonder drug, penicillin, in the Pathology Department's Sterile Solutions Unit in 1949. The 'factory' made solutions and drugs to sell around the country. Pathology professor Eric D'Ath kept it going in the hope it would prove useful for a future pharmacy department and it was duly handed over in the 1960s.

PRIME MINISTER'S DEPARTMENT PHOTOGRAPH, BOX-184-007, S16-102A, HOCKEN COLLECTIONS.

chemist Roy Gardner and Dunedin Hospital chief pharmacist John Conroy – 'came to the rescue' and became part-time lecturers for the specialist pharmacy subjects. The old Dental School Annexe was converted to provide specialised labs for the pharmacy programme and sterile solutions unit, which pharmacy took over from the Pathology Department.[118]

Pharmacy teaching began in 1963, with one student admitted to the third year of the course and five to second year. They immediately formed the Otago University Pharmacy Students Association; there weren't enough of them to enable a full student 'bash', so a cocktail party became their main annual social function. The first students to complete a BPharm, in 1965, were Margaret Sumich, Kenneth Taylor and Robert Tribe, and Taylor became the first MPharm graduate in 1967. All had already completed the CIT diploma course; the best students from CIT provided a steady stream of applicants to Otago.[119] Graduates found good positions and there was plenty of interest in the course, especially after the Pharmaceutical Society of Great Britain stopped reciprocal registration for the CIT's pharmacy diploma in 1968 but retained it for the Otago degree. By 1975 the degree admitted 25 students annually, making it less financially precarious. It split from pharmacology in 1970 and moved to the Science Faculty because of financial concerns. The 'detachment' of pharmacy from its 'real roots' in medicine was unfortunate, Fastier noted, but the medical dean made it clear that pharmacy was expendable if the troubled Medical School did not attract more funding.[120] Fastier remained 'caretaker' of the Pharmacy Department until the arrival of its first professor, Harry Taylor – formerly head of the CIT programme – late in 1971. Taylor led the Otago programme through 10 years of quiet consolidation. Despite his best efforts, the university was unable to provide pharmacy with a new building and it expanded into a series of makeshift premises; a 1981 retirement tribute to Taylor reported that he saw pharmacy flourish 'in the most decrepit building in the university, with his administrative work performed in an office no bigger than a commodious cupboard'.[121]

The department underwent big changes in the 1980s, sparked by Canadian Donald Perrier's whirlwind three years as professor. Perrier revamped Otago's curriculum; pharmacy

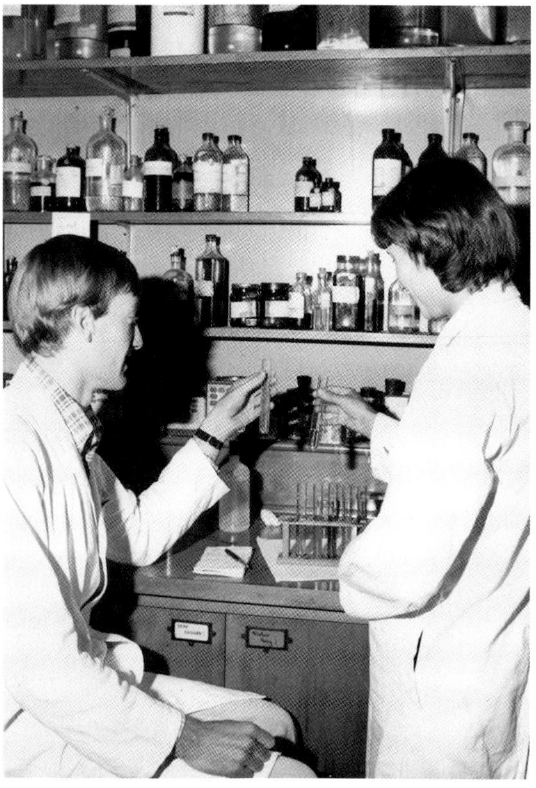

Pharmacy student Alan McClintock and technician Sandra Barkman identifying 'unknown' chemical compounds in Rob McKeown's pharmaceutical chemistry lab, c. 1983.

UNIVERSITY OF OTAGO PHOTOGRAPHIC UNIT RECORDS, MS-4368/085, S16-669C, HOCKEN COLLECTIONS.

traditionally centred on the product rather than the patient, but as more graduates shifted into retail pharmacy they needed better preparation for primary health care. Students enjoyed spending more time in hospital wards, where they learned to work with other health professionals and experienced the clinical applications of their knowledge. In line with his vision of the pharmacist as clinician as well as scientist, Perrier oversaw the department's transfer back to the Medical Faculty at the beginning of 1985. He attracted more funding for equipment to further the department's research and for a larger student intake, which rose to 30 in 1985.[122]

DEVELOPMENTS IN MEDICINE

In 1958, in his final annual report as medical dean, Hercus commented on the 'phenomenal expansion and widening of scope of medicine' in his 21 years in charge. In addition to the developments in the medical sciences, the clinically oriented specialties were evolving. There were now 'sub-departments' headed by full-time staff and 'approaching independent status' within the medicine and surgery departments: paediatrics, psychiatry, neurology, orthopaedics, neurosurgery, thoracic surgery, ophthalmology and anaesthesia.[123] Clinical research was boosted in 1961 when the dean, Edward (Ted) Sayers, negotiated a Wellcome Trust grant to construct a research building. It was a tribute to Smirk's high-profile hypertension research and came with the condition that the university appoint a research professor; it duly appointed Smirk to a new chair. In 1963 all of the Medicine Department's scattered research workers moved into their modern facility.[124] Cardiologist John Hunter took over from Smirk as professor of medicine in 1962. Psychological medicine finally got its own department that year, with Wallace Ironside as first professor, and paediatrics and child health got its first professor, James Watt, in 1967. Hunter built up the remainder of the Medicine Department, establishing units in various specialties, such as endocrinology and gastroenterology. There was quite a changing of the guard, which helped with Sayers' mission to modernise the undergraduate curriculum: there were fewer lectures in favour of clinical and small group teaching, and more emphasis on psychiatry, social medicine, radiology and clinical pathology.[125]

By the late 1960s, the Medical School was in trouble: it had too many students and not enough staff, patients or money. After the University of New Zealand was disestablished the UGC allocated all funding at university level; the Medical School lost its independent funding and had to compete with other rapidly growing faculties for a share of Otago's far from generous

Staff of the Wellcome Research Institute mark Horace Smirk's retirement in 1968. Smirk is seated at the centre of the second row from the front, holding a pair of glasses. PAULINE FRASER COLLECTION.

grant. Otago's plea to the UGC for additional funding failed; its chair, Canterbury's former 'iron vice-chancellor' Frederick Llewellyn, referred to 'rampant special schools' in a meeting with Otago representatives. The Medical School resented coming under the university administration, when it had once dealt directly with government. It was unhappy with its allocation, but Otago VC Arthur Beacham had no more to offer; he and Sayers remained at daggers drawn.[126]

The committee appointed in 1967 to recommend a replacement dean on Sayers' retirement convinced VC Robin Williams to get an external report into the size and structure of the Medical School. Ronald Christie, dean of medicine at McGill University, Canada, spent three months at Otago and presented his report in 1968. He concluded that Otago's faculty was 'one of the most economical in the English speaking world. This economy has been carried to the point when the future of the Medical School is in jeopardy.' Facilities at Dunedin Hospital were inadequate and the school was 'unique in that its teaching hospitals are administered by an elected board which has no University representation.' Salaries were 'far below the rest of the English speaking world' and understaffing meant insufficient time for research. Christie recommended more funding, the appointment of a dean with greater authority, and various improvements to the curriculum. To ensure adequate clinical training the school needed either to halve its student intake – an unlikely option when New Zealand had an increasing demand for doctors that the newly opened medical school in Auckland could not yet fill – or open a second clinical school, preferably in Christchurch.[127]

The UGC, government and hospital board were more willing to listen to an overseas expert than the previous complaints of the school and university. Implementing changes fell to the next dean, anatomy professor Bill Adams, supported by Robin Irvine in the new position of clinical dean; and they received good support from the Otago administration. By the end of 1968 the university had several representatives on the Otago Hospital Board, a rise in medical and dental salaries, a special grant to fund additional positions and promises of further buildings.[128] In 1969 Irvine presented the University Council with a report on the further implementation of Christie's recommendations, and this became the blueprint for the school's future. The school's intake rose in two stages, and both Christchurch and Wellington became clinical schools, taking students at fourth-year level from 1973 and 1977 respectively. The development of the 'northern' schools was a major project (see chapter 10).[129]

MEDICAL EXPANSION

The increase in students and staff and in buildings in the 1970s restored the morale of Medical School staff in Dunedin. Clinical departments expanded. Alan Alldred was appointed foundation professor in orthopaedics in 1972, Barry Baker became New Zealand's first professor of anaesthesia in 1975 and Stuart Heap took up a chair of radiology in 1978; and those fields, previously under the Surgery Department, all gained independent department status in 1977 and 1978.[130] Teaching and research in general practice emerged initially in the Preventive and Social Medicine Department, where Dixon was 'visionary in recognising that general practice had no academic base, even though 50% of New Zealand's doctors were GPs'.[131] Dixon appointed George Emery, who had established the country's first group general practice in South Dunedin in the 1950s, as half-time lecturer in 1962, and in the early 1970s a small cluster of general practice staff emerged. The department led planning for the Mosgiel Health Centre, which opened in 1974 to house an array of Hospital Board health professionals alongside private GPs; it became a teaching centre for medical students. A few years later, the general practice academics transferred to the Medicine Department. In 1983 Campbell Murdoch took up a general practice chair, endowed by Auckland doctor Elaine Gurr, an Otago medical graduate of 1923.[132] Another emerging specialty within the Medicine Department was care of the elderly; John Campbell became foundation professor of geriatric medicine in 1984.[133]

The biggest expansion was in the medical sciences: the discovery of the structure of DNA in the 1950s had captured the public imagination and attracted students to related fields. Petersen, who became biochemistry professor in 1968, recalls that the department 'grew like a mushroom'. Medical students were the department's 'bread and butter', but much of the growth came through science students. Extra staff were funded but finding qualified people was challenging; the shift in 1973 into a new building, generously equipped with the latest technology, made recruitment easier.[134] The Microbiology Department experienced a surge in numbers of students interested in genetics. John Loutit, one of the first Australasians to work in bacterial genetics, was recruited from Adelaide in 1956 to pioneer work in that field in New Zealand. His wife Margaret Loutit, also a microbiologist, recalls that when she started studying biology it was largely a descriptive field, but genetic techniques revolutionised that. Early genetic techniques were 'complex, slow and difficult'; possibilities for research arose as technology advanced and the department attracted many research students.[135]

Physiology was 'in a more precarious position than any other preclinical department in the Medical School,' Christie reported in 1968 – it had 'several distinguished physiologists' but they had too little time for research.[136] The authorities took note and by the mid-1970s the department had half a dozen more permanent academic staff. James Robinson, who arrived at Otago in 1957 and succeeded McIntyre as head of department in 1961, and Tony Macknight, who followed Robinson as head in 1980, led the research in other directions with renal, electrolyte and epithelial physiology as a focus. Neurophysiology was not forgotten, though; in 1972 John Hubbard returned to Otago to lead a new phase of work on neurotransmitters. John Harris and team – later

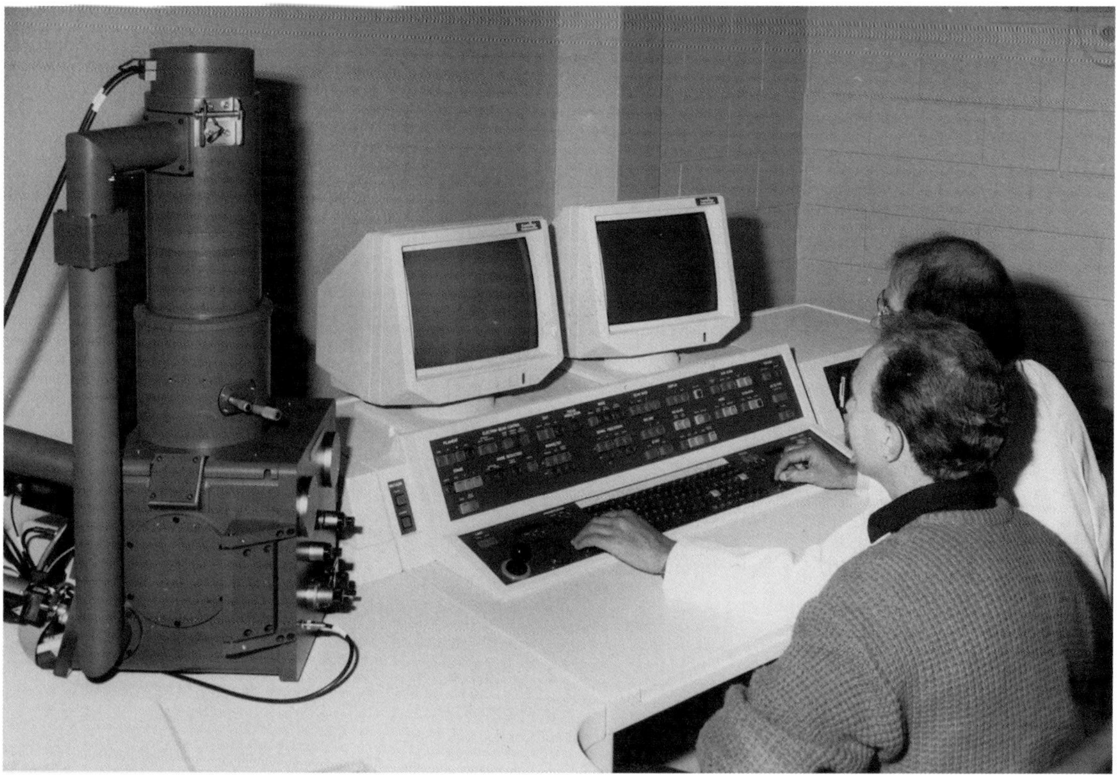

Zygmunt Poczwa (left) and Colin Geary with the Pathology Department's new computer-controlled scanning electron microscope, 1988.
DEPARTMENT OF PATHOLOGY RECORDS, MS-1364/200, S17-610G, HOCKEN COLLECTIONS.

the Developmental Biology Unit – researched the development of the nervous and muscular systems, and others worked on respiratory physiology. It was one of the most research-active departments at the university.[137]

The Anatomy Department did not teach science undergraduates and so did not experience the explosive growth of the other medical sciences, but it kept busy with the enlarged medical classes and evolving technology. Electron microscopy revolutionised anatomy research, according to Bill Trotter, a local graduate who started teaching in the department in the late 1940s and became professor in 1969.[138] The Dental School installed Otago's first electron microscope in 1958, and the Medical School got access to another in the 1960s when the MRC set up a Microscopy Unit and employed David Rayns to run it. Anatomists and others used it 'to explore previously unattainable structural features of the organ systems in which they were interested'. Cell membranes, which appeared 'boringly uniform' under ordinary transmission electron microscopy, became more interesting when Otago acquired a Baltec BAF 300 freeze-fracture machine in 1970. It was used for over 30 years, by which time the university had acquired a collection of increasingly sophisticated scopes.[139] When Gareth Jones took over as professor in 1983 the Anatomy Department changed its ethos 'from a medically oriented department to a science oriented one'. A half unit in anatomy for science students was introduced in 1978 and in 1986 it became a full BSc major. A name change to the Department of Anatomy and Structural Biology in 1991 reflected the changes technology had brought: it still taught and researched gross anatomy, but it also explored biology at the cellular level.[140]

Pharmacology remained a small department, but under the leadership of Garth McQueen, who came to Otago in 1954 to work on hypertension with Smirk, it developed innovative programmes. The New Zealand National Poisons Information Centre started in 1964 as a one-man operation run from the Dunedin Hospital Emergency Department, and eventually became a busy 24/7 public service with an enormous knowledge base. Alongside it McQueen developed New Zealand's Centre for Adverse Drug Reactions and the Intensive Medicines Monitoring Programme. Developed in the wake of the thalidomide tragedy, the valuable public service these programmes offered was recognised with dedicated government funding from 1982. McQueen also directed the Medical Research Council Toxicology Unit for some years.[141] Pharmacology taught only medical and pharmacy students and a few science postgraduates until the early 1980s, when it allowed some science students to join undergraduate classes; many were psychology majors, interested in the effects of drugs on the brain. A paper was developed for the BSc in neuroscience and in 1994 pharmacology became a BSc major.[142]

'Good research some of which is outstanding is to be found in most departments, and the incidence of mediocre research is less than in most of the medical schools I have visited,' Christie wrote in 1968.[143] Much of that research was in the MRC units, which by 1975 included biochemistry, immunopathology, virus and toxicology; the Ministry of Agriculture and Fisheries funded a Hydatid Unit and the Cancer Society supported the Hugh Adam Department of Cancer Research.[144] Later the MRC closed its own units and most of the research projects were absorbed into academic departments.

Several of the clinical departments were hives of research, too. In 1953 Michael Woodruff took up a full-time chair in surgery, established to promote further research (as the full-time medical chair had been for medicine). Woodruff left for Edinburgh in 1957 – in an era of slow communication he found the isolation from experts in other countries frustrating – but his short stay at Otago was inspirational. He was a pioneer in transplantation and later performed Britain's first successful kidney transplant. At Otago he worked on transplant rejection and acceptance, including collaborative experiments with Peter Medawar, who visited from London in 1956 and who shared the Nobel Prize with Macfarlane Burnet in 1960 for their discovery of acquired immunological tolerance. After Woodruff's departure, transplant immunology research continued under orthopaedic surgeon Norman Nisbet. Local graduate Barbara Heslop, a pathologist, joined the research team in 1958 and kept it going after Nisbet left in the mid-1960s; it later transferred from the Surgery Department to pathology.[145]

In the early 1970s the Department of Paediatrics and Child Health embarked on a project that was to become internationally renowned and valued – the Dunedin Multidisciplinary Health and Development Study, widely known as 'the Dunedin Study'. It began with paediatricians and neonatologists interested in the long-term wellbeing of tiny babies who survived in infancy thanks to improvements in technology, and it grew into a major multidisciplinary project that followed a cohort of Dunedin babies through life. Directed for many years by Phil Silva and later by Richie Poulton, the ongoing Dunedin Study made – and continues to make – many important findings that have influenced health and social policy in New Zealand and around the world.[146] In 1998, with the study subjects well into adulthood, it moved from the Paediatrics Department into the Preventive and Social Medicine Department, an attractive home because of its research strength.

By the 1970s the Preventive and Social Medicine staff had a wide range of research underway, from smallpox to noise-induced deafness. With the arrival of epidemiologist David Skegg as a young professor in 1980, research reached another level. Skegg urged more study of the epidemiology of diseases that were especially prevalent in New Zealand, such as heart disease and some cancers – areas 'where there was a special opportunity or public health need'. Skegg carried out significant work in cancer epidemiology, contraceptive and drug safety and multiple sclerosis. He had talented collaborators in the department, including fellow epidemiologist Charlotte Paul. When AIDS emerged in the 1980s they and Nigel Dickson established an AIDS Epidemiology Group. By the end of the century the department was home to the Hugh Adam Cancer Epidemiology Unit, the Injury Prevention Research Unit, the Ngāi Tahu Māori Health Research Unit, the National Occupational and Environmental Health Research Centre (a collaboration with the University of Auckland), the National Poisons Centre and the New Zealand Pharmacovigilance Centre. Alongside its research, the department's teaching responsibilities grew as it introduced epidemiology, community health, biostatistics and Māori health into the undergraduate medical course in the 1980s.[147]

ENGAGING WITH MĀORI

Otago had been educating Māori doctors since the 1890s, but never in great numbers. The Medical School recognised that New Zealand and the Pacific needed more Indigenous doctors and established a 'preference' system in 1951: it offered priority entry to two Māori or Pacific Island students.[148] In 1975 it extended the preference to New Zealand-resident Pacific Islanders and raised the quota to six people, but just one person was admitted to the 201-strong class through the system in 1976. Removal of the '50 per cent blood' requirement the following year increased admissions, but Māori and Pacific people were still seriously underrepresented in medical classes. In 1980 dean Geoffrey Brinkman expressed the faculty's concern at 'the inadequate response of Maoris to opportunities in Medicine'; it was 'taking active steps to promote interest among influential Maori groups'.[149] Recruiting more Māori students was not just a Māori responsibility: the Medical School needed to change if it was to qualify more Māori doctors.

Change was also needed to provide better education on things Māori to all medical students. A 1988 Medical Council review of medical education at Otago and Auckland noted that early attempts to bring 'taha Maori and multi-cultural understanding' into the programmes, along with initiatives on communication and ethics and gender issues, were regarded as 'somehow marginal to the curriculum as a whole'.[150] The criticism of the 'apparent mono-cultural ethos' within the school added momentum to initiatives already underway. In 1988 a working party that included members of the Māori community stated that a Māori health lecturer was 'essential to effective implementation of a bicultural perspective in our curriculum'.[151] A couple of years earlier John Broughton (Ngāti Kahungunu, Ngāi Tahu), a part-time lecturer in the Dental School, began giving a few classes on Māori health to medical students; in 1989 his position became permanent through the university's 'new blood' scheme to introduce new academic fields. Meanwhile, funding from the National Heart Foundation enabled Otago to appoint Papaarangi Reid (Te Rarawa) as half-time Māori health lecturer at Wellington. Māori health academia was 'in its infancy', Broughton recalls; most Māori doctors were 'busy in their own communities'. He started out based mainly in the Preventive and Social Medicine Department with a small amount of time in the Dental School; later, with the appointment of Joanne Baxter (Ngāi Tahu, Ngāti Apa ki te Rā Tō) to teach medical students, he could devote more time to dentistry.[152]

The Māori health lecturers served as role models, provided support to Māori students, ensured that graduates of all ethnicities had some understanding of Māori health, and worked on recruitment. University-wide initiatives such as the Māori Centre improved support for Māori students, and Māori medical and dental students established their own associations. Numbers accelerated after a big push in the 2000s to recruit and support Māori through to graduation; Health Sciences PVC Don Roberton was a strong advocate for such efforts. Associate deans for Māori were appointed at each of the three campuses in 2010.

Baxter was appointed to the Dunedin post and led a Health Sciences Māori Workforce Development Unit. One of its programmes – a 'gem in the crown,' says Broughton – tackled a barrier for Māori: many had not studied science to the necessary level at high school. When Tū Kahika provided a foundation studies year for up to 20 students as preparation for health sciences first year, the intake of Māori students to medicine more than doubled.[153]

'We are changing the face of the medical workforce,' Health Sciences PVC Peter Crampton noted in 2014. Otago's 'overall guiding policy' was to educate health professionals who would reflect the diversity of the society they worked in. As well as increasing Māori engagement, the Medical School targeted the recruitment and support of Pacific Islands students. Fa`afetai Sopoaga, an Otago medical graduate who had lectured in the Preventive and Social Medicine Department since 1999, was appointed to the role of associate dean (Pacific) for the Health Sciences Division in 2009 and headed a new Pacific Islands Research and Student Support Unit. In 2011, in collaboration with the Student Learning Centre, Pacific Islands Health Professional Students' Association, Pacific Islands Centre and local Pacific community, she established the Pacific Orientation Programme at Otago (POPO), and it and other initiatives boosted Pacific entry.[154] In 2015 VC Hayne celebrated the big jump in Pacific Island and Māori students in the health sciences: 'The social implications of this are enormous and, over time, will change the face of health-care provision in this country'.[155]

REFORMING THE CURRICULUM

The Māori and Pacific associate deans in the health sciences were all women, and this reflected another change. Women accounted for less than 20 per cent of entries to Medical School until 1973. There was a noticeable rise from that year until, in 1985, women made up half the class for the first time.[156] Women academics were still rare, partly because many medical specialties required years of further full-time training with little wriggle room for parental responsibilities.[157] Heslop, one of the few professorial women, commented: 'It was only when the numbers of women in the medical classes started to increase that the necessity to arrange jobs a little more imaginatively than had been done previously occurred to the administration.' Heslop had completed her Otago medical training in 1948; she wrote that 'active encouragement' of medical women was then rare; 'I guess that all reasonably intelligent women of my vintage got used to being patronised by men whom they regarded as rather stupid.'[158] Continuing advocacy and more women graduates led to a steady rise in women on staff.

One of them was Katrina Varian, who in 1989 commenced as a clinical lecturer in general practice with special responsibility for teaching women's health. It was a growing field, promoted by women's organisations and highlighted by the inquiry into alleged malpractice in the treatment of women with cervical cancer at National Women's Hospital. Silvia Cartwright's damning 1988 report into the 'unfortunate experiment' in Auckland sparked reforms to the health system and brought new responsibilities in ethics, informed consent and patients' rights.[159] The Medical School responded quickly with the introduction of teaching on informed consent. It already had ethics in the programme – it was a particular interest of Brinkman, the dean from 1978 to 1983, who instigated the campaign for a bioethics centre at Otago. In 1986 ethicist Alistair Campbell of Edinburgh came as visiting professor – a 'dynamic presence', he promoted ethics and commenced formal teaching of the subject in 1987. In 1988 the university approved a Bioethics Research Centre, which put Otago in the vanguard of an emerging field. The centre received funding from various churches and the health board.[160] It expanded to include staff from varied backgrounds – from neurosurgery and philosophy to Chinese medicine and English; the Master of Bioethics and Health Law degree, begun in 1995, reflected its interdisciplinary nature.[161] Ethics was taught to medical undergraduates and 'woven into all training' in the late 1990s; this 'integration of medical ethics' was 'probably unique to any medical school in the world,' bioethics director Donald Evans noted.[162]

Not everybody approved of subjects like communication and ethics – some people still thought that students absorbed these qualities by observing clinical teachers at the bedside. However, the Cartwright report had revealed deficiencies and the public expected better: medical education had to include explicit teaching in these subjects. Overall there was an ever-increasing body of knowledge in the biosciences and clinical medicine, but there was a limit to what could be fitted into the programme. The course was highly didactic – medical students spent countless hours in lectures and in the dissection room. 'The teaching was very good; most of it was excellent ... it was just that they tried to teach too much,' recalls Skegg, who entered second-year medicine in 1967. Anatomy was the worst offender: 'We didn't actually need to know why every little groove was in every bone.'[163] During the 1980s some departments reduced the lecture load in favour of self-directed learning, and shifted from the delivery of facts to problem-based learning. These changes laid the foundation for a more radical curriculum shift in 1997, when the second- and third-year course became 'integrated' rather than discipline-based: it included modules based on organ systems as well as 'Patient, doctor and society', a course that incorporated early clinical contact and covered topics like ethics and communication skills; and 'systems integration', a case-based course that brought together clinical material from the other modules. Similar reforms were later made to the fourth- and fifth-year courses.[164]

The curriculum changes highlighted anomalies in the intermediate year. As early as 1946 dental dean John Walsh noted that 'the present tendency for the Medical Intermediate course to drift towards Stage I Science, and to be regarded as an elimination test rather than a year of preparation for future professional studies, is not in the best interests of dental education.'[165] The same problem applied to medicine. The list of intermediate subjects was modified over time but the course content of those subjects was controlled by science and arts faculties of the various universities; the health sciences could not introduce more relevant material or shift some of their crowded syllabus back into first year. Proposals in the early 1980s for tailored courses for medical intermediate students attracted controversy at Otago and, especially, at other universities which would lose intermediate students. The UGC negotiated a compromise: Otago would continue to admit students from other universities, but it would direct which of those universities' courses intermediate students should take.[166]

In 1998, in a less regulated era, Otago introduced a Health Sciences First Year (HSFY) programme. The course had to be taken in Dunedin, and this caused a loss of goodwill from other universities. Cynics noted that HSFY increased Otago's student numbers and funding. But there was more to it than that: it allowed a fairer comparison between applicants, and courses were purpose-designed for the health professions.[167] HSFY underwent various modifications over time, but it remained the common intermediate year for medicine, dentistry, pharmacy, medical laboratory science and physiotherapy degrees. It attracted many enrolments and competition for entry to second-year classes in the professional degrees was always intense. Selection methods were still debated – and probably always will be. Grades were still the top criterion, but some courses added the widely used Undergraduate Medicine and Health Sciences Admission Test – a psychometric test devised in Australia. The test became part of Otago's admission process for medicine in 2003, for dentistry in 2005 and for medical laboratory science in 2007; and the Dental School interviewed prospective students from 2005.[168]

AN AGE OF HEALTH REFORMS

During the 1980s and 90s New Zealand's health system experienced 'incessant reforms and changes,' writes Robin Gauld. The 1993 restructuring of the public sector in New Zealand was 'one of the most radical … in the world', and it had serious effects on clinical education.[169] Hospitals became crown health enterprises (CHEs) that were contracted to provide health services and make a profit. Funding was tight, especially in the south, where the new population-based funding system had the effect of cutting budgets. For the business managers running CHEs, educating health professionals was not a priority; joint clinical staff were burdened with growing workloads as hospitals reduced staff. A long-running dispute between the Dunedin School of Medicine and Healthcare Otago over who was costing whom money was resolved by a 1997 report: to the surprise of the CHE managers, it revealed that Medical School staff were giving more service to the hospital than their remuneration warranted; the university was thus bearing a cost, however 'insignificant'. The report, alongside further modifications to the health system and a changing of the guard at the CHE, improved relationships and morale.[170]

Government reforms did offer opportunities in health science education. In 1979, in the midst of the oil shock, the government cut entry to medical schools. Otago's three clinical schools were structured around an annual entry of 200 students and when that dropped to 150, survival became difficult. Brinkman eventually persuaded the government to raise the intake to 170 from 1986. There was some relief, too, from the freer tertiary market of the 1990s: although the domestic cap in enrolments was not raised, Otago started enrolling international health science undergraduates through arrangements with other governments. It began with a group from Malaysia in 1992 and added others, including the first group from Saudi Arabia in 2000; at one point Warwick Brunton, associate dean (international), had 300 students from the International Student Special Scheme under his care.[171] In 2004 the government, anxious to recruit more doctors into rural areas and into mental health, boosted the domestic intake to 190; students who committed to working in those fields were given priority. Subsequently admissions increased to cope with New Zealand's changing demography, and reached 282 in 2017.[172]

With more students and shorter patient stays in hospitals it became trickier to arrange clinical experience for students, especially in Dunedin. The solution was to spread further afield. The Medical School worked with the Southland Hospital Board from the 1970s: students could undertake their final year or complete their obstetrics diploma at Kew Hospital in Invercargill, and the university appointed local part-time clinical lecturers to the hospital.[173] A medical trust established by Southland's Gilmour family funded a distance learning centre at Kew, which allowed Southland doctors and students to participate in Dunedin events through links with the Barnett Lecture Theatre and the Department of General Practice.[174] Fourth-year student surgery attachments in Invercargill were offered from 1988 and were a popular option. Other clinical fields were added, and in 2005 orthopaedic surgeon Gordon Veale became the first associate dean for Southland.[175]

Otago set up hubs in smaller centres – Oamaru, Balclutha, Gore, Frankton, Dunstan and Greymouth – from 2001 with the aim of recruiting more doctors into rural practice. All Dunedin fifth-year students spent five weeks at one of the hubs – described as 'one of the best learning experiences during medical training'.[176] The Department of General Practice established the Te Waipounamu Research Unit to investigate rural practice in 2002; the director, Queenstown GP Pat Farry, was a driving force in rural programmes. Farry also directed the Rural Medicine Immersion Programme, a bold initiative in which some students spent most of their fifth year in a rural setting. A 2007 pilot programme was 'an outstanding success' and it expanded to include students from all three campuses, with rural teaching centres around the country; graduates of the programme gravitated to rural practice.[177] A change of name to the Department of General Practice and Rural Health in 2009 signalled the importance of rural health in the Dunedin school.

Medicine had to diversify to survive when its undergraduate intake was low. Postgraduate courses became more important.[178] The specialist colleges still provided the main qualifications for medical specialists, but the Medical School built up its vocational postgraduate courses. By 1986 there were students enrolled in diplomas in obstetrics, child health, community health, industrial health, child psychotherapy, clinical pathology and microbiology. Otago's undergraduate Diploma in Occupational Health Practice, introduced in 1987, was the first to take advantage of teleconferencing technology, and other successful distance-taught courses followed. Some, such as public health, attracted people from other health professions, and that gathered momentum after the government set up the Clinical Training Agency (CTA) as part of the 1990s health reforms, to fund post-entry clinical training in the sector.[179]

Funding for research was always tight, though medicine benefited more from public philanthropy than most other fields. Otago's Leading Thinkers scheme added health science research centres and chairs in the 2000s. The initiative started well in 2003 with a donation from the charitable trust of Dunedin businessman Eion Edgar, Otago's chancellor, which funded the Edgar National Centre for Diabetes and Obesity Research. The Karitane Products Society added funding to endow a research fellowship in early childhood obesity.[180] Other Leading Thinkers donations secured existing projects with precarious income; for instance, Cure Kids funded a chair in child health, which enabled Otago to retain Stephen Robertson, a gifted paediatrician and clinical geneticist whose work had previously been funded on 'soft' money. Cure Kids also funded a second chair in paediatric research, awarded to Christchurch neonatologist Brian Darlow.[181] The Mercy Sisters endowed a chair in international health, and Stuart and Marylyn McKinlay endowed a chair in global health: the two professors led the Centre for International Health, based in the Department of Preventive and Social Medicine.[182]

Other initiatives covered a range of clinical and bioscience fields: the Carney Centre for Pharmacogenomics (Christchurch), the Gama Research Fellowship in Bipolar Disease (Christchurch), the McKenzie Chair in Clinical Science, and the New Zealand Institute for Cancer Research Trust Chair in Cancer Pathology. Robert Webster and family endowed a chair in viral pathogenesis; Webster completed an MSc in microbiology at Otago in 1957 and went to the United States, where he developed vaccines and researched the links between avian and human influenza. American philanthropist John Thrash's donation established a state-of-the-art laboratory for molecular research in infectious diseases, led by Kurt Krause. The two initiatives became part of the Webster Centre for Infectious Diseases, which brought together researchers from around the university and beyond it in a 'virtual centre dedicated to supporting basic research in infectious diseases throughout New Zealand'.[183]

EXPANDING BEYOND MEDICINE

In 1995, after an Australian Medical Council accreditation review found that the Otago Medical School's 'decision-making pathways' were unclear, it restructured. The new Dunedin School of Medicine, comprising the clinical departments, sat alongside the Christchurch and Wellington schools, and the departments of anatomy, biochemistry, microbiology, pharmacology and physiology became the Otago School of Medical Sciences (later renamed Biomedical Sciences).[184] The Medical School had already been incorporated, along with the Dental School, into the Division of Health Sciences when the university was arranged into divisions in 1989. The school was no longer a powerful realm of its own, and some regretted that; but Otago's expansion into other health programmes kept the Medical School 'safe', as David Stewart recalled. During the troubled 1980s when it seemed one of the clinical schools might have to close, or on the various occasions Christchurch or Wellington threatened to split off, other programmes gave Otago resilience. During Stewart's watch as medical dean and AVC, physiotherapy returned to the university, pharmacy gained in status, a medical laboratory science programme was introduced and planning began for expansion into various dental occupations. Those programmes were enabled by reforms in the tertiary and health sectors and took advantage of 'an enormous resource being underutilised' in the medical sciences and pathology departments. The rest of this chapter explores their development.[185]

PHARMACY TAKES OFF

In pharmacy, the whirlwind started by Perrier in the early 1980s continued under his successor. Australian Mike Roberts was 'a real mover and shaker', said Stewart; indeed, he 'shook a bit too hard' but did 'get things going'. Soon after his 1986 arrival, Roberts gained council approval to double pharmacy's annual intake to 60 students and to develop distance postgraduate qualifications targeted at working pharmacists. He added his voice to the long campaign to make a degree mandatory for registration.[186] The CIT diploma came close to gaining degree status in the early 1980s, after the Pharmaceutical Society negotiated for the programme's affiliation with one of the universities. Massey agreed to accept the CIT diploma as an external degree, but the UGC denied approval. In 1986 CIT came up with another proposal, for a four-year degree taught jointly with Victoria; and Otago recommended that, instead, all New Zealand pharmacy education should be at Otago. The UGC preferred the single pharmacy school at Otago option, but referred the decision to the Ministry of Education. In 1988 the minister commissioned a report to identify the training needs of pharmacists that noted that Otago had a high staff turnover, Roberts had just resigned and resources were stretched, but it had a 'commendable' research output and a committed head in Peter Coville, registrar of the Pharmaceutical Society and a former head of the CIT programme.[187]

In 1989 the government announced that from 1991 the CIT programme would close and all prospective pharmacists would complete the four-year Otago degree, with an intake of 100 students a year. It was a blow to CIT, but a boost to Otago and to the profession.[188] Alongside the expanded undergraduate intake Otago had plenty of postgraduates: in 1992 there were over 100 people enrolled in distance-taught postgrad courses, in addition to internal students; many were international students, including some enrolled through a special arrangement with Hong Kong University.[189] Expansion earned the Pharmacy Department an upgrade in status – in 1991 it became the School of Pharmacy, with Coville as dean. The leadership of 'Papa Smurf', as he was affectionately known, helped ease the growing pains as the school expanded and integrated some of the former CIT staff.[190]

Otago did not have the field to itself for long. Although Pharmaceutical Society president Earle Shaw said in 1989 that having one Pharmacy School would 'prevent the duplication of vital resources' and made 'economic sense', a decade later, with demand for more pharmacists and an increasingly competitive tertiary sector, the government approved another degree course at the University of Auckland. Otago lost one of its best staff, John Shaw, who became head of the Auckland programme, but the southern school still flourished. Ian Tucker, the Otago dean from 1999 to 2010, nurtured and developed its research culture. In 2013, as pharmacy celebrated its 50th anniversary at Otago, Tucker's successor Stephen Duffull noted that it enrolled 145 new undergrads each year, had around 40 PhD students, was rated in the top 100 schools in the world and attracted 'extraordinarily high quality staff'.[191]

PHYSIOTHERAPY RETURNS

After the Otago Hospital Board took over control of the massage therapy programme from the university in 1915, there were many developments. By the early 1940s students spent two years at the Dunedin school, followed by a six-month clinical placement in one of the main centre hospitals. World War II created more demand for the 'rehabilitative professions' and physiotherapists were still in short supply; by 1960 the school was accepting around 70 students each year into a course that was now three years.[192] It retained close links with the university: students attended anatomy and physiology classes at the Medical School and staff from physics, pathology and psychological medicine taught for the programme at various times. Physio students socialised with other Otago students, some lived in the residential colleges and in 1950 they joined OUSA en masse so they could retain access to its canteen, social facilities and sports teams. Many physiotherapists wanted to enhance the status of the profession, which needed more research and specialist education. Decades of requests for Otago to establish a chair of physiotherapy and a diploma course bore no fruit, though they came close in the 1960s.[193] In 1965 the University Council approved in principle a proposal from the Physiotherapy Board and a year later the Medical Faculty expressed support: its report claimed that physiotherapy was particularly deserving among the 'paramedical' professions of 'the type of training provided by the University concept', since it was 'therapeutic and not merely supportive'.[194]

That support came to nothing when the UGC refused funding. Instead, in 1976 the university link with the Physiotherapy School was broken and the course was transferred to Otago Polytechnic. A second school of physiotherapy had opened at Auckland Institute of Technology (AIT) in 1973. The move into technical institutes reflected broader national policy. The Department of Health decided in the 1960s to transfer the training of health professionals to the education sector. Professions whose members aspired to a university education – physiotherapy and nursing, for example – were caught up in the Department of Education's enthusiasm for technical institutes. The Physiotherapy Board, backed by the Medical Association, rejected a proposal to locate a national physiotherapy school at CIT; the board wanted physiotherapy education to remain close to a medical school. The government then directed the Otago school to transfer to Otago Polytechnic. The government was already funding three tertiary institutions in the city, and it rejected a popular alternative proposal from the hospital board for a College of Health Sciences in Dunedin.[195]

In 1976 physiotherapy became, overnight, the largest department of Otago Polytechnic and its first health science course. The polytech entered the venture in good faith, but for the profession it was 'little more than a stepping stone towards its ultimate goal', a university education.[196] It achieved that in two stages. In 1985 the medical dean set up a group of interested parties and eventually a senate working party presented a proposal for a four-year Bachelor of Physiotherapy (BPhty): the teaching would be split 50:50 between the university for the science components and the polytech for the professional and clinical aspects. The degree would be awarded by the university, since polytechs were not yet authorised to award degrees. In 1989 the UGC gave its approval but, as it was about to disband, the funding decision rested with the Ministry of Education – which was only prepared to fund a three-year degree. Those planning the programme believed the funding for four years would eventually come through and started the course in 1991; a group that was fast-tracked because of prior medical sciences study became the first graduates at the end of 1993.[197]

One motive for upgrading to a degree was to access postgraduate education and research. Physiotherapists completed projects under the umbrella of other disciplines, but the profession was seriously under-researched in this country. There was 'a paucity of data to support the value of physiotherapy', noted Robin McKenzie at the 1994 official launch of the university's postgraduate programmes in physiotherapy, which had begun the previous year and already had 19 students enrolled.[198] Meanwhile, the undergraduate programme hit a snag: the government still refused funding for the BPhty's fourth year and, until it relented at the end of 1997, physio students had to pay much higher fees in their final year of study.[199]

In 1994 incoming VC Graeme Fogelberg set up an independent review of the Physiotherapy School, which recommended that the university take sole charge of the joint operation. The

The government at first refused to fund the fourth year of the physiotherapy degree and the university was not prepared to cross-subsidise students; it also faced major problems with inadequate funding for dentistry education. The high fees charged to fourth-year students prompted protests, like this one in the Octagon in 1995.

OUSA RECORDS, MS-4225/291, S17-611G, HOCKEN COLLECTIONS.

polytech agreed to that, though it lost students and had an expensive redundancy round – it was what physiotherapists had been working towards for decades. From 1996 the Physiotherapy School sat alongside the other professional schools within the Division of Health Sciences. Peter Milburn, acting dean, reported at the end of the year that they were 'interesting times' but that the move was positive; it brought together 'all aspects of physiotherapy and research' and the school could 'develop a seamless curriculum throughout the full spectrum of academic programmes'. Some of the former polytech staff were appointed to the university and enrolled for higher degrees, and this became the norm for physiotherapy educators. John Sullivan was appointed Otago's inaugural physiotherapy professor and dean at the end of 1996; he had studied at Otago's Physical Education School and then in Canada, and had become an expert on physical rehabilitation following brain injury. A plan to lease and refurbish the old physio building from the hospital board fell through, so the school took up temporary premises in the Hercus Building until, to the envy of many other parts of the university, it moved into a new building in 1997.[200]

From 1998 prospective physiotherapists joined the hordes of aspiring health professionals in Health Sciences First Year. Some in the profession were unhappy at the loss of direct entry and specialist education at first-year level, but Sullivan pointed out the boost in status that HSFY gave; it sent 'the wonderful message that doing Physiotherapy is the same as any other Health Science profession'. Specialist papers and clinical experience began at second year and, as with the previous joint degree, the fourth year was in clinical centres, with the class divided between Wellington, Christchurch and Dunedin.[201]

RADIOGRAPHY INTERLUDE

For several decades the Physiotherapy School had a sibling – the Otago School of Radiography, also run by the hospital board and associated with the university. Southern doctor Harry de Lautour acquired an X-ray apparatus in 1899, just four years after Wilhelm Roentgen's discovery of that technology; he used it to image fractures and bone deformities, a fragment of steel in a man's eye and 'numerous hands and feet exposing needles in the bones, and others showing the presence of glass, shot, etc.'[202] Dunedin Hospital acquired its first machine in 1904 and its first specialist radiologist, Percy Cameron, in 1910; by the next year he was treating cancers with radium and diagnosing patients using X-ray technology. In 1914 Cameron became the Medical School's first radiology lecturer. Arthur Otway, 'a gentleman impeccably dressed in morning coat and striped trousers', became 'X-ray operator' at the hospital in 1920. Like other early radiographers Otway learned his skills on the job: Health Department plans for registration and a national school for radiographers fell through. The technology was revolutionary but also dangerous and for many early users, including Cameron, exposure to radiation had debilitating or even fatal results.[203] For expert advice on the science of radiation, radiologists turned to physicists: Otago's physics professor, Robert Jack, advised the hospital board on matters such as replacing a tube of radium after Cameron accidentally broke it in 1923.[204]

By the 1940s there was enough work to appoint a medical physicist at Dunedin Hospital. Warren Sinclair, who had just completed an MSc at Otago, took on the role, though he had 'some trepidation at this new type of career'. Medical specialists pushed for two courses that began in 1946: a University of Otago Diploma of Diagnostic Radiology for qualified doctors, and a course run by the Otago School of Radiography for technicians. Hospitals in all the main centres set up their own radiography schools during the 1940s and their trainees sat the exams of the Society of Radiographers in London.[205] Each hospital found its lecturers where it could, but for Dunedin the Medical School was an obvious source, and from 1946 radiography students joined physiotherapy students at anatomy lectures and dissections.[206] Hugh Jamieson became lecturer in radiological physics at the university in 1948 alongside the hospital medical physics post. He completed his MSc 'using a gas X-ray tube and a primitive X-ray spectrometer. These had been bought the year I was born and had lurked in a Physics Department cupboard awaiting my arrival in Dunedin, to be dusted off and given to me with a vague suggestion that I get them to work, and use them'; by contrast he found the hospital equipment 'marvellous!' The university had better teaching facilities, however,

Celebrating the first Otago School of Radiography graduation in 1948. Back row, from left: Hugh Jamieson (physicist), Ian Grant (student), Keith Buckley (staff radiographer). Front row: Jessie Borrie (student), William Sowerby (head of department), Mervyn Allan (student). Ken Campbell-Board also graduated.
IAN GRANT COLLECTION.

and Jamieson conducted demonstrations and experiments in the Physics Department with the radiography and radiology students. The hospital's charge radiographer served as tutor for the other classes.[207]

Radiography students were kept on the university's books until physiotherapy training moved to Otago Polytechnic in 1976. Radiography training was on the move from the health sector, too. A national course in therapeutic radiography began at CIT in 1978. The radiation therapy course evolved from that, and later transferred to Otago's Wellington campus (see chapter 10). Training in diagnostic radiography continued at hospitals, including Dunedin, until a national 1990 review led to it moving to three technical institutes – the closest one was in Christchurch.[208] The university lost its formal link with radiography training. But in 1983 it introduced a specialist MSc in medical physics – as did Waikato the following year.[209] This was timely, as the extent and complexity of radiation oncology services mushroomed in the late 1980s. Diagnostic radiology also became more complex, with advancing scanning technology and invasive techniques such as angiography. However, medical physics remained a niche course for a small profession and was difficult to sustain; there were just 24 medical physicists employed in New Zealand in 1999. Canterbury developed a programme that included a registrar component to fit new professional accreditation requirements. Otago quietly dropped its medical physics degree, which disappeared from its calendar after 1998; the final thesis was submitted early in 2003.[210]

ENTER MEDICAL LABORATORY SCIENCE

Medical laboratory science was another profession that joined the great migration of training from the health sector to the education sector in the late twentieth century. In 1987 Colvin Campbell, president of the New Zealand Institute of Medical Laboratory Technology (NZIMLT), reflected on the changes to medical lab work. In the 1950s technologists worked manually, had 'a small test repertoire' and no lab assistants; they did 'all the work from collection to reporting'. The 'age of technology' arrived with semi-automation, then fuller automation, in the 1960s and 1970s. The booming New Zealand economy supported 'new and bigger laboratories, with more staff and better equipment and more laboratory assistants'; the latter were needed 'to feed the voracious analysers'. Training was not so progressive: 'we continued to train able seamen and master mariners in the age of jets and space rockets', as Campbell put it.[211]

In the 1920s the Department of Health offered a Certificate of Proficiency in Bacteriological Technique to lab technicians who passed an exam after a five-year apprenticeship. This later broadened into other aspects of medical laboratory work, and from 1949 trainees passed a Basic Training Certificate three years into their apprenticeship. Training was provided by the labs where they worked. The Auckland Hospital Board, with several major hospitals and numerous laboratory personnel, set up a school in 1961 with a full-time tutor to train its medical technologists, along with a shorter course for assistants. In 1970 the Basic Training Certificate was replaced with a New Zealand Certificate of Science; trainees attended part-time courses at their local tech, or a longer block course at CIT. The Certificate of Proficiency, which became the Diploma in Medical Laboratory Technology in 1982, remained an advanced qualification.[212]

In 1973 medical laboratory technology joined the list of health occupations that required official registration.[213] It was a profession on the rise and the NZIMLT wanted better education. A proposal for a degree at Massey in the early 1980s fell through when it was rejected by the Hospital Boards Association, but the campaign did not stop.[214] The NZIMLT reported recruitment problems, a fragmented training system 'inappropriate for the modern medical laboratory' and, for those who had not obtained a BSc before training, a lack of access to postgraduate education or overseas registration; New Zealand was out of step with comparable countries.[215] AIT offered a four-year diploma from 1989 and CIT started a similar programme in 1990, but those did not fulfil the profession's aspirations.[216]

By 1989 the NZIMLT was in serious discussions with Otago about a degree programme. Dunedin Hospital technologists had a good relationship with the Medical School and Stewart, the dean, was keen to bring medical laboratory science into the university. After consulting widely, Colin Watts from the Clinical Biochemistry Department and Colin Geary, head of the Pathology Department, came up with a proposal for a four-year Bachelor of Medical Laboratory Science (BMLSc) degree and, in an era that was supportive of bold educational ventures, it received government approval. It was also an era of free market competition, and when others were informed of Otago's proposal they came up with their own schemes: Massey received approval to commence a degree from 1992 and in 1994, after technical institutes were permitted to award degrees, the AIT programme was upgraded

Second-year medical laboratory science students Alice Gee and Philip Shaw completing a transfusion science protocol, 2015.
LISA GALLAGHER PHOTOGRAPH, DEPARTMENT OF PATHOLOGY COLLECTION.

to a degree. The CIT diploma programme did not survive, but the approval of three professional degree courses left Otago, Massey and AIT (which became Auckland University of Technology in 2000) competing for a limited pool of students.[217]

The Otago medical laboratory science programme started well, although it did not reach its desired quota of 60 students. The first students entered second year in 1992; most had completed HSFY, though a few had taken other pathways.[218] The second-year course included anatomy, biochemistry, microbiology, physiology and a practical intensive course in laboratory technology, and in third year they studied clinical biochemistry, health microbiology, haematology and immunohaematology and general pathology. In the fourth year they dispersed to laboratories around the country where they completed advanced study in their two chosen specialty fields.[219] Watts, the inaugural director, was a good teacher and popular with students, and his 'friendly charm' as he travelled the country negotiating with laboratories helped smooth their path. Watts died a couple of months before the graduation of the first 23 students in December 1994; he endowed a prize for the top graduate.[220] Though medical laboratory science was an interdisciplinary programme with its own board of study, it found a de facto home in the Pathology Department, into which the smaller Clinical Biochemistry Department had merged in 1991. Another clinical biochemist, Chris Lovell-Smith, succeeded Watts as part-time director, and subsequent directors had backgrounds in related sciences. In 1995 the government approved a postgraduate diploma and master's degree in medical laboratory science, fulfilling a goal the profession had worked towards for decades.[221]

EXPANDING DENTAL EDUCATION

In the 1990s the Otago Dental School expanded into other areas of oral health – dental technology, therapy and hygiene. Its previous ventures beyond dental surgery had not survived. From 1929 it had offered an 18-month 'special mechanical dentistry course', which aimed to prepare students 'to be a capable laboratory assistant to a practitioner', but the course was abandoned in 1942. Women in particular were attracted to the course: Pickerill's biographer suggests he preferred them in the role because they were less likely to extend themselves into clinical work in competition with dentists – a perennial concern for dentists.[222] In the first half of the twentieth century many dental technicians, who manufactured prosthetics, effectively practised as dentists or worked independently of them, despite this being banned by the 1936 Dentists Act. The technicians campaigned for legal 'chairside rights' – direct access to patients – but they had a powerful opponent in the New Zealand Dental Association. Technicians trained on the job, often through an apprenticeship, and their training was haphazard until the introduction of registration in 1969. From then dental technology became part of the shift into technical institutes: in 1974 CIT commenced a part-time course, which developed into a three-year full-time Diploma in Dental Technology during the 1980s. It was 'almost entirely divorced from the direct influence of dentists'.[223]

Dentists were also worried that dental nurses might encroach on their territory. The profession was deeply divided over the innovative school dental scheme introduced in 1921. The state, anxious to improve the oral health of New Zealand children, had established dental treatment in schools; and rather than using dentists to provide the service it introduced what would become an iconic figure, the school dental nurse. Dental nurses trained for two years at their own school in Wellington; they worked alone, but under the direction of a public health dentist. All were women – they were cheaper to employ and were supposedly better suited to dealing with children than men were. Other training schools opened in Auckland and Christchurch in the 1950s, and by 1972 there were 1350 dental nurses practising in New Zealand. A decline in demand led to the closure of the Christchurch and Auckland training schools in 1980. Dental nurses were rebranded as dental therapists in 1995, by which time health and education reforms were bringing big changes to the school dental scheme. In 1991 they became one of the last health occupations to have their training moved from the health sector to the education sector when Wellington Polytechnic took over the course.[224]

The Dental School also had 'nurses' whose role was to provide chairside assistance to dentists. In 1946 Sister Wilson became the first matron of the school's nursing staff; she took over from the senior nurse, Miss Hutton, who had been in charge. The nursing staff expanded with the Dental School, but turnover was rapid. A two-year course for 'dental assistants' was established in 1962, supervised by the matron. In 1964 six young women – only females were admitted – received their certificates and badges on completion of the first course. Walsh wrote that the next 'logical development' was to provide enough qualified assistants 'so that the final year students can be taught to work with a chairside assistant'. Turnover was still high, though – perhaps because trained assistants were in demand with local dentists. The local branch of the Dental Association, the Dental School matron and Otago Polytechnic devised a nationally recognised course for dental assistants. The Dental School programme closed and the polytechnic course began in 1970, 'leading after examination to a nationally recognized certificate and badge'.[225]

In the 1960s there was much discussion about dental 'auxiliaries' who might take over some of the 'routine menial work' of dentists. New Zealand had dental therapists but not hygienists, though Americans had been training dental hygienists since the 1910s and Britain since the 1950s. New Zealand had high rates of periodontal disease, and Dental School professor William Cunningham urged that hygienists be introduced here after he had observed their work overseas in the late 1960s. The Dental Association was wary; and legislation did not allow for hygienists, though some were trained by the Defence Force from 1973. Support slowly grew and by the mid-1980s a few dentists employed hygienists illegally. The Dental Act of 1988 allowed dentists to delegate tooth-cleaning and oral health advice, and this freed the way for hygienists. On the advice of the Health Department, overseas hygienists were denied entry to New Zealand; the department believed that unemployed school dental nurses could take on those duties, and in 1989 the dental nurse training

Wenchao Zhou (also known as Tom), a first-year Bachelor of Dental Technology student, works on setting up dentures in 2004.

JOHN AARTS PHOTOGRAPH, FACULTY OF DENTISTRY COLLECTION.

school offered a two-week 'conversion' course to train dental therapists in hygienist skills. But the Dental Association wanted something more. In 1990 it set up a committee chaired by Angela Pack, associate professor of periodontology at Otago, to prepare a curriculum for hygienist training. After delays in obtaining funding, in 1994 a 15-month course for a National Certificate in Dental Hygiene commenced at Otago Polytechnic, and students gained some of their clinical experience at the Dental School.[226]

Peter Innes returned to New Zealand as dean of the Dental School in 1992. He found it rather old-fashioned, and introduced some changes, the most controversial of which was to bring education for all dental health practitioners into the Otago school. To him that made sense. Dentists trained at the university, technicians in Upper Hutt, therapists in Wellington and hygienists at Otago Polytechnic – and each course required costly equipment; having everything in one location would save the country money. That wasn't the only consideration: practitioners had to work cooperatively, so it was to their advantage to study alongside one another. Innes had support from the Health Sciences Division and from the university administration, which was keen to attract more students and develop more programmes; the 1996 review of the Dental School supported such expansion. The Ministry of Education was keen and recommended that integration of the programmes at Otago begin at once. Winning the support of the professions wasn't so easy. Dentists, including dental academics, did not like the idea of their school educating other dental workers, and the suggestion they might receive degrees was particularly provocative: Innes was a lone voice on the Dental Association Board. Dental therapists, who had a tradition of regimented training, were also wary of the change.[227]

Because of the resistance to degrees, Otago introduced its new programmes in 1999 as diplomas, starting with a two-year Diploma in Dental Therapy for 20 students and a one-year Diploma in Clinical Dental Technology for three students. It was a 'radical' move for the Dental School, Innes admitted. He had a vision of integrated dental centres in the future, saying, 'It doesn't make sense to train a person for five years at University and then have them do simple fillings, which a dental therapist can do after two years' training.'[228] A two-year Diploma in Dental Hygiene started the following year. Otago Polytechnic had few regrets about transferring its course, which it had found difficult to staff, and CIT was happy to offload its dental technology course, which was expensive to run. From 2001 Otago offered a three-year dental technology degree, and a two-year diploma option was added in 2002. Integration of the courses was not straightforward, but some of the teaching was shared between the 'auxiliary' programmes and occasionally with the dental students.[229]

The Clinical Dental Technology Diploma was especially controversial, since it provided the advanced training for existing technicians to deal directly with patients, as mandated under the 1988 Act. An earlier attempt to set up the required course at CIT fell through because of funding woes. After urging from the Dental Technicians Board, the Dental School went through 'a long bureaucratic procedure' to create the diploma, which attracted plenty of applicants for the few places available. In December 1999 Robert Pollard, Brent Norton and Simon Ford graduated; Innes and fellow dental academic Gordon Carter observed that it was 'the first time students other than students of dentistry had graduated with a clinical qualification from the School of Dentistry. It was an historical moment to savour at the end of the millennium.' Not everybody approved: the students enjoyed their course but experienced a 'lack of appreciation' from some staff, who retained the attitudes of their former 'legally protected monopoly' and were reluctant 'to relinquish patient care to professionals complementary to dentistry'.[230]

Once the courses were all located in the Dental School, further upgrades were made to qualifications. In 2002 the Bachelor of Health Sciences became the vehicle for the first degrees in dental therapy and dental hygiene. The 2003 Health Practitioners Competence Assurance Act awarded dental therapists the right to work in private practice, though most continued as school dental therapists. The Act also introduced registration for hygienists. In 2007, on the recommendation of the Dental Council's accreditation team, hygienists and therapists switched to a Bachelor of Oral Health, and the diplomas were phased out; graduates of the new degree could practise as both hygienists and therapists. The Dental Technology Diploma was phased out from 2008, leaving all the practitioners with a degree as their sole entry-level qualification.

As hygienists became more widely accepted, demand for qualifications rose; and Otago lost its monopoly on oral health education when AUT started a Bachelor of Oral Health programme in 2002.[231] With degrees came the opportunity for postgraduate education. Otago added a Postgraduate Diploma in Dental Therapy in 2002 and a Master of Dental Technology in 2006. Postgraduate opportunities to 'evaluate and develop the discipline and extend its expertise' were 'of great satisfaction to those in the profession', noted oral health professionals Julie Satur and Barbara Dewson.[232] Dental technicians, whose work changed rapidly with innovations in materials and computer-aided design and manufacture, seized the opportunity for higher qualifications: by 2012 just over half of New Zealand's practising dental technicians were clinical dental technicians.[233]

Meanwhile, a growing cohort of dental graduates obtained higher degrees. The 1988 Dental Act created a register of dental specialists who were required to have a postgraduate qualification – and that attracted more students to Otago's existing Master of Dental Surgery programme. In 2007 that degree, which included clinical coursework and a thesis and required considerably more time and effort and skill than most master's degrees, was upgraded to a Doctor of Clinical Dentistry; Australia had already introduced professional doctorates and Otago needed to keep up. The master's degree was still available for students in fields that were not part of the specialist registration scheme, as was the Master of Community Dentistry degree, introduced in 1985 and completed for the most part by dentists working in public health.[234]

The clinical doctorate was one of several innovations overseen by Gregory Seymour, who became dean in 2005. Innes had restructured the school from nine departments into three;

Greg Seymour, John Ward (Otago chancellor) and John Broughton at Waitangi after signing a memorandum of agreement with Ngāti Hine Health in 2011.
JOHN BROUGHTON COLLECTION.

it was not a popular move with staff, and only happened after 'a great deal of fuss'.[235] Seymour realigned some of the disciplines and restructured the school's management. General staff and the 'hospital' functions of the school became the responsibility of an operations manager, leaving the departments as 'true academic units whose role is focused on teaching and research'. Research was an increasing focus and the Sir John Walsh Research Institute was established in 2007, the school's centenary year.[236]

Another development as the Dental School reached its centenary was its increasing engagement with Māori. Broughton wrote in 2000 that Māori did 'not enjoy the same dental health status as non-Māori across all age groups. The evidence for this is plain to see wherever Māori happen to be.' Affordability and accessibility were big barriers to dental care, as was an 'important but often overlooked' factor: 'the tapu of the head', which led some people to avoid 'this very tapu part of the body being invaded'.[237] In addition to pioneering Māori health teaching at Otago, Broughton improved Māori access to oral health through national policy advisory work and practical schemes that involved the Dental School. He booked the staff clinic to provide dental care for the local Māori community – a move that met with some initial resistance within the school. When it became a teaching clinic, students enjoyed working with children from the local kura kaupapa. In 2000 Broughton and a few student volunteers travelled to Rotorua where they provided dental treatment to parents in a Te Arawa programme for mothers and babies; the local community housed and looked after them. It was a great success and was repeated in subsequent years until, eventually, more students volunteered than could be accommodated. The scheme inspired similar programmes that took senior dental students to the Pacific Islands to volunteer and gain experience.[238]

Broughton wanted to incorporate work in Māori communities into the regular academic year. That fitted with Seymour's plan to introduce outplacements for students – something that had been done in other countries for years. New Zealand dentists were not, on the whole, keen to take students in their practices, but Māori health providers embraced the idea, so it started there. After a successful trial in 2010 in which students spent a week with Māori providers giving supervised dental care, from 2011 a five-week placement became part of the curriculum. Considerable work went into preparing students and developing relationships with providers. The Dental School signed formal memoranda of understanding with several iwi and the relationships that were built up, together with other initiatives, helped attract more Māori into dental careers. Furthermore, the scheme meant that all professionals graduating from the Otago Dental School now had an understanding of Māori cultural frameworks, and experience working with Māori communities.[239]

The expansion of the Dental School beyond dental surgery did not downgrade the school, as some had feared. Indeed, when QS World University Rankings included dentistry as a subject area for the first time in 2015, Otago came in eighth in the world, just ahead of Harvard; it was the first time any subject in any New Zealand

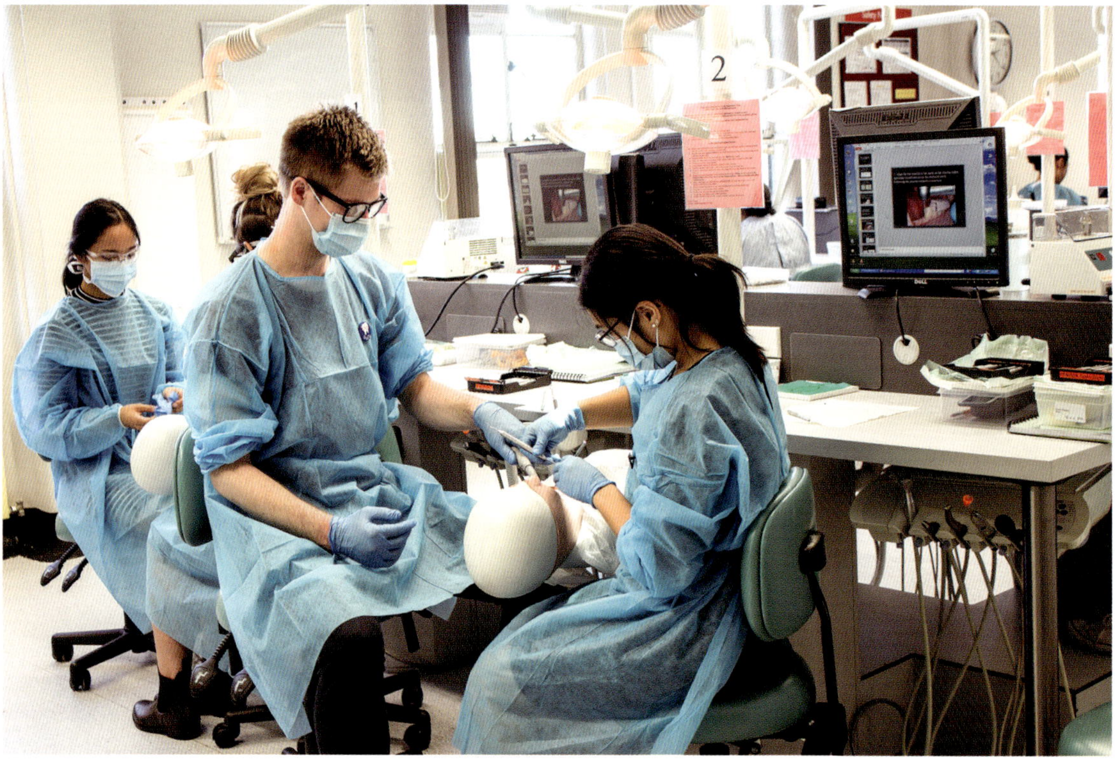

Bachelor of Oral Health students working in the Faculty of Dentistry's simulation clinic in 2016.
FIONA MCDONALD PHOTOGRAPH, FACULTY OF DENTISTRY COLLECTION.

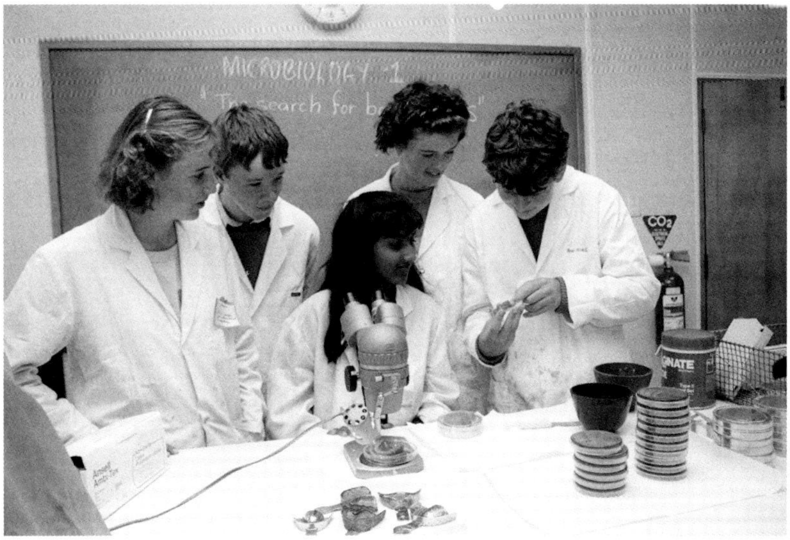

High-school students work on a microbiology project during the university's first Hands on Science summer camp in 1990. The popular and successful programme later expanded to include humanities and commerce subjects as well as science.
UNIVERSITY OF OTAGO PHOTOGRAPHIC UNIT RECORDS, MS-4185/042, S15-500D, HOCKEN COLLECTIONS.

university earned a top 10 ranking. Dean Paul Brunton, recently appointed, commented: 'I was formulating a five year strategic plan for the faculty to get us in the top 20, and now I'm going to have to rewrite that.'[240] The school was tight for space – though plans were underway to remedy that – but it had embraced technology. In 2009 it invested over $3 million in a 73-chair simulation lab where students worked on mannequins with removable jaws, and an individual video screen allowed them to follow a teaching demonstration.[241] Such advances enabled students to hone practical skills before they were let loose on real people. Some digital technology was created locally, such as ImpressDent, a web-based computer simulation that allows students to practise the tricky procedure of making an accurate dental impression; it was developed in 2014 by Otago dental lecturer Sunyoung Ma, working with a programmer and designers from the Higher Education Development Centre.[242] Founding director Pickerill, who predicted in 1908 that the Dental School had 'great possibilities, and will before long become one of the most important and well-paying departments of this University', would be pleased at its progress.[243]

EDUCATING HEALTH SCIENTISTS

Beginning with a handful of medical students in the 1870s, Otago developed a broad range of programmes to educate health professionals: it produced thousands of graduates and contributed enormously to the health sector in New Zealand and beyond. In the last decade the Health Sciences Division has taken over from humanities as the university's largest, measured by student enrolments – but that is just part of its contribution. It has enhanced human wellbeing through its research, not just in the health professions but in the biomedical sciences. Those sciences have grown from small parts of the Medical School into a powerhouse of the university, and it is fitting that they eventually developed their own degree, the Bachelor of Biomedical Science. Commenced in 2002, the BBiomedSc includes a range of interdisciplinary majors, from infection and immunity to drugs and human health. For some students it is a springboard to one of the health professions and, for others, into a research career. An honours programme introduced in 2005 includes a research thesis.[244] It is a fitting place to end this chapter: the health sciences at Otago have incorporated both pragmatism and 'blue sky' thinking.

CHAPTER TEN

Beyond Dunedin

In the late twentieth century government reforms enabled New Zealand universities to be more entrepreneurial and to expand territories. Massey was most ambitious: it opened a campus in Albany, in the same city as the University of Auckland, in 1993, and it merged with Wellington Polytechnic, not far from Victoria, in 1999.[1] Otago's first move beyond its Dunedin base had come decades earlier, when universities were under strict central control; its motive was to improve clinical education for senior students at New Zealand's only medical school.

EXPANDING MEDICINE

In 1923 the Medical School had a problem: 40 of its finalists failed their exams. They needed to spend another six months in clinical settings before they resat finals, but there was no room for them in Dunedin. Christchurch Hospital authorities offered to cater for them, so in 1924 they headed north. At the same time the Medical School was phasing in its new six-year programme. The sixth year was entirely clinical, but finding sufficient experience in Dunedin was difficult. It was New Zealand's largest urban centre when the school opened in the 1870s, but by the 1920s Auckland, Wellington and Christchurch all had bigger populations. In 1926 the regular practice of sending some of the final-year class to Christchurch began, and Wellington and Auckland were added as destinations in 1927. At first the medical superintendents took charge of any teaching programme, delivered by local medical staff. No money changed hands but the system was popular at the northern hospitals, as Hercus and Bell explained: 'The presence of students had an immediately stimulating effect on the whole hospital. Patient care improved both in diagnosis and treatment. The spirit of enquiry so fundamental to medical teaching, and indeed, to the whole work of the modern hospital, was greatly strengthened.'[2]

In 1937 the university entered into a formal agreement with each of the hospital boards concerned: it set up 'joint relationship committees' and established branch faculties, each with a subdean. In 1955 it secured government funding to strengthen teaching and research in each branch faculty with medical units that got underway in 1959 and 1960, though not without resistance from locals. Each unit was headed by a physician who led the clinical work, teaching and research. Otago was fortunate to attract three of its own outstanding graduates to the positions: Derek North in Auckland, Ian Prior in Wellington and Don Beaven in Christchurch.[3]

The 1968 Christie report into the troubled Medical School recommended either halving the school's intake or opening a second clinical school, preferably in Christchurch. Another report by clinical dean Robin Irvine recommended developing clinical schools in Christchurch and Wellington to take students from fourth year upwards. The schools would require considerable investment in staff, but with extensive building projects planned at Christchurch and Wellington hospitals, academic facilities could be embedded mainly within them. Even without the development of full clinical schools, Wellington and Christchurch needed to enlarge their faculties to deal with a larger sixth-year class – the Auckland branch could not take Otago sixth-years after 1972 when the first University of Auckland medical class reached that stage.[4]

After considerable negotiation Christchurch and Wellington became clinical schools of the University of Otago in 1971 and 1973 respectively, and took their first fourth-year students in 1973 and 1977. Irvine wrote in his original proposal that 'neither Clinical School would be regarded as the beginning of a full medical school'; he wrote this amid fears 'in some quarters' that the Christchurch or Wellington schools might join with their local universities to offer a complete medical education independent of Otago.[5] That did not happen, but it was always a possibility.

CHRISTCHURCH BEGINNINGS

Otago's Christchurch campus dates its origins back to 1850, when the London-based Canterbury Association produced a scheme for a college in its colony in New Zealand, to be associated with a hospital: 'One of the Fellows of the college (being a medical man) will have the superintendence of the hospital, which may be opened generally as a medical school, under proper regulations.'[6] But early attempts to launch a medical school failed; there was no hospital until 1862 and the colonists had other priorities. The establishment of Otago's Medical School fired provincial rivalries and in 1875 the Canterbury Provincial Council committed £300 to help set up a local school. The hospital staff were keen and in 1876 provincial superintendent William Rolleston proclaimed the existence of the Christchurch Medical School in the Canterbury gazette, complete with a list of lecturers appointed. The proclamation was later declared legally null and void, as such an institution needed an Act or ordinance behind it; furthermore, the University of New Zealand Senate refused to recognise the school. The school negotiated to become a faculty of Canterbury University College, but there were further hurdles. Provincial government ended just two months after Rolleston's proclamation, so the project's survival depended on central government support. Although some politicians expressed sympathy, they did not come up with funding and the Christchurch Medical School 'lay dead in the waters of the Avon River', as the school's first historians described it.[7]

Canterbury developed its health services and in the 1920s medical authorities were happy to take senior Otago medical students. They were less receptive to later suggestions by the Otago medical dean and University of New Zealand Senate that clinical instruction would be improved through academic staff, partly because such staff might compete for patients; the existing faculty were 'visiting' staff, working in private practice in addition to their hospital consultancies.[8] There was a strong conservative element in the Christchurch medical world, reflecting a wider Canterbury ethos derived from the region's Tory High Anglican colonial beginnings. When James Ng went to Christchurch Hospital as a sixth-year student in 1959 he found it more hierarchical than Dunedin. It was 'full of Christ's College types', he recalls. 'They fought each other like cats and dogs', but united against outsiders. It wasn't a welcoming environment for somebody with origins in a Chinese laundry in Ashburton, but Ng proved himself and eventually won the branch faculty's prize.[9]

It no doubt helped Beaven, Otago's first senior academic at Christchurch, that he was a

Christ's College old boy, albeit one less privileged than most; he had grown up in poverty and had attended the elite private school and medical school on scholarships. Beaven returned to Christchurch from postgrad study in England in 1955 and became senior resident physician at the hospital and clinical tutor for the Medical School. In 1960, newly returned to Christchurch from a fellowship at Harvard, he became founding director of Otago's academic unit in medicine with the status of senior lecturer. There was 'staunch opposition' from hospital staff, Beaven later recalled; they thought appointing a doctor who was not in private practice was 'a creeping form of socialism'. The Medical School dean, together with Leslie Averill, the physician who chaired the Hospital Board, persuaded the board to approve the unit by suggesting that without it Christchurch risked losing its medical students and junior medical staff.[10]

The Medical Unit's work dispelled doubts. In 1966, when the government approved a new medical school at Auckland, Christchurch began preparing for a larger influx of sixth-years from the Dunedin school. A working party dubbed 'the gang of four' – Beaven, surgeon Pat Cotter, paediatrician Fred Shannon and radiologist George Rolleston, who headed the branch faculty as subdean – recommended adding further academic units in surgery and obstetrics and gynaecology, and more accommodation (the top floor of the St Andrew's Sunday School building served as a lecture room from 1951 until 1962, when a hospital ward was converted into offices and teaching spaces). They were soon making larger plans: when Christie visited in 1968, the branch faculty and hospital board welcomed his suggestion that Christchurch become a clinical school. Any dreams of establishing a full local medical school were stymied by the University of Canterbury's lack of interest: VC Neville Phillips informed Rolleston that 'medical schools were far too costly and were invariably a financial embarrassment to any university which had one'.[11]

THE CHRISTCHURCH CAMPUS

The Christchurch Clinical School officially came into being on 28 April 1971 when the University of Otago and North Canterbury Hospital Board ratified the constitution of its council. The council, with half its members appointed by the university and half by the hospital board, replaced the previous joint relationships committee. It had both advisory and executive powers and various subcommittees, considered necessary for a school distant from its parent university. It did valuable work, but as health and education reforms sped up and new management systems became the fashion it was increasingly bypassed; it came to an end in 1989 after the introduction of the State Sector Act, when the dean became, in effect, the school's chief executive.[12]

The dean was always a key figure. Rolleston, who led the Clinical School through its first 10 years, was 'a Cantabrian through and through', Dorothy Page notes.[13] 'Gentleman George', as many knew him, was a descendant of early Canterbury gentry and his mana in the wider community helped win support for the venture. Like many Christchurch staff over the years, Rolleston's primary loyalty was to the region rather than to the university; many locals were blissfully unaware that their Medical School was part of the University of Otago. Relationships with other Canterbury institutions were cordial and researchers collaborated – for instance, Beaven worked with Lincoln University staff on insulin and the pancreas in sheep, using Lincoln's animal and laboratory facilities.[14] Rolleston was cautious, according to Beaven, and lacked experience in a large teaching hospital, but other professors with experience helped balance that.[15] The school had eight departments – medicine, obstetrics and gynaecology, paediatrics, pathology, preventive and social medicine, psychological medicine, radiology and surgery – together with the Dean's Department, 'the school's administrative heart'.[16] Some hospital staff wanted to become part of the university but 'didn't have capacity for research'; bringing in outsiders created tension in fields

A dinner at the Christchurch Club in the early 1970s, probably to mark a milestone in the life of the Christchurch Clinical School, since many of those present were on its council. Max Panckhurst, Otago chemistry professor and a member of the Clinical School Council, is closest to the camera with fair curly hair. Clockwise from him are: L.M. Berry (North Canterbury Hospital Board medical superintendent), Carl Perkins (council), George Rolleston (Christchurch dean), Robin Williams (Otago VC), Leslie Averill (North Canterbury Hospital Board chair), Alan Burdekin (Christchurch Club manager, standing), Bill Adams (Otago Medical School dean), L.A. Bennett (council), Robin Irvine (Otago Medical School clinical dean), unknown, unknown, Pat Cotter (partly obscured, council), D. Horne, Don Beaven (medicine professor), unknown, Fred Shannon (paediatrics professor), Athol Mann (council), J.L. Laurenson.

IRVINE FAMILY PAPERS, MS-4207/006, S16-669A, HOCKEN COLLECTIONS

where there were already clinical specialists.[17]

One difficulty was the physical layout of Christchurch Hospital, which lacked facilities for research. In 1970 the hospital board, university and UGC came to an agreement over buildings. An extensive hospital redevelopment was still in the early planning stages, so the university undertook to immediately build a facility, known as the Medical Centre, to house the school's administration, teaching facilities, library, student spaces, animal facility and laboratories; as well as some hospital service departments that were in urgent need of an upgrade. The centre opened in 1973, conveniently located next to Christchurch Hospital on Riccarton Avenue. The hospital redevelopment was much slower, and academic departments were squeezed into unsatisfactory spaces for years to come. Departments that had no link to the hospital were housed in older buildings that the university acquired, such as the Cambridge Terrace property that became the Preventive and Social Medicine Department. The Education Department gifted some old houses in the vicinity that were formerly part of the University of Canterbury to the Clinical School; some of these became student accommodation.[18] Otago's Christchurch campus thus resembled Dunedin's, with a mixture of purpose-designed buildings and older premises acquired and adapted as more space was required. The original 1970s plans for the university building had envisaged a future 'wraparound' development, but that 'completion' of the building failed to eventuate; it was a sore point with Christchurch that projects

The University of Otago's Christchurch building in 2010. The glass-fronted 'clip-on' extension, added in 2006, 'completed' the building in 'a somewhat different form' from the 1970s plan.

ALEX LOVELL-SMITH PHOTOGRAPH, UNIVERSITY OF OTAGO MARKETING AND COMMUNICATIONS COLLECTION.

in Dunedin took precedence. Finally, in 1998, the Christchurch campus celebrated its 25th anniversary with the opening of an extension that provided extra space for research, conferences, a foyer and café; a local fundraising campaign contributed to the $3 million cost.[19]

By 1977 the Clinical School Council felt it had 'successfully come through its initiation to the point of being a young but stable institution'. By then it had welcomed its fifth intake of fourth-year students; the first group of 42 had arrived in 1973.[20] Students in Christchurch, Wellington and Dunedin sat the same exam at the end of their fifth year, but each school approached the curriculum differently. Alan Clarke made a dramatic change as Christchurch dean in 1988 when he abolished the interdisciplinary clinical science course as few students attended the lectures, yet they performed well in exams. When he taught at Dunedin in the 1960s he thought the clinical science course 'just the bee's knees', but he now looked back on it as 'an example of over teaching, big time. We were forced to do that because of the shortage of patients.' In Christchurch, students' time was better spent in clinical settings, he believed.[21]

Some curricular changes were directed from above, but each campus developed them differently. In the 2000s, for instance, faculty dean Don Roberton allocated funding for each of the campuses to upgrade clinical skills teaching, and he directed a minimum time to be spent on hauora Māori (Māori health). Christchurch developed a clinical simulation centre with teaching spaces set up as a clinic room, resuscitation bay and two-bed hospital room; a range of mannikins, including sophisticated human simulators, gave students the opportunity to practise skills.[22] Christchurch was more than 10 years behind the other campuses in appointing specialist lecturers in Māori health; they developed the Māori/Indigenous Health Institute (MIHI), supported by the Māori community. Christchurch's developments in simulated learning and hauora Māori were superior to those in other centres, said dean Peter Joyce, and that claim was backed up when MIHI director and associate dean (Māori) Suzanne Pitama was presented with the 2015 Prime Minister's Supreme Award for Tertiary Teaching Excellence.[23]

GROWING AND DIVERSIFYING

In its first 10 years, 650 students entered the Christchurch clinical programme.[24] Undergraduate medicine was still the main programme but postgraduate students, some of them doctors and some other health professionals or scientists, soon outnumbered the undergraduates. The name changed to reflect a broadening remit: in 1986 it dropped the 'clinical' and became the Christchurch School of Medicine; in 2001 it became the Christchurch School of Medicine and Health Sciences; and, in 2007, simply the University of Otago, Christchurch.[25] Andrew Hornblow, dean from 1994 to 2002, represented the shift: unusually for the head of a medical school, he was not medically qualified – he was a psychologist. He started as a senior lecturer in the Psychological Medicine Department then moved to the Public Health and General Practice Department, where he became professor of community health.[26] Both departments expanded their programmes. The Certificate in Community Psychiatric Care, begun in 1988, was open to those with experience but no degree; it was funded by the Health Workforce Development Fund 'in response to dramatic changes in the care of the mentally ill'. The Postgraduate Diploma in Mental Health was introduced in 1994.[27] The Public Health Diploma, a joint offering with the Wellington and Dunedin campuses and (for a few years) the University of Auckland, attracted a range of health workers. In the 1990s the Orthopaedic Surgery and Musculoskeletal Medicine Department expanded its Diploma in Musculoskeletal Medicine – originally designed for medical general practitioners – to include behavioural psychology and pain management, and opened it to other professions such as physiotherapists.[28]

From the 1990s there was more demand for postgraduate education from all health professions, sparked by the availability of new funding from the Clinical Training Agency. The Christchurch campus, with the large Canterbury health workforce to cater for, became, as Hornblow noted, 'a fairly major provider of advanced training for people who were moving into leadership positions, other than those that were medically qualified'. That raised the school's budget by around a third and enabled the appointment of more staff.[29] The Rural Health Unit of the Public Health and General Practice Department offered an innovative primary rural health care programme that attracted nurses as well as doctors; it ended when the Nursing Council ruled that nursing postgraduate programmes must be offered from specialist nursing departments.[30]

NURSING

After the collapse of the Nursing Diploma in the 1920s, Otago did not offer nursing education for decades. In 1970 Helen Carpenter of Toronto reviewed nursing education in New Zealand on behalf of the World Health Organization, and her report led to extensive reforms. Technical institutes established nursing schools – the first were in Wellington and Christchurch in 1973 – and hospital-based programmes were gradually phased out. Technical institutes also took over the role of the School of Advanced Nursing Studies in developing advanced diploma courses.[31] Carpenter recommended that some nurses receive higher education at universities: she suggested that Otago's Preventive and Social Medicine Department, along with the Education Departments at Victoria, Massey and Canterbury, start by appointing a nurse to their academic staff with a view to building up research and courses later.[32] Victoria and Massey offered a few BA papers in nursing studies but plans at Otago came to nothing: proposals for a diploma in nursing administration and, later, a bachelor's degree leading to nursing registration, did not make it past the UGC. In 1979, faced with various proposals, the UGC appointed a special committee on nursing education, which recommended turning down proposals from Otago, Massey and Auckland; instead it recommended that Victoria develop its existing programme into a full nursing degree and Massey continue its existing courses.[33]

Robyn Beach presenting to students enrolled in Nursing – High Acuity at the Centre for Postgraduate Nursing Studies premises in Oxford Terrace, Christchurch, 2012.
AMANDA CLIFFORD PHOTOGRAPH, CENTRE FOR POSTGRADUATE NURSING STUDIES COLLECTION.

Victoria approached Otago's Wellington Clinical School, which agreed to teach five of the 16 courses to be offered in a Victoria nursing degree. The course began in 1986, and Otago's Wellington dean Tom O'Donnell reported that the 'first class of Nursing degree students in Applied Medical Science … gave very favourable feedback on their programme and achieved good results'. Staff from several of the Wellington departments taught in the programme, and Jocelyn Keith, who lectured in Otago's Community Health Department, was also on the staff of the Victoria Nursing Department. The programme ended because of political problems and poor enrolments. Some leaders in nursing were unhappy about the involvement of medicine and there were tensions within the Victoria department. Victoria disestablished the degree and the department in 1993 (it later built up a postgraduate school of nursing).[34] In Dunedin the push for an undergraduate programme ended when Otago Polytechnic opened its Nursing School in 1984.[35]

In 1997 Otago's Centre for Postgraduate Nursing Studies opened in Christchurch. Christchurch Polytechnic (now Ara Institute of Canterbury), which offered an undergraduate nursing programme, chose not to develop postgraduate programmes, so there was an unmet call for further nursing education in the region. The Christchurch centre's flexible teaching methods, which included block courses and distance education, attracted students from all over the South Island and a few from further afield: students could complete a postgraduate diploma or master's degree in health sciences, endorsed in nursing, or shorter certificates in specialist fields. From 2006 students could choose a 'clinically applied research practicum' in place of a thesis for a master's endorsed in 'nursing – clinical'. That fitted the qualification for registration as a nurse practitioner – an advanced level of practice that included prescribing rights.[36]

There were developments in nursing research, too. The centre attracted grants from the Health Research Council and elsewhere; and it benefited from Tertiary Education Commission funding targeted at developing research capability in nursing and other health professions that did poorly under the PBRF system. In 2008

Lisa Whitehead received the university's Early Career Award for Distinction in Research in recognition of her achievements in research on the management of long-term conditions – a field of particular interest to the Nursing Centre. As its research capability improved the centre attracted PhD students from both New Zealand and overseas; by 2012 it had 10 PhD candidates among its 350 students and was the largest postgraduate programme on the Christchurch campus.[37]

The Nursing Centre was never short of initiative. In 2016 it enrolled the first students in its boldest venture yet: the Master of Nursing Science, which allowed people with a bachelor's degree in any discipline to complete a concentrated two-year programme for registration as a nurse. This was a scheme that had been offered in North America for decades, and in Australia for several years, but it was new to New Zealand and required additional regulations from the Nursing Council. Finally, some 90 years after the first ill-starred attempt, the University of Otago was offering a course that led to the registration of nurses.[38]

MEDICAL RESEARCH

Research flourished in other Christchurch departments, too, as it had from the beginning. The work in diabetes and endocrine research (started by Beaven in the Branch Faculty days) continued, and several other projects were going strong. Paediatrics professor Fred Shannon was interested in the impact of the rise in single-parent families on child health and wellbeing. He obtained MRC funding to employ social researcher David Fergusson and statistician John Horwood, who set up the Christchurch Child Development Study to collect data on around 1200 babies born in Christchurch in 1977 and follow them through life. The study later shifted to the Psychological Medicine Department and was renamed the Christchurch Health and Development Study. As with the Dunedin longitudinal study begun a few years earlier, the results influenced social and health policy in New Zealand and beyond. Important findings ranged from the effects on children of parental smoking and of lead exposure, to the role of strong cultural bonds of attachment in Māori wellbeing. Half of the study cohort experienced the Canterbury earthquakes of 2010 and 2011 and half did not: this prompted investigation of the impact of disasters on wellbeing.[39]

Other enduring research projects had a biomedical focus. Robin Carrell was already working on haemoglobin when he became associate professor in the clinical school in 1973. Christine Winterbourn, who joined his research group in 1971, became 'one of the first scientists to demonstrate [that] our cells produce free radicals as part of their normal function', her colleague Tony Kettle explained, and she then explored some of the chemistry of free radicals that occur in disease. The work of the Free Radical Research Group attracted research students and scientists, and the principal investigators received many awards; in 2011 Winterbourn was the first woman to receive the Royal Society of New Zealand's highest honour, the Rutherford Medal.[40] The Christchurch Heart Institute is now the largest research group on the Christchurch campus, with 45 research staff. The institute traces its origins to the Branch Faculty Medical Unit of the 1960s, which went on to become a group with 'a formidable capacity in basic and clinical research in hypertension and heart failure'. The institute's goal was 'to generate original knowledge from "bench to bedside", ie from DNA to the management of the heart patient' – epitomised in the widely used diagnostic blood tests developed from its research into cardiac hormones.[41]

Bioengineering research flourished in the twenty-first century. In 2009 Otago received TEC seed funding to develop its bioengineering programme; the resulting research hubs included the Christchurch Centre for Bioengineering, directed by Anthony Butler. The funding required the Universities of Canterbury and Otago to work together to enhance their respective strengths in engineering/physics and medical research; and later the centre became part of the larger multi-institutional centre of research excellence, MedTech CoRE. The Christchurch centre brought together two projects that were already showing results: a new form of medical imaging, the Medipix All Resolution System, developed by radiologist and physicist Butler and his team in collaboration with the University of Canterbury; and innovative devices for joint repairs, created using stem cells, 3D printing and other technologies by the Christchurch Regenerative Medicine and Tissue Engineering Group (CReaTE), led by Tim Woodfield.[42]

Alongside these prominent projects there were many other research studies carried out in Christchurch, ranging from depression to the development of blood supply to cancer cells. Many of the research projects were supported by the MRC/HRC and the Canterbury Medical Research Foundation. The Heart Foundation was another big supporter: from 1996 it funded a chair in cardiovascular studies, held by Mark Richards, long-time director of the Heart Institute. The Heart Institute also received a multimillion-dollar gift from a philanthropist. Christchurch attracted three large donations through Otago's Leading Thinkers scheme in the early 2000s: the Cure Kids Chair in Paediatric Research supported Brian Darlow's work in newborn medicine; the Jim and Mary Carney Trust endowed a Centre for Pharmacogenomics, which brought together the clinical pharmacology work of Evan Begg and Martin Kennedy's genetic work to investigate genes and responses to drugs; and the GAMA Foundation endowed a research fellowship in bipolar disorder, with Virginia Maskill as inaugural fellow.[43]

Researchers in Christchurch made the most of commercial opportunities. In the 1970s clinical biochemist Carrell set up a protein lab that enabled diagnostic testing on haemoglobin, and other centres sent patient samples for special testing. Carrell and his team also produced control samples that were in demand, and they set up Canterbury Scientific to recoup costs. It became a registered company in 1985, and moved from being a small enterprise to a larger one after contracting with multinational corporation Bayer in 1998 to supply controls for a glycated haemoglobin analyser. Canterbury Scientific continued to develop products that were in demand in international markets. It moved into a dedicated facility in 2002, and to a larger, purpose-built one in 2011.[44] In 2007 the Free Radical Research Group won the first annual Otago Innovation Proof of Concept competition for its project to develop a tool to measure oxidative stress in biological samples.[45] In 2015, after years of work by Otago Innovation and researcher Chris Pemberton, the university and venture capitalists launched Upstream Medical Technologies to refine, test and market the diagnostic tests developed at the Christchurch Heart Institute.[46]

Christchurch's academic departments, originally tiny, expanded along with their research and postgraduate education. In 1986 the anaesthesia and orthopaedic surgery departments, which already had specialist professors in John Gibb and Bill Gillespie, both became independent of the Surgery Department. The Orthopaedic Surgery and Musculoskeletal Medicine Department represented a productive alliance between medical and surgical experts teaching and researching in the field. Surgery was still a large department that specialised in several areas, old and new. In 1991 the department appointed Anne-Marie Kelly to Australasia's first university post in emergency medicine, and Michael Ardagh was promoted to the country's first chair in emergency medicine in 2001. Two members of the department, Randall Allardyce and Philip Bagshaw, were prime movers behind the Canterbury Charity Hospital Trust, established in 2004 to assist with unmet needs in the community; the hospital provided free day surgery and medical consultations, using donations and volunteer labour. *North and South* magazine honoured Bagshaw as New Zealander of the Year in 2009 for his humanitarian work.[47]

The department that started in 1974 as Preventive and Social Medicine went through several name changes; by 1994 it was the Public Health and General Practice Department. General practice became an important field in both undergraduate and postgraduate medical education, though it wasn't until 1997 that Les Toop became Christchurch's first professor in the field. As at Dunedin and Wellington, the general practice chair was funded externally: two Canterbury community trusts and the Pegasus Medical Group guaranteed five years of support. The department was interdisciplinary from the beginning – it employed two MRC-funded biostatisticians, who provided a service to researchers throughout the school. In addition to general practice and public health physicians and epidemiologists, heads of department and professors included a psychologist (Hornblow), health economist (Jane Chetwynd), medical sociologist (Peter Davis) and biostatistician (Philip Schluter). In 1995 it was the first Christchurch department to appoint a nurse, Linda Bullock, to an academic role; she taught health promotion. By the end of the 1990s the department had around 70 staff. At that point nursing and MIHI became independent units, and in 2014 the core programmes separated into two departments, general practice and population health.[48] Christchurch's other founding departments also grew, but continued under the format of their original disciplines.

TROUBLED TIMES

The health reforms of the 1980s and 90s were challenging for all New Zealand teaching hospitals but particularly difficult in Christchurch. In 1990 an anonymous staff member commented that hospital managers at Christchurch Hospital 'seem hell-bent on making our institution into a superbly efficient, gigantic cottage hospital'.[49] Clinical care at the hospital deteriorated further. The concerns of many health professionals, including some of Otago's senior academics, prompted an official enquiry by health and disability commissioner Robyn Stent. The enquiry reported in 1998 that there was 'a preoccupation with efficiency, funding and financial performance', forced on the health board from above, and that 'unnecessary deaths occurred'. Later that year the Association of University Staff presented its inaugural Academic Freedom Award to Otago staff Gary Nicholls, Richards and Bagshaw and to another medical colleague, Stuart Gowland – all of whom were on the executive of the Christchurch Hospitals Medical Staff Association – for calling the safety practices of the hospital to account. As Nicholls and Peter Moller later reflected, measuring the effects of the health reforms on the Christchurch school wasn't easy. There was 'no clear effect on research productivity', but many clinical staff 'spent long hours over some years contemplating, discussing and taking action for or against effects of the reforms in the Christchurch hospitals – time that would otherwise have been spent with patients, teaching, undertaking research or getting on with their personal/family lives'.[50]

In September 2010 a large earthquake struck Canterbury. The main building on the Otago campus had superficial damage and was closed for only a few days, but the brick St Elmo's Court building, the leased home of MIHI and the Public Health and General Practice Department, was badly damaged and was condemned. Kim Thomas, the campus communications adviser, noted a few weeks later that 'people just want to try and move on and get back to normal'. The frightening experience of the original quake and ongoing aftershocks had 'solidified the sense of community on the Christchurch campus', said Thomas.[51]

Worse was to come: the big quake of February 2011 caused far more destruction in Christchurch. Otago dietetics student Sisi Xin and politics PhD student Didem Yaman died in the quake; and although no staff or students from the Christchurch campus lost their lives, some had family or friends who were killed or badly injured, and many had serious damage to their homes. As Joyce, the dean, remarked, 'No one was unaffected.' Five years later about 20 per cent of staff still had unresolved issues relating to insurance and home repairs. The university's buildings had varying levels of damage; the main building performed better than others because of its strong central core, but it was coded off-limits except for urgent

Beverley Burrell and Paul Saunders, co-convenors of Nursing – Leadership and Management, presenting a lecture to students in 2011. The class was held in the Christchurch Philatelic Society rooms, one of many temporary premises used by the university after the usual venues were closed because of earthquakes. Several university buildings were damaged and there were years of disruption as offices, labs and library shifted from one temporary location to another, some of them remote.

AMANDA CLIFFORD PHOTOGRAPH, CENTRE FOR POSTGRADUATE NURSING STUDIES COLLECTION.

business and did not reopen until 2013, after a multimillion-dollar repair and strengthening project.[52]

Christchurch medical students coped remarkably well: a comparison with fifth-year exam results from the other campuses revealed 'a small negative impact' from earthquake disruption in 2010, but 'no detectable adverse impact' in 2011.[53] David Palmer, one of the 2011 fifth-years, noted that students lost access to their usual work and recreation areas – with unanticipated results: they 'met in spare rooms all around the hospital and have as a result become "citizens of the hospital" and mixed far more with regular medical staff than before the earthquake'. The fact that there were no available regular teaching spaces 'forced an amount of innovation and creativity in teaching'.[54] The disruption to research and postgraduate students was worse, and there was a marked increase in time taken to complete theses.[55] Still, few staff left Christchurch. Some used the disaster they were experiencing as a research topic and published studies on the psychological impact of the earthquakes on Otago's staff and students.[56] Joyce, who retired in 2016, is a proud Cantabrian whose association with the Christchurch campus stretches back to its 1973 beginnings; he reflected with satisfaction on its outstanding history of research and education, which survived major natural disasters.[57] The University of Otago's first 'northern' campus did it proud.

WELLINGTON BEGINNINGS AND VICTORIA UNIVERSITY

Each of the Otago campuses developed a different culture, reflecting their region. The Wellington campus was less interested in its early origins than Christchurch: there are three published histories of the Christchurch campus, but none for Wellington. Still, as founding professor of medicine Tom O'Donnell noted in a 1975 article, early on there were schemes for medical education in Wellington: the New Zealand Company's 1839 plans for its Wellington settlement included hospitals and sites for a 'College of Surgeons' and a 'College of Physicians'.[58] Wellington established a public hospital in the 1840s, but plans for medical education there went no further until a new hospital opened in Newtown in 1881. In 1882 the hospital committee approved the admission of medical students to Wellington Hospital, provided they passed a matriculation exam and paid an annual fee. The regulations allowed doctors on staff to have two pupils each. It is unclear whether any students actually attended the hospital in what amounted to an apprenticeship, but not one that offered the prospect of a medical degree.[59] In 1889 there was a proposal to establish a local 'preliminary School of Medicine and Practical Science' where students could complete the first year or two of their medical studies in Wellington before proceeding to Otago, but this did not eventuate.[60]

Medical education began in earnest in Wellington in 1926 when the Hospital Board agreed to take Otago students for their final clinical year. Like Christchurch and Auckland, in 1937 Wellington became a branch faculty of the Otago Medical School, and a couple of decades later it launched an academic Medical Unit. The reaction of locals to the Medical Unit was 'lukewarm', as it had been in the south; the existing physicians had no interest in further teaching or research, and initial plans for a 30-bed unit were foiled. Instead, in 1959 cardiologist Ian Prior was appointed head of a 12-bed unit. Prior developed an interest in the epidemiological side of cardiovascular disease; he was known as the 'father of epidemiology' in New Zealand and the Pacific.[61] In 1969, as epidemiology research grew and attracted MRC funding, the hospital board and the branch faculty set up a separate Epidemiology Unit. After earlier failed attempts, they also started a Surgical Unit in 1970 and recruited Australian surgeon Ian Hulme-Moir as first director. Wellington appointed another star Otago graduate, Ken North, to take over the Medical Unit from Prior; but Warren Austad filled in for a year while North completed another task: he was seconded by a joint committee of the Wellington Hospital and Victoria University of Wellington to 'prepare the case for the establishment of a third medical school in Wellington, in the context of medical education requirements in New Zealand'.[62]

It was here that the histories of medical education in Christchurch and Wellington diverged. Both centres had advocates for a full medical school but the University of Canterbury was not interested; Victoria University of Wellington felt disadvantaged because of its lack of special schools and was anxious to secure one. In the early 1950s the University of New Zealand investigated setting up a second medical school, but Wellington lost out to Auckland. By the late 1960s it was evident that the new Auckland school and the existing Otago school could not cater for New Zealand's future medical workforce needs. As Otago came up with alternative ways of expanding, Wellington devised a project for another full medical school. The campaign was launched in 1965 by John Mercer, chair of the Medical Council and national president of the Medical Association; he was also director of pathology at Wellington Hospital and a former subdean of the Branch Faculty. Mercer urged Wellington doctors 'to determine whether they feel this community has a claim' to a third medical school; if so, it would be strengthened by a 'close association between university and medical authority'.[63] Wellington Hospital medical staff approached Victoria, which said it was interested so long as the basic science course was provided on its own campus. A working party carried out further planning in 1967.[64]

When Christie presented his report the following year, 'medical people in Wellington felt aggrieved', according to Brian Corkill of the Wellington group: they believed 'an assessment of the national needs for medical education, not merely those of the Otago Medical School, should have been considered'.[65] Irvine's 1969 report, which recommended Otago set up a clinical school in Wellington as well as in Christchurch, was partly prompted by the threat of another medical school opening in the capital. A later faculty dean, John Hunter, reflected that running three clinical schools was 'taking on too much', but 'it's better that it's part of Otago than part of Victoria'.[66] A majority of the Wellington Hospital Board agreed with its senior medical staff that, while it would welcome more students as in Irvine's plan, it still had a strong case for a full medical school. It joined with the Victoria University Council in commissioning North to 'prepare the case'.[67] His October 1970 report recommended a third school be developed 'as soon as possible' in the 'only centre with a large enough university and hospital, not already fully committed to medical teaching'. Wellington had space 'available at the university and the hospital to proceed with the development' and 'could be admitting students by 1975–76'; the cost was 'likely to be of the same order as that involved by the Minister's plan to expand the Otago preclinical school and set up a clinical school at Wellington hospital'. North argued that separating 'preclinical and clinical teaching', as in Otago's proposed scheme, was 'educationally unsound'.[68]

By the time North's report came out it was evident the UGC was not going to fund another medical school at Victoria, and in December 1970 the Wellington Hospital Board agreed to set up a clinical school with the University of Otago.[69] Victoria's hopes of a medical school were not entirely dashed: the UGC gave vague promises to consider later the transfer of the Wellington Clinical School from Otago to Victoria. That did not happen, but the idea was revived from time to time. Discussion of the prospect was especially lively during Ian Axford's brief reign as Victoria's VC, from 1982 to 1985. Axford was keen for Victoria to take over the Clinical School, and he had the backing of some of the staff at the school; this was a period when Wellington staff felt they were 'not getting a fair share' of university resources from the Otago administration. However, Victoria's biological sciences staff were wary of taking on a full medical course, and the government wasn't prepared to fund it.[70]

THE WELLINGTON CAMPUS

In 1971 Otago University and the Wellington Hospital Board started preparing for the first intake of fourth-years in 1977. Frank Hall, a respected and popular Wellington physician with considerable administrative experience, was appointed first dean, but within a couple of years he developed serious health problems and had to take long periods of leave. He resigned in 1976, and much of the planning work fell to his assistant, Corkill, head of Wellington's Obstetrics and Gynaecology Department and another efficient administrator.[71]

Converting the substandard Wellington Hospital into a modern teaching facility, let alone one that suited the needs of the Wellington public, was a major project. By the mid-1960s the hospital board had committed to 'a massive rebuilding programme', but progress was slow. The advent of the Clinical School slowed it further, since plans had to be modified to integrate clinical and academic facilities. At the university's suggestion, Auckland firm Cutter and Pickmere, which had recently designed its Christchurch building, took over as architects – and that created even more delays. The university committed to building an academic block, to be linked to a clinical services block housing both hospital and university services. The initial scheme for a 1200-bed hospital was downsized as the country ran into financial difficulties in the late 1970s; and the intended clinical services building became wards instead. The academic building went ahead, though behind schedule. Ewan Coleman, a microbiologist who began a 40-year career at the Medical School in 1976, recalls that the building was still a hole in the ground when he arrived. The UGC funded a small building – O'Donnell referred to it as 'a temporary block', but it was better known as the 'tin shed' – to house offices and a seminar room for the Medicine Department until the main building was finished.[72]

Other than the dean, the first academic appointment to the school was the professor of medicine. North, the Medical Unit director, departed for England in 1972, disappointed at the failure of the full medical school scheme. Otago replaced him with respiratory specialist O'Donnell, who was already a professor in Dunedin and moved to Wellington late in 1973.[73] Most of the professors arrived in 1975 to set up their departments amid the construction chaos. Not everyone got along: Linda Holloway, a future dean who started her Wellington career as a senior lecturer in pathology in 1979, recalled that the professor, Bill Stehbens, was 'convinced that everyone in public health and psychological medicine was by definition a communist'. There was a steady turnover of pathology staff – and not only because of the substandard conditions in the old mortuary where they worked: there were 'cats and kittens living in ducting and things like that', Holloway recalled.[74] Building good relationships with existing hospital clinicians was a delicate business, and some managed it better than others. Corkill recalled that 'at the time there was a definite excess of general surgeons in the hospital', and this made surgeons wary of the new department: Bill Isbister, the professor, had

The Wellington campus was still a building site when the first fourth-year medical students commenced there in 1977. The main academic block is on the left, with the link block joining it to the ward support block that is under construction on the right.
WELLINGTON HOSPITAL PROGRESS SHOTS, K.E. NIVEN AND CO COMMERCIAL NEGATIVES, 1/2-240760-F, ALEXANDER TURNBULL LIBRARY.

difficulty negotiating patient beds and theatre time. The 'situation slowly improved', but Isbister never acquired the larger surgical unit he hoped for; he departed for Saudi Arabia in 1990.[75]

Isbister was not the first professor to depart Wellington out of frustration over resources: psychiatrist John Roberts headed back to England in 1979. There was a shortage of psychiatrists in the region, the hospital's Psychiatry Unit was still in its infancy and, while existing psychiatrists were 'delighted' at the development of an academic unit, suitable clinical arrangements and spaces for administration and teaching took a long time to appear. The chair was vacant until Graham Mellsop was recruited from Melbourne in 1982, and under his able leadership the department increased its resources.[76] The Community Health Department began under the charismatic Ken Newell, whose presence could always be detected by the smell of tobacco. He started out alongside the Epidemiology Unit in a former nurses' home in Coromandel Street and soon had a lively department going. Unfortunately for New Zealand, he was enticed away to the prestigious tropical community health chair in Liverpool in 1983.[77]

Wellington did not live up to the expectations of the second dean, Ralph Johnson – an English neurologist who took up the post in 1977. He was 'assured, confident and extremely articulate', according to Corkill.[78] Johnson was eager to develop the Wellington school and expected it to become a full medical school – but he got offside with the hierarchy in Dunedin by liaising with other bodies before consulting his superiors. Eventually he lost the support of his Wellington colleagues, too, and by 1985 'an overwhelming majority did not want his contract renewed'. Johnson stayed on in Wellington as a professor for a couple of years, before taking a senior job at Oxford.[79] O'Donnell replaced Johnson as dean and remained there until his retirement in 1991.

Despite the challenges, the Wellington Clinical School was effective from the beginning, especially in its core business of educating undergraduate students. Staff were conscious that students had a choice of clinical schools and they made Wellington an attractive destination. The 47 students who commenced fourth-year medicine in 1977 established a good culture: they 'cooperated damn well and damn hard to make the show go',

The deans of the Medical School met regularly. Having a cup of tea in 1986 are, from left: David Stewart (Dunedin), Tom O'Donnell (Wellington), John Hunter (faculty dean) and Alan Clarke (Christchurch).
UNIVERSITY OF OTAGO PHOTOGRAPHIC UNIT RECORDS, MS-4368/092, S17-612A, HOCKEN COLLECTIONS

O'Donnell recalled. Some arrived a week early and assisted with the move into the available two floors of the uncompleted building.[80] Puddles, planks and tarpaulins proved no deterrent to education – the first students performed well in their exams.[81] The school already had a history of staff and student social events – Hall and his wife regularly hosted dinners for sixth-year students and staff – but the addition of fourth-years prompted another event: the annual staff versus student volleyball game, followed by a humorous debate, usually adjudicated by a local identity.[82]

The school had a good relationship with the Hospital Board, for which taking on the Medical School was a big administrative and financial commitment. Wellington escaped the worst of the toxic difficulties that plagued Christchurch and Dunedin teaching hospitals during the health reforms of the 1990s.[83] Like Christchurch, until the 1990s Wellington had a Clinical School Council; and it had a succession of influential chairs. The first was Otago graduate and retired politician Arnold Nordmeyer, one of the architects of New Zealand's state-funded health system. He was followed by Gordon Robb, the retired head of the New Zealand branch of chemical giant ICI, and then William Scollay, an influential businessman and pioneer of trade links with Japan. Scollay's interest in the Medical School was sparked when he received treatment from Isbister; as chair he worked to raise awareness of the value of the Medical School to Wellington.[84]

Two days after the first fourth-year class began at Wellington, Johnson hosted an open day: 'it was time Wellingtonians understood what the School was doing', he said.[85] An article in the university newsletter describing the official opening ceremony at Wellington in 1979 revealed a Dunedin view of that 'most remote outpost'. The author noted that 'the Otago flag is kept flying' and that staff and students retained an affinity with the university, but that there was a 'feeling of remoteness from wider academic contact' and a 'sense of isolation'.[86] Wellington campus leaders worked hard to ensure they were not forgotten in Dunedin and that they received their fair share of resources and support; building strong local networks added to campus resilience.

Members of the Asthma Research Group in 2008: (from left) Richard Beasley, Julian Crane, Carl Burgess, Neil Pearce. A Wellington family affected by the use of fenoterol commissioned the painting by Keila Martin, entitled *Inhaler Pile*, to celebrate the lifesaving impact of the group's research. RICHARD BEASLEY COLLECTION.

SUPPORTING RESEARCH

One important form of local support was money. The Wellington Medical Research Foundation was a key source of research funds; together with the Wellington branch of the Cancer Society it agreed to fund part of the salary of the pathology professor, provided he directed the Wellington Cancer and Medical Research Institute they were developing.[87] Stehbens duly became director of that institute, which was formally opened in leased space in the Medical School building in 1979. The institute's trust had already, in 1974, granted $35,000 towards an electron microscope for the Pathology Department.[88] Stehbens researched the development of atherosclerosis: he argued that it was disturbances to blood flow rather than high blood lipid levels that first prompted the development of plaque in blood vessels.[89] The institute was renamed the Malaghan Institute in 1986 in honour of its founding donors, Len and Ann Malaghan (Len had made his fortune as founder of the Tip-Top ice-cream business). Graham Le Gros succeeded Stehbens as director in 1994 and established projects in immunology and asthma. In 2004 the Malaghan Institute left the Wellington campus, where Otago was unwilling to provide the additional space it needed – and Victoria created a purpose-built facility on its Kelburn campus.[90]

Respiratory illness was a leading research field at Wellington, starting with O'Donnell and another early member of his department, Peter Holst. In 1978 the MRC became concerned about New Zealand's high asthma death rate and appointed a special taskforce to investigate; O'Donnell was chair of the taskforce, and Holst was another key member. It was, however, some of the younger researchers at Wellington who solved the puzzle of the epidemic of asthma fatalities. Physicians Julian Crane and Richard Beasley and pharmacologist Carl Burgess, all from the Medicine Department, were suspicious that a popular asthma drug, fenoterol, might be a problem. They asked epidemiologist Neil Pearce of the Community Health Department to join them in a study. The Asthma Task Force had investigated asthma deaths. The new Asthma Research Group now took the original data, gathered further information on people's drug use and added control patients to the design. Their results, published in the *Lancet* in 1989, were explosive: they revealed a link between asthma deaths and fenoterol. The drug manufacturer, Boehringer Ingelheim, conducted a campaign to discredit the study. It was a tense time for the Wellington campus, as O'Donnell and others resisted suggestions that fenoterol was dangerous. Other studies confirmed the Asthma Research Group's findings and, after considerable delay, government subsidies for fenoterol were withdrawn.[91] Those responsible for the lifesaving project continued as the Wellington Asthma Research Group and on other projects, and all became professors on the Wellington campus. In 2001 Beasley established an independent research organisation, the Medical Research Institute of New Zealand. He became an Otago adjunct professor, working in collaboration with many others. In 2016 he received the Royal Society's Sir Charles Hercus Medal in recognition of 'his wide ranging contributions to advancing respiratory medicine and health science research in New Zealand'.[92]

The Wellington campus lost the Malaghan Institute, but a few years later it developed the Centre for Translational Physiology, intent on 'translating science into health'. In 2012 a staff taskforce suggested that researchers needed more space and core capabilities to enhance biomedical research, and it recommended that 'bringing together both clinicians and academics' would help 'decrease the time from scientific discovery to clinical application'. The centre opened in 2013 under the directorship of Shieak Tzeng, an Otago graduate in medicine and physiology. It had shared laboratory spaces for human physiology studies, together with adjoining clinics. Collaborative research projects were soon underway. In 2015 the centre acquired the Global Energetics and Environmental Simulation Suite (GEnESIS), which enabled 'gold standard assessments of energy expenditure' – useful in research into obesity, diabetes, and responses to extreme environments. It was New Zealand's first facility of the type and a boon to the Wellington region for more than just health research: elite athletes, including Wellington's Hurricanes rugby team, used it for simulated high-altitude training.[93]

Wellington dean John Nacey said in 2006 that improving technology made biomedical research more successful, but more expensive, too. Public health research provided 'more bang for your buck' and was easier to fund in a small economy like New Zealand's.[94] Public health teaching and research flourished at Wellington. The fact that it was in the capital city was important. Staff often worked on issues that had a bearing on government policy, and the Department (later Ministry) of Health valued that; it provided funding towards the foundation community health chair, some staff worked for both organisations and others collaborated on research.[95] The Community Health Department (renamed Department of Public Health in 1994) became Wellington's largest, with expertise in a range of fields besides medicine, including sociology, biostatistics, health services organisation, economics and health promotion. Its staff appeared frequently in the media – such as infectious disease epidemiologist Michael Baker talking about contaminated chicken, and Philippa Howden-Chapman on the need for warm, dry, safe housing.[96] Howden-Chapman, a clinical psychologist with an interest in social aspects of health, joined the staff in 1991; she led the He Kainga Oranga/Housing and Health Research Programme, which won the Prime Minister's Science Prize in 2014.[97]

The department was also home to Te Rōpū Rangahau Hauora a Eru Pōmare, the Eru Pomare Māori Health Research Centre, named in honour of its first director after his untimely death in 1995. Pomare was one of the Department of Medicine's founding staff; he succeeded O'Donnell as Wellington dean in 1992. In addition to his work in gastroenterology, he championed Māori health. He established the Māori Health Research Centre, originally known as Te Manawa Hauora, with funding from the HRC in 1992. It built on the work already being done by Pomare and Papaarangi Reid, the public health physician appointed to teach Māori health in 1989. Reid

Eru Pomare (medicine) lecturing in the Small Lecture Theatre, Wellington.
UNIVERSITY OF OTAGO, WELLINGTON COLLECTION.

assumed leadership of the centre after Pomare's death and it continued to grow. In 2000 Tim Rochford was appointed to a full-time position teaching Māori health, and this freed Reid up to concentrate on the centre's expanding research programme. Reid later left to head the University of Auckland's Te Kupenga Hauora Māori and her colleague Bridget Robson became director of the Wellington centre.[98]

EXPANDING TEACHING

As on the other campuses, Public Health offered postgraduate qualifications that appealed to a range of people besides doctors. Otago's Public Health Diploma had developed a tropical medicine focus. In 1981 Newell initiated a Wellington-based replacement, the Diploma in Community Health, with a wider brief. A more flexible Public Health Diploma, offered at all three campuses and at the University of Auckland, replaced it a decade later. The Wellington department also reached a broader group through its distance-taught undergraduate Certificate in Health Promotion, begun in 1993.[99]

Another innovation was the Public Health Summer School, first run in 1997: it offered a range of one- to three-day courses that disseminated the latest research and provided professional development. It quickly became a popular fixture and in 2013 it passed 500 enrolments. Baker, one of the school's directors, noted that year that the programme was continually updated and responded to emerging public health issues; it played 'a key role in helping connect New Zealand researchers and practitioners with leading international thinkers'.[100]

In 1983 John Durham joined the Medicine Department to teach general practice and convene medical student placements in the community, starting with one-week attachments for final-year students. Other general practice staff joined him and in 1989 they set up as a separate unit in the 'tin hut'.[101] In 1992 Wellington GPs set up a trust to raise funds for a chair; the Accident Compensation Corporation (ACC), which wanted to 'ensure GPs are training in the area of vocational rehabilitation', was a principal sponsor.[102] General practice earned full departmental status in 1997, when the inaugural professor, Tony Dowell, arrived from

Leeds.[103] It expanded into a five-week module in the fourth year of the medical degree and four weeks at sixth year. The department took over the diplomas in travel medicine and in emergency medicine, and added further qualifications in health science and primary health care. A change of name in 2005 to Department of Primary Health Care and General Practice reflected the growth of 'inter-professional learning and research'; staff came from a range of professional groups in the primary health sector.[104]

Undergraduate medical students increasingly ventured beyond Wellington Hospital for acute as well as community clinical experience. From the early days some attended nearby Hutt Hospital and in 1978 the Clinical School built a teaching facility there.[105] The expense of providing facilities was a hurdle: in 2006 Nacey noted his frustration at funding problems that delayed expansion into Hawke's Bay, where the health board wanted to take 50 students.[106] Eventually regional undergraduate sites opened in Palmerston North in 2008 and Hastings in 2010. Palmerston North Hospital doctors were 'delighted to work with students and eager to teach without any signs of the so-called "student fatigue" often encountered in larger teaching hospitals', the MidCentral District Health Board declared.[107] Groups of final-year students spent their entire year there or in Hastings, and often stayed on as house surgeons.

Wellington developed rural teaching centres in Tararua and Wairarapa as part of the rural medicine immersion programme. If it was not so expensive, Wellington could make even more use of the opportunities in its hinterland, says Sunny Collings, who became dean in 2010. The university had to employ people to teach and look after students and provide learning facilities such as videolinks back to the main campus. In locations where students went for shorter placements there was a need for accommodation.[108] External funding from Health Workforce New Zealand enabled Otago to commence an interprofessional education programme in the Gisborne and East Coast region in 2012, in conjunction with the Tairāwhiti District Health Board. Eastern Institute of Technology nursing students and Otago students in dentistry, dietetics, medicine, pharmacy and physiotherapy worked and lived together on five-week clinical placements with the largely Māori rural communities on the East Coast. An analysis of the first few years, led by programme director Sue Pullon, showed that a well-supported rural setting was highly suitable for preparing senior students for collaborative practice; immersion in a Māori community provided valuable learning, and students loved the experience.[109]

RADIATION THERAPY

In 2001 Otago's Wellington campus took over New Zealand's sole course in radiation therapy. Radiation therapy was originally taught alongside radiography in the main centre hospitals. CIT commenced a radiation therapy course in 1978 under which students spent half the programme in hospitals, which paid them a stipend; the stipend continued through subsequent course changes until 2016.[110] The course evolved into a degree in the late 1990s, but by then radiation therapists believed their course was 'outgrowing' the 'polytechnic environment', as head of department Karen Coleman later wrote. CIT had financial difficulties and eventually became a regional rather than a national provider, so it was no longer a suitable home for a national course. In 2000 a committee representing radiation therapists set about finding another provider. Its choices were limited to institutions in Auckland, Wellington or Christchurch, which had the necessary hospital radiation therapy facilities, and the unanimous preference was for Otago's Wellington campus, thanks to its central location, established postgraduate opportunities and international standing. In August 2000 CIT signed a memorandum of understanding with the university. Otago also planned to take over CIT's national podiatry course, but later withdrew when it emerged the course would need large financial subsidies; the course went instead to AUT. As

CIT's financial troubles worsened, the government announced in April 2001 that it would close in two months, halfway through the academic year; the remnants of CIT merged with Hutt Valley Polytechnic to become Weltec. The transfer of radiation therapy had to be sped up. It remained at its existing Heretaunga premises for the rest of the year, but under the auspices of the University of Otago. The course then relocated – physically as well as institutionally, as Coleman explained: 'Three prefab buildings from the CIT Health Sciences site were literally chopped in half, put on trucks and moved during the night, 35kms to the new location' on the Otago campus.[111]

Radiation therapy was the university's first undergraduate health science degree taught entirely away from Dunedin. It was a small and specialised programme and its staff and students had little in common with those in Wellington's other departments. In 2002 radiation therapy had 82 students; it attracted more applications and increased its intake from its CIT years.[112] Moving premises during southerly gales and translating the curriculum and documentation into 'Otago "speak"' were tricky tasks – but one of the biggest challenges of the shift to the university was developing a research culture.[113] As with other new university programmes, one of the first priorities was to upgrade the qualifications of staff. When anatomy and physiology lecturer Patries Herst graduated PhD in 2006 it was an encouraging development: for her PhD Herst had researched the use of oxygen by cancer cell membranes, through the Malaghan Institute.[114] In 2008 she became research coordinator and director of an honours programme that offered a pathway to higher research degrees, and a few years later she reported 'increased awareness amongst NZ RTs [radiation therapists] that evidence-based practice requires clinically relevant research in which RTs can play a pivotal role'.[115] In 2012 the department introduced a postgrad certificate offered through distance education that catered to a growing interest in 'advanced practice', where experienced radiation therapists with advanced qualifications could extend their roles.[116] With stronger confidence in the profession, the departmental name changed in 2011 from Medical Radiation Therapy to Radiation Therapy, and the Bachelor of Health Sciences endorsement became the Bachelor of Radiation Therapy.[117]

Radiation therapy 'is a technology-driven, ever-changing profession', a 2012 review noted, but the department's facilities did not reflect that technical sophistication.[118] That changed in 2013 when Otago acquired a virtual environment radiation therapy training system (VERT), something like 'a flight simulator for radiation therapy'. It was already a standard tool in some countries, but the expense of the system delayed its adoption in New Zealand. After several years of lobbying the $1 million cost was met by the government, and the university and the Cancer Society funded its installation and integration into the degree programme. As patient numbers rose, the radiation technology in clinical areas was less available for teaching, so VERT was an essential learning tool that was available to medical physicists and radiation oncologists as well as radiation therapists.[119] The acquisition of VERT helped Otago with its mission to educate a profession that may have been small, but that was 'an essential element of the management of cancer in New Zealand'.[120]

BUILDING WELLINGTON

As the Wellington campus expanded its education and research, accommodation became crowded. In 2007 Prime Minister Helen Clark opened an $18 million upgrade that incorporated building additions as well as refurbishment of some older facilities. Nacey expressed the staff and students' appreciation of the 'significant improvement to the ambience and facilities … We wanted a physical heart and that's what we now have.' The 'fantastic working environment' included the library, computer laboratories, teaching spaces and café.[121]

The expansion of the Wellington campus spelled the end of one shortlived venture, the Wellington Stadium Centre. When the stadium

Students working in the new Wellington campus library in 2007. The building renovations and addition, squeezed into 'the awkward leftover spaces between existing buildings', won Athfield Architects an award for interior architecture.

UNIVERSITY OF OTAGO MARKETING AND COMMUNICATIONS COLLECTION.

opened in 2000 the university needed more space for physiotherapy students who were completing clinical training in Wellington. The stadium trust suggested that Otago build a facility there. The NZ Institute of Sport entered into a collaboration with Otago, Victoria and CIT to run a high-performance sports academy; Otago's strengths in sports medicine and sports science suited the project. Otago invested $2 million in the stadium centre, which opened in 2001 with great hopes for the use of its modern teaching and conference facilities; it also became the home of the local Schools Liaison Office. Unfortunately, as Graeme Fogelberg says, the sports academy did not attract the numbers it should have, and once physiotherapy had the opportunity to move to the expanded main Wellington campus, conveniently close to the other health science programmes, it did so. In 2009 Otago closed its stadium centre and the Institute of Sport took over the facility; Otago liaison staff shifted to central Wellington offices.[122]

OTAGO IN AUCKLAND

Like Christchurch and Wellington, Auckland – New Zealand's largest city – hosted Otago medical students from the 1920s onwards, and in 1959 Otago set up a Medical Unit there. It was led by Derek North who, like his younger brother Ken at the Wellington campus, was an Otago graduate and Rhodes Scholar.[123] Auckland had always had aspirations for its own medical school: in 1886 it offered anatomy lectures but, without the support of the Hospital Board and the University of New Zealand Senate, the course died. The dream survived, though, and by the time Otago established its Medical Unit in Auckland, the University of New Zealand had ruled there would be a second medical school there.

Otago's operations in Auckland helped set up the clinical infrastructure for the new school. North was involved in planning it, and became the foundation professor of medicine and later dean. In 1973, when Auckland's first medical students reached their final year, Otago bowed out of its clinical commitments in the city. Keith Sinclair, in his history of the University of Auckland, remarked that it was striking 'how rarely the Auckland medical men, almost all of whom were Otago graduates, turned to Otago for advice. That was partly because Otago was hostile or unhelpful, but partly because the Aucklanders wanted to do something different.'[124] North claimed that the 'competitive rivalry' between the two schools was 'all in good fun' and benefited both; Auckland had a blank page to implement fresh ideas and Otago followed some that were successful.[125]

Otago and Auckland had no difficulty filling places in their medical programmes, but attracting good students to universities in general became competitive in the 1990s, driven by the government's 'bums on seats' EFTS funding model. Warwick Johnson, who became Otago's schools liaison officer in 1989, recalls that Irvine informed him late in 1992 that they needed an additional 500 students for the following year. Johnson and John Scandrett, the commercial activities director, set up a successful marketing

Otago leased just part of the former IBM premises in Upper Queen Street, but secured the naming rights; that gave it a highly visible presence in central Auckland. According to Eric Walton, who joined the Auckland Centre in 2008 as enterprise manager, businesses observed that Otago had invested in quality facilities that demonstrated a seriousness about engagement with Auckland. UNIVERSITY OF OTAGO MARKETING AND COMMUNICATIONS COLLECTION.

campaign; this started a trend that other institutions followed, and marketing campaigns ramped up across the country. But the liaison officers were always the key people on the ground, visiting schools and advising prospective students. Earlier liaison officers had worked in their own regions, advising school pupils on courses that were available in all the universities. Otago's first liaison officer was Basil Howard, appointed in 1943; he famously approved the course of every Otago student, and was later appointed dean of students. Ian Page, Johnson's predecessor, made a few forays to Auckland schools, but only after seeking permission from the local liaison officer. That all changed in the competitive environment of the 1990s. Otago appointed more officers in Dunedin, as well as staff based in Auckland from 1996 and Wellington from 1998. The schools liaison service eventually set up twice-yearly visits to almost every school in New Zealand.[126]

Grant Hopkins, the first Auckland-based liaison officer, recalls that he 'scurried around' the whole North Island at first, but after Helen Ridley took on the Wellington post he concentrated on the area from Taupō north. Hopkins was based in Otago's Auckland Centre, opened in 1996 as part of a strategic plan to establish Otago as a truly national university: it was visible in Dunedin, Christchurch and Wellington, but there was 'a big void in the biggest centre of population', Fogelberg recalls. The centre, with Adrienne Molloy as coordinator, had office, conference and teaching facilities. Otago had no designs on the Auckland undergraduate scene, but it hoped to offer continuing education and postgraduate programmes there.[127] The Auckland project flourished early: the Commerce Division started an executive MBA there in 1997. The original accommodation at 47 Wakefield Street became crowded, so in 1999 the centre moved to larger premises in Queen Street.[128]

The Auckland Centre had sophisticated audio and videoconferencing technology and the potential of a large Otago graduate pool in the city, but Dunedin-based academics were slow to use it – apart from the dentistry, dietetics and pharmacy programmes. After the Auckland executive MBA ended in 2004, academic use dropped, but it still provided a useful venue for alumni functions, public lectures and summer school courses, and was a convenient base for enterprise activities. Above all, it was still the base for schools liaison services in the north, and many open days and other functions were held on site. The Auckland liaison staff increased to three, including a specialist Māori liaison officer, and when Mike Wilson became national coordinator for schools liaison in 2003 he based himself in Auckland. The liaison team was critical in recruiting students from the populous north to Dunedin.[129]

SOUTHLAND

Nearer its home base, the university had an older relationship with the deep south, and some of its foundation students were Southlanders.[130] Southland was not highly populated, but Otago was its regional university and southern students made an important contribution to the roll: in the 1970s they made up around 12 per cent of Otago students.[131] Southlanders were avid consumers of continuing education – they had one of the earliest WEA (Workers' Educational Association) groups from 1915, and they made the most of the university outreach programmes. In the 1930s many women participated in Home Science Extension activities with a tutor resident in Gore. After the war, continuing education expanded into other fields, and by 1950 Otago's Invercargill-based tutor, Vivian Powley, was beetling around Southland in a Ford Prefect, giving and organising classes. That year Invercargill residents could attend tutorials on public speaking, photography, 'makers of history', art appreciation, industrial relations, popular science and flower arrangement. The drama tutor travelled to Invercargill to organise events, including a play at the borstal and popular poetry recitals. The big drawcard of the year was a lecture by geology professor Noel Odell on his Everest exploits. Otago was a leading supplier of continuing education in Southland until Southland Polytechnic took over in the late 1900s.[132]

Southlanders were also keen on local courses that contributed to a formal university qualification. The University of New Zealand allowed students to sit exams as 'external' students. Some were self-taught and others had private tutors; and some communities arranged classes to assist local students. After the University of New Zealand ended, students could still obtain an 'exemption' from attending lectures at one of the universities. Most of Otago's exempted students were in commerce, often based in Invercargill. Academics did not like these exemptions, but they agreed to give the occasional seminar or tutorial to Invercargill students. The students had an advocate in feisty local MP Norman Jones – a commerce teacher who was 'always, at times forcefully, insistent that the service and connection be maintained', according to Commerce AVC Lyall McLean.[133]

The university and Southland Polytechnic (later the Southern Institute of Technology (SIT)) had a good relationship, and it became even better when Otago built an extension centre on the polytech grounds in Invercargill in 1975.[134] A couple of years later the two organisations, together with Massey University, were the first to take advantage of legislation that enabled polytechs to provide university studies in association with a university. Ron Walker, who ran Otago's extension programmes in Southland, became director of the Centre for University Studies: he coordinated study assistance for Massey and Otago extramural students along with the continuing education

Teaching students Dayle Herewini and Shari Frengley at work in a visual arts class on the Southland campus in 2009.
MARNI STONE PHOTOGRAPH, SOUTHLAND CAMPUS COLLECTION.

programme.[135] Commerce Faculty staff ran end-of-year seminars in Invercargill and supplied the staff there with teaching materials that were used throughout the year. Advanced papers were not offered extramurally – students had to complete their degree in Dunedin – but the fact that they could complete a considerable portion of their degree in Invercargill created goodwill towards Otago. The Southland community had its own plans for regional development, however, and at the heart of those lay SIT. An innovative zero-fees scheme, introduced in 2001, attracted many students to Invercargill. SIT continued to support some Otago BCom papers, but eventually it developed its own full BCom and the arrangement ended.[136]

Although the Southland extension and commerce programmes died, Otago retained links with Invercargill through its medical education programme from the 1970s onwards, with more students heading south for clinical placements and a distance learning centre set up at Kew Hospital.

In 2007 the university acquired professional programmes in teacher education and a campus in Invercargill through the merger with the Dunedin College of Education. The college set up the 'outpost' because of a shortage of secondary teachers in Southland; it provided local training options for people who wanted to stay in the south or could not readily move to Dunedin. Twenty-one students attended the first course in 1980 – the start of a tradition of training teachers with strong ties to their region. Like its Dunedin parent, the Southland campus faced possible closure in the mid-1980s, but it survived through government reforms to expand in the freer education market of the 1990s. From 1990 primary and early childhood education qualifications were added to the Southland programme. The innovative Te Pōkai Mātauranga o te Ao Rua programme evolved from the desire of the Invercargill campus to reach out to the local Māori population, initially through a specialised six-month foundation course that began in 1991, and then through an enhanced Māori cultural element in the primary and early childhood programmes. The programme later developed into specialised bilingual courses, which became the jewel in the crown of the Southland campus; the 2012 college review noted their 'very high local and national profile amongst the Māori population'.[137]

2017 education students (from left) Andrew Boutillier, Kyllee Munro and Megan Baird walk towards *Te Puka a Ahuahu* (*The Anchorstone of Ahuahu*), a 1992 carving by Oti Murray that reflects the Southland campus's strong links with Māori. The back of the work is left untouched and the front is finely finished, representing the students' journey from chaos to knowledge and understanding; and the marriage of indigenous Oamaru stone carving and the exotic radiata pine base symbolises the college's commitment to biculturalism. Later gifts of Pacific Island and Malaysian artworks symbolise the participation of students from other cultures.

JOANIE RONNFELDT PHOTOGRAPH, SOUTHLAND CAMPUS COLLECTION.

A NATIONAL INSTITUTION

If the University of Otago had remained quietly at home in Dunedin it would be a very different institution at 150 years. Its developments in other centres changed it irrevocably. Reaching out to the bigger cities in the north secured the future of the Otago Medical School in Dunedin and, at the same time, benefited the 'northern' centres. Purely from a financial perspective, in 2012 the university had an estimated 'direct economic impact' of $47.1 million in Wellington and $46.2 million in Christchurch, with over 700 full-time equivalent staff in each of those cities.[138] The positive influence on regional health services was important, too: Otago established teaching centres for the health sciences from Invercargill to Tairāwhiti. The far south had its teacher education programmes and a special relationship with the Commerce Division, and Otago had even established a foothold in the centre of the Auckland metropolis, although that was principally administrative. The University of Otago was very much at home in Dunedin, but its operations elsewhere gave it resilience and made it a significant national institution.

CHAPTER ELEVEN

Support services

THE LIBRARY

A library is 'of prime importance' to any university, Ernest Duncan wrote in the 1939 *Otago University Review*; it 'has been said that the library is more important in the modern University than the teaching staff, and in New Zealand, where we have no tutorial system and books are our only reliable link with the important thought and life of the world, this may prove to be true'.[1] According to the 1959 Parry Report, library collections were 'of great importance to all students', but a university library was especially necessary for arts students – it needed to have 'adequate working space for those who use it as their "laboratory"'.[2] As more of its resources were accessed digitally, the library remained an indispensable physical space for study. It was at the heart of university life.

The University of Otago Library had modest beginnings. In 1872 it had 500 volumes, some purchased by the founding professors in Britain and others donated by the public; it fitted into a bookcase in the council chamber. The cash-strapped university spent little on the library in its early years: the collection grew to around 8000 volumes in its first 20 years thanks to public gifts, the contribution of a shortlived independent reference library committee and the donation of the Otago provincial government library after the provinces were abolished in 1876. Not all the books were relevant, and they were kept in locked shelves to which the registrar, who served as librarian, held the keys.[3]

In 1907 Thomas Morland Hocken, a Dunedin doctor, donated his collection of early New Zealand books, pictures and manuscripts to the people of New Zealand, on condition that they be managed by the University of Otago. A wing was added to the museum to house the collection and the university employed its first full-time librarian, William Trimble, to catalogue and care for it. The Hocken, as it came to be known, was expensive to run, and some later questioned its relevance to the university, but it went on to become one of Otago's greatest assets. Further donations and a policy of actively collecting New Zealand and Pacific materials maintained the significance of the Hocken as one of the country's major collections. It contributed to the university's public service and each year dozens of theses, books, journals, exhibitions and other productions made use of the Hocken's resources. 'There is no doubting the Hocken's pivotal position in Otago's research culture', history professor Tony Ballantyne noted in 2015.[4]

Trimble's successor, Beatrice Howes, was appointed in 1913 to work half-time at the Hocken and half-time in the main library, and this finally relieved the registrar of library duties.

History professor Angus Ross, a student in the early 1930s, recalled that the library's collection then 'scarcely deserved the name of a university library, so small and so poor was it'.[5] In 1931 the Carnegie Corporation offered each of New Zealand's university colleges a large book grant, on condition that they sent a graduate to study library science in the US and then appointed them university librarian. Otago's existing librarian, Ngarita Gordon, was ineligible as she hadn't graduated. In 1934, with the offer about to expire, Otago advertised the position and John Harris was selected. There was a hitch when the US vice-consul refused Harris a visa because of his left-wing political activism; and the police commissioner informed the University Council of Harris's political activities in Auckland, too. But the council did not back down from its appointment. Harris's establishment background presumably helped: his grandfather was an Anglican archdeacon and headmaster of Christ's College, which Harris attended before completing a degree at Oxford; and he believed his descriptions of rugby and sailing activities helped win him the position. The Carnegie Corporation permitted Harris to complete his fellowship at the University of London instead, and he returned to New Zealand in 1936. Better funding and a qualified director transformed the library. By 1948, when Harris departed to serve in university libraries in Nigeria and later Ghana, Otago had several qualified librarians on staff, subscribed to 1200 serials, and that year added 6000 books and loaned out over 26,000 volumes from the main library.[6]

The library expanded through the Clocktower Building, forcing various departments out, but eventually it outgrew available space.[7] A new library building opened in 1965, but once it was full it had no potential for extensions. Jock McEldowney, university librarian from 1961 to 1987, planned beyond its capacity even before the building went up. 'Controlled decentralisation' in six locations, each with a senior librarian, was a pragmatic solution that took advantage of libraries that had developed in an ad hoc fashion elsewhere on campus – along with a new Science Library.[8]

Because of the frugal funding of the central library, many departments had developed their own. When the Medical School moved to Great King Street in 1917, the Medical Library was born and all the medical books in the central library were transferred there. It built a considerable collection thanks to the generosity of the medical profession, and in 1929 it received a 'dazzling collection' of rare books and manuscripts that had belonged to three generations of a distinguished Edinburgh family of anatomists, the Monro family.[9] Medical School administrators took charge of the medical collection in 1917 and appointed their own librarian – initially an honorary post. The librarian remained independent of university library control until 1965, when the VC ruled that allocation of the bulk library grant would be controlled by the university librarian.[10]

The Dental and Law libraries gained status under McEldowney's structure. The Law Library got an improved home when the faculty moved into the Hocken (now Richardson) Building in 1979 – also the new home of the Hocken Library. As a heritage collection the Hocken did not throw out 'old' items, and it always needed more space. Some of its collections were stored in the former vehicle testing station in Leith Street, before all were reunited in a refurbished dairy factory in Anzac Avenue in 1998.[11] The final library in the controlled decentralisation programme – the Science Library – was created from the collections of several departments ('they weren't libraries, just collections', according to McEldowney). Some,

Students at work in the library's main reading room (now the council chamber) in the Clocktower Building, 1949. Neil Howard, a 1950s student, recalled that the 'most terrifying place was the upper Oliver at the northern end where the real swots worked. Here silence reigned supreme, dropped books, coughs, sneezes, splutters were greeted with angry eyes appearing above the top of books while a spoken word suggested the imminent appearance of a bouncer.' Later generations fired off complaints about noisy freshers – or sighed over their library crush – via anonymous social media app Yik Yak.
PRIME MINISTER'S DEPARTMENT PHOTOGRAPH, BOX-184-012, S15-199E, HOCKEN COLLECTIONS.

18 March 1970 was a rather unusual day at the central library: Queen Elizabeth and Prince Philip chatted to students. They and Prince Charles and Princess Anne toured several parts of the university.

UNIVERSITY OF OTAGO REGISTRY RECORDS, AG-180-072/021, S14-561C, HOCKEN COLLECTIONS.

especially chemistry, were reluctant to lose their individual libraries; but botanist Ann Wylie, who had to visit several departments for resources she needed for genetics, was one supporter. After years of negotiation the Science Library opened in 1977: collections from seven locations merged in a purpose-built space in the science campus. Under the capable management of Philip Kidd, it soon won over most critics.[12]

The clinical schools in Christchurch and Wellington added 'another interesting complication' – everybody wanted staff and students there to receive a standard of library service equivalent to that in Dunedin.[13] Both cities had existing medical libraries, supported by their hospital boards: the Christchurch library had grown from a postgraduate medical subscription library started in 1934; and doctors at Wellington Hospital began a reference library of medical journals in 1928.[14] In 1971, after 'complicated negotiations', the university and North Canterbury Hospital Board agreed to pool their resources. The existing library became the basis of a jointly funded service. The university provided a purpose-built space in its building and employed a specialist librarian.[15] The Christchurch arrangement set a pattern that was followed in Wellington. Shortly before the first fourth-year students arrived in 1977, a rugby team that was raising money spent a weekend shifting books into the partially completed university building, with the library as the priority in the whole operation.[16] The arrangements for the northern schools prompted the University Library to develop closer arrangements with the Otago Hospital Board, whose staff had always used the Medical Library. In 1975 medical and dental librarian Don Jamieson became honorary librarian to the board.[17] In 1993, when health boards were replaced with crown health enterprises, the university took sole responsibility for the medical libraries and contracted with other organisations that used their services.[18]

The card catalogue was a revolutionary development in its time: later it was computing that transformed the organisation of libraries. In the 1960s library computing systems were at the 'garbage in, garbage out' stage, McEldowney believed, but by the 1970s good technology was available. Convincing the university to invest in it wasn't easy, but in 1980 the library took its first step along the information superhighway and installed a computer terminal to 'dial up' databases overseas; library staff used it to carry out searches of the literature for researchers.[19] In 1981, with grants from the Lottery Board and a Medical School centennial trust, Otago acquired access to health science database Medline; the first search took place in the Christchurch Medical Library.[20] Another technology introduced that year was less popular – 'tattle tape', which set off an alarm if people removed books from the central library without authorisation.[21] Computerising the catalogue was a much bigger investment. In 1985 Otago joined the New Zealand Bibliographic Network, which gave it access to an international computer database of cataloguing records, making cataloguing easier. There were no more

Librarians (from left) Alan Edwards, Max Broadbent and Lindsay Henderson hard at work behind the scenes in the Orders Department of the Central Library, early 1970s.

UNIVERSITY LIBRARY RECORDS, 96-111/018, S17-611C, HOCKEN COLLECTIONS.

additions to the card catalogue: updates appeared on microfiche as an interim measure until library users gained online access.[22]

University librarian Michael Wooliscroft oversaw the next technological advances. Years of planning culminated in the online public catalogue going live in 1989, and book circulation was automated from 1990. The old card catalogue wasn't yet redundant – it took years for old records to be digitised – but searching for newer items became easier.[23] The library acquired its first CD-ROM software in 1989, which enabled local access to searches that had previously required expensive international telecommunications. Before the internet, software such as this was popular; it created a surge in interloans as researchers looked up articles published in journals that were not held in the library.[24]

By the time Wooliscroft retired in 2005 the library was scarcely recognisable from the organisation he had joined in 1987. Technology had evolved, and library users had access to 62,000 journals, mostly in electronic format. The central library building had undergone a revolution, too. The decentralisation policy eased things for a while, but eventually the burgeoning student roll made a larger building essential; by 1998 the 1965 building was coping with twice the books and more than twice the reader places it was designed for. One of Fogelberg's top priorities as VC was to do something about the facility, which was 'a total disgrace'.

In 2001 the Information Services Building (ISB) opened. The name indicated that this was more than a traditional library – it was designed to incorporate computing services and to adapt to future technologies not yet imagined.[25] There were other, less dramatic developments under Wooliscroft's successors, Sue Pharo and Howard Amos. Management was restructured, digital resources expanded, and the university acquired two more libraries with the 2007 merger to form the University of Otago College of Education:

the small education library on the Southland campus, and the Bill Robertson Library, which held broader collections as the joint library of the former Dunedin College of Education and Otago Polytechnic. The Robertson Library dated from 1981, and brought together the collections of the two institutions: DCE had needed to replace its small, damp prefab library and the polytech needed a library for its Forth Street campus, and the government had forced the marriage as a joint facility to save costs.[26] The university took over management of the library in 2007 and supplied services under contract to Otago Polytechnic. The university's existing education collection was moved from the ISB and merged into the Robertson Library. It underwent an extensive refurbishment in 2010 – one in a round of renovations of library branches to equip them for the latest technology and to modernise their study spaces.[27]

OTAGO UNIVERSITY PRESS

One offshoot of the library was the university's publishing arm, the University of Otago Press (from 2004 Otago University Press), which provided an outlet for academics when there were few publishing opportunities in New Zealand. The press was set up in the 1950s to publish inaugural lectures but it soon progressed to more substantial works. The first book published by the press, in 1959, was T.B.L. Webster, *Greek Art and Literature, 700–530 BC: The beginnings of a modern civilization*. The university librarian was in charge, working in conjunction with local printer and publisher John McIndoe.[28] The press published a regular trickle of books, some of which were hits – notably John Parr's *Introduction to Ophthalmology*, first published in 1976 and reprinted many times and in various editions.[29] 'The time when the job could be done as a spare-time hobby passed many years ago,' McEldowney reported when he retired in 1985; 'until the appointment of the first Assistant Editor, Dr J.M. Harris, three years ago the Press was languishing.'[30]

In 1986 the press became 'autonomous' within the university and moved from its library cupboard to a room in the Arts Building. It acquired a Macintosh Plus word processor for administrative tasks, and it used Otago's VAX computer to prepare camera-ready copy. Some things didn't change with technology: editor Bill Sewell encountered 'delays caused by attempts to negotiate joint publication agreements with publishers in the UK, and delays in receiving copy from authors'.[31] The publishing market became more crowded and Otago 'needed to increase production to stay in the game'. Its output took a leap from 1993 when Wendy Harrex was appointed as editor and the first full-time employee. As the press developed into a 'professional publishing house' with several staff, it expanded its list: it needed 'a mix of academic and general books, so that we have income earners as well as worthy slow sellers', said Harrex in 2006.[32] At Otago University Press's 50th birthday celebrations in 2008, Harrex noted, 'we have done more regional natural history publishing than anyone else in New Zealand and we have also tried to publish books about Southern Māori'. By then it had published 300 books, and it took pride in its association with literary journal *Landfall*, which it had published from 1994. In 2013 Harrex handed over to Rachel Scott, formerly publisher at Canterbury University Press, and Otago University Press has flourished under her direction.[33]

INFORMATION TECHNOLOGY SERVICES

The transformation of the library into the Information Services Building demonstrated the evolution of information technology. The Computer Centre of the 1960s had become an expanding juggernaut that, in 1983, split into academic and service departments. The centre itself – renamed the Computing Services Centre (CSC) in 1985 – was the proud owner of a two-year-old Burroughs B5930 computer, a three-year-old VAX 11/780 system and a new VAX-11/750;

Robin Skeggs, an assistant lecturer in the Accounting and Finance Department, working on an IBM personal computer around 1985.

ACCOUNTANCY AND FINANCE DEPARTMENT COLLECTION.

in 1985 it added another VAX 11/750 (with 6 megabytes of memory – large for the time) and the VAX machines were 'clustered' to create a larger system with terminals around campus.[34] The CSC also hosted a laboratory of 64KB Microprocessor Developments Ltd 'microcomputers', but in 1985 it sold the few that were still serviceable after years of heavy usage and invested in the latest thing, the Apple Macintosh.[35] The 'Mac', released in 1984, wasn't the first mass market personal computer, but it was easy to use and demand rocketed; by the end of 1985 there were over 400 around the university. Word processing was 'a major preoccupation with many departments', CSC director Neil James reported in 1985; it made computing almost as important to staff dealing with words as to those dealing with numbers.[36] Computer-assisted learning (CAL) emerged in the mid-1980s and Otago became a New Zealand leader as its early adopters – anatomy, clinical biochemistry, economics, maths, microbiology and pharmacology – were joined by other departments.[37]

The CSC ran a non-profit sales service for hardware and software, but it remained expensive. In 1989 the university set up three CAL labs with a total of 45 computers loaded with standard software, and several departments had small sets. Students could use those computers when they weren't booked for a class, though demand meant permits were limited to senior students and they were not available for simple word processing.[38] 'One thing seems constant about computing in this University – the demand outstrips the supply', James wrote in 1990; there was 'fierce competition for the available resources'.[39]

Like most universities Otago was an early adopter of networking; it started with local area networks, but links beyond campus soon emerged. Around 1985 a VAX was connected to the Post Office's Pacnet service and in 1987 the Wellington and Christchurch campuses joined it; there was 'a steady increase in the use of electronic mail', the CSC reported.[40] By 1990 work was underway to increase bandwidth through Kawaihiko, the New Zealand universities' networking organisation; access to the internet came through the gateway established by Waikato University in 1989.[41] A project to network personal computers on the Otago campus also began in 1989; the Novell network was 'at the cutting edge of microcomputer networking technology, world-wide'. David Harris, who set it up, expected between 200 and 300 machines to be connected by 1991.[42]

A future where 'the computer on the desk' was 'the main method of access to information' was 'not far away', James declared in 1991. More capacity was required so people could participate in this 'second Gutenburg revolution'; it was unlikely most students would 'be able to afford a machine of their own within the near future'.[43] In 1993 and 1994 four computer resource rooms were added and existing labs increased capacity; some were open 24 hours a day. That expansion was critical: students needed computers for the growing use of CAL, to access email and to complete assignments that required internet access. They could print assignments and theses for a small fee on the laser printers which replaced the 'ancient noisy dot matrix printers' that had frustrated users of the labs.[44] Otago boasted it was 'a leader in the ease of use of access to various resources and in the universal training that it offers students'. CSC ran a driving licence system for computer users: students completed a self-teaching package and sat competency tests for various programs.[45] Training for staff was a big responsibility as computing became pervasive: CSC developed 'courses on how to do things properly in the first place, rather than to provide help after things have been done incorrectly'.[46]

As the price of computers dropped, provision became less of a burden and there was better access. New generations of students arrived at university clutching laptops and already confident computer users; they seldom needed basic training. The challenge now was to meet demand for bandwidth, for everything from big data transfers for high-powered researchers to online video viewing for film students. In 1995 work began on an ethernet network to replace the existing 'incomplete, piecemeal and outdated' system; two years and $5.2 million later the upgrade was complete and Otago had 'the largest, fastest and most flexible internal network in New Zealand', with around 5000 personal computers connected on the Dunedin, Christchurch and Wellington campuses. Information Services director Martin Anderson noted the network was 'a key strategic asset to the university'; an outlet was standard in every office, teaching space or other facility.[47]

Anderson's role was created by Fogelberg in his 1995 restructuring of administration. The Information Services Division incorporated both library and computing services; its director was on the Vice-chancellor's Advisory Group, and this gave the division strategic representation at the highest level.[48] James continued to manage the CSC. In 1996 the centre became Information Technology Services (ITS), 'which better represents the extended variety of services we provide'.[49] When Anderson's 2005 retirement coincided with that of the librarian who reported to him, VC David Skegg restructured. The library moved back to the Academic Division and ITS and University Print carried on as the Division of Information Technology Services.[50]

ITS director Mike Harte and George Benwell of the School of Business took a tour of US universities in 2005 to investigate the latest campus technology. They reported that 'our services and facilities here at Otago are second to none', with one exception: wireless networking had 'fallen into a black hole here'.[51] A couple of years earlier the Information Science Department trialled wireless for its students to experiment with; and by 2007 the staff newsletter declared Otago 'wireless and proud'. Students could 'break free from their desks' and access the student network in the ISB link, Commerce Building or Executive Residence, and it was gradually rolled out elsewhere.[52] The arrival of wireless was timely as smartphones surged in popularity; by 2016, 98 per cent of students owned a laptop and most had a smartphone.[53] James's 1999 vision that IT networking would become like electricity – 'taken for granted' and 'almost invisible' – had been realised. And as with electricity, people noticed if the network failed.[54] In 2012 the University Council approved a 'future state network project' that replaced the 1990s infrastructure with high-speed fibre and expanded wireless. The project took longer and cost more than anticipated; installing cables into walls of older buildings sometimes became a bigger job involving asbestos removal, updated fire protection and earthquake strengthening.[55] The ITS team kept the essential service going. Their roles ranged from customer services to information security and from infrastructure management to provision of teaching and learning facilities.

Technology revolutionised teaching. In 2000 Otago ran a pilot of web-based software CourseInfo, from US company Blackboard. Before long it became a standard teaching tool, with staff posting announcements, readings and multimedia resources for students. Distance students and students with impairments found it especially useful. Later, recordings of entire lectures were posted; in the first semester of 2016 students viewed or downloaded close to a million lectures.[56] The university also adopted technology for marketing and wider communication. Croydon Paton became first full-time website coordinator in 1999 and soon there were several people developing a multipronged web presence.[57] In 2008 Otago launched a channel on iTunes U, giving public access to inaugural professorial lectures, library tours and appealing examples of student work, such as clips from the natural history filmmaking course.[58] The appointment of Susan Baxter as Otago's first social media adviser in 2015 signalled a desire to make better use of the multiple social platforms already embraced by many parts of the organisation.[59]

Computing received nary a mention in the university's centenary history; now campus life would be unthinkable without it.

STUDENT HEALTH

During the twentieth century the university developed various student support services. The first was Student Health, established in 1946 as the brainchild of medical dean Charles Hercus. The Medical School had been carrying out medical examinations of its own students, but decided to open a general practice health service for all students, the first of its kind in Australasian universities. It was partly funded by a social security grant allocated for each student who signed up; it aimed to combine 'preventive and therapeutic work' and it helped in the clinical teaching of medical students. Student Health started with two part-time doctors – preventive medicine lecturer Archie Douglas (the director) and microbiology lecturer Molly Marples – plus a part-time nutrition worker and a secretary, and the public health nurse lent a hand. Clinics were held in the department until 1962, when it became an independent service.[60]

Preventive medicine lecturer Archie Douglas in the department's health clinic, which also hosted Student Health. Douglas was the first director of Student Health.

UNIVERSITY OF OTAGO MEDICAL SCHOOL ALUMNUS ASSOCIATION RECORDS, MS-1537/601, S17-610B, HOCKEN COLLECTIONS.

By the end of its first year Student Health had signed up 736 of the 2440 students on the Otago roll, completed 963 consultations in the clinic and made 144 home visits. Students most commonly sought help for skin complaints, digestive problems, flu or colds, and 'the possible appendix was constantly calling for diagnosis and treatment'. The threat of tuberculosis – for which the first effective drug treatment was not discovered until 1944 – loomed large in the clinic's early years; screening was mandatory for students in some courses.[61] In 1980 Russell Kippax, the physician in charge, noted that compulsory screening continued, but that he believed it to be 'a waste of time'.[62] The decline in tuberculosis had seriously reduced one of the main threats to the health of young people.

Other health issues were more persistent. Glandular fever 'was again responsible for a great deal of acute and chronic ill-health', Douglas reported in 1951, and other infectious diseases, skin conditions and accidents were common. He was concerned about poor student diet and housing, including at some residential colleges: Studholme featured 'fire-risks, antiquated buildings, defective provision for food storage, over-crowding in bed-rooms, poor design, dangerous steps and generally inadequate amenities to mention only some of the faults'.[63] Residential colleges had improved by the time director Kim Ma`ia`i wrote a report on Student Health in 2010, but the 'aging and often poorly insulated housing stock, in which the majority of students are housed' remained a concern. Research showed 'direct correlation between low ambient room temperature and increased incidence of acute respiratory illness', and Ma`ia`i said the workload of Student Health during winter supported this correlation.[64]

In 1975 David Strang, retiring from Student Health after 14 years in charge, noted trends over the previous decade. The 'pattern of medical work' was 'not unusual for this age group', but there was a 'spectacular increase in one particular aspect of the work, i.e. gynaecological and urogenital conditions and contraceptive advice'.[65] Probably the main reason for the surge in sexual health work was that the contraceptive pill hit the market and it required a prescription. The Medical Association's ethical committee ruled in 1966 that prescribing contraceptives to 'unmarried persons, thereby facilitating extra-marital relationships, is not in keeping with the highest principles of the medical profession'.[66] However, Student Health was more liberal. In 1965 Strang reported: 'the social code is changing … and some apparently mature and responsible people are making free decisions which do not accord with society's religious and ethical standards'. He wrote that Student Health 'prescribes oral contraceptives only for married students and those about to be married', but students were getting prescriptions somewhere: 'many women students are taking the "pill" regularly, and this can only be regarded as prudent in their particular circumstances'.[67] Students of the late 1960s recall they had little difficulty persuading Student Health to prescribe the pill for 'medical' reasons; the doctors had seen too many unwanted pregnancies.[68]

PSYCHOLOGICAL SUPPORT

Student Health was concerned for students' mental as well as physical wellbeing. 'In all our dealings with students we endeavour to promote their all round fitness', Douglas noted, and that included 'mental hygiene'. In 1949 he reported concern at 'the number of students who come with either frank anxiety or depression conditions, or who come with symptoms which might be those of organic trouble but which are really of nervous origin'.[69] As the roll grew there was a call for specialised psychological support. In 1964 and 1965 Basil James of the Psychological Medicine Department spent half a day a week at Student Health, which gave time 'to see only the most urgent and pressing problems'. Among 'the reservoir of emotional problems' in students, he noted 'a percentage of serious disorders which is remarkably high when compared with available statistics from other countries'. Student life was

Student Health had a strong preventive focus: it encouraged students to balance their studies with physical and social activities. Director Archie Douglas and Philip Smithells of the School of Physical Education were instigators of the Trotter's Gorge Hut, photographed during construction in 1951. Douglas 'hoped many students would spend weekends at this beautiful place as a change from town and life in halls of residence', though Smithells wrote in 1967 that the hut had 'never been used as much as was originally hoped'.
PHILIP SMITHELLS PAPERS, MS-1001/218, S13-559B, HOCKEN COLLECTIONS.

challenging for some, he explained. 'Not only are students in a vulnerable age group, and subjected to stresses which are peculiar to undergraduate life, but also any degree of psychiatric incapacity can prove very disrupting to the performance of an individual engaged in competitive academic work.' He urged the provision of 'an expanded psychiatric service', and thought 'non-psychiatric counselling' would be 'a very valuable addition'.[70]

After a gap of five years another part-time psychiatrist was appointed and in 1971 the university appointed its first counsellor, Lewis Lowery. Otago had already benefited from Lowery's counselling skills as university chaplain. The SCM employed part-time chaplains on campus from the 1940s, but in the 1960s, 'an era of high ecumenical hopes', the SCM, local Anglican bishop and the National Council of Churches advocated for an official university chaplain. The post was overseen by a university committee, and the Otago Tertiary Chaplaincy Trust Board eventually took over responsibility. The Catholic Church appointed its own chaplain to students, but during the early 1970s that, too, became 'an honorary appointment to University staff'.[71] Lowery, a Baptist trained in counselling as a minister and through the Justice Department, anticipated that those skills might be useful when he became chaplain in 1964, but suspected 'the ecclesiastical image' would deter some students from seeking assistance. However, the great need for counselling overcame any such barrier; in 1968, for instance, Lowery had 717 counselling sessions with over 200 people. As he put it, 'the extent of human suffering now known to exist on the campus' showed a need for more support.[72] From 1971 he was freed up to devote himself full-time to counselling.

By 1989 the counselling service employed one full-time and seven part-time counsellors, including interns. Still, there was no shortage of demand.[73] When Lowery retired in 1993 he reflected on changes in the challenges students faced. There was greater pressure 'not only to pass

Student Health started out in the Preventive and Social Medicine Department, then moved to an old house in Union Street and, in 1979, to the Clocktower Building. In 1996, when this photograph was taken, 'the largest young adult and sexual health centre in New Zealand' moved into custom-built premises in Albany Street, with ample room for its 22 staff. They included the traditional doctors, nurses, counsellors and support staff, together with a new role, a dedicated health educator.
IAN PRESTIDGE PHOTOGRAPH, STUDENT HEALTH COLLECTION.

their exams but to get top marks' – a trend he had noted earlier during times of economic downturn. Student loans added another level of stress. On the other hand, he noted that 'a change in patterns of sexual relationships, both heterosexual and homosexual', was 'very positive'. Young people were 'much less troubled with sexual fantasy and sexual interaction is based on choice not fear'; and women were 'increasingly strong in relationships and will no longer simply fit in with a man'.[74]

Like Student Health, which it worked with and later merged into, the counselling service had a preventive mission. In 1976 it commenced popular 'help yourself' courses in a range of topics from 'rapid reading' and 'coping with exam stress' to 'developing social skills' and 'flatting'.[75] Marianne Quinn, a clinical psychologist, began alcohol education in 1986. With a group at Arana she ran 'Thinking about drinking' – a 'discussion with staff, wardens of halls, students, the proctor and others about the role alcohol plays in campus life, and changes we would like to see'.[76] David Gerrard, director of Student Health, reported: 'Alcohol is our major drug problem and I lend my full support to any on-campus agencies sharing this concern.'[77] Like unplanned pregnancies, problems with alcohol and exam panic would never disappear from the student population, but the health and counselling services worked hard to educate and support students, and they encouraged preventive programmes run by other parts of the university, including the residential colleges and OUSA. And when prevention failed, Student Health was there to pick up the pieces.

THE STUDENT LEARNING CENTRE

By the 1990s counsellors could no longer meet demand for their learning skills courses. Terry Crooks, director of the Higher Education Development Centre (HEDC), assisted with those courses. He proposed that Otago invest in a dedicated learning centre: widening participation in higher education was bringing more students with learning difficulties to universities and Otago was falling behind other tertiary institutions in terms of support for learning.[78] Proposals in 1990 and 1993 didn't progress far because of the expense. But when Phil Meade arrived as DVC (Academic) in 1995 he brought change. A 'champion of the need for student learning assistance', Meade commissioned surveys that showed 'students were eager'. The Student Learning Centre opened in 1999. It was part of HEDC but had its own coordinator – Carol Hunter – along with a teaching fellow and senior lecturer, who served as academic director. The centre operated out of an old house, and later moved to the ISB Building. It offered free workshops such as 'exam technique' and 'effective reading and note making' and, later, a fuller service that included one-on-one assistance. Crooks' and Meade's predictions about demand were correct; within a year there were 320 students, from first-years to postgrads, signed up for workshops and other assistance.[79] The centre rebranded as HEDC Student Learning Development in 2017; by then it had teaching fellows at the Wellington, Christchurch and Southland campuses as well as Dunedin, and offered an array of services, including 'peer learning and support programmes' led by student volunteers and tutors.[80]

EXPANDING OPPORTUNITIES

In the 1980s and 90s 'equal opportunities' became an important issue on campus. Jennifer Child's 1988 EEO report made wide-ranging recommendations. Although these dealt primarily with employment, many also applied to students – such as suggestions for greater consultation with Māori and Pacific communities and disability groups and to establish programmes to improve access to tertiary education.[81] It was in this environment that Otago developed support for disadvantaged students, backed up by equity funding from the government. Three of these initiatives are discussed here.

The Disability Information and Support team in 2011. Back row from left: Emma Holt, Eileen O'Regan, Helen Ingrams. Front: Jenny Week, Donna-Rose McKay, Kim Daufratshofer. By 2010 there were around 850 Otago students with a disability that affected their study, and 25,500 hours of learning assistance was provided. McKay led the service effectively for many years; her death in 2013 was a great loss to Otago.

GRAHAM WARMAN PHOTOGRAPH, UNIVERSITY OF OTAGO MARKETING AND COMMUNICATIONS COLLECTION.

Disability support

Stories from the late twentieth century reveal how many barriers there were for students with impairments; and for earlier generations it was even more difficult to complete a qualification. Barry Kirkland was Otago's first profoundly deaf graduate: he completed a BSc and BCom (Hons) in 1993. At lectures he relied on visual presentations and handouts. During his second degree he got a special grant to buy a portable computer, which other students used to type lecture notes for him. He appreciated their help – but what deaf students really needed, he said, was interpreters. He noticed there was considerable prejudice against deaf people in the community: deafness was often equated with a lack of intelligence. Kirkland hoped his achievements would encourage others to enrol at university.[82] Donna-Rose Harris, who used a wheelchair, began her studies in the late 1970s. She later recalled: 'My long-suffering friends pulled me up two or three flights of stairs twice a week to the top of the Quad Geology Building to my stats lecture because [organisers] refused to move the lecture to somewhere more accessible.'[83]

The university's first serious efforts to support people with impairments came in 1982, when a 'useful booklet for disabled students' was produced for the Student Services Committee, assisted by Works and Services. Among other things, the booklet listed wheelchair-accessible toilets and buildings with ramps around campus. As the staff newsletter reported, 'there is a formidable list of areas where wheelchairs cannot be propelled', but 'the future for the disabled student looks bright'. Some existing facilities were being upgraded to remove barriers, and new building design incorporated more provision for people with disabilities.[84] The Disabled Action and Support Group, established in 1987, provided a support mechanism for students, and it established a fund to pay for individual assistance such as extra tutoring – though not for equipment.[85]

There was growing demand for support. In 1990 Coralie Kirkland, appointed to report on existing students with disabilities at Otago, found that about a third of students with impairments had mobility problems, and another third had vision loss, hearing loss or specific learning disabilities. The most common difficulties were an inability to read overhead transparencies or to hear lecturers. Kirkland recommended the appointment of a permanent liaison officer for disabilities, and the establishment of a student learning centre.[86] In response to this and to the first EEO management plan, the university appointed Rachel Ford as a temporary part-time disabilities facilitation officer in 1991, and in 1992 it appointed Harris (later McKay) as the first permanent staff member dedicated to people with disabilities. From those tentative beginnings the support service grew into an impressive operation. In 1998 a project officer and administrator were added: this enabled the service to be strategic about making the campus more inclusive, rather than merely responding to the immediate needs of students. Staff advocated for students, and supported them to achieve as much independence as possible. Coordinating learning support was a key task, with many casual staff – mostly fellow students – employed as notetakers, interpreters and tutors.[87]

Māori liaison and the Māori Centre

Until the late twentieth century there were only a few Māori students at Otago. By the 1980s there were more, but they were still seriously underrepresented. Students, the community and Māori Studies staff campaigned for university authorities to improve Māori participation. When the government released special equity funding in response to the 1987 Watts Report, Otago used its share to put in place a Māori liaison officer and a Māori Centre. Khyla Camp (later Russell), a 'prominent member of the Kai Tahu tribe', became Māori liaison officer in 1988.[88] It was essentially a 'browning up' of the existing liaison officer's role, she recalls; when she visited schools, Māori students were set apart for her to meet. After a while, she and Huata Holmes of DCE decided to invite interested students to a marae instead, starting with a hui at Te Rūnanga o Waihōpai marae in Invercargill; people of all ages and tribal backgrounds came along. Recruiting Māori students was a big task, but it didn't end there. Russell was dealing with 'the emotional, financial, academic and career problems of students', sometimes in a very practical way: she had an emergency food cupboard, stocked by the Ōtākou branch of the Maori Women's Welfare League. Pioneering the Māori liaison role was exhausting – in addition to her work with students she was appointed as a Māori voice on numerous university committees. She was often 'literally in the middle' between students and the institution and there were 'no limits to the engagement'. In 1992, suffering from burnout, she left. Others took over her role and eventually there were several people dedicated to Māori liaison and support.[89]

The Māori Centre, opened in 1989, was an important place for many of the Māori students. Te Hunga Mātauranga – later changed to Te Huka

Outside the Māori Centre in 2002. The centre started in one old Castle Street house and eventually expanded into two adjacent houses, linked together and refurbished with an attractive entrance; a third house was shared with Te Roopu Māori (the Māori Students Association).
MĀORI CENTRE TE HUKA MĀTAURAKA COLLECTION.

Mātauraka to reflect the local dialect – was in an old house in Castle Street; it quickly became 'a hive of activity' as the first administrator, Winsome Dacker, reported. The centre had three main roles: to assist and retain existing students; to provide a link between the university and the Māori community; and to work with Māori school students 'to stimulate a desire for further study' and help them qualify for entrance (the Watts Report had identified the small proportion of Māori completing higher secondary qualifications as a key factor in low university enrolment). In addition, many people turned to the centre for advice on things Māori, such as establishing a bicultural approach.[90] For 15 years the Māori Centre was also home to Araiteuru Kōhanga Reo. The preschool language nest started at Araiteuru marae, then moved to the Otago Polytechnic Māori Centre. The move to the university suited parents who were staff or students, and it 'enriched the centre with the living Maori language'. The kōhanga children provided 'an obvious source of potential students who are completely "au fait" with the University', and it drew in other Māori who had never been on campus. And as a bonus, kaiako (teachers) Nanny Aya and Mereana Smith assisted university students with their reo. The kōhanga moved to Ravensbourne in 2004.[91]

Tutorials were at the heart of the centre's work – assisting with study skills and specific university courses. Tutors came from varied backgrounds: 'We look for the best', regardless of ethnicity, says manager Pearl Matahiki.[92] Among the first were Mua and Linda Strickson-Pua, who were tutoring in the Department of Education and saw a need for additional support for Māori. Mua was a New Zealand Samoan studying theology; Linda was of English descent but raised among Māori in Ruatoria. 'It is no mean feat dealing with students who are daunted by the University,' *Mea Maori* reported, but 'this pair made study enjoyable and stimulating. Laughter was a feature of their group.'[93] In 1991 administrator Miria Thorn reported that 60 students had used the tutorials in the previous year; and a survey by the Department of Māori Studies reported a rise in Māori pass rates.[94] Results were impressive given the shoestring budget – the tutors were volunteers. A tutor coordinator was appointed in 1990 and a part-time secretary in 1991; from 1991 the Māori liaison officer, previously based in the registry, moved to the Māori Centre.[95]

By 1994 there were 877 Otago students who identified as Māori. Godfrey Pohatu of Māori studies was delighted: he gave kudos to Māori liaison, which took 'the University of Otago to the

A welcome for Māori students at Kāti Huirapa Marae, Karitane, as part of Māori orientation in February 2007.
MĀORI CENTRE TE HUKA MĀTAURAKA COLLECTION.

people and to potential Maori students', and 'the excellent support networks'. Māori liaison officer Luella Narayan said that 'much of the credit should go to the Maori Centre Administrator who gives academic, psychological and social support to Maori students'.[96] Celebrating Māori achievement was part of the centre's ethos and from 1996 it arranged pre-graduation celebrations for Māori graduates and whānau.[97]

In 2000 the centre was restructured and permanent staff replaced contract positions. The dynamic Matahiki became manager and the staff expanded to include a community liaison officer and counsellor as well as administrative staff. Two programmes were introduced in 2002 with Ministry of Education special grants to support Māori students: Turaka Hou (Māori orientation) and Ka Rikarika a Tāne (a mentoring programme); later, funding for the programmes was added to the university's regular budget. The orientation programme aided students' transition to university with tours and advice and a chance to meet local Māori, including pōwhiri on local marae.[98] In 2015 Te Huka Mātauraka marked its first 25 years in joint anniversary celebrations with Te Tumu. The centre had plenty to celebrate – it had played a big role in the massive growth of Māori participation at Otago. It provided students with a 'home away from home' or a 'whānau on campus'.[99]

Pacific Islands Centre

Pacific Islanders were another group underrepresented among students, despite a long history at Otago. DVC Phil Meade set David Richardson, director of student services, to investigate how Otago could improve access and achievement for Pacific students. They decided to establish a dedicated support centre run and led by Pacific people. It was a model that had proved itself with the Māori Centre and that fitted the mood

A celebration for Pacific graduates in August 2011. Nini Kirifi-Alai, director of the Pacific Islands Centre, is in the centre (with purple lei).

GRAHAM WARMAN PHOTOGRAPH, UNIVERSITY OF OTAGO MARKETING AND COMMUNICATIONS COLLECTION.

of the times: New Zealand Pacific communities wanted to improve their future through education.[100] The Pacific Islands Centre (a name carefully chosen to avoid favouring one Pacific language or ethnic group) got underway in 2001. Project officer Pesamino Tili set up a room and an office in an old Leith Street house that was shared with disability support; he provided pastoral care and extra tutorials for Pacific students. In 2002 Nina Kirifi-Alai, who had recently graduated as a mature student in law and had been involved in student politics in Auckland, was appointed as the centre's manager on an 18-month fixed contract. She was an ideal fit; she loved the job and became a fixture at the university. She had standing in the Pacific community, and in 2007 her family in her home village of Iva Savaii, Samoa, gave her the high chief title Tofilau.[101]

The centre provided a cultural home for students, with study space, mentoring and extra tutorials in a relaxed environment. A support group for postgraduate students, set up in 2002, was popular; it met monthly and held an annual Pacific Voices Symposium, where students presented their work. Sports events and social gatherings added to the support on offer. Like the Māori Centre, the Pacific Islands Centre celebrated graduations and ran orientation programmes that offered 'a warm Pacific welcome' to newcomers. The centre moved into larger premises in an old house in Leithbank in 2006. Rooms in the house were named after early Otago graduates who became high-achieving Pacific leaders – Fijian Ratu Sir Kamisese Mara and Cook Islander Sir Tom Davis – and one of the courtyards was named after an Otago law graduate and first New Zealand Pacific Judge A`e`au Semi Epati. Dunedin's Pacific communities, who had been supporting Pacific students from out of town for generations, were involved in the centre from the beginning.[102]

As Kirifi-Alai notes, early Pacific students at Otago were selected by their countries as the best; they were well prepared and well funded. That continued to be the case for students from the Pacific Islands, but students who had been raised in New Zealand were often ill-prepared for university – their families had little experience of tertiary education and they hadn't always taken the right school subjects for their career aspirations. The university needed to recruit more Pacific students, but it also needed to ensure they were properly prepared, and assist their transition. In 2006 the Pacific Islands Centre began bringing groups of secondary students to a three-day on-campus experience, to help demystify student life. A liaison officer joined the centre's staff in 2008 and was soon busy travelling the country, as many Pacific students came from Auckland or Wellington. From 2010 the centre brought Pacific leaders from around New Zealand to visit the Dunedin campus; they returned to their communities prepared to advise prospective students and their families about Otago.

As the list of Pacific graduates lengthened, university education was more visible in the community and became an increasingly achievable aspiration.[103] The Pacific Islands Centre ran homework centres: the Dare to Succeed programme was for Pacific students in Dunedin high schools, with current Pacific students at Otago as tutors. Further afield, minister Victor Pouesi and his wife Salome Pouesi set up a homework programme in Mangere, supported by the Otago centre, in 2011. These schemes were an outreach to the community rather than a recruitment tool, though some of the participants ended up studying at Otago.[104] The Pacific Islands Centre was a great force for good at Otago, and contributed to growth in the university's engagement with the Pacific community: the number of students identifying as Pacific tripled between the mid-1990s and the mid–2010s.[105] In 2016 the roll included over 800 Pacific students. Otago had come a long way since 1929, when Tom Dovi started his medical degree as the only Pacific person on campus.

CHAPTER TWELVE

Teaching

HOW TO TEACH

The University of Otago's Scottish heritage was displayed in its dependence on the formal lecture. It was a frugal system: the professor did all the teaching, except in the sciences, which employed assistants for laboratory classes. Humanities subjects had no tutorials until the 1940s. Angus Ross recalled that history professor John Elder told a young lecturer whose students showed marked progress after he introduced seminar discussions: 'These young men like to hear themselves talk but you're paid to lecture and you'll therefore lecture. So long as I'm head of this department, there'll be no discussions.'[1] Tutorials sneaked into arts subjects as the government funded them for World War II returned service people, and after that they became standard. In 1948 Frank Mitchell, the education professor, reported: 'this year the Honours students on their own initiative organised tutorials for students taking Education I. I hope that it will soon be possible to conduct regular tutorials for all stages.' In the same year departing philosophy professor David Raphael pointed out that tutorials were 'not just a desirable luxury' in that subject – they were 'essential for adequate training. Philosophy is a way of doing things with one's mind, not a set of facts to be learned, and consequently the student must be in a position to practise the accomplishment in question.'[2] Tutorials required a bigger investment in staff, but the climbing student roll justified that; small-group teaching eventually supplemented lectures in all fields.

Teaching styles varied greatly. John Murdoch recalled meeting some of classics professor George Sale's honours students after a lecture in 1907: 'They had just received their corrected Latin proses, and the most successful had gained a mark of "minus 300". Sale deducted marks, 10, 50, 100 or more for a mistake, according to his estimate of its seriousness.' Murdoch had little respect for the methods of his professors: 'Otago University as I knew it was in effect a glorified coaching school.' Staff were 'capable and well-qualified', but with centrally set courses, examined abroad, 'inspirational teaching' was 'almost hopeless if not quite impossible' – at least in English, 'a notoriously difficult subject to teach.'[3] Future high-school principal Muriel May, an Otago student of the 1910s and 20s, recalled that Thomas Gilray, the English professor, 'taught by dictating at a relentless pace to his benches of scribbling students in the Lower Oliver classroom … at the prearranged dates we regurgitated. There were no seminars, no discussions, originality was not fostered nor were personal opinions encouraged.' There were always, of course, some inspiring teachers. May remembered George Thompson's French lectures as 'invariably stimulating and enjoyable.'[4]

EXAMINING METHODS

To ensure its degrees had credibility, the University of New Zealand appointed overseas examiners: scripts in the arts and sciences went to Britain, to be graded by scholars who knew nothing of the students' circumstances. That caused delays and carried risks: the hard work of 1897 students was wasted when their scripts were lost in the wreck of the steamship *Mataura* on its way to England.[5] 'Very varied were the emotions students felt on receipt of this news,' the *Review* reported.[6] The external examining system retained its supporters despite the disaster. The *ODT* commented in the aftermath that marking by eminent British scholars 'gives the New Zealand degree distinct and special value, and the New Zealand University is the only one outside Britain that subjects its students to this severe test'.[7] Others wanted reform, but the University of New Zealand Senate was slow to agree. From the mid-1920s Stage 1 and 2 BA and BSc exams were set and marked in New Zealand; professors took turns acting as national examiners. Only World War II, with its high risk to shipping, finally ended the practice of sending advanced scripts to Britain.[8]

The next reform was for professors to set exams for their own students, to fit local adaptations of the curriculum. The Medical School used the 'external–internal' system from the 1890s: its own professors set and graded exams, with an external examiner as quality controller.[9] Arts and science professors won that privilege in gradual steps until, by 1949, all arts and science exams were external–internal. It was part of a wider devolution of powers; in the 1950s each tertiary institution won the right to set its own courses, though they had to be approved nationally.[10]

The next reform came after pressure from students who were concerned about the burden of exams. Students had to fulfil 'terms' in order to sit exams, meaning they had to reach a minimum standard in their coursework, but other than that their year's work counted for nothing. After a widely backed OUSA campaign, in 1973 the Arts Faculty introduced internal assessment; at least 15 per cent of final grades came from work completed during the year. Internal assessment was soon widely adopted and its weighting in final grades gradually increased.[11] OUSA regretted the change: 'C.I.A. continuous internal assessment: Our greatest bungle?', the 1977 student handbook queried. 'Now EVERYONE has to work all through the year and cannot afford to make mistakes or slack for a few weeks because otherwise they may have virtually failed the course!'[12] Final exams still mattered enough to be stressful, but students now had less time for the other distractions of campus life.[13] Frank Forster, OUSA president in 1981, wrote: 'Since I began my University experience in 1975, there has been a perceptible trend for students to devote themselves more to study and less to activity.'[14] However, the genie was out of the bottle and internal assessment was there to stay.

TEACHING BEYOND CAMPUS

From the beginning, Otago staff did not confine their teaching to students; they reached out to the wider public too. It was an element of the community service that sat alongside the key functions of teaching and research as part of the role of the academic – later taken into consideration for promotion. The inaugural lectures given by the founding professors were popular events, and they and their successors were often called on as speakers. Thomas Parker, biology professor in the 1880s and 1890s, is a good example: he spoke on evolution and other topics to the Oamaru Athenaeum and Mechanics' Institute, the Wesleyan Literary and Debating Society, the Congregational Mutual Improvement Society and the Dunedin Field Naturalists' Club, all community organisations devoted to learning; and at a fundraiser for the Technical Classes Association.[15] His lectures, like most public presentations of the day, received detailed reports in newspapers, though words could not convey the full effect of their scientific props. Later generations of academics took advantage of new technology to reach the public. Otago physics

Radio offered a new opportunity to reach out beyond the walls of academia. This was clearly the goal of Robert Bell, maths professor from 1919 to 1948, in his 1940 broadcast on 4YA Dunedin, on 'The human side of mathematics'. As the *Listener* commented, figures may at first seem dull, but Bell 'knows very well how to make them interesting'. Its cartoon of the clichéd 'hoary old beaver' of a mathematician bore little resemblance to Bell, a dapper Scotsman renowned for his clear thinking and his warm nature.

NZ LISTENER, 9 AUGUST 1940, P.35, S14-177A, HOCKEN COLLECTIONS.

professor Robert Jack broadcast New Zealand's first radio programme in 1921, and thereafter university staff frequently shared their expertise on public broadcasts. Although other forms of media later joined it – notably television, blogs and social media – radio is still a popular means of disseminating some of the scholarship coming out of the university.[16]

WEA AND UNIVERSITY EXTENSION

The first formal involvement of the university in adult education came through the Workers' Educational Association (WEA), which was set up in 1902 in Britain as a joint effort of labour leaders and university staff to educate working people. In 1915 Meredith Atkinson and David Stewart, two 'missionaries' from the New South Wales WEA, toured New Zealand and organisations were set up in five centres, including Dunedin and Invercargill. The goal of WEA, Atkinson explained, was 'to convey to the workers higher education in all its forms'; it wanted to cultivate 'an educated democracy'.[17] The University of New Zealand provided grants to support tutorial classes, which were organised by local committees of labour and university representatives. Classes selected their own topic of study; at each meeting the tutor lectured for an hour, followed by an hour of class discussion.[18]

The first Dunedin class, like many elsewhere, selected economics for its subject and Otago's economics and history professor Harry Bedford was appointed tutor. At the end of the 1915 session Bedford reported that he had 'never had a more intelligent body of students, and never before have I had so enthusiastic a class'.[19] Invercargill went one better with two classes – in economics, tutored by Baptist minister and Christian socialist John Archer; and English literature, tutored by Oliver Duff, a school teacher.[20] Modern history, social history and natural history were added to the Invercargill programme in 1916. The *Southland Times* reflected that the inauguration of the WEA was 'perhaps the most striking cultural revival this town has yet experienced … men and women of all ages and all conditions attended the lectures' and it 'was the most unequivocal success'.[21]

The WEA flourished and classes developed in smaller towns as well as in the main centres. Some used the 'box scheme' whereby lecture notes, books and other educational aids were sent to classes that had no tutor.[22] By 1930 Dunedin had WEA classes in economics, philosophy, literature, music and drama, all held at the university, along with 'Mrs Benson's class at the YWCA'; the former home science professor ran that class especially for women, but women also attended and, in some cases, tutored, other classes. John Beaglehole, recently returned to New Zealand from postgraduate study in England, spent 1930 as Otago's WEA tutor organiser – or 'commercial travelling in miscellaneous wisdom', as he later called the work. He and another tutor ran classes at Milton, Sawyers Bay, Waikouaiti,

Hampden, Outram, Warrington, and at Sargood's Boot Factory and the Roslyn Woollen Mills in Dunedin.[23] Meanwhile, Otago's Home Science School started its own extension work. The Carnegie Corporation, which helped fund the home science extension work, also kept the WEA going through the depression, when discussion groups and box schemes, rather than tutored classes, became more common.[24]

The Labour government restored funding and in 1938 established the Council of Adult Education to coordinate it. In 1943 Ralph Souter, one of a succession of Otago economics staff who directed WEA for the region, reported membership of 1275 people, despite the disruption of war.[25] In 1948 the government devoted additional funding and directed university councils to set up Regional Councils of Adult Education. For the first time Otago had sufficient funding to appoint a full-time director of adult education: David Hall took charge of the home science extension and WEA operations.[26] The team included 'specialist' tutors in home science, drama and music, along with several 'general' tutors, and there was an office and resident tutor in Invercargill. Tutors, who had in 1930 rejoiced at 'the improved winter railway time table, which makes possible the saving of three hours' travelling for classes north of Dunedin', now sped around in a motley collection of motor vehicles: the 1949 selection included, 'in order of age', a 'Ford V8, Morris 10, Ford Van, Humber 10, Vauxhall 12, and Hillman 10'.[27]

The end of the University of New Zealand and developments in adult education, including the growth of evening classes in high schools, prompted a government restructure in 1964. The regional councils were wound up and individual universities ran adult education as they saw fit. Otago, like the others, converted its adult education service into a full academic department, known as University Extension, and its tutors became lecturers.[28] While 'continuing education', as it was increasingly styled, remained the central focus, the department developed formal qualifications, too – notably its certificates in social work and in Māori.

LEARNING AIDS

Visual aids were a feature of some early university classes: the anatomical drawings of John Scott, a skilled artist as well as first dean of the Medical School, were used at Otago for decades.[29] Others used glass slides and a 'magic lantern' to show images. John Mackie recounted how Noel Benson used this device in first-year geology lectures in 1929: the 'projector incorporated an arc-lamp which spluttered, fizzed and made other dangerous noises, although as a source of light it was quite spectacular'. The professor occasionally tripped over its wires 'and the whole contrivance would crash to the floor'; that also happened on the day he rushed to extinguish the light after discovering students had replaced his slide with a slide of a nude.[30] Slides were a popular teaching tool – shown through a more compact slide projector from the mid-twentieth century, and the slides themselves went from glass to film and then to digital format.

In 1940 arts and sciences dean Robert Bell reported that several departments took advantage of a scheme for borrowing 'sound-films' and found them 'an extremely valuable and effective addition' to teaching.[31] The Medical School, concerned about managing its enlarged student intake, urged that an Audio Visual Learning Centre (AVLC) be set up in 1973 and provided space for its academic director David Teather and team.[32] Not every academic liked new technology: John Howells, who retired from the Economics Department in the 1990s, said, 'my major advancement in the technology area stopped with the biro pen'.[33] The emergence of the AVLC 'was regarded with suspicion by some staff members who had visions of classes being handed over to various mechanical gadgets', the staff newsletter reported in 1977. By then, the 'prejudice' was declining: 30 departments were using the centre, with projects ranging from 'tape/slide/workbook programmes' for anatomy courses to a 'film providing "evidence" for a simulated Supreme Court trial' for law students.[34]

Top: W.R. Morris lecturing in the 'old anatomy lecture theatre' – now the Gowland Lecture Theatre – in the Lindo Ferguson Building, 1949. Anatomical drawings and skeletons were popular visual aids right from the Medical School's earliest classes.

PRIME MINISTER'S DEPARTMENT PHOTOGRAPH, UNIVERSITY OF OTAGO MEDICAL SCHOOL ALUMNUS ASSOCIATION RECORDS, MS-1537/441, S17-550C, HOCKEN COLLECTIONS.

Above: A class underway in the late 1980s or early 1990s in the Castle Lecture Theatres. The overhead transparency was a popular teaching tool for many years, later overtaken by Powerpoint digital slides.

UNIVERSITY OF OTAGO PHOTOGRAPHIC UNIT RECORDS, MS-4185/060, S17-550A, HOCKEN COLLECTIONS.

LEARNING ABOUT TEACHING

New technology accelerated discussion of teaching and learning. In 1971 the Lecturers' Association ran a well-attended seminar on teaching methods, and it proposed that the university set up a research centre on higher education. Two years later Otago appointed Terry Crooks as a lecturer in the Education Department, with half his time devoted to research and advice on university teaching. Crooks, the Lecturers' Association and the AVLC ran occasional sessions on teaching methods. A 1976 session, for instance, looked at the use of film; staff discussed films produced at Otago that they had used in anthropology, physical education and medicine. Psychology lecturer Louis Leland 'introduced a film which demonstrated the training of laboratory rats'. He said he made 'a similar film each year with rats trained by the current year's students' and used it to demonstrate to the following year's students that 'training rats is within their capability'.[35] In 1976 the senate established a Higher Education Research and Advisory Centre (HERAC) committee. HERAC and the AVLC often worked together and in 1978 they merged under another name, this one destined to last: the Higher Education Development Centre (HEDC).[36]

HEDC raised awareness of the need for 'stimulating teaching', as Teather reported in 1983. A two-day seminar on 'helping students succeed' attracted 140 staff and 'there was now hardly a department which did not make regular use of the resources at HEDC' for producing teaching aids.[37] In 1986 the centre appointed Graham Webb to advise staff on using computers in education.[38] Otago's Computing Services developed a team with expertise in computer-assisted learning and, in the 1990s, HEDC's audiovisual production section joined them as part of Information Technology Services. HEDC continued to research and disseminate information on tertiary teaching, provide advice and run courses; from 1996 it offered a Postgraduate Diploma in Tertiary Teaching.[39] To 'enhance' learning and teaching, the university, through the senate's Committee for the Advancement of Learning and Teaching, offered special grants for research and innovation in teaching.[4]

HEDC did not confine its attentions to staff: it developed a Student Learning Centre, opened in 1999, and it gave students an opportunity to provide feedback on their courses that staff could use to identify areas where they could improve or as validation of their abilities when seeking promotion. In an era of quality assurance, student evaluations became part of the evidence for departments that were undergoing review.[41] The centre's 2010 review stated that HEDC now had 'a significant institution-focused service component', and its research, teaching and service roles were 'integrally linked' as it worked 'in partnership with staff and students to advance, preserve and promote the ideals, knowledge and values of higher education'.[42] With a growing body of research on higher education from staff and postgraduates and a range of courses and support services for academics who sought to make their teaching more effective, Otago had travelled a long way from the days of Sale scoring papers at 'minus 300' and Gilray 'dictating at a relentless pace'.

TEACHING AT A DISTANCE

University Extension led Otago's first ventures into formal distance education. It had long supplied learning to groups beyond Dunedin using its box scheme, and the home science section was one of the first AVLC clients, creating sets of scripts, tape recordings and slides of lectures for country groups, but offering distance education for formal qualifications was trickier.[43] Massey had a monopoly on university distance education in New Zealand. It founded its extramural service in 1960 as a Palmerston North branch of Victoria, teaching papers via mail and with 'vacation' block courses; by 1984 it had over 10,000 distance students.[44] Peter McMechan, director of University Extension from 1979, drove Otago's campaign for the UGC to approve it as a supplier of distance education for credit. McMechan was a local graduate who

Elizabeth Purdie of University Extension's Distance Teaching Unit in the audioconference control room around 1988 or 1989. Otago's distance teaching technology, christened Unitel, was the brainchild of Jack Salmon, a former post office technician. Claire Matthewson, who took on the role of getting distance-learning programmes started, recalled meeting Salmon for the first time in 1984. He had a workshop 'full of wires, metal strips and tools' and there she 'saw the shoebox-size prototype of what became the 4-wire Unitel. Four had just been placed for a network trialling around the region – one each in Oamaru, Alexandra, Balclutha, and Invercargill.'

UNIVERSITY OF OTAGO PHOTOGRAPHIC UNIT RECORDS, MS-4185/028, S15-656D, HOCKEN COLLECTIONS.

had worked at the University of the South Pacific, which pioneered distance education by satellite in 1972. In 1984 Otago welcomed news of its official recognition as 'a South Island extramural centre'.[45] It devised its own fixed-line audioconferencing network, Unitel, to offer 'real-time' teaching at distant centres, supplemented with written packages.[46]

Otago started its distance programme with a Certificate in Humanities, building on University Extension's experience teaching liberal arts to mature students. Peter Leech ran a pilot course on the culture and politics of Renaissance Italy in 1985, and in 1986 there were four certificate courses.[47] Students loved it and some were inspired to enrol for degrees at Otago. In 1987 the Unitel network became national: students could link in to teaching sessions from 30 centres around the country, often hosted by other institutions. That helped distance learning reach McMechan's ambitious goal of 1000 credit enrolments in its first five years. Theology was an early starter, establishing its own certificate and diploma courses. The humanities certificate courses eventually wound up, but theology distance courses flourished and it developed a full distance degree. Other early courses were more vocational, such as social work and clinical dentistry; distance learning was a convenient vehicle for continuing education qualifications for people already in

Occupational health specialist Bill Glass (centre) of the Department of Preventive and Social Medicine conducts an audioconference session in the University Extension Department conference room, 1991.

UNIVERSITY OF OTAGO PHOTOGRAPHIC UNIT RECORDS, MS-4185/027, S16-669B, HOCKEN COLLECTIONS.

the workforce.[48] Claire Matthewson, who led the fledgling distance programmes, realised that 'there seems to be nothing that cannot somehow be taught and learned at a distance. The subject range in those first five years was astonishingly wide.' One reason for the programme's success was its 'self-selection': only interested departments and academics participated.[49]

Computer technology supplemented Unitel from the late 1990s, allowing visual as well as audio interaction. The dietetics distance programme trialled interactive computer learning: students reviewed content placed on a web page and completed tasks before chatting with a tutor and other students. Distance computer-based learning could be frustrating, as some participants had slow internet connections and low-capacity computers, so audioconferencing via the robust Unitel system remained the default. The possibilities for computer interactions expanded when Otago acquired Blackboard software in 2000, and in 2009 it invested in new web conferencing technology and most distance teachers abandoned Unitel.[50] Occupational and aviation medicine, which started its distance programme from the Preventive and Social Medicine Department in 1987 and shifted to the Medicine Department on the Wellington campus in 1993, was notable for its embrace of technology. Led by the entrepreneurial Rob Griffiths, it sought 'total world domination on reputation (since we cannot compete on price)', with students and teaching staff all over the world, including in the Middle East and North America. By 2016 it was using Moodle and other applications to offer various online learning tools, from webinars (seminars conducted over the internet), podcasts, blogs and discussion forums to 'virtual reality platforms for air ambulance simulations and occupational medicine site visits'.[51]

THE END OF UNIVERSITY EXTENSION

As distance learning developed, Otago continued holding non-credit extension courses, mostly on campus or at regional centres and led by extension staff or by academic departments, which found it was a good place to trial programmes. Under pressure to bring in income, the continuing education section became more entrepreneurial. Brian O'Rourke, who headed the section, ran preparation for retirement courses for the police and DCC; and from 1986 Otago designed summer schools for the Elderhostel organisation, which ran 'learning adventures' that combined travel and continuing education for retired Americans.[52] The well-off Americans epitomised the transformation of Otago's adult education from its origins as a scheme for the working class with little education. O'Rourke comments that continuing education participants did 'not fit a bell curve'; they may not have attended university, but most had made it well through high school.[53] That was a feature of community education around New Zealand: studies from the 1970s revealed 'a fairly homogeneous group of white, middle-class and relatively well-educated people – with women tending to dominate in non-vocational areas'.[54]

The University Extension Department focused increasingly on its distance credit courses. In 1984 it offered 50 'general' continuing education courses and 15 summer schools; by 1992 that had dropped to 16 courses and four 'special' schools.[55] There were tensions between the different functions of the department; it underwent several restructurings, with a rapid turnover of directors and constant alterations in government funding. In 1994 VC Robin Irvine appointed a panel to review University Extension: it reported 'very high levels of satisfaction expressed with the work of University Extension', but recommended extensive changes.[56] Instead, under Fogelberg as new VC, Otago disestablished its University Extension Department in 1995.

That was not the end of distance teaching at Otago, but its administration was devolved to divisions and departments and ITS took over the technical side.[57] As Fogelberg explained, that meant the 'substantial' income from distance teaching would go directly to the academic divisions instead of being 'largely absorbed by the extension administration'.[58] Senate established a Distance Learning Committee to promote and oversee distance education (later absorbed into the Committee for the Advancement of Learning and Teaching).[59] Distance teachers felt isolated: in 2000 they set up a Distance Learning Reference Group. Matthewson, director of Summer School and continuing education, was appointed distance learning adviser, though there was a limit to what she could achieve in one day a week. In 2008 Bill Anderson became director of distance learning, a post designed to provide 'central leadership, coordination, facilitation and dissemination of good practice'. Distance learning thus became a small central department again, with an advisory board.[60] Face-to-face teaching was still Otago's first priority, but high-quality distance learning programmes had a firm place on the curriculum.

Continuing education also devolved to departments, and some offered the occasional short course. The Politics Department ran a successful Foreign Policy School in 1966 that became an annual event. The school, which emerged from extension courses on current events, provided a forum where students and the public met experts in foreign policy.[61] On the Wellington campus the Public Health Summer School, founded in 1997, quickly became a popular annual event. Otago's engagement with the community did not come to a halt with the demise of University Extension: there were many public events on its campuses, including public lectures and seminars, and music and drama performances. Eventually the Summer School office took responsibility for promotion and oversight of continuing education, but the old-style community-based extension course was over. The University of the Third Age (U3A), which offers continuing education for 'the retired and semi-retired', picked up some of the slack: it established a Dunedin branch in 1994 and developed a close relationship with the university, with Otago staff often leading its courses.[62]

REARRANGING THE YEAR

Among many changes at the university in the 1990s, one of the most dramatic was the restructuring of the academic year. It started in 1992 when Otago replaced its 'unit' system, introduced by the University of New Zealand in the 1920s, with degrees based on papers. Most units were already made up of groups of two or three papers; under the revised system students had more flexibility to include single papers in their degree.[63]

Breaking the academic year into two semesters attracted greater controversy; senate approved it narrowly 'after considerable debate' in 1992 and it came into force in 1994.[64] Under the semester system students had a mid-year break and an allocated exam time. Although at first many academics believed it impossible to adapt their papers to fit a single semester, it gradually became the norm – for the humanities, science and commerce at least. In the first year, single semester papers attracted large enrolments. The system appealed to students as they could start or finish a degree or completely change direction mid-year; and they could repeat a paper they had failed in the first semester in the second (many commerce papers were offered twice).[65] Organising the year into semesters helped attract international exchange students who no longer had to enrol for a full academic year that did not coincide with that of the northern hemisphere.

SUMMER SCHOOL

In 1996 maths professor Derek Holton identified what he saw as a problem with semesters: they provided an opening for a 'three semester year'; the 'temptation to add an extra teaching period over summer might at some stage be irresistible to some future administrator'.[66] He was right – and it didn't take long. Otago had been offering continuing education courses over summer for a long time already, but not many were for credit. There were some early experiments – for instance, in 1971 and 1972 the English Department ran a paper for four weeks in January, with written work in February and March and a weekend school in April; students sat the exam during the May vacation. The Arts Faculty 'approved the holding of such courses in the future', but enthusiasm died and later proposals failed to win staff support.[67] By 1999 Otago was the only New Zealand university without a summer school, and this put it at a disadvantage in the contest for students. There was a clear demand: some Otago students attended other universities during summer to further their learning. Fogelberg set up a committee to investigate extending Otago's teaching year. It quickly ruled out the idea of three equal teaching semesters and became the Summer School Working Party. Its final report, in February 2000, recommended that a summer school be introduced for a trial period of two or three years. Students could complete a paper through an intensive six-week course rather than the usual 13-week semester. One paper was considered a full-time commitment, though a few enthusiasts tackled two.[68]

In January 2001, 700 students arrived on campus to study the 23 papers on offer at Otago's first formal Summer School. That was more than anybody hoped for: 'it went off like a rocket', recalls Merv Smith, formerly head of the Biochemistry Department, who was the first director. Departments were permitted to keep 80 per cent of the income from Summer School papers to use as they wished, which gave them the motivation to participate and the funds to employ additional staff. After a second successful year, with over 1000 enrolments, Summer School became a permanent fixture on the Otago calendar.[69] Effective writing, computer programming, criminal justice, introductory economics and introductory business management featured among the most popular papers in the early years of Summer School; they were compulsory for some degrees and enabled students to make a headstart or to repeat a paper they had failed.[70] Some departments tried quirkier courses, such as 'the vampire on screen'. Others introduced new subjects into the

Otago curriculum: disabilities studies, Arabic language and – one of the most popular choices – forensic biology. Some papers were taught at the Wellington campus and the Auckland Centre, and a few were offered through distance learning.[71]

Enrolments for Summer School surpassed 2000 in 2005. This was small by comparison with most New Zealand universities, but it had advantages: 'its current size is one of its key attractions', the director noted in 2007. The extended year improved services for staff and postgrad students as libraries, cafés and OUSA services that had previously operated on reduced hours or had closed over January and February stayed open and available.[72] Nevertheless, the school had to battle against 'the deeply embedded Otago view that summer is a time for research or annual leave'. Not all departments participated. The humanities and commerce divisions were the most enthusiastic and were rewarded for their efforts – not just financially: 'Summer School provides a great learning experience for students and a very satisfying teaching experience for staff', reported a 2007 review.[73] Summer School came of age in 2014 when it lost its unusual funding model; it was no longer an 'add-on' but a core part of the university.[74]

FOUNDATION STUDIES

In the 1990s, in a bid to attract more international students, Otago embarked on a new teaching venture: Foundation Studies. As Fogelberg says, the university 'couldn't bring someone straight out of Kuwait and plonk them into a first-year class'. Young international students needed support to adjust to an unfamiliar culture and to courses that built on skills that were expected of New Zealand school leavers. Various Australian universities had bridging programmes, and DVC Ian Smith proposed that Otago partner with one of them rather than starting from scratch. He negotiated an agreement with the University of New South Wales and in 1997 Otago welcomed its first students to a Foundation Studies Certificate course, allied with the Australian programme and recognised for university entry at several institutions.[75] The partnership simplified the project and gave the course more appeal to international students. The arrangement continued until 2009, when Otago's programme became independent.[76]

Otago set up a limited liability company, wholly owned by the university, to run Foundation Studies. That reduced financial risk in the volatile international education market. It also served to keep Foundation Studies separate from the normal requirements of an academic department; it had no research obligations and employed staff with qualifications in secondary or ESOL teaching.[77] The programme started with 34 students from 11 different countries; all took courses in academic English and maths, and additional subjects depending on their chosen stream – arts/commerce or health sciences/sciences. Foundation Studies arranged homestay accommodation and offered a range of support services; it organised regular social, cultural and sporting events, from a fishing expedition to a visit to the art gallery. Not every student completed the programme, not all gained university entry and not all chose Otago, but in the first three years 74 students enrolled at the university after finishing a foundation year, and others enrolled at other institutions.[78] An early venture to offer one stream in Auckland, at private tertiary institution Auckland Institute of Studies St Helens, did not last long; thereafter it focused on its home in Dunedin. The programme was initially based at 533 Castle Street but soon moved into a brand-new building, St David II, and in 2011 to another shiny new home in the University Plaza.[79]

Foundation Studies was associated with another project aimed at international students, the Otago Language Centre (OLC). OLC was established in 1991 as a joint venture – 'unprecedented in tertiary education in New Zealand' – between the university, DCE and Otago Polytechnic, with backing from the DCC. It ran short intensive English courses, with the aim of attracting private overseas students who might proceed to other courses.[80] Foundation Studies contracted OLC to run its academic English course, and in 2000 it purchased the centre outright. It offered courses for beginners as well as more advanced English speakers, including prospective university students who met academic qualifications but needed to improve their English.[81] International demand for OLC and Foundation Studies programmes varied, along with immigration policy, exchange rates and changing preferences in 'the important China market', and there was intense competition between language schools. A growing contingent of domestic students helped sustain Foundation Studies: some were recent migrants; others were born and raised in New Zealand. The programme filled gaps in their schooling to help them to university entrance standard; raising of that standard bumped up domestic enrolments in Foundation Studies in 2015.[82]

In the late 2000s the government became concerned about universities' involvement in foundation studies because of 'the subsequent performance of [foundation year] graduates'.[83] In 2010 Skegg reported that Otago would be 'scaling back … the domestic student component of its Foundation Studies programme' in line with its 'strategic focus on advanced study'.[84] However, both government and university subsequently renewed their commitment to Foundation Studies as it became a valued tool for improving tertiary access for educationally disadvantaged groups. It already had some history of that. In 2001 the first Māori students completed the programme. They were sponsored by Te Tapuae o Rēhua, a collaboration between Te Rūnanga o Ngāi Tahu and various southern tertiary institutions, established in 1998 in the wake of Ngāi Tahu's Treaty of Waitangi settlement to improve Māori access to higher education.[85] From 2010 Foundation Studies introduced programmes, funded by the Ministry of Health, to prepare Māori and Pacific Island students for Otago's health science courses, and those students contributed to a surge in Māori and Pacific students in the health sciences.[86]

REWARDING TEACHING

In 2002 the Ministry of Education established Tertiary Teaching Excellence Awards to recognise excellence and enhance good practice and career development for teachers. They came with a sizeable monetary reward. Each institution could nominate two people. Otago invited staff to submit portfolios; Markus Milne from accountancy and Tim Wilkinson from medicine (Christchurch) were selected in the first year. In 2003 Fogelberg proposed that Otago give excellence awards to its nominees for the national honours, and in 2004 Ann Richardson of public health (Christchurch) and Murray Skeaff of human nutrition were the inaugural recipients.[87] Various parts of the university also instituted prizes for teaching, beginning with the Christchurch and Dunedin schools of medicine.[88] Discussion of the teaching awards in the Committee for the Advancement of Learning and Teaching sparked another recognition of good teaching: the OUSA tertiary teaching awards.[89] The OUSA awards had little monetary value but carried kudos, since teachers did not apply but were nominated by students, with votes calibrated according to class size. Ruth Fitzgerald, a medical anthropologist, topped the poll and received the inaugural award in 2002.[90] OUSA later added other awards to the mix, including research supervisor of the year and an inclusive teaching award, sponsored by Disability Support.[91]

That teaching awards emerged in the early twenty-first century was no accident: their timing coincided with the arrival of the Performance-Based Research Fund, which measured academics' research performance. They served as a reminder that the government, the university and, above all, the students valued teaching. Gordon Sanderson created a stir when, on winning the Prime Minister's Supreme Award for Teaching Excellence in 2013, he said Otago was 'not very enthusiastic about teaching' and staff wanting to 'get ahead' had to focus on research at the expense of teaching. In response, the local branch of the Tertiary Education Union expressed concern at the 'national refocus on PBRF'.[92] Similar concerns emerged from the report

Some teaching staff appeared on OUSA's top 10 list multiple times: the remarkable Tony Zaharic was OUSA's teacher of the year in 2007, 2009 and 2010. Zaharic was a teaching fellow responsible for helping stressed health science first-years through their 'mindnumbing' biochemistry course; he won plaudits for his 'empathetic and approachable manner' as well as his humour and effective teaching and, to his embarrassment, earned a fan page on Facebook. In 2011 he received a national award for 'sustained excellence' in teaching. Photographed in 2011.

UNIVERSITY OF OTAGO MARKETING AND COMMUNICATIONS COLLECTION.

on tertiary education released by the government's Productivity Commission in 2017: it suggested that PBRF and international rankings 'incentivise providers to focus on particular kinds of research, and to prioritise investment in research over investment in teaching'. Harlene Hayne defended Otago's commitment to teaching: 'Given that our teaching revenue stream is 2.3 times greater than our research revenue stream, the financial incentive is to prioritise teaching … In fact, at a world-class university, teaching and research are interdependent, so it is not a case of prioritising one or the other, it's a case of maximising the synergies between the two.' She observed that Otago 'clearly excelled at teaching': its staff had won the top national teaching award for the previous five years.[93] Of the flurry of top prizes, three went to Māori women nominated in the kaupapa Māori category. When law lecturer Jacinta Ruru was nominated in 2015 she expressed her pleasure that Otago recognised the importance of culturally inclusive teaching methods that valued Māori students. 'There are so many amazing Māori teachers at Otago,' Ruru said; 'it's great to have this recognition for what we do in supporting students, particularly Māori students, to succeed at Otago.'[94] Ruru was a leading researcher into indigenous people's legal rights and the natural world, and codirector of Ngā Pae o te Māramatanga, New Zealand's Māori Centre of Research Excellence; she thus epitomised the 'research-led teaching' ideal. In 2016 she became New Zealand's first Māori professor of law.[95]

Otago winners of the Prime Minister's supreme award for tertiary teaching excellence

Year	Name	Subject
2003	Peter Schwartz	Pathology (Dunedin)
2009	Selene Mize	Law
2012	Rhiannon Braund	Pharmacy
2013	Gordon Sanderson	Ophthalmology (Dunedin)
2014	Karyn Paringatai	Te Tumu – School of Māori, Pacific and Indigenous Studies
2015	Suzanne Pitama	Māori Indigenous Health Unit (Christchurch)
2016	Jacinta Ruru	Law
2018	Fa`afetai Sopoaga	Pacific Islands Research and Student Support Unit (Health Sciences Division)

CHAPTER THIRTEEN

Buildings

Universities are mostly about people, but people need buildings to work in. Otago has constructed or repurposed many buildings through its history (see Appendix 3). Its first home was in a building of Oamaru stone, designed in neoclassical style by William Mason for a post office.[1] As the building neared completion in 1867, provincial superintendent James Macandrew suggested it 'might be turned to much better account than that of a Post Office'.[2] He convinced the government to turn the building over to the province in exchange for a more modest post office building. Locals put the 'new post office' to good use for meetings and balls before the Otago Museum took over as its first long-term tenant. The university saw its potential and in 1871 it moved in.

The building wasn't perfect. The University Council spent 'a large sum in providing a new roof for the hall, in altering the staircase, and in adapting the building generally to the purposes of a University',[3] but it was cheaper and quicker than starting from scratch. Some parents were dubious about the university's Princes Street location amid 'the temptations and seductions of a town life'. But the chief drawback of the building was that there was no room for expansion: the university shared the building with the museum and art school and, in addition, there were constant requests from citizens to use the hall. The council wanted to develop residential accommodation for students; that didn't happen for several decades, but it prompted the university to make plans to move.[4]

A HOME BY THE LEITH

In 1874 the Otago Provincial Council granted the university a site in part of the 'old cemetery reserve' (subsequently used for Arthur Street School and Otago Boys' High School).[5] A few months later, however, when the museum was allocated a site in Great King Street, the Arthur Street location seemed less ideal; University Council member Donald Stuart argued 'it was absolutely necessary that the Museum be situated in close proximity to the University, on account of the zoological, botanical, and medical classes'.[6] In 1875 the cemetery reserve land was exchanged for a site known as the botanical garden reserve that was conveniently close to the museum and the hospital, and the council began construction in 1878, once it had finally secured a buyer for its original building.[7]

The land was, like all of the region, traditional Kāi Tahu Whānui land. The river flowing through it, Ōwheo, was named for Waitaha chief Wheo, and there was a kaik or settlement of the same

The University of Otago's original premises in the centre of town were fitting for a university that modelled itself on urban foundations such as Edinburgh and London rather than 'the sleepy cloisters' of Oxbridge. The 'footpath before its door was a favourite resort for loungers', George Thompson wrote when pointing out the building's failings in the university's jubilee history. After the university moved out, the building housed a bank and later the Stock Exchange; it was demolished in 1969.

PHOTOGRAPH c.1877. UNIVERSITY OF OTAGO LIBRARY RECORDS. 96-111/15. S17-612B. HOCKEN COLLECTIONS.

The future site of the university in 1867. This view is looking south from what was Tanna Hill, where Marama Hall is today. The riverbed of the Leith is visible at the base of the hill (right) and the circle in the middle distance is a garden bed, part of the Botanic Garden. The two towers in the distance are part of the 1865 Exhibition Building, which became Dunedin Hospital.

J.W. ALLEN PHOTOGRAPH, ALBUM 347, P1990-015/24/013, S17-182A, HOCKEN COLLECTIONS.

The back of the Dental School (now the Staff Club) in the aftermath of the 1923 flood. A one-storey addition of galvanised iron that nestled into the back corner was completely washed away; parts of it were found in the harbour as far away as Ravensbourne. Contents of the building, which housed the mechanical room, students' common room and dark room, were fished out of the Leith and the harbour; somebody found a dental case with a full set of instruments on the peninsula side of the harbour. The recently constructed addition at the back was left hanging over the Leith.

PHOTO 334/9, 1923 FLOODS – LANTERN SLIDE COLLECTION, DUNEDIN CITY COUNCIL ARCHIVES.

name at what is now the junction of Leith and Howe streets. The Ōwheo originally ran into the harbour at Harbour Terrace. Like all major waterways, it provided Māori with access to inland areas, and the lower reaches of the river supplied food and other resources.[8]

The Water of Leith, as settlers named the Ōwheo, helped make the campus what was later described as one of 'the world's most beautiful universities'.[9] But it was not always benign: in 1868 its raging floodwaters washed away several bridges and about an acre of cultivated land in the original Dunedin Botanic Garden, along with flood defences then under construction. That led the Botanic Garden to move, freeing its former site for the university.[10] The university initially planned to build on a prominent knoll on Tanna Hill, south of Union Street, but DCC quarrying activities had lowered the hill to the point where it would require expensive earthworks. Instead the first buildings went up on the flatter section of the site, north of Union Street. The Leith flowed through the site 'in a somewhat unruly course over a bed of boulder and shingle'; attempts were made to 'confine' it 'in its original bed' using wooden breastwork, constructed using prison labour, but the protection was swept away and the land was scoured out 'by the force of successive floods'.[11] In the 1890s the university reclaimed some of the riverbed: it blasted away rocks that obstructed the flow of the stream, built a concrete retaining wall from Union to Leith Street and filled the space behind. By 1906 there were 16 houses on the reclaimed land and the wall had withstood several floods.[12]

Of course, the Leith still flooded from time to time.[13] In April 1923 all low-lying parts of Dunedin and the Taieri Plains flooded. The Leith was 'a striking sight', the *ODT* reported, 'the groynes churning the waters into what was a veritable seething cauldron'. The floodwaters undermined the Union Street bridge foundations and scoured out parts of the road. The Dental School came off the worst: the flooding made it clear that its site was not suitable for expansion and in 1926 the school moved to another building.[14] University buildings escaped serious damage from the more severe flood of 1929, but a memorial walk that had been planted beside the Leith in 1927 disappeared as the river washed away its banks for a distance of about 150 metres. Nearby, the wooden bridges at Leith and Clyde streets were also washed away.[15] The 1929 flood prompted improvements to Leith flood defences, and these were gradually upgraded over the years. A recent scheme involves major landscaping works for beautification as well as flood protection: the stretch near the Clocktower Building was completed in 2014, and work is underway further downstream.[16] Students saw the flooding Leith as a challenge and in 2010, when it ran especially high, a few daredevils tried surfing it.[17]

The newly completed university buildings around 1879. The clocktower lacked a clock for its first few decades. The council planned to install the clock from its original premises, but failed to make that clear in the contracts when selling the building and the Colonial Bank insisted on keeping it; the indebted council could not afford to purchase another. In 1930 Thomas Sidey, the chancellor, donated funds for a clock that was installed the following year; it was a fitting gift by 'Summertime' Sidey, the politician who succeeded, after a long campaign, in introducing daylight saving time to New Zealand.
BURTON BROTHERS PHOTOGRAPH, C.012077, TE PAPA TONGAREWA.

BUILDING IN STONE

In 1877 the council held an architectural competition to design new buildings for the university. The prize went to Maxwell Bury, an English engineer who had been designing buildings in Nelson and Christchurch for some years.[18] His design for the main building, chemistry and anatomy divisions, boarding establishment and six professorial houses was 'by far the most suitable', said the Professorial Board, because it was 'more conveniently arranged than any of the others, and gives more accommodation. It also admits of easy extension or diminution if the expense be found too great.'[19] The council asked Bury to modify his plans from classical to Gothic style and include a clocktower. In his evidence to the 1879 Royal Commission on the University of New Zealand, Stuart noted that 'the Professorial Board were right in saying that style was not the first thing to seek after; but, at the same time, we had some old-world notions, and liked to have the University with some style about it'. The council wanted the academic buildings in stone rather than brick; as Stuart reported: 'In this town we find there is scarcely a brick building that is sound. The brick is so inferior that it soon wastes.'[20] The initial budget of £17,000 was inadequate – some local architects did not enter the competition because of this – and a 'diminution' had to be made.[21] Even after excluding the boarding establishment, two of the professors' houses and the south wings of the two main buildings, the project cost over £30,000; part of the overrun was from unanticipated extra expenses for the foundations. The university was left owing a large sum to the contractors, McGill and Forrest, who refused to hand over one building. Eventually the council secured a loan, but the awkwardness over finances meant there was no grand opening of

An 1890s view of the university, including the new School of Mines building (right), quickly christened 'the Tin Shed'. It cost £1000 and was 'well provided with the requisite furnaces and fittings for practical work, and the necessary appliances for class-teaching'. As Gordon Parry later wrote, it 'was more like a foundry than a University department, a total incongruity on a site where every effort was being made to perpetuate the Gothic style'. It wasn't long before the corrugated-iron building became dilapidated, with a leaking roof and rotting timber framing.

H.J. GILL PHOTOGRAPH, BOX-140-001, S17-172A, HOCKEN COLLECTIONS.

the Main (Clocktower) Building when it came into use in 1879. The Chemistry and Anatomy Building had been completed the year before, also without fanfare.[22]

The council extended the buildings in stages to fit Bury's original scheme. The Chemistry and Anatomy Building acquired another wing in 1883, giving 'ample and suitable accommodation for the Faculty of Medicine, the Chemistry Classes, and the School of Mines'.[23] Louis Salmond designed a southern extension for the Physiology Department, completed in 1905, and in 1914 extensions designed by Edmund Anscombe were added at either end for the Medical School. The last addition, in 1943, extended the building on its longest axis, towards Leith Street; by then the Medical School had moved out but the Chemistry Department needed more room. When chemistry moved out in the 1970s the Geology Department was left as sole tenant.[24] The building was rundown and refurbishment of the old Chemistry Department was tricky, Richard Norris recalled; mercury had collected between the floorboards.[25] The building was a good fit for geology, as Rick Sibson pointed out in 1995: 'Built largely of basaltic lava and vent-breccia from the long extinct Dunedin Volcano, it's almost everything a Geology Department should be, even if the heating doesn't work much of the time!'[26] In 2003 Gwyneth Paltrow (playing Sylvia Plath) was filmed lecturing there in a scene for the biopic *Sylvia*, and Daniel Craig (playing Ted Hughes) read poetry in a scene set in Marama Hall.

The quadrangle, between the clocktower and geology buildings, photographed by chemist Arthur Campbell in 1970. The 'quad' was 'horticulturally challenged', recalls Elizabeth Whitcombe of her 1950s student days. During the 1970s Campbell and botanists Geoff Baylis and Alan Mark planted trees and more planning went into improvements to the expanding campus, sparked by the street closure programme. The university also acquired its first full-time gardener; previously the janitor had mowed the lawns but obviously had little time for gardening.
ARTHUR CAMPBELL COLLECTION

The original Main Building ended just south of the clocktower. A 1914 extension provided large classrooms for English lectures, which had outgrown the existing spaces.[27] The new wing was named in honour of Richard Oliver, a former Dunedin resident who made a fortune as a merchant and in railways, banking, shipping and farming before he returned to England in 1899; a donation from his widow enabled the building to go ahead. Anscombe, who altered Bury's plans for the addition, also designed another wing for the Physics Department, completed in 1922, that doubled the building's capacity. In 1966, with new buildings completed or scheduled for the library, arts and physics, the Clocktower Building was adapted for its next long-term tenant: university administration. At that point it was extended a further 4 metres to the east.[28]

That last extension might never have happened: Otago came close to losing its clocktower in the 1950s. The government's education and works experts wanted the tower or, preferably, the entire building demolished as its masonry had deteriorated and it presented an earthquake risk. The university came up with a scheme to strengthen the building and the Ministry of Works reluctantly agreed.[29] Otago's annual report for 1962 expressed relief: 'The preservation of the university clock tower after a threat of demolition has given much satisfaction to those many generations who over the years have been associated with the university. The heavy stone ornamentation has been replaced without changing the general appearance, copper sheathing substituted for the slate roof and the tower itself strengthened by cross-ties.'[30] This was not the last time the university had to strengthen a fragile older building. In 1995 Sibson warned a complacent university that Dunedin had earthquakes; he reported that 'casual visits' to various departments and, 'I'm ashamed to say, the dim recesses of the Geology Building', had revealed 'many instances of unsecured bookcases … and, probably worse, a very limited awareness of seismic hazard in chemical and biological laboratories'.[31] Dunedin was not at the epicentre of the disastrous earthquakes of 2010 and 2011, but they heightened the awareness of hazards. In 2011, in accordance with new DCC and government requirements, the university began strengthening existing buildings to a high standard, with residential colleges the first priority.[32] One building – the aquarium at Portobello – was closed to the public immediately and slated for demolition.[33]

BREAKING NEW GROUND

Several building projects arose from the development of the special schools in the early twentieth century. Louis Salmond designed the Dental School, described by the *ODT* at its 1908 official opening as 'a scholastic-looking edifice'. Situated on the busy corner of Union and Castle streets, it was 'well lighted, but at present rather bare': that was probably because building costs, including 'protection of the riverbank', absorbed most of the budget. At the opening, Thomas Sidey suggested the school 'was an institution which was destined to grow into large proportions', and his prophecy soon came true.[34] Extensions were built to accommodate growing student and patient numbers, but the big 1923 flood forced the school to find a larger home. The original building became the Registry, then the Law School and subsequently the Staff Club.[35]

In 1909 the School of Mines moved from its 1890 'tin shed' into a new bluestone building. The building incorporated the latest technology – electric lighting – and director James Park declared it would 'rank among the best equipped and commodious mining schools in Australasia'.[36] The architectural competition to design the building was won by Anscombe, a local recently returned from several years in the US learning his profession. The School of Mines initially stood alone, but Anscombe designed it as the west wing of a larger building that extended to Leith Street, with an archway flanked by octagonal towers over the university's main Union Street entrance.[37] The council must have been impressed, because it used Anscombe for most design projects over the next two decades. The rest of the Archway Building, together with the adjoining Allen Hall, became the first Student Union, opened in 1914. One of its more playful aspects was the Gothic-style grotesques carved over the archway, representing different branches of learning.[38] For generations of students the walk beneath the archway was a place of mixed emotions, known to some as the 'tunnel of tears': exam results were posted on its noticeboards until 1994, when the Privacy Act and volume of information ended the practice.[39]

Another Anscombe-designed bluestone building was constructed nearby in 1920: the Home Science School. When it started in 1911 the school inherited the miners' decrepit tin shed, 'renovated for the purpose' and 'fitted with a convenient Chemical Laboratory'.[40] After years of badgering the government, the university received funding to replace this 'temporary' arrangement with purpose-built premises. The new building, erected on part of the excavated Tanna Hill, faced east, 'opening from what will later on be a quadrangle, it being proposed at some future date to erect other buildings on this site'.[41] For a long time the Home Science School looked out only onto tennis courts, although it quickly ran out of room. In 1947 an army hut containing 10 kitchens was 'a very valuable addition to the School' and in 1961 it at last acquired another wing, the Gregory Building, on the southern side of the proposed quadrangle.[42] Any thoughts of a quadrangle disappeared when the Archway Lecture Theatres were built in 1974, 'unnervingly close' to the Home Science Building. By then the stone building was in line for demolition, which explains why the design of the lecture theatres building took little account of its position. But some people realised its heritage value; it was given a reprieve from demolition, listed as an historic place in 1988 and extensively refitted in the 1990s.[43] Ironically, when a 25-year campus master plan was produced in 2010 it was the Archway Lecture Theatres that were on the demolition list, together with the Gregory Building, which was considered 'of limited architectural merit'; and the idea of a quadrangle was resurrected.[44]

After the Home Science School moved out the tin shed was demolished and another Anscombe bluestone building went up in its place. The Maheno and Marama Hospital Ships

Architect Edmund Anscombe in his Dunedin office around 1911. His work had a strong influence on Otago's appearance, including on the original buildings, for which he designed several extensions. Architectural historian Peter Entwisle suggested that Anscombe's 'reconception of Bury's design … turned a modest, balanced, clock tower building into the noble, asymmetrical range we see today. He made a playful arched and battlemented quadrangle where his predecessor had envisaged nothing more than a rather simple plan of parallel buildings.'
JOHN PENLINGTON COLLECTION.

Surplus Fund Memorial Hall – soon abbreviated to Marama Hall – was a relic of the recent war. In 1915 the government chartered the *Maheno* and the *Marama* from the Union Steam Ship Company and converted them into floating military hospitals; the public gave generously to a fund to fit them out. At the end of the war there was money left in the fund and, following a suggestion by the military surgeon-general, it was spent on a drill hall for Otago medical students.[45] The foundation stone for the building, which included a gymnasium, apparatus room, office and committee room, was laid in 1919, but by the time the building opened in 1923 the Medical School's training corps was inactive. The building was used for other activities for several years, including as a boxing venue. When military training was revived in 1927, sweaty medical and dental students used the drill hall for its intended purpose.[46] It later

Below: The School of Home Science in 1962, with the new wing next to the 1920 building. The wing acquired two more floors in 1968, when it was christened the Gregory Building after the former dean.
FRANZ BARTA PHOTOGRAPH, P1997-156-09-220, HOCKEN COLLECTIONS.

The main Medical School buildings along Great King Street were eventually named after former deans: from right, the Lindo Ferguson Building (opened 1927), Scott Building (1917) and Hercus Building (1948).
UNIVERSITY OF OTAGO MEDICAL SCHOOL ALUMNUS ASSOCIATION RECORDS, MS-1537/637, S17-517C, HOCKEN COLLECTIONS.

became an extension of the crowded Student Union, and when OUSA acquired a new building in 1960, Marama Hall became the home of the Education Department and, later, the Music Department. Carved into its stonework is the badge of the New Zealand Army Medical Corps (and the coats of arms of the governors-general who opened it and laid the foundation stone); that and its name are a reminder of its function as a memorial to those who served on the hospital ships.[47]

A MEDICAL CAMPUS

As well as the bluestone buildings by the Leith, the university was establishing a presence in Great King Street. In 1914 the Medical Faculty won government approval for further extensions to the anatomy and physiology departments, plus a building for pathology and bacteriology. The site of this building, opposite the hospital, was controversial. Some councillors wanted all developments to be on the existing campus, but medical academics wanted to be closer to the hospital.[48] Sydney Champtaloup argued that senior medical students were 'intimately associated with the Hospital. At present students attend some classes at the University, and have then to proceed to the Hospital for others, and to return to the University later. This involves a great waste of time and energy.'[49] A public appeal raised £8000 (over $1 million in 2018 values), including £2000 from William Dawson, who made a fortune through

The new South Block – later the Hercus Building – in 1949. It was a striking example of streamline moderne style, designed by Eric Miller. Hercus recounted how the minister of education, Rex Mason, 'turned down our original severely utilitarian plan with the statement, "This is not a factory, but a national building of great importance, and it must bear the marks of its function"'. The design incorporated various artworks, including a sculptured marble panel by Richard Gross above the main Hanover Street entrance, and there were plaster murals inside. The building, with 210 rooms, became the home for the preventive medicine, pathology and bacteriology departments. PRIME MINISTER'S DEPARTMENT PHOTOGRAPH, BOX-184-034, S17-111A, HOCKEN COLLECTIONS.

Speight's brewery, and £1000 from members of the Medical Faculty; and this was matched by the government. However, the project ran considerably over budget due to 'the presence of subterranean water, later found to characterise the whole area', along with rising prices because of war conditions.[50] The building opened in 1917. This was just the beginning: medical dean Lindo Ferguson had ambitious plans to expand the school along the entire block. There was another battle over the anatomy and physiology extensions: in 1919 the council decided they should be on the main campus, and this provoked a successful campaign by the Medical Faculty, Medical Association and *ODT* to construct a large building adjoining the 1917 one.[51] After considerable delays in raising funds, the building was opened in 1927. Designed by Anscombe to complement its neighbour, it housed anatomy (including histology), physiology, biochemistry and pharmacology, and had the 'necessary classrooms, laboratories, and research rooms for a school averaging an annual class of 50 students'.[52]

Ferguson's successors took up his scheme and, in the midst of World War II, work began on the South Block. Construction was challenging because of labour and supply shortages; four Dunedin building firms – Love, Naylor, Mitchells and McLellans – formed the Associated Builders consortium to complete the project (now known as the Hercus Building).[53] The next new building was less imposing and not destined to last: a single-storey brick building, completed in 1956 next to the Lindo Ferguson Building, provided space for the surgery and obstetrics and gynaecology departments. The Wellcome Research Institute appeared on the corner of Frederick and Great King streets in 1963. In 1972 the Medical Library

The Wellcome Research Institute was a tribute to medical professor Horace Smirk's important research on hypertension. It provided space for various research teams. Designed by Niel Wales, its simple forms and lack of ornamentation reflected the international style of the period. It soon developed the nickname 'Hori's whare'; the Dental School was 'Jack's shack' after dental dean John Walsh, and the Pharmacology Department in the old Knox Sunday school was 'Fred's shed' after its professor, Fred Fastier.

FRANZ BARTA PHOTOGRAPH, P1997-156/09-284, HOCKEN COLLECTIONS.

moved into the Sayers Building, which replaced the 1950s surgery and obstetrics and gynaecology building; it also housed the Medical School administration. A year later the multistorey Adams Building emerged behind the Sayers Building, with an entrance from Frederick Street; it provided space for the preventive and social medicine, pharmacology, pharmacy and surgery departments, along with HEDC.[54]

With the 1970s buildings completed, Ferguson's 1910s vision of a Medical School encompassing the whole block was fulfilled. It was a showcase of twentieth-century architecture, from neoclassicism to brutalism. Across the road Dunedin Hospital, whose presence had drawn the Medical School to that location, also went through several developments. The largest of these was the ward block, opened in 1980; at the

time it was 'the largest and most important single community building authorised by a New Zealand Government'. The university was heavily involved in its planning, as the south wing incorporated Medical School facilities and the project was funded by both education and health budgets; a publicity booklet hailed its 'ideal integration' of academic and clinical facilities, 'achieved for the first time in Australasia within this complex'. The development included a lecture theatre block, completed in 1974, with a pedestrian bridge to the Sayers Building.[55] In 2017, as debate raged over the future of the hospital complex, which had deteriorated after years of 'shamefully deferred maintenance', David Skegg reminded Dunedinites of the 'spirit of euphoria' at the ward block's opening and the critical involvement of the university in its development.[56]

The new Sayers (front) and Adams buildings in the 1970s. The Sayers Building was designed by Alan Neil of Fraser Oakley Pinfold. A 1994 exhibition on University of Otago architecture suggested his 'use of fair-faced concrete is an essay in Brutalism'. The Adams Building was designed by Miller White and Dunn and the design was recycled in the Microbiology Building, opened in 1974 on Cumberland Street. The 1994 exhibition noted its utilitarian architecture: it 'appears to have been designed from the inside out' and 'no thought appears to have been given to the external appearance … Built in the tradition of tower blocks in a park-way, it does not invite inspection of detailing.'
UNIVERSITY OF OTAGO MEDICAL SCHOOL ALUMNUS ASSOCIATION RECORDS, MS-1537/665, S17-517D, HOCKEN COLLECTIONS.

The second Dental School was built of brick and concrete with Oamaru stone facings; at its 1926 opening the *ODT* noted that its 'facade is skilfully worked up in such a way as to give an imposing appearance and minimise the narrowness'. In his typical style, Anscombe included various crests and ornamentations along with a 'bronze figure of Saint Apollonia' which gave 'a touch of vivacity and colour' to the neoclassical design.
BOX-238-002, S17-111C, HOCKEN COLLECTIONS.

DENTISTRY MANOEUVRES

The Dental School was expanding, too. Ferguson foiled suggestions the second Dental School should be immediately next to the Medical School because he wanted the entire block.[57] Instead it found a site along the road, ideal because it supplied the 'great desideratum' of '180 feet of unobstructed light'.[58] Within two decades the 1926 building became cramped and dean John Walsh began campaigning for a replacement. After delays due to competing demands for government funding, shortages of labour and materials, and changes of government, construction started in 1956. Problems with the foundations caused further delays. The Walsh Building, as it was later renamed, eventually opened in 1961.[59] It, too, soon became cramped, and in 1984 a redevelopment, including an additional west wing, was completed.[60] As the school expanded its research and courses, space again became tight. In 2015 the University Council approved a major development. The Walsh Building's heritage listing meant care was needed. The plans, by Auckland architects Jasmax, involved demolishing the west wing and the nearby Barningham Building and replacing them with an 8000-square-metre clinical building with an atrium and social space linking it

Above: The third Dental School, designed in the Government Architect's Office by Ian Reynolds and Gordon Wilson, featured sleek modern design with glass curtain walls and bright colours; it incorporated art, including mosaics and Frederick Staub sculptures. Like its contemporary, the nearby Queen Mary Maternity Hospital (now Hayward College), it polarised public opinion. Formal recognition of its significance as 'an outstanding example of international style Modernist architecture' came with its listing as a Category I historic place in 2005.
PETER INNES COLLECTION.

Left: Student hijinks featured at the 1961 opening of the Dental School. Blair Tennent, the minister of education who did the honours, had once been a dental student himself, and laughed as he was carried shoulder-high on a litter from the Octagon to the new building; a group of about 150 students dressed as Arabs had prostrated themselves on the ground before the ministerial car and forced it to stop. The procession was led by a goat, which normally resided in a student flat; as the *New Zealand Dental Journal* wrote, its 'well timed bleats later punctuated the formal addresses in a highly amusing manner'.
OTAGO DAILY TIMES PHOTOGRAPH, PETER INNES COLLECTION.

The former resident doctors' quarters, across Frederick Street from the hospital, were transformed into the Hunter Centre – a health sciences learning centre with teaching and social spaces and café – in 2008 (photographed here in 2017). Like the Te Pā project, it won an architectural award for Parker Warburton Team Architects.

UNIVERSITY OF OTAGO MARKETING AND COMMUNICATIONS COLLECTION.

to the refurbished Walsh Building.[61] Few regretted the demise of the Barningham Building, which had been part of an old foundry complex before it was taken over by the university; as early as the 1980s it was described as 'cramped' and 'decrepit'.[62]

The 1926 Dental School, meanwhile, found another purpose. In 1963 the Zoology Department moved in 'reluctantly'; by the end of that year the zoologists were finding that 'the building itself was very satisfactory, although the surroundings left much to be desired'.[63] Until 1963 the department was housed at the back of the Otago Museum, along with the Botany Department; this was a natural arrangement when the early biology professors were museum directors. The university handed the museum over to a new trust board in 1955, but it continued to occupy part of the building. When zoology moved out, botany expanded into its former space, and it remained in those increasingly 'antiquated and unsatisfactory premises' until 1993. By then it had outgrown them and the museum wanted the space.[64] Zoology initially shared its new premises with the Commerce Division, but it soon took over the whole building. It also colonised surrounding buildings; by 2002 it occupied 'adjacent buildings that were once premises of ironfounders ("444 George St"), undertakers (McLean Building), glassblowers and dental nurses (Annexe)'. However, head of department Carolyn Burns had much 'anticipatory pleasure' at the sight of 'an enormous hole in the parking lot between the main Zoology building and the Captain Cook Hotel'; in 2003 that hole transformed into a three-storey building, named in honour of former biology professor William Benham.[65]

A GROWING CAMPUS

Other departments occupied collections of old buildings as the university acquired premises to meet its demand for space. Some were later moved or demolished to make way for developments, but others survived, occasionally in a seriously modified form. An extreme example appeared in 2014 in Castle Street where Te Pā, a new building for the Childcare Association, retained the façades of a row of wooden villas. Preservation added to the cost, as architect Simon Parker explained, but it was 'worthwhile to retain our unique heritage and adds significantly to the character of the buildings and the streetscape'.[66] Other houses survived with little alteration, including the oldest building on the Dunedin campus, built before anyone imagined a university in the neighbourhood.[67] Thomas Calcutt, a printer, court clerk and land speculator who arrived in Otago in 1858, acquired all of the land in the block bounded by Clyde Street, Union Street, Leith Street and the river; his wife Mary gave birth to their son Arthur in Leith Cottage, their new house there, in October 1862. Baby Arthur died at just four months and the Calcutts sold Leith Cottage not long after to George and Ann Cook, whose child was born there in January 1864. The Cooks, a family of lawyers, owned the cottage for eight decades.[68]

Brothers Alfred and George Cook in the garden of the Union Street home purchased by their parents George and Ann around 1863. George Cook senior, who died in 1898, was 'an upright, estimable lawyer of the old English school – a man who brought with him to the colony all the traditions and all the prejudices of the English bar, and who resented all innovations'. The Cooks lived in splendid isolation on the block until 1902, when other houses were added; some of them also survived. The Cook home became Mellor House.
ELIZABETH MACAVOY COLLECTION.

The university purchased Leith Cottage after the deaths of the elderly Alfred and Margaret Cook in 1945; it wanted houses for student accommodation during a postwar influx. The six-bedroom home was renamed Mellor House in honour of chemist Joseph Mellor, one of Otago's most successful graduates. The upstairs space became accommodation for Arana Hall residents, and downstairs became the home of the Geography Department. Two rooms were knocked together to create a classroom, and tea on the veranda became a departmental tradition. Geography gradually took over the entire house and a prefab hut in the garden; when it moved into the Library/Arts Building in 1964, Mellor House became home to the Psychology Department.[69]

The university's acquisition of existing buildings was often ad hoc, but it had strategic plans for the campus. In the mid-twentieth century there was debate about the direction of expansion. Eventually the campus grew larger than most anticipated and spread in all directions, but initially there were two alternatives: to expand east towards Logan Park, or between the Clocktower and the medical and dental campus in Great King Street (the 'diagonal plan'). In 1945 the University Council gave general approval to the diagonal scheme. Frederick Soper later wrote that 'the Union was the key building that helped to determine the siting of other University buildings'; the projected plan showed it 'on the site of the Otago Tennis Club, the grounds of which had been bequeathed to the University in the Allen bequest'.[70] OUSA fought a losing battle against that site.[71] There were long delays raising funds and convincing the government to provide support,

An aerial view of the campus in November 1947, before major expansion began. The tennis courts that became the site of the University Union, the first major building in the diagonal plan, are at centre right. At the top left of the photograph is the teachers' college, which moved to that Union Street site in 1939. Its large wooden buildings were destroyed in a 1968 fire and were replaced with buildings that are still used by the College of Education.
WHITES AVIATION PHOTOGRAPH, WA-10707-F, ALEXANDER TURNBULL LIBRARY.

but eventually two key buildings – the University Union (opened in 1960) and Library/Arts Building (1965) – emerged in line with the diagonal plan; those common facilities were 'equidistant from the furthest extremity of the old campus to the north and the Medical School to the south'.[72]

As the need for buildings grew, so did doubts about the diagonal plan. Works and Services later reported it 'was abandoned primarily because it was incompatible with the city traffic system, and with a larger campus envisaged it was likely to produce an unsatisfactory geographic arrangement of buildings'.[73] In 1964 Otago consulted assistant government architect John Blake-Kelly and adopted his 'very attractive long-term development plan' that included development both south and west of the original buildings.[74] Historian William Morrell wrote in 1969 that the 'height of some of the projected buildings came as a shock at first, but as they rise they inspire confidence that the completed university, dominating the landscape of north and central Dunedin, will give the city new cause for pride'.[75] What strikes a twenty-first-century viewer of Blake-Kelly's proposal is not the tall buildings but his solution for dealing with heavy foot traffic

A late-1970s view reveals the expansion of the 1960s and 70s. In the distance the curving diversions of the one-way street system along State Highway 1 are visible; they permitted the eventual closure of Castle Street, which is in the centre of the photo. Part of Union Street is already closed, and the Archway Lecture Theatres have been built over some of the former roadway. In the distance, the large footprint of the low-rise Library/Arts Building is visible. BOX-237-003, S13-217F, HOCKEN COLLECTIONS.

over the busy streets of several city blocks: a series of buildings linked by first-floor aerial walkways. Some buildings – Arts, Biochemistry and Science I and II – included large first-floor circulation areas to allow for these walkways, but the cost and practical difficulties led the university to instead advocate a traffic-free campus. That required the closure of several busy streets and rerouting Dunedin's one-way street system. Ted Dews, the engineer who headed Otago's Works Department, 'got alongside the city engineer' and the UGC funded a traffic study. In 1968 the DCC agreed in principle to close and divert streets, giving a main campus of around 16 hectares free from public traffic. With that greater flexibility, Blake-Kelly and Otago staff architect Ernest Snow came up with a revised campus plan. Buildings came and went but the street deviation project, which became reality in the 1970s, survived as one of the campus's most significant developments.[76]

The campus plan of the 1960s underwent many minor changes and a few larger reviews. A 1980 revision recommended that 'buildings must blend with adjoining residential areas, at least in scale, with tall buildings confined to the centre of the campus'.[77] Before long, rapid growth meant the university needed to make the most of available land, and larger buildings began to appear at the campus edge, notably the Commerce Building (completed in 1992) – the advance guard of development to the east. There was expansion west and along the old diagonal route, too, with construction of the Physical Education, Student Health and Physiotherapy buildings in the 1990s. The Executive Residence joined the Commerce Building to the east in 1994. But the biggest change came with the merger with DCE in 2007, when Otago acquired an entire block of buildings in Union Street. Adjacent to that was Dunedin's Forsyth Barr stadium, completed in 2011 amid controversy over the cost to ratepayers. The stadium had an advocate in VC David Skegg, who saw its strategic potential to the university; 'it wouldn't have gone ahead without his support', suggests former chief operating officer John Patrick. The university committed to its own building alongside the stadium, and it 'reenergised that part of the city', says Patrick.[78] Under Skegg's watch Otago undertook another major planning exercise, completed in 2010, that mapped projected developments for the next 25 years on all of its campuses.[79]

BUILDING IN THE 1960s AND 70s

Skegg noted that an aspect of the 2010 campus plan that might be 'controversial' was the fact that several buildings were proposed for demolition 'on the grounds that they are no longer fit for purpose or are located in the wrong place'.[80] Most were not ancient; they were from the 1960s and 70s.

The 1965 Library/Arts Building was constructed around the property of elderly storekeeper William Matthews, who refused to move. His property on the corner of Albany and Castle streets was demolished after he died in 1967, aged 91.

ARTHUR CAMPBELL PHOTOGRAPH, ARTHUR CAMPBELL COLLECTION.

The Arts Building, c. 1970. Architect John Aimers placed seminar rooms in the central portion of each floor, meaning staff offices were in 'quiet cul-de-sacs which are desirable in a Faculty of Arts'. Those cul-de-sacs were not always quiet: Ninian Smart, a distinguished religious studies scholar who visited Otago in 1971, recalled 'the former dean of arts, reprimanded by the registrar for playing cricket on the matted corridors of the new arts building'. The two-storey section at the front fitted the Blake-Kelly plan for aerial walkways, with a large circulation area at the centre of the first floor. In 1977, after confusion between the names of the 'arts lecture theatres' and new 'archway lecture theatres', lecture theatres in the Arts Building became the Burns lecture theatres – and thereafter, people often mistakenly referred to the entire building as the 'Burns building'.
ARTHUR CAMPBELL PHOTOGRAPH, ARTHUR CAMPBELL COLLECTION.

Some construction methods from that period did not stand the test of time; for example, spalling (crumbling of concrete panels caused by rusting reinforcing rods) required expensive remedial work on several Otago buildings. Opinions varied about the design of the buildings: some appreciated their modern aesthetic; others were not fans of the brutalist style.[81] One 1960s building – the Library/Arts Building – had already gone by 2010. Auckland architectural students Rolland Adams and Brian Dodd won a competition for its design; to meet the restrictive budget they chose a large low-rise building, just two storeys tall, with a courtyard in the centre. Construction was relatively economical but the building was not a good long-term investment; the foundations could not support another storey and there was no space to expand outwards.[82] Part of the 1965 building was incorporated into the 2001 Information Services Building.

Most university buildings were constructed with tight budgets, and this was particularly so in the 1960s. The Interim Science Building, opened in 1965, was 'interim' in usage rather than construction. It provided temporary additional space for the physical sciences until their other buildings were completed in the 1970s, meaning Otago could avoid restricting entry into subjects whose labs were cramped into every attic and basement available. The two-storey light steel-frame construction was built quickly with existing plans that had already been used for buildings at Auckland and Massey universities. With no space readily available for the long design, it was built to span the Leith. True to schedule,

The Richardson Building (originally the Hocken Building), at left, was the tallest building on campus, completed in 1979. Designed by Ted McCoy, it was a 'monumental example of late Modernism' and received a Category I historic places listing in 2011; in his report for Heritage New Zealand, Michael Findlay suggested it 'was a critical success with the architectural profession but public resistance to its particular aesthetic has not greatly diminished over time'.

BOX-237-008, S17-182F, HOCKEN COLLECTIONS.

the geology, physics and chemistry departments moved in within a year. The building was ideal for the university's new computer as its cables could be fitted underneath, where the building crossed the river; the story goes that people waiting for the computer to churn through a program sometimes passed the time fishing out the window.[83] Another long building of the period was the 1969 Arts Building, structured to use minimal space while providing for 'Staff Studies, Seminar Rooms and Research Rooms requiring good daylighting and aspect'.[84] Not all of the Arts Faculty could fit into the building: geography, anthropology and education, as well as the Law

Faculty, moved into the 1979 Hocken Building, which had custom-designed space for the Hocken Library in its southern wing. In 1998 the Hocken Library was rehoused in a refurbished former dairy factory in Anzac Avenue, and its space in the Hocken Building was later redesigned for Te Tumu. To avoid confusion with the new Hocken site, the former building was renamed after John Richardson, an early Otago chancellor.[85]

Most new buildings of the 1970s were monochromatic, designed to complement the original bluestone buildings. Ted McCoy's Archway Lecture Theatres, opened in 1974, broke that mould. The four theatres, which seated between 120 and 260 people each, featured the latest in technology, with airconditioning and wiring for television. They featured striking exterior graphic designs, which faded over the years but seemed particularly bright in 1974. McCoy explained to the *ODT* that he aimed to introduce 'a bit of colour' onto the campus. 'There has been criticism that many university buildings are grey and forbidding. We have tried to liven this one up with strong primary colours and graphics – to inject a little playfulness in the building.' The designs had no particular meaning, McCoy said; people could 'interpret them in any way they liked'.[86] The building's cruciform shape, placed diagonally, made the most of the tight site and provided an open courtyard at each of the four entrances.[87] It bewildered generations of students and lecturers, who frequently lost their bearings coming out of the building; it was handy for testing robotic navigation algorithms.[88]

A new science precinct began with the demolition of existing buildings on the land bounded by Cumberland, St David, Castle and Union streets that had once accommodated around 100 low-cost dwellings, crowded together along alleyways.[89] In late 1968 construction started on the first building, Science I (now the Mellor Laboratories), and the Chemistry Department

The first buildings in the science precinct, Science I (left) and Biochemistry, under construction around 1970.
ARTHUR CAMPBELL PHOTOGRAPH, ARTHUR CAMPBELL COLLECTION.

moved in early in 1971.[90] Next out of the ground was a building for the Biochemistry Department, previously squeezed into the Lindo Ferguson Building with much of the Medical School.[91] Then came the chemistry research building (Science II), a 10-storey construction that towered over the campus; it was occupied in 1973.[92] Special attention was paid to the appearance of the fourth building in the precinct, the Microbiology Building. 'We are taking particular care with the external treatment of the façade and the over-all form of the building,' Dews explained. 'We want it to look a particularly attractive building since it is to be the focal point for the approach to the university.' There was a plan, later abandoned, to make a road from that point of Cumberland Street to the clocktower, making the building the 'front door' of the campus. The Microbiology Building was completed in 1974; the project had been accelerated to cater for an increase in medical students.[93] The foundations of the final building in the science complex, Science III, required 'one of the largest single [concrete] pours to be laid on a Dunedin site'. It opened in 1977 to house the Physics Department and Science Library, and mathematics moved in a little later. Original plans to extend Science III across St David Street and to include room for botany were dropped because of funding constraints. It was neither the first nor the last time that botany had plans for a new building dropped, and it is still scattered around several older premises.[94]

THE END OF THE BUILDING BOOM

The opening of the Hocken Building marked the end of a period of building expansion.[95] Otago reported in 1979 that 'Dunedin architects and builders have noted the slow-down with considerable concern as the rolling programme of development at the university has been an important source of employment in recent years'.[96] In the 1970s alone, eight large buildings were completed on the main campus, and two in Great King Street; in addition the hospital block and OUSA's Clubs and Societies Building were about to open, and the university's first buildings in Christchurch and Wellington were completed. Student enrolments levelled out in the 1970s and early 80s, and this made it difficult to convince government that yet more buildings were needed. Projects continued at a slower rate, including new premises for the Animal Breeding Station on the Taieri, a laboratory annexe for physical education and a marine laboratory building at Portobello.[97]

The Castle Lecture Theatre complex was completed in two stages in 1988 and 1991 as government funding became available. The UGC paid for the main building and teaching equipment, and Otago funded the 'performance/conference appurtenances'. One large lecture theatre doubled as an opera venue, with an orchestra pit under a removable floor.[98] This was another building by McCoy, the renowned Dunedin architect who had already influenced the look of the campus through UniCol, the Archway Lecture Theatres and the Hocken Building. The Castle complex, which he described as relating 'back to the early university clocktower buildings, with precast concrete bluestone-faced panels and deeply recessed precast window surrounds', was his last big project for the university. However, when Otago merged with DCE it gained another McCoy building – the Owheo Building, completed in 1991. Built around an open courtyard, it was 'designed to embrace the site rather than commandeer it', he later wrote; its 'semi-domestic undercurrent … was probably a reaction to doctrinaire modern, a feeling I had at the time'.[99]

In the second half of the 1980s the university roll again rose rapidly. This created a squeeze on accommodation, and frustrations with sourcing government funding ran high. 'Botany, Consumer and Applied Sciences and Psychology are still using World War II huts and in addition about 30 old houses are being used by various departments', the 1987 Otago annual report noted.[100] The mushrooming Commerce Faculty felt particularly hard done by. It had been campaigning for its own building for some time and staff were spread around various premises. It was, perhaps, 'a sign of the times', suggested the university's 1986 annual report, when the Marketing Department took over the School of Mines Building (Archway West) after mineral technology moved to Auckland.[101]

The frustrations of the Commerce Faculty over accommodation resulted in this 'new commerce building' in 1986. When the booking for a suitable venue for course approval was cancelled, the dean hired a large marquee for the lawn next to the Arts Building. Accounting professor Lyall McLean, who undertook the decoration, recalled that 'it was good fun the first day but it rained the next and the lawn in front of the Arts Building became quite muddy'. LYALL MCLEAN COLLECTION.

POSTMODERN DEVELOPMENTS

With the devolution of funding for capital projects the Commerce Building finally got underway. The council did not have unlimited resources but it could set its own priorities and no longer needed UGC approval for each project. In 1990, as it prepared for the change in funding system, Otago developed a capital works programme with a Commerce Building top of the list. 'Although this building will commit a very large part of the available capital,' the annual report noted, 'it is a multipurpose design, and the space to be vacated by the Commerce Division is urgently needed by the three other academic Divisions on the central campus.'[102] Events moved quickly: construction commenced in 1990, some departments moved into their new premises at the end of 1991 and work was complete by the end of 1992. John Blair, who won the architectural competition for the building, later noted that he and his team had just 46 working days after approval from the University Council to produce working drawings and call for tenders.[103]

Blair's striking postmodern design won an architectural award, but the commerce dean's use of a tent labelled 'The new commerce building' in 1986 turned out to be prophetic. Wind and rain entered the central atrium through its partial glass covering, and the 'non-slip' atrium floor tiles did not perform as expected. In 1997 the glass cover of the atrium was extended. This was an improvement, but the building was still exposed to the elements. Other modifications followed, including repairs after earthquakes in 2004 caused the atrium structure to move.[104] There were ongoing problems despite various safety improvements. In 2015 a woman who had slipped and sustained serious injuries in the building two years earlier took a private prosecution against the university; records shown in evidence revealed that a dozen people had suffered serious injury from falls in the building. The university pleaded guilty: it paid reparation to the complainant, apologised and assured her that plans were well advanced for a 'major refit' of the building.[105]
A temporary fix was made in time for the 2016 academic year: it involved resurfacing steps in the atrium and laying marine-grade carpet, since the roof still leaked.[106] Later that year work began on an extensive upgrade, designed by Hamish Blair of Mason and Wales: it included a full roof for the atrium, with different entrances and remodelling of the internal spaces. The refurbished building was renamed the Otago School of Business Building. A striking feature of the redevelopment was the incorporation of design and artworks by Ngāi Tahu artists Simon Kaan and Ross Hemera that referenced Māori trade and enterprise in early Otago. These cultural components, the result of the combined efforts of the dean, Office of Māori

The Psychology Department initially occupied the university's oldest building, Mellor House (1862), and in 2010 it became the proud owner of one of its most innovative, the William James Building. Designed by Tim Heath to fit New Zealand Green Building Council criteria, the building included solar panels and other energy-efficient features; it used sustainable building materials, harvested rainwater for toilets, and came complete with a roof garden of Otago native plants, designed and maintained by the Botany Department.
GRAHAM WARMAN PHOTOGRAPH, UNIVERSITY OF OTAGO MARKETING AND COMMUNICATIONS COLLECTION.

Development, architects and artists, indicated how far the university had advanced in its respect for tikanga.[107]

Other projects in the 1990s were more successful as a new generation of architects transformed the campus. The Psychology Department occupied a collection of old houses; they had their charms but, with their associated prefabs, struggled to accommodate one of Otago's largest departments. It took a long time 'to convince the university that decent facilities were really desperately needed', recalls Geoffrey White. Psychology had six separate animal labs, including one in a Nissen hut with a leaky roof.[108] In 1990 the department acquired its first 'permanent' building, the Goddard Laboratories. Architect Tim Heath won an award for the 'low-key, high-tech, friendly building' that housed the department's electronic and computing workshops and some of its undergrad labs.[109] Twenty years later the department's accommodation problems were 'finally resolved' with another Heath design, the William James Building, with more laboratory, office and teaching space.[110]

Mason and Wales, Dunedin's oldest architectural firm, designed two projects that harked back to the older buildings in their vicinity: the Executive Residence (completed 1994) and the Student Health Building (1996). The Executive Residence was a Commerce Division project to accommodate executives attending short-term courses. That scheme was a financial failure but the residence became a successful university-wide facility used as a guesthouse and function venue.[111] Two other 1990s buildings – a physical education block designed by Lindsay Gillies and the Physiotherapy Building, a McCoy and Wixon design – were postmodern in style.[112] McCoy and Wixon also designed the Marine Studies Centre, perched above the aquarium and marine laboratory at Portobello. Financed by the university's 1990 Development Appeal Fund and the Community Trust of Otago, it provided facilities for short courses and a range of users. It featured a 5000-litre aquarium centrepiece, which became important for teaching after the 1960s aquarium was closed to the public as an earthquake risk. That building was demolished in 2016 and a teaching laboratory, research aquarium and seawater system were installed in its place. This was a 'medium term replacement for space lost'; a long-term plan proposed building another marine science facility, preferably in the upper harbour.[113]

ENTERING A NEW MILLENNIUM

New buildings in St David Street reflected changes in the university sector in the late twentieth century. Lecture theatres were 'a pressing need' as the student roll grew; some Stage 1 science lectures were repeated three times for want of a larger theatre. The 550-seat St David Lecture Theatre, opened in 2000, provided a solution. The designer was John McCoy, son of Ted McCoy. The building, which included other teaching spaces, a café and a large lobby linked through to Science III, demonstrated McCoy's characteristic 'clean simple lines and sharp definition'.[114] The Centre for Innovation across the road, completed in 2001, was dominated by glass, described as an 'asymmetric shiny glass Rubik's cube'; its boldness fitted a space intended 'to showcase the University's applied research'.[115] A building next door highlighted another aspect of Otago's changing commercial arrangements: St David II, opened in 1998, was custom-built for Foundation Studies and the Otago Language School. When they moved to the University Plaza in 2011, St David II became available for other departments – though it had to be closed for seismic strengthening, completed in 2015. Further redevelopment of the building to incorporate administration offices began in 2017.[116]

The St David Street developments highlighted that entrance to the university, and in 2014 a corner of the lecture theatre complex was converted into a visitors' centre.[117] A large Oamaru stone sign appeared on the corner of Cumberland and St David streets, signalling the entrance to the campus to visitors arriving from the north. Graduates posed in front of the sign for photographs, as well as in the traditional setting with the Leith and the clocktower in the background.

The view of the Clocktower Building across the Leith survived unspoiled thanks to years of protests over schemes to build a vehicle bridge to the clocktower, including Blake-Kelly's 1960s plan for an aerial walkway and the vehicle bridge envisaged in the 1970s street diversion scheme.[118] A 1991 bridge crossing scheme fell through, as did others in 1997 and 2003. The Historic Places Trust and the university reached agreement in 2003 that the existing footbridge would be moved five metres north and replaced with a 'vehicle capable' bridge. Resource consent came through early in 2004 but opposition continued and an appeal was lodged in the Environment Court. When David Skegg became VC later that year one of his first actions was to urge the council to abandon the bridge plans. This brought an end to 'a long-running and sometimes acrimonious debate, and delighted advocates for the retention of the bridge', he reported.[119]

The St David Street buildings were impressive, but in scale they were outdone by the Information Services Building (ISB), completed in 2001 to replace the overcrowded library. In a move that attracted some criticism the university looked internationally for architects in what was a complex project, because the library had to remain open during construction. Otago selected Los Angeles firm Hardy Holzman Pfeiffer Associates, who had already demonstrated their ability to 'take an existing building … and configure a new one around it'. The east end of Otago's 1960s library was demolished to make way for the largest part of the new building, and once that was complete the old portion was extensively remodelled. The finished product was named the ISB rather than the library; it

included a large 'information commons' computer area and was extensively wired to 'future proof' for advances in technology. The project included spaces for student support and university administration services as well as the Link, a social and food and retail area that joined the building to the University Union.[120] Fogelberg was delighted, and declared it 'a magnificent, world-leading facility'.[121]

Alongside the ISB the Arts Building looked tired, especially after it was surrounded by scaffolding and netting to protect passersby from falling concrete; its balconies were removed to reduce the hazard in 2016. A humanities precinct was scheduled to take its place eventually.[122] Property Services in Albany Street was another building destined to be demolished to make way for the new precinct. It started as a small brick premises built for engineers J. & A.P. Scott in 1912. The firm expanded through the years, with projects ranging from servicing Leyland trucks to making mortar shells during World War II, when the government paid for a large extension. The university purchased the building for its Works and Services Department in 1974; at the official opening Studholme warden Mary Dunn supplied 'a handsome cake iced in the University colours and bearing a message which began "Help! Dial 405 ..."' – the department was essential to the university.[123] By 1976 it had 80 Works staff, '60 of whom are fully occupied on construction and maintenance activity', responsible for building floor space (excluding residential accommodation) equivalent to 1200 houses.[124] And as the university's land and buildings expanded, so did its property team: in addition to maintenance, it undertook building alterations and the occasional larger project. For example, Otago asked its Property Services team to design the 2017 building for the Dunedin Study.[125] The Property Services website summed up its responsibilities neatly: 'From overseeing the design and construction of award-winning buildings, fixing broken light bulbs, booking office space, cutting the grass and trimming hedges, we're the highly-trained men and women who help keep the five University of Otago campuses humming'.[126] In 2017 chief operating officer Stephen Willis restructured Property Services into two divisions: Property Services and Campus Development. With the 'most complex and most expensive' capital programme in Otago's history underway, a dedicated team could concentrate on the major projects.[127]

Opposite and above: Exterior and interior of the ISB, photographed in 2013 and 2004 respectively. The 'celebrity squares' reader spaces (right) were among several interesting features of the building. Architect Stephen Johnson and his team were 'mindful to create large memorable spaces as well as smaller nooks and crannies', as Johnson explained. 'It is a large building, and we have sought to make it as transparent and porous as possible through the use of glass, perforated metal and portals.' As well as books, computer services and study spaces, the ISB accommodated the Student Learning Centre, audioconferencing, registry's student information desk, cafés and social spaces. UNIVERSITY OF OTAGO MARKETING AND COMMUNICATIONS COLLECTION.

CHAPTER FOURTEEN

Otago's place in the world

'Your place in the world' was the tagline of a University of Otago marketing campaign launched in 2008.[1] Otago's own place in the world was, and is, significant. Its origins were provincial and it was located far from the world's largest population centres as one of the southernmost universities on the planet.[2] That location had advantages: it was ideal for marine science and tourism research and as a centre for natural history filmmaking courses, and it attracted strong local support. Otago's founders were entrepreneurial and ambitious and most of their schemes succeeded; the most remarkable was to found a university at all at a time when leaders in other parts of New Zealand thought it premature. Otago proved them wrong: it attracted talented professors and founding students who might otherwise have been lost to New Zealand or lacked opportunity to develop their intellectual capacities. And it sparked the development of the University of New Zealand, making tertiary education available in other centres.

Being first mover advantaged Otago in later developments, especially with the special schools. In its first decade the university set up schools of medicine and mining, in the early twentieth century the dental and home science schools, and later the schools of physical education, pharmacy and surveying. By today's standards each was a reckless venture, starting with few students, but the university stuck with them and they developed into highly regarded schools. Boldness paid off: after a plan to establish home science at Canterbury fell through, Otago took it on – albeit somewhat reluctantly – and developed a school that educated thousands of women and shared its expertise with homes and communities everywhere; its twenty-first century legacy included Otago's strength in human nutrition and food science. Mining departed in the 1980s but the other special schools continued. Otago did not remain sole New Zealand supplier of qualifications in all those fields, though it educated all of New Zealand's medical graduates until the 1970s and still produces all of its home-grown dental and surveying graduates; in that alone its significance to the country was enormous.

In other fields where the task was shared with other tertiary institutions, Otago made a big contribution. Many professionals, from lawyers and linguists to social workers and statisticians, obtained an excellent education at Otago, as did various politicians, including a couple of the country's prime ministers in Robert Stout and Bill English. Although it became more cautious, the university continued to launch new programmes, such as New Zealand's first MBA in the 1970s when other institutions believed there was no demand for it.

Various Pacific Island staff and students with senior university managers at the launch of the Pacific Academic Caucus in 2016. Tasileta Teevale, Otago's first director of Pacific Development, is seated at right.
SHARRON BENNETT PHOTOGRAPH, PACIFIC DEVELOPMENT OFFICE COLLECTION.

EDUCATING THE WORLD

Otago's influence spread beyond New Zealand as it welcomed international students: Fijian Tom Dovi and South African Clarence Piliso in the 1920s and 30s; the Colombo Plan students of the 1950s, 60s and 70s; and the Middle Eastern health science students, Asian language students, US exchange students, postgraduates from continental Europe and online MBA students of the twenty-first century. Future leaders of Fiji (Kamisese Mara; Timoci Bavadra), the Cook Islands (Tom Davis), Tuvalu (Tomasi Puapua) and East Timor (Rui Araujo) all attended Otago, as did other influential politicians, including several Malaysian cabinet ministers.

The university's role in the Pacific was especially noteworthy: many Pacific Islanders used their Otago education to improve lives in the region. Those graduates gave Otago strong links with Pacific countries, strengthened later both formally and informally, in part through the growing number of Otago staff with Pacific connections. After the 2009 tsunami in Samoa, for example, the university and its Pacific Islands Centre supported staff members Fa`afetai Sopoaga and Kim Ma`ia`i who travelled to Samoa for medical relief work, and a couple of students who assisted with the aid effort.[3] The links extended to institutions: in 2004 Otago signed memoranda of understanding with the University of the South Pacific and National University of Samoa (NUS), enabling student exchanges and research collaboration.[4] The relationship with NUS developed with various high-level delegations to and from the Pacific, and in 2010 NUS gifted a house on its campus where Otago staff and postgraduates who were researching or working in Apia could stay.[5] When NUS established its own Faculty of Medicine in 2014, Otago lent important support.[6]

The university's role in the Pacific gained standing through its Pacific Strategic Framework, endorsed by the council in 2012 after consultation with Pacific community leaders. The framework was 'at heart, an equity response', DVC Vernon Squire noted in the introduction; it aimed at 'improved rates of access, retention and completion among New

Zealand students of indigenous Pacific descent'. The framework was 'broad in scope' and included the goal of 'contributing to the Pacific region and international progress'.[7] In 2013 Tasileta Teevale became Otago's first director of Pacific Development. Her links with the institution were strong: 'My family migrated from Samoa in the 1980s when my father received a scholarship to study at Otago. We left our Island shores for this very university,' she explained. She graduated in physical education and headed north for further study and work.[8] Teevale remarked a couple of years later on the progress Otago had made since her student days, with 'a lot more Pacific students' and the development of 'specific Pacific student services', including 'the Pacific Islands Centre, the Pacific Islands Research Students' Support Unit in the Health Sciences Division, and Pacific student support personnel in each of the four academic divisions'.[9]

WORKING WITH MĀORI

The Pacific Strategic Framework took inspiration from Otago's Māori Strategic Framework and the Office of Māori Development, established several years earlier. They were important steps in integrating 'the support and progression of "things Māori"' into all aspects of the university.[10] It represented a mindshift from the university's early decades, when it essentially ignored Māori except as the occasional subject of academic research. As a powerful institution, the university formed part of the machinery of colonisation. Attitudes started changing in the 1970s with the Māori cultural, social and political renaissance. More Māori attended university and a handful joined the academic staff, and there was a surge in interest in Māori language and culture. The university was slow to respond and there were numerous delays getting Māori studies going, but eventually many departments incorporated material relating to Māori into their teaching and research. The rise of EEO policies and legislation in the 1980s prompted the university to take equity issues seriously. With funding from government, it began initiatives to recruit and support Māori students. The Māori liaison officer and Māori Centre contributed to a notable growth in Māori engagement and success.

This increasing engagement with Māori led Otago to take note, at last, of its relationship with mana whenua. 'We were sitting in the midst of a Māori community which had very little contact with the University,' registrar Douglas Girvan later reflected; 'it became apparent we had to have a formal contact'. In 1988 the university established a Māori Affairs Board to advise it 'on matters of policy and protocol affecting the Māori community and the University, including the Māori Centre'. The board included people nominated by the council, Māori community and students, along with the registrar, the head of Māori studies and the Māori liaison officer. However, board members, including convener Alva Kapa, were unhappy with its limits: it didn't meet often enough and lacked any real influence, and its membership was problematic: 'How can a non-Māori person give advice about policy and protocol to the University about Māori things?'[11] The frustrated rūnanga representatives eventually withdrew. One of Ranginui Walker's findings in his 1998 Treaty of Waitangi review of the university was that the 'Māori Affairs Board has been ineffective and should be replaced with a Council linking mana whenua into the University in a meaningful way that gives substance to the principle of partnership under the Treaty of Waitangi'. He praised Otago's charter and strategic plan for their definitions of its Treaty obligations, but noted that its practice 'falls short of what is happening in other universities'; it needed to 'implement the kaupapa' of those documents and 'embrace the bicultural world of the University's Māori Treaty partner'.[12]

The 1998 review wasn't all bad: Walker commended the Ngāi Tahu Māori Health Research Unit as 'an example of best practice in forming a partnership with tāngata whenua to help meet the University's obligations to Māori'; its director, John Broughton, was 'a key player' and of much value to the university 'in getting the relationship right'. Another exemplar of 'best practice' was the Zoology Department, which negotiated with Ngāi Tahu 'on matters of mutual interest in the flora and fauna of the Otago region' and, in 1997, appointed Matapura Ellison to the part-time academic position of pouhere tāngata.[13] Walker's hard-hitting review encouraged change, and slowly Otago built a healthier relationship with mana whenua. In 2000 the university and Te Rūnanga o Ngāi Tahu signed a memorandum of understanding, renewed in 2007 and 2013.[14] In 2001 a newly formed council Treaty of Waitangi Committee began meeting and Darryn Russell was appointed full-time Māori affairs adviser, reporting directly to the VC.[15] After 'vigorous discussion', in 2003 Otago developed a policy for research consultation with Māori, which had previously been carried out in an ad hoc manner if at all. Local rūnanga formed the Ngāi Tahu Research Consultation Committee, external to the university, to provide a single point of consultation, and the university appointed a facilitator to manage its policy and liaise with the committee.[16]

Otago undertook another Treaty of Waitangi 'stocktake' in 2005. It refined 'six expectations with regard to the University's Treaty of Waitangi obligations, aspirations and responsiveness': leadership, partnership, Māori research, growth and development, quality programmes and language and culture; they were developed into a Māori Strategic Framework, approved in 2007.[17] The Office of Māori Development, established in 2008 with Russell as director, oversaw the framework's implementation and provided centralised leadership for Māori development at Otago.[18]

Once Otago committed to its Treaty obligations the results were impressive. Tuari Potiki, who succeeded Russell and acting director Janine Kapa-Blair in 2012, commented that 'support for Māori development has been strong because it was implemented carefully and gently, and in a uniquely polite Kāi Tahu way'.[19] With its relationship with mana whenua and appropriate cultural leadership in place, Otago could develop its relationships with other Māori people and organisations; that was a shift from the 1990s when, as Walker described it, the rituals of encounter were 'fraught with cultural nervousness, uncertainty, and a feeling of being unsafe'.[20] The university developed memoranda of understanding with various iwi and Māori organisations, including a 2008 agreement with Ngāti Toa Rangatira, one of the mana whenua iwi in the Wellington campus region, formalising an existing 'long-standing relationship'.[21]

'The relationship with iwi is the foundation we stand on,' said Potiki. 'Beyond that, I see *the* core objective as increasing Māori student achievement.'[22] Throughout the twentieth century, Māori who studied at Otago took on important roles in Māori health, education and development. In the twenty-first century that contribution accelerated. When 45 Māori medical students graduated in 2016 it marked 'a significant inflection point', said health sciences PVC Peter Crampton; 'we expect at least this number of Māori doctors to graduate each year from now on'.[23] Otago's commitment to Māori development, in alliance with Māori students, whānau and communities, contributed to a new era in health and other sectors of New Zealand life. Within the university a transformation was evident not just in its teaching and research, but in its entire ethos. On the recommendation of the Māori Affairs Board, Otago adopted the name Te Whare Wānanga o Otāgo in 1990. Eventually every part of the organisation had both Māori and English names, with bilingual signage prominent around the campuses and te reo Māori part of university documents and branding.[24] Kāi Tahu Whānui tikanga was incorporated into events, from formal welcomes at graduations and conferences to blessing buildings. Māori history and culture was a visible force, epitomised in the design and artworks in the 2017 redevelopment of the Business School building.

TOWN AND GOWN

On 5 July 1871 Dunedin shops and offices closed so citizens could attend the university's official opening, marking the beginning of a 'town and gown' relationship critical to both parties. Following the 1876 abolition of the provincial government that founded it, the university's strongest local relationship was with its host city. Dunedin was proud of its status as the home of New Zealand's first university. Residents could consult professors for expert advice and attend public lectures (good entertainment in an era before radio or television), and their children could obtain a tertiary education without leaving town. The university attracted skilled professionals to the city, from teachers and medical specialists to nutritionists and dentists, and locals benefited from their presence. The university also benefited from the citizens of Dunedin, who provided a captive audience on whom future professionals could practise their skills; local residents cheered on graduates, bought students' dubious capping magazines and tolerated some of their pranks.

The university was important to Dunedin's economy, especially as other industries declined. When Otago experienced a downturn in the student roll in 1981, the mayor Cliff Skeggs commented that the implications were serious for Dunedin: 'The University is a major employer of academic and non-academic staff, a major source of revenue for small businesses; and the students themselves form an important consumer section of the population.'[25] Fortunately for the city, that decline was temporary. The university later produced annual economic impact reports that measured its financial worth to Dunedin and other cities where it had campuses. In 1997 the university spent $225.7 million and its students an estimated $145 million, excluding fees; when the 'downstream impact' was added the university's impact totalled $630.2 million, $584 million of it in Dunedin.[26] In 2004 the total economic impact in all centres broke the billion-dollar mark for the first time.[27] As Otago planning and funding director David Thomson pointed out in 2016, the university's impact was 'far-reaching across many sectors of the economy, with the institution and its staff and students spending widely in local businesses'. It was 'among the top 50 largest employers in New Zealand'.[28] Those who weren't employed by the university but made a living through it ranged from the widows who took in student lodgers in the early twentieth century to the three generations of the Chin family, headed by Kum Yuen 'Kim' Chin, a.k.a. Mr Tui, who kept student bellies full with greasies at the Tui Café.[29] Then there were the people who rolled ice creams at the Rob Roy Dairy, a popular student destination that topped national charts for icecream sales; the teachers who educated the children of university staff; and the construction workers who built the buildings.[30]

The DCC valued the university and the relationship between them was close; the mayor was on the University Council from 1911 to 2015, when legislation reduced the number of councillors. In addition to the generosity of local individuals, organisations and businesses, the university profited from several joint ventures with the DCC, including the Otago Language School, City College and the Dunedin City Chair in Entrepreneurship; and both were big players in the stadium project. As in any relationship there were occasional difficulties: citizens in general appreciated the prosperity and opportunities the university brought to Dunedin and enjoyed the liveliness of thousands of intelligent young people, but some were concerned about the spread of the university and the transformation of residential areas into student enclaves. Students sometimes tested community tolerance: Peter Chin, the Otago law graduate who became mayor of Dunedin, recalls how 'devastated' he felt when he saw the destruction caused by the Undie 500 riots of the mid-2000s. The troublemakers were a tiny proportion of students but created much angst, and the city and university were frustrated at the constant media attention on any student misbehaviour in Dunedin. University and city were of one mind in discouraging the Undie 500 event, which eventually ended.[31]

CREATING CULTURE

New Zealand governments increasingly viewed universities as engines of economic growth, but their value went beyond that. The university enriched Dunedin's cultural life: students and staff from around the world brought diversity to the city, with more choices in food, entertainment, religious worship and a multitude of other things. University people were also creators and consumers of the arts. If it wasn't for the university, Chin notes, Dunedin would become 'like Milton', a quiet town to the south; 'the Fortune Theatre would die, the Southern Sinfonia would die, the art gallery; all the cultural things in this city would die bit by bit'.[32] One of the most influential cultural movements to arise in southern New Zealand, the indie music style sometimes called the 'Dunedin sound', might not have flourished without student musicians and audiences, orientation gigs and student radio.

Cultural production was the day-to-day business of some of the university's programmes, such as music, theatre studies, English and dance. They honed the talents of artists and actors, and brought colour and illumination and pleasure to the city. From 1959 the university became a patron of the arts through a series of fellowships; the recipients read like a who's who of the country's finest writers, artists and composers.[33] It started with a gift from an anonymous 'group of citizens' to fund a literary fellowship named after Robert Burns; it marked the bicentenary of the birth of the Scottish poet, whose nephew, Thomas Burns, was Otago's first chancellor.[34] Alan Horsman, the English professor, discussed the plan for the fellowship with the principal donor, 'whom I knew and was never expected to divulge'. He was 'a generous man', Horsman says, 'with the means to help New Zealand authors, and it was considerable help'. He adds that the success of the fellowship 'is plain in the work which these people have produced'.[35] When the fellowship was established there was little infrastructure to support New Zealand writers. The Burns Fellowship provided 'the first and most substantial literary residency'.

Burns fellows received a year's salary, a room in the English department and complete freedom to write. Not all writers found the year easy, but others thrived during their first opportunity to write full-time. Cilla McQueen, the 1985 and 1986 Burns Fellow, is photographed in contemplative mood in the fellow's office at the 50th anniversary celebrations of the fellowship in 2008 – when Sue Wootton held the fellowship.
ENGLISH AND LINGUISTICS DEPARTMENT COLLECTION.

Other opportunities 'for a full year's writing with a decent income' surfaced later, but the Burns was always the most prestigious.[36] In 1959, as Ian Cross began his year as the first Burns fellow, poet and editor Charles Brasch wrote in *Landfall* that 'part of a university's proper business is to act as nurse to the arts, or, more exactly, to the imagination as it expresses itself in the arts and sciences. Imagination may flourish anywhere. But it should flourish as a matter of course in the university, for it is only through imaginative thinking that society grows, materially and intellectually.'[37] The fellowship was valuable to the university as much as it was to the recipients – and society in general. 'It was a very good thing for the department to have practising writers around, available to be talked with,' says Horsman. Some, like 1966 and 1967 Burns Fellow James K. Baxter, participated in classes. He 'would come to a class occasionally and make his experience available. He would speak

Michael Illingworth, photographed here in his studio in 1968, was the first Frances Hodgkins Fellow in 1966. He made the news a year earlier when his painting *As Adam and Eve*, on show at the Barry Lett Galleries in Auckland, sparked an obscenity complaint to the police – an incident that cemented the painter's frustration with conservative middle-class New Zealand.

MAX OETTLI PHOTOGRAPH, P2011-027, S16-102C, HOCKEN COLLECTIONS.

to the class about prosody in a way which, from a practising poet, was authoritative.'[38]

The success of the Burns Fellowship inspired another anonymous gift to set up the Frances Hodgkins Fellowship, a similar scheme for painters and sculptors. From 1966 it offered the recipient the opportunity to live in Dunedin for a year with a secure income and studio space provided; as with the Burns, the Hodgkins fellow had complete freedom of expression to work on projects of their choice.[39] The rules stated that fellows needed to have 'executed sufficient work' to demonstrate talent as a painter or sculptor, but there was no requirement for applicants to have any formal education in fine arts – ensuring that mavericks would not be cut out. The selection committee demonstrated it was willing to support innovative and controversial artists.[40] There was an unfortunate start when Michael Illingworth left halfway through his 1966 tenure; he claimed he couldn't work in the studio provided.[41]

Otago does not, like some universities, have a fine arts programme; the Dunedin School of Art, established in 1870, is now part of Otago Polytechnic.[42] That meant the university struggled to understand the needs of artists, as Priscilla Pitts noted on the fellowship's 50th anniversary: 'In the early days, they didn't realise how artists work. They can be noisy and messy and have particular needs that writers or musicians might not.'[43] Finding a suitable space for the studio was challenging and it moved around various old houses and prefabs. The second holder, sculptor Tanya Ashken, found Dunedin more congenial than Illingworth had. Among the friends she made was Philip Smithells, director of the Phys Ed School; she joined the students in his gymnastic classes and used her observations of their movements and poses in her sculpture. When her tenure as fellow ended the Hocken Library held an exhibition of her work.[44] Exhibitions at the Hocken became a regular feature of the fellowship, as did the cross-fertilisation with other scholars and creative people.

In 1970 Anthony Watson became the first recipient of the Mozart Fellowship, funded by another anonymous gift 'to aid and encourage the composition of music in New Zealand and by associating active composers with the life of the University, to foster interest in contemporary music within the University' – the 'contemporary' referred to contemporary classical music, not rock music. At a 2007 reunion Anthony Ritchie, Mozart Fellow in 1988 and 1989, reflected on 'the freedom it provides, allowing a composer to think beyond the day-to-day worries of earning a crust, and to reflect on their musical language or style. It gives them a chance to experiment with new approaches, try writing in new genres.' Many of the fellows 'were cutting edge in their day, creating thought-provoking work that often presented challenges to audiences'.[45] They were hosted by the Music Department and some chose to teach – such as Gillian Bibby, the 1976 and 1977 fellow, who also conducted an opera, Monteverdi's *L'Orfeo*, directed by music professor John Drummond.[46] The 1976 Arts Faculty report noted Bibby's influence: 'Electronic music is developing, with the beginnings of a well-equipped studio under the direction of Gillian Bibby, the Mozart Fellow.'[47]

Other fellows collaborated widely. Jeremy Mayall, the 2014 and 2015 fellow, brought a chef into one project: his work *Flutter*, performed in the Otago Museum's tropical rainforest butterfly enclosure, was a 'multisensory experience' of music, sights, feels, smells and tastes; at certain points in the performance the audience ate flavoured macarons. Mayall later worked with the Food Science Department on the link between taste and sound; and he collaborated with psychology professor David Bilkey on the relationship between music and the brain. Mayall found the university environment stimulating: 'I try to make the most out of interdisciplinary projects – there are so many brilliant people in such a wide variety of fields here,' he said.[48]

A dance fellowship had different origins. After anthropology postgraduate Caroline Plummer died of cancer in 2003, her parents raised funds for a fellowship in her honour, and the government matched the funds through the Leading Thinkers scheme. Plummer, who completed a Diploma for Graduates in dance at Otago, was passionate about 'the power of dance as a medium for healing, education, cultural understanding and artistic expression'.[49] The Caroline Plummer Fellowship in Community Dance offered a six-month residency. It was 'a landmark opportunity' and 'a unique fellowship unmatched anywhere else in the world', noted Lyne Pringle, the 2011 fellow, who worked on a project with St Clair and St Kilda beach communities.[50] Unlike the older arts fellowships it was open to international applicants; the first fellow, in 2005, was Petra Kuppers, a German resident in the US who 'gained her dance qualification from a wheelchair'.[51] Subsequent fellows were a mix of New Zealanders and international community dance practitioners. They worked on a wide range of projects, from Georgina White's work on social dance (2006) to Sean Curham on walking and dancing with dogs (2009).[52]

The University of Otago acquired another arts fellowship in 2007 when it merged with DCE. In 1992 DCE established a residency for children's writers, funded jointly with the Queen Elizabeth II Arts Council (later Creative New Zealand).[53] Anna Marsich, one of the brains behind the residency, noted that DCE had 'always been involved in promoting children's literature'; it was 'important that teachers know what books are being produced and who the authors writing children's literature in New Zealand are'. There were 'not many awards for children's and young people's literature in this country and children's authors are often overlooked', she said – so the half-year residency was important. It later came with free accommodation in the 1909 Titan Street cottage that playwright Robert Lord, a former Burns Fellow, had left in trust for other writers on his death in 1992. Eleanor Orwin, who worked on a post-apocalyptic novel for teenagers during her 2009 residency, noted the advantage of having access to the university's libraries, and the joy of collegiality with the College of Education lecturers, 'Not because we are talking about what I'm doing, just because I know they are people who believe in children's books. I feel I don't have to justify what I do.'[54] As with the community dance fellowship, one of the great merits of the children's literature residency was in raising the profile of an underappreciated art.

The arts fellowships fostered a remarkable flow of creativity. Some fellows found the environment congenial and settled long-term in the south. Ralph Hotere came to Dunedin in 1969 as the Hodgkins Fellow and stayed on; he lived and worked in Port Chalmers and gave support and encouragement to subsequent fellows until his death in 2013.[55] Hone Tuwhare, Burns Fellow in 1969 and 1974, remained in the south and eventually settled at Kaka Point in the Catlins.[56] Popular playwright Roger Hall, Burns Fellow in 1977 and 1978, stayed on at the English Department as a half-time teaching fellow until 1994; his presence enlivened the theatre scene on campus and in the city.[57] Such people ensured support for the fellowships in the south. Although the original gifts were intended to endow the Burns, Hodgkins and Mozart fellowships permanently, by the late 1970s inflation had eroded their value and the university held a successful fundraising appeal to boost fellowship funds.[58]

In its Hocken Collections the University of Otago holds one of New Zealand's finest collections of art, archives and publications. Hocken's original gift included over 400 pictures, and the library purchased and was given more. In keeping with the original collection most of the earlier additions were acquired for their historical interest, but they included many fine drawings and paintings.[59] From the 1950s the pictorial collection took a new direction. Brasch headed a pictures subcommittee and, against some opposition, shifted the acquisitions focus from history to aesthetics, and to include modern works. His friend Rodney Kennedy made the first of many generous gifts to the Hocken in 1956, of 23 drawings by Colin McCahon. Brasch and Kennedy both donated other important artworks during their lifetime and by bequest. McCahon added works of his own, and his parents bequeathed other McCahon works to the collection. By 2007 the Hocken held some 14,000 pictures.[60] They included works by the Hodgkins fellows, some of which were inspired by art held in the Hocken Collections. Some of the Burns fellows spent time among the books and manuscript treasures of the Hocken: Tuwhare delved into the Māori manuscripts and Alison Wong, the 2002 fellow, sought out sources of information on New Zealand's Chinese past. Many of the fellows eventually donated their own literary papers to the Hocken's collection of treasures.

A CRITIC AND CONSCIENCE OF SOCIETY

The Education Amendment Act (1989) mandated that New Zealand universities 'accept a role as critic and conscience of society'. That mandate reassured critics of the neoliberal reforms of the era that the traditional liberal ideals of a university were not completely overturned by the drive towards competition and privatisation. Ironically, the increased accountability and endless measurement required of universities to underpin competition prevented them from adopting the most extreme forms of free market ideology. A group of Otago academics noted in 2010: 'NZ universities tend to benchmark themselves against the elite research-intensive Western universities that have managed to retain a strong liberal character and they must compete in this international market to attract and retain high-quality academic staff. Moving too far from the values of the elite institutions risks diminishing NZ's universities on the world stage.' The values of 'disinterested knowledge, critical reason and openness' survived, albeit sometimes with difficulty.[61]

The creative arts, and the humanities more generally, was an arena where Otago fulfilled its

Librarian Donald Jamieson in the Hocken pictures stack, 1965. He is looking at works donated in 1961 by Charlton Edgar, who taught at the Dunedin School of Art in the 1930s. This gift of nearly 400 works, known as the Mona Edgar collection in honour of Edgar's wife, 'update[d] the Hocken with thirty years worth of modern New Zealand art', wrote curator Linda Tyler; it 'changed the historical orientation of the collection irrevocably'.

BOX-240-004, S16-102B, HOCKEN COLLECTIONS.

'critic and conscience' role. But it was not the only one: public health, one of the university's largest research fields, uncovered some of New Zealand's worst social problems and suggested solutions, and occasionally governments took notice. The Wellington campus He Kainga Oranga/ Housing and Health Research Programme, led by Philippa Howden-Chapman, did not hesitate to publicise its findings, no matter how inconvenient that was for landlords and government housing policy.[62] In 2005 geology professor Dave Craw and student Laura Haffert visited Waiuta on the West Coast, the site of a former mine and processing plant that had closed 50 years earlier and had been turned into a reserve. While they were eating lunch they noticed distinctive crystalline material on the ground and took samples that later revealed 'incredibly high' levels of arsenic; they had uncovered one of New Zealand's most contaminated former industrial sites. The Department of Conservation closed access to the worst affected area. Haffert's PhD investigated the extent of contamination and made recommendations for dealing with it. These findings led to an extensive clean-up of Waiuta and other mining sites in the vicinity.[63]

The 'critic and conscience' role was closely tied to other mandated roles of the university: 'to develop intellectual independence', to 'meet international standards of research and teaching' and to serve as 'a repository of knowledge and expertise'.[64] In the expansion of knowledge Otago was a prominent player. The list of recipients of the university's medals for research, set up in 2007 'to promote research and to give recognition to outstanding performance', reveals the broad sweep of research areas, ranging from anatomy, philosophy, history and chemistry, to medicine, English, law and zoology.[65] A sample of winners of the Distinguished Research Medal demonstrates the abundance of expertise: Sally Brooker (chemistry), who designed and built 'molecular-scale self-assembling systems that could ultimately be used as nano components'; Lisa Matisoo-Smith (anatomy), who uses evolutionary genetics to study Pacific migrations; Allan Herbison (physiology), who made important findings on the brain's control of fertility; and Robert Poulin (zoology), a 'world leader in the study of parasite ecology and evolution'.[66]

Otago researchers have changed the world in dramatic ways, as a few examples demonstrate. The Dunedin and Christchurch longitudinal studies have accumulated a storehouse of knowledge that has influenced social policy in New Zealand and internationally. One outcome made headlines: Tennessee killer Bradley Waldroup escaped the death penalty thanks to research by the Dunedin Study team that revealed that the combination of a particular gene and childhood abuse made some men prone to violence.[67] The study's injury research team prevented deaths and injuries by advocating the installation of safety mats under playground equipment, and recommending shorter cords on electric jugs.[68] An epidemic in asthma deaths was halted when researchers at the Wellington campus in the 1980s uncovered a link between the epidemic and the asthma drug fenoterol.[69] Biochemist Parry Guilford and his team from the Cancer Genetics Laboratory worked with a Māori whānau afflicted with high rates of stomach cancer to develop a genetic test to identify those at risk; early intervention prevented the cancer and the test is now used around the world.[70] Otago medical researchers in earlier times changed lives through their research into problems that are now largely eradicated, such as endemic goitre and hydatids disease. And looking to the future, we can only speculate on how many lives may be spared through the Centre for Peace and Conflict Studies' work on conflict resolution and peace movements.

The University of Otago's founders selected as its motto 'sapere aude', often translated as 'dare to be wise'. They may have chosen it from a letter by the Roman poet Horace in which he states: 'Starting a task is as good as accomplishing half of it. Dare to know. Begin!' Some Otago scholars pointed out that 'sapere aude' also appeared in Immanuel Kant's 1784 essay on the enlightenment, where its sense is 'Have courage to make use of your own understanding'.[71] Whatever the case, the phrase, which has formed the theme of many a graduation address, encapsulates the spirit of New Zealand's first university. Its founders had the audacity to set up a university in the farthest reaches of the British Empire and to build it into a world-class institution; its staff used their talents to create, support and share new knowledge; and its students dared to make the most of their intellectual capabilities. Long may it continue!

Timeline

	Administration	Roll	Major new courses	External events
1869	*University of Otago formally created*			
1870				*University of New Zealand created by statute*
1871	*Classes started*	*Opening roll 81 students*	*Arts and Sciences*	
1872	*First women students*			
1873			*Law*	
1874	*First Otago graduate (Alexander Williamson, BA); Otago joined University of New Zealand*	*Roll of 50*		
1875			*Medicine*	*Canterbury University College opened*
1876				*Otago Normal School Training Department opened (start of Dunedin College of Education)*
1878	*Move to new buildings on current Dunedin campus*			
1879		*Roll passed 100*	*Mining*	
1880				*Lincoln College opened*
1883				*Auckland University College opened*
1886	*First woman graduate (Caroline Freeman, BA)*			
1890	*Otago University Students' Association created*			
1897		*Roll passed 250*		
1899				*Victoria University College opened*
1904	*First Māori graduate (Peter Buck/Te Rangi Hīroa, MB ChB)*		*Education*	

	Administration	Roll	Major new courses	External events
1907			*Dentistry*	
1911			*Home science*	
1912		*Roll passed 500*	*Commerce*	
1913			*Physiotherapy*	
1914				*World War I began*
1915	*Formal adult education commenced (through WEA)*			
1920		*Roll passed 1000*		
1924	*First senior medical students in Christchurch*			
1925	Critic *commenced publication*			
1926			*Music*	
1927	*First PhD graduate (Rudolf Penseler); first senior medical students in Wellington and Auckland*			
1928				*Massey Agricultural College opened*
1929	*First Chinese graduate (Kathleen Pih, MB ChB)*			
1935	*First (probably) Pacific Islands graduate (Tom Dovi, MB ChB)*			
1937	*Branches of Faculty of Medicine established in Christchurch, Wellington and Auckland*			
1939				*World War II began*
1946	*Student Health Service opened*	*Roll passed 2000*	*Theology*	
1948	*First full-time vice-chancellor (Robert Aitken)*		*Physical education*	
1951	*First Colombo Plan international students*			

	Administration	Roll	Major new courses	External events
1959	*First book published by Otago University Press; first Burns fellow (Ian Cross)*			
1962				*University of New Zealand dissolved*
1963			*Surveying and Pharmacy*	
1965				*University of Waikato opened*
1966	*First computer purchased; first Frances Hodgkins fellow (Michael Illingworth)*			
1967	*Mixed flatting controversy*			
1968				*University of Auckland Medical School opened*
1970	*First Mozart fellow (Anthony Watson)*	*Roll passed 5000*		
1971	*Christchurch Clinical School established (first 4th-year students in 1973)*			
1973	*Wellington Clinical School established (first 4th-year students in 1977)*			
1983	*First woman president of OUSA (Phyllis Comerford)*			
1985	*Distance education credit courses commenced*			
1986		*Female students outnumbered males*		
1987	*Mining courses moved to University of Auckland*			
1989	*9 faculties restructured into 4 academic divisions; Māori Centre opened*	*Roll passed 10,000*		*Education Act 1989 – major education reforms commenced*
1990				*University Grants Committee abolished*

	Administration	Roll	Major new courses	External events
1992			*Medical laboratory science*	*Government student loan scheme commenced; first children's writer in residence at Dunedin College of Education (Ruth Corrin)*
1993	*First woman chancellor (Judith Medlicott)*			
1994	*Semester system commenced*			
1996	*Auckland Centre opened*			
1997			*Nursing (Christchurch)*	
1998			*Teaching*	
1999			*Dental therapy*	
2000				*Tertiary Education Advisory Commission established; Auckland Institute of Technology became Auckland University of Technology*
2001	*Summer School commenced; Pacific Islands Centre opened*		*Radiation therapy (Wellington), Dental technology, Dental hygiene*	
2002				*Performance-Based Research Fund established*
2003	*Leading Thinkers scheme gained government support*			*Tertiary Education Commission established*
2004				
2005	*First Caroline Plummer fellow (Petra Kuppers)*	*Roll passed 20,000*		
2007	*Merger with Dunedin College of Education; Campus Watch commenced*			
2010		*Roll peaked at 22,139*		*Darfield earthquake*
2011	*First woman VC (Harlene Hayne)*			*Christchurch earthquake*
2017	*Support services restructured*			

Appendix 1

COMPOSITION OF THE UNIVERSITY OF OTAGO COUNCIL

Year	Legislation	No. of members	Appointed by
1869	*University of Otago Ordinance*	12	*Provincial superintendent (later the governor); clause for election by a senate composed of graduates (court of convocation) not activated*
1891	*University of Otago Council Election Act*	12	*Governor (6), professors (2), graduates (4)*
1911	*University of Otago Council Act*	16+	*Governor (2), professorial board (2), court of convocation (4), Otago Education Board (1), Southland Education Board (1), school committees (1), DCC (1), Otago Hospital and Charitable Aid Board (1), secondary school governing bodies (1), primary teachers (1), secondary teachers (1); grandparenting clause for members appointed before 1891*
1946	*University of Otago Council Act*	20–22	*Governor-general (2), professorial board (2), lecturers (1), court of convocation (5), Otago Education Board (1), Southland Education Board (1), school committees (1), secondary school governing bodies (1), primary teachers (1), secondary teachers (1), OUSA executive (1, not a current student, graduate of at least 2 years), DCC (1), OHB (1), VC (ex officio); council may co-opt up to 2 more members*
1961	*University of Otago Amendment Act*	20–22	*Governor-general (3), court of convocation (6), senate (4), lecturers (1), DCC (1), OHB (1), OUSA executive (1, not a current student, graduate of at least 2 years), secondary school governing bodies (1), secondary teachers (1), VC (ex officio); council may co-opt up to 2 more members*
1969	*University of Otago Amendment Act*	22–24	*Governor-general (3), court of convocation (6), senate (4), lecturers (2), DCC (1), OHB (1), OUSA executive (2), secondary school governing bodies (1), secondary teachers (1), VC (ex officio); council may co-opt up to 2 more members*
1977	*University of Otago Amendment Act*	25–27	*Governor-general (3), court of convocation (6), senate (4), lecturers (2), DCC (1), OHB (1), OUSA executive (2), governing bodies of secondary schools (1), secondary teachers (1), Otago Polytechnic Council (1), DCE Council (1), VC (ex officio), pro-VC (ex officio); council may co-opt up to 2 more members*

Year	Legislation	No. of members	Appointed by
1990	*Education Amendment Act*	*17–20*	*Minister of education (4), VC (ex officio), academic staff (1–3), general staff (1–3), students (1–3), central organisation of employers (1), central organisation of workers (1), other council appointments; council total 12–20 members. At Otago this became: minister of education (4), VC (ex officio), academic staff (3), general staff (1), OUSA (2), central organisation of employers (1), central organisation of workers (1), DCC (1), court of convocation (3), plus up to 3 others*
2015	*Education Amendment Act*	*12*	*Minister of education (3–4), council (5–8), council total 8–12 members. At Otago: minister of education (4), academic staff (1), general staff (1), VC (ex officio), OUSA president (ex officio), other council appointments (4)*

Appendix 2

OTAGO RESIDENTIAL COLLEGES

Name	Location	Former name/s	Year open'd	Orig'l res intake	2018 capacity	Owner
Selwyn College	*Castle Street*	—	*1893*	*6*	*188*	*Anglican Church*
Knox College	*Arden Street*	—	*1909*	*40*	*262*	*Presbyterian Church*
St Margaret's College	*Leith Street*	—	*1911*	*15*	*224*	*Presbyterian Church*
Studholme College	*Clyde Street (originally Leith Street)*	*Studholme, House, Studholme Hall*	*1915*	*15*	*187*	*University*
Arana College	*Clyde Street*	*Arana Hall*	*1943*	*40*	*404*	*University (previously Stuart Residence Halls Council)*
Carrington College	*Heriot Row*	*Carrington Hall*	*1945*	*37*	*243*	*University (previously Stuart Residence Halls Council)*
Aquinas College	*Gladstone Road*	*Aquinas Hall, Dalmore House*	*1954*	*72*	*152*	*University (previously Dominican Order)*
University College	*Leith Street*	—	*1969*	*324*	*507*	*University*
Salmond College	*Knox Street*	*Salmond Hall*	*1971*	*140*	*260*	*Presbyterian Church*
Cumberland College	*Castle Street*	*Cumberland House*	*1989*	*145*	*327*	*University*
Hayward College	*Frederick Street*	*Hayward Hall*	*1992*	*150*	*162*	*University*
Toroa College	*Regent Road*	*Toroa Internat'l House*	*1996*	*105*	*152*	*University*
Caroline Freeman College	*Cumberland Street*	*City College*	*2000*	*189*	*201*	*University (previously Dunedin City Tertiary Accommodation Trust)*
Abbey College	*Cumberland Street*	—	*2008*	*72*	*75*	*University*
Te Rangi Hīroa College	*Castle Street*	—	*2014*	*125*	*125*	*University*

FORMER OTAGO RESIDENTIAL COLLEGES

Name	Location	Year open'd	Final year	Orig'l res intake	Highest capacity	Owner
Stuart House	*Cumberland Street*	*1941*	*1946 (became flats)*	*29*	*48*	*Stuart Residence Halls Council*
Dominican Hall	*Park Street*	*1946*	*1978*	*20*	*50*	*Dominican Sisters*
Wesley Hall	*Park Street*	*1958*	*1970*	*14*	*14*	*Dunedin Central Methodist Mission*
Helensburgh House	*Taieri Road*	*1984*	*1991*	*105*	*200+*	*University (leased from OHB)*

Appendix 3

BUILDINGS CONSTRUCTED FOR THE UNIVERSITY (EXCLUDING RESIDENTIAL COLLEGES)

Name	Location	Former name/s	Year open'd	Architect/s (lead architect)	Main building contractor	Extensions
Geology Building	*Leith Walk*	*Chemistry and Anatomy Building*	*1878*	*Maxwell Bury*	*McGill & Forrest*	*1883, 1905, 1914, 1943*
Clocktower Building	*Leith Walk*	—	*1879*	*Maxwell Bury*	*McGill & Forrest*	*1914, 1922, 1966*
Scott/Shand House and Black/Sale House	*St David Street*	*Professorial houses*	*1879*	*Maxwell Bury*	*McGill & Forrest*	—
'Tin Shed' (demolished)	*Leith Walk*	*School of Mines, School of Home Science*	*1890*	*Henry Hardy*	*?*	—
Staff Club	*Union Place*	*Dental School, Registry, Law Faculty*	*1908*	*Louis Salmond*	*McKinnon & Hamilton*	*1909, 1921, 1923*
Archway West Building	*Union Place*	*School of Mines*	*1909*	*Edmund Anscombe*	*Gabriel Hodges*	—
Allen Hall & Archway Building	*Union Place*	*Student Union*	*1914*	*Edmund Anscombe*	*Fletcher Bros*	—
Scott Building	*Great King Street*	*Medical School*	*1917*	*Mason & Wales (P.Y. Wales)*	*Fletcher Bros*	—
Applied Sciences Building	*Union Place*	*Home Science Building*	*1920*	*Edmund Anscombe*	*Orr Campbell*	—
Marama Hall	*Leith Walk*	*Marama & Maheno Hospital Ships Surplus Fund Memorial Hall*	*1923*	*Edmund Anscombe*	*Wood & McCormack*	—
Marples Building	*Great King Street*	*Dental School, Zoology Building*	*1926*	*Edmund Anscombe*	*W.H. Naylor*	—

Name	Location	Former name/s	Year open'd	Architect/s (lead architect)	Main building contractor	Extensions
Lindo Ferguson Building	*Great King Street*	*Medical School*	*1927*	*Edmund Anscombe*	*William McLellan*	—
Hercus Building	*Hanover Street*	*Medical School South Block*	*1948*	*Miller & White*	*Associated Builders*	—
University Union	*Castle Walk*		*1960*	*Miller White & Dunn (Ian Dunn)*	*Mitchell Bros*	*1969, 1986*
Walsh Building	*Great King Street*	*Dental School*	*1961*	*Government Architects (Ian Reynolds & Gordon Wilson)*	*C.S. Luney*	*1984*
Gregory Building	*Leith Walk*	—	*1961*	*Miller White & Dunn (Geoffrey White)*	*James Donaldson & Son*	*1967*
Trustbank Aquarium (demolished)	*Portobello*	*Portobello Marine Biological Research Station*	*1962*	*Miller White & Dunn*	*M.F. Taylor*	—
Wellcome Research Institute	*Frederick Street*	—	*1963*	*Mason & Wales (Niel Wales)*	*W.H. Naylor Ltd & William McLean Ltd*	—
Library/ Arts Building (demolished)	*Albany Street*	—	*1965*	*Rolland Adams & Brian Dodd*	*Fletcher Construction*	—
Information Technology Services Building	*Leith Walk*	*Interim Sciences Building, Computing Services Centre*	*1965*	*Beatson, Rix-Trott, Carter & Co*	*Mitchell Brothers*	—
Arts Building	*Albany Street*	—	*1969*	*Mason & Wales (John Aimers)*	*Mitchell Brothers*	—
Smithells Gymnasium	*Cumberland Street*	—	*1970*	*Mason & Wales (John Aimers)*	*Mitchell Brothers*	—
Mellor Laboratories	*Union Street*	*Science I Building*	*1971*	*Ministry of Works*	*Fletcher Construction*	—
Biochemistry Building	*Cumberland Street*		*1971*	*Allingham & Harrison (John Harrison)*	*Fletcher Construction*	*1996*

Name	Location	Former name/s	Year open'd	Architect/s (lead architect)	Main building contractor	Extensions
Sayers Building	*Great King Street*	—	*1972*	*Architects Engineers Partnership (Alan Neil)*	*Fletcher Construction*	—
Science II Building	*Union Street*	—	*1973*	*Mason & Wales (John Aimers)*	*Fletcher Construction*	—
University of Otago, Christchurch	*Riccarton Avenue*	*Christchurch Clinical School Medical Centre*	*1973*	*Thorpe, Cutter, Pickmere & Douglas*	*Fletcher Construction*	*1998, 2006*
Adams Building	*Frederick Street*	*Medical Sciences Building*	*1973*	*Miller White & Dunn (Ian Dunn)*	*Naylor Love*	*1996*
Archway Lecture Theatres	*Union Place*	—	*1974*	*McCoy & Wixon (Ted McCoy)*	*Atkinson & Forbes*	—
Microbiology Building	*Cumberland Street*	—	*1974*	*Miller White & Dunn (Ian Dunn)*	*Naylor Love*	—
Dunedin Hospital Lecture Theatres (Colquhoun and Barnett Theatres)	*Great King Street*	—	*1974*	*Stephenson & Turner*	*Downers*	—
Science III Building	*Cumberland Street*	—	*1977*	*Allingham Harrison & Partners (John Harrison)*	*Naylor Love*	—
University of Otago, Wellington	*Mein Street*	*Wellington Clinical School Academic Block*	*1979*	*Cutter, Pickmere & Douglas*	*Fletcher Construction*	*2007*
Richardson Building	*Castle Walk*	*Hocken Building*	*1979*	*McCoy & Wixon (Ted McCoy)*	*Fletcher Construction*	—
Clubs and Societies Centre	*Albany Street*	*Recreation Centre*	*1980*	*Mason & Wales (Ashley Muir)*	*Fletcher Construction*	—
Dunedin Hospital Ward Block & Associated Medical School Facilities	*Great King Street*	—	*1980*	*Stephenson & Turner*	*Fletcher Construction*	—

Name	Location	Former name/s	Year open'd	Architect/s (lead architect)	Main building contractor	Extensions
Animal Breeding Station	*Taieri*	—	*1982*	*McAllum & Warburton*	*?*	*1985*
Physical Education Laboratory Annexe	*Cumberland Street*	—	*1986*	*Allingham Harrison Partnership*	*Mitchell Almet*	—
Portobello Marine Laboratory	*Portobello*	—	*1986*	*Oakley, Pinfold, Turvey & Co (Bob Oakley)*	*Downer & Co*	—
Castle Lecture Theatres	*Castle Walk*	—	*1988*	*McCoy & Wixon (Ted McCoy)*	*Mitchell Almet*	*1991*
Goddard Laboratories	*Union Street*	—	*1990*	*Tim Heath*	*Fletcher Construction*	
Otago Business School Building	*Union Street*	*Commerce Building*	*1992*	*John Blair*	*Naylor Love*	—
Physical Education Building	*Union Street*	—	*1994*	*Harrison & Gillies (Lindsay Gillies)*	*Naylor Love*	—
Executive Residence	*Union Street*	—	*1994*	*Mason & Wales (Ashley Muir)*	*Naylor Love*	—
Student Health Centre	*Walsh Street*	—	*1996*	*Mason & Wales (Ashley Muir)*	*Naylor Love*	—
New Zealand Marine Studies Centre	*Portobello*	—	*1997*	*McCoy & Wixon*	*Stevenson & Williams*	—
Physiotherapy Building	*Great King Street*	—	*1997*	*McCoy & Wixon*	*Naylor Love*	—
St David II	*St David Street*	—	*1998*	*Salmond Anderson Heath (Tim Heath)*	*Naylor Love*	—
St David Lecture Theatre	*St David Street*	—	*2000*	*McCoy & Wixon (John McCoy)*	*Naylor Love*	—
Information Services Building	*Albany Street*	—	*2001*	*Hardy Holzman Pfeiffer Associates (Stephen Johnson); Opus International Consultants*	*Naylor Love*	—
Centre for Innovation	*St David Street*	—	*2001*	*Mason & Wales (Ashley Muir)*	*Naylor Love*	—

Name	Location	Former name/s	Year open'd	Architect/s (lead architect)	Main building contractor	Extensions
OUSA Aquatic Centre	*Magnet Street*	—	*2002*	*Architectural Ecology (Tim Heath)*	*Amalgamated Builders*	—
Benham Building	*Great King Street*	—	*2003*	*McCoy & Wixon*	*Naylor Love*	—
Botany Research Building	*Union Street*	—	*2005*	*Ashby Building Designs*	*Naylor Love*	—
Parker Building	*Great King Street*	—	*2009*	*Parker Warburton Team Architects (Simon Parker)*	*Lund South*	—
William James Building		—	*2010*	*Architectural Ecology (Tim Heath)*	*Naylor Love*	—
University Plaza	*Anzac Avenue*	—	*2011*	*Warren & Mahoney (Blair Johnston), McCoy & Wixon*	*Naylor Love*	—
Te Pā	*Castle Street*	—	*2014*	*Parker Warburton Team Architects (Simon Parker)*	*Amalgamated Builders*	—
Dunedin Multidisciplinary Health and Development Research Unit Building	*Anzac Avenue*	—	*2017*	*University of Otago Property Services (Murray Goldfinch)*	*Cook Brothers*	—
Portobello Teaching Laboratory	*Portobello*	—	*2017*	*McCoy & Wixon*	*Cook Brothers*	—
Dental School	*Great King Street*	—	*Under constr'n*	*Jasmax Joint Venture*	*Leighs Cockram*	—
Research Support Facility	*Great King Street*	—	*Under constr'n*	*Jacobs*	*Naylor Love*	—

COLLEGE OF EDUCATION BUILDINGS MERGED WITH UNIVERSITY IN 2007

Name	Location	Former name/s	Year open'd	Architect/s	Builders	Extensions
Administ'n Block	*Union Street*	—	*1972*	*Otago Education Board (Eoin Davidson)*	*Fletcher Construction*	*1976?*
Teaching Wing	*Union Street*	—	*1972*	*Otago Education Board (Eoin Davidson)*	*Fletcher Construction*	*1976*
Music, Soft Technology and Science Building	*Union Street*	*Student Centre*	*1972*	*Otago Education Board (Eoin Davidson)*	*Fletcher Construction*	—
Tower Block	*Union Street*	—	*1976*	*Oakley Pinfold Turvey & Neil (Gib Pinfold)*	*Downer & Co*	—
Auditorium	*Union Street*	—	*1976*	*Oakley Pinfold Turvey & Neil (Gib Pinfold)*	*Atkinson & Forbes*	—
Gymnasium	*Union Street*	—	*1976*	*Oakley Pinfold Turvey & Neil (Gib Pinfold)*	*Stevenson & Williams*	—
Southland Campus	*Nelson Street, Invercargill*	—	*1980*	*Government Architect*	*W.E. Mathieson*	—
(former Ministry of Works office complex, used by College of Education from 1992)						
Robertson Library	*Union Street*	*Bill Robertson Library*	*1981*	*Oakley Pinfold Turvey & Co (Bob Turvey)*	*Stevenson & Williams*	*1989, 2010*
Owheo Building	*Union Street*	—	*1991*	*McCoy & Wixon (Ted McCoy)*	*Naylor Love*	—
Education Centre	*Union Street*	—	*1993*	*Salmond Anderson Heath*	*Amalgamated Builders*	—
Drama Centre	*Union Street*	—	*1993*	*Oakley Gray (Norman Oakley)*	*Mitchell Almet*	—

EXISTING BUILDINGS ACQUIRED BY THE UNIVERSITY (EXCLUDING OLD HOUSES & SMALLER BUILDINGS)

Name	Location	Year opened (OU)	Original use
University of Otago, later Colonial Bank, Stock Exchange (demolished)	*Princes Street*	*1871*	*'New Post Office'*
Physical Education Building	*Cumberland Street*	*1948 (initially shared)*	*Teachers' Training College*
Portobello Marine Biological Station (demolished)	*Portobello*	*1951*	*Portobello Marine Fish Hatchery and Biological Station*
Barningham Building (demolished)	*Great King Street*	*1953*	*Foundry*
Botany Building (previously Surveying)	*Great King Street*	*1964*	*Wright's Bakery*
Property Services	*Albany Street*	*1974*	*J. & A.P. Scott (engineers)*
Botany Annexe (formerly Surveying)	*Union Street*	*1977*	*Woodwork and cookery rooms for North Dunedin schools*
Information Science Laboratories (formerly Hocken Library)	*Leith Street*	*1987*	*Vehicle Testing Station*
Union Court	*Union Street*	*1988*	*Castle Flats*
Unipol (former)	*Anzac Avenue*	*1990*	*Williamson Jeffrey Ltd (stationery factory)*
Marine Science Department/ Surveying School	*Castle Street*	*1993*	*Queen Mary Maternity Hospital*
Hocken Library	*Anzac Avenue*	*1998*	*Otago Co-operative Dairy Co*
Music Building	*Albany Street*	*2007*	*New Zealand Broadcasting Corporation studio*
Hunter Centre	*Great King Street*	*2008*	*Hospital resident doctors' quarters*
71 Frederick Sreet	*Frederick Street*	*2009*	*Bowling Green Hotel*
Marsh Study Centre	*Castle Street*	*2013*	*Gardens Tavern*

Year opened (original)	Original architect/s	Original builders	Notes
1868	*Mason & Clayton*	*McKay & Goodfellow*	
1909	*Otago Education Board (James Rodger)*	*F.W. Lyders*	
1904	?	*R. Bauchop & Co*	
1883–84	?	?	
1952	?	*Sabiston & Hutton*	*Wright's operated from this site from the 1860s*
1912	?	*Farquharson*	*Extended several times, including major additions in 1919 and during World War II*
1910	*Department of Education*	*John White*	
1963	*Dunedin City Corporation Engineers Office*	*W. Camp Builders*	
1930	*W.H. Dunning*	*Frank & George Lawrence*	
1947	*McDowell Smith*	*Fletcher Construction*	
1937	*Mason & Wales*	*Naylor*	*Extended in 1940s*
1954	*L.W.S. Lowther*	*Love Construction*	
1968	*Government Architect*	*Stevenson & Williams*	
1972	?	*Walker & Hasler*	
1880–81	?	?	
1969	*Murray Cockburn*	*Wix & Fairhurst*	

Notes

ABBREVIATIONS

AJHR	*Appendices to the Journals of the House of Representatives*
DNZB	Dictionary of New Zealand Biography
ES	*Evening Star*
HC	Hocken Collections
OB	*Otago Bulletin*
ODT	*Otago Daily Times*
OUR	*Otago University Review*
OW	*Otago Witness*
UOAR	*University of Otago Annual Report*
UOC	*University of Otago Calendar*
UOM	*University of Otago Magazine*
UON	*University of Otago Newsletter*

INTRODUCTION

1. The previous histories are G.E. Thompson, *A History of the University of Otago (1869–1919)* (Dunedin: Wilkie, 1919) and W.P. Morrell, *The University of Otago: A centennial history* (Dunedin: University of Otago Press, 1969).
2. Sam Elworthy, *Ritual Song of Defiance: A social history of students at the University of Otago* (Dunedin: Otago University Students' Association, 1990). A new history of the OUSA by Philippa Keaney was in progress at the time of writing this book.
3. Thompson, *University of Otago* and Morrell, *University of Otago* both include long accounts of Otago's foundation and relationship with the University of New Zealand. W.J. Gardner, *Colonial Cap and Gown: Studies in the mid-Victorian universities of Australasia* (Christchurch: University of Canterbury, 1979) provides a useful overview of the foundation of Otago and other Australasian universities. The two detailed histories of the University of New Zealand are J.C. Beaglehole, *The University of New Zealand: An historical study* (Wellington: New Zealand Council for Educational Research, 1937) and Hugh Parton, *The University of New Zealand* (Auckland: Auckland University Press/University Grants Committee, 1979).
4. J.C. Beaglehole to Norman Richmond, 4 October 1948, in Tim Beaglehole (ed.), *'I Think I am Becoming a New Zealander: Letters of J.C. Beaglehole* (Wellington: Victoria University Press, 2013), 237.
5. The people interviewed formally by Dorothy Page and Alison Clarke are listed in the bibliography.
6. University of Otago 1869–2019: writing a history, https://otago150years.wordpress.com/

1: FOUNDING AND ADMINISTRATION

1. Arthur S. Thomson, *The Story of New Zealand: Past and present – savage and civilized* (London: John Murray, 1859), vol. 2, 229–30. On Thomson, see Michael Belgrave, 'Thomson, Arthur Saunders', from the Dictionary of New Zealand Biography (DNZB): www.teara.govt.nz/en/biographies/1t95/thomson-arthur-saunders
2. 'Statistics of the Province of Otago, 1859–60', *Otago Witness* (*OW*), 21 July 1860, 6.
3. Atholl Anderson, *The Welcome of Strangers: An ethnohistory of southern Maori A.D. 1650–1850* (Dunedin: University of Otago Press/Dunedin City Council, 1998); Bill Dacker, *Te Mamae me te Aroha, The Pain and the Love: A history of Kai Tahu Whānui in Otago, 1844–1994* (Dunedin: University of Otago Press/Dunedin City Council, 1994); Waitangi Tribunal, *The Ngai Tahu Report, 1991 (Wai 27)* (Wellington: Brooker & Friend, 1991).
4. *Statistics of New Zealand*, 1864, Table 1; 1867, Table 3; *Results of a Census of the Colony of New Zealand*, 1871, Table 3. None of these statistics included Māori, whose population in Dunedin itself was probably very small, though there were several dozen living on the Otago Peninsula at the settlement of Ōtākou in the 1860s: see Anderson, *Welcome of Strangers*, 168.
5. W.J. Gardner, *Colonial Cap and Gown: Studies in the mid-Victorian universities of Australasia* (Christchurch: University of Canterbury, 1979), 11.
6. R.D. Anderson, *Education and Opportunity in Victorian Scotland: Schools and universities* (Oxford: Clarendon, 1983), 27–28.
7. Ian Carter, *Ancient Cultures of Conceit: British university fiction in the post-war years* (London: Routledge, 1990), 267.
8. G.E. Thompson, *A History of the University of Otago (1869–1919)* (Dunedin: Wilkie, 1919), 7–12. Thompson's history has a detailed account of the foundation of the university. See also A.H. McLintock, *The History of Otago: The origins and growth of a Wakefield class settlement* (Dunedin: Otago Centennial Historical Publications, 1949), 508–18.
9. Report of the Select Committee on the Establishment of University Scholarships, *Appendix to the Journals of the House of Representatives* (*AJHR*), 1867, F-01; 'Simmons, Frank Churchill', in G.H. Scholefield (ed.), *A Dictionary of New Zealand Biography* (Wellington: Department of Internal Affairs, 1940), vol. 2, 303. On debates in Otago over the merits of scholarships or a local university, see Mark Galvin, 'Here or there? The founding of the University of Otago', in The Time Keepers, *Tower Turmoil: Characters and controversies at the University of Otago*

(Dunedin: Department of History, University of Otago, 2005), 13–27.

10. J.C. Beaglehole, *The University of New Zealand: An historical study* (Wellington: New Zealand Council for Educational Research, 1937), 21–23; Hugh Parton, *The University of New Zealand* (Auckland: Auckland University Press/University Grants Committee, 1979), 15.
11. Erik Olssen, 'Macandrew, James', from DNZB: www.teara.govt.nz/en/biographies/1m1/macandrew-james
12. Select Committee on Scholarships.
13. *University of Otago Annual Report* (*UOAR*), 1887, 1.
14. 'Report of Select Committee on College', *Otago Daily Times* (*ODT*), 1 June 1868, 5; Thompson, *University of Otago*, 17–18.
15. University of Otago Ordinance, 1869; Mark Hill, Russell Sandberg & Norman Doe, *Religion and Law in the United Kingdom* (Alphen aan den Rijn, Netherlands: Kluwer Law International, 2011), 180.
16. 'The Otago University', *ODT*, 11 November 1869, 2.
17. *ODT*, 14 October 1869, 2; Jane Thomson (ed.), *Southern People: A dictionary of Otago Southland biography* (Dunedin: Longacre Press, 1998), 84, 213, 417–18; 'Ward, Charles Dudley Robert', in Scholefield, *Dictionary of New Zealand Biography*, vol. 2, 458; 'Obituary: Mr C.C. Graham', *Wairarapa Daily Times*, 28 December 1915, 5; 'Death of Dr Burns', *Evening Star* (*ES*), 8 April 1907, 3; Margaret Morgan, 'Stuart, Donald McNaughton', from DNZB: www.teara.govt.nz/en/biographies/2s50/stuart-donald-mcnaughton; Tom Brooking, 'Burns, Thomas', from DNZB: www.teara.govt.nz/en/biographies/1b52/burns-thomas; Olive Trotter, 'Richardson, John Larkins Cheese', from DNZB: www.teara.govt.nz/en/biographies/1r8/richardson-john-larkins-cheese; Sherwood Young, 'Strode, Alfred Rowland Chetham', from DNZB: www.teara.govt.nz/en/biographies/1s26/strode-alfred-rowland-chetham; Michael Belgrave, 'Hulme Edward', from DNZB: www.teara.govt.nz/en/biographies/1h37/hulme-edward; Blain Biographical Directory of Anglican Clergy in the South Pacific: http://anglicanhistory.org/nz/blain_directory/
18. 'The Otago University: Meeting of the council', *ODT*, 11 November 1869, 2.
19. W.P. Morrell, *The University of Otago: A centennial history* (Dunedin: University of Otago Press, 1969), 14.
20. Anderson, *Education and Opportunity*, 29–36.
21. James Macandrew to University of Otago Council, 10 November 1869, published in *ODT*, 11 November 1869, 2; 'Provincial Council', *ODT*, 31 May 1870, 2; editorial, *ODT*, 3 June 1870, 2; 'Provincial Council', *ODT*, 9 June 1870, 2; 'University of Otago', *ODT*, 20 July 1870, 3. The original Otago Provincial Council motion to support the chair financially was lost, but a second vote a few days later was won.
22. 'Shipping', *ODT*, 22 June 1871, 2; 'University of Otago', *ODT*, 20 July 1870, 3.
23. Thompson, *University of Otago*, 44–57.
24. Opinion of the Attorney-General as to the power of the University of Otago to confer degrees, *Journals and Appendix to the Journals of the Legislative Council of New Zealand*, 1872, 5.
25. The beginnings of the University of New Zealand are recounted in detail in the following works, on which this and the next four paragraphs are based: Beaglehole, *University of New Zealand*; Parton, *University of New Zealand*; and Thompson, *University of Otago*.
26. Parton, *University of New Zealand*, 17.
27. The Queen was not prepared to empower the University of New Zealand to grant more degrees than Melbourne or Sydney, so the New Zealand University Act of 1874 was amended to remove references to degrees in science and 'such other departments of knowledge, except Theology' that the senate 'shall from time to time determine'.
28. 'Otago University', *ODT*, 14 March 1877, 5; Thompson, *University of Otago*, 77–78.
29. James Macandrew to University of Otago Chancellor, 16 May 1878, cited in 'Otago University', *ES*, 8 June 1878, 2; Thompson, *University of Otago*, 78–81.
30. Report of the Royal Commission appointed by His Excellency to inquire into and report upon the operations of the University of New Zealand and its relations to the secondary schools of the colony, *AJHR*, 1880, H-01, 23–24.
31. Beaglehole, *University of New Zealand*, 139.
32. Beaglehole, *University of New Zealand*, 140–56; Parton, *University of New Zealand*, 21–23.
33. Thompson, *University of Otago*, 83–84.
34. 'The Otago University: Meeting of the council', *ODT*, 11 November 1869, 2.
35. Royal Commission on the University of New Zealand, xi.
36. University of Otago Council Election Act, 1891. Existing council members remained in place, with vacancies to be filled by one of the three bodies in set order.
37. 'Meeting of graduates', *ODT*, 5 October 1903, 7; 'University Council', *ODT*, 6 October 1903, 2.
38. 'Otago University Council', *OW*, 10 June 1908, 12; 'University Council', *ODT*, 11 June 1908, 2; 'Reconstructing Otago University Council', *ES*, 24 August 1911, 4; 'Otago University Council', *OW*, 18 October 1911, 7, 9; University of Otago Council Act, 1911.
39. For instance, the Society of Accountants sought representation: see 'Society of Accountants annual meeting', *ODT*, 31 August 1911, 4.
40. Sam Elworthy, *Ritual Song of Defiance: A social history of students at the University of Otago* (Dunedin: Otago University Students' Association, 1990), 56.
41. Muriel May, *Freshly Remembered: Half a century of school* (Christchurch: Whitcombe & Tombs, 1975), 132; Eileen Wallis, 'May, Muriel Wallace', in Thomson, *Southern People*, 335.
42. *University of Otago Calendar* (*UOC*), 1966–1967.
43. Elworthy, *Ritual Song of Defiance*, 106–07, 114–15; University of Otago Amendment Act, 1969.
44. OUSA Executive Annual Report, 1970, OUSA records, MS-0641/0507, Hocken Collections (HC).
45. Interviews with Graeme Fogelberg, David Skegg, Jan Flood.

46. University of Otago Amendment Act, 1977; *UOC*, 1979.
47. Education Amendment Act, 1990; *UOC*, 1990–1995; D W Girvan to Lockwood Smith, 5 October 1994, Vice Chancellor's Office records, MS-4394/439, HC.
48. John Hartevelt, 'Reform eyes cuts to university councils', Stuff, 5 May 2012: www.stuff.co.nz/national/politics/6866103/Reform-eyes-cuts-to-university-councils; Philip Matthews, 'Will sweeping changes improve university?', *Press*, 30 November 2013: www.stuff.co.nz/the-press/news/9460750/Will-sweeping-changes-improve-university
49. Vaughan Elder, 'Labour joins students to protest changes to university governance', *ODT*, 9 October 2013: www.odt.co.nz/news/dunedin/labour-joins-students-protest-changes-university-governance; Jan Flood interview.
50. Laura Munro, 'Council protest fails to retain student voice', *Critic*, 20 July 2015, 6; Carla Green, 'Backlash over university council amendments', *Critic*, 23 February 2015, 11; Joe Higham, 'The backwards step for uni councils', *Critic*, 30 March 2015, 18–19; Timothy Brown, 'Rallying for university council role', *ODT*, 20 March 2015: www.odt.co.nz/news/dunedin/rallying-university-council-role
51. *UOAR*, 2015, 10; 'New University Council meets', Otago Bulletin Board, 9 February 2016: www.otago.ac.nz/otagobulletin/news/otago535401.html
52. Education Amendment Act 1990, 856.
53. *UOC*, 1990, 1992.
54. John Gibb, 'Gender balance queried', *ODT*, 1 November 2015: www.odt.co.nz/news/dunedin/gender-balance-queried; Carla Green, 'University council gender imbalance questioned', *ODT*, 27 January 2016: www.odt.co.nz/news/dunedin/university-council-gender-imbalance-questioned. In accordance with Ward's statement, the next of the council's own appointments was a woman, Carrie Hobson: Sam Stevens, 'A place for all', *University of Otago Magazine* (*UOM*), no. 45, 2017, 36–38.
55. Graeme Fogelberg interview.
56. 'A look at the role of vice-chancellors', *University of Otago Newsletter* (*UON*), May 1981, 1–2.
57. Thompson, *University of Otago*, 144.
58. Robert D. Anderson, Michael Lynch & Nicholas Phillipson, *The University of Edinburgh: An illustrated history* (Edinburgh: Edinburgh University Press, 2003); Clifford Turney, Ursula Bygott & Peter Chippendale, *A History of the University of Sydney*, vol. 1 (Sydney: University of Sydney, 1991); Geoffrey Blainey, *A Centenary History of the University of Melbourne* (Melbourne: Melbourne University Press, 1957); Gardner, *Colonial Cap and Gown*, 12–26; John R. Thelin, *A History of American Higher Education* (Baltimore: Johns Hopkins University Press, 2004), 75–79.
59. *UOAR*, 1870–1876; Thompson, *University of Otago*, 142–44.
60. *Ngai Tahu Report*, xiv-xv.
61. Buddy Mikaere, *Te Maiharoa and the Promised Land* (Auckland: Reed, 1988); Ross Somerville, 'Te Maiharoa, Hipa', from DNZB: www.teara.govt.nz/en/biographies/1t48/te-maiharoa-hipa; D.C. McDonald, 'Campbell, Robert', from DNZB: www.teara.govt.nz/en/biographies/2c4/campbell-robert; 'University Council', *OW*, 17 July 1875, 8.
62. *Treaty of Waitangi Review of the University of Otago* (Dunedin: University of Otago, 1998), 3, 11.
63. Morrell, *University of Otago*, 59–86. William ('Willie') Morrell, Otago history professor, was the son of William Morrell, formerly the chancellor.
64. *UOAR*, 1872–1903; Thompson, *University of Otago*, 143–46.
65. 'Otago University funds: A handsome offer to the university medical school', *ODT*, 2 June 1903, 5; 'Obituary: Mr Wolf Harris', *ODT*, 23 March 1926, 7. Harris, who had been based in London for many years, was well known for his philanthropy to Dunedin causes. All equivalents to historic values in this book are calculated using the Reserve Bank of New Zealand Inflation Calculator: www.rbnz.govt.nz/monetary-policy/inflation-calculator
66. 'Obituary' [James Lothian], *ES*, 30 October 1888, 2; 'Personal items', *OW*, 13 April 1904, 21.
67. Morrell, *University of Otago*, 87–90; Thompson, *University of Otago*, 147–54.
68. R.J. MacLachlan, Director-General of Lands, to Minister of Lands, 11 June 1963, University of Otago Reserves and Endowments file, Department of Education records, R7243084, Archives New Zealand, Wellington. Other documents in this file reveal the ups and downs of income from the endowments, along with plans for the Mararoa and Benmore runs.
69. Thompson, *University of Otago*, 227–28.
70. MacLachlan to Minister of Lands, 11 June 1963.
71. Parton, *University of New Zealand*, 163–78, 242–48; Morrell, *University of Otago*, 223–26; *UOAR*, 1900; and Graham Scott & Simon Smelt, 'Ownership of universities: A paper for consideration by the New Zealand Vice-Chancellors' Committee', 1995, Vice-Chancellor's Office records, MS-4394/437, HC.
72. University Grants Committee Annual Report, *AJHR*, 1975, E-01, 5.
73. *UOAR*, 1979.
74. *UOAR*, 1982.
75. University Grants Committee Annual Report, *AJHR*, 1986–1987, E-03; Ron Crawford, *History of Tertiary Education Reforms in New Zealand* (New Zealand Productivity Commission, 2016); Wendy Larner & Richard Le Heron, 'Neo-liberalizing spaces and subjectivities: Reinventing New Zealand universities', *Organization*, vol. 12, no. 6, 2005, 843–62; Cris Shore, 'The reform of New Zealand's university system: "After neoliberalism"', *Learning and Teaching*, vol. 3, no. 1, 2010, 1–31.
76. *UOAR*, 1990.
77. University Grants Committee Annual Report, *AJHR*, 1990, E-03.
78. *UOAR*, 1880, 1900, 1989; Parton, *University of New Zealand*, 175.
79. Ron Chambers, *Justice and Jellybeans: From Ulster*

policeman to Otago University proctor (Dunedin: Missing Stocks Press, 2006), 137–65.

80. Kyle Matthews, speech at OUSA 125th anniversary celebration, 2015.
81. 'Campus diary', *Otago Graduate*, 1993, 12.
82. Graeme Fogelberg, 'Between a rock and a hard place', *UON*, September 1996, 2. On the registry occupations, see Chambers, *Justice and Jellybeans*, 167–71.
83. Interviews with Graeme Fogelberg and Peter Innes; Jo Galer, 'Crisis looms in dentistry', *UOM*, no. 2, 2002, 10–15; Lisa Allison, 'Dentistry fees may triple', *ODT*, 1 July 1994, 1; John Gibb, 'Failure to consult over dentistry cuts criticised', *ODT*, 6 July 1994, 4; John Gibb, '"Wild-ranging harm" result of dental cuts', *ODT*, 8 July 1994, 5; Tony Smith, 'Dental protest gains support', *ODT*, 18 July 1994, 1; Nicole Jellard, 'High fees seen as a kick in the teeth', *Sunday Star-Times*, 20 October 1996, supplement, 5; John Gibb, 'Dentistry students "outraged" at report', *ODT*, 15 March 1999, 4; John Gibb, 'Dentistry students protest', *ODT*, 19 March 1999, 5.
84. Kyle Matthews, speech at OUSA 125th anniversary celebration, 2015.
85. *UOAR*, 2000, 10, 77.
86. Faculty of Science Annual Report, 1970 to 1972, Records of Registry and Central Administration, AG-180-7/10 and 7/11, HC.
87. 'Developing role for TACS', *UON*, June 1977, 1–2.
88. 'BDC progress', *UON*, June 1979, 5; 'New home for BDC', *UON*, March 1982, 6; 'New director for Business Development Centre', *UON*, October 1986, 5.
89. *UOAR*, 1984; 'Building bridges through ACS', *UON*, January 1986, 1–2.
90. *UOAR*, 1987; 'Commercial activity', *UON*, December 1987, 4–5.
91. David Reade, 'Otago University moves into private research', *Export News*, 9 April 1992, 5–6; John Irving, 'Fuel for thought', *NZ Business*, May 1989, 44–46.
92. 'Commercial activities restructured', *UON*, November 1989, 4–5; 'Commercial activities', *UON*, July 1992, 4; 'Commercial activities', *UON*, April 1993, 5.
93. *UOAR*, 2000, 70.
94. *UOAR*, 2001, 9.
95. 'People, promotion and design crucial to Centre's success', *UON*, May 1999, 1–2.
96. *UOAR*, 2002, 13.
97. 'What is this thing called the Centre for Innovation?', *Otago Bulletin* (*OB*), 6 October 2006, 11.
98. 'First grant awarded by Otago Innovation', *OB*, 23 March 2007, 4; Mark Wright, 'Point to prove', *UOM*, no. 41, 2015, 20–21.
99. Wright, 'Point to prove'.
100. Dorothy Page, *Anatomy of a Medical School: A history of medicine at the University of Otago 1875–2000* (Dunedin: Otago University Press, 2008), 127.
101. Faculty of Medicine Annual Report, 1985 and 1986, Records of Registry and Central Administration, AG-180-7/15, HC; J.V. Hodge, 'Fifty years of health research', *New Zealand Medical Journal*, vol. 100, 1987, 449–52.
102. Derek Dow, 'Medical research', Te Ara – the Encyclopedia of New Zealand: www.teara.govt.nz/en/medical-research; Page, *Anatomy of a Medical School*, 266–67; Dorothy Page interview with George Petersen.
103. Page, *Anatomy of a Medical School*, 85–86, 267.
104. Dow, 'Medical research'; 'Our history', Canterbury Medical Research Foundation: www.cmrf.org.nz/About/; 'About the foundation', Otago Medical Research Foundation: www.omrf.org.nz/about/
105. John Jillett interview; '£43,500 for marine research trawler', *ODT*, 15 November 1963; 'Marine research', *ES*, 18 November 1963; 'Lyttelton firm will build 46ft research trawler', *ODT*, 30 September 1964; 'Marine biology trawler ready this year', *ODT*, 20 October 1965; 'University trawler to be called Munida', *ODT*, 24 November 1965; 'Marine biology: New trawler big aid for research', *ES*, 7 December 1965; 'New skipper joins research trawler', *ODT*, 30 March 1966; all clippings in Portobello Marine Laboratory clippings books, Department of Marine Science records, MS-3302/196 and 199, HC. On the Golden Kiwi lottery, see David Grant, *On a Roll: A history of gambling and lotteries in New Zealand* (Wellington: Victoria University Press, 1994), 220–35.
106. Medical School Annual Report, 1961 and 1963, Records of Registry and Central Administration, AG-180-7/07 and 7/08, HC.
107. *Sci-Tech*, no. 1, 1990 (newsletter of the Ministry of Research, Science and Technology), cited in 'Univord', *UON*, June 1990, 6; *UOAR*, 1992, 5.
108. *UOAR*, 1993, 10.
109. *UOAR*, 1995, 11.
110. *UOAR*, 1999, 11.
111. 'Big grant for university unit', *UON*, August–September 1997, 4.
112. *UOAR*, 1992, 5.
113. Aidan Curzon-Hobson, 'The marginalization of higher learning: An interpretation of current tertiary reform policy in New Zealand', *Teaching in Higher Education*, vol. 9, no. 2, 2004, 211–24; Crawford, *Tertiary Education Reforms*.
114. *A History and Overview of the PBRF* (Wellington: Ministry of Education, 2012): www.education.govt.nz/assets/Documents/Further-education/Policies-and-strategies/Performance-based-research-fund/PBRFHistoryAndOverview.pdf
115. David Skegg interview.
116. John Patrick interview; *UOAR*, 2009; Dene Mackenzie, 'Science, innovation roles for academics', *ODT*, 6 January 2011: www.odt.co.nz/business/science-innovation-roles-academics; John Gibb, 'Big Otago role in science challenges', *ODT*, 2 April 2014: www.odt.co.nz/news/dunedin/big-otago-role-science-challenges; Timothy Brown, '$14.6m grant, and "more to come" for university': *ODT*, 5 March 2015, www.odt.co.nz/news/dunedin/146m-grant-and-more-come-university; Vaughan Elder, 'Further boost for Otago health sciences', *ODT*, 24 November 2015: www.odt.co.nz/news/dunedin/further-boost-otago-health-sciences; Vaughan Elder,

'Magnitude of health challenge highlighted', *ODT*, 5 December 2015: www.odt.co.nz/news/dunedin/magnitude-health-challenge-highlighted. The funding for Centres of Research Excellence and National Science Challenges came through the Ministry of Business, Innovation and Employment, whose predecessor, the Department of Science and Innovation, had taken over the operation of public good science funding previously run by FoRST.

117. John Patrick interview.
118. Interviews with Graeme Fogelberg and David Skegg; 'Advancement campaign on the go', *OB*, 12 June 2003, 1; 'Funding boost recognises Otago's research strength', *OB*, 12 December 2003, 1–2; 'Leading thinkers programme celebrated', *OB*, 30 November 2007, 13; Alison Finigan (ed.), *Partnerships for Excellence: Celebrating 10 years of the Leading Thinkers initiative* (Dunedin: Development & Alumni Relations Office, University of Otago, 2014). See chapters 6 to 10 for discussion of the various projects funded.
119. Morrell, *University of Otago*, 160–61; Yvonne Wilkie, *Weaving Vision, Heritage and Hope: 150 years of the Presbyterian Synod of Otago and Southland 1866 to 2016* (Dunedin: Synod of Otago & Southland, Presbyterian Church of Aotearoa New Zealand, 2016), 145–51; Dorothy Page to author, 23 November 2017.
120. 'The Otago University: Meeting of the council', *ODT*, 11 November 1869, 2; 'Departmental', *ES*, 9 August 1871, 2; Council minutes, 15 May 1873, University of Otago Records of Registry and Central Administration, AG-180-1/01, HC.
121. Simon Wilson, 'A useable collection: The origins and growth of the University of Otago library', in *Culture of Change: Beginnings at the University of Otago* (Dunedin: Departments of English & History, University of Otago, 2006), 1–19.
122. 'Educational', *ODT*, 16 June 1873, 4; 'The late Henry Clapcott', *ES*, 21 September 1897, 2; 'The late Mr W.H. Mansford', *ODT*, 24 May 1890, 4.
123. G.S. Parsonson, 'Hamilton, Augustus', in Thomson, *Southern People*, 207; R.K. Dell, 'Hamilton, Augustus', from DNZB: www.teara.govt.nz/en/biographies/2h8/hamilton-augustus
124. Richard Boast, 'Garrow, James Mitchell Ellis', from DNZB: www.teara.govt.nz/en/biographies/3g3/garrow-james-mitchell-ellis
125. *ES*, 26 December 1912, 4.
126. Thompson, *University of Otago*, 216; 'A look at the role of vice-chancellors', *UON*, May 1981, 1–2.
127. *UOAR*, 1914, 25.
128. See chapters 6 to 8 for details of these developments.
129. Report of the Faculty of Arts, Science and Music, 1943; Joint report of the Faculty of Arts and Music and Faculty of Science, 1944, Records of Registry and Central Administration, AG-180-7/02 and 7/03, HC.
130. Morrell, *University of Otago*, 157–58; 'A look at the role of vice-chancellors'.
131. Geoffry Billing to Allan Fisher, 25 April 1946, Allan Fisher papers, MS-4304/282, HC.
132. *UOAR*, 1945 and 1947.
133. Raymond Hoffenberg, 'Robert Stevenson (Sir) Aitken', Munk's Roll, http://munksroll.rcplondon.ac.uk/Biography/Details/49; 'Sir Robert Aitken dies', *UON*, June–July 1997, 7.
134. 'Of vice-chancellors', *Otago University Review* (*OUR*), 1953, 4.
135. Arts Faculty Annual Report, 1953, Records of Registry and Central Administration, AG-180-7/05, HC.
136. Page, *Anatomy of a Medical School*, 151–52.
137. Hoffenberg, 'Robert Stevenson (Sir) Aitken'.
138. 'New Vice-Chancellor', *OUR*, 1954, 12; F.G. Soper, 'University of Otago: Ten years as vice-chancellor 1954 to 1963', Frederick Soper papers, 90–161, Box 2, HC; 'Obituary: Professor F.G. Soper', *UON*, February 1982, 2; Joy Soper, 'Soper, Frederick George', in Thomson, *Southern People*, 472.
139. Vaughan Elder, 'Courage of convictions was a mark of the man', *ODT*, 25 August 2012, 36; 'University mourns passing of Arthur Beacham', Murdoch University: http://media.murdoch.edu.au/university-mourns-passing-of-arthur-beacham; Tim Gray interview; Morrell, *University of Otago*, 227–33.
140. 'Leading NZ scientist worked on development of atomic bomb', *Dominion Post*, 23 March 2013, C15; John Gibb, 'From medical school to Manhattan project', *ODT*, 28 June 2013, 32; Dorothy Page interview with Robin Williams; George Petersen interview.
141. Page, *Anatomy of a Medical School*, 179; '... and New Year honours', *UON*, February 1989, 3; Judith Medlicott, 'Sir Robin Irvine', *UON*, October 1996, 8; J.D. Hunter, 'Irvine, Robin Orlando Hamilton', Royal Australasian College of Physicians College Roll, http://members.racp.edu.au/page/library/college-roll/college-roll-detail&id=14
142. 'New year – new management system', *UON*, February 1989, 1–2; *UOAR*, 1989.
143. Interviews with John Patrick, George Petersen, David Richardson, Alan Musgrave, Jim Flynn, Lyall McLean, Alan Geare.
144. Graeme Fogelberg interview; Anne French, 'Profile of a strategist: Graeme Fogelberg', *New Zealand Strategic Management*, vol. 1, no. 2, 1994, 13–19.
145. Proposal for restructuring the senior management of the University of Otago, Vice-Chancellor's Office records, MS-4394/409, HC.
146. *UOC*, 1965–1992; 'Richard Mulgan: Acting vice-chancellor', *UON*, September 1986, 3–4; 'Second Pro-Vice-Chancellor', *UON*, February 1992, 2.
147. Proposal for restructuring the senior management.
148. 'DVC Research and International has client focus', *UON*, February 1995, 1; 'Quality – the key word of the new DVC (Academic)', *UON*, December 1994, 1; 'Quality teaching to quality retirement', *OB*, 3 December 2004, 2.
149. 'The end of an era', *UON*, December 1974, 1–2; 'Change of registrar', *UON*, February 1975, 2–5; 'Dr John Waddell Hayward', *UON*, October 1996, 8; 'On rocks, rolls and rapid change', *UON*, July 1995, 10; 'Highly regarded former registrar dies', *OB*, 4 November 2005, 5.

150. Interviews with Tim Gray and Jan Flood; 'Former registrar committed for trial', *ODT*, 24 June 1999, 8; 'Former registrar to do 200 hours' community service', *ODT*, 4 December 1999, 4; Blair Mayston, 'Former registrar notes change', *ODT*, 5 February 2002, 6.
151. 'New administrative post', *OB*, 3 December 2004, 9.
152. 'New head of international announced', *OB*, 17 November 2006, 1; 'Farewell: Deputy vice-chancellor, Dr Ian Smith', *OB*, 23 April 2004, 4.
153. David Skegg interview; Nicola Mutch, 'Rhodes 1972: David Skegg', *UOM*, no. 3, 2002, 20; David Skegg, 'VC highlights', interview notes for *UOM*, 3 May 2011; Nicola Mutch, 'Leaving legend', *UOM*, no. 29, 2011, 13–16.
154. Harlene Hayne interview; 'Next Deputy Vice-Chancellor', *OB*, 5 Sept 2008, 2; Harlene Hayne to University of Otago staff, 22 January 2015; Timothy Brown, 'Key urges students to give it 100%', *ODT*, 18 February 2015: www.odt.co.nz/news/dunedin/key-urges-students-give-it-100; 'Vice-Chancellor among Marsden recipients', Otago Bulletin Board, 5 November 2015: www.otago.ac.nz/otagobulletin/news/otago272601.html
155. Mark Wright, 'Rules of engagement', *UOM*, no. 42, 2016, 13–15.
156. 'Support Services Review: Final decision overview', 12 October 2017 and 'FAQs': www.otago.ac.nz/support-services-review/index.html; Margot Taylor, 'Uni job cut plan labelled "drastic"', *ODT*, 13 October 2017: www.odt.co.nz/news/campus/university-of-otago/uni-job-cut-plan-labelled-'drastic'
157. 'Farewell: Deputy vice-chancellor, Dr Ian Smith', *OB*, 23 April 2004, 4.
158. John Patrick interview.

2: THE STUDENTS

1. David Hamer, 'Stout, Robert', from DNZB: www.teara.govt.nz/en/biographies/2s48/stout-robert; Margaret Tennant, 'MacGregor, Duncan', from DNZB: www.teara.govt.nz/en/biographies/2m7/macgregor-duncan. For the date of Stout's admission to the bar, see *ODT*, 5 July 1871, 2. Stout himself claimed to be the first student to enrol and Thompson recognised him as the first; see G.E. Thompson, *A History of the University of Otago (1869–1919)* (Dunedin: Wilkie, 1919), 62.
2. 'University of Otago', *ODT*, 6 December 1871, 2. There are no surviving lists of students for the early years in the university archives, though there is a tally for 1871 which includes some names: 'Students of 1871 classed', Inwards Letters, Records of Registry and Central Administration, AG-180-27/02, HC. Some names (but not of those who paid fees in a timely fashion) appeared in the university cash book and others are in surviving letters to the university council secretary, where they stated their intention to enrol.
3. D.M. Stuart to J.L.C. Richardson, 6 November 1871, Toitū Otago Settlers Museum, cited in W.P. Morrell, *The University of Otago: A centennial history* (Dunedin: University of Otago Press, 1969), 42.
4. 'Students of 1871 classed'.
5. *ES*, 1 April 1878, 2; Gustav Hirsch, letter to the editor, *ES*, 2 April 1878, 2.
6. 'Death of the Engineer-in-Chief', *Bruce Herald*, 21 March 1907, 5; Peter Lowe, 'Hay, Peter Seton', from DNZB: www.teara.govt.nz/en/biographies/2h24/hay-peter-seton (this essay states that Hay was the first graduate of the University of Otago, but that honour belongs to Alexander Williamson).
7. 'The varsity's "one and only" graduate', *ES*, 3 February 1920, supplement, 5; Amy Coleman, 'Otago's first graduate: 1874', in Stuart Strachan & Linda Tyler (eds), *Kā Taoka Hākena: Treasures from the Hocken Collections* (Dunedin: Otago University Press, 2007), 48.
8. 'Students of 1871 classed'.
9. Thomas Hutchison obituary, *Press*, 7 September 1929, 15.
10. 'The late Sir John Denniston', *Star* (Christchurch), 22 July 1919, 4; 'Stewart, William Downie (1842–1898) and family', in Jane Thomson (ed.), *Southern People: A dictionary of Otago Southland biography* (Dunedin: Longacre Press, 1998), 483–84.
11. *Register (Fasti) of New Zealand Presbyterian Ministers, Deaconesses & Missionaries 1840 to 2015*, Archives Research Centre, Presbyterian Church of Aotearoa New Zealand: www.presbyterian.org.nz/archives/page143.htm
12. Alexander Watt Williamson papers, Misc-MS-0454/001, HC; F.O. Bennet, 'Mary Cuddie', in G.J. Griffiths (ed.), *The Advance Guard: Series II* (Dunedin: Otago Daily Times, 1974), 151–78.
13. Bennett, 'Mary Cuddie'.
14. 'The Otira tunnel: Peter Seton Hay, MA, MICE – An appreciation by "X"', *OW*, 21 August 1923, 59.
15. *Register (Fasti) of New Zealand Presbyterian Ministers*; 'News of the week', *OW*, 15 July 1871, 14; *ODT*, 2 May 1872, 2.
16. 'Cecil Yates Biss', *British Medical Journal*, no. 2666, 3 February 1912, 282; 'Cecil Yates Biss', *Royal College of Physicians: Lives of the fellows*: http://munksroll.rcplondon.ac.uk/Biography/Details/411; Family information thanks to Alan Biss, Peter Lineham to author, 16 October 2016.
17. Selina Chapman and 148 others to University of Otago council, 31 July 1871, Inwards letters, Records of Registry and Central Administration, AG-180-27/02, HC; 'The Otago University', *ES*, 12 August 1871, 2.
18. W.J. Gardner, *Colonial Cap and Gown: Studies in the mid-Victorian universities of Australasia* (Christchurch: University of Canterbury, 1979), 73.
19. Eileen Wallis, *A Most Rare Vision: Otago Girls' High School – the first 125 years* (Dunedin: Otago Girls' High School Board of Trustees, 1995), 9–23; Dorothy Page, 'The first lady graduates: Women with degrees from Otago University, 1885–1900', in Barbara Brookes, Charlotte Macdonald & Margaret Tennant (eds), *Women In History 2* (Wellington: Bridget Williams Books, 1992), 98–128; Dorothy Page, 'Dalrymple, Learmonth White', from DNZB: www.teara.govt.nz/en/biographies/1d2/dalrymple-learmonth-white

20. John Richardson to Selina Chapman, 10 August 1871, Records of Registry and Central Administration, Letter book, AG 180-30/01, HC.
21. Felicity Hunt & Carol Barker, *Women at Cambridge: A brief history* (Cambridge: University of Cambridge Press, 1998), ii.
22. Gardner, *Colonial Cap and Gown*, 79–81.
23. *ODT*, 3 May 1872, 2; 4 May 1872, 2; 9 May 1872, 2.
24. 'University of Otago', *ODT*, 31 October 1872, 2; 'The varsity's "one and only" graduate'; 'University of Otago', *ODT*, 31 October 1873, 2.
25. 'The late Mr George Elliott Barton', *ES*, 4 June 1903, 7; S.A. Prentice, 'Barton, Edward Gustavus Campbell (1857–1942)', Australian Dictionary of Biography: http://adb.anu.edu.au/biography/barton-edward-gustavus-campbell-9445/text16607. Edward Barton appeared among the successful students listed in *ODT*, 31 October 1872, 2 and 25 November 1874, 2.
26. 'University of Otago', *ODT*, 1 November 1872, 2; 'University of Otago', *ODT*, 31 October 1873, 2. An obituary of John Langmuir senior (*ES*, 2 March 1877, 2) notes that he arrived from Victoria in 1863; the index to Victoria shipping records shows the family party which arrived in Otago on the *Ceylon* in 1863 included John junior, aged 7 years, and Margaret, aged 11 years.
27. 'University of Otago', *ODT*, 17 November 1875, 2; Page, 'First lady graduates'; Dorothy Page, 'Freeman, Caroline', from DNZB: www.teara.govt.nz/en/biographies/2f26/freeman-caroline
28. Page, 'First lady graduates'.
29. John Hislop to Mr Paterson, 31 March 1871, Letter book, Records of Registry and Central Administration, AG-180-30/01, HC.
30. *UOAR*, 1873. The University of New Zealand took over control of matriculation from 1880.
31. A. Livingston to Benjamin Wells, 22 March 1872, Letter book, Records of Registry and Central Administration, AG-180-30/01, HC.
32. Henry Clapcott to Professors Sale, MacGregor, Shand and Black, 30 May 1873 and 2 June 1873, Letter book, Records of Registry and Central Administration, AG-180-30/01, HC; 'Otago University Council', *ODT*, 5 November 1895, 3.
33. *UOAR*, 1885, 1901.
34. *UOC*, 1882, 27–29; 'University of Otago', *OW*, 6 May 1871, 17; 'Centenary of Sir Walter Scott', *ODT*, 10 August 1871, 2–3; 'Higher education for women', *OW*, 8 June 1872, 2; *UOAR*, 1893; Page, 'First lady graduates'.
35. 'Presentations to pupil teachers', *Bruce Herald*, 4 March 1879, 5; 'Matriculation: successful candidates', *ES*, 5 May 1879, 2.
36. Thompson, *University of Otago*, 57–58.
37. M.P.K. Sorrenson, 'Buck, Peter Henry', from DNZB: www.teara.govt.nz/en/biographies/3b54/buck-peter-henry; Irwin K. Jackson, 'Wi Repa, Tutere', from DNZB: www.teara.govt.nz/en/biographies/3w12/wi-repa-tutere; D.W. Carmalt Jones, *Annals of the University of Otago Medical School 1875–1939* (Wellington: Reed, 1945), 114–16; Dorothy Page, *Anatomy of a Medical School: A history of medicine at the University of Otago 1875–2000* (Dunedin: Otago University Press, 2008), 52–53.
38. Sean Ellison & Thomas Brons, 'Ellison, Edward Pohau', from DNZB: www.teara.govt.nz/en/biographies/4e9/ellison-edward-pohau
39. 'A Maori funeral', ODT, 20 January 1908, 2; Rei Owens, 'Taiaroa family', in Thomson, *Southern People*, 493–94.
40. John Broughton, 'Evans, Ani Parata', in Thomson, *Southern People*, 151; John Broughton interview.
41. Mere Montgomery, *Otago University Maori Club 1972 to 1975* (Dunedin: M. Montgomery, 1993); interviews with John Broughton and Mere Montgomery.
42. 'A Maori health nurse: The health work of Emere Makere Waiwaha Kaa Mountain', in Sandra Coney, *Standing in the Sunshine: A history of New Zealand women since they won the vote* (Auckland: Viking, 1993), 102–3; A.G. Strong, *History of the Development of University Education in Home Science in New Zealand 1911–1936* (Dunedin: University of Otago, 1937), 38.
43. John Harré, 'A survey of the performance of Maori students at the University of Otago', 1967, Records of Registry and Central Administration, AG-180-7/09, HC.
44. *Roll of the Graduates of the University of Otago* (Dunedin: University of Otago, 1989); 'Ratu Dr J.A.R. Dovi', *Pacific Islands Monthly*, December 1971, 112; Kamisese Mara, *The Pacific Way: A memoir* (Honolulu: University of Hawai`i Press, 1997); Anand Satyanand, 'Mutyala Satyanand', *New Zealand Medical Journal*, vol. 116, no. 1168, 2003, 318; Nicola Mutch, 'Distant education', *UOM*, no. 18, 2007, 22–24.
45. 'Honorary doctorate for former Cook Islands PM', *OB*, 20 May 2005, 1.
46. Heather Young Leslie, 'Pushing children up: Maternal obligation, modernity, and medicine in the Tongan ethnoscape', in Victoria Lockwood (ed.), *Globalization and Culture Change in the Pacific Islands* (Upper Saddle River, New Jersey: Pearson, 2004), 390–412.
47. Overseas students by country of origin, University Grants Committee records, R12485704, Archives New Zealand, Wellington.
48. University of Otago enrolment statistics, 1986–89, courtesy of University of Otago Planning and Funding Office; *UOAR*, 1996–2016.
49. Christine Berry, *The Zealand Student Christian Movement, 1896–1996: A centennial history* (Christchurch: Student Christian Movement of Aotearoa, 1998), 3; 'Student from Africa', *New Zealand Herald*, 17 January 1931, 12; 'Negro student to enter medical school', *Press*, 13 March 1931, 13; Darrell M. Newton, *Paving the Empire Road: BBC television and black Britons* (Manchester: Manchester University Press, 2011); David Killingray, 'Rights, land, and labour: Black British critics of South African policies before 1948', *Journal of Southern African Studies*, vol. 35, 2009, 375–98. Piliso also received support from the University of New Zealand Senate, which excused him from examination fees, and from Knox College, which provided subsidised accommodation. The minister of education was happy

with Piliso's admission but not willing to fund a bursary: 'we have no responsibility either direct or indirect with regard to the South African native, and I do not see how the education of such a native should be a charge against New Zealand'. See Statement from Minister of Education, 9 January 1931, Students from Overseas Attending New Zealand Universities, Remission of Fees, Education Department records, R18178076, Archives New Zealand, Wellington.

50. *UOAR*, 1961.
51. 'Arrival of African students', *External Affairs Review*, vol. 11, no. 2, 1961, 26; Benedict Okagbue Mba, 'The evolution of Nigerian independence (with reference to British contributions) 1945–1960', MA thesis in history, University of Otago, 1965; Moses Siyanbola Olayinka, 'Review of the education of teachers in England, New Zealand and Nigeria (with special reference to the problems of teacher education in Nigeria)', MA thesis in education, University of Otago, 1965.
52. Overseas students by country of origin; Sam Elworthy, *Ritual Song of Defiance: A social history of students at the University of Otago* (Dunedin: Otago University Students' Association, 1990), 89, 114; 'Ebraima Manneh is Gambia's new ambassador to America', The Point, 14 March 2017: http://thepoint.gm/africa/gambia/article/ebraima-manneh-is-gambias-new-ambassador-to-america
53. Georgina Sargison, 'Saris in a cold climate: Colombo Plan students at the University of Otago', in *Culture of Change: Beginnings at the University of Otago* (Dunedin: Department of History, University of Otago, 2006), 95–118; Jenny Collins, 'Perspectives from the periphery? Colombo Plan students in New Zealand universities, 1951–1975', *History of Education Review*, vol. 41, no. 2, 2012, 128–46.
54. Eva Wong Ng, 'Pih-Chang, Kathleen (1903–1991)', in Thomson, *Southern People*, 389.
55. Interviews with James Ng and Peter Chin.
56. James Ng, *Windows on a Chinese Past*, Vol. 3 (Dunedin: Otago Heritage Books, 1999), 222–23; James Ng interview.
57. University of Otago enrolment statistics, 1986.
58. *The Colombo Plan at 50: A New Zealand perspective* (Wellington: New Zealand Official Development Assistance, Ministry of Foreign Affairs & Trade, 2001); John Gerritsen, 'Fruits of the plan', *New Zealand Education Review*, 10 August 2001, 10–11; Sargison, 'Saris in a cold climate'.
59. Overseas students by country of origin.
60. Sargison, 'Saris in a cold climate'.
61. Gerritsen, 'Fruits of the plan'; Nigel Zega, 'Being different', *UOM*, no. 25, 2010, 14–16; *Colombo Plan at 50*, 15–16.
62. *Colombo Plan at 50*, 18–19.
63. John Mackie to Gill Parata, 14 December 1997, Vice-Chancellor's Office records, MS-4394/174, HC.
64. 'Tribute: Dr Sulaiman Daud', *UOM*, no. 26, 2010, 44.
65. David Thomson to author, 2 November 2016.
66. University of Otago Student Headcount by Division 1920–2010, statistics courtesy of David Thomson, Director, Planning and Funding.
67. Science completions by gender, 18 February 2016, statistics courtesy of David Thomson, director, Planning and Funding.
68. David Thomson to author, 2 November 2016.
69. Figures on the gender of students from the 2015 annual reports of Auckland, AUT, Lincoln, Otago, Victoria and Waikato universities. Canterbury statistics courtesy of Business Insight Reporting, University of Canterbury, 7 November 2016. Figures for Massey were not available.
70. Elworthy, *Ritual Song of Defiance*, 131–38. On the tensions resulting from the OUSA's creation of a women's room, see also Kiri Cochrane, 'A room of one's own: A feminist space at the University of Otago', in *Culture of Change*, 119–33.
71. Malcolm McKinnon, *Independence and Foreign Policy: New Zealand in the world since 1935* (Auckland: Auckland University Press, 1993), 266–68.
72. McKinnon, *Independence and Foreign Policy*, 266–68; Nicholas Tarling, *International Students in New Zealand: The making of policy since 1950* (Auckland: New Zealand Asian Institute, University of Auckland, 2004), 9–100; Andrew Pieter Butcher, 'No place like home: The experiences of South-East Asian international university students in New Zealand and their re-entry into their countries of origin', PhD thesis, Massey University, 2002, 25–45.
73. 'Overseas students', *UON*, June 1979, 6.
74. University of Otago enrolment statistics, 1981–89; *UOAR*, 1990–99.
75. Tarling, *International Students*, 101–221; Neville Bennett, *Asian Students in New Zealand* (Wellington: Institute of Policy Studies, Victoria University of Wellington, 1998), 24–37; Butcher, 'No place like home', 59–64.
76. University Grants Committee Annual Report, *AJHR*, 1987–1990, E3, 6.
77. *UOAR*, 2000.
78. *UOAR*, 1996, 2003; 'Preliminary enrolment figures', *OB*, 21 April 2006, 4.
79. Vaughan Elder, 'Joyce urges action on student numbers', *ODT*, 12 September 2012: www.odt.co.nz/news/dunedin/joyce-urges-action-student-numbers; 'Preliminary enrolment figures', *OB*, 21 April 2006, 4; Carla Green, 'Increase in new overseas students', *ODT*, 23 April 2015: www.odt.co.nz/news/dunedin/increase-new-overseas-students. For the impact of the drop in international students at Waikato, for instance, see Noeline Alcorn, *Ko te Tangata: A history of the University of Waikato, the first fifty years* (Wellington: Steele Roberts, 2014), 261.
80. Statistics from *UOAR*, 1995–2015; 'Malay millions at risk', *Times Higher Education Supplement*, 14 November 1997, 1.
81. 'Study Abroad students helping offset decline in Malaysian numbers at Otago', *UON*, May 1999, 7. Bannister subsequently became president of Hawai`i Pacific University: see 'Otago graduate elected university president', *ODT*, 24 January 2011: www.odt.co.nz/news/dunedin/otago-graduate-elected-university-president

82. Harlene Hayne, 'Vice-Chancellor's comment', *UOM*, no. 43, 2016, 4.
83. 'Obituary: Gill Parata, 1947–2003', *OB*, 17 October 2003, 6; 'More than recruitment' and 'Varied role for new PVC', *OB*, 20 March 2008, 6; Mark Wright, 'Rules of engagement', *UOM*, no. 42, 2016, 13–15.
84. Nancy Swarbrick, 'Primary and secondary education', Te Ara – the Encyclopedia of New Zealand: www.teara.govt.nz/en/primary-and-secondary-education
85. John Hislop to R. Cameron, 26 July 1871, Letter book, Records of Registry and Central Administration, AG-180-30/01, HC.
86. *UOC*, 1920–1989.
87. OUSA circular to members, 1990, OUSA records, MS-4240/529, HC; Stephen Hamilton, *A Radical tradition: A history of the Victoria University of Wellington Students' Association 1899–1999* (Wellington: Steele Roberts, 2002), 208–10. Fees were determined by the University Council each year and changed so often that they were no longer published in the *UOC* but in separate fees brochures.
88. *UOAR*, 1993, 7.
89. 'Who are our students?', text of radio talk by Lindsay Wright, broadcast on YC-9.43, 27 August 1970, OUSA records, MS-0641/640, HC.
90. *Report of the Committee on New Zealand Universities, December 1959* (Wellington: Government Printer, 1960).
91. Report of Royal Commission on University Education in New Zealand, *AJHR*, 1925, E–7a; 'The night school on the Leith', *ODT*, 18 June 1923, 9.
92. University Grants Committee Annual Report, *AJHR*, 1962, E–3; Elworthy, *Ritual Song of Defiance*, 99, 124; Otago statistics from *UOAR* and enrolment data.
93. Kerryn Pollock, 'Tertiary sector reform from the 1980s', Te Ara – the Encyclopedia of New Zealand: www.teara.govt.nz/en/tertiary-education/page–4; Katie Kenny, 'The birth of student loans', *Critic*, 7 May 2012: www.critic.co.nz/features/article/1925/the-birth-of-student-loans; Laura Munro, 'Government offers 90c to solve rent crisis', *Critic*, 30 March 2015, 4; Joe Higham, 'Student loans: Past and present', *Critic*, 27 April 2015, 6–7; Otago statistics from *UOAR*.
94. Calculated for figures for 2013 to 2015 from University of Auckland Annual Report, 2015, 8; *UOAR*.
95. *UOAR*, 2000 and 2016.
96. *UOAR*, 1871–2010.
97. *UOAR*, 2005, 13.
98. *UOAR*, 2006, 13.
99. *UOAR*, 2010, 14; 2011, 13.
100. Jo Moir, 'Higher entrance standards result in fewer students', Stuff, 30 January 2015: www.stuff.co.nz/national/education/65575139/higher-entrance-standards-result-in-fewer-students
101. 'Enrolments for 2015 announced', Otago Bulletin Board, 1 April 2015: www.otago.ac.nz/otagobulletin/news/otago089838.html
102. 'Canterbury University offers generous incentives to attract students', Stuff, 19 October 2015: www.stuff.co.nz/national/73134982/canterbury-university-offers-generous-incentives-to-attract-students
103. John Gibb, 'University boosts scholarship values', *ODT*, 15 July 2015: www.odt.co.nz/news/campus/university-of-otago/university-boosts-scholarship-values
104. *UOAR*, 2015, 14.
105. Ibid.
106. *UOAR*, 2009, 15.
107. *UOAR*, 2007, 13; 'Otago breaks 1000 PhD barrier', *OB*, 10 September 2007, 1; 'PhD 1000 Gala Ball', *OB*, 5 October 2007, 5.
108. J.C. Beaglehole, *The University of New Zealand: An historical study* (Wellington: New Zealand Council for Educational Research, 1937), 278–79; Hugh Parton, *The University of New Zealand* (Auckland: Auckland University Press for the University Grants Committee, 1979), 185–86; *UOAR*, 2008, 15.
109. 'Snippets', *UON*, February 1995, 20.
110. *UOAR*, 1995; 'By degrees', *UON*, August 1994, 13.
111. 'Graduation milestone', *UON*, June 1996, 8. The count began in 1962, following the abolition of the University of New Zealand.
112. Personal communication with David Murray, who graduated with PhD number 2006 in December 2005; *UOC*, 2015.

3: STUDENT LIFE

1. Cathrin Schaer, 'Academy awards', *More*, January 1993, 51–56.
2. Sam Elworthy, *Ritual Song of Defiance: A social history of students at the University of Otago* (Dunedin: Otago University Students' Association, 1990), 9, 19–20.
3. 'The varsity's "one and only" graduate', *ES*, 3 February 1920, supplement, 5.
4. Elworthy, *Ritual Song of Defiance*, 19–24.
5. Ibid., 24–27; 'The Otago University Students' Association', in *Otago University Review (Special Number): A history of the Otago University during its minority* (Dunedin: OUSA, 1893), 43–48.
6. Elworthy, *Ritual Song of Defiance*, 26–28, 36. On the 1983 women's room, see Kiri Cochrane, 'A room of one's own: A feminist space at the University of Otago', in *Culture of Change: Beginnings at the University of Otago* (Dunedin: Departments of English & History, University of Otago, 2006), 119–33.
7. M.A. Jennings, *Aunt Pearl's Story* (Suva: M. Jennings, 1981), 10.
8. Elworthy, *Ritual Song of Defiance*, 35; 'Executive notes', *OUR*, May 1902, 12–13.
9. Agnes Blackie, 'Student days', Blackie family papers, MS–4443/002, HC.
10. Elworthy, *Ritual Song of Defiance*, 47, 51.
11. 'OUSA life members', OUSA: http://ousa.org.nz/home/history/ousa-life-members/
12. 'History', OUSA: http://ousa.org.nz/home/history/
13. *UOAR*, 1908.

14. 'University of Otago: Opening of Oliver wing and students' building', *ODT*, 8 April 1914, 2.
15. 'University bazaar', *ODT*, 12 August 1909, 5.
16. 'University of Otago: Opening'.
17. 'New look union', *UON*, January 1986, 10; 'Starting the year with a fizz', *UON*, March 1987, 7; 'University Union ... looking better than ever', *UON*, March 1995, 10–11.
18. Papers relating to the University Book Shop, Harold Turner papers, MS-1431-002/659, HC; 'University Bookshop taken over', *ODT*, 13 April 1962, 3; Kyle Matthews, speech at OUSA 125th anniversary celebration, 2015; Elworthy, *Ritual Song of Defiance*, 129.
19. Neil Howard, 'Life at university – fifties style', unpublished reminiscences.
20. 'Cafeteria', *University of Otago Students' Handbook*, 1960, 16.
21. University of Otago Union price list, 1976, OUSA records, MS-4233/011, HC.
22. 'University Union ... looking better than ever'.
23. Sylvia Keane, 'Memories of home science in the twenties', School of Consumer and Applied Sciences records, MS-3890, Box 12, HC.
24. Interview with Nancy and Melville Carr.
25. 'Eating out', *OUSA Orientation Handbook*, 1975, 59–60.
26. Elworthy, *Ritual Song of Defiance*, 130.
27. Christine Berry, *The New Zealand Student Christian Movement, 1896–1996: A centennial history* (Christchurch: Student Christian Movement of Aotearoa, 1998), 1–3.
28. Blackie, 'Student days'.
29. Elworthy, *Ritual Song of Defiance*, 33. I have heard the SCM and TSCF 'alternative' meanings through people in my own family who met their partners through these organisations.
30. Stuart Lange, *A Rising Tide: Evangelical Christianity in New Zealand 1930–65* (Dunedin: Otago University Press, 2013), 42–48.
31. 'Catholic Students' Club', *New Zealand Tablet*, 15 December 1921, 23; 'Dunedin Catholic Students' Club', *ODT*, 5 October 1922, 8.
32. Anna Davin, 'Community, life-cycle, diaspora: A daughter's view', in Barbara Brookes & Dorothy Page (eds), *Communities of Women: Historical perspectives* (Dunedin: Otago University Press, 2002), 13–26.
33. 'Religious needs of students', Vice-Chancellor's Office records, MS-4394/612, HC; Cathy Heenan, 'Muslim students make transition to university campus', *ODT*, 27 July 1995, 22; Glenda Price, 'Muslims get into games', *ODT*, 6 July 1996, 5; 'Muslim Students Assn', OUSA: http://ousa.org.nz/recreation/clubs/club-details/123/; 'What I wish you knew', *Critic*, 7 September 2015, 20–23. The room set aside for prayer seems to have moved around, and in 2009 students welcomed the setting aside of a 'permanent' prayer space by the university: see 'Prayer space welcomed', *OB*, 20 February 2009, 3.
34. 'Our association', Otago Muslim Association: https://otagomuslimassociation.wordpress.com/about/
35. *Otago Students' Almanac*, 1980, 130, 139–40.
36. 'OUSA clubs', OUSA: http://ousa.org.nz/recreation/clubs/
37. *Otago University Rugby Football Club 1886–1969* (Dunedin: Light Blues Association, 1969), 5–9.
38. George Griffiths, *Otago University at Cricket: Its history, records and statistics* (Dunedin: Otago Heritage Books, 1978).
39. 'The Otago University Lawn Tennis Club', in *OUR: A history of Otago University during its minority*, 62–63.
40. 'Basket ball', *ES*, 11 May 1914, 6.
41. 'Basket ball', *ODT*, 16 August 1915, 3; 'Basket ball tournament', *ES*, 19 October 1915, 9; Suzanne McFadden, 'Netball', Te Ara – the Encyclopedia of New Zealand: www.teara.govt.nz/en/netball
42. 'Tramping club', *OUR*, 1930, 78.
43. 'Tramping club', *OUR*, 1947, 65.
44. Arthur Porritt to Sam Elworthy, 23 May 1989, OUSA centenary file, OUSA records, MS-4240/319, HC.
45. Diana Beaglehole, 'Porritt, Arthur Espie', from DNZB: www.teara.govt.nz/en/biographies/5p34/porritt-arthur-espie
46. 'The Inter-'Varsity Athletic Tournament', *OUR*, May 1902, 23–28.
47. Elworthy, *Ritual Song of Defiance*, 32.
48. Otago University Amateur Athletic Association minute book, 1902–1916, 82–145, HC; 'The Inter-'Varsity Athletic Tournament', *OUR*, May 1902, 23–28.
49. 'University sport', *OUR*, September 1923, 72.
50. 'Harrier Club', *OUR*, September 1930, 76.
51. Roger Robinson, 'Lovelock, John Edward', from DNZB: www.teara.govt.nz/en/biographies/4l14/lovelock-john-edward
52. 'Affiliated clubs to OUSA 1991', OUSA records, MS-4240/687, HC.
53. OUSA clubs list: www.ousa.org.nz/recreation/clubs/
54. Interviews with Rex Thomson and Doug Booth.
55. 'Otago's captaincy treble', *UON*, July 1998, 12.
56. Craig Page, 'Aquatic centre launched', *ODT*, 27 May 2002, 10; 'New berth for scarfie scullers', *Architecture New Zealand*, March/April 2003, 24–27; Mark Wright, 'Winning strokes', *UOM*, no. 39, 2014, 26–27; 'Outstanding result for Otago rowers', Otago Bulletin Board, 24 April 2015: www.otago.ac.nz/otagobulletin/news/otago091065.html
57. OUSA President Report on Williamson and Jeffrey Building, 1988, OUSA records, MS-4240/349, HC; 'Works progress report', *UON*, August 1990, 3.
58. 'The surf's always up at Recreation Services', *OB*, 22 April 2005, 9; 'A day in the life of Karen Wells, Programme Coordinator, Recreation Services', *OB*, 17 October 2003, 5.
59. Vaughan Elder, 'Room for everyone in Unipol at the Plaza', *ODT*, 27 April 2012: www.odt.co.nz/news/dunedin/room-everyone-unipol-plaza; 'OUSA sells Unipol share for cash monies', *Critic*, 22 April 2012: www.critic.co.nz/news/article/1834/ousa-sells-unipol-shares-for-cash-monies; 'OUSA Recreation Centre officially opened', *Critic*, 13 July 2014: www.critic.co.nz/news/article/4080/ousa-recreation-centre-officially-opened

60. 'Uni bank-rolls thugby', *Critic*, 23 February 2014: www.critic.co.nz/news/article/3548/uni-bank-rolls-thugby; 'University's rugby sponsorship', *ODT*, 13 February 2014: www.odt.co.nz/news/campus/university-of-otago/universitys-rugby-sponsorship
61. 'Presentation of diplomas', *ES*, 9 August 1879, 3.
62. Elworthy, *Ritual Song of Defiance*, 21–23, 29–30; 'The students' saturnalia', *OUR*, August 1899, 63.
63. The formal ceremony and its history are described in the booklet published for each graduation.
64. Elworthy, *Ritual Song of Defiance*, 30, 53–54, 122, 139.
65. 'Scarfies capping procession returns', Press release, 5 May 2000, Scoop: www.scoop.co.nz/stories/ED0005/S00009/scarfies-capping-procession-returns.htm
66. John Gibb, 'Procession to precede graduation ceremony', *ODT*, 7 May 1998, 2; Stephen Hall-Jones interview.
67. *Knox Collegian*, 1987, 31.
68. Vivien Pullar, 'Whatever happened to … the Selwyn Ballet', *UOM*, no. 8, 2004, 43.
69. David Cole, 'Down memory lane once more', *Otago Graduate*, 1988, 23; Elworthy, *Ritual Song of Defiance*, 70–72.
70. Loulou Callister-Baker, 'Right in the nutcracker', *Critic*, 21 July 2014, 19–21; Zane Pocock, 'Editorial: The good of crushed expectations', *Critic*, 21 July 2014, 3.
71. Tecwyn Evans 'The University of Otago capping sextet 1903–1993', MusB (Hons) research project, University of Otago, 1993, MS-3253, HC; 'The university students' capping carnival', *ODT*, 30 June 1905, 3.
72. 'Sextet sings through the decades', *Otago Graduate*, 1991, 13.
73. Allison Rudd, 'Capping Show offends', *ODT*, 3 June 2010, 8.
74. Rebecca Tansley, 'Whatever happened to … the Sextet?', *UOM*, no. 33, 2012, 49–51.
75. Elworthy, *Ritual Song of Defiance*, 136.
76. David Large, 'Capping it all off: A change of scene for the capping show', in *Culture of Change*, 167–86; 'New-style capping show', *UON*, April 1984, 12; Margot Taylor, 'Capping show balances both its humour and cutting edge', *ODT*, 28 February 2016: www.odt.co.nz/news/dunedin/capping-show-balances-both-its-humour-and-cutting-edge
77. Elworthy, *Ritual Song of Defiance*, 54, 79, 135–36, 139; Ben Hutchison, 'A cover and cliques', in The Time Keepers, *Tower Turmoil: Characters and controversies at the University of Otago* (Dunedin: Department of History, University of Otago, 2005), 155–73.
78. Taylor, 'Capping show balances'.
79. University of Otago Graduation Programmes; Elaine Donaldson interview.
80. Jennings, *Aunt Pearl's Story*, 10.
81. Stephen Hall-Jones interview.
82. J.H. Murdoch, 'Teaching reminiscences', 30, New Zealand Council for Educational Research: Educational reminiscences, 88-005-10, Alexander Turnbull Library.
83. Keane, 'Memories of home science'.
84. Interview with Nancy and Melville Carr; *University of Otago Freshers' Handbook*, 1957, 25.
85. 'Bill and Mary English's private love story', *Women's Weekly*, 15 February 2017: www.msn.com/en-nz/lifestyle/familyandrelationships/bill-and-mary-englishs-private-love-story/ar-AAmZzra?li=BBqdb1S
86. Elworthy, *Ritual Song of Defiance*, 52; Alison Clarke, *A Living Tradition: A centennial history of Knox College, Dunedin 1909–2009* (Dunedin: Knox College, 2009), 137–44; Ben Fahy, 'Rituals create ties that bind', *ODT*, 4 March 2006, magazine, 1, 4; John Gibb, 'Filthiest fun in Leith run', *ODT*, 5 March 2010: www.odt.co.nz/news/dunedin/filthiest-fun-leith-run
87. *University of Otago Students' Handbook*, 1964, 9.
88. *Otago University Student Handbook*, 1966, 64.
89. *OUSA Orientation Handbook*, 1975, 79; *Otago Students' Almanac*, 1980, 31–32.
90. *OUSA Handbook*, 1984, 93.
91. Amy Joseph, 'Changes on the air: Radio One, 91FM', in *Culture of Change*, 135–54.
92. Stephen Hall-Jones interview; *OUSA Orientation Handbook*, 1979, 28; 1990, 19; 1991, 19.
93. 'On parade', *2001: A Speight's Odyssey Orientation*, 10.
94. 'Students' toga parade turns ugly', *ODT*, 25 February 2009, 1; Allison Rudd, '3 expulsions following toga parade', *ODT*, 4 July 2009, 1.
95. Emily Menkes, 'No toga parade but students will still party', *ODT*, 8 March 2010: www.odt.co.nz/news/campus/university-of-otago/no-toga-parade-students-will-still-party; Bella Macdonald, 'Zombie spotted at toga party', *Critic*, 24 February 2013: www.critic.co.nz/news/article/2560/zombie-spotted-at-toga-party
96. Harlene Hayne to all University of Otago staff, 22 January 2015.
97. *Ori16 Magazine*.
98. 'Don't swallow the "culture" bait', *OUR*, 1946, 47–49.
99. 'University Dramatic Club', in *OUR*: *A history of Otago University during its minority*, 51–56; Alister McDonald, 'The history of OUDS at Allen Hall', in Lisa Warrington & Alison Finigan (eds), *Allen Hall: 100 years, 100+ voices* (Dunedin: Department of Music, Theatre Studies Programme, University of Otago, 2014), 48–70.
100. McDonald, 'History of OUDS'.
101. Jocelyn Harris interview; 'Idols hit in "Yes or No"', *ODT*, 19 June 1963, 3; 'Yes and no', *Critic*, 27 June 1963, 7.
102. McDonald, 'History of OUDS'.
103. Mason Durie, 'The ownership of health', in Nigel Beckford & Michael Fitzsimons (eds), *Te Paruhi a nga Takuta* (Wellington: FitzBeck Publishing, 2013), 98–103.
104. Mere Montgomery, *Otago University Maori Club 1972 to 1975* (Dunedin: M. Montgomery, 1993); interviews with John Broughton and Mere Montgomery.
105. Montgomery, *Otago University Maori Club*; interviews with John Broughton and Mere Montgomery; Melani Anae, Lautofa Iuli & Leilani Burgoyne (eds), *Polynesian Panthers: The crucible years 1971–74* (Auckland: Reed, 2006), 102–03.

106. 'About Te Roopū', Te Roopū Māori: www.otago.ac.nz/teroopu/about.html
107. 'International Club', *OUR*, 1951, 37; Agnes Blackie, 'The spare time of a lecturer', Blackie family papers, MS–4443/005, HC.
108. Georgina Sargison, 'Saris in a cold climate: Colombo Plan students at the University of Otago', in *Culture of Change*, 95–118.
109. Blackie, 'The spare time of a lecturer'.
110. 'Here's a cul-chuh page!', *OUSA Orientation Handbook*, 1975, 15; 'Clubs and Societies', *Otago Students' Almanac*, 1980, 13–142.
111. Elworthy, *Ritual Song of Defiance*, 127.
112. Stephen Hall-Jones interview.
113. Stephen Hall-Jones interview; Heather Jackson, 'Videos with wings: The Mothra competition takes flight', in *Culture of Change*, 155–65; Tim Lindsay, 'MOTHRAs: The iconic festival that slowly withered away', *Critic*, 29 July 2013, 40.
114. Elworthy, *Ritual Song of Defiance*, 87, 129; interviews with Bridget Rennie and Donna Jones.
115. Elworthy, *Ritual Song of Defiance*, 24–27; 'The Otago University Students' Association', in *OUR: A history of Otago University during its minority*, 43–48; 'Students' Association', *ES*, 9 May 1891, 2; 'Death of Mr W.E. Spencer', *Evening Post*, 31 May 1927, 10.
116. 'Whatever happened to … the OUSA presidents?', *UOM*, no. 28, 2011, 49–51; interviews with Bridget Rennie, Donna Jones, Stephen Hall-Jones; Elworthy, *Ritual Song of Defiance*, 114, 135–37.
117. Sharon Dooley, 'Ivory tower idyll: Students at the University of Otago in the depression, 1929–1936', BA (Hons) dissertation, University of Otago, 1983, 58.
118. Angus Ross, 'The university and the community: The University of Otago from within, since 1930', 9, script for Faculty of Arts Open Lectures – centennial series, 1969, MS-0835, HC; Dooley, 'Ivory tower idyll', 71–79.
119. 'He died for freedom: A. Maclure killed in Spain', *Workers Weekly*, 7 January 1938, 1.
120. Elworthy, *Ritual Song of Defiance*, 64, 108–14, 121–28, 131–41; interviews with Bridget Rennie, Donna Jones, Stephen Hall-Jones.
121. Dougal McLachlan, 'Students behaving badly: Student discipline at the University of Otago', in *Culture of Change*, 21–37.
122. Elworthy, *Ritual Song of Defiance*, 57–60.
123. Ibid., 74–75.
124. Ibid., 116–21; 'Discipline regulations', *UOC*, 1971, 45–55; 1973, 495–506.
125. Interviews with Peter Chin and David Skegg.
126. *UOAR*, 2006, 14; 'Discipline regulations', *UOC*, 2008, 221–29.
127. David Skegg interview; Allison Rudd, '"More proactive" university expected', *ODT*, 7 November 2009: www.odt.co.nz/news/dunedin/more-proactive-university-expected; Allison Rudd, 'Conduct code conflict continues', *ODT*, 10 December 2009: www.odt.co.nz/news/dunedin/conduct-code-conflict-continues; Mark Price, 'OUSA drops appeal against code of conduct ruling', *ODT*, 16 March 2010: www.odt.co.nz/news/dunedin/ousa-drops-appeal-against-code-conduct-ruling; Matthew Haggart, 'OUSA opposition softened', *ODT*, 9 June 2011: www.odt.co.nz/news/dunedin/ousa-opposition-code-softened
128. 'Office of the Proctor', K.N. Houghton (Registrar) to Vice-Chancellor, 10 June 1998, Vice-Chancellor's Office records, MS–4394/433, HC; Ron Chambers, *Justice and Jellybeans: From Ulster policeman to Otago University proctor* (Dunedin: Missing Stocks Press, 2006), 37; 'University to remember former Proctor Ron Chambers', Otago Bulletin Board, 11 November 2014: www.otago.ac.nz/otagobulletin/people/otago082524.html
129. 'Police presence secured on campus', *UON*, February/March 1997, 3.
130. David Richardson interview; David Richardson, 'Creating cultural change – Campus Watch: A most fortunate experiment', paper for Campus and Student Security Conference, 2014; Olivia Collier, 'Campus Watch confessions', *Critic*, 11 May 2015, 20–23.
131. Kimberly Cousins, 'Evaluation of Campus Watch: A community-based initiative to reduce alcohol-related harm and social disorder in a university setting', PhD thesis, University of Otago, 2012, iv.
132. Paul Christoffel, 'Liquor laws', Te Ara – the Encyclopedia of New Zealand: www.teara.govt.nz/en/liquor-laws; David Richardson interview.
133. Kypros Kypri, Melanie L. Bell, Geoff C. Hay and Joanne Baxter, 'Alcohol outlet density and university student drinking: A national study', *Addiction*, vol. 103, 2008, 1131–38.
134. Richardson, 'Creating cultural change'; Ellie Constantine, 'Pub owners warned over Cookathon', *ODT*, 17 September 2009: www.odt.co.nz/news/dunedin/pub-owners-warned-over-cookathon; 'University buys the "Bowler"', *ODT*, 12 March 2009: www.odt.co.nz/news/dunedin/university-buys-bowler; Allison Rudd, 'Varsity buying, closing bar', *ODT*, 19 April 2010: www.odt.co.nz/news/dunedin/varsity-buying-closing-bar; Mark Wright, 'Whatever happened to … the Cook?', *UOM*, no. 40, 2015, 51; Vaughan Elder, 'Captain Cook sets sail on new voyage', *ODT*, 18 May 2016: www.odt.co.nz/news/dunedin/captain-cook-sets-sail-new-voyage-video
135. *UOAR*, 2009, 16; Allison Rudd, 'University bans alcohol promotion', *ODT*, 29 October 2009: www.odt.co.nz/news/dunedin/university-bans-alcohol-promotion
136. University of Otago Council papers relating to voluntary student membership, 1997, Vice-Chancellor's Office records, MS–4394/065, HC; Education (Tertiary Students Association Voluntary Membership) Amendment Act 1998; Chris Barton, 'Students pay high price for freedom', *New Zealand Herald*, 18 December 2010: www.nzherald.co.nz/nz/news/article.cfm?c_id=1&objectid=10695053
137. *UOAR*, 2011, 14.
138. Callum Fredric, 'Business time', *Critic*, 24 February 2012: www.critic.co.nz/features/article/1546/business-time
139. Callum Fredric, 'It's voluntary Jim, but not as we know it', *Critic*, 1 April 2012: www.critic.co.nz/news/article/1768/its-voluntary-jim-but-not-as-we-know-it

140. Margot Taylor, 'VSM changed face of student politics', *ODT*, 25 October 2016: www.odt.co.nz/news/dunedin/vsm-changed-face-student-politics; Carla Green, 'Where have the student radicals gone?', *ODT*, 20 September 2015: www.odt.co.nz/news/dunedin/where-have-student-radicals-gone
141. 'The "Otago University Review"', in *OUR: A history of Otago University during its minority*, 48–50.
142. Stephen Hamilton & Nelson Wattie, 'Otago University Review', in Roger Robinson and Nelson Wattie (eds), *The Oxford Companion to New Zealand Literature* (Auckland: Oxford University Press, 1998), 421; H. Tohill, 'Seventy years of student publications', *OUR*, 1957, 45–49. Publication details for the *OUR* and its successors from the University of Otago library catalogue.
143. *A Canterbury Tale: The autobiography of Dr Francis Bennett* (Wellington: Oxford University Press, 1980), 109.
144. 'Editorial', *Critic*, 2 April 1925, 1.
145. 'Angela Burns against Critic Te Arohi', New Zealand Press Council Ruling, May 2013: www.presscouncil.org.nz/rulings/angela-burns-against-critic-te-arohi
146. 'Otago Mental Health Support Trust against Critic–Te Arohi', New Zealand Press Council ruling, October 2010: www.presscouncil.org.nz/rulings/otago-mental-health-support-trust-against-critic-te-arohi
147. Stu Oldham, 'Student "rape guide" banned', *ODT*, 2 February 2006, 1.
148. 'Article in Critic held back', *ODT*, 11 July 1952, 8; Paul Oestreicher to author, 20 March 2016.
149. '80: Critic Te Arohi 1925–2005', *Critic*, 15 August 2005, 19–24.
150. 'Obituary: Sir Geoffrey Cox', *Guardian*, 4 April 2008, 37.
151. Tohill, 'Seventy years of student publications'. Tohill wrote that there was just one issue of *Challenge*, but there are two issues, published by Stevens, in the Hocken Collections; 'Critique 1980', *Otago Students' Almanac*, 1980, 32.
152. John Robson to Jocelyn Harris, 20 August 1994, 94–116, HC.
153. Robbie Fitzgerald, 'What's in a name: The burning of *Falus*', in *Tower Turmoil*, 141–54; Elworthy, *Ritual Song of Defiance*, 103–09.
154. Dorothy Page, *Anatomy of a Medical School: A history of medicine at the University of Otago 1875–2000* (Dunedin: Otago University Press, 2008), 107–08, 183–84, 283–84; 'SOULS publications', Society of Otago University Law Students: https://soulsotago.com/publications/
155. Hamilton & Wattie, 'Otago University Review'.
156. 'The Wind and the Rain', *Auckland Star*, 26 April 1935, 3; 'Doctor-playwright's death in Dunedin', *ODT*, 10 October 1958.
157. The term 'scarfie' derives from the popular student practice of wearing blue and gold scarves, part of students' 'common identity' since the 1950s. See Elworthy, *Ritual Song of Defiance*, 78. It later became synonymous with a cultural identity of drunken misbehaviour that not all students approved of: see 'Brand scarfie', *Critic*, 11 July 2010: www.critic.co.nz/features/article/333/brand-scarfie

4: A PLACE TO LIVE: LODGINGS, COLLEGES AND FLATS

1. William Hutchison to John Hislop, 13 April 1871, Inwards Letters, Records of Registry and Central Administration, AG-180-27/02, HC.
2. John Hislop to William Hutchison, 2 May 1871, Letter book, Records of Registry and Central Administration, AG-180-30/01, HC.
3. 'The Otago University', *OW*, 6 December 1873, 11.
4. G.E. Thompson, *A History of the University of Otago (1869–1919)* (Dunedin: Wilkie, 1919), 87–97.
5. A. Livingston to Benjamin Wells, 22 March 1872, Letter book, Records of Registry and Central Administration, AG-180-30/01, HC. Wells replied with a letter enclosing a money order for the fees of his two sons, Charles Archer Wells and Benjamin Wells, who were about to depart for Dunedin: Benjamin Wells to A. Livingston, 20 April 1872, Inwards Letters, Records of Registry and Central Administration, AG-180-27/03, HC.
6. 'University boarding-houses', *ODT*, 6 July 1877, 3.
7. Such attitudes persisted in Scotland, as Knox College master Hubert Ryburn discovered when he paid a visit there in 1958. See Alison Clarke, *A Living Tradition: A centennial history of Knox College, Dunedin, 1909–2009* (Dunedin: Knox College, 2009), 2.
8. 'Modi Viviendi', *OUR*, 1946, 32–33.
9. *OW*, 8 March 1862, 8; Mrs Muir to University of Otago Council, 23 June 1871, Inwards Letters, Records of Registry and Central Administration, AG-180-27/02, HC.
10. Alexander Watt Williamson papers, Misc-MS-0454/001, HC; Thomas Cuddie funeral notice, *ODT*, 4 September 1871, 2.
11. *ODT*, 28 March 1881, 3.
12. *ODT*, 14 April 1896, 5.
13. Judith Nathan & Simon Nathan, *My Dearest Georgie: Transcriptions of 24 letters from James Hector to his wife Georgiana* (Wellington: Geoscience Society of New Zealand, 2015), 8–19.
14. Agnes Blackie, 'The spare time of a lecturer', Blackie family papers, MS-4443/005, HC; *UOAR*, 1932. For details of the disciplinary row, see Sam Elworthy, *Ritual Song of Defiance: A social history of students at the University of Otago* (Dunedin: Otago University Students' Association, 1990), 59–60.
15. Maurice Matich, *From Beacon Point: My journey, my story* (Wellington: Phantom House, 2013), 75.
16. H.W. Turner, *Halls of Residence* (Wellington: New Zealand Council for Educational Research, 1953), 20–21.
17. Dorothy Page interview with Chris Heath.
18. 'Diocesan synod', *ODT*, 28 October 1886, 4; Ken Booth, 'Nevill, Samuel Tarratt', from DNZB: www.teara.govt.nz/en/biographies/2n8/nevill-samuel-tarratt; Ray Hargreaves, *Selwyn College's First Century: A history and list of residents 1893–1992* (Dunedin: Centennial Committee, Selwyn College Board of Governors, 1993), 8–11.

19. Hargreaves, *Selwyn College's First Century*, 11–30; Barbara Fountain, 'Good old days at Selwyn recalled', *ODT*, 15 May 1993, 3.
20. Hargreaves, *Selwyn College's First Century*, 13–14, 18–19, 30–31.
21. Arthur Porritt to Sam Elworthy, 23 May 1989, OUSA centenary records, MS-4240/319, HC.
22. Clarke, *Living Tradition*, 2–9, 21–22.
23. Ibid., 43–54, 105–06, 147–50, 193.
24. Susannah Grant, *Vision for the Future: A centennial history of St Margaret's College, Dunedin 1911–2011* (Dunedin: St Margaret's College, 2010), 3–23.
25. A.G. Strong, *History of the Development of University Education in Home Science in New Zealand 1911–1936* (Dunedin: University of Otago, 1937), 29–31; *UOC*, 1917, 221.
26. *School of Home Science History, 1911–1961* (Dunedin: University of Otago, School of Home Science, 1962), 20–21; Sadie Andrews interview.
27. Interviews with Sadie Andrews and Nancy Carr.
28. *School of Home Science History*, 21–26; Rebecca Tansley, *Studholme: A century of life and learning* (Dunedin: University of Otago, 2015), 25, 56–58.
29. Turner, *Halls of Residence*, 13–14; G.A. Macaulay, *A Triumph of Improvisation: The Stuart Residence Halls Council, Stuart House, Arana Hall, Carrington Hall 1941–1991* (Dunedin: Stuart Residence Halls Council, 1991), 3–6, 11.
30. Harold W. Turner, Address at opening of Turner Wing, Arana Hall, 4 June 1994, copy courtesy of Bill Dawson.
31. Ian McGibbon, 'Allen, James', from DNZB: www.teara.govt.nz/en/biographies/3a12/allen-james; Lois Voller, papers relating to Sir James Allen and the Allen family, AG-458-4, HC; *School of Home Science History*, 20.
32. Macaulay, *Triumph of Improvisation*, 8–9.
33. Ibid., 8–12; Peter Holland, Hugh Kidd & Richard Welch (eds), *From Mellor to Hocken: Fifty years of geography at the University of Otago* (Dunedin: Department of Geography, University of Otago, 1995), 19–20, 31–33, 44–45.
34. Melville Carr interview; Sam Stevens, 'Whatever happened to … Stuart House (aka Arana Hall)?', *UOM*, no. 36, 2013, 50–51; 'Irreverent to the Reverends: Arana celebrates 70 years', Otago Bulletin Board, 22 November 2013: www.otago.ac.nz/otagobulletin/news/otago059638.html; Macaulay, *Triumph of Improvisation*, 12, 17–18.
35. Macaulay, *Triumph of Improvisation*, 6, 23–26.
36. Ibid., 26, 31; Bill Dawson interview; Peter Walker (Carrington warden), personal communication, 22 May 2015.
37. Turner, *Halls of Residence*, 57–59.
38. Mary Augustine McCarthy, *Star in the South: The centennial history of the New Zealand Dominican Sisters* (Dunedin: St Dominic's Priory, 1970), 273–74; Heritage New Zealand listing for Transit House: www.heritage.org.nz/the-list/details/367; Lois Galer, *Houses of Dunedin: An illustrated collection of the city's historic homes* (Dunedin: Hyndman, 1995), 60–62.
39. Rosie Manins, 'When we all lived at Dominican Hall', *ODT*, 9 October 2012: www.odt.co.nz/news/dunedin/when-we-all-lived-dominican-hall
40. McCarthy, *Star in the South*, 273–74; 'Transit House visit', *Southern Heritage Trust Newsletter*, no. 18, 2015, 1; W.P. Morrell, *The University of Otago: A centennial history* (Dunedin: Otago University Press, 1969), 219. Turner, *Halls of Residence*, 8, records it then had 30 residents. 'Roll Call 1949', *Dominican*, 1959, 22, lists 42 residents. An OUSA list of residential halls and colleges for c. 1964 notes that Dominican Hall has accommodation for 46 (OUSA records, MS-0641/0115, HC), while another for 1967 states its capacity as 48 (OUSA records, MS-0641/0140, HC). The 1976 OUSA questionnaire completed by hall president Bernadette Ford recorded 39 residents that year; extras had been squeezed into some of the shared bedrooms, with the warden saying 'she accepted so many … because there was evidently no other place for many of the girls to get in' (OUSA records, MS-0641/0604, HC).
41. M.D., 'Dormitory Diary', *Dominican*, 1960, 7. The only resident in the roll call for 1960 with the initials M.D. was Maureen Donnelly.
42. James Whyte to G.M. Cussen, 7 March 1948, cited in Morrell, *University of Otago*, 214.
43. *Stepping Up: A celebration of six decades of history at Aquinas College* (Dunedin: Development & Alumni Relations Office, University of Otago, 2011).
44. 'Hostel roundup', *OUR*, 1957, 23–26.
45. *Stepping Up*, 3.
46. 'Statistical information on halls of residence at Otago', OUSA records, MS-0641/0140, HC.
47. *Stepping Up*, 7, 51.
48. 'Statistical information on halls of residence at Otago'.
49. Elsie Maclean to D.B. Gordon, 30 November 1961, Wesley Residential Hall records, Methodist Central Mission (Dunedin) records, AG-640-045-025/009, HC.
50. Elsie Maclean to D.B. Gordon, 18 September 1961, Wesley Residential Hall records, Methodist Central Mission (Dunedin) records, AG-640-045-025/002, HC.
51. Kenneth Thomson to D.B. Gordon, [1963]; J.J. Reid, report for 1964; both in Wesley Residential Hall records, Methodist Central Mission (Dunedin) records, AG-640-045-025/007, HC.
52. D.B. Gordon to J.W. Hayward, 18 September 1970; D.B. Gordon to Director General of Health, 12 November 1970; H.de R. Flesher to D.B. Gordon, 22 June 1971; all in Wesley Residential Hall records, Methodist Central Mission (Dunedin) records, AG-640-045-025/011, HC.
53. Elworthy, *Ritual Song of Defiance*, 99; Student Accommodation Officer Annual Report, 1965; Assistant Registrar (Accommodation) Annual Report, 1976, Records of Registry and Central Administration, AG-180-7/08 and 7/13, HC; 1955 figures from *University of Otago: Submissions to the Committee of Enquiry on New Zealand Universities* (Dunedin: University of Otago, 1959), 14 (calculated using the total roll for consistency with the figures available for other years).

54. John Gardiner, *Student Digs Known as the Bach* (Auckland: J. Gardiner, 1996); Ian Breward, *Grace and Truth: A history of Theological Hall, Knox College, Dunedin 1876–1975* (Dunedin: Theological Education Committee, Presbyterian Church of New Zealand, 1975), 47; 'Miller, Rev Dr Alexander (Lex)', Register (Fasti) of New Zealand Presbyterian Ministers, Deaconesses & Missionaries 1840 to 2015: www.presbyterian.org.nz/archives/Page183.htm
55. *Submissions to the Committee of Enquiry*, 14 (calculated using the total roll for consistency with the figures available for other years).
56. Melville Carr interview; 'The "Shambles" as Murdoch Mackenzie knew it', *Otago School of Mines and Metallurgy 1950s Graduates Newsletter*, October 2004, John Neilson papers, MS-2842/001, HC.
57. *Submissions to the Committee of Enquiry*, 16.
58. Student Accommodation Officer Annual Report, 1965; Assistant Registrar (Accommodation) Annual Report, 1976, Records of Registry and Central Administration, AG-180-7/08 and 7/13, HC.
59. Elworthy, *Ritual Song of Defiance*, 99.
60. Janet Mitchell interview.
61. James K. Baxter, 'A small ode on mixed flatting', *Falus*, no. 10, 1967. *Falus* was an anti-establishment student paper that first broke the story about the mixed flatting incident. One of the producers of this 'tawdry little rag', John Robson, later recalled that the threatened student 'had not been able to get *Critic* interested in his plight'. See John Robson to Jocelyn Harris, 20 August 1994, 94–116, HC.
62. 'Long live democracy!', *Falus*, no. 7, [1967]; '"Get out of mixed flats" demand', *Critic*, 4 July 1967, 1; '"Live in" plan by students', *ODT*, 6 July 1967, 1; 'The story so far', *Critic*, 19 July 1967, 1–2; Dorothy Page interview with Robin Williams, 2008; David Wilson, 'The student revolt against paternalism: Student protest and the mixed flatting controversy at the University of Otago', *Flinders Journal of History and Politics*, vol. 22, 2001–2002, 141–62; Debby Foster, 'No mixing by students', in The Time Keepers, *Tower Turmoil: Characters and controversies at the University of Otago* (Dunedin: Department of History, University of Otago, 2005), 127–40.
63. Dorothy Page interview with Robin Williams.
64. Morrell, *University of Otago*, 242.
65. Wilson, 'Student revolt against paternalism'. Though it was perhaps not widely known at the time, the flatmates were drawn together by their shared Jewish identity, according to Michael MacAvoy (personal communication, 31 May 2015).
66. 'The story so far', *Critic*, 19 July 1967, 1–2; Wilson, 'Student revolt against paternalism'.
67. Elworthy, *Ritual Song of Defiance*, 104–07.
68. Gardiner, *Student Digs*.
69. Sarah Gallagher, personal communication; Sarah Gallagher, 'Hanging out: Preserving an ephemeral print culture in Dunedin', paper presented at Library and Information Association of New Zealand Aotearoa conference, 2010; Dunedin Flat Names Project: https://dunedinflatnames.co.nz/
70. Matthew Bannister, *Positively George Street* (Auckland: Reed, 1999), 90–91, 110–20; Bronwyn, comments on University of Otago 1869–2019: Writing a history blog, 10 and 11 March 2014: https://otago150years.wordpress.com/2014/03/10/naming-flats/
71. Shane Gilchrist, 'Moving on from Six60 Castle', *ODT*, 8 October 2011: www.odt.co.nz/entertainment/music/moving-six60-castle; Shawn McAvinue, 'You're in Six60's world', *ODT*, 24 February 2014: www.odt.co.nz/news/dunedin/youre-six60s-world; '"Overloading" caused balcony collapse', *ODT*, 24 May 2016: www.odt.co.nz/news/dunedin/overloading-caused-balcony-collapse; Rhys Chamberlain, 'Castle St flat fire suspicious', *ODT*, 22 June 2016: www.odt.co.nz/news/dunedin/castle-st-flat-fire-suspicious
72. Joe Higham, 'Student flats or student slums?', *Critic*, 6 March 2016: www.critic.co.nz/features/article/5562/student-flats-or-student-slums
73. 'Wanted: Best student flat', *ODT*, 5 September 2008: www.odt.co.nz/news/dunedin/wanted-best-student-flat; Teuila Fuatai, 'Rodent-infested shithole to rent, must supply own rodents', *Critic*, 11 October 2010: www.critic.co.nz/news/article/624/-rodent-infested-shithole-to-rent-must-supply-own-; Ellie Constantine, 'Worst flat complete with rats', *ODT*, 27 September 2010: www.odt.co.nz/news/campus/university-of-otago/worst-flat-complete-rats; Emily Draper, 'OUSA awards: Hypothermic students rejoice', *Critic*, 20 July 2014: www.critic.co.nz/news/article/4120/ousa-awards-hypothermic-students-rejoice--
74. Olivia Caldwell, 'Students say many flats not worth rental', *ODT*, 15 July 2013: www.odt.co.nz/news/dunedin/students-say-many-flats-not-worth-rental; Kim Dungey, 'Transforming the house of horrors', *ODT*, 10 November 2013: www.odt.co.nz/news/dunedin/transforming-house-horrors; Josie Cochrane, 'Dunedin flats to be rated, warranted and starred', *Critic*, 19 May 2014: www.critic.co.nz/news/article/3986/dunedin-flats-to-be-rated-warranted-and-starred
75. 'O.U. centennial project appeal', *ES*, 25 November 1964, 1; 'Hall of residence for 300 students planned', *ES*, 25 November 1964, 3; 'University College', *UON*, August 1974, 8.
76. L.C. Baker & D.F. Symon, *Report on the Early Establishment Years of University College* (Dunedin: University College Council, 1972); Chris Addington, personal communication, 4 September 2015.
77. Morgan Cook, '"If I cannot get some more help, I cannot change it": Student culture and change at University College, Dunedin 1969–2007', BA (Hons) dissertation, University of Otago, 2010, 11, 37–44; Taryn Tait, 'Living together: The beginnings of co-educational halls of residence at Otago', in *Culture of Change: Beginnings at the University of Otago* (Dunedin: Departments of English & History, University of Otago, 2006), 75–93.
78. Ron Chambers, *Justice and Jellybeans: From Ulster policeman to Otago University proctor* (Dunedin: Missing Stocks Press, 2006), 105–12; Cook, '"If I cannot get some more help"', 55–58.

79. Cook, '"If I cannot get some more help"', 60–70.
80. 'UniCol's new wings officially opened', *OB*, 26 March 2004, 4.
81. Breward, *Grace and Truth*, 116, 164–68; 'New residential hall for women at Knox', *ODT*, 6 November 1963, 1; 'Appeal for women's hostel is launched', *ODT*, 10 June 1965, 3; Clarke, *Living Tradition*, 26–29; Grant, *Vision for the Future*, 112–15.
82. 'Hostel plans delayed', *ODT*, 15 March 1967, 1; 'Residential hall tender let', *ODT*, 16 November 1968, 1.
83. Knox College Council Annual Report, *Proceedings of the General Assembly of the Presbyterian Church of New Zealand*, 1965, 34a–35a; *Presbyterian Church of New Zealand: Reports of committees and other papers to be presented to General Assembly*, 1971, 22–24; Nan Burgess, 'Salmond, Sarah and family', in Jane Thomson (ed.), *Southern People: A dictionary of Otago Southland biography* (Dunedin: Longacre Press/Dunedin City Council, 1998), 439–40.
84. Clarke, *Living Tradition*, 28–30.
85. Student Accommodation Officer Annual Report, 1965; Assistant Registrar (Accommodation) Annual Report, 1976, Records of Registry and Central Administration, AG-180-7/08 and 7/13, HC.
86. Tait, 'Living together'.
87. Student Accommodation Officer Annual Report, 1974, Records of Registry and Central Administration, AG-180-7/12, HC; 'Male invasion', *UON*, March 1974, 6.
88. Tansley, *Studholme*, 74.
89. 'Male invasion', *UON*, March 1974, 6.
90. Tait, 'Living together'.
91. Knox College Council Annual Report, *Reports of Committees and Other Papers to be Presented to General Assembly*, 1976, 16–19.
92. Council of Knox College and Salmond Hall Annual Report, *Reports of Committees and Other Papers to be Presented to General Assembly*, 1979, 84–86.
93. 'Dominican Hall being closed', *ODT*, 19 December 1978, 1.
94. 'Aquinas closing', *UON*, August 1980, 10; *Stepping Up*, 26, 41.
95. Clarke, *Living Tradition*, 79.
96. Macaulay, *Triumph of Improvisation*, 22.
97. 'Sky rocket battle for discussion', *ES*, 2 November 1977; 'Student rocket battles have "cooled down"', *ES*, 3 November 1977; '"Stupid, childish" student minority blamed for hall upsets', *ES*, 3 November 1977, all in newspaper cuttings book, Records of Registry and Central Administration, AG-180-034/040, HC.
98. Tait, 'Living together'; Grant, *Vision for the Future*, 136–47, 163–67.
99. Clarke, *Living Tradition*, 77–79. There was one mature woman student who lived at Knox in 1982, a year before the first undergraduate women residents were admitted.
100. Tait, 'Living together'.
101. 'Selwyn College elects first woman president', *ODT*, 13 November 1993, 5. On the culture wars on campus, see Elworthy, *Ritual Song of Defiance*, 131–38.
102. *Knox Collegian*, 1989, 9.
103. Accommodation Office Annual Report, 1984, Records of Registry and Central Administration, AG-180-7/15, HC; 'Student housing concern', *Dunedin Star Midweek*, 15 February 1984, 1; Bill Dawson interview.
104. J.T. Jennings to D.W. Girvan, 13 January 1984 and D.W. Girvan to D.C.J. Pearce, 30 January 1984, Records of Registry and Central Administration, MS-3747, Box 107, HC.
105. Accommodation Office Annual Report, 1984, Records of Registry and Central Administration, AG-180-7/15, HC.
106. Glenys Roome interview; 'An interview with Glenys Roome, warden of Hayward Hall', *University of Otago General Staff Association Newsletter*, December 1993.
107. 'The proctor', *Star*, 23 June 1999, 2; Chambers, *Justice and Jellybeans*, 81.
108. 'Helensburgh House', *Critic*, 21 February 1984, 3.
109. Glenys Roome interview; Andrew A., Marie S., Matt, alliekiwi, Mark, Nathan Tane and Graeme P., comments on University of Otago 1869–2019: Writing a history blog, 6 August 2012 to 12 May 2015: https://otago150years.wordpress.com/2013/08/04/the-vanishing-hall-of-residence/
110. Accommodation Office Annual Report, 1984–1987, Records of Registry and Central Administration, AG-180-7/15, HC.
111. Accommodation Office Annual Report, 1988, Records of Registry and Central Administration, AG-180-7/15, HC.
112. *Stepping Up*, 41–43.
113. Ibid.; Ashley Day interview; Self-review, University of Otago Review of Aquinas College, 2011, 3–4.
114. 'Nurses home slated for demolition', *ODT*, 15 April 1988, 1; 'University to lease hostel for students', *ODT*, 9 September 1988, 5.
115. Cumberland House Annual Report, 1989, Records of Registry and Central Administration, MS-3747, Box 108, HC.
116. 'University gets lease of hostel', *ODT*, 23 August 1991, 5; Self-review, University of Otago Review of Cumberland College, 2009, 6.
117. Morag McGlinchy & Natasha Gowan, comments on University of Otago 1869–2019: Writing a history blog, 16 and 23 September 2014: https://otago150years.wordpress.com/2014/09/15/25-years-of-cumberland/
118. 'Seismic strengthening projects at the University': www.otago.ac.nz/seismicprogramme/projects/otago043859.html; Matthew Haggart, 'Strengthening starts', *ODT*, 25 November 2011: www.odt.co.nz/news/dunedin/strengthening-starts
119. Debbie Porteous, 'The end is nigh', *ODT*, 14 July 2011: www.odt.co.nz/news/dunedin/end-nigh
120. Callum Fredric, 'The Cumberland ghost', *Critic*, 21 May 2012, 6; Vaughan Elder, '"Ghost" frightens college students', *ODT*, 22 May 2012: www.odt.co.nz/news/dunedin/ghost-frightens-college-students
121. 'University gets lease of hostel', *ODT*, 23 August 1991, 5; Glenys Roome interview.
122. Glenys Roome interview; 'Student hostel work to begin next month', *ODT*, 14 September 1991, 4; 'Hall honours Haywards', *ODT*, 24 October 1991, 1; 'New hostel popular

with students', *ODT*, 31 March 1992, 24; 'Hayward Hall proves a big hit with students', *UON*, October 1993, 12; Report of University of Otago Review of Hayward College, 2014, 23; 'Update: Heading to Rio Paralympics 2016', Otago Connection: www.otago.ac.nz/otago-connection/otago621008.html

123. Bill Dawson interview.
124. 'New complex for overseas students', *Star Midweek*, 28 June 1995, 1.
125. Self-review, University of Otago Review of Toroa International House, 2006, 3; Self-review, University of Otago Review of Toroa College, 2011, 5; Kim Dungey, '"League of nations" eases culture shock', *ODT*, 21 February 2003, 17.
126. Self-review, University of Otago Review of Toroa International House, 2006, 3–6; Report of University of Otago Review of Toroa College, 2011, 6–7.
127. 'More bedrooms, new facilities for Toroa College', *ODT*, 22 August 2013, 4; Toroa College website: www.otago.ac.nz/toroa/index.html
128. Accommodation Office Annual Report, 1983–1985, Records of Registry and Central Administration, AG-180-7/15, HC; 'More rental accommodation is on the way', *UON*, September 1984, 1–2.
129. Self-review, University of Otago Review of University Flats, 2009, 5–6; 'Host has "friends all over the world"', *Star*, 8 August 2013, 9.
130. Report of University of Otago Review of Cumberland College, 2009, 12.
131. Self-review, University of Otago Review of University Flats, 2009, 5; Emily Draper, 'Cumberland Courts no more', *Critic*, 2 March 2015, 13.
132. Report of University of Otago Review of University Flats, 2016.
133. 'University joins new hostel working party', *UON*, July 1998, 10.
134. Self-review, University of Otago Review of City College, 2009, 6–7; Report on the first planning meeting for a new hall of residence, Vice-Chancellor's Office records, MS-4394/247, HC; Kim Dungey, 'Flatting meets hostel living', *ODT*, 4 February 2000, 11.
135. 'City College name change', Otago Bulletin Board, 27 November 2017: www.otago.ac.nz/otagobulletin/news/otago669137.html
136. John Gibb, 'February target for Abbey College', *ODT*, 28 December 2007, 4.
137. 'A new landmark in Dunedin: Abbey Lodge Motel', *ODT*, 22 December 1979, supplement; 'Abbey College proving popular option', *OB*, 1 May 2009, 1.
138. Report of University of Otago Review of Abbey College, 2014, 6–8; 'Purchase of Abbey Lodge opens gateway to postgraduate college', *OB*, 24 August 2007, 1; 'Abbey College proving popular option', *OB*, 1 May 2009, 1; Vaughan Elder, 'House bought to add rooms for students', *ODT*, 23 April 2014, 5.
139. 'Abbey College head retires', Otago Bulletin Board, 5 June 2013: www.otago.ac.nz/otagobulletin/people/otago047950.html
140. Vaughan Elder, 'House bought to add rooms for students', *ODT*, 23 April 2014, 5.
141. Ashley Day interview; 'Living Space, Dunedin', *ODT*, 24 January 2012: www.odt.co.nz/living-space-dunedin; 'More Henderson companies seized', *Press*, 18 June 2010: www.stuff.co.nz/the-press/business/3829079/More-Henderson-companies-seized; Martin van Beynen, 'Henderson bankrupt', *Press*, 29 November 2010: www.stuff.co.nz/the-press/news/4402869/Henderson-bankrupt; Vaughan Elder, 'Uni buys hotel for student digs', *ODT*, 17 April 2013: www.odt.co.nz/news/dunedin/uni-buys-hotel-student-digs; Vaughan Elder, 'LivingSpace conversion for students begins soon', *ODT*, 10 October 2013: www.odt.co.nz/news/dunedin/livingspace-conversion-students-begins-soon
142. M.P.K. Sorrenson, 'Buck, Peter Henry', from DNZB: www.teara.govt.nz/en/biographies/3b54/buck-peter-henry
143. Aaron Smale, 'In the shadow of a totara', *Mana*, no. 117, 2014, 48–53; 'Te Rangi Hiroa whanau and tribe special guests at new college opening', Otago Connection: www.otago.ac.nz/otago-connection/archives/past-issues/otago070256.html; Vaughan Elder, 'Maori theme makes latest college unique', *ODT*, 7 February 2014: www.odt.co.nz/news/dunedin/maori-theme-makes-latest-college-unique
144. 'Long-serving college warden retires, again', Otago Bulletin Board, 7 September 2016: www.otago.ac.nz/otagobulletin/people/otago620943.html; Ashley Day interview.
145. 'Creating first-year identity for locals', Otago Bulletin Board, 13 February 2014: www.otago.ac.nz/otagobulletin/news/otago065167; 'Inaugural Director of First-Year Experience appointed', Otago Bulletin Board, 27 November 2015: www.otago.ac.nz/otagobulletin/news/otago341801.html
146. 'Major artwork unveiled', Otago Bulletin Board, 28 November 2016: www.otago.ac.nz/otagobulletin/news/otago627845.html
147. *UOAR*, 2006, 14

5: THE STAFF

1. Staff numbers for 1979 from J.M. Child, *Equal Employment Opportunities, University of Otago* (Dunedin: University of Otago, 1988), 20.
2. Rex Wright-St Clair, 'Ferguson, Henry Lindo', from DNZB: www.teara.govt.nz/en/biographies/3f3/ferguson-henry-lindo
3. W.A. Watters, 'Ulrich, George Henry Frederick', from DNZB: www.teara.govt.nz/en/biographies/2u1/ulrich-george-henry-frederick
4. University Laboratory Annual Report, *Otago Provincial Council Votes and Proceedings*, 1876.
5. *UOC*, 1905 (lists of former staff and graduates).
6. N.T.M. Wilsmore, 'John Kenneth Harold Inglis. 1877–1935', *Journal of the Chemical Society*, 1937, 700–1; 'Obituary: Dr F.W. Dunlop', *New Zealand Herald*,

18 October 1932, 12; *Register (Fasti) of New Zealand Presbyterian Ministers, Deaconesses & Missionaries 1840 to 2015*, Archives Research Centre, Presbyterian Church of Aotearoa New Zealand: http://www.presbyterian.org.nz/archives/Page159.htm

7. Gregory Lee, 'White, David Renfrew', from DNZB: www.teara.govt.nz/en/biographies/2w15/white-david-renfrew
8. Michael Gill, 'Bedford, Harry Dodgshun', from DNZB: www.teara.govt.nz/en/biographies/3b21/bedford-harry-dodgshun; 'Personal', *ES*, 20 September 1916, 4; 'Dr G.E. Thompson', *Auckland Star*, 24 May 1944, 3.
9. Lucy S. Adams, *Thomas Dagger Adams: Professor of Classics at the University of Otago* (Wellington: A.H. & A.W. Reed, 1954), 18–24.
10. 'Otago University: Chair of history', *ODT*, 25 June 1920, 6; 'Chair of economics', *ES*, 16 November 1920, 3; 'Otago University: Chair of economics', *ODT*, 1 December 1920, 4; Matthew Littlewood, 'The curious case of Professor Pringle', in The Time Keepers, *Tower Turmoil: Characters and controversies at the University of Otago* (Dunedin: Department of History, University of Otago, 2005), 51–63.
11. *UOC*, 1915–1929.
12. 'A distinguished woman graduate: Miss Gladys Cameron', *ODT*, 13 February 1928, 11.
13. Heath McDonald, 'Boys-Smith, Winifred Lily', from DNZB: www.teara.govt.nz/en/biographies/3b41/boys-smith-winifred-lily; J.D. Campbell, 'Benson, Gertrude Helen and Benson, William Noel', from DNZB: www.teara.govt.nz/en/biographies/4b24/benson-gertrude-helen. On the significance of the School of Home Science as a place for women academics, see Tanya Fitzgerald, 'Academic housework? Women professors at the University of New Zealand 1911–1961', *New Zealand Journal of Education Studies*, vol. 42, nos 1 & 2, 115–28; Tanya Fitzgerald, 'An absent presence: Women professors at the University of New Zealand 1911–1961, *Journal of Educational Administration and History*, vo. 39, no. 3, 2007, 239–53.
14. 'Three professors retiring', *UON*, December 1990, 2; 'Woman professor arrives', *UON*, July 1992, 1.
15. 'University Women's Association', *ODT*, 21 May 1914, 11.
16. 'Otago University Women's Association', *OUR*, June 1918, 33; June 1920, 48–49.
17. Helen Benson, 'Federation of women', *OUR*, 1937, 7; 'What it means to be a university woman', *OUR*, 1928, 49–51; *History of the New Zealand Federation of University Women* (Dunedin: New Zealand Federation of University Women, Otago Branch, 1954); 'Otago on location: The academic dress hire rooms', Otago Connection, 7 December 2016: www.otago.ac.nz/otago-connection/otago628782.html
18. Ann Wylie interview; 'Who we are', Graduate Women New Zealand: www.gwnz.org.nz/about-us/
19. Lynley Hood to author, 30 December 2016 (including a copy of the original invitation).
20. Leah Taylor, 'Strong, Ann Monroe Gilchrist', from DNZB: www.teara.govt.nz/en/biographies/4s51/strong-ann-monroe-gilchrist
21. K. Turner, 'The art of home making', *New Zealand Tablet*, 27 December 1923, 25.
22. For an example of public belief that Strong was widowed, see 'Tribute to professor: Dean of home science', *New Zealand Herald*, 24 May 1937, 3.
23. Mark Donoghue, 'Ralph William Souter (1897–1946)', in J.E. King (ed.), *A Biographical Dictionary of Australia and New Zealand Economists* (Cheltenham: Edward Elgar Publishing, 2007), 261–64.
24. *UOC*, 1951; Arthur Campbell interview; Li Zhang, 'Sah, Peter P.T.', in *Complete Dictionary of Scientific Biography*, vol. 24 (Detroit: Charles Scribner's Sons, 2008), 321–24.
25. *UOC*, 1951; Department of Physiology Annual Report, 1951, Records of Registry and Central Administration, AG-180-7/04, HC.
26. Dorothy Page, *Anatomy of a Medical School: A history of medicine at the University of Otago 1875–2000* (Dunedin: Otago University Press, 2008), 116, 118–20, 128; 'Obituary: Walter Edwin Griesbach', *New Zealand Medical Journal*, vol. 68, 1968, 187–88; Viola Angelika Schwarz, *Walter Edwin Griesbach (1888–1968): Life and work*, trans. John S. Dawson (Dunedin: J.S. Dawson, 2002).
27. 'Obituary: Franz David Bielschowsky', *New Zealand Medical Journal*, June 1965, 338–39; C.M. Goodall, P. Shubik & J.H. Weisburger, 'Dr Franz David Bielschowsky: 1902–1965: An appreciation', *Cancer Research*, vol. 26, 1966, 346–48; Jean Kennedy to author, 21 July 2016.
28. Felix Grayeff, *Migrant Scholar: An autobiography* (Druck: Universitatsbibliothek Freiburg i. Br., 1986).
29. Schwarz, *Griesbach*; Paul Oestreicher to author, 15 and 16 March 2016.
30. *UOC*, 1990–91.
31. *UOC*, 1962; 'Tireless treaty champion dies', *Waatea News*, 11 June 2015: www.waateanews.com/waateanews/x_story_id/OTcxMw==/National/x_story/Tireless-treaty-champion-dies; Bill Dacker, *Te Mamae me te Aroha, the Pain and the Love: A history of Kai Tahu Whānui in Otago, 1844–1994* (Dunedin: University of Otago Press/Dunedin City Council, 1994), 132.
32. John Broughton to author, 19 April 2017; School of Physical Education Annual Report, 1973, Records of Registry and Central Administration, AG-180-7/12, HC.
33. *Treaty of Waitangi Review of the University of Otago* (Dunedin: University of Otago, 1998), 25.
34. 'About us', Te Poutama Māori: www.otago.ac.nz/te-poutama-maori/about/index.html
35. 'Caucus formalised for Pacific academic staff', Otago Bulletin Board, 12 July 2016: www.otago.ac.nz/otagobulletin/people/otago617173.html
36. Dorothy Page, 'Soper, Eileen Louise', from DNZB: www.teara.govt.nz/en/biographies/4s37/soper-eileen-louise
37. Ian Church, 'Stevenson, Isaac' and 'Annie Elizabeth Stevenson', in Jane Thomson (ed.), *Southern People: A dictionary of Otago Southland biography* (Dunedin: Longacre Press/Dunedin City Council, 1998), 482.
38. F.G. Soper, 'University of Otago: Ten years as vice-chancellor 1954 to 1963', 20–21, Frederick Soper papers, 90–161, Box 2, HC.

39. Sheila Ward, Hilary Hunt & Quentin Furlong, *Otago University Staff Families Association 1910–2000* (Dunedin: Otago University Staff Families Association, 2008); Eileen L. Soper, *The Leaves Turn* (Dunedin: John McIndoe Ltd, 1973), 56; 'Staff families', *UON*, September 1987, 13.
40. Campbell, 'Benson, Gertrude Helen and Benson, William Noel'.
41. Margaret Loutit interview.
42. Gina Donnelly, 'Women and children first and last', BA (Hons) dissertation, University of Otago, 1994, 20–25, 33.
43. University Nursery Association Annual Report, 1969, OUSA records, MS-0641/0622, HC.
44. Donnelly, 'Women and children', 26–27.
45. Rosemarie Smith to author, 7 April 2017.
46. Donnelly, 'Women and children', 28–37.
47. Ibid., 16–17, 28–41; 'Te Pā opens', *UOM*, no. 39, 2014, 38–39.
48. Barbara Brookes, 'Academic motherhood' [in press].
49. Jocelyn Harris interview; Dorothy Page, 'Horsman, Dorothea', in Thomson, *Southern People*, 235–36.
50. Helen Leach interview.
51. Harlene Hayne interview.
52. 'Women staff caucus', *UON*, March 1983, 7; 'Staff women's caucus', *UON*, March 1987, 14–15.
53. Brookes, 'Academic motherhood'.
54. 'Equal employment policy', *UON*, May 1987, 4; 'Equal employment opportunity officer', *UON*, September 1987, 3.
55. Child, *Equal Employment Opportunities*.
56. *UOAR*, 1988, 1989; 'EEO co-ordinator', *UON*, February 1990, 3.
57. 'Equal employment opportunities management plan approved for implementation', *UON*, July 1991, 1; 'EEO report 1992', *UON*, June 1993, 10–11.
58. 'Women's way to leadership', *UON*, March 1996, 3; 'Getting women's careers on the cards', *UON*, July 1996, 6;
59. Jocelyn Harris interview.
60. *UOAR*, 2000, 106.
61. 'Women encouraged to pursue academic careers', *OB*, 5 September 2008, 4.
62. 'General staff women feel disadvantaged', *UON*, May 1993, 8.
63. Andrew McNaughton, 'University life', *OB*, 2 December 2005, 9.
64. Child, *Equal Employment Opportunities*.
65. E.J. Godley, 'Biographical notes: Alexander Callender Purdie (1824–1899) and Alex Purdie (c. 1861–1905)', *New Zealand Botanical Society Newsletter*, no. 78, 2004, 16–19; 'Obituaries', *ES*, 26 June 1899, 2; 'University council', *OW*, 4 May 1893, 15.
66. *UOAR*, 1894. The number of attendants is not specified, but in the balance sheet £392 was spent on attendants' salaries and £70 on 'retiring allowance to janitor' (a year's salary).
67. *UOAR*, 2000–2015.
68. Shirley Kelly interview.
69. Child, *Equal Employment Opportunities*, 19.
70. *UOAR*, 2000, 2015.
71. *Treaty of Waitangi Review*, 25; *University of Otago Equity Demographics: Annual HR Equity Report*, 2015, 11–12.
72. *UOC*, 2015.
73. 'Non-academic staff', *UON*, September 1974, 13.
74. Nicholas Tarling, *Professionals and Unionists: A history of the Association of University Staff 1923–98* (Wellington: Association of University Staff, 2000), 12, 20–22.
75. Agnes Blackie, 'The spare time of a lecturer', Blackie family papers, MS–4443/005, HC.
76. Peter Franks, *The Reluctant Unionists – From Ivory Tower to the Real World: A history of the New Zealand University Technicians Union, 1971–1991* (Wellington: Association of University Staff of New Zealand, 1993), iii.
77. Tarling, *Professionals and Unionists*, 40–41, 62–66, 109–12.
78. 'History', Tertiary Education Union: http://teu.ac.nz/about/history/
79. 'Inaugural general staff award winners', *OB*, 9 September 2005, 2.

6: THE HUMANITIES

1. John Barsby, 'Sale, George Samuel', from DNZB: www.teara.govt.nz/en/biographies/2s1/sale-george-samuel
2. Margaret Tennant, 'MacGregor, Duncan', from DNZB: www.teara.govt.nz/en/biographies/2m7/macgregor-duncan
3. 'University of Otago', *ODT*, 11 July 1871, 2.
4. 'Bachelor of Arts. Latin as degree subject no longer compulsory. Decision of the senate', *New Zealand Herald*, 24 January 1917, 9.
5. John O'Shea, 'Recollections of my student days', *The Otago University Jubilee 1869–1919: Ceremonies and celebrations* (Dunedin: Evening Star, 1920), 54.
6. 'University of Otago', *ODT*, 11 July 1871, 2; *UOAR*, 1873.
7. 'University of Otago', *ODT*, 11 July 1871, 2.
8. *ODT*, 19 October 1871, 2.
9. The original syllabus for Otago degrees is outlined in the report of the University Council meeting, *ODT*, 28 April 1871, 2–3. For the senior class course, see 'University of Otago', *ODT*, 31 October 1872, 2.
10. 'Professor MacGregor's lecture', *Wellington Independent*, 20 July 1871, 3; *UOAR*, 1873.
11. In 1878 conservatives on Synod who were upset over views published by MacGregor swayed the vote on a proposed new chair to be endowed by the church, deciding it should be in moral philosophy and political economy; MacGregor would remain professor of psychology and logic only. The University Council refused the offer of this chair. See Tennant, 'MacGregor, Duncan'; Kim Sullivan, 'Divinity, Darwinism and the curse of the chair', in The Time Keepers, *Tower Turmoil: Characters and controversies at the University of Otago*, (Dunedin: Department of History, University of Otago, 2005), 29–49; Editorial, *ODT*, 17 January 1876, 2; Editorial and 'The new professorship', *ODT*, 14 January 1878, 2–3; 'The synod and the University Council', *ODT*, 23 January 1879,

supplement, 1. On MacGregor as a lecturer, see D.R. White, 'Impressions of university life in the early days' and James Johnson, 'The university and the training of teachers', in *Otago University Jubilee*, 33, 81. For a detailed account of the dispute over the church-endowed chairs, see G.E. Thompson, *A History of the University of Otago (1869–1919)*, (Dunedin: Wilkie, 1919), 124–41.

12. *UOAR*, 1874; John Smillie, 'Law at Otago: 1873–1998', *Otago Law Review*, vol. 9, no. 2, 1998, 187–94; David Hamer, 'Stout, Robert', from DNZB: www.teara.govt.nz/en/biographies/2s48/stout-robert. On the many changes to legal qualifications and degrees through the years, see Michael Cullen, *Lawfully Occupied: The centennial history of the Otago District Law Society* (Dunedin: Otago District Law Society, 1979), 111–41.
13. Carol Brown, 'Benjamin, Ethel Rebecca', from DNZB: https://teara.govt.nz/en/biographies/2b18/benjamin-ethel-rebecca; 'Ethel Benjamin Address', Otago Women Lawyers' Society: https://otagowomenlawyerssociety.com/ethel-benjamin/
14. *UOAR*, 1875.
15. Obituary, *OW*, 11 September 1901, 29; Keith Sinclair, *A History of the University of Auckland 1883–1983* (Auckland: Auckland University Press, 1983), 79.
16. Individual class sizes were published in the *UOAR* up to 1889.
17. For instance, from 1876 Buechler taught German at the Otago Boys' and Otago Girls' high schools in addition to his university work; he later added French classes for teacher trainees to his portfolio. He left his various Dunedin positions to become a master at Timaru High School in 1881. 'Education Board', *ODT*, 11 February 1876, 3; 'Timaru High School', *Timaru Herald*, 4 November 1880, 7.
18. J.B. Callan, 'Some teachers of twenty years ago', in *Otago University Jubilee*, 51.
19. 'Otago University – the opening address', *OW*, 6 May 1882, 11.
20. *ODT*, 15 December 1888, 2; 'The Manapouri expedition', *ODT*, 27 December 1888, 3; *UOAR*, 1889; D. Colquhoun, 'Reminiscences of the university, 1884', in *Otago University Jubilee*, 39.
21. 'University council', *ODT*, 5 January 1889, 4; 'Presbyterian synod', *ODT*, 1 February 1889, 3.
22. Peter Matheson, 'Salmond, William', from DNZB: www.teara.govt.nz/en/biographies/2s3/salmond-william; Callan, 'Some teachers'; O'Shea, 'Recollections'; Violet Greig, 'The university in a democracy', in *Otago University Jubilee*, 44–47.
23. *UOAR*, 1902, 1911; Smillie, 'Law at Otago'; Richard Boast, 'Garrow, James Mitchell Ellis', from DNZB: www.teara.govt.nz/en/biographies/3g3/garrow-james-mitchell-ellis. Law student numbers were published in the *UOAR*.
24. Carol Morton Johnston & Harry Morton, *Dunedin Teachers College: The first hundred years* (Dunedin: Dunedin Teachers College, 1976), 1–13; J.S. Tennant, 'The university and the teacher', in *Otago University Jubilee*, 43; *UOAR*, 1902.
25. Thomas Gilray, 'Otago University: A thirty years' retrospect', in *Otago University Jubilee*, 17–26.
26. 'Cloak-room notes', *OUR*, vol. 12, no. 1, 1898, 11–12.
27. *UOAR*, 1902.
28. 'The University Senate', *ODT*, 28 February 1902, 4; 'University Senate', *Evening Post*, 27 February 1904, 6.
29. 'Education: Training of teachers', *AJHR*, 1906, E–1C, 1; 'University Council', *ODT*, 3 May 1904, 7; 'University Council', *OW*, 15 June 1904, 13; Report of the Principal of the Training College, *AJHR*, 1905, E–1C, 4; *UOC*, 1905, 84.
30. *UOAR*, 1909, 1910; Annual Report of the Minister of Education, *AJHR*, 1910, E–1, 16.
31. 'University Council', *ODT*, 18 December 1901, 7; *UOAR*, 1902. On Watt, see John Collie, *The Story of the Otago Free Church Settlement 1848 to 1948* (Dunedin: Presbyterian Bookroom, 1948), 79.
32. *UOAR*, 1913.
33. *UOAR*, 1915 [31 March], 1915 [31 December], 1917.
34. Annual report of the Minister of Education, *AJHR*, 1911, E–7, 3.
35. *UOAR*, 1908; Thompson, *University of Otago*, 200.
36. University of Otago council minutes, 15 June 1915, 16 October 1917 and 3 December 1918, Records of Registry and Central Administration, AG-180-1/06, HC; *UOAR*, 1918, 1919.
37. *UOAR*, 1899.
38. Council minutes, 16 March 1915, Records of Registry and Central Administration, AG-180-1/06, HC.
39. Thompson, *History of the University of Otago*, 199; *OUR*, June 1918, 14–15.
40. *UOC*, 1907–1917; *UOAR*, 1917, 1920; Michael Gill, 'Bedford, Harry Dodgshun', from DNZB: www.teara.govt.nz/en/biographies/3b21/bedford-harry-dodgshun
41. 'The history of the department, with special attention to the development of the curriculum', Self-review, University of Otago Review of the Department of History, 1994, 1–2.
42. *UOAR*, 1918; 'Fels, Willi (1858–1946)', in Jane Thomson (ed.), *Southern People: A dictionary of Otago Southland biography* (Dunedin: Longacre Press/Dunedin City Council, 1998), 157. Willi Fels was the grandfather of Charles Brasch, a future generous benefactor to the university.
43. Atholl Anderson, 'Skinner, Henry Devenish', from DNZB: www.teara.govt.nz/en/biographies/4s29/skinner-henry-devenish
44. *UOC*, 1920, 141; 1929, 195–96.
45. Arts and Science Faculty Annual Report, 1930, Records of Registry and Central Administration, AG-180-7/01, HC.
46. W.J. Hamilton, 'James Herries Beattie (1881–1972)', in Thomson, *Southern People*, 34–35. This work was published much later as H. Beattie & Atholl Anderson, *Traditional Lifeways of the Southern Maori: The Otago University Museum ethnological project, 1920* (Dunedin: Otago University Press/Otago Museum, 2009).
47. Arts and Science Faculty Annual Report, 1935, Records of Registry and Central Administration, AG-180-7/01, HC.

48. Arts and Science Faculty Annual Report, 1939, Records of Registry and Central Administration, AG-180-7/02, HC.
49. University of Otago council minutes, 17 August and 14 December 1926, Records of Registry and Central Administration, AG-180-1/08, HC; John Blair obituary, *ODT*, 11 September 1913, 8; John Drummond, 'Galway, Victor Edward', from DNZB: www.teara.govt.nz/en/biographies/5g3/galway-victor-edward
50. Department of Music Annual Report, 1949 (25th anniversary report), Records of Registry and Central Administration, AG-180-7/03, HC; *UOC*, 1929, 197–98.
51. Honor McKellar interview.
52. *UOC*, 1923.
53. Elizabeth Mason, 'Cockabully story: The memoirs of Elizabeth Mason (nee Mabel McIndoe)', Misc-MS–1400/001, HC.
54. John Barsby, 'Classics at Otago 3: The Manton period (1949–65)', *Australasian Society for Classical Studies Proceedings*, vol. 32, 2011, 5.
55. Arts and Science Faculty Annual Report, 1930, Records of Registry and Central Administration, AG-180-7/01, HC.
56. Arts and Science Faculty Annual Report, 1932, Records of Registry and Central Administration, AG-180-7/01, HC.
57. Johnston & Morton, *Dunedin Teachers College*, 74–96, 155–56; Arts and Science Faculty Annual Report, 1933, 1935, Records of Registry and Central Administration, AG-180-7/01, HC; *UOAR*, 1921, 1922.
58. Arts and Science Faculty Annual Report, 1942, Records of Registry and Central Administration, AG-180-7/02, HC; Cullen, *Lawfully Occupied*, 131–32.
59. 'Impending retirement of Professor Ross', *UON*, June 1976, 3.
60. *UOC*; Felix Grayeff, *Migrant Scholar: An autobiography* (Druck: Universitatsbibliothek Freiburg i. Br., 1986).
61. Hugh Parton, *The University of New Zealand* (Auckland: Auckland University Press/University Grants Committee, 1979), 144–45; Simon Rae, *Challenge and Change: An account of theological education and ministry training at Knox College, Dunedin, 1976–2010* (Dunedin: Knox Centre for Ministry & Leadership, Presbyterian Church of Aotearoa New Zealand, 2011), 112; David Hamer, 'Stout, Robert', from DNZB: www.teara.govt.nz/en/biographies/2s48/stout-robert
62. Ray Hargreaves, *Selwyn College's First Century: A history and list of residents 1893–1992* (Dunedin: Centennial Committee, Selwyn College Board of Governors, 1993); Ian Breward, *Grace and Truth: A history of Theological Hall, Knox College, Dunedin 1876–1975* (Dunedin: Theological Education Committee, Presbyterian Church of New Zealand, 1975); Peter Norris, *Southernmost Seminary: The story of Holy Cross College, Mosgiel (1900–97)* (Dunedin: Holy Cross Seminary, 1999); Murray Savage, *Haddon of Glen Leith: An ecumenical journey* (Dunedin: Associated Churches of Christ in New Zealand, 1970), 31–43.
63. *UOAR*, 1946; Parton, *University of New Zealand*, 144–45; Rae, *Challenge and Change*, 112–14.
64. Arts and Music Faculty Annual Report, 1946 and 1948, Records of Registry and Central Administration, AG-180-7/03, HC.
65. Peter Holland, Hugh Kidd & Richard Welch (eds), *From Mellor to Hocken: Fifty years of geography at the University of Otago* (Dunedin: Department of Geography, University of Otago, 1995), vii, 1–5, 7–8, 15–18. On the Thomas Report and the changing secondary school curriculum, see Roger Openshaw, Greg Lee & Howard Lee, *Challenging the Myths: Rethinking New Zealand's educational history* (Palmerston North: Dunmore Press, 1993), 162–76; and Ian Cumming & Alan Cumming, *History of State Education in New Zealand 1840–1975* (Wellington: Pitman, 1978), 279–82.
66. 'History of the department', 3.
67. Arts and Music Faculty Annual Report, 1948, Records of Registry and Central Administration, AG-180-7/03, HC; *UOC*, 1948, 130 and 1949, 142.
68. *UOC*; Austin Mitchell, *The Half-Gallon Quarter-Acre Pavlova Paradise* (Christchurch: Whitcombe & Tombs, 1972).
69. Arts and Music Faculty Annual Report, 1948, Records of Registry and Central Administration, AG-180-7/03, HC.
70. Arts and Music Faculty Annual Report, 1961, Records of Registry and Central Administration, AG-180-7/07, HC.
71. *UOC*; Margaret Dalziel, 'Looking back', in Greg Waite, Jocelyn Harris & Heather Murray (eds), *World and Stage: Essays for Colin Gibson* (Dunedin: Department of English, University of Otago, 1998), 6–14; Angus Ross, 'The University of Otago from within, since 1930', script for talk for Arts Open Lectures Centennial Series, 4 June 1969, 13, MS-0835, HC; 'Chair of English: New professor for Otago University', *ODT*, 23 November 1950, 6.
72. R.T. Robertson, 'Our literature in the English prescriptions', *OUR*, 1956, 28–30.
73. Alan Horsman interview.
74. Lawrence Jones, 'New Zealand studies at Otago', *Kite: Newsletter of the New Zealand Literature Association*, no. 2, 1992, 4–5.
75. Arts and Music Faculty Annual Report, 1961 and 1970, Records of Registry and Central Administration, AG-180-7/07 and 7/10, HC.
76. Law Faculty Annual Report, 1959, 1966–1967, Records of Registry and Central Administration, AG-180-7/07 and 7/09, HC; Smillie, 'Law at Otago'.
77. Olessia Kirchik, Yves Gingras & Vincent Larivière, 'Changes in publication languages and citation practices and their effect on the scientific impact of Russian science (1993–2010), *Journal of the American Society for Information Science and Technology*, vol. 63, no. 7, 2012, 1411–19.
78. *UOC*, 1960–1975.
79. Peter Stupples interview.
80. *UOC*, 1967–1976; Arts and Music Faculty Annual Report, 1968, 1970, 1971 and 1973, Records of Registry and Central Administration, AG-180-7/09 to 7/12, HC.

81. Theology Faculty Annual Report, 1969–1972, Records of Registry and Central Administration, AG-180-7/10 and 7/11, HC; Norris, *Southernmost Seminary*, 95–101.
82. Arts and Music Faculty Annual Report, 1961, Records of Registry and Central Administration, AG-180-7/07, HC.
83. Arts and Music Faculty Annual Report, 1963, Records of Registry and Central Administration, AG-180-7/08, HC.
84. Peter Anthony Jackson, 'The mind of a nation: A philosophical and historical critique of psychology in New Zealand', PhD thesis, Massey University, 1998, 103–05. On Bernadelli's background, see also 'Husband and wife to join university', *New Zealand Herald*, 28 September 1961, 3.
85. *UOC*, 1964–1966.
86. Anderson, 'Skinner, Henry Devenish'; Neil Howard, 'Life at university – fifties style'; Helen Leach & Peter Wilson, 'History of the Anthropology Department at the University of Otago', Self-review, University of Otago Review of Department of Anthropology, 1992.
87. Arts and Music Faculty Annual Report, 1959, 1962–1965, Records of Registry and Central Administration, AG-180-7/07 and 7/08, HC; Peter Gathercole, 'Otago 1958–1968', *Archaeology in New Zealand*, vol. 43, nos 3 & 4, 2000, 206–19 and 283–96; Helen Leach interview.
88. Helen Leach interview; Helen Leach, *The Pavlova Story: A slice of New Zealand's culinary history* (Dunedin: Otago University Press, 2008).
89. Arts and Music Faculty Annual Report, 1967–1968, Records of Registry and Central Administration, AG-180-7/09, HC; Gathercole, 'Otago 1958–1968'; 'Cambridge College honours archaeologist', *OB*, 11 July 2008, 9.
90. Arts and Music Faculty Annual Report, 1970 and 1975, Records of Registry and Central Administration, AG-180-7/10 and 7/13, HC; Leach & Wilson, 'History of the Anthropology Department'; 'News in brief', *UON*, October 1975, 12.
91. Janet Davidson, review of Atholl Anderson, Brian Allingham & Ian Smith (eds), *Shag River Mouth: The archaeology of an early southern Maori village* (Canberra: Research School of Pacific & Asian Studies, Australian National University, 1996), in *Journal of the Polynesian Society*, vol. 106, no. 2, 1997, 185–87.
92. *University of New Zealand Calendar*; *UOC*; Self-review, University of Otago Review of Department of Geography, 1993, 5–6; Subjects in which degrees were obtained, University Grants Committee statistics files, R12485703, Archives New Zealand, Wellington; University of Otago Graduation programmes, 1966–1967.
93. Jim Flynn interview; Arts and Music Faculty Annual Report, 1968 and 1969, Records of Registry and Central Administration, AG-180-7/09 and 7/10, HC; 'Otago honours Jim Flynn', *OB*, 14 May 2010, 3. For an example of the popular attention paid to Flynn's research on intelligence, see Sally Blundell, 'Mind gains', *New Zealand Listener*, 9 July 2016, 12–19.
94. 'New language laboratory', *UON*, March 1982, 4–5; 'New Language Learning Centre', *UON*, April 1990, 6; 'State of the art language laboratories open this month', *UON*, September 1994, 1–2.
95. Interviews with Roger Collins, Alyth Grant and Peter Stupples.
96. Arts and Music Faculty Annual Report, 1973, Records of Registry and Central Administration, AG-180-7/12, HC.
97. 'Thoughts on imbalance', *UON*, April 1976, 1–4; *UOC*, 1972–1973.
98. 'Thoughts on imbalance'.
99. 'Classics news', *UON*, May 1979; *UOC*, 1968–1976.
100. John Barsby interview; *UOC*, 1979, 182.
101. 'Thoughts on imbalance'.
102. 'History of the department', 5–6; *UOC*, 1974–1975.
103. 'Personal chair', *UON*, November 1983, 3; '"Inspiring" history teacher and HOD retires', *UON*, September 2000, 6; Tony Ballantyne, 'Obituary: W.H. McLeod: New Zealand scholar and an authority on the history of Sikhism', *Guardian*, 4 September 2009, 39.
104. 'Benefactors have helped in many fields', *UON*, August 1982, 1–2; *UOC*.
105. *UOC*; *UON*, March 1975, 5; 'Geography growth', *UON*, June 1978, 5; Emmet Maclaurin, 'Otago University student interest in growing environmental problems between 1968 and 1984', History 353 essay, 2014.
106. *UOC*; Self-review, University of Otago Review of Department of Geography, 1993, 6; 'Honour for Ron Lister', *UON*, October 1983, 2; 'Regional planning', *UON*, April 1978, 4; 'Planning course', *UON*, July 1985, 5–6; Alyce Melrose, 'Ali Memon, great planning lecturer, researcher and winner of the New Zealand Planning Institute's Premier Award in April 2011', *Lincoln Planning Review*, vol. 3, no. 2, 2012, 62–64.
107. Arts and Music Faculty Annual Report, 1971, 1975 and 1979, Records of Registry and Central Administration, AG-180-7/11, 7/13 and 7/14, HC; *UOC*, 1971–1979; Self-review, University of Otago Review of the Department of English, 2009, 8; 'Professor devoted life to debunking myths', *ODT*, 21 September 2002: www.otago.ac.nz/anthropology/Linguistic/donn.html
108. *UOC*, 1985.
109. *UOC*; Self-review, University of Otago Review of the Department of English, 2009, 8–9; 'Linguistics takes off!', *Otago Humanities Review*, Semester 1, 1999, 9.
110. Arts and Music Faculty Annual Report, 1944, Records of Registry and Central Administration, AG-180-7/03, HC; 'University drama: Presentation of three plays', *ODT*, 23 July 1945, 8; *Roll of the Graduates of the University of Otago* (Dunedin: University of Otago, 1989), 467; Oswald Counsell Stephens biography, Historic Cemeteries Conservation Trust of New Zealand: www.cemeteries.org.nz/stories/stephensoswaldcounsell210407.pdf
111. 'The teaching staff and Allen Hall', in Lisa Warrington & Alison Finigan (eds), *Allen Hall: 100 years, 100+ voices* (Dunedin: Department of Music, Theatre Studies Programme, University of Otago, 2014), 153, 158–60.
112. Peter Entwisle, 'Kennedy, Rodney Eric', from DNZB: www.teara.govt.nz/en/biographies/5k7/kennedy-rodney-eric
113. Arts and Music Faculty Annual Report, 1971 and 1973, Records of Registry and Central Administration, AG-180-

7/11 and 7/12, HC; *UOC*, 1973, 135; Sam Eckett, 'Toward performance: The development of the University of Otago music department', in *Culture of Change: Beginnings at the University of Otago* (Dunedin: Departments of English & History, University of Otago, 2006), 57–74.

114. 'Teaching staff and Allen Hall', 153–57, 163, 165–73.
115. Arts and Music Faculty Annual Report, 1964, Records of Registry and Central Administration, AG-180-7/08, HC.
116. *UOC*, 1966, 73; Arts and Music Faculty Annual Report, 1967, Records of Registry and Central Administration, AG-180-7/09, HC.
117. Arts and Music Faculty Annual Report, 1971, Records of Registry and Central Administration, AG-180-7/11, HC; John Drummond, 'Honor McKellar: A voice unique', *Music in New Zealand*, no. 26, 1994, 32–36, no. 27, 1994–1995, 33–39; 'Maurice Till', SOUNZ: Centre for New Zealand Music Toi te Arapuoru: http://sounz.org.nz/contributor/performer/1389
118. Arts and Music Faculty Annual Report, 1973, Records of Registry and Central Administration, AG-180-7/12, HC.
119. Bruce McMillan to author, 30 January 2014.
120. Johnston & Morton, *Dunedin Teachers College*, 140, 166–69, 173–75; Arts and Music Faculty Annual Report, 1967, Records of Registry and Central Administration, AG-180-7/09, HC.
121. *Report of the Commission on Education in New Zealand* (Wellington: Government Printer, 1962), 488–511; Johnston & Morton, *Dunedin Teachers College*, 211–12; David Keen, *In a Class of its Own: A Dunedin College of Education anniversary history* (Dunedin: Dunedin College of Education, 2001), 69–70.
122. Arts and Music Faculty Annual Report, 1972, Records of Registry and Central Administration, AG-180-7/11, HC.
123. Keen, *In a Class of its Own*, 70–73; *UOC*, 1977, 208; Jim Flynn interview.
124. Joint Board of Studies in Education Annual Report, 1977, Records of Registry and Central Administration, AG-180-7/13, HC; Keen, *In a Class of its Own*, 74, 90, 95.
125. Arts and Music Faculty Annual Report, 1977, Records of Registry and Central Administration, AG-180-7/13, HC.
126. 'Computers in education', *UON*, May 1982, 3; *UOC*, 1983, 191–92.
127. 'Computer hand-on week a success', *UON*, March 1988, 8.
128. 'A view into education', *UON*, August 1988, 1–2.
129. Keen, *In a Class of its Own*, 127–31; *UOC*, 1991, 51–2; 'Support between the people a rare thing', *UON*, September 1996, 5.
130. Regional Council of Adult Education Annual Report, 1957, Records of Registry and Central Administration, AG-180-7/06, HC. On H.T. Wesley, see obituary, *Te Ao Hou*, no. 60, September 1967, 2: http://teaohou.natlib.govt.nz/journals/teaohou/image/Mao60TeA/Mao60TeA002.html. Information on his language skills from Michael Stevens (email to author, 19 June 2014) and Robert Montgomery (personal communication, 21 July 2014).
131. Enrolment forms, Department of University Extension records, 93-080, Box 8, HC; Department of University Extension Annual Report, 1972 and 1973, Records of Registry and Central Administration, AG-180-7/11 and 7/12, HC.
132. Report to the Faculty of Arts, Faculty of Arts minutes, 5 April 1972, Records of Registry and Central Administration, AG-180-9/02, HC.
133. Faculty of Arts minutes, 5 April 1972, 3 May 1972, Records of Registry and Central Administration, AG-180-9/02, HC.
134. Academic Staffing Committee minutes, 17 June 1975, Records of Registry and Central Administration, MS–1423/004, HC.
135. 'Serious and satiric', *Critic*, 2 September 1975; 'Maori Club protest about appointment', *ODT*, 6 August 1975; Petition, Notes on meeting with representatives of Maori Graduates Association, and 'Maori course at University of Otago', press release, all in Maori Studies general file, Records of Registry and Central Administration, MS–3747, Box 134, HC.
136. Faculty of Arts minutes, 4 July 1979, Records of Registry and Central Administration, AG-180-9/06, HC. Those who declined the position included Toby Rikihana in 1976 (he initially accepted, but withdrew shortly afterwards) and Tipene O'Regan in 1979. I haven't identified the third person. See Academic Staffing Committee minutes, 6 July 1976 and 19 June 1979, Records of Registry and Central Administration, MS–1423/005 and MS–1423/006, HC; *UON*, July 1976, 6.
137. Faculty of Arts minutes, 16 April 1980, Records of Registry and Central Administration, AG-180-9/06, HC; *UON*, July 1980, 2. Though the Faculty of Arts remained committed to filling the other position, it was frozen by the academic staffing committee in 1980 for financial reasons, along with many other university posts: Academic Staffing Committee minutes, 13 July 1980, Records of Registry and Central Administration, MS–1423/007, HC.
138. 'Developing Maori heritage', *UON*, March 1986, 7–8; Godfrey Pohatu, 'The university, Maori Studies and Treaty praxis', PhD thesis, University of Otago, 1999; 'Obituary – Dr Godfrey Pohatu', *OB*, 13 August 2004, 9; 'Maori Studies', *UON*, March 1988, 3; Michael Reilly, 'A history of Maori, Pacific and Indigenous studies at Otago University, 1969–2008: A personal view', unpublished paper, 2.
139. 'Maoritanga and New Zealand Studies', *UON*, July 1986, 4; David Thomson, 'Our most popular papers', *UON*, October 1994, 7.
140. 'Maori cultural successes', *UON*, August 1989, 5.
141. 'Obituary – Dr Godfrey Pohatu'; Reilly, 'History of Maori, Pacific and Indigenous Studies', 3–6; 'Huge increase in Maori Studies Department numbers', *Te Maori News*, 3, 4 (March 1994), 13.
142. Report of University of Otago Review of the Department of Maori Studies, 1995, 2.
143. Report of University of Otago Review of Te Tumu, the School of Maori Studies, 2002, 12–13, 22; Reilly, 'History of Maori, Pacific and Indigenous Studies', 6–7.

144. *The History of Te Tumu* (Dunedin: Te Tumu, School of Maori, Pacific & Indigenous Studies, 2006), 8; Reilly, 'History of Maori, Pacific and Indigenous studies', 11.
145. Report of University of Otago Review of Te Tumu, the School of Maori Studies, 2002, 9, 11–13.
146. Reilly, 'History of Maori, Pacific and Indigenous studies', 14–18; Stu Oldham, 'Professor stood down', *ODT*, 13 April 2007, 1; Allison Rudd, 'Family support for academic', *ODT*, 14 April 2007, 2; Amy Gibb, 'Tenacious dean stood down', *Critic*, 23 April 2007, 4; Allison Rudd, 'Maori academic quits', *ODT*, 16 June 2007, 4; John Lewis, 'ERA rejects former academic's request', *ODT*, 10 January 2008, 1; John Gibb, 'Academics drop employment claim', *ODT*, 19 April 2008: www.odt.co.nz/campus/university-otago/3654/academics-drop-employment-claim; John Gibb, 'New head for Maori studies', *ODT*, 20 May 2008: www.odt.co.nz/campus/university-otago/6403/new-head-maori-studies
147. Reilly, 'History of Maori, Pacific and Indigenous studies', 12–13, 22.
148. Humanities Division Annual Report, 1990, Records of Registry and Central Administration, AG-758/085, HC; *UOAR*, 1990–2017; David McKenzie interview.
149. 'Partnerships for excellence: The future of language study at the University of Otago. Report of the review panel for the School of Languages', June 1996, 12, George Petersen papers, r.6975, Box 38, HC.
150. 'Asian Studies at Otago: Report of the working party set up to investigate the introduction of teaching and research in Asian Studies at the University of Otago', September 1991, Records of Registry and Central Administration, MS-3786, Box 12, HC.
151. 'A boost for Asian Studies', *UON*, July 1993, 1; 'Focus on Asian Studies', *UON*, July 1993, 2.
152. 'Partnerships for Excellence', 9–10.
153. 'Humanities restructuring on track', *UON*, July 1998, 10.
154. 'Humanities to adopt flatter management structure', *OB*, 19 May 2006, 5.
155. 'Report of the working party on the Humanities', July 1997, George Petersen papers, r.6975, Box 38, HC.
156. Graeme Fogelberg interview.
157. Peter Stupples interview.
158. Graeme Fogelberg interview; 'Report of the review panel for the School of Languages', 21, 45; John Gibb, 'Popularity of Spanish paper "unprecedented"', *ODT*, 31 March 2001, 21; Self-review, University of Otago Review of Department of Languages and Cultures, 2008.
159. *UOC*; Bruce Munro, 'Portuguese popular', *Star*, 22 May 2008, 9.
160. Self-review and Report, University of Otago Review of Department of Languages and Cultures, 2008; *Performance-Based Research Fund, Evaluating Research Excellence – the 2012 Assessment: Final Report* (Wellington: Tertiary Education Commission, 2013).
161. Theology Faculty Annual Report, 1985, Humanities Division Annual Report, 1992, Records of Registry and Central Administration, AG-180-7/15 and AG-758/085, HC; 'Faculty of theology', *UON*, July 1992, 2; Rae, *Challenge and Change*, 115–18.
162. *UOC*, 1991–1993; 'Religious studies professor appointed', *UON*, March 1992, 3.
163. 'Milestone in the religious studies department', *UON*, July 1994, 4.
164. Rae, *Challenge and Change*, 84.
165. Ibid., 75–125; Norris, *Southernmost Seminary*, 131–37; 'New department emerges', *UON*, July 1996, 3; 'Eminent theologian appointed to foundation chair', *UON*, October 1996, 2.
166. Report of University of Otago Review of Department of Theology and Religious Studies, 2008; Report of University of Otago Review of Department of Theology and Religion, 2014; *UOC*, 2010–2011; 'Debut for Arabic language at Summer School', *OB*, 28 January 2005, 7; 'Arabic course adds international flavour', *OB*, 26 January 2007, 5; Elaine Webster to author, 29 April 2015.
167. D.W. Girvan, Memorandum to deans and heads of department: New blood lectureships, 20 June 1988, Jocelyn Harris papers, r.8044, HC.
168. Proposal for new blood appointment in women's studies, 18 July 1988, Jocelyn Harris papers, r.8044, HC; Academic staffing committee minutes, 16 August 1988, 6 September 1988 and 20 September 1988, Records of Registry and Central Administration, MS-1423/011, HC.
169. *UOC*, 1990–1994; 'About people', *UON*, August 1989, 11; 'Women's studies: A new beginning!', *Critic*, 20 February 1990, 7; Annabel Cooper interview; Report of University of Otago Review of Department of Anthropology, 2006, 23.
170. Jude Barback, 'The "decline" of women's studies', *New Zealand Education Review*, vol. 2, no. 2, 2011, 44–45 (note also the comment in response to this article from the Otago gender studies staff).
171. *UOC*, 1994–2008; Report of University of Otago Review of Department of Anthropology, 2006, 23; Annabel Cooper interview.
172. Academic Staffing Committee minutes, 20 September 1988, Records of Registry and Central Administration, MS-1423/011, HC.
173. 'Developments in Gender and Women's Studies since 1998', Self-review, University of Otago Review of Department of Anthropology, 2006; Report of University of Otago Review of Department of Anthropology, 2006, 22.
174. Report of University of Otago Review of Department of Sociology, Gender and Social Work/Children's Issues Centre, 2014, 10.
175. *Social Work Education in New Zealand Universities: A report* (Palmerston North: University Grants Committee, 1981), 1981, 44; Angeline Barretta-Herman, 'Development of social work in New Zealand: 1969–1988', *Social Work Review*, vol. 5, no. 4, 1993, 4–8, vol. 5, no. 5, 1993, 30–35, vol. 6, no. 3, 1994, 12–18.
176. Regional Council of Adult Education/Department of University Extension Annual Reports, 1959–1967, Records of Registry and Central Administration, AG-180-7/07 to 7/09, HC.

177. Mary Nash, 'People, policies and practice: Social work education in Aotearoa/New Zealand from 1949–1995', PhD thesis, Massey University, 1998, 272–73, 453; Warwick Brunton, *The Medicine of the Future: A history of the Department of Preventive and Social Medicine, University of Otago 1886–2011* (Dunedin: Department of Preventive and Social Medicine, 2011), 157.
178. Department of University Extension Annual Report, 1974 and 1976, Records of Registry and Central Administration, AG-180-7/12 and 7/13, HC.
179. *UOC*, 1980, 383; *Social Work Education in New Zealand Universities*, 34; Department of University Extension Annual Report, 1983, Records of Registry and Central Administration, AG-180-7/15, HC.
180. *UOC*, 1976–1981.
181. Consumer and Applied Sciences Faculty Annual Report, 1987, Records of Registry and Central Administration, AG-180-7/15, HC; *UOC*, 1988–1990.
182. Consumer and Applied Sciences Faculty Annual Report, 1988, Records of Registry and Central Administration, AG-180-7/15, HC.
183. *UOC*, 1990–1993.
184. Pam Jemmett, personal communication, 3 July 2015; Report of University of Otago Review of Department of Community and Family Studies, 2003.
185. 'Certification of social work programmes', *OB*, 16 May 2003, 9.
186. Report of University of Otago Review of Department of Community and Family Studies, 2003.
187. 'New name for community and family studies', *OB*, 27 January 2006, 7; 'Changing of the guard in social work', *OB*, 5 October 2007, 7.
188. Report of University of Otago Review of Department of Sociology, Gender and Social Work/Children's Issues Centre, 2014, 19; *UOC*, 2007–2013; Barbara Gilray, 'Social worker registration: A decade of development, debate and delivery', *Aotearoa New Zealand Social Work*, vol. 25, no. 3, 2013, 25–34; Liz Beddoe, 'Continuing education, registration and professional identity in New Zealand social work', *International Social Work*, vol. 58, no. 1, 2015, 165–74.
189. Chris Brickell, 'Those "other sociologists": Social analysis before sociology', *New Zealand Sociology*, vol. 22, no. 1, 2007, 4–27.
190. Chris Brickell, Martin Tolich & Bonnie Scarth, 'Sociology before sociology at Otago University', *New Zealand Sociology*, vol. 29, no. 4, 2014, 27–44; David Skegg to author, 31 July 2017.
191. Brickell, Tolich & Scarth, 'Sociology before sociology'; 'Major status for sociology', *OB*, 8 October 2004, 11; Report of University of Otago Review of Department of Sociology, Gender and Social Work/Children's Issues Centre, 2014.
192. John Gibb, 'Criminology papers on offer at Otago', *ODT*, 14 February 2015: www.odt.co.nz/news/dunedin/criminology-papers-offer-otago; 'Criminology minor exciting addition to Otago', Otago Connection, 2015: www.otago.ac.nz/news/otagoconnection/otago088723.html
193. Keen, *In a Class of its Own*, 45–46, 78–79; Noeline Alcorn, 'Teacher education policy in New Zealand since 1970', *Waikato Journal of Education*, vol. 18, no. 1, 2015, 37–48; Louise Shaw, *Making a Difference: A history of the Auckland College of Education 1881–2004* (Auckland: Auckland University Press, 2006), 213–16.
194. Keen, *In a Class of its Own*, 79–86; *UOAR*, 1997, 12; 1998, 13–14; 'Teaching degree change has implications for the University', *UON*, August–September 1997, 2; Bruce McMillan to author, 30 January 2014.
195. 'Distinctive teaching programme', *UON*, October 1999, 5.
196. Report of University of Otago Review of Faculty of Education, University of Otago, 2004, 9, 18–28.
197. Keen, *In a Class of its Own*, 82–85.
198. 'Proposed merger of college and university', *OB*, 20 May 2005, 3; 'Councils approve college merger', *OB*, 27 January 2006, 5; 'Merger confirmed between university and college', *OB*, 25 August 2006, 1.
199. 'First Otago college of education dean appointed', *OB*, 20 October 2006, 1.
200. *UOC*, 2007–2009.
201. Report of University of Otago Review of College of Education, 2012, 9, 11–12; Allison Rudd, 'Fifteen jobs go at College of Education', *ODT*, 4 September 2010: www.odt.co.nz/news/dunedin/124480/fifteen-jobs-go-college
202. John Lewis, 'Prospects bleak for Otago teacher graduates', *ODT*, 22 December 2011: www.odt.co.nz/news/dunedin/191868/prospects-bleak-teacher-graduates
203. Vaughan Elder, '20% decrease in workforce', *ODT*, 23 January 2015: www.odt.co.nz/news/dunedin/330849/20-decrease-workforce; Enrolment figures compiled for university library by student data warehouse.
204. 'Postgraduate teaching course doubles in size', Division of Humanities news and events, 17 March 2015: www.otago.ac.nz/humanities/news/otago088892.html; Enrolment figures compiled for university library by student data warehouse.
205. *Performance-Based Research Fund – the 2012 Assessment*, 89–28.
206. Report of the University of Otago Review of College of Education, 2012, 16–17.
207. 'From the AVC's desk', *Otago Humanities Review*, no. 1, 1998, 2.
208. *UOC*, 1977–1979
209. Arts and Music Faculty Annual Report, 1979, Records of Registry and Central Administration, AG-180-7/14, HC; 'Art history popular', *UON*, April 1982, 3.
210. 'Art history', *UON*, October 1987, 11.
211. *UOC*, 1990–2008; Report of University of Otago Review of Department of History, 2008, 9–10; Report of University of Otago Review of Department of History and Art History, 2013, 10–11.
212. 'About people', *UON*, September 1990, 8; *UOC*, 1991.
213. 'The rise of film studies', *UON*, April-May 1995, 10; *UOC*, 1996.
214. 'Alumni memories with Lisa Scott', *UOM*, no. 39, 2014, 44.
215. Self-review, University of Otago Review of Department of Media, Film and Communication, 2011, 4.

216. 'New major in communication studies', *Otago Humanities Review: On the move*, no. 1, 1999, 9.
217. Self-review, University of Otago Review of Department of Media, Film and Communication, 2011, 3–4, 11–12.
218. 'Communication "literacies" vital to Otago's future', *UON*, July 2000, 5.
219. Report of the University of Otago Review of Department of Media, Film and Communication, 2011, 2–3, 10–11; Self-review, University of Otago Review of Department of Media, Film and Communication, 2011, 1–2, 7, 9–16.
220. *UOC*, 2013–2015.
221. Alison Finigan (ed.), *Partnerships for Excellence: Celebrating 10 years of the Leading Thinkers initiative* (Dunedin: Development & Alumni Relations Office, University of Otago, 2014); 'New profs advance Otago's research and teaching', *OB*, 8 October 2004, 4; 'Ron Lister Fellow', *OB*, 24 March 2006, 4; 'We don't know how lucky we are', *OB*, 18 May 2007, 7; *UOC*.
222. 'Anonymous donors fund new philosophy chair', *OB*, 24 March 2005, 1; Finigan, *Partnerships for Excellence*; Charles Pigden, 'Philosophical history: The Otago department': www.otago.ac.nz/philosophy/history.html
223. 'Children's Issues Centre a coup for Otago', *UON*, November 1994, 1; 'Trust cements future of Children's Issues Centre', *OB*, 16 June 2006, 1; Finigan, *Partnerships for Excellence*; 'McMillan, Alexander (1884–1967)', in Thomson, *Southern People*, 317.
224. 'Children's Issues Centre appoints director', *UON*, April-May 1995, 1; 'First professor of Childhood Studies', *OB*, 11 July 2008, 2; Finigan, *Partnerships for Excellence*.
225. 'Children's Centre up and running', *UON*, September 1995, 1; 'PGSF kick starts research programmes', *UON*, July 1996, 2; 'Children's Issues Centre launches new journal', *UON*, February/March 1997, 1; 'Courses will meet professionals' needs', *UON*, March 2000, 5; 'A decade of children's issues', *OB*, 2 December 2005, 8.
226. Report of University of Otago Review of Department of Sociology, Gender and Social Work/Children's Issues Centre, 2014, 14–15.
227. 'Chair in Irish studies for Otago', *OB*, 3 December 2004, 1; 'New chair arrives with eyes smiling', *OB*, 6 October 2006, 3; 'Scottish studies gains two professors', *OB*, 8 February 2008, 2; 'Irish and Scottish Centre', *OB*, 9 July 2010, 3; Finigan, *Partnerships for Excellence*.
228. 'English 124: The first year', *UON*, November 1993, 4; 'Otago teaching fellow breaks new ground', *UON*, March 1995, 18; Self-review, University of Otago Review of Department of English, 2009, 9; *UOC*.
229. Law Faculty Annual Report, 1966 to 1980, Records of Registry and Central Administration, AG-180-7/09 to 7/13, HC.
230. Law Faculty Annual Report, 1983, Records of Registry and Central Administration, AG-180-7/15, HC.
231. Law Faculty Annual Report, 1985 to 1987, Records of Registry and Central Administration, AG-180-7/15, HC; 'Limit on numbers imposed in law faculty', *UON*, August 1985, 1–2; Rachel Barrowman, *Victoria University of Wellington 1899–1999: A history* (Wellington: Victoria University Press, 1999), 238–40.
232. Law Faculty Annual Report, 1988, Records of Registry and Central Administration, AG-180-7/15, HC.
233. 'Down memory lane once more', *Otago Graduate*, 1988, 23–27. Women at other New Zealand law schools faced similar experiences. An example is Shirley Smith, who studied at Victoria in the 1950s: https://shirleysmithaddress.org/shirley-smith/
234. Smillie, 'Law at Otago'.
235. *UOC*, 1988–1995; 'Lecturers join forces for new paper on gender and the law', *UON*, November 1994, 9; Self-review, University of Otago Review of Faculty of Law, 2007, 51–52.
236. 'Student success', Faculty of Law: http://www.otago.ac.nz/law/about/success/index.html; Rebecca Tansley, 'Law of the land', *UOM*, no. 45, 2017, 24–27.
237. Report of University of Otago Review of Faculty of Law, 2013, 12–15; 'Otago Law Review', Faculty of Law: www.otago.ac.nz/law/research/journals/otago036503.html
238. 'New Zealand Law Foundation chair in emerging technologies', *OB*, 5 October 2007, 6. On the human genome project, see Self-review, University of Otago Review of Faculty of Law, 2007, 81–82; 'Genome project team's "extraordinary" job', *Law Talk*, 30 March 2009, 5.
239. Finigan, *Partnerships for Excellence*.
240. 'Law centre launched', *OB*, 20 April 2007, 4; Finigan, *Partnerships for Excellence*; 'New director of Legal Issues Centre', LawTalk, 16 June 2016: www.lawsociety.org.nz/lawtalk/lawtalk-archives/issue-890/new-director-of-legal-issues-centre
241. 'New Karitane post and theology research centre', *OB*, 18 May 2007, 7; Finigan, *Partnerships for Excellence*.
242. Report of University of Otago Review of Department of Theology and Religion, 2014, 17.
243. 'National centre for peace studies established', *OB*, 2 November 2007, 3; 'Otago fills position of peace and conflict', *OB*, 3 October 2008, 3; Report of the University of Otago Review of National Centre for Peace and Conflict Studies, 2014; Finigan, *Partnerships for Excellence*.
244. *UOAR*, 2016, 23.
245. Humanities Aronui Medal, Royal Society Te Apārangi: https://royalsociety.org.nz/what-we-do/medals-and-awards/humanities-aronui-medal/; Jock Phillips, 'New Zealand history moves south', NZHistoryJock, 17 December 2014: https://nzhistoryjock.wordpress.com/2014/12/17/new-zealand-history-moves-south/
246. Atholl Anderson, 'Wairau Bar: Ancestors and archaeology', in Atholl Anderson, Judith Binney & Aroha Harris, *Tangata Whenua: An illustrated history* (Wellington: Bridget Williams Books, 2014), 100–1; Nicola Mutch, 'Voyage of discovery', *UOM*, no. 34, 2013, 6–9.
247. *UOAR*, 2010–2016.
248. Sandra Grey, 'Uni doing little about Govt neglect of humanities', *ODT*, 5 October 2016: www.odt.co.nz/opinion/uni-doing-little-about-govt-neglect-humanities. For an opinion piece on humanities cuts in the US and many countries, see Francine Prose, 'Humanities

teach students to think. Where would we be without them?', *Guardian*, 12 May 2017: www.theguardian.com/commentisfree/2017/may/12/humanities-students-budget-cuts-university-suny
249. *UOAR*, 2016, 13.
250. Margot Taylor, 'Uni staff payouts of $1m', *ODT*, 20 December 2016: www.odt.co.nz/news/dunedin/uni-staff-payouts–1m; Margot Taylor, 'Anthropologists axed as part of humanities cull', *ODT*, 23 December 2016: www.odt.co.nz/news/campus/university-of-otago/anthropologists-axed-part-humanities-cull

7: THE SCIENCES

1. 'The university course', *ES*, 12 July 1871, 3.
2. University of New Zealand Annual Report, *AJHR*, 1885, E-05; *University of New Zealand Calendar*, 1885–1919.
3. P.C. Fenton, 'Shand, John', from DNZB: www.teara.govt.nz/en/biographies/2s17/shand-john
4. D.R. White, 'Impressions of university life in the early days', Violet Greig, 'The university in a democracy' and T.D. Pearce, 'Our professors: some personal recollections', all in *The Otago University Jubilee 1869–1919: Ceremonies and celebrations* (Dunedin: Evening Star, 1920), 33, 46, 60.
5. 'University of Otago', *OW*, 8 November 1873, 23; *UOAR*, 1874–1877.
6. 'Natural philosophy', *Oxford English Dictionary*: www.oed.com. The term 'natural philosophy' persisted longer in Scotland; that was perhaps why Otago retained 'natural philosophy' in the title for its professor until the 1920s.
7. *UOAR*, 1882–1887; *UOC*, 1881–1886; 'University Council', *ES*, 21 December 1886, 2.
8. D.V. Fenby, 'Black, James Gow', from DNZB: www.teara.govt.nz/en/biographies/2b24/black-james-gow
9. *ODT*, 12 January 1872, 2. Class numbers appear in the *UOAR*, 1874.
10. *ES*, 12 January 1872, 2.
11. 'University of Otago', *ES*, 2 May 1872, 2; Fenby, 'Black, James Gow'.
12. Greig, 'University in a democracy'; Pearce, 'Our professors'; Fenby, 'Black, James Gow'.
13. *UOAR*, 1874; Jeffery Parker, 'The Otago University Museum', in *Otago University Review (Special Number): A history of the Otago University during its minority* (Dunedin: OUSA, 1893), 30–32.
14. *UOC*, 1877. For student numbers for each subject see *UOAR*, 1879. Class honours lists also appeared in the local press at the end of the year: see *OW*, 17 November 1877, 17 and 16 November 1878, 20.
15. *UOAR*, 1877.
16. Editorial, *ODT*, 20 January 1877, 2; H.N. Parton, 'Hutton, Frederick Wollaston', from DNZB: www.teara.govt.nz/en/biographies/2h59/hutton-frederick-wollaston; B.I. Brewin, 'Former professors of zoology at the University of Otago', *Science Record*, vol. 4, 1954, 8. On further controversy over the choice of subject for the chair, see Chapter 6, note 11.
17. Brewin, 'Former professors', A. Warwick Don, 'Parker, Thomas Jeffery', from DNZB: www.teara.govt.nz/en/biographies/2p7/parker-thomas-jeffery; Rosi Crane, '"A dangerous visionary"? The lectures of the evolutionist T.J. Parker', *Journal of New Zealand Studies*, vol. 15, 2013, 36–49; Rosi Crane, 'A "strange fauna": T.J. Parker (1850–1897) and the creation of zoological knowledge in Otago', *New Zealand Journal of History*, vol. 49, 2015, 60–80.
18. Gordon Parry, *The Otago School of Mines 1879–1979: An historical sketch* (Dunedin: Otago School of Mines, University of Otago, 1979), 1.
19. James Macandrew to University of Otago Council, 10 November 1869, published in *ODT*, 11 November 1869, 2.
20. 'University of Otago', *ODT*, 9 May 1872, 5; 'The government quartz-crushing machine', *ODT*, 3 July 1872, 7.
21. 'Provincial Council', *ES*, 16 June 1875, 3; 'The University', *ES*, 8 July 1875, 3.
22. 'The General Assembly', *ODT*, 29 September 1876, 2.
23. W.J. Gardner, E.T. Beardsley & T.E. Carter, *A History of the University of Canterbury 1873–1973* (Christchurch: University of Canterbury, 1973), 131–32.
24. 'Professor Ulrich's lecture', *ODT*, 10 April 1880, 1; 'The Kaitangata disaster, 1879', in A.H. McLintock (ed.), *An Encyclopaedia of New Zealand*, originally published 1966: www.teara.govt.nz/en/1966/disasters-and-mishaps-coal-mining
25. *UOC*, 1882.
26. John La Roche, 'Thames School of Mines', report for the Institution of Professional Engineers New Zealand, 2012: www.ipenz.org.nz/heritage/itemdetail.cfm?itemid=2478
27. *UOAR*, 1880–1893; 'Otago University', *ODT*, 9 November 1887, 4.
28. *ES*, 28 May 1900, 2; 'U' (George Ulrich), 'Matters relating to the School of Mines', in *OUR*: *A history of Otago University during its minority*, 32–34.
29. Thomas Gilray, 'Otago University: A thirty years' retrospect', in *Otago University Jubilee*, 21; 'Mining', *ODT*, 13 June 1900, 6; W.A. Watters, 'Ulrich, George Henry Frederick', from DNZB: www.teara.govt.nz/en/biographies/2u1/ulrich-george-henry-frederick; Parry, *Otago School of Mines*, 2–3.
30. John Morton, 'Benham, William Blaxland', from DNZB: www.teara.govt.nz/en/biographies/3b27/benham-william-blaxland; Gavin McLean, 'Park, James', from DNZB: www.teara.govt.nz/en/biographies/3p8/park-james
31. *UOAR*, 1901; W.A. Watters, 'Marshall, Patrick', from DNZB: www.teara.govt.nz/en/biographies/3m44/marshall-patrick
32. 'The capping ceremony', *ES*, 7 July 1900, 3.
33. W.P. Morrell, *The University of Otago: A centennial history* (Dunedin: University of Otago Press, 1969), 88, 102; 'Mr Beverly's bequest to the university', *ODT*, 1 November 1907, 2; Hardwicke Knight and L.E.S. Amon, 'Beverly, Arthur', from DNZB: www.teara.govt.nz/en/biographies/1b20/beverly-arthur

34. 'Otago University claim for assistance', *ODT*, 13 September 1913, 4. This reflected the advice provided by the professorial board to an enquiry into the university's finance and organisation in 1912 that 'assistance will certainly be required shortly in Chemistry, Mathematics and Biology'. See Professorial Board minutes, 6 May 1912, Records of Registry and Central Administration, AG-180-15/04, HC.
35. *UOC*, 1917, 5; 'Royal Flying Corps': www.airhistory.org.uk/rfc/home.html; University Council minutes, 16 July 1918, 20 August 1918, 14 October 1918, Records of Registry and Central Administration, AG-180-1/06, HC.
36. 'University Council', *ODT*, 19 June 1918, 10.
37. 'University Council', *ES*, 18 April 1917, 2; University Council Minutes, 16 October 1917, Records of Registry and Central Administration, AG-180-1/06, HC.
38. 'New professor for the Otago University', *ODT*, 26 February 1907, 5; Agnes Blackie, 'The university half a century ago', Blackie family papers, MS-4443/001, HC.
39. University council minutes, 18 September and 26 October 1917, Records of Registry and Central Administration, AG-180-1/06, HC; Report of a meeting of the finance committee, 26 September 1917, Committee reports, Records of Registry and Central Administration, AG-180-2/02, HC. Both council and press maintained a veil of secrecy over the circumstances of Richards' departure. The decision to give him notice did not appear in the local papers and the *ES* simply reported on 11 December 1917: 'On dit that Professor Richards is about to resign the chair of mathematics at the Otago University'.
40. A.G. Hocken, *Geology at Otago: The first 100 years* (Wellington: Geological Society of New Zealand, 2003), 39.
41. Ibid., 34–47; McLean, 'Park, James'; J.B. Mackie, 'Further reminiscences with a geological flavour', *Geological Society of New Zealand Newsletter*, no. 61, 1983, 51–53; John Mackie interview, 2009, Development and Alumni Relations Office, Otago School of Mines oral history project, MS-4126/001, HC; Watters, 'Marshall, Patrick'.
42. *OW*, 13 April 1904, 21; Hocken, *Geology at Otago*, 40–41; N.De B. Hornibrook, 'Thomson, James Allan', from DNZB: www.teara.govt.nz/en/biographies/3t33/thomson-james-allan
43. Hocken, *Geology at Otago*, 50–63; Wolf Mayer, 'William Noel Benson (1885–1957): Insights into the life and work of an eminent geologist', *Earth Sciences History*, vol. 32, no. 1, 2013, 55–85; J.D. Campbell, 'Benson, Gertrude Helen and Benson, William Noel', from DNZB: www.teara.govt.nz/en/biographies/4b24/benson-gertrude-helen
44. W.B. Benham, 'Natural history in the University of Otago', in *Otago University Jubilee*, 40–42.
45. University Council minutes, 21 May 1918; 19 May 1919, 19 August 1919, 12 September 1919; Committee reports, 10 June 1918, Records of Registry and Central Administration, AG-180-2/02, HC.
46. Benham, 'Natural history'.
47. 'Cawthron Lecture', *Nelson Evening Mail*, 24 July 1919, 5; *Colonist* (Nelson), 16 May 1917, 12.
48. J.M. Whittaker, 'Aitken, Alexander Craig (1895–1967)', rev. Anita McConnell, in *Oxford Dictionary of National Biography*: www.oxforddnb.com/view/article/30357
49. W.H. Lang, 'John Ernest Holloway 1881–1945', *Obituary Notices of Fellows of the Royal Society*, vol. 5, 1947, 425–44; Geoff Baylis, 'Holloway, John Ernest', from DNZB: www.teara.govt.nz/en/biographies/4h33/holloway-john-ernest; Ann Wylie interview; reminiscences of Gordon Johnston and J or B Fitzgerald, Department of Botany records, MS-4387/012, HC.
50. 'Otago University', *ES*, 10 August 1909, 7.
51. 'A distinguished soldier: Colonel Studholme's death', *Press*, 28 May 1934, 12.
52. Gardner, Beardsley & Carter, *History of the University of Canterbury*, 116–17.
53. John Studholme to James Allen, cited in 'University council', *ES*, 5 June 1909, 11. For the final council debate and decision, see 'Otago University. Another chair. Domestic science. A divided council', *ES*, 10 August 1909, 7.
54. Barbara Brookes, 'King, Frederic Truby', from DNZB: www.teara.govt.nz/en/biographies/2k8/king-frederic-truby; Erik Olssen, 'Truby King and the Plunket Society: An analysis of a prescriptive ideology', *New Zealand Journal of History*, vol. 15, no. 1, 1981, 3–23; 'Batchelor, Ferdinand Campion', in Jane Thomson (ed.), *Southern People: A dictionary of Otago Southland biography* (Dunedin: Longacre Press/Dunedin City Council, 1998), 31; Dorothy Page, 'Dissecting a community: Women medical students at the University of Otago, 1891–1924', in Barbara Brookes & Dorothy Page (eds), *Communities of Women: Historical perspectives* (Dunedin: University of Otago Press, 2002), 111–27.
55. 'Promotion of health of women and children', *ES*, 19 May 1909, 4. For Truby King's speech at the same meeting, see *ES*, 20 May 1909, 6.
56. Jenny Collins, 'Glorified housekeepers or pioneering professionals? The professional lives of home science graduates from the University of New Zealand', *History of Education Review*, vol. 37, no. 2, 2008, 40–51.
57. On the significance of the school of home science as a place for women academics, see Tanya Fitzgerald, 'Academic housework? Women professors at the University of New Zealand 1911–1961', *New Zealand Journal of Education Studies*, vol. 42, nos 1 & 2, 115–28; and Tanya Fitzgerald, 'An absent presence: Women professors at the University of New Zealand 1911–1961', *Journal of Educational Administration and History*, vol. 39, no. 3, 2007, 239–53.
58. Heath McDonald, 'Boys-Smith, Winifred Lily', from DNZB: www.teara.govt.nz/en/biographies/3b41/boys-smith-winifred-lily; Campbell, 'Benson, Gertrude Helen and Benson, William Noel'; A.G. Strong, *History of the Development of University Education in Home Science in New Zealand 1911–1936* (Dunedin: University of Otago, 1937), 8–9.
59. Blackie, 'University half a century ago'.
60. Strong, *University Education in Home Science*, 10.

61. 'Typescript of tapes recording reminiscences of early graduates, recorded 197[illegible]', School of Consumer and Applied Sciences records, MS–3890, Box 12, HC.
62. *UOAR*, 1913.
63. 'Notes on life at Studholme by Miss J.C.A. Rudall written probably in late 1970s', OUSA centenary file, OUSA records, MS–4240/319, HC.
64. *UOAR*, 1912.
65. *UOAR*, 1913; Strong, *University Education in Home Science*, 29.
66. 'Extract from the Report of the Professor in Charge, Home-science Department, University of Otago', in 'Education: Manual and Technical Instruction annual report', *AJHR*, 1914, E-05, 90; Minister of Education Annual Report, *AJHR*, 1917, E-01, 42; Melanie Nolan, 'Putting the state in its place: The domestic education debate in New Zealand', *History of Education*, vol. 30, no. 1, 2001, 13–33; Strong, *University Education in Home Science*, 34–35; Jenny Collins, 'Beyond the domestic sphere? A home science education at the University of New Zealand, 1911–1936', *Journal of Educational Administration and History*, vol. 41, no. 2, 2009, 115–30.
67. *UOAR*, 1919, 1920. For a table of student enrolments by faculty for 1920 to 1968, see Morrell, *University of Otago*, 244–45.
68. Campbell, 'Benson, Gertrude Helen and Benson, William Noel'; Leah Taylor, 'Strong, Ann Monroe Gilchrist', from DNZB: www.teara.govt.nz/en/biographies/4s51/strong-ann-monroe-gilchrist; A.G. Strong, *University Education in Home Science*, 13–18.
69. Sylvia Keane, 'Memories of home science in the twenties', School of Consumer and Applied Sciences records, MS–3890, Box 12, HC.
70. Strong, *University Education in Home Science*, 12–13, 19–20; 'E. Neige Todhunter (1901–1991)', *Journal of Nutrition*, vol. 123, no. 4, 1993, 603–09.
71. John Studholme to James Allen, 22 May 1909, cited in Strong, *University Education in Home Science*, 6; *School of Home Science History, 1911–1961* (Dunedin: University of Otago, School of Home Science, 1962), 14.
72. Strong, *University Education in Home Science*, 6; *School of Home Science History*, 14.
73. School of Home Science and Home Science Extension Bureau Annual Reports, 1930, Records of Registry and Central Administration, AG-180-7/01, HC.
74. Strong, *University Education in Home Science*, 37.
75. 'A Maori health nurse: The health work of Emere Makere Waiwaha Kaa Mountain', in Sandra Coney, *Standing in the Sunshine: A history of New Zealand women since they won the vote* (Auckland: Viking, 1993), 102–03; Strong, *University Education in Home Science*, 38; Collins, 'Glorified housekeepers'. The quote comes from the *New Zealand Free Lance*, 2 October 1935, 18, as cited in Coney, *Standing in the Sunshine*.
76. Military personnel file of Daniel Black Waters, WW1 4/1220, Archives New Zealand: www.archway.archives.govt.nz/; University Council minutes, 20 November 1917, Records of Registry and Central Administration, AG-180-1/06, HC.
77. *UOAR*, 1915.
78. University council minutes, 21 September 1915 and 21 March 1916, Records of Registry and Central Administration, AG-180-1/06, HC; Professorial board minutes, 16 September 1915, Records of Registry and Central Administration, AG-180-15/05, HC.
79. University council minutes, 17 April 1917, Records of Registry and Central Administration, AG-180-1/06, HC; 'Mining and science faculty', *OUR*, October 1918, 73; 'A professor's work: Fighting the bacilli', *Evening Post*, 1 February 1917, 8; 'Death of professor, Dr John K.H. Inglis, services in war epidemic', *New Zealand Herald*, 21 September 1935, 15. Hicks, who became a respected physiologist in Australia, later earned fame for directing the Australian army catering service during World War II. See Heather Nash, 'Hicks, Sir Cedric Stanton (1892–1976)', Australian Dictionary of Biography: http://adb.anu.edu.au/biography/hicks-sir-cedric-stanton–10499/text18627
80. 'The life and times of James Park: Geologist, explorer, university dean', MS-0233, HC.
81. Blackie, 'University half a century ago'.
82. 'Stan Hughes recollections of the physics department, University of Otago', 24–25, MS–1675/001, HC; Jim Sullivan, 'Jack, Robert', from DNZB: www.teara.govt.nz/en/biographies/4j1/jack-robert
83. N.T.M. Wilsmore, 'John Kenneth Harold Inglis. 1877–1935', *Journal of the Chemical Society*, 1937, 700–01.
84. Arts and Science Faculty Annual Report, 1931, 1935, Records of Registry and Central Administration, AG-180-7/01, HC.
85. Arts and Science Faculty Annual Report, 1937, Records of Registry and Central Administration, AG-180-7/02, HC.
86. 'Cockabully story: The memoirs of Elizabeth Mason (née Mabel McIndoe)', Misc-MS–1400/001, HC.
87. '100 years of zoology', *UON*, May 1977, 1–2; Ewan Fordyce, 'Brian John Marples BA MA MSc FRSNZ FAZ 1907–1997', *Royal Society of New Zealand 2000 Academy Yearbook*: www.royalsociety.org.nz/publications/reports/yearbooks/year2000/obituaries/brian-marples/
88. *UOC*; Science Faculty Annual Report, 1963, Records of Registry and Central Administration, AG-180-7/08, HC; G.L. Rapson, 'Obituary: Ella Orr Campbell, DipTch, MA (Hons), DSc, DNZM, 1910–2003', *New Zealand Journal of Botany*, vol. 42, 2004, 695–708; 'Marion Liddell Fyfe', *UON*, September 1986, 5; Agnes Blackie obituary, *UON*, March 1975, 13.
89. Arts and Science Faculty Annual Report, 1941, Records of Registry and Central Administration, AG-180-7/02, HC.
90. Arts and Science Faculty Annual Report, 1941; Sullivan, 'Jack, Robert'.
91. F.G. Soper, 'Chemistry in New Zealand', *Chemistry in New Zealand*, vol. 39, 1975, 97–101; 'Chemists in World War II', *UON*, October 1975, 3–5.
92. School of Home Science Annual Report, 1939, Records of Registry and Central Administration, AG-180-7/02, HC; *School of Home Science History*, 27–28.

93. Arts and Science Faculty Annual Report, 1945, Records of Registry and Central Administration, AG-180-7/03, HC.
94. Arts and Science Faculty Annual Report, 1945 and 1946, Records of Registry and Central Administration, AG-180-7/03, HC.
95. Science Faculty Annual Report, 1946, Records of Registry and Central Administration, AG-180-7/03, HC.
96. Science Faculty Annual Report, 1950, Records of Registry and Central Administration, AG-180-7/04, HC.
97. Soper, 'Chemistry in New Zealand'.
98. Gregor Macaulay, Biographical notes on Rudolf Penseler, unpublished paper.
99. University of Otago graduation booklets; Registers of submitted PhD and master's theses, PhD office, Academic Services, Records of Registry and Central Administration, r.6864, HC.
100. Philip Smithells, 'The first twenty years 1948–1967 (an attempt at an assessment)', 1–2, Philip Smithells papers, MS-2617/009, HC; Warwick Brunton, *The Medicine of the Future: A history of the Department of Preventive and Social Medicine, University of Otago, 1886–2011* (Dunedin: Department of Preventive & Social Medicine, 2011), 83–84; Hugh Parton, *The University of New Zealand* (University Grants Committee, 1979), 135–36. On the Thomas Report and the changing secondary school curriculum, see Roger Openshaw, Greg Lee & Howard Lee, *Challenging the Myths: Rethinking New Zealand's educational history* (Palmerston North: Dunmore Press, 1993), 162–76; and Ian Cumming & Alan Cumming, *History of State Education in New Zealand 1840–1975* (Wellington: Pitman, 1978), 279–82. On the history of physical education in New Zealand more generally, see Robert A. Stothart, *The Development of Physical Education in New Zealand* (Auckland: Heinemann, 1974).
101. School of Physical Education Annual Report, 1949–1955, Records of Registry and Central Administration, AG-180-7/03, 7/04 and 7/05, HC; *UOC*, 1948–1955; Dennis McEldowney, 'Smithells, Philip Ashton', from DNZB: www.teara.govt.nz/en/biographies/5s30/smithells-philip-ashton
102. Smithells, 'First twenty years'.
103. Tribute to Martin Holdsworth on his retirement, Department of Botany records, MS-4387/123, HC.
104. J. & B. Fitzgerald to Department of Botany, 12 August 2004, Department of Botany records, MS-4387/012, HC.
105. Science Faculty Annual Report, 1960, Records of Registry and Central Administration, AG-180-7/07, HC; Ann Wylie, 'Geoff and the Botany Department: The long haul', *New Zealand Botanical Society Newsletter*, 76, 2004, 11–12; Alan Mark, 'Geoff and the Hellaby Indigenous Grasslands Research Trust', *New Zealand Botanical Society Newsletter*, 76, 2004, 18–19; Peter Bannister, 'Otago's "Botanic Man" retires', *UON*, March 1998, 12.
106. Ann Wylie interview; Science Faculty Annual Report, 1960 and 1971, Records of Registry and Central Administration, AG-180-7/07 and 7/11, HC; *UOC*, 1973, 204.
107. Science Faculty Annual Report, 1977, Records of Registry and Central Administration, AG-180-7/13, HC; *UOC*, 1979, 272–73.
108. Science Faculty Annual Report, 1969, Records of Registry and Central Administration, AG-180-7/10, HC.
109. Subjects in which degrees were obtained, University Grants Committee records, R12485703, Archives New Zealand, Wellington.
110. *UOC*, 1972, 170–71.
111. Carolyn Burns, 'One hundred and twenty-five years of zoology', speech notes, 2002; Science Faculty Annual Report, 1971, Records of Registry and Central Administration, AG-180-7/11, HC.
112. 'Praise for Portobello', *UON*, May 1974, 9. See also 'Marine laboratory in the public eye', *UON*, June 1976, 7–8.
113. Christopher J. Glasby & Geoffrey B. Read, 'A chronological review of polychaete taxonomy in New Zealand', *Journal of the Royal Society of New Zealand*, vol. 28, no. 3, 1998, 347–74; *OW*, 26 November 1886, 9.
114. George M. Thomson & Thomas Anderton, *History of the Portobello Marine Fish-hatchery and Biological Station* (Wellington: Dominion of New Zealand Board of Science and Art, 1921), 9–20; E.J. Batham, 'History of the Portobello Marine Biological Station', *Australian Journal of Science*, vol. 19, 1956, 87–91; 'Portobello changes', *UON*, April 1974, 4–6.
115. Batham, 'History of the Portobello Marine Biological Station'; *UOAR*, 1962; Ann Wylie interview. On Betty Batham, see John Jillett, 'Batham, Elizabeth Joan', from DNZB: www.teara.govt.nz/en/biographies/5b13/batham-elizabeth-joan
116. John Jillett interview; '£43,500 for marine research trawler', *ODT*, 15 November 1963; 'Marine research', *ES*, 18 November 1963; 'Lyttelton firm will build 46ft research trawler', *ODT*, 30 September 1964; 'Marine biology trawler ready this year', *ODT*, 20 October 1965; 'University trawler to be called Munida', *ODT*, 24 November 1965; 'Marine biology: New trawler big aid for research', *ES*, 7 December 1965; 'New skipper joins research trawler', *ODT*, 30 March 1966; all clippings in Portobello Marine Laboratory clippings books, Department of Marine Science records, MS-3302/196 and 199, HC; Science Faculty Annual Report, 1965, 1968, Records of Registry and Central Administration, AG-180-7/08 and 7/09, HC.
117. 'Marine laboratory in the public eye', *UON*, June 1976, 7–8.
118. Science Faculty Annual Report, 1967 and 1970, Records of Registry and Central Administration, AG-180-7/09 and 7/10, HC; R.M. Williams, 'Looking ahead in higher education', in F.W. Mitchell (ed.), *Looking Ahead in New Zealand Education* (Wellington: Reed, 1971), 100–12.
119. Science Faculty Annual Report, 1972, Records of Registry and Central Administration, AG-180-7/11, HC.
120. Don Warrington interview.
121. Science Faculty Annual Report, 1973, Records of Registry and Central Administration, AG-180-7/12, HC.
122. *UOC*, 1980, 249–50.
123. Science Faculty Annual Report, 1977, Records of Registry and Central Administration, AG-180-7/13, HC.

124. Hocken, *Geology at Otago*, Figure 28; *UOC*, 1960, 1975; Richard Norris interview.
125. Neil Howard, 'Life at university – fifties style', unpublished reminiscences.
126. Grant Hunter, 'Noel Odell: A Kiwi perspective of an Everest veteran', *New Zealand Alpine Journal*, 2014, 124–29; Hocken, *Geology at Otago*, 75–76.
127. Hocken, *Geology at Otago*, 76; Retirement tribute in *UON*, December 1989, 4.
128. Richard Norris interview; Hocken, *Geology at Otago*, 86–87, 100.
129. 'Geology talk', *UON*, December 1979, 6.
130. Richard Norris interview.
131. *UOC*, 1960, 1975.
132. R. Edward Corbett, Denis R. Lauren & Rex T. Weavers, 'The structure of Laurenene, a new diterpene from the essential oil of *Dacrydium cupressinum*. Part 1', *Journal of the Chemical Society, Perkin Transactions I*, 1979, 1774–90; Nigel Perry, 'Plant extracts – Unique plants and chemicals', Te Ara – the Encyclopedia of New Zealand: www.TeAra.govt.nz/en/diagram/14462/laurenene
133. Arthur Campbell interview; 'Campbell lab', *UON*, September 1987, 14.
134. Soper, 'Chemistry in New Zealand'; Barrie M. Peake, 'The last 25 years of chemistry in Otago and Southland', *Chemistry in New Zealand*, vol. 75, no. 3, 2011, 141–46; 'Personal professors', *UON*, December 1984, 2; interviews with Arthur Campbell and Melville Carr.
135. *UOC*, 1920, 141; 1941, 178.
136. Science Faculty Annual Report, 1950, Records of Registry and Central Administration, AG-180-7/04; Garry J. Tee, 'Nineteenth and early twentieth century statistics: Some New Zealand connections', *Australian and New Zealand Journal of Statistics*, vol. 44, no. 1, 2002, 3–12; David Vere-Jones, Murray J. MacKinnon & Brian Silverstone, 'Harold Silverstone: A perspective', *Australian and New Zealand Journal of Statistics*, vol. 43, no. 4, 2001, 393–98.
137. G.H. Jowett, 'The introduction of statistics at Otago', *Science Record*, vol. 14, 1964, 47–48.
138. Subjects in which degrees were obtained, University Grants Committee records, R12485703, Archives New Zealand, Wellington; *UOC*, 1965, 101.
139. John Gibb, 'Nothing dry about a life in statistics', *ODT*, 24 April 2016: www.odt.co.nz/campus/university-otago/380728/nothing-dry-about-life-statistics
140. Brunton, *Medicine of the Future*, 131–33; Science Faculty Annual Report, 1970, Records of Registry and Central Administration, AG-180-7/10.
141. Science Faculty Annual Report, 1971, 1974 and 1975, Records of Registry and Central Administration, AG-180-7/11, 7/12 and 7/13; 'Biometrics unit', *UON*, April 1974, 12; 'Centre for Applications of Statistics and Mathematics': www.maths.otago.ac.nz/?contact_casm
142. S. Verblunsky, 'Robert Mark Gabriel', *Journal of the London Mathematical Society*, vol. 33, no. 1, 1958, 125–28.
143. H.C. Levy, 'Professor William Davidson', *New Zealand Mathematical Society Newsletter*, no. 30, 1984, 15–16.
144. David Hill, 'Professor Desmond Sawyer', *New Zealand Mathematical Society Newsletter*, no. 32, 1984, 19; Vere Jones, MacKinnon & Silverstone, 'Harold Silverstone'; H.S. Roberts, 'Harold Silverstone (1915–1974)', in H.S. Roberts (ed.), *A History of Statistics in New Zealand* (Wellington: New Zealand Statistical Association, 1999), 88–90.
145. S.J. Bernau, 'Postgraduate mathematics in New Zealand', *Science Record*, vol. 17, 1967, 4–5.
146. Science Faculty Annual Report, 1974, Records of Registry and Central Administration, AG-180-7/12. The theses were: A.B. Evans, 'On Newtonian and relativistic cosmology'; and N.V. Zotov, 'A comparison of cosmological models with observational data'.
147. Brian Cox interview; Jack Schofield, 'Sir Maurice Wilkes obituary', *Guardian*, 30 November 2010: www.theguardian.com/technology/2010/nov/30/sir-maurice-wilkes-obituary. On Taylor, 'one of the most notable scientists of this century', see G.K. Batchelor, 'Geoffrey Ingram Taylor', *Biographical Memoirs of Fellows of the Royal Society*, vol. 22, 1976, 565–633.
148. Brian Cox interview; Gardner, Beardsley & Carter, *History of the University of Canterbury*, 395; Rachel Barrowman, *Victoria University of Wellington 1899–1999: A history* (Wellington: Victoria University Press, 1999), 184; 'Computing history displays: First floor – the IBM 1620', University of Auckland, Department of Computer Science: www.cs.auckland.ac.nz/historydisplays/FirstFloor/IBM1620/IBM1620Main.php
149. B.G. Cox, 'A university computing centre', *Science Record*, vol. 15, 1965, 40–41.
150. Brian Cox interview; Science Faculty Annual Report, 1964, Records of Registry and Central Administration, AG-180-7/08.
151. Brian Cox interview; Cox, 'A university computing centre'.
152. Brian Cox and Tim Gray interviews.
153. Brian Cox and Hank Wolfe interviews; *UOC*, 1966, 108; 1968, 211.
154. *UOC*, 1969, 215; Science Faculty Annual Report, 1970, 1973, 1976, 1977, 1978 and 1979, Records of Registry and Central Administration, AG-180-7/10, 7/12, 7/13 and 7/14, HC; Brian Cox interview.
155. 'Computing centre', *UON*, April 1980, 8.
156. 'Welcome to VAX', *UON*, June 1981, 12.
157. 'Computer review', *UON*, July 1983, 8–9; 'Personal professors', *UON*, February 1978, 3; *UOC*, 1984, 27.
158. *UOC*, 1965, 108; Geoffrey White interview.
159. Science Faculty Annual Report, 1967, Records of Registry and Central Administration, AG-180-7/09, HC.
160. Subjects in which degrees were obtained, University Grants Committee records, R12485703, Archives New Zealand, Wellington.
161. Science Faculty Annual Report, 1973, Records of Registry and Central Administration, AG-180-7/12, HC.
162. 'Emeritus Professor Michael Charles Davison': https://unidirectory.auckland.ac.nz/profile/m-davison
163. 'Emeritus Professor K Geoffrey White': www.otago.ac.nz/psychology/staff/geoffwhite.html; 'Respected academic appointed to senior research role', *OB*, 26 March 2004, 4.

164. *UOC*, 1974, 226; 1975, 246; 'Psychology progress', *UON*, March 1979, 3; Geoffrey White interview.
165. Science Faculty Annual Report, 1973, Records of Registry and Central Administration, AG-180-7/12, HC.
166. 'Psychology progress', *UON*, March 1979, 3.
167. David Marks & Richard Kammann, *The Psychology of the Psychic* (New York: Prometheus Books, 1980), 44.
168. 'About people', *UON*, May 1986, 11; Warwick Don, 'The first 21 years', *NZ Skeptics*, 1 August 2006: http://skeptics.nz/journal/issues/80/the-first-21-years
169. Nic MacArthur & Michael Buckenham to author, 29 May 2017; John Mackie, *Captain Jack, Surveyor and Engineer: The autobiography of John Mackie* (Wellington: New Zealand Institute of Surveyors, 2007), 314–15.
170. School of Mines Annual Report, 1940, 1942, Records of Registry and Central Administration, AG-180-7/02, HC; Kari Wilson-Allan, '"Although my country is against you [...] I still remain the same to you as before." Words of gratitude and uncertainty: Thai students' wartime communications in New Zealand', The Hocken Blog: https://blogs.otago.ac.nz/thehockenblog/2011/12/05/although-my-country-is-against-you-i-still-remain-the-same-to-you-as-before-words-of-gratitude-and-uncertainty-thai-students-wartime-communications-in-new-zeal/
171. John Mackie interview.
172. *School of Mines and Metallurgy Bulletin*, 1947, 11–13.
173. *School of Mines and Metallurgy Bulletin*, 1947, 11–15; 1949, 3–4, 8–10; 1951, 3–4; 1952, 3–4; 1955, 8–9; G.S. Parsonson, *A Brief History of the Otago School of Mines 1871–1971* (Dunedin: University of Otago, 1971), 7; John Mackie interview.
174. *Faculty of Technology Bulletin*, 1960, 6.
175. *School of Mines and Metallurgy Bulletin*, 1954, 9–10.
176. School of Mines and Metallurgy Annual Report, 1955, Records of Registry and Central Administration, AG-180-7/05, HC.
177. *Report of the Committee on New Zealand Universities, December 1959* (Wellington: Government Printer, 1960), 83.
178. *UOAR*, 1961.
179. 'Mining school history', *Otago School of Mines and Metallurgy 1950s Graduates Newsletter*, November 2001, John Neilson papers, MS-2842/001, HC (citing Jack Mackie); *Department of Mineral Technology Bulletin*, 1964–1965, 6–7; Parsonson, *Otago School of Mines*, 8–9; *UOAR*, 1965.
180. *Department of Mineral Technology Bulletin*, 1964–1965, 6–9.
181. 'Mining school history'; *Department of Mineral Technology Bulletin*, 1971, 6.
182. Science Faculty Annual Report, 1970, Records of Registry and Central Administration, AG-180-7/10, HC.
183. *Department of Mineral Technology Bulletin*, 1971, 5–6; Science Faculty Annual Report, 1969, Records of Registry and Central Administration, AG-180-7/10, HC.
184. 'Mining school history' (citing Michael Buckenham).
185. *Department of Mineral Technology Bulletin*, 1980.
186. University Grants Committee Annual Report, 1981, *AJHR*, 1982, E3.
187. University Grants Committee Review Committee, *Discussion Paper 5: Engineering* (Wellington: University Grants Committee, 1982), 10.
188. University Grants Committee Annual Report, 1982, *AJHR*, 1983, E3.
189. University Grants Committee Annual Report, 1984, *AJHR*, 1984–1985, E3; Karin Warnaar, 'Strip mining: The fight for a faculty', in *Tower Turmoil: Characters and controversies at the University of Otago* (Dunedin: Department of History, University of Otago, 2005), 189–206; Basil Jones interview.
190. 'University blamed', *ODT*, 26 October 1984, 1; Basil Jones interview.
191. Michael Buckenham, 'Mining degree programme to cease', *ODT*, 10 August 1995, 8; *University of Auckland Annual Report*, 1995, 20.
192. For instance, see *UOC*, 1894, 93.
193. John Mackie interview.
194. *A Salute to the Captain: Celebrating the 100th birthday of Emeritus Professor J.B. Mackie, 3 September 2010* (Dunedin: Development and Alumni Relations Office, University of Otago, 2010). The quote is from Luke Martin, 'Memories of Molesworth', 129–31.
195. John Mackie interview.
196. John Mackie, 'Survey school development', in Mick Strack (ed.), *Survey Marks: A 2013 celebration, 50 years of the School of Surveying at Otago University, 125 years of the New Zealand Institute of Surveyors* (Dunedin: School of Surveying, University of Otago & New Zealand Institute of Surveyors, 2013), 29–35.
197. Mackie, 'Survey school development'.
198. John Mackie interview.
199. Warren Garlick, 'First days of the Otago Surveying School', and Bhuwan Dutt, 'A great leader', in *Salute to the Captain*, 119–22.
200. Allan Blaikie, 'Field camps', in Strack, *Survey Marks*, 63–68.
201. Laura B. Coll McLaughlin, 'Women in New Zealand surveying', in Strack, *Survey Marks*, 101–06.
202. Self-review, University of Otago Review of Department of Surveying, 1996, 2; Mick Strack, 'Surveyors, Māori land and Te Tiriti o Waitangi', in Strack, *Survey Marks*, 95–99.
203. Mackie, in Science Faculty Annual Report, 1971 and 1973, Records of Registry and Central Administration, AG-180-7/11 and 7/12, HC ; *UOC*, 1975 and 1976.
204. Basil Jones interview.
205. Science Faculty Annual Report, 1975, Records of Registry and Central Administration, AG-180-7/13, HC.
206. John Mackie interview.
207. Basil Jones interview.
208. Self-review, University of Otago Review of Department of Surveying, 2005, 6; 2011, 6.
209. Science Faculty Annual Report, 1982, Records of Registry and Central Administration, AG-180-7/14, HC; Self-review, University of Otago Review of Department of Surveying, 2005, 6; 2011, 6.

210. Mark Wright, 'Surveying the past … and the future', *UOM*, no. 35, 2013, 15–17; 'Exploring the Ross Ice Shelf', University of Otago Division of Sciences: www.otago.ac.nz/sciences/research/highlights/otago599378.html
211. School of Home Science Annual Report, 1940–1980, Records of Registry and Central Administration, AG-180-7/02 to 7/14, HC.
212. *School of Home Science Prospectus*, c. 1956; interviews with Nancy Carr, Sadie Andrews, Janet Mitchell and Raechel Laing.
213. School of Home Science Annual Report, 1973, Records of Registry and Central Administration, AG-180-7/12, HC.
214. School of Home Science Annual Report, 1962, 1967, 1969 and 1973, Records of Registry and Central Administration, AG-180-7/07, 7/09, 7/10 and 7/12, HC; Home Science roll books, School of Consumer and Applied Sciences records, MS–3890, Box 4, HC.
215. Brookes, 'King, Frederic Truby'.
216. James R. Robinson, 'Malcolm, John', from DNZB: www.teara.govt.nz/en/biographies/4m33/malcolm-john
217. Philippa Mein Smith, 'Bell, Muriel Emma', from DNZB: www.teara.govt.nz/en/biographies/4b21/bell-muriel-emma
218. *School of Home Science History*, 53–54.
219. Leah Taylor, 'Gregory, Elizabeth', from DNZB: www.teara.govt.nz/en/biographies/5g19/gregory-elizabeth
220. 'Professor Marion Robinson', *UON*, December 1988, 8; 'Emeritus Professor Marion Frances Robinson', *OB*, 13 June 2003, 10; School of Home Science Annual Report, 1968, Records of Registry and Central Administration, AG-180-7/09, HC; Jim Mann, 'Marion Frances Robinson 1923–2003', *Royal Society of New Zealand Yearbook*, 2003: www.royalsociety.org.nz/publications/reports/yearbooks/year2003/obituaries/marion-robinson/
221. 'Chair of Human Nutrition', *UON*, March 1975, 3–4.
222. Janet Mitchell interview.
223. Raechel Laing interview.
224. Home Science Faculty Annual Report, 1986, Records of Registry and Central Administration, AG-180-7/15, HC.
225. Consumer and Applied Sciences Faculty Annual Report, 1987, Records of Registry and Central Administration, AG-180-7/15, HC; 'Clothing and textile consultancy service', *UON*, June 1989, 3; 'Building bridges through ACS', *UON*, January 1986, 1–3; 'Firefighters shape up for study', *UON*, April 1993, 3.
226. 'The winds of change', *UON*, July 1986, 5; 'Whipping up the media', *UON*, August 1986, 9.
227. 'Home science talk', *UON*, October 1974, 3–4; 'New name, new image for home science', *UON*, August 1987, 1.
228. Interviews with Jim Mann and Raechel Laing; Consumer and Applied Sciences Faculty Annual Report, 1987, Records of Registry and Central Administration, AG-180-7/15, HC; *UOC*, 1988, 372–73.
229. Home Science Faculty Annual Report, 1986, Records of Registry and Central Administration, AG-180-7/15, HC; 'Home science', *UON*, April 1979, 3.
230. Consumer and Applied Sciences Faculty Annual Report, 1987, Records of Registry and Central Administration, AG-180-7/15, HC.
231. *UOAR*, 1969, 1977.
232. School of Physical Education Annual Report, 1974, Records of Registry and Central Administration, AG-180-7/12, HC.
233. 'Physical education', *UON*, September 1974, 7; School of Physical Education Annual Report, 1975, Records of Registry and Central Administration, AG-180-7/13, HC.
234. School of Physical Education Annual Report, 1975, 1980, 1981, 1984 and 1988, Records of Registry and Central Administration, AG-180-7/13, 7/14 and 7/15, HC.
235. 'New director', *UON*, April 1974, 3–4. 'Director talks of physical education', *UON*, July 1976, 4; interviews with Rex Thomson and Doug Booth; School of Physical Education Annual Report, 1978, Records of Registry and Central Administration, AG-180-7/14, HC.
236. School of Physical Education Annual Report, 1979 and 1981, Records of Registry and Central Administration, AG-180-7/14, HC.
237. School of Physical Education Annual Report, 1981, Records of Registry and Central Administration, AG-180-7/14, HC.
238. Physical Education Faculty Annual Report, 1982, Records of Registry and Central Administration, AG-180-7/14, HC.
239. Physical Education Faculty Annual Report, 1987, Records of Registry and Central Administration, AG-180-7/15, HC.
240. Rex Thomson interview.
241. Physical Education Faculty Annual Report, 1982 and 1983, Records of Registry and Central Administration, AG-180-7/14 and 7/15, HC.
242. 'The phys ed stir', OUSA archives, MS-4240/034, HC.
243. Interviews with Rex Thomson and Doug Booth.
244. School of Physical Education Annual Report, 1973, Records of Registry and Central Administration, AG-180-7/12, HC.
245. School of Physical Education Annual Report, 1970, Records of Registry and Central Administration, AG-180-7/10, HC; 'Personal chairs', *UON*, December 1984, 2–3; 'Outgoing dean looks back on an enjoyable and satisfying tenure', *UON*, March 2000, 11.
246. Doug Booth interview.
247. Brendan Hokowhitu, 'Te mana Māori: Te tātari i ngā kōrero parau', PhD thesis, University of Otago, 2002; 'From Canada to Waikato, new dean is coming home', University of Waikato: www.waikato.ac.nz/news-events/media/2015/from-canada-to-waikato-new-dean-is-coming-home
248. Doug Booth interview; Physical Education Faculty Annual Report, 1984, Records of Registry and Central Administration, AG-180-7/15, HC.
249. Rex Thomson, *School of Physical Education 50th Reunion 1948–1998* (Dunedin: School of Physical Education, 1998), 28; Self-review, University of Otago Review of School of Physical Education, 2003, 2–3.
250. 'Outgoing dean looks back on an enjoyable and satisfying tenure', *UON*, March 2000, 11; interviews with Rex Thomson and Doug Booth. The intake rose to 200 in 1992.
251. 'Science link highlighted in new name', Otago Bulletin

Board, 4 June 2013: www.otago.ac.nz/otagobulletin/news/otago047900.html

252. 'Otago's sports-related disciplines shine in world rankings', Otago Bulletin Board, 15 March 2017: www.otago.ac.nz/otagobulletin/news/otago638489.html; Vaughan Elder, 'Phys Ed School job cuts', *ODT*, 7 March 2017: www.odt.co.nz/news/dunedin/phys-ed-school-job-cuts
253. Self-review, University of Otago Review of School of Surveying, 2011, 6.
254. *UOC*, 1990–1993.
255. Raechel Laing interview.
256. Report of Review of Clothing, Textile Science, Design and Community Studies in the School of Consumer and Applied Sciences, 1990, 5–10.
257. Division of Sciences Annual Report, 1992, Records of Registry and Central Administration, AG-758/085, HC; *UOC*, 1993–1994.
258. *UOC*, 1929, 302–03.
259. *School of Home Science History*, 37, 39, 45–47; School of Home Science Annual Report, 1948, Records of Registry and Central Administration, AG-180-7/03, HC.
260. *UOC*, 1980, 326–28; 1990, 377.
261. 'Designs for the future', *UON*, May 1994, 5.
262. Report of University of Otago Review of Department of Design Studies, 2005.
263. David Loughrey, '$1.9m for design unit', *ODT*, 24 April 2008: www.odt.co.nz/news/dunedin/3924/19m-design-unit; Dene Mackenzie, 'Dunedin to get design institute', *ODT*, 11 October 2008: www.odt.co.nz/news/dunedin/26788/city-set-get-design-institute; Dene Mackenzie, 'Design Institute deal welcomed', *ODT*, 14 October 2008: www.odt.co.nz/news/dunedin/27175/design-institute-deal-welcomed; 'Shared design centre gains funding', *OB*, 31 October 2008, 2; Allison Rudd, 'Funding withdrawn for design institute', *ODT*, 6 May 2009: www.odt.co.nz/on-campus/otago-polytechnic/54305/funding-withdrawn-design-institute?page=0%2C1
264. *UOAR*, 2010, 14; John Gibb, 'Varsity not in financial crisis: Skegg', *ODT*, 11 May 2010: www.odt.co.nz/on-campus/university-otago/105411/varsity-not-financial-crisis-skegg
265. John Lewis, 'Varsity merger proposal puzzles staff', *ODT*, 29 January 2010: www.odt.co.nz/on-campus/university-otago/90985/varsity-merger-proposal-puzzles-staff; John Lewis, 'Professor quits over plan', *ODT*, 30 January 2010: www.odt.co.nz/on-campus/university-otago/91158/professor-quits-over-plan; John Lewis, 'Design students strongly oppose merger', *ODT*, 8 February 2010: www.odt.co.nz/on-campus/university-otago/92254/design-students-strongly-oppose-merger; Rebecca Fox, 'Move to axe design studies shocks students', *ODT*, 29 April 2010: www.odt.co.nz/on-campus/university-otago/103768/move-axe-design-studies-shocks-students; Allison Rudd, 'All over for department of design', *ODT*, 12 May 2010: www.odt.co.nz/on-campus/university-otago/105582/all-over-department-design
266. Report of University of Otago Review of Department of Applied Sciences, 2014.
267. Carla Green, 'Design school move opposed', *ODT*, 15 July 2015: www.odt.co.nz/campus/university-otago/349081/design-school-move-opposed; 'Opportunities and challenges', editorial, *ODT*, 18 July 2015: www.odt.co.nz/opinion/editorial/349496/opportunities-and-challenges; Carla Green, 'Attack on plan for uni department', *ODT*, 20 July 2015: www.odt.co.nz/campus/university-otago/349628/attack-plan-uni-dept; Michael Findlay, 'Design graduates in great demand', *ODT*, 23 July 2015: www.odt.co.nz/opinion/opinion/350000/design-graduates-great-demand; Joe Higham, 'Closure of department of applied sciences', *Critic*, 7 September 2015, 8; Raechel Laing interview.
268. Report of University of Otago Review of Department of Applied Sciences, 2014.
269. Raechel Laing interview; 'Textile tests for the real world', *He Kitenga*, 2009: www.otago.ac.nz/research/hekitenga2009/textiletests.html; 'International medal for Otago textile expert', Otago Bulletin Board, 7 December 2015: www.otago.ac.nz/otagobulletin/people/otago367806.html
270. 'The outlook for the new Centre for Materials Science and Technology', Otago Bulletin Board, 13 May 2016: www.otago.ac.nz/otagobulletin/news/otago611557.html
271. Tim Miller, 'Science centre plans upheld by university', *ODT*, 3 November 2017: www.odt.co.nz/news/campus/university-of-otago/science-centre-plans-upheld-university; Mike Houlahan, 'Materials Science will close', *ODT*, 13 December 2017: www.odt.co.nz/news/dunedin/materials-science-will-close
272. 'Professor of food science appointed', *UON*, October 1994, 7; 'Food for thought', *UON*, March 1995, 2; 'Flavour feast returns', *UON*, April-May 1997, 3; 'Respected brewing expert known for his skill and personal style', *OB*, 23 March 2007, 3.
273. Janet Mitchell interview; 'Food science takes on international flavour', *OB*, 8 August 2008, 3; 'New Otago professors named', Otago Bulletin Board, 24 November 2009: www.otago.ac.nz/news/news/otago006216.html
274. Report of University of Otago Review of Department of Food Science, 2012, 6; Self-review, University of Otago Review of Department of Food Science, 2012, 3–6.
275. Dion Crooks, *A History: New Zealand Dietetic Association (Inc) and dietetics in New Zealand* (Wellington: New Zealand Dietetic Association, 1993).
276. Strong, *University Education in Home Science*, 20–21.
277. Elizabeth Gregory, 'The development of dietetics in New Zealand', *Nutrition*, vol. 6, no. 4, 1952, 22–24; Muriel Bell, *Nutrition in New Zealand: Forty years' history, 1920–60*, 15–16 (supplement to *Journal of the New Zealand Association of Home Science Alumnae (N.Z.)*, vol. 31, 1962); Training of Dieticians, Dean's Department, Faculty of Medicine records, MS-4324/102, HC.
278. 'Dietetic training programme at full steam', *UON*, April 1994, 7; Self-review, University of Otago Review of Dietetics Programme, 2010, vii; Jim Mann interview.

279. Report of University of Otago Review of Dietetics Programme, 2010; Self-review, University of Otago Review of Dietetics Programme, 2010, 3, 9–10; 'NZ's first Master of Dietetics graduates', Otago Bulletin Board, 6 May 2013: www.otago.ac.nz/otagobulletin/postgraduate/otago046367.html; Jim Mann interview. Massey University's Albany campus offers an MSc (Nutrition and Dietetics) and the University of Auckland a Master of Health Sciences in Nutrition and Dietetics: www.massey.ac.nz/massey/learning/programme-course-paper/programme.cfm?study_year=2014&prog_id=92431&major_code=2867; www.fmhs.auckland.ac.nz/en/faculty/for/future-postgraduates/postgraduate-study-options/programmes/masters/master-of-health-sciences/mhsc-nutrition-dietetics.html
280. Jim Mann interview.
281. 'Emeritus Professor Christine Thomson', Department of Human Nutrition: www.otago.ac.nz/humannutrition/staff/otago063250.html; 'Personal chair in human nutrition', *UON*, April–May 1995, 4; 'New Zealand's iron lady', *UON*, August-September 1997, 6.
282. Jim Mann interview; 'World Health Organization status for Otago', *OB*, 26 March 2004, 1, 3.
283. 'Official opening for National Diabetes Centre', *OB*, 12 August 2005, 6; Alison Finigan (ed.), *Partnerships for Excellence: Celebrating 10 years of the Leading Thinkers initiative* (Dunedin: Development and Alumni Relations Office, University of Otago, 2014).
284. Jim Mann interview.
285. Jim Mann interview.
286. Interviews with Nancy Carr, Raechel Laing, Janet Mitchell.
287. Sadie Andrews interview; 'Dear Miss Carpenter', *New Zealand Listener*, 23 October 1953, 8; 'Sadie Andrews – last of a long line', *UON*, November 1987, 9; 'The end of a long and valued association with the University of Otago', *UON*, June 1994, 15.
288. *UOC*, 2012, 384–89.
289. Report of University of Otago Review of Applied Science Programme, University of Otago, 2006, 11.
290. 'New degree matches Government plans for developing a broader-based economy', *UON*, December 2006, 6.
291. 'New programmes meeting industry needs', *UON*, September–October 1998, 9.
292. Lyall McLean, *A History of Economics and the Development of Commerce Degrees at the University of Otago 1871–2009* (Dunedin: L. McLean, 2011), 130, 178–82.
293. *UOC*, 2001–2016.
294. 'Applied science programme: Bridging to industry', *OB*, 11 July 2003, 4; 'Transpower applied sciences scholarships', *OB*, 13 June 2003, 3.
295. Report of University of Otago Review of Applied Science Programme, 2014, 11.
296. Science Faculty Annual Report, 1965, Records of Registry and Central Administration, AG-180-7/08, HC; *UOC*, 1965; 'Postgrad diploma in wildlife management: On the wild side', *OB*, 26 March 2004, 7; Self-review, University of Otago Review of Department of Zoology, 2008, 14–15.
297. Self-review, University of Otago Review of Department of Zoology, 2008, 15; 'Otago announces professorial promotions', 20 December 2012: www.otago.ac.nz/news/news/otago040382.html
298. Nick Grant, 'Interview: The natural history of Michael Stedman III', *OnFilm*, October 2010, 10.
299. 'High interest in new filmmaking course', *UON*, July 2000, 6.
300. Ibid.
301. 'Chair in science communication to be established', *OB*, 22 September 2006, 1; 'First professor of science communication', *OB*, 10 August 2007, 7; 'Otago committed to science communication', *OB*, 2 November 2007, 6; Nicola Mutch, 'New centre taking science to the people', *OB*, 22 February 2008, 3; 'Talking the walk', *UOM*, no. 20, 2008, 10–12.
302. Self-review, University of Otago Review of Department of Zoology, 2008, 16.
303. Finigan, *Partnerships for Excellence*.
304. Report of University of Otago Review of Centre for Science Communication, 2012, 11–12; Matthew Haggart, 'Science meets art at festival', *ODT*, 14 November 2011: www.odt.co.nz/campus/university-otago/186441/science-meets-art-festival; Shane Gilchrist, 'A natural partnership', *ODT*, 12 November 2011: www.odt.co.nz/entertainment/film/186230/natural-partnership
305. Self-review, University of Otago Review of Neuroscience Programme, 2008, 6.
306. 'Cognitive science at Otago', *UON*, November 1989, 6; D.W. Girvan, Memorandum to deans and heads of department: New blood lectureships, 20 June 1988, Jocelyn Harris papers, r.8044, HC; *UOAR*, 1989.
307. Colin Townsend interview; Self-review, University of Otago Review of Ecology Programme, 2008, 1.
308. 'Genetics major could be exciting for the university', *UON*, October 1999, 8; Self-review, University of Otago Review of Genetics Programme, 2007, 3–4.
309. Interviews with Colin Townsend and Ann Wylie.
310. Science Faculty Annual Report, 1981 and 1984, Records of Registry and Central Administration, AG-180-7/14 and 7/15, HC; *UOC*, 1982, 246; 'Marine laboratory's role growing in importance', *UON*, August 1984, 1–2; 'Chair in marine science', *UON*, September 1989, 2; 'The growth of marine science and aquaculture at Otago', *UON*, October 1990, 1–2.
311. 'New department consolidates marine science strengths', *UON*, August 1992, 1; Self-review, University of Otago Review of Department of Marine Science, 1993, 1.
312. Self-review, University of Otago Review of Department of Marine Science, 2009, 6; Report of University of Otago Review of Department of Marine Science, 2009, 9–12; Richard Norris interview; *UOC*, 1998–2007.
313. 'Undergraduate study in marine science', Department of Marine Science: www.otago.ac.nz/marinescience/study/undergraduate/; *UOC*, 2015.
314. Research Centre for Oceanography: http://iron.otago.ac.nz/index.html; 'Ocean explorers', *He Kitenga: Horizons*:

www.otago.ac.nz/hekitenga/horizons/otago064697.html; 'Top oceanography ranking', *OB*, 20 May 2011, 3.
315. 'The sciences put to sea in a beautiful pea green boat', *OB*, 14 July 2006, 1; Mark Wright, 'Cresting the waves ... and plumbing the depths', *UOM*, no. 38, 2014, 19–21; Finigan, *Partnerships for Excellence*.
316. Self-review, University of Otago Review of Department of Mathematics and Statistics, 2009, 1–5, 25; Peter Fenton interview.
Self-review, University of Otago Review of Department of Physics, 2009, 5; Report of University of Otago Review of Department of Physics, 2009, 7. The textbook, written by the teaching fellows and professional practice fellows working on the course, was initially produced by the department and was taken up by a large international publisher soon afterwards: Kirsten Franklin, Paul Muir, Terry Scott, Lara Wilcocks & Paul Yates, *Introduction to Biological Physics for the Health and Life Sciences* (Chichester: Wiley, 2010).
317. Self-review, University of Otago Review of Department of Physics, 2009, 5.
318. Peter Fenton interview; Report of University of Otago Review of Department of Mathematics and Statistics, 2009, 11, 14–15.
319. 'Search for the new state of matter', *UON*, April–May 1997, 3; 'Hot time for ultracold atoms group', *OB*, 9 September 2005, 10; 'Major funding for Otago research programmes announced', *OB*, 27 July 2007, 3; 'The physics of success', *OB*, 29 October 2010, 6–7; 'Dodd-Walls Centre celebration', Otago Bulletin Board, 12 September 2014: www.otago.ac.nz/otagobulletin/news/otago079133.html; Self-review, University of Otago Review of Department of Physics, 2009, 6; Don Warrington interview.
320. Richard Norris interview.
321. 'Southern hemisphere's first new geology research facility', *OB*, 16 May 2003, 6.
322. Å. Fagereng, V.G. Toy & J.V. Rowland (eds), *Geology of the Earthquake Source: A volume in honour of Rick Sibson* (London: Geological Society, 2011); 'Richard Sibson', The Royal Society: https://royalsociety.org/people/richard-sibson-12274/
323. 'Otago appoints first Professor of Earthquake Science', University of Otago media release, 20 May 2015: www.otago.ac.nz/geology/news/archive/2015/otago107251.html; David Skegg to author, 31 July 2017; Nigel Zega, 'Seismic science', *UOM*, no. 43, 2016, 21–23.
324. Richard Norris interview.
325. Report of University of Otago Review of Department of Chemistry, 2012, 25.
326. Report of University of Otago Review of Department of Computer Science, 2010, 9; Hank Wolfe interview; Self-review, University of Otago Review of Department of Computer Science, 1993, 7; 2004, 4; Self-review, University of Otago Review of Department of Information Science, 2008, 1–3.
327. 'Computer course tops popularity stakes', *UON*, June–July 1997, 3.
328. Self-review, University of Otago Review of Department of Computer Science, 2004, 3; Report of University of Otago Review of Department of Computer Science, 2010, 10, 16.
329. Self-review, University of Otago Review of Department of Computer Science, 1993, 3; 2004, 18–20; 2010, 27–28.
330. Self-review, University of Otago Review of Department of Computer Science, 1993, 4.
331. 'Black Albatross creates innovative web site for Toyota NZ', *UON*, March 1998, 10; Self-review, University of Otago Review of Department of Computer Science, 2004, 5; 2010, 6.
332. 'Computer graphics – intensive creativity with commercial spin-off', *UON*, May 1989, 4; Self-review, University of Otago Review of Department of Computer Science, 1993, 4; 'ARL history', Animation Research Ltd: http://arl.co.nz/index.php/arl-company/arl-history; 'World class New Zealand: A roll call of top Kiwis', *New Zealand Management*, June 2013, 6.
333. Geoffrey White interview; K. Geoffrey White, 'Obituary: Graham Valentine Goddard (1938–1987)', *New Zealand Journal of Psychology*, vol. 16, no. 1, 1987, 42–43; David Skegg to author, 31 July 2017.
334. Geoffrey White interview.
335. 'Respected academic appointed to senior research role', *OB*, 26 March 2004, 4; 'Next Deputy Vice-Chancellor (R and E)', *OB*, 5 September 2008, 2.
336. 'Respected academic appointed to senior research role', *OB*, 26 March 2004, 4.
337. Geoffrey White interview; Report of University of Otago Review of Department of Psychology, 2004, 15.
338. Report of University of Otago Review of Department of Psychology, 2011, 8.

8: COMMERCE

1. T.K. Cowan, *Commerce at Otago 1912–1987: A personal perspective*, abridged edn (Dunedin: University of Otago, 1988), 3–4.
2. Conrad Blyth, 'Early academic economics in New Zealand (Notes on its history from the 1870s to the 1950s)', University of Auckland Department of Economics Working Papers Series, no. 266, 2008, 4–5.
3. The original syllabus for Otago degrees is outlined in the report of the University Council meeting, *ODT*, 28 April 1871, 2–3. For the senior class course, see 'University of Otago', *ODT*, 31 October 1872, 2. On MacGregor, see chapter 6.
4. *UOC*, 1882, 78. On Brown, see chapter 6.
5. *UOAR*, 1889, 1890, 1894, 1895, 1896; Violet Greig, 'The university in a democracy', J.B. Callan, 'Some teachers of twenty years ago', and John O'Shea, 'Recollections of my student days', all in *The Otago University Jubilee 1869–1919: Ceremonies and celebrations* (Dunedin: Evening Star, 1920), 46, 49, 56.
6. 'University training for captains of industry', *Auckland Star*, 3 July 1902, 4.
7. 'President's address', *New Zealand Society of Accountants Year Book*, 1913, 46–47. Barr cited H.S. Morgan, 'The universities and a business diploma', *Review of Reviews*, July 1913.

8. Lyall McLean, *A History of Economics and the Development of Commerce Degrees at the University of Otago 1871–2009* (Dunedin: L. McLean, 2011), 19–22; Blyth, 'Early academic economics', 8–9; Keith Sinclair, *A History of the University of Auckland 1883–1983* (Auckland: Auckland University Press, 1983), 113; W.J. Gardner, E.T. Beardsley & T.E. Carter, *A History of the University of Canterbury 1873–1973* (Christchurch: University of Canterbury, 1973), 117.
9. Blyth, 'Early academic economics', 8–9.
10. McLean, *Economics and the Development of Commerce Degrees*, 23–25; Bernadette F. Devonport, 'An introduction to the interaction between the universities and the Institute of Chartered Accountants of New Zealand, 1910 to the present day', *Pacific Accounting Review*, vol. 21, no. 2, 2009, 150–69. The NZSA was known from 1996 as the New Zealand Institute of Chartered Accountants; in 2014 it merged with the Australian institute to become Chartered Accountants Australia and New Zealand.
11. Cowan, *Commerce at Otago*, 4; Donald G. Trow & Stephen A. Zeff, *Accounting Education and the Profession in New Zealand: Profiles of the pioneering academics and the early university accounting departments 1900–1970* (Wellington: New Zealand Institute of Chartered Accountants, 2010), 32. After the five years was up, the NZSA provided £75 per year for another 3 years, with Otago raising another £75 per year from local businesses: see Cowan, *Commerce at Otago*, 4.
12. McLean, *Economics and the Development of Commerce Degrees*, 24–25, 29, 34; *UOAR*, 1913.
13. 'Summary of the proceedings of the sixth annual general meeting', *New Zealand Society of Accountants Year Book*, 1914–1915, 83.
14. Devonport, 'Interaction between the universities and the Institute of Chartered Accountants'. For an example of Banks' Commercial College advertising, see *ODT*, 14 January 1916, 1.
15. Cowan, *Commerce at Otago*, 15; Trow & Zeff, *Accounting Education*, 35.
16. President's address, *New Zealand Society of Accountants Year Book*, 1913, 47.
17. 'Alphabetical roll of the graduates of the University of New Zealand that have kept terms in the University of Otago', *UOC*, 1920, 13–35; 'Personal', *ODT*, 21 December 1914, 6; 'Off to the front', *ODT*, 10 February 1915, 8; Alfred Owen Wilkinson military file, R22019340, Archives New Zealand: www.archway.archives.govt.nz/ViewFullItem.do?code=22019340&digital=yes
18. Commerce Faculty Annual Report, 1920, Records of Registry and General Administration, AG-180-31/0047, HC; *UOC*, 1920, 146. Total commerce student numbers were reported in the *UOAR*; sometimes, though not always, they gave the separate figures for men and women.
19. T.K. Cowan, 'The commerce course – retrospect and prospect', in R.A. Sinclair (ed.), *The Commerce Review* (Dunedin: Otago Commerce Students' Association, 1969), 23–24.
20. 'Commerce', *OUR*, 1946, 9–10.
21. 'Deans', in Sinclair, *Commerce Review*, 25–26; McLean, *Economics and the Development of Commerce Degrees*, 30.
22. J.M. Paterson to University of Otago Registrar, 20 June 1947, Commerce Faculty general file, Records of Registry and Central Administration, AG-180-3/436, HC.
23. 'Some prominent lecturers', in Sinclair, *Commerce Review*, 27.
24. Trow & Zeff, *Accounting Education*, 36.
25. Commerce Faculty Annual Report, 1920, Records of Registry and General Administration, AG-180-31/0047, HC; 'University Senate', *ODT*, 22 January 1921, 10; *UOC*, 1920; 'Graduates of the Year', *Otago University Capping Carnival Book*, 1929, 3. Otago calendars listed some of the subjects required for the Diploma in Banking and stated that 'These subjects may be taken by Banking candidates at the University of Otago' (*UOC*, 1929, 206). Banks Commercial College in Wellington, which offered correspondence courses, boasted in its advertising that, for the Diploma in Banking, 'over 80 per cent of the successful candidates in the Dominion were Banks's' (*ODT*, 18 February 1930, 11).
26. Cowan, *Commerce at Otago*, 11–12.
27. Hugh Parton, *The University of New Zealand* (Auckland: Auckland University Press/University Grants Committee, 1979), 143.
28. 'Some prominent lecturers'; Trow & Zeff, *Accounting Education*, 37; 'Obituary: Mr L.D. McIver, B.Com., A.P.A.N.Z.', *Accountants' Journal*, vol. 47, no. 8, 1969, 339.
29. *UOAR*, 1917, 1920; Michael Gill, 'Bedford, Harry Dodgshun', from DNZB: www.teara.govt.nz/en/biographies/3b21/bedford-harry-dodgshun; McLean, *Economics and the Development of Commerce Degrees*, 34–37.
30. Matthew Littlewood, 'The curious case of Professor Pringle', in The Time Keepers, *Tower Turmoil: Characters and controversies at the University of Otago* (Dunedin: Department of History, University of Otago, 2005), 51–63.
31. McLean, *Economics and the Development of Commerce Degrees*, 36–38; Warren Hogan, 'Allan George Barnard Fisher (1895–1976)', in J.E. King (ed.), *A Biographical Dictionary of Australia and New Zealand Economists* (Cheltenham: Edward Elgar Publishing, 2007), 99–102.
32. Testimonial for G.C. Billing, 21 June 1946, A.G.B. Fisher papers, MS-4304/168, HC.
33. *UOC*, 1922–1947; Gill, 'Bedford, Harry Dodgshun'.
34. Blyth, 'Early Academic Economics', 27–31; Hogan, 'Allan George Barnard Fisher'.
35. Walter James Boraman, 'History of public finance in New Zealand: From the earliest times to the year 1890', PhD thesis, University of New Zealand, 1929; McLean, *Economics and the Development of Commerce Degrees*, 42.
36. Blyth, 'Early academic economics', 29–30; Mark Donoghue, 'Ralph William Souter (1897–1946)', in King, *Australia and New Zealand Economists*, 261–64; Testimonial for R.W. Souter, 5 December 1929, A.G.B. Fisher papers, MS-4304/168, HC.
37. 'Benefactors have helped in many fields', *UON*, August

1982, 1–2; Ralph Reid, 'Reid, Donald (1833–1919)', in Jane Thomson (ed.), *Southern People: A dictionary of Otago Southland biography* (Dunedin: Longacre Press/ Dunedin City Council, 1998), 414.
38. Geoffry Billing to A.G.B. Fisher, 9 December 1947, A.G.B. Fisher papers, MS-4304/282, HC; Blyth, 'Early academic economics', 31.
39. Geoffry Billing to A.G.B. Fisher, 25 April 1946, A.G.B. Fisher papers, MS-4304/282, HC; *UOC*, 1946, 113–14; 1950, 16.
40. Cowan, *Commerce at Otago*, 109–10.
41. Commerce Faculty Annual Report, 1959, Records of Registry and Central Administration, AG-180-7/07, HC.
42. Cowan, *Commerce at Otago*, 19–22.
43. Commerce Faculty Annual Report, 1959, 1960 and 1970, Records of Registry and Central Administration, AG-180-7/07 and 7/10, HC.
44. Cowan, *Commerce at Otago*, 43.
45. *Report of the Committee on New Zealand Universities, December 1959* (Wellington: Government Printer, 1960), 37–42.
46. Cowan, *Commerce at Otago*, 44.
47. J.A. Valentine, 'Education for the accountancy profession', *Accountants' Journal*, vol. 47, no. 7, 1969, 261–67; Devonport, 'Interaction between the universities and the Institute of Chartered Accountants'.
48. Commerce Faculty Annual Report, 1960 and 1970, Records of Registry and Central Administration, AG-180-7/07 and 7/10, HC.
49. Cowan, *Commerce at Otago*, 24–27, 44.
50. Commerce Faculty Annual Report, 1962, Records of Registry and Central Administration, AG-180-7/07, HC; *UOC*, 1963, 231–32.
51. Commerce Faculty Annual Report, 1963–1966, Records of Registry and Central Administration, AG-180-7/08, HC; *UOC*, 1963–1966.
52. Cowan, *Commerce at Otago*, 24–27; 'Some prominent lecturers'; Commerce Faculty Annual Report, 1969, Records of Registry and Central Administration, AG-180-7/10, HC.
53. Commerce Faculty Annual Report, 1962, Records of Registry and Central Administration, AG-180-7/07, HC.
54. Commerce Faculty Annual Report, 1965, Records of Registry and Central Administration, AG-180-7/08, HC.
55. *OUSA Orientation Handbook 1975*, 46.
56. Cowan, *Commerce at Otago*, 55.
57. *UOC*, 1975, 347–49; 'Chair of marketing', *UON*, February 1976, 4; Guenther Mueller-Heumann, 'The marketing course at Otago 1966–1990: A case study in curriculum technology, university fashions and politics', 1990, revised 2007, 2–3: https://ourarchive.otago.ac.nz/handle/10523/1460
58. Rob Lawson interview. On the growth of the department, see also 'The phenomenal development of marketing', *Otago Graduate*, 1988, 29–31.
59. Commerce Faculty Annual Report, 1966, Records of Registry and Central Administration, AG-180-7/09, HC.
60. Commerce Faculty Annual Report, 1970, Records of Registry and Central Administration, AG-180-7/10, HC; *UOC*, 1970, 312.
61. McLean, *Economics and the Development of Commerce Degrees*, 172–74; Cowan, *Commerce at Otago*, 80.
62. Commerce Faculty Annual Report, 1969 and 1970, Records of Registry and Central Administration, AG-180-7/10, HC.
63. McLean, *Economics and the Development of Commerce Degrees*, 133.
64. Commerce Faculty Annual Report, 1970, Records of Registry and Central Administration, AG-180-7/10, HC.
65. McLean, *Economics and the Development of Commerce Degrees*, 132–37.
66. Cowan, *Commerce at Otago*, 80–81.
67. Alan Geare interview.
68. McLean, *Economics and the Development of Commerce Degrees*, 118, 137, 162, 189.
69. Commerce Faculty Annual Report, 1978 and 1983, Records of Registry and Central Administration, AG-180-7/14 and 7/15, HC; 'Professor selected', *UON*, June 1981, 2; Cowan, *Commerce at Otago*, 79; McLean, *Economics and the Development of Commerce Degrees*, 106–07, 114–15.
70. 'New home for BDC', *UON*, March 1982, 6; Commerce Faculty Annual Report, 1972, Records of Registry and Central Administration, AG-180-7/11, HC.
71. Commerce Faculty Annual Report, 1975, Records of Registry and Central Administration, AG-180-7/13, HC.
72. Cowan, *Commerce at Otago*, 84, 107; 'BDC loses director', *UON*, January 1986, 5; 'Acting for BDC', *UON*, February 1986, 5; 'New director for Business Development Centre', *UON*, October 1986, 5.
73. Cowan, *Commerce at Otago*, 75, 77–79.
74. McLean, *Economics and the Development of Commerce Degrees*, 103, 146, 176; Alan Geare interview.
75. Enrolment statistics compiled from Commerce Faculty Annual Reports and *UOAR*.
76. Michelle Emery, Jill Hooks & Ross Stewart, 'Born at the wrong time? An oral history of women professional accountants in New Zealand', *Accounting History*, vol. 7, no. 2, 2002, 7–34; Beverley Lord & Alan Robb, 'Women students and staff in accountancy: The Canterbury Tales', *Accounting History*, vol. 15, no. 4, 2010, 529–58; Rosalind H. Whiting & Christine Wright, 'Explaining gender inequity in the New Zealand accounting profession', *British Accounting Review*, vol. 22, 2001, 191–222. I am grateful to Hilary Smith for these references.
77. Cowan, *Commerce at Otago*, 87; Commerce Faculty Annual Report, 1986, Records of Registry and Central Administration, AG-180-7/15, HC.
78. Subjects in which degrees were obtained, University Grants Committee records, R12485703, Archives New Zealand, Wellington; Whiting & Wright, 'Explaining gender inequity'.
79. Commerce Faculty Annual Report, 1979, Records of Registry and Central Administration, AG-180-7/14, HC; McLean, *Economics and the Development of Commerce Degrees*, 81–82.

80. 'Accounting by computer' and 'Commerce computer', *UON*, August 1979, 4, 11–12.
81. Commerce Faculty Annual Report, 1980–1984, Records of Registry and Central Administration, AG-180-7/14 and 7/15, HC.
82. McLean, *Economics and the Development of Commerce Degrees*, 82–83; Lyall McLean interview.
83. Cowan, *Commerce at Otago*, 103.
84. 'Otago has enlightened approach to computing', *UON*, June 1987, 7–8.
85. Report of University of Otago Review of Department of Information Science, 2008, 9. The self-review document prepared for that review is a good example of the explanations provided by the departments. See also the 2008 Memorandum of Understanding between the two departments, which is reproduced in McLean, *Economics and the Development of Commerce Degrees*, 180–82. Under the new EFTS-based government funding system, science students attracted 51% more money than those in commerce or arts (Otago's information science department shared some of this additional funding with the rest of the commerce division). Hank Wolfe interview; McLean, *Economics and the Development of Commerce Degrees*, 176–77.
86. McLean, *Economics and the Development of Commerce Degrees*, 190–93.
87. Self-review, University of Otago Review of Department of Information Science, 2008, 4, 10–12; Hank Wolfe interview.
88. Cowan, *Commerce at Otago*, 27.
89. Commerce Faculty Annual Report, 1959, Records of Registry and Central Administration, AG-180-7/07, HC.
90. Cowan, *Commerce at Otago*, 69.
91. D.S. Wright, 'MBA – Master of Business Administration – its history and meaning', *Management*, vol. 26, no. 8, 1979, 42–44.
92. Cowan, *Commerce at Otago*, 69–70.
93. *UOC*, 1973, 325.
94. Cowan, *Commerce at Otago*, 79–80, 91–91; 'New research chair', *UON*, July 1975, 6; *UON*, December 1975, 10; 'MBA degree', *UON*, April 1977, 5; 'Professor of Management', *UON*, September 1984, 2.
95. 'MBA graduates', *UON*, February 1979, 5; Commerce Faculty Annual Report, 1978, Records of Registry and Central Administration, AG-180-7/14, HC.
96. 'MBA programme', *UON*, April 1980, 3; 'Must aspiring managers be masochists?', *UON*, October 1980, 1–2; Cowan, *Commerce at Otago*, 91–92.
97. Cowan, *Commerce at Otago*, 91–92; 'Obituary: Dr David Wright', *UON*, March 1983, 4; Interviews with Alan Geare and Hank Wolfe.
98. 'MBA programme', *UON*, April 1983, 8.
99. Commerce Faculty Annual Report, 1980, 1982 and 1984, Records of Registry and Central Administration, AG-180-7/14 and 7/15, HC; Alan Geare interview.
100. 'Business school visitors', *UON*, May 1985, 9–10; 'Internationalising the MBA', *UON*, March 1992, 5.
101. 'New MBA course in Auckland', *UON*, June–July 1997, 3.
102. McLean, *Economics and the Development of Commerce Degrees*, 227–28; Proposal for new Executive MBA, Division of Commerce records, MS-4183/021, HC.
103. 'Otago MBA responds to market needs', *UON*, October 1996, 1.
104. 'MBA guide 2010', *NZ Business*, September 2009, 31–38.
105. Kevin Kevany, 'Degrees of flavour', *NZ Business*, September 2012, 24–26.
106. McLean, *Economics and the Development of Commerce Degrees*, 228; interviews with Lyall McLean, Rob Lawson and Alan Geare.
107. 'Otago MBA goes online', Otago Bulletin Board, 17 September 2014: www.otago.ac.nz/otagobulletin/news/otago079512.html
108. 'Online MBA hitting the right note', Otago Bulletin Board, 20 August 2015: www.otago.ac.nz/otagobulletin/news/otago120873.html; 'New Zealand's only Online MBA ranked among the world's best', Otago Bulletin Board, 6 April 2017: www.otago.ac.nz/news/news/otago642513.html
109. McLean, *Economics and the Development of Commerce Degrees*, 229–31; Lyall McLean interview.
110. 'Tourism programme mooted', *UON*, September 1986, 9.
111. 'New Diploma in Tourism', *UON*, October 1988, 5.
112. Geoff Kearsley, 'New course developments in tourism', *UON*, December 1994, 18.
113. 'Director of tourism studies', *UON*, May 1993, 5.
114. 'Tiki tour', *UON*, March 1996, 8; Self-review for University of Otago Review of the Department of Tourism, 2006, 12.
115. Self-review, University of Otago Review of Department of Tourism, 2006, 12; Geoff Kearsley, 'New course developments in tourism', *UON*, December 1994, 18.
116. 'Tiki tour', *UON*, March 1996, 8.
117. Self-review, University of Otago Review of Department of Tourism, 2006, 12; McLean, *Economics and the Development of Commerce Degrees*, 212–13.
118. University of Waikato: www.waikato.ac.nz/study/subjects/tour.shtml; Victoria University of Wellington: www.victoria.ac.nz/explore/study-areas/tourism-management/about; Lincoln University: www.lincoln.ac.nz/Study/Qualifications/Qualification/?QualCode=b.tourism%20management&major=false; Auckland University of Technology: www.aut.ac.nz/study-at-aut/study-areas/hospitality--tourism/undergraduate-courses/bachelor-of-international-tourism-management-overview
119. Self-review, University of Otago Review of Department of Tourism, 2011, 6, 29–30; *UOC*, 2011–2012; McLean, *Economics and the Development of Commerce Degrees*, 212.
120. John Howells interview.
121. Self-review, University of Otago Review of Department of Economics, 2011, 5–6.
122. 'About people', *UON*, February 1992, 8.
123. Gavin McLean, 'Premiers and prime ministers: Support services and statues', Te Ara – the Encyclopedia of New Zealand: www.teara.govt.nz/en/cartoon/33206/heather-simpson
124. 'Winning with economics: It's not cricket!', *UON*, December 1990, 4; 'About people', *UON*, April 1991, 17;

Stephen Knowles & John McCombie, 'Erkin Bairam 1958–2001: His contribution to economics', University of Otago Economics Discussion Papers, no. 0212, 2002; 2, 14–15; John Howells interview.

125. Knowles & McCombie, 'Erkin Bairam'; Erkin I. Bairam, 'Research productivity in New Zealand university economics departments, 1988–1995', *New Zealand Economic Papers*, vol. 30, no. 2, 1996, 229–41.
126. Self-review, University of Otago Review of Department of Economics, 2006, 1–3; 2011, 6.
127. Self-review, University of Otago Review of Department of Economics, 2011, 6; Lesley Elliott with William J. O'Brien, *Sophie's Legacy: A mother's story of her family's loss and their quest for change* (Auckland: Longacre, 2011), 152–71. Lesley Elliott, the mother of victim Sophie Elliott, was unsurprisingly angry that the university had failed to protect Sophie. The event prompted a review of the ethical behaviour policy as it concerned staff–student relationships, but Lesley Elliott believed the resulting changes were 'merely tinkering around the edges' (Elliott & O'Brien, 246).
128. Report of University of Otago Review of Psychological Medicine, Dunedin School of Medicine, 2009, 9; Vincent Marks & Caroline Richmond, 'Colin Bouwer: Professor of Psychiatry and murder', *Journal of the Royal Society of Medicine*, vol. 101, no. 8, 2008, 400–08.
129. *Performance-Based Research Fund, Evaluating Research Excellence – the 2012 Assessment: Final Report* (Wellington: Tertiary Education Commission, 2013), 89–14, 89–35, 89–37, 89–64, 89–65.
130. Report of University of Otago Review of Department of Finance and Quantitative Analysis, 2007, 7–8.
131. Report of University of Otago Review of Department of Accountancy and Business Law, 2007, 4.
132. Report of University of Otago Review of Department of Accountancy and Finance, 2014, 9; Elspeth McLean, 'University council approves department mergers', *ODT*, 15 July 2010: www.odt.co.nz/campus/university-otago/115933/university-council-approves-department-mergers; Allison Rudd, 'Business school might be about to lose 10 jobs', *ODT*, 6 August 2010: www.odt.co.nz/campus/university-otago/119509/business-school-might-be-about-lose-10-jobs
133. McLean, *Economics and the Development of Commerce Degrees*, 240–41.
134. Alison Finigan (ed.), *Partnerships for Excellence: Celebrating 10 years of the Leading Thinkers initiative* (Dunedin: Development and Alumni Relations Office, University of Otago, 2014); 'Otago appoints new Chair in Entrepreneurship', *OB*, 27 July 2007, 4; *UOC*, 2011, 534.
135. Report of University of Otago Review of Centre for Entrepreneurship, 2013, 15; Finigan, *Partnerships for Excellence*.
136. 'Professor Brendan Gray is retiring but not giving up on entrepreneurs', Otago Bulletin Board, 26 May 2016: www.otago.ac.nz/otagobulletin/people/otago612730.html
137. 'Global focus for new commerce major', *UON*, September–October 1998, 4.
138. 'International business programme has great potential', *UON*, May 2000, 8; Self-review, University of Otago Review of International Business Programme, 2007, 7. Students whose first language was not English or Māori were exempted from language study but still studied another culture.
139. *International Business Course Information*, 2016, 18.
140. McLean, *Economics and the Development of Commerce Degrees*, 58–60.

9: HEALTH SCIENCES

1. Erik Olssen, 'Macandrew, James', from DNZB: www.teara.govt.nz/en/biographies/1m1/macandrew-james. See chapter 1 for discussion of Macandrew and his role in the founding of the university.
2. James Macandrew to Colonial Secretary, July 1871, cited in G.E. Thompson, *A History of the University of Otago (1869–1919)* (Dunedin: Wilkie, 1919), 99.
3. D.W. Carmalt Jones, *Annals of the University of Otago Medical School 1875–1939* (Wellington: Reed, 1945), 48–51; Charles Hercus & Gordon Bell, *The Otago Medical School Under the First Three Deans* (Edinburgh: Livingstone, 1964), 8–9; Dorothy Page, *Anatomy of a Medical School: A history of medicine at the University of Otago 1875–2000* (Dunedin: Otago University Press, 2008), 18–19; Thompson, *University of Otago*, 99–101.
4. Geoffrey Blainey, *A Centenary History of the University of Melbourne* (Melbourne: Melbourne University Press, 1957), 25–35.
5. *UOAR*, 1874.
6. *UOAR*, 1875; Millen Coughtrey to James Gow Black, 28 January 1874, cited in Carmalt Jones, *Annals*, 53–54.
7. Page, *Anatomy of a Medical School*, 20–21; Carmalt Jones, *Annals*, 49–52.
8. *UOAR*, 1876; Carmalt Jones, *Annals*, 56–65.
9. Millen Coughtrey, *The Introductory Address in the Faculty of Medicine of Otago University* (Dunedin: Mackay, Risk, Munro & Co., 1875), 3.
10. *UOAR*, 1876. I have not been able to locate details of this course or its students in other sources, either.
11. Carmalt Jones, *Annals*, 63–64. Solomon became a prominent barrister: see Jennifer Brice, 'Solomon, Saul (1857–1937)', in Jane Thomson (ed.), *Southern People: A dictionary of Otago Southland biography* (Dunedin: Longacre Press/Dunedin City Council, 1998), 470.
12. 'Obituary: Dr Charles A. Low', *New Zealand Herald*, 23 November 1925, 10; 'Obituary: Dr Charles Archibald Low', *Lake County Press*, 12 November 1925, 2.
13. Carmalt Jones, *Annals*, 66–68; Page, *Anatomy of a Medical School*, 22–24.
14. Page, *Anatomy of a Medical School*, 22.
15. Carmalt Jones, *Annals*, 69–71.
16. Carmalt Jones, *Annals*, 82–85 (including reminiscences of Scott by Barnett); Rex Wright-St Clair, 'Scott, John Halliday', from DNZB: www.teara.govt.nz/en/biographies/2s7/scott-john-halliday; Page, *Anatomy of a Medical School*, 29.

17. *ODT*, 20 December 1877, 2; 21 December 1877, 2; Carmalt Jones, *Annals*, 75; Page, *Anatomy of a Medical School*, 27–28.
18. Carmalt Jones, *Annals*, 75–80; Page, *Anatomy of a Medical School*, 31–32.
19. Carmalt Jones, *Annals*, 86–90, 95–96; Page, *Anatomy of a Medical School*, 32–33.
20. Page, *Anatomy of a Medical School*, 28–29; *UOAR*, 1893, 1899.
21. Millen Coughtrey, *The Graduation Address, on the Occasion of the Conferring, for the First Time in New Zealand, of the Degrees of LL.D and M.B. of the New Zealand University* (Dunedin: Otago Daily Times, 1887), 8.
22. Page, *Anatomy of a Medical School*, 34–38; John Angus, *A History of the Otago Hospital Board and its Predecessors* (Dunedin: Otago Hospital Board, 1984), 85–89; Report of the Dunedin Hospital Inquiry Commission, *AJHR*, 1891, H-01.
23. *UOAR*, 1901.
24. Robert D. Anderson, Michael Lynch & Nicholas Phillipson, *The University of Edinburgh: An illustrated history* (Edinburgh: Edinburgh University Press, 2003), 109, 140–41. There was an exception: a woman completed medical training at Edinburgh in the 1820s, disguised as a man. Sophia Jex-Blake and colleagues, determined on a medical education but foiled in attempts to enter the Edinburgh faculty, opened an independent medical school for women in that city in 1886.
25. Page, *Anatomy of a Medical School*, 48–52; Dorothy Page, 'Dissecting a community: Women medical students at the University of Otago, 1891–1924', in Barbara Brookes & Dorothy Page (eds), *Communities of Women: Historical perspectives* (Dunedin: Otago University Press, 2002), 111–27; Patricia A. Sargison, 'Siedeberg, Emily Hancock', from DNZB: www.teara.govt.nz/en/biographies/3s16/siedeberg-emily-hancock
26. T.W.H. Brooking, *A History of Dentistry in New Zealand* (Dunedin: New Zealand Dental Association, 1980), 23–30.
27. R.F. Stockwell, *The Origins of the Dental Profession in New Zealand* (Dunedin: New Zealand Dental Association, 1977), 6–8.
28. Brooking, *History of Dentistry*, 22.
29. Stockwell, *Origins of the Dental Profession*, 12–17.
30. Ibid., 16–19; *UOAR*, 1904, 1907.
31. *UOAR*, 1907. On Davies, see Stockwell, *Origins of the Dental Profession*, 21–22.
32. R. Harvey Brown, 'Pickerill, Henry Percy', from DNZB: www.teara.govt.nz/en/biographies/3p25/pickerill-henry-percy; Harvey Brown, *Pickerill: Pioneer in plastic surgery, dental education and dental research* (Dunedin: Otago University Press, 2007).
33. 'University Council', *OW*, 16 October 1907, 16.
34. *UOAR*, 1909; 'Local and general', *OW*, 11 November 1908, 27; 'University council', *ES*, 4 July 1911, 8.
35. *UOAR*, 1908.
36. H.P. Pickerill, 'Impressions on first arrival in New Zealand', *New Zealand Dental Journal*, vol. 3, 1907, 47–48.
37. *UOAR*, 1908; Brown, *Pickerill*, 151–55.
38. *UOAR*, 1908.
39. *UOAR*, 1911.
40. *UOAR*, 1915.
41. Brooking, *History of Dentistry*, 74–78.
42. Brown, *Pickerill*, 119–44.
43. 'Dental School: Annual Report', *ODT*, 16 June 1920, 6.
44. Brooking, *History of Dentistry*, 96–99.
45. 'Dental School: Annual Report', *ODT*, 16 June 1920, 6.
46. Roy Hanan, *A Dentist at Large* (Christchurch: G. Hanan, 1977), 29.
47. Dental School Annual Report, 1921, Records of Registry and Central Administration, AG-180-31/0055, HC.
48. *UOC*, 1920, 190–96.
49. Angela R.C. Pack, 'Women in New Zealand dentistry, 1880–1980', *New Zealand Dental Journal*, vol. 77, 1981, 19–25.
50. Brown, *Pickerill*, 156, 188–203; Brooking, *History of Dentistry*, 111–17.
51. Louise Shaw, *In Our Hands: 100 years of the School of Physiotherapy in Otago 1913–2013* (Dunedin: University of Otago School of Physiotherapy, 2013), 15–36; Leah Taylor, *Dunedin School of Massage: The first ten years of physiotherapy training in New Zealand* (Dunedin: L. Taylor, 1988), 2–8; 'University Council', *ES*, 19 March 1913, 7; 'University Council', *ES*, 16 April 1913, 7; 'Training in massage', *ODT*, 30 June 1913, 4; 'School of Massage', *Kai Tiaki*, vol. 6, no. 3, 1913, 114.
52. Shaw, *In Our Hands*, 30–36, 46. Armstrong is named as Lily in Shaw's history, but Shaw later discovered her correct name was Lizzie: Louise Shaw to author, 17 November 2014.
53. Shaw, *In Our Hands*, 37–39; Taylor, *Dunedin School of Massage*, 7–16.
54. Shaw, *In Our Hands*, 38–44; Taylor, *Dunedin School of Massage*, 17–23.
55. 'University Council', *ES*, 7 June 1904, 3; 'A veterinary college', *ES*, 1 November 1904, 2.
56. 'University Council', *ODT*, 8 October 1907, 2; *UOAR*, 1907–1914.
57. Hugh Parton, *The University of New Zealand* (University Grants Committee, 1979), 136–38; Eric Shortridge, Catherine Smith & Earle Gardner, *'And While You're Here': A brief history of the New Zealand veterinary profession* (Wellington: New Zealand Veterinary Association, 1998), 73–74; Bill Dawson interview.
58. Marie E. Burgess, *Nursing in New Zealand Society* (Auckland: Longman Paul, 1984), 60–63; E. Beatrice Salmon, *A Profession in Transition: Issues in nursing in New Zealand over two decades, 1961–1981* (Wellington: C.L. Bailey Nursing Education Trust, 1982), 60–64.
59. Diploma in Nursing file, 1923, Faculty of Medicine, Dean's Department records, MS-4324/020, HC; 'Diploma of Nursing', *ODT*, 4 October 1924, 16; 'Diploma of Nursing', *ODT*, 27 March 1926, 19; 'University Council', *ODT*, 18 May 1927, 5; A.G. Strong, *History of the Development of University Education in Home Science in New Zealand 1911–1936* (Dunedin: University of Otago,

1937), 35; Beryl Hughes, 'Nursing education: The collapse of the Diploma of Nursing at the University of Otago, 1925–1926', *New Zealand Journal of History*, vol. 12, no. 1, 1978, 17–33; Mary Lambie, *My Story: Memoirs of a New Zealand nurse* (Christchurch: N.M. Peryer Ltd, 1956), 53.

60. Hughes, 'Nursing education'; Lambie, *My Story*, 61–66.
61. Hercus & Bell, *Otago Medical School*, 191, 231–32; Page, *Anatomy of a Medical School*, 40–41; 'Obituary: Mr Wolf Harris', *ODT*, 23 March 1926, 7. Harris, who had been based in London for many years, was well known for his philanthropy to Dunedin causes.
62. Page, *Anatomy of a Medical School*, 41, 43.
63. Ibid., 44.
64. *UOAR*, 1910.
65. Page, *Anatomy of a Medical School*, 44.
66. Roy Porter, *The Greatest Benefit to Mankind: A medical history of humanity from antiquity to the present* (London: Harper Collins, 1997), 428–61.
67. 'Obituary: Dr W.S. Roberts', *Press*, 11 September 1937, 16; Hercus & Bell, *Otago Medical School*, 241–42.
68. Warwick Brunton, *The Medicine of the Future: A history of the Department of Preventive and Social Medicine, University of Otago 1886–2011* (Dunedin: Department of Preventive & Social Medicine, University of Otago, 2011), 21–39.
69. Carmalt Jones, *Annals*, 141–42; Hercus & Bell, *Otago Medical School*, 241–42, 251–53, 257–58. Drennan was appointed in 1915 but was held up by war service.
70. Brunton, *Medicine of the Future*, 41–63, 120–21; Page, *Anatomy of a Medical School*, 125.
71. First Annual Report by Professor J.G. Black on the University Laboratory, *Otago Provincial Council Votes and Proceedings*, 1875, 297–302.
72. Hercus & Bell, *Otago Medical School*, 278; Macdonald obituary, 'Personal', *ES*, 25 August 1902, 6.
73. Carmalt Jones, *Annals*, 100.
74. Hercus & Bell, *Otago Medical School*, 278–79; Page, *Anatomy of a Medical School*, 44–45, 90–91; F.N. Fastier, 'Pharmacology', in Edwin R. Nye (ed.), *Medical Research in Otago 1922–1997: As portrayed by 75 years of the Proceedings of the University of Otago Medical School* (Dunedin: Otago Medical School Research Society, 1998), 49–58.
75. Hercus & Bell, *Otago Medical School*, 279, 364–68
76. *UOC*, 1894, 74–75.
77. Page, *Anatomy of a Medical School*, 80–82.
78. Ibid., 67–70.
79. Hercus & Bell, *Otago Medical School*, 127–28; Christopher Moore, George Rolleston, John Riminton & Andrew Hornblow, *A Vision Realised: The Christchurch School of Medicine, University of Otago 1972–1997* (Christchurch: Christchurch School of Medicine, 1998), 4–5; Page, *Anatomy of a Medical School*, 87.
80. Eric D'Ath, Reminiscences concerning the Pathology Department, Medical Library Historical Collection, MS–1623/023, HC.
81. Fred Fastier interview.
82. Norman Edson, 'Some notes on the past', Medical Library Historical Collection, MS–1623/023, HC; F.N. Fastier, *Recollections of an Old Scarfie* (Dunedin: Amidine Publications, 2004), 45–48.
83. Hercus & Bell, *Otago Medical School*, 273–77.
84. John C. Eccles, 'My scientific odyssey', *Annual Review of Physiology*, vol. 39, 1977, 1–18.
85. Edson, 'Some notes on the past'.
86. L.G. Brock, J.S. Coombs & J.C. Eccles, 'Action potentials of motoneurones with intracellular electrode', *Proceedings of the University of Otago Medical School*, vol. 29, 1951, 14–15; Edson, 'Some notes on the past'; David R. Curtis & Per Anderson, 'Sir John Carew Eccles, A.C. 27 January 1903–2 May 1997: Elected F.R.S. 1941', *Biographical Memoirs of Fellows of the Royal Society*, vol. 47, 2001, 159–87.
87. Wilfrid Rall, 'Spatial summation and monosynaptic input-output relations in the mammalian spinal cord', PhD thesis, University of New Zealand, 1953; Margaret Elaine di Menna, 'Yeasts of the human body: Their nature and relationships', PhD thesis, University of New Zealand, 1953 (graduated 1954). Lyle Brandon Fastier also completed his PhD thesis, 'An experimental study of the mouse encephalomyelitis group of viruses', in 1953. Three researchers – Douglas Shaw, Barrie Cousins and Alexander Arcus – completed biochemistry PhDs in the mid-1950s.
88. Page, *Anatomy of a Medical School*, 127, 133; Hercus & Bell, *Otago Medical School*, 140–43.
89. Edson, 'Notes on the past'; *UOC*; Hercus & Bell, *Otago Medical School*, 235–40, 251–56. While Hercus and Bell state that microbiology was taught to science students from 1950, the Science Faculty Annual Report for that year notes that the new Stage 2 and 3 courses were replacing an existing course in bacteriology for science. All three subjects were listed as available for science students in the calendar from 1943 (though not initially at advanced level).
90. Science Faculty Annual Report, 1950, Records of Registry and Central Administration, AG-180-7/04, HC.
91. George Petersen and Mervyn Smith interviews; Hercus & Bell, *Otago Medical School*, 238; 'Norman Lowther Edson', *Lancet*, vol. 295, no. 7659, 1970, 1296.
92. Donald Bacon, 'Personal memories associated with the introduction of microbiology at the University of Otago 1946 to 1955', 2005, MS–2523, HC; J.A.R. Miles, Retirement tribute to Associate Professor M.J. Marples, Faculty of Medicine, Dean's Department records, MS–4326/054, HC; *The First 50 Years: A brief history of the New Zealand Microbiological Society* (Dunedin: New Zealand Microbiological Society, 2005), 5–8; Brunton, *Medicine of the Future*, 74–75, 92–95, 108–17, 124–25.
93. 'University of Otago past year's graduates', *ODT*, 12 July 1928, 7.
94. 'Chair of Dentistry', *ODT*, 14 December 1927, 10.
95. Dental Faculty Annual Report, 1929, *ODT*, 12 February 1930, 2; 1930–1945, Records of Registry and Central Administration, AG-180-7/01, 7/02 and 7/03, HC; 'Dental students: Registrations about half number needed', *Press*, 10 December 1941, 6.
96. 'The Dental School: Year's operations reviewed', *ODT*, 27 April 1927, 5; John H. Peat, 'Eighty years ago …', *New*

Zealand Dental Journal, vol. 103, no. 4, 2007, 108–09.
97. Dental Faculty Annual Report, 1927, 1942–1944, Records of Registry and Central Administration, AG-180-31/0124, AG-180-7/02 and 7/03, HC.
98. Page, *Anatomy of a Medical School*, 117–23.
99. Medical Faculty Annual Report, 1939 and 1943, Records of Registry and Central Administration, AG-180-7/02, HC; Page, *Anatomy of a Medical School*, 118–21.
100. Medical Faculty Annual Report, 1940, Records of Registry and Central Administration, AG-180-7/02, HC.
101. Dental Faculty Annual Report, 1947, Records of Registry and Central Administration, AG-180-7/03, HC.
102. Brooking, *History of Dentistry*, 157.
103. J.P. Walsh, 'Initial report of the Dean of the Dental Faculty to the Council of the University of Otago', May 1946, Records of Registry and Central Administration, AG-180-7/03, HC.
104. Dental Faculty Annual Report, 1951–1963, Records of Registry and Central Administration, AG-180-7/04 to 7/08, HC.
105. Page, *Anatomy of a Medical School*, 116, 118–20; Susannah Williams, 'The Jewish doctors in New Zealand 1933–1945', 2008: www.holocaustcentre.org.nz/remember/refuge-in-nz/jewish-doctors. A total of 68 refugee doctors were granted permits, though only 34 arrived and completed retraining.
106. Paul Oestreicher to author, 16 March 2016.
107. Williams, 'Jewish doctors'.
108. Hercus & Bell, *Otago Medical School*, 159–65; Page, *Anatomy of a Medical School*, 144–45, 150, 294–97, 345–46.
109. Elaine Donaldson interview; Pack, 'Women in New Zealand dentistry'.
110. Page, *Anatomy of a Medical School*, 145.
111. 'A hard act to follow', *Mana*, no. 59, 2004, 71–80.
112. 'Frederick Te Tiwha Bennett', *Te Ao Hou*, no. 60, 1967, 2; 'Nga Rara Rangatahi (The Young Doctors)', *Tihei Mauri Ora!*, no. 2, 1999, 6–9.
113. John Broughton interview.
114. Susan Heydon & Stephen Duffull, *Pharmacy at Otago: The first 50 years: The school, the profession and the people* (Dunedin: New Zealand's National School of Pharmacy, University of Otago, 2013), 4–5; Reg Coombes, *Pharmacy in New Zealand: Aspects and reminiscences*, (Auckland: Ray Richards for the Pharmaceutical Society of New Zealand, 1981), 125, 132; Astrid Baker, 'An unlimited liability: Free medicines and Labour's Social Security Act 1938', *New Zealand Journal of History*, vol. 32, no. 2, 1998, 143–62.
115. Pharmacy Board to all pharmaceutical chemists, 1966, cited in Coombes, *Pharmacy in New Zealand*, 129–34.
116. Heydon & Duffull, *Pharmacy at Otago*, 3–6; Coombes, *Pharmacy in New Zealand*, 121–27; F.N. Fastier, *Pharmacy Teaching at Otago University: How it began* (Dunedin: Amidine Publications, 1992), 11.
117. Coombes, *Pharmacy in New Zealand*, 127–37; Fastier, *Pharmacy Teaching*, 11–20; Ian Dougherty, *Central Institute of Technology 1960–2001: A brief history* (Upper Hutt: Central Institute of Technology, 2001), 4; William Renwick, 'Beeby, Clarence Edward', from DNZB: www.teara.govt.nz/en/biographies/5b17/beeby-clarence-edward
118. Fastier, *Pharmacy Teaching*, 20–26.
119. Heydon & Duffull, *Pharmacy at Otago*, 9–14.
120. Fastier, *Pharmacy Teaching*, 37–40.
121. 'Professor H. Taylor', *UON*, December 1981, 4.
122. Heydon & Duffull, *Pharmacy at Otago*, 28–35; *UOC*, 1984–1985; 'Significant events from the past year', *UON*, February 1985, 1–2.
123. Medical Faculty Annual Report, 1958, Records of Registry and Central Administration, AG-180-7/06, HC.
124. Medical Faculty Annual Report, 1961 and 1963, Records of Registry and Central Administration, AG-180-7/07 and 7/08, HC.
125. Medical Faculty Annual Report, 1960, Records of Registry and Central Administration, AG-180-7/07, HC; Page, *Anatomy of a Medical School*, 162–64.
126. Page, *Anatomy of a Medical School*, 164–71. On Llewellyn, see W.J. Gardner, E.T. Beardsley & T.E. Carter, *A History of the University of Canterbury 1873–1973* (Christchurch: University of Canterbury, 1973), 366–67.
127. Ronald V. Christie, *Report on the Medical School* (Dunedin: University of Otago, 1968); Page, *Anatomy of a Medical School*, 168–75; J.D. Hunter, 'The dean speaks!', *Medical Digest*, 1977, 4–7.
128. Page, *Anatomy of a Medical School*, 176–80.
129. R.O.H. Irvine, 'The future of the Medical School: A report on the future of the Medical School with particular reference to the implementation of proposals made in the Christie report', Records of Registry and Central Administration, AG-180-7/10, HC.
130. Medical Faculty Annual Report, 1975–1978, Records of Registry and Central Administration, AG-180-7/13 and 7/14, HC; *UOC*, 1972–1978.
131. Self-review, University of Otago Review of Department of General Practice, Dunedin School of Medicine, 2008, 6; Medical Faculty Annual Report, 1978 and 1982, Records of Registry and Central Administration, AG-180-7/14, HC.
132. Brunton, *Medicine of the Future*, 133–34, 136–37, 161–62.
133. Medical Faculty Annual Report, 1984, Records of Registry and Central Administration, AG-180-7/15, HC.
134. Interviews with George Petersen and Mervyn Smith; George Petersen to author, 28 October 2013.
135. Margaret Loutit interview; John Gibb, 'Influential, respected, scientific teacher and researcher: John Stuart Loutit', *ODT*, 30 March 2013, 40.
136. Christie, *Report on the Medical School*.
137. J.R. Robinson, 'Physiology', in Nye, *Medical Research in Otago*, 59–83.
138. W.D. Trotter, 'Advances in anatomy 1922–97', in Nye, *Medical Research in Otago*, 9–19; 'Professors to retire', *UON*, November 1982, 3.
139. Dental Faculty Annual Report, 1959, Records of Registry and Central Administration, AG-180-7/07, HC; 'Electron microscope', *UON*, September 1974, 6; Trotter, 'Advances

in anatomy'; Richard Easingwood, 'Freeze fracture in Otago', *Microscopy in Focus*, no. 18, 2008, 7; 'Inside the Centre for Electron Microscopy', *OB*, 2 October 2009, 6.
140. Self-review, University of Otago Review of Department of Anatomy and Structural Biology, 1998, 1–2; *UOC*, 1978 and 1986.
141. E.G. McQueen, 'Toxicology and the research unit', in Nye, *Medical Research in Otago*, 125–34; R. Laverty, 'Ewen Garth McQueen', Lives of the Fellows, Royal College of Physicians: http://munksroll.rcplondon.ac.uk/Biography/Details/3042; Sean Flaherty, 'Poised for poisonings', *UOM*, no. 12, 2005, 20–22; 'History of the centre', New Zealand National Poisons Centre: www.poisons.co.nz/history.php; Ian Dougherty, 'Indispensable vigilance', *UOM*, no. 43, 2016, 5–7.
142. Self-review, University of Otago Review of Department of Pharmacology and Toxicology, 2008; *UOC*, 1994.
143. Christie, *Report on the Medical School*.
144. *UOC*, 1975.
145. B.F. Heslop, 'Surgery: Transplantation research in Dunedin', in Nye, *Medical Research in Otago*, 153–61; Peter Morris, 'Sir Michael Francis Addison Woodruff', *Biographical Memoirs of Fellows of the Royal Society*, vol. 51, 2005, 455–71.
146. 'Major research project', *UON*, December 1974, 6; Phil A. Silva & Michelle McCann, 'An introduction to the Dunedin study', in Phil A. Silva & Warren R. Stanton (eds), *From Child to Adult: The Dunedin Multidisciplinary Health and Development Study* (Auckland: Oxford University Press, 1996), 1–23.
147. Brunton, *Medicine of the Future*, 158–84, 190–94.
148. *UOC*, 1951, 219.
149. *UOC*, 1975, 283; Medical Faculty Annual Report, 1976, 1977 and 1980, Records of Registry and Central Administration, AG-180-7/13 and 7/14, HC.
150. *The Education of Medical Undergraduates in New Zealand: Report of the review committee set up by the Medical Council of New Zealand* (Wellington: Medical Council of New Zealand, 1988), 4, 31.
151. Medical Faculty Annual Report, 1988, Records of Registry and Central Administration, AG-180-7/15, HC.
152. Brunton, *Medicine of the Future*, 171; John Gibb, 'To lecture in Maori health', *ODT*, 29 May 1989, 9; D.W. Girvan, Memorandum to deans and heads of department: New blood lectureships, 20 June 1988, Jocelyn Harris papers, r.8044, HC; *UOAR*, 1989, 49; John Broughton interview.
153. John Broughton interview; Joanne Baxter and Peter Crampton interview, *Te Ahi Kaa*, Radio New Zealand National, 7 September 2014: www.radionz.co.nz/national/programmes/teahikaa/audio/20148535/dr-joanne-baxter-and-dr-peter-crampton; 'Associate Māori Dean', *OB*, 11 June 2010, 10; Joanne Baxter, 'From inspiration to graduation', *UOM*, no. 39, 2014, 36–37; Louise Ihimaera & Kirsty Maxwell-Crawford, *Whakapuāwaitia Ngāi Māori 2030, Thriving as Māori 2030: Māori health workforce priorities* (Hamilton: Reanga New Zealand Consultancy, 2012), 53–54.
154. Baxter & Crampton, *Te Ahi Kaa*; Peter Crampton, Naomi Weaver & Andrea Howard, 'Holding a mirror to society? The sociodemographic characteristics of the University of Otago's health professional students', *New Zealand Medical Journal*, vol. 125, no. 1361, 2012, 12–28; 'Pacific Dean', *OB*, 2 October 2009, 3; Fa`afetai Sopoaga, Tony Zaharic, Jesse Kokaua, Alec J. Ekeroma, Greg Murray & Jacques van der Meer, 'Pacific students undertaking the first year of health sciences at the University of Otago, and factors associated with academic performance', *New Zealand Medical Journal*, vol. 126, no. 1384, 2013, 96–108; Fa`afetai Sopoaga & Jacques van der Meer, 'Investigating factors that influence success of Pacific students in first-year health sciences at university in New Zealand', *New Zealand Medical Journal*, vol. 125, no. 1352, 2012, 28–38; Fa`afetai Sopoaga & Jacques van der Meer, 'Building a Pacific health workforce in New Zealand: Initial findings from a transition project in first year health sciences at university. A practice report', *International Journal of the First Year in Higher Education*, vol. 2, no. 2, 61–68.
155. *UOAR*, 2015, 15.
156. J.D. Hunter to Helen Clark, Minister of Health, 28 July 1989, copy courtesy of Barbara Heslop.
157. *Education of Medical Undergraduates*, 37–39.
158. Barbara Heslop, 'Some reflections', unpublished reminiscences.
159. Barbara Brookes, *A History of New Zealand Women* (Wellington: Bridget Williams Books, 2016), 415–21.
160. Medical Faculty Annual Report, 1986–1988, Division of Health Sciences Annual Report, 1989 and 1990, Records of Registry and Central Administration, AG-180-7/15 and AG-758/085, HC; Dorothy Page interview with John Campbell, Chris Heath, David Skegg and David Stewart; Dorothy Page interview with John Hunter.
161. 'A new venture in bioethics and health law' and 'BITC 301 in review', *UON*, October 1994, 5; 'Three chairs!', *UON*, December 1994, 3; 'New staff will help meet centre's increasing role in the Medical School', *UON*, May 2000, 7.
162. 'Integration of bioethics into Medical School curriculum a world first', *UON*, November–December 1998, 5.
163. David Skegg interview.
164. Page, *Anatomy of a Medical School*, 211–12, 254–63.
165. Dental Faculty Annual Report, 1946, Records of Registry and Central Administration, AG-180-7/03, HC.
166. Medical Faculty Annual Report, 1981 and 1983, Records of Registry and Central Administration, AG-180-7/14 and 7/15, HC; Dorothy Page interview with David Stewart.
167. Dorothy Page interviews with David Stewart, Andrew Hornblow, Graham Mortimer, George Petersen & David Jones.
168. *UOC*, 1998–2007; Peter Innes & Alison Rich, 'Changes in the selection of dental students in New Zealand', *New Zealand Dental Journal*, vol. 101, no. 1, 2005, 19–21; Rebecca Walker, Rachel Spronken-Smith, Carol Bond, Fiona McDonald, John Reynolds & Anna McMartin, 'The impact of curriculum change on health sciences first year students' approaches to learning', *Instructional Science*, vol. 38, 2010, 707–22.

169. Robin Gauld, *Revolving Doors: New Zealand's health reforms – the continuing saga*, 2nd edn (Wellington: Health Services Research Centre & Institute of Policy Studies, Victoria University of Wellington, 2009), 1, 77.
170. Page, *Anatomy of a Medical School*, 237–46.
171. Medical Faculty Annual Report, 1979 and 1985, Records of Registry and Central Administration, AG-180-7/14 and 7/15, HC; 'Medical intake', *UON*, December 1985, 5–6; Dorothy Page interviews with David Stewart, Chris Heath, Graham Mortimer & George Petersen; 'Malaysian students in health sciences', *UON*, November 1991, 2; 'Vice-Chancellor's Brunei visit pays dividends for the university', *UON*, July 1998, 11; Dorothy Page interview with John Adams; Page, *Anatomy of a Medical School*, 279–80; Warwick Brunton to author, 11 October 2016.
172. 'Senate report', *OB*, 17 October 2003, 2; Medical Training Board, *The Future of the Medical Workforce: First annual report November 2007–December 2008* (Wellington: Ministry of Health, 2009), 32; *UOC*, 2005–2012; Division of Health Sciences, Medicine entry requirements: www.otago.ac.nz/healthsciences/students/professional/medicine/index.html#application-process
173. Faculty of Medicine Annual Report, 1976 and 1977, Records of Registry and Central Administration, AG-180-7/13, HC.
174. 'Medical trust', *UON*, August 1985, 5–6; Dorothy Page interview with John Adams.
175. Medical Faculty Annual Report, 1988, Records of Registry and Central Administration, AG-758/085, HC; Dorothy Page interview with John Adams; *UOAR*, 2004, 21; *UOC*, 2006.
176. Patrick Farry, John Adams, Lucie Walters, Paul Worley & Susan Dovey, 'Development of the Rural Immersion Programme for 5th-year medical students at the University of Otago', *New Zealand Medical Journal*, vol. 123, no. 1323, 2010, 16–23; Dorothy Page interview with John Adams.
177. Self-review, University of Otago Review of Department of General Practice, Dunedin School of Medicine, 2008, 26; 'RMIP: The legacy of Dr Pat Farry', Department of General Practice and Rural Health: www.otago.ac.nz/dsm-gprh/rmip/pat-farry/index.html; Farry, Adams, Walters, Worley & Dovey, 'Rural Immersion Programme'; William Shelker, Tony Zaharic, Branko Sijnja & Paul Glue, 'Influence of rural background and rural medical training on postgraduate medical training and location in New Zealand', *New Zealand Medical Journal*, vol. 127, no. 1403, 2014, 12–16.
178. Dorothy Page interview with Linda Holloway.
179. Medical Faculty Annual Report, 1986, Records of Registry and Central Administration, AG-180-7/15, HC; Brunton, *Medicine of the Future*, 172–74, 182–84; Beverley Burrell interview.
180. Peter Joyce & Tim Wilkinson, 'The future', in Peter Joyce, Gary Nicholls, Kim Thomas & Tim Wilkinson (eds), *The Christchurch Experience: 40 years of research and teaching* (Christchurch: University of Otago, Christchurch, 2015), 184–86; Graeme Fogelberg interview; 'Funding boost recognises Otago's research strength', *OB*, 12 December 2003, 1–2; Alison Finigan (ed.), *Partnerships for Excellence: Celebrating 10 years of the Leading Thinkers initiative* (Dunedin: Development and Alumni Relations Office, University of Otago, 2014).
181. 'Child health research chair established', *OB*, 11 August 2006, 3; 'Cure Kids chair in paediatric research announced', *OB*, 5 October 2007, 3.
182. Brunton, *Medicine of the Future*, 202–04; Finigan, *Partnerships for Excellence*.
183. Finigan, *Partnerships for Excellence*; 'Webster Centre: about us': www.otago.ac.nz/webster/about/index.html; 'Robert G. Webster: Influenza innovator': www.otago.ac.nz/webster/about/otago049748.html
184. Page, *Anatomy of a Medical School*, 251–53.
185. Dorothy Page interviews with John Campbell and David Stewart.
186. 'Major expansions planned in pharmacy course', *UON*, December 1986, 1–2; M.S. Roberts, 'The changing nature of pharmacy in the New Zealand health care system', *New Zealand Medical Journal*, vol. 100, 1987, 522–23; Heydon & Duffull, *Pharmacy at Otago*, 35–37; Dorothy Page interview with David Stewart.
187. Heydon & Duffull, *Pharmacy at Otago*, 25–26, 37–40; 'Otago opposes pharmacy course', *UON*, April 1986, 2.
188. 'Society welcomes Goff's decision on education', *New Zealand Pharmacy*, vol. 9, no. 6, 1989, 14; 'New Zealand pharmacy education to be concentrated at Otago', *UON*, June 1989, 1–2; Dougherty, *Central Institute of Technology*, 8–10.
189. Peter Coville, 'Pharmacy practice in Dunedin', *New Zealand Pharmacy*, vol. 12, no. 4, 1992, 20–21; 'Pharmacy heads to Hong Kong', *UON*, October 1990, 5.
190. 'Two new health sciences deans', *UON*, February 1991, 2; 'Former pharmacy dean honoured in Relay for Life', *OB*, 7 March 2003, 1; Heydon & Duffull, *Pharmacy at Otago*, 42–44, 50–51.
191. 'Society welcomes Goff's decision'; Heydon & Duffull, *Pharmacy at Otago*, 52–55, 70–72.
192. Shaw, *In Our Hands*, 68–73, 80, 82–83; Joan Derbidge, 'Physiotherapy teaching', *New Zealand Journal of Physiotherapy*, vol. 4, no. 1, 1972, 3–4.
193. Shaw, *In Our Hands*, 68, 75, 83, 87–88.
194. 'Report of the committee to advise on the proposal to place the physiotherapy school under university control', Faculty of Medicine, Dean's Department records, MS-4318/086, HC.
195. Shaw, *In Our Hands*, 88–90; Ian Dougherty, *Continuing Education of Quality: A history of Otago Polytechnic and its predecessors 1870–2006* (Dunedin: Otago Polytechnic, 2006), 29–30.
196. Shaw, *In Our Hands*, 90–93; Dougherty, *Continuing Education*, 29–30.
197. Medical Faculty Annual Report, 1984, Records of Registry and Central Administration, AG-180-7/15, HC; 'Physiotherapy degree?', *UON*, October 1987, 15; Shaw, *In Our Hands*, 97–105; Dougherty, *Continuing Education*, 56.

198. 'Postgraduate physiotherapy programmes officially opened', *UON*, November 1994, 3; 'News from the Otago Polytechnic School of Physiotherapy, Dunedin', *New Zealand Journal of Physiotherapy*, vol. 21, no. 2, 1993, 5.
199. Shaw, *In Our Hands*, 108–09.
200. Peter D. Milburn, 'School of Physiotherapy, University of Otago: The year in review', *New Zealand Journal of Physiotherapy*, vol. 24, no. 3, 1996, 25–26; 'Conversation in a cold climate', *UON*, February/March 1997, 7; 'New physio building opens', *UON*, August–September 1997, 5; Shaw, *In Our Hands*, 105–08.
201. 'Conversation in a cold climate'; *UOC*, 1998, 291–95; Shaw, *In Our Hands*, 107–10.
202. 'Otago Institute', *ES*, 13 May 1899, supplement, 3; *Oamaru Mail*, 30 August 1899, 2.
203. 'Hospital board's reports', *ODT*, 17 May 1920, 5; James Ryan, Keith Sutton & Malcolm Baigent, *Australasian Radiology: A history* (Sydney: McGraw-Hill, 1996), 297–99, 303–4; John C. Probert & Christopher H. Atkinson, 'New Zealand: One small country's history of radiation oncology', *International Journal of Radiation Oncology, Biology, Physics*, vol. 36, 1996, 481–86.
204. 'Hospital board reports', *ODT*, 20 January 1923, 7.
205. Probert & Atkinson, 'History of radiation oncology'; *UOC*, 1946, 49; J.F. Borrie, 'Radiography training in New Zealand: An historical survey', *Radiography*, vol. 40, 1974, 2–8; Ryan, Sutton & Baigent, *Australasian Radiology*, 315–16.
206. Phone interview with Ian Grant, 28 October 2016.
207. Borrie, 'Radiography training'; Hugh Jamieson (ed.), *The Development of Medical Physics and Biomedical Engineering in New Zealand Hospitals 1945–1995*, 2nd edn (Dannevirke: H. Jamieson, 1995), 23–25.
208. Peter Elliott, 'Diagnostic radiography training in New Zealand 1970–1995' and Janfrey Doak, 'Radiation therapy', both in Jan Palmer (ed.), *Shadows: Röntgen Centenary Journal*, November 1995. After its own students completed in 1993, Dunedin Hospital became a clinical experience centre for radiography students from Christchurch Polytechnic.
209. *UOC*, 1983, 258; Jamieson, *Medical Physics and Biomedical Engineering*, 58–59, 148.
210. L. Oliver, R. Fitchew & J. Drew, 'Requirements for radiation oncology physics in Australia and New Zealand', *Australasian Physical and Engineering Sciences in Medicine*, vol. 24, 2001, 1–18; W.H. Round et al., 'Brief histories of medical physics in Asia–Oceania', *Australasian Physical and Engineering Sciences in Medicine*, vol. 38, 2015, 381–98.
211. Colvin Campbell, 'Presidential address', *New Zealand Journal of Medical Laboratory Technology*, vol. 41, no. 4, 1987, 140–41.
212. University of Otago proposal for degree of Medical Laboratory Science, New Zealand Institute of Medical Laboratory Science records, MS-3620/189, HC; Colvin Campbell & Anne Paterson, 'Education', *New Zealand Journal of Medical Laboratory Science*, vol. 50, no. 4, 1996, 195–203; M. Jeannette Grey, 'Silver jubilee of the Auckland Hospital Board School of Medical Laboratory Technology 1961–1986', *New Zealand Journal of Medical Laboratory Technology*, vol. 40, no. 4, 1986, 164–65.
213. Des Philip & Helen Robertshaw, 'Registration and the Medical Laboratory Technologists' Board', *New Zealand Journal of Medical Laboratory Science*, vol. 50, no. 4, 1996, 204–16.
214. Paul McLeod, 'Presidential address', *New Zealand Journal of Medical Laboratory Science*, vol. 46, no. 4, 1992, 131–32.
215. 'Technologist education – a discussion paper', New Zealand Institute of Medical Laboratory Science records, MS-3620/180, HC.
216. Proposal for degree of Medical Laboratory Science; Campbell & Paterson, 'Education'.
217. Campbell & Paterson, 'Education'; Anne Paterson, 'Obituary: Colin Watts', *New Zealand Journal of Medical Laboratory Science*, vol. 48, no. 4, 1994, 182; Colin Geary interview; 'History of the Medical Laboratory Science programme': www.otago.ac.nz/medlabsci/about/otago609026.html
218. 'Education committee', *New Zealand Journal of Medical Laboratory Science*, vol. 46, no. 3, 1992, 102.
219. *UOC*, 1992–1994.
220. Paterson, 'Obituary: Colin Watts'; Colin Geary interview; Les Milligan, 'Graduation report: BMLSc course, Otago University, December, 1994', *New Zealand Journal of Medical Laboratory Science*, vol. 49, no. 1, 1995, 21.
221. Colin Geary interview; 'History of the Medical Laboratory Science programme'.
222. Brown, *Pickerill*, 200. The first mention of students in this 'special mechanical dentistry course', all of them women, appears in the annual report for 1929 (published in the *ODT*, 12 February 1930, 2). The course – subsequently known as the dental technicians' course – continued until 1942 and most of its students were women (see Dental Faculty Annual Reports, 1930–1942, Records of Registry and Central Administration, AG-180-7/01 and 7/02, HC). See *UOC*, 1941, 257–58 for a description of this 18-month course.
223. Dentists Act 1936; Brooking, *History of Dentistry*, 151–53, 178–80; Peter Davis, 'Jurisdictional disputes in New Zealand dentistry: Controlling access to the mouth and entry to the market', in Linda Bryder (ed.), *A Healthy Country: Essays on the social history of medicine* (Wellington: Bridget Williams Books, 1991), 25–43; Dougherty, *Central Institute of Technology*, 4–5; Stanley C. Cowman, *Towards a Place in the Health Family: Dental technicians and their work* (Upper Hutt: Department of Dental Technology, CIT, 1998); John Newton, 'The changing role of dental technicians in New Zealand', *New Zealand Dental Journal*, vol. 85, 1989, 21–22.
224. Brooking, *History of Dentistry*, 101–05, 171; Helen R. Tane, 'A qualitative study of dental therapy in New Zealand', *New Zealand Dental Journal*, vol. 105, no. 3, 2009, 82–86; Julie Satur & Barbara Dewson, 'A history of the dental and oral health therapy profession in Australia and New Zealand', *Australian and New Zealand Journal of Dental and Oral Health Therapy*, vol. 1, no. 1, 2012, 13–16.

225. Dental Faculty Annual Report, 1946 1947, 1960, 1962, 1964, 1969–1970, Records of Registry and Central Administration, AG-180-7/03, 7/07, 7/08 and 7/10, HC.
226. Angela R.C. Pack, 'Hygienists and their role in dental practice', *New Zealand Dental Journal*, vol. 91, 1995, 57–61; Brooking, *History of Dentistry*, 204–07, 219; Dougherty, *Continuing Education*, 67.
227. Peter Innes interview.
228. 'New courses a "radical" move for the Dental School', *UON*, September–October 1998, 7.
229. Peter Innes interview; Dougherty, *Continuing Education*, 67; *UOC*, 2000–2002; Peter B. Innes, 'Integration of the work force', *New Zealand Dental Journal*, vol. 96, 2000, 101.
230. Peter Innes interview; 'The new era begins', *New Zealand Dental Journal*, vol. 85, 1989, 1; Newton, 'Changing role of dental technicians'; Gordon MacF. Carter & Peter B. Innes, 'The Postgraduate Diploma in Clinical Dental Technology', *New Zealand Dental Journal*, vol. 96, 2000, 53–56.
231. *UOC*, 1999–2008; Self-review, University of Otago Review of Faculty of Dentistry, 2007, 2; Satur & Dewson, 'Dental and oral health therapy profession'; Susan M. Moffat & Dawn E. Coates, 'New Zealand's oral health students: Education and workforce implications', *New Zealand Dental Journal*, vol. 107, no. 2, 2011, 51–56; Kathryn M.S. Ayers, Alison M. Meldrum, W. Murray Thomson & J. Timothy Newton, 'The working practices and job satisfaction of dental hygienists in New Zealand', *Journal of Public Health Dentistry*, vol. 66, no. 3, 2006, 186–91.
232. Satur & Dewson, 'Dental and oral health therapy profession'.
233. Saeed Salem Alameri, 'Dental technology services and industry trends in New Zealand', Master of Dental Technology thesis, University of Otago, 2013, 23; Owen Poland, 'Wide open for change', *Engineering Insight*, vol. 15, no. 2, 2014, 6–12.
234. Dental Faculty Annual Report, 1989, Records of Registry and Central Administration, AG-758/085, HC; Self-review, University of Otago Review of Faculty of Dentistry, 2007, 1, 39–40; *UOC*, 1988, 2007, 2014; Peter Innes interview.
235. Peter Innes interview.
236. Self-review, University of Otago Review of Faculty of Dentistry, 2007, 2–4; Peter Innes interview; Richard Cannon, 'The Sir John Walsh Research Institute: A national institute for oral health research in New Zealand', *New Zealand Dental Journal*, vol. 103, 2007, 17.
237. John Broughton, 'Oranga niho: Māori oral health services', *New Zealand Dental Journal*, vol. 96, 2000, 97–100.
238. John Broughton interview; Report of University of Otago Review of Faculty of Dentistry, 2007, 20; 'Agreement signed with Te Arawa health provider', *OB*, 13 July 2007, 1; 'Dental students extract learning from Samoa visit', *OB*, 15 July 2005, 7; 'Island trek', *OB*, 11 August 2006, 4.
239. John Broughton interview; Report of University of Otago Review of Faculty of Dentistry, 2014, 14–15.
240. Vaughan Elder, 'School of Dentistry welcomes top 10 ranking', *ODT*, 30 April 2015: www.odt.co.nz/news/dunedin/school-dentistry-welcomes-top-10-ranking
241. 'Dental simulation lab', *OB*, 30 October 2009, 3.
242. Sunyoung Ma, Gala Hesson, Richard Zeng & Swee-Kin Loke, 'ImpressDent: Learning how to make dental impressions with a computer simulation', in B. Hegarty, J. McDonald & S.-K. Loke (eds), *Rhetoric and Reality: Critical perspectives on educational technology* (Dunedin: Ascilite2014, 2014), 378–82; Gemfire Design portfolio: https://gemfiredesign.com/portfolio/impressdent/
243. *UOAR*, 1908.
244. Report of University of Otago Review of Biomedical Sciences Programme, 2016, 6.

10: BEYOND DUNEDIN

1. Michael Belgrave, *From Empire's Servant to Global Citizen: A history of Massey University* (Auckland: Massey University Press, 2016).
2. Charles Hercus & Gordon Bell, *The Otago Medical School Under the First Three Deans* (Edinburgh: Livingstone, 1964), 127–28.
3. Ibid., 128–30; Christopher Moore, George Rolleston, John Riminton & Andrew Hornblow, *A Vision Realised: The Christchurch School of Medicine, University of Otago 1972–1997* (Christchurch: Christchurch School of Medicine, 1998), 4–5; Medical Faculty Annual Report, 1955, 1959, Records of Registry and Central Administration, AG-180-7/05 and 7/07, HC; Eric Espiner, 'Medical Unit (1960–75)', in Peter Joyce, Gary Nicholls, Kim Thomas & Tim Wilkinson (eds), *The Christchurch Experience: 40 years of research and teaching* (Christchurch: University of Otago, Christchurch, 2013), 113–16; Dorothy Page, *Anatomy of a Medical School: A history of medicine at the University of Otago 1875–2000* (Dunedin: Otago University Press, 2008), 270.
4. Ronald V. Christie, *Report on the Medical School* (Dunedin: University of Otago, 1968); R.O.H. Irvine, 'The future of the Medical School: A report on the future of the Medical School with particular reference to the implementation of proposals made in the Christie report', Records of Registry and Central Administration, AG-180-7/10, HC.
5. Irvine, 'Future of the Medical School'.
6. 'Plan of college', *Lyttelton Times*, 20 September 1851, 5. These 1850 origins are outlined in Moore, Rolleston, Riminton & Hornblow, *A Vision Realised*, 1–2; and on the campus website: www.otago.ac.nz/christchurch/about/history/
7. Moore, Rolleston, Riminton & Hornblow, *A Vision Realised*, 2; J.C. Beaglehole, *The University of New Zealand: An historical study* (Wellington: New Zealand Council for Educational Research, 1937), 235–37; James Hight & Alice M.F. Candy, *A Short History of the Canterbury College (University of New Zealand)* (Auckland: Whitcombe & Tombs, 1927), 46–50; W.J. Gardner, E.T. Beardsley & T.E. Carter, *A History of the University of Canterbury 1873–1973* (Christchurch: University of Canterbury, 1973), 48–49.

8. Moore, Rolleston, Riminton & Hornblow, *A Vision Realised*, 4–7.
9. James Ng interview.
10. Dorothy Page interview with Don Beaven; Mike Crean, 'Sir Donald Ward Beaven', *New Zealand Medical Journal*, vol. 122, 2009, 129–32. On Averill, see Geoffrey W. Rice, 'Averill, Leslie Cecil Lloyd', from DNZB: www.teara.govt.nz/en/biographies/5a25/averill-leslie-cecil-lloyd
11. Moore, Rolleston, Riminton & Hornblow, *A Vision Realised*, 7–14.
12. Ibid., 23–29, 40–41, 49.
13. Page, *Anatomy of a Medical School*, 192.
14. Peter Joyce interview; Dorothy Page interviews with Don Beaven and Andrew Hornblow.
15. Dorothy Page interview with Don Beaven.
16. Moore, Rolleston, Riminton & Hornblow, *A Vision Realised*, 29–32.
17. Dorothy Page interview with Don Beaven.
18. Moore, Rolleston, Riminton & Hornblow, *A Vision Realised*, 15–21, 26–32.
19. Ibid., 50–51, 58–61; 'News from the Wellington and Christchurch schools of medicine', *UON*, 7 March 1998, 7; 'Clip-on boosts space in Christchurch', *OB*, 11 August 2006, 8; 'Wellington and Christchurch building programmes update', *OB*, 26 January 2007, 8; 'Redesigned lecture theatre impresses', *OB*, 22 February 2008, 7; 'Rolleston upgrade completed', *OB*, 20 February 2009, 2. For an example of Christchurch's frustration at the delay in 'completing' the building, see Medical Faculty Annual Report, 1986, Records of Registry and Central Administration, AG-180-7/15, HC.
20. 'Christchurch note', *UON*, September 1977, 7.
21. Moore, Rolleston, Riminton & Hornblow, *A Vision Realised*, 34, 45–46; Page, *Anatomy of a Medical School*, 259–60; Dorothy Page interview with Alan Clarke; Division of Health Sciences Annual Report, 1990, Records of Registry and Central Administration, AG-758/085, HC.
22. Peter Joyce interview; MaryLeigh Moore, 'Clinical simulation centre', in Joyce, Nicholls, Thomas & Wilkinson, *Christchurch Experience*, 146–53.
23. Suzanne Pitama, 'Māori/Indigenous Health Institute (MIHI)', in Joyce, Nicholls, Thomas & Wilkinson, *Christchurch Experience*, 17–21; Peter Joyce interview; 'Suzanne Pitama wins NZ's top teaching award', Otago Bulletin Board, 12 August 2015: www.otago.ac.nz/otagobulletin/people/otago119433.html
24. *The Christchurch Clinical School of Medicine: After ten years* (Christchurch: Christchurch Clinical School of Medicine, 1982), 17.
25. Peter Joyce interview; Dorothy Page interview with Andrew Hornblow; Peter Joyce, 'An historical overview', in Joyce, Nicholls, Thomas & Wilkinson, *Christchurch Experience*, 4–9; 'What's in a name', *UON*, October 1986, 3; *UOAR*, 2001, 18; 'Names changes for Wellington and Christchurch', *OB*, 18 May 2007, 6.
26. Moore, Rolleston, Riminton & Hornblow, *A Vision Realised*, 114–15, 118–19.
27. Ibid., 115, 117; Roger Mulder, 'Psychological medicine', in Joyce, Nicholls, Thomas & Wilkinson, *Christchurch Experience*, 50–52.
28. Gary Hooper, 'Orthopaedic surgery and musculoskeletal medicine', in Joyce, Nicholls, Thomas & Wilkinson, *Christchurch Experience*, 38–40; Peter Joyce interview.
29. Dorothy Page interview with Andrew Hornblow.
30. Les Toop, 'Public health and general practice', in Joyce, Nicholls, Thomas & Wilkinson, *Christchurch Experience*, 53–55.
31. Helen Carpenter, *An Improved System of Nursing Education for New Zealand* (Wellington: Department of Health, 1971); Marie E. Burgess, *Nursing in New Zealand Society* (Auckland: Longman Paul, 1984), 60–70, 73, 76–78; M. Patricia Carroll, 'Basic nursing education', in Margaret Gibson Smith & Yvonne T. Shadbolt (eds), *Objects and Outcomes: New Zealand Nurses' Association 1909–1983, commemorative essays* (Wellington: New Zealand Nurses' Association, 1984), 64–78.
32. Carpenter, *Nursing Education*, 24–26.
33. Diploma in Nursing Administration file, 1972–1978, Faculty of Medicine, Dean's Department records, MS-4300/080, HC; Wellington Division file, 1979–1980, Faculty of Medicine, Dean's Department records, MS-4305/049, HC; Beatrice Salmon, 'New Zealand universities and nursing education: The first seven decades', in P. Carroll, A. Fieldhouse & S. Shaw (eds), *A Profession in Transition: Issues in nursing in New Zealand over two decades, 1961–1981* (Wellington: C.L. Bailey Nursing Education Trust, 1982).
34. Tom O'Donnell interview; Rachel Barrowman, *Victoria University of Wellington 1899–1999: A history* (Wellington: Victoria University Press), 192–95, 366; Medical Faculty Annual Report, 1986, Records of Registry and Central Administration, AG-180-7/15, HC; '1980 proposal for a School of Nursing Studies in Wellington: Victoria University & Wellington School of Medicine', in 'Wellington School of Medicine: Comments, historical data and abstracts up to 1991', unpublished compilation, courtesy of University of Otago, Wellington.
35. Ian Dougherty, *Continuing Education of Quality: A history of Otago Polytechnic and its predecessors 1870–2006* (Dunedin: Otago Polytechnic, 2006), 30–31.
36. 'New nursing studies centre a winner for all parties', *UON*, May 1998, 7; 'New centre for postgraduate nursing opens', *OB*, 25 February 2005, 1; Lisa Whitehead, 'Centre for postgraduate nursing studies', in Joyce, Nicholls, Thomas & Wilkinson, *Christchurch Experience*, 30–32; Beverley Burrell interview.
37. Whitehead, 'Centre for postgraduate nursing studies'; Beverley Burrell interview.
38. Beverley Burrell interview; 'Master nursing with any graduate degree', Otago Bulletin Board, 10 July 2015: www.otago.ac.nz/otagobulletin/news/otago114698.html; 'Intensified masters programmes launched', *Kai Tiaki Nursing New Zealand*, vol. 22, no. 1, 2016, 8.
39. *Christchurch Clinical School of Medicine*, 22–23; David Fergusson & John Horwood, 'Christchurch health and development study', in Joyce, Nicholls, Thomas &

Wilkinson, *Christchurch Experience*, 79–87; 'Longitudinal studies: A national taonga', He Kitenga, 14 May 2013: www.otago.ac.nz/healthsciences/news/media/hekitenga/otago045632.html; 'Professor's long career in Christchurch celebrated', Otago Bulletin Board, 24 August 2015: www.otago.ac.nz/otagobulletin/people/otago121447.html

40. 'Christchurch's leading woman of science honoured', University of Otago, Christchurch, News and Events, 7 December 2015: www.otago.ac.nz/christchurch/news/archive/otago368401.html; Christine Winterbourn & Tony Kettle, 'Centre for free radical research', in Joyce, Nicholls, Thomas & Wilkinson, *Christchurch Experience*, 75–78.
41. Mark Richards, Richard Troughton, Eric Espiner, Vicky Cameron, Leigh Ellmers, Anna Pilbrow, Chris Charles, Miriam Radmaker, Chris Pemberton & Tim Yandle, 'Christchurch heart institute', in Joyce, Nicholls, Thomas & Wilkinson, *Christchurch Experience*, 68–74; Peter Joyce interview.
42. 'Spectral difference', He Kitenga, 14 May 2013: www.otago.ac.nz/healthsciences/news/media/hekitenga/otago043322.html; Anthony Butler, 'Centre for bioengineering', in Joyce, Nicholls, Thomas & Wilkinson, *Christchurch Experience*, 109–12.
43. Peter Joyce interview; 'Otago wins heart chair', *UON*, October 1996, 3; Richards, Troughton, Espiner, Cameron, Ellmers, Pilbrow, Charles, Radmaker, Pemberton & Yandle, 'Christchurch heart institute', 68–74; Alison Finigan (ed.), *Partnerships for Excellence: Celebrating 10 years of the Leading Thinkers initiative* (Dunedin: Development and Alumni Relations Office, University of Otago, 2014); Brian Darlow, 'Neonatal health', in Joyce, Nicholls, Thomas & Wilkinson, *Christchurch Experience*, 88–95; Martin Kennedy, Peter Joyce & Evan Begg, 'Carney centre for pharmacogenomics', in Joyce, Nicholls, Thomas & Wilkinson, *Christchurch Experience*, 100–04; Peter Joyce, 'Mental health clinical research unit', in Joyce, Nicholls, Thomas & Wilkinson, *Christchurch Experience*, 96–99.
44. Maurice Owen, 'Canterbury Scientific Limited', in Joyce, Nicholls, Thomas & Wilkinson, *Christchurch Experience*, 117–21; Fiona Summerfield, 'Successful innovation takes time: The story of Canterbury Scientific', in Rebecca Hurrell, Andrew Muscroft-Taylor, Glyn Strange & Bryan Williamson (eds), *Scientific Sleuthing: Chemical discoveries made in New Zealand* (Christchurch: Clerestory Press, 2017), 193–201.
45. 'First grant awarded by Otago Innovation', *OB*, 23 March 2007, 4.
46. Kim Thomas, 'Heart breakthrough', *UOM*, no. 42, 2016, 16–17.
47. Moore, Rolleston, Riminton & Hornblow, *A Vision Realised*, 46–47; Frank Frizelle, 'Surgery', in Joyce, Nicholls, Thomas & Wilkinson, *Christchurch Experience*, 60–66; 'Charity hospital founder named NZer of the year', Stuff, 1 January 2009: www.stuff.co.nz/national/165527/Charity-hospital-founder-named-NZer-of-year
48. Moore, Rolleston, Riminton & Hornblow, *A Vision Realised*, 118–23; Les Toop, 'Public health and general practice', in Joyce, Nicholls, Thomas & Wilkinson, *Christchurch Experience*, 53–55; *UOC*, 1974–2015.
49. Division of Health Sciences Annual Report, 1990, Records of Registry and Central Administration, AG-758/085, HC.
50. Gary Nicholls & Peter Moller, 'Health reforms and the Stent inquiry', in Joyce, Nicholls, Thomas & Wilkinson, *Christchurch Experience*, 158–68.
51. 'Earthquake: Christchurch campus moves on from quake', *OB*, 29 October 2010, 8.
52. Ellie Constantine, 'Otago students still missing', *ODT*, 5 March 2011: www.odt.co.nz/news/dunedin/otago-students-still-missing; Joyce, 'Historical overview'; Peter Joyce interview; Fiona Clarkson, 'A better future …', *UOM*, no. 34, 2013, 21–23.
53. Peter Joyce, 'Historical overview'.
54. David Palmer, 'A student's experience', in Joyce, Nicholls, Thomas & Wilkinson, *Christchurch Experience*, 154–56.
55. Peter Joyce interview.
56. Frances A. Carter, Caroline J. Bell, Anthony N. Ali, Janice McKenzie & Timothy J. Wilkinson, 'The impact of major earthquakes on the psychological functioning of medical students: A Christchurch, New Zealand study', *New Zealand Medical Journal*, vol. 127, 2014, no. 1398, 54–66; Caroline Bell, Frances Carter, Joseph Boden, Tim Wilkinson, Jan McKenzie & Anthony Ali, 'Psychological impact of the Canterbury earthquakes on university staff', *New Zealand Medical Journal*, vol. 129, no. 1430, 2016, 18–28; Frances A. Carter, Caroline J. Bell, Anthony N. Ali, Janice M. McKenzie, Joseph M. Boden & Timothy J. Wilkinson, 'Predictors of psychological resilience amongst medical students following major earthquakes', *New Zealand Medical Journal*, vol. 129, no. 1434, 2016, 17–22.
57. Kim Thomas, 'On reflection', *UOM*, no. 43, 2016, 24–25.
58. T.V. O'Donnell, 'A University Department of Medicine in Wellington', *New Zealand Medical Journal*, vol. 81, 1975, 142–46.
59. 'City Council', *Evening Post*, 7 February 1882, 2; L.H. Barber & R.J. Towers, *Wellington Hospital 1847–1976* (Wellington: Wellington Hospital Board, 1976), 155.
60. Hercus & Bell, *Otago Medical School*, 16; B.M. Corkill, 'Wellington School of Medicine – origins', in 'Wellington School of Medicine: Comments, historical data and abstracts'.
61. Corkill, 'Wellington School of Medicine'; Page, *Anatomy of a Medical School*, 270; 'Ian Ambury Miller Prior', Munk's Roll, Royal College of Physicians: http://munksroll.rcplondon.ac.uk/Biography/Details/6136
62. Corkill, 'Wellington School of Medicine'; 'Hulme-Moir, Francis Ian (1938–1980)', Plarr's Lives of the Fellows Online, Royal College of Surgeons: http://livesonline.rcseng.ac.uk/biogs/E006590b.htm; 'Kenneth Alfred Kingsley North', Munk's Roll, Royal College of Physicians: http://munksroll.rcplondon.ac.uk/Biography/Details/7023; K.A.K. North, *Report on Medical Education*

in New Zealand and the Need for a Third Medical School (Wellington: Victoria University of Wellington, 1970).
63. Barrowman, *Victoria University of Wellington*, 191–92; Hugh Parton, *The University of New Zealand* (University Grants Committee, 1979), 124; J.O. Mercer to Dr Park, chair of Wellington Hospital medical staff, 8 November 1965, in Corkill, 'Wellington School of Medicine'.
64. Corkill, 'Wellington School of Medicine'.
65. Ibid.
66. Dorothy Page interview with John Hunter.
67. Corkill, 'Wellington School of Medicine'.
68. North, *Report on Medical Education*, 1.
69. Corkill, 'Wellington School of Medicine'.
70. Tom O'Donnell interview; Dorothy Page interview with John Nacey; Barrowman, *Victoria University of Wellington*, 192.
71. *UOAR*, 1971; Corkill, 'Wellington School of Medicine'; Page, *Anatomy of a Medical School*, 195–96; Graeme Sharp & Adrian Stewart, 'Brian Morrison Corkill', *New Zealand Medical Journal*, vol. 118, no. 1217, 2005, 1526; Thomas V. O'Donnell, 'The development of the Wellington School of Medicine – A personal view', 1–2, in 'Wellington School of Medicine: Comments, historical data and abstracts'.
72. Barber & Towers, *Wellington Hospital*, 112–15; Corkill, 'Wellington School of Medicine', 15–20, 28; O'Donnell, 'Development of the Wellington School of Medicine', 2; Ewan Coleman interview.
73. Corkill, 'Wellington School of Medicine', 19, 21–22; Tom O'Donnell interview.
74. Dorothy Page interview with Linda Holloway.
75. Corkill, 'Wellington School of Medicine', 21–22; O'Donnell, 'Development of the Wellington School of Medicine', 3; Tom O'Donnell interview.
76. Corkill, 'Wellington School of Medicine', 23; O'Donnell, 'Development of the Wellington School of Medicine', 4–5; Tom O'Donnell interview; Dorothy Page interview with Linda Holloway; Self-review, University of Otago Review of Department of Psychological Medicine, Wellington, 2009, 5.
77. Clare Salmond, *The First 25 Years of the Department of Public Health (Formerly, Department of Community Health) at the Wellington School of Medicine and Health Sciences* (Wellington: Wellington School of Medicine & Health Sciences, 2004), 5; Corkill, 'Wellington School of Medicine', 25; Dorothy Page interview with Linda Holloway.
78. Corkill, 'Wellington School of Medicine', 27–28.
79. O'Donnell, 'Development of the Wellington School of Medicine', 10–11; Page, *Anatomy of a Medical School*, 213; Dorothy Page interviews with John Hunter, David Stewart and David Skegg.
80. Tom O'Donnell interview. Student headcount from Medical Faculty Annual Report, 1977, Records of Registry and Central Administration, AG-180-7/13, HC.
81. Corkill, 'Wellington School of Medicine', 28.
82. O'Donnell, 'Development of the Wellington School of Medicine', 11.
83. Ibid., 6, 12–13; Page, *Anatomy of a Medical School*, 241, 245–46.
84. Wellington School of Medicine: Comments, historical data and abstracts, 6–8; O'Donnell, 'Development of the Wellington School of Medicine', 13–14; Bruce Brown, 'Nordmeyer, Arnold Henry', from DNZB: www.teara.govt.nz/en/biographies/5n12/nordmeyer-arnold-henry; 'NZ–Japan trade pioneer dies', *Evening Post*, 10 January 1990, 4.
85. 'Wellington Clinical School', *UON*, March 1977, 4.
86. 'Otago flag kept flying in Wellington', *UON*, December 1979, 1–2.
87. Corkill, 'Wellington School of Medicine', 20–21.
88. 'A timeline of the Malaghan Institute's history of innovation and discovery', Malaghan Institute of Medical Research: www.malaghan.org.nz/news/a-timeline-of-the-malaghan-institute-s-history-of-innovation-and-discovery/; 'Gifts and bequests', *UON*, September 1974, 6.
89. Robert E. Olson & Enid Gilbert-Barness, 'In memoriam: William E. Stehbens', *Fetal and Pediatric Pathology*, vol. 25, 2006, 131–35.
90. Brian O'Brien, 'Malaghan, Leonard Aloysius Patrick', from DNZB: www.teara.govt.nz/en/biographies/5m29/malaghan-leonard-aloysius-patrick; 'Timeline of the Malaghan Institute'; Tom O'Donnell interview.
91. Neil Pearce, *Adverse Reactions: The fenoterol story* (Auckland: Auckland University Press, 2007); Linda Holloway interview with Dorothy Page.
92. 'Milestone for Wellington research group', *UON*, November–December 1998, 5; Royal Society of New Zealand media release, 23 November 2016: http://royalsociety.org.nz/2016/11/23/sir-charles-hercus-medal-advancing-respiratory-medicine-and-health-science-research-in-new-zealand/; 'Who are we', Medical Research Institute of New Zealand: www.mrinz.ac.nz/Whoarewe
93. 'Histories' and 'Facilities', Centre for Translational Physiology: www.otago.ac.nz/uow-physiology/about/otago053169.html and www.otago.ac.nz/uow-physiology/facilities/index.html; John McKenzie, 'Defending super rugby champion Hurricanes find new way to get even fitter', *One News*, 24 January 2017: www.tvnz.co.nz/one-news/sport/rugby/defending-super-rugby-champion-hurricanes-find-new-way-get-even-fitter
94. Dorothy Page interview with John Nacey.
95. Corkill, 'Wellington School of Medicine', 24–25; Salmond, *Department of Public Health*, 19.
96. For example, Susan Edmunds, 'Superbug found in chicken "dangerous"', Stuff, 22 November 2015: www.stuff.co.nz/national/health/74173066/Superbug-found-in-chicken-dangerous; 'Contaminated chicken the biggest food safety issue in NZ', *Morning Report*, Radio New Zealand National, 12 December 2016: www.radionz.co.nz/national/programmes/morningreport/audio/201827328/contaminated-chicken-the-biggest-food-safety-issue-in-nz; 'Cold homes, not P, the health culprit, says academic', Radio New Zealand National, 18 March 2016: www.radionz.co.nz/news/national/299308/cold-homes,-not-p,-the-health-culprit-academic; Rob Stock, 'Philippa Howden-Chapman highlights NZ's

increasingly embarrassing housing crisis', Stuff, 25 November 2015: www.stuff.co.nz/business/74391434/philippa-howdenchapman-highlights-nzs-increasingly-embarrassing-housing-crisis

97. 'The Prime Minister's Science Prize 2014': www.pmscienceprizes.org.nz/previous-winners/2014-science/
98. Page, *Anatomy of a Medical School*, 248–49, 267; 'Medical community mourns WSM dean', *UON*, February 1995, 12; Salmond, *Department of Public Health*, 9.
99. Salmond, *Department of Public Health*, 6–10, 12–14, 19; Brunton, *Medicine of the Future*, 167–69, 182–83.
100. Karyn Ammundsen, 'Healthy engagement', *UOM*, no. 36, 2013, 21–23.
101. Self Review, University of Otago Review of Department of Primary Health Care and General Practice, 2009, 1.
102. 'Wellington school announces new chair in general practice', *UON*, March 1996, 1.
103. 'Wellington school appoints professorial trio', *UON*, October 1996, 3; 'Professor Tony Dowell', University of Otago, Wellington: www.otago.ac.nz/wellington/departments/primaryhealthcaregeneralpractice/staff/otago039310.html; 'Primary solutions', He Kitenga, 2009: www.otago.ac.nz/research/hekitenga2009/primarysolutions.html
104. Self-review, University of Otago Review of Department of Primary Health Care and General Practice, 2009, 1.
105. Medical Faculty Annual Report, 1978, Records of Registry and Central Administration, AG-180-7/14, HC.
106. *UOAR*, 2004, 21; Dorothy Page interview with John Nacey.
107. Dates courtesy of Phillip Kane, Business and Operations Manager, University of Otago, Wellington; 'Palmerston North option', MidCentral District Health Board: www.midcentraldhb.govt.nz/WorkingMDHB/WorkingWith/WgtnSON/Pages/Palmerston-North-Option.aspx
108. Sunny Collings interview.
109. Ainslie Talbot, 'Working together, learning together', *UOM*, no. 35, 2013, 36–37; Susan Pullon, Christine Wilson, Peter Gallagher, Margot Skinner, Eileen McKinlay, Lesley Gray & Patrick McHugh, 'Transition to practice: Can rural interprofessional education make a difference? A cohort study', *BMC Medical Education*, 16, 2016, 154–65.
110. J.F. Borrie, 'Radiography training in New Zealand: An historical survey', *Radiography*, vol. 40, 1974, 2–8; Janfrey Doak, 'Radiation therapy', in Jan Palmer, ed., *Shadows: Röntgen Centenary Journal*, November 1995, 38–43; Ian Dougherty, *Central Institute of Technology 1960–2001: A brief history* (Upper Hutt: Central Institute of Technology, 2001), 4; Damian George, 'Students fear "insurmountable" costs as stipend axed', *ODT*, 1 July 2015: www.odt.co.nz/news/dunedin/students-fear-insurmountable-costs-stipend-axed
111. Karen Coleman, 'Relocating radiation therapy: The true story', *Shadows: The New Zealand Journal of Medical Radiation Therapy*, vol. 45, no. 3, 2002, 12–14; Vice-Chancellor's Office file, MS-4394/958, HC.
112. Wellington branch report, *Shadows*, vol. 45, no. 1, 2002, 29–31; Julie Burbery, 'Department of Radiation Therapy Wellington School of Medicine and Health Sciences', *Shadows*, vol. 45, no. 3, 2002, 37.
113. Report of University of Otago Review of Department of Radiation Therapy, 2012, 20; Coleman, 'Relocating radiation therapy'.
114. 'Medical course radiates in glow of first PhD', *OB*, 16 June 2006, 4; Patries Herst, 'Trans-plasma membrane electron transport: Physiological importance in the p^0 model of aerobic glycolysis', PhD thesis, University of Otago, 2006.
115. Patries Herst, 'An overview of RT-led research in New Zealand', *Shadows*, vol. 54, no. 1, 2011, 31.
116. Karen Coleman, 'Education reports: Department of Radiation Therapy University of Otago, Wellington', *Shadows*, vol. 54, no. 3, 2011, 62–63; vol. 55, no. 1, 2012, 59; Karen Coleman, Marieke Jasperse, Patries Herst & Jill Yielder, 'Establishing radiation therapy advanced practice in New Zealand', *Journal of Medical Radiation Sciences*, vol. 61, 2014, 38–44.
117. Karen Coleman, 'Education reports: Department of Radiation Therapy University of Otago, Wellington', *Shadows*, vol. 54, no. 1, 2011, 51–52.
118. Report of University of Otago Review of Department of Radiation Therapy, 2012, 17–18, 28.
119. 'New radiation therapy training system benefits both patients and students', Otago Medical School media release, 13 March 2013: www.otago.ac.nz/medical-school/news/archive/otago043213.html; Paul Kane, 'The impact of the VERT virtual reality system on teaching and learning associated with radiation therapy planning skills in the second year of the Bachelor of Radiation Therapy', Master of Health Science (Clinical Education) thesis, University of Otago, 2014, 3; 'New radiation therapy training systems big on benefits', *New Zealand Health and Hospital*, vol. 65, no. 1, 2013, 16.
120. Report of University of Otago Review of Department of Radiation Therapy, 2012, 7.
121. 'Prime minister opens $18m addition', *OB*, 21 September 2007, 1.
122. *UOAR*, 2000, 12, 15; 2001, 10, 14, 18; 'New centre will raise Otago's profile in Wellington', *UON*, December 2000, 3; 'Stadium centre closing', *OB*, 30 October 2009, 5; 'Capital centre', *OB*, 19 February 2010, 3; Self-review, University of Otago Review of School of Physiotherapy, 2007, 41; Graeme Fogelberg interview.
123. Page, *Anatomy of a Medical School*, 270.
124. Keith Sinclair, *A History of the University of Auckland 1883–1983* (Auckland: Auckland University Press, 1983), 37–38, 270–84.
125. Catherine Gunn, 'Rhodes 1950: Derek North', *UOM*, no. 3, 2002, 18.
126. Warwick Johnson and Grant Hopkins interviews; 'Otago in the city of sails', *UON*, June 1996, 2; 'New liaison officer', *UON*, November–December 1998, 10. On Howard, see Neil Howard, 'Howard, Basil Hillyer', in Jane Thomson (ed.), *Southern People: A dictionary of Otago Southland Biography* (Dunedin: Longacre Press/Dunedin City Council, 1998), 236–37.

127. Interviews with Grant Hopkins and Graeme Fogelberg; 'Otago in the city of sails'; 'Opening night in Auckland', *UON*, September 1996, 3.
128. 'New base for Auckland centre', *UON*, October 1999, 9; 'Auckland centre opening a big hit in the city of sails', *UON*, September 2000, 8.
129. Interviews with Grant Hopkins, Eric Walton & Mike Wilson; 'Auckland centre available for use', *OB*, 3 October 2008, 5.
130. In 1871 the council secretary fielded enquiries from prospective students in Bluff and Winton, among other places. Early student records are patchy, but it seems at least one of those southerners – Morrison – paid fees and presumably joined the foundation students. G.F. South, Bluff, to John Hislop, 4 May 1871, Inwards Letters, Records of Registry and Central Administration, AG-180-27/02, HC; John Hislop to R. Cameron, Winton, 26 July 1871, Letter book, Records of Registry and Central Administration, AG-180-30/01, HC. Cameron enquired on behalf of Morrison; that name is listed paying fees on 20 September 1871 in the University of Otago cash book, Records of Registry and Central Administration, AG-180-048/001, HC.
131. University of Otago Student Headcount by Division 1920–2010, statistics courtesy of David Thomson, director, Planning and Funding.
132. Regional Council of Adult Education Annual Report, 1950, Records of Registry and Central Administration, AG-180-7/04, HC. On home science extension, see chapter 6; and on other extension activities see chapter 12.
133. Lyall McLean, *A History of Economics and the Development of Commerce Degrees at the University of Otago 1871–2009* (Dunedin: L. McLean, 2011), 60–61. On Jones, see Peter Muller, 'Jones, Norman Philip', in Thomson, *Southern People*, 261.
134. University of Otago Extension Centre, Invercargill, Report to Board of Studies, 27 June 1975, Department of University Extension records, MS-3884-4-5, HC; 'The Southland scene', *UON*, June 1974, 1–2.
135. A Proposal to establish a Centre for University Studies within the Southland Polytechnic, 1977, Commerce Division records, MS-4183/051, HC; Ian Dougherty, *Bricklayers and Mortarboards: A history of New Zealand polytechnics and institutes of technology* (Palmerston North: Dunmore Press, 1999), 238.
136. McLean, *Economics and the Development of Commerce Degrees*, 60–62. On SIT, see Joanne Harris, 'Don't dream it's over', *Education Review*, vol. 12, no. 46, 2007, 7–9.
137. Report of University of Otago Review of College of Education, 2012, 28; David Keen, *In a Class of its Own: A Dunedin College of Education anniversary history* (Dunedin: Dunedin College of Education, 2001), 146–52.
138. 'Economic impact of university grows', Otago Bulletin Board, 14 May 2013: www.otago.ac.nz/otagobulletin/news/otago047091.html

11: SUPPORT SERVICES

1. E.R. Duncan, 'Library lapses', *OUR*, September 1939, 26–28. On Duncan, see his obituary, *New York Times*, 28 November 1990, D22.
2. *Report of the Committee on New Zealand Universities* (Wellington: Government Printer, 1960), 71.
3. *UOAR*, 1873; Simon Wilson, 'A useable collection: The origins and growth of the University of Otago library', in *Culture of Change: Beginnings at the University of Otago* (Dunedin: Departments of English & History, University of Otago, 2006), 1–19.
4. Stuart Strachan & Linda Tyler (eds), *Kā Taoka Hākena: Treasures from the Hocken Collections* (Dunedin: Otago University Press, 2007); Tony Ballantyne, *Archives, Public Memory and the Work of History: The 2015 Hocken lecture* (Dunedin: Hocken Collections Uare Taoka o Hākena, University of Otago, 2015), 9.
5. Angus Ross to Sam Elworthy, 7 May 1989, OUSA records, MS-4240/319, HC.
6. Dave Robertson, 'John Harris, librarian and alien anarchist', in The Time Keepers, *Tower Turmoil: Characters and controversies at the University of Otago* (Dunedin: Department of History, University of Otago, 2005), 65–79; Library Annual Report, 1948, Records of Registry and Central Administration, AG-180-7/03, HC.
7. *UOAR*, 1961.
8. 'New building is impressive', *ODT*, 7 April 1965, 11; Library Annual Report, 1965 and 1986, Records of Registry and Central Administration, AG-180-7/08 and 7/15, HC; Jock McEldowney interview.
9. Dorothy Page, *Anatomy of a Medical School: A history of medicine at the University of Otago 1875–2000* (Dunedin: Otago University Press, 2008), 98–101.
10. Jock McEldowney interview.
11. Library Annual Report, 1979, Records of Registry and Central Administration, AG-180-7/14, HC; 'Law library expands', *UON*, July 1989, 6; 'Hocken archives, manuscripts and photographs in new premises', *UON*, July 1989, 7; Stuart Strachan, 'The Hocken Collections 1910 to 2007', in Strachan & Tyler, *Kā Taoka Hākena*, 21–26.
12. Interviews with Jock McEldowney and Ann Wylie; University Librarian's Annual Report, 1977, Records of Registry and Central Administration, AG-180-7/13, HC.
13. Library Annual Report, 1986, Records of Registry and Central Administration, AG-180-7/15, HC.
14. 'Wellington Hospital: Additions and alterations', *Evening Post*, 29 November 1928, 9; Christopher Moore, George Rolleston, John Riminton & Andrew Hornblow, *A Vision Realised: The Christchurch School of Medicine, University of Otago 1972–1997* (Christchurch: Christchurch School of Medicine, 1998), 131.
15. Library Annual Report, 1971, 1972, 1975, and 1986, Records of Registry and Central Administration, AG-180-7/11, 7/13 and 7/15, HC.
16. Library Annual Report, 1973 and 1974, Records of Registry and Central Administration, AG-180-7/12, HC; 'New staff members', *UON*, March 1975, 16; B.M.

Corkill, 'Wellington School of Medicine – origins', 28, in 'Wellington School of Medicine: Comments, historical data and abstracts up to 1991', unpublished compilation, courtesy of University of Otago, Wellington.

17. Library Annual Report, 1975, Records of Registry and Central Administration, AG-180-7/13, HC.
18. Moore, Rolleston, Riminton & Hornblow, *Vision Realised*, 134–37.
19. Jock McEldowney interview ; 'Library information services take a step forward', *UON*, September 1980, 1–2.
20. 'Medline service', *UON*, July 1981, 11.
21. 'Tattle tape', *UON*, April 1981, 5.
22. Library Annual Report, 1985, Records of Registry and Central Administration, AG-180-7/15, HC; 'New library catalogue', *UON*, March 1985, 10.
23. 'Contract for local system signed', *UON*, April 1989, 6; 'Online catalogue update', *UON*, November 1989, 8; 'Circulation system in operation', *UON*, April 1990, 4.
24. 'CD-ROM', *UON*, April 1989, 6; 'Interlibrary loans and CD-ROMs', *UON*, April 1994, 16.
25. 'On the move: Influential librarian retires', *OB*, 22 April 2005, 4; Michael Wooliscroft, 'Background notes for Information Services Building working party', April 1995, Vice-Chancellor's Office records, MS–4394/428, HC; 'New ISB building will be state-of-the-art facility', *UON*, May 1998, 1; 'ISB project reaches its first major milestone', *UON*, July 2000, 8; Graeme Fogelberg interview.
26. David Keen, *In a Class of its Own: A Dunedin College of Education anniversary history* (Dunedin: Dunedin College of Education, 2001), 178–82.
27. 'An uplifting redevelopment', *OB*, 15 October 2010, 1; 'Law library makeover', *OB*, 4 September 2009, 5; 'Dental library e-affected', *OB*, 22 January 2010, 3. The Wellington and Christchurch renovations were part of larger projects on those campuses, discussed in chapter 10.
28. 'University Press turns 50', *OB*, 23 January 2009, 6–7; Jock McEldowney interview; 'What's in a name?', *OB*, 16 June 2006, 4.
29. Jock McEldowney interview.
30. University of Otago Press Annual Report, 1985, Records of Registry and Central Administration, AG-180-7/15, HC.
31. University of Otago Press Annual Report, 1986, Records of Registry and Central Administration, AG-180-7/15, HC.
32. 'What's in a name?'
33. 'University Press turns 50'; 'Publisher leaves Otago University Press in good heart', Otago Bulletin Board, 16 May 2013: www.otago.ac.nz/otagobulletin/people/otago047207.html
34. 'History', *University of Otago Computing Services Newsletter*, March/April 1984; Donald Ellis, 'Dialup facility – Vax 11/780', *University of Otago Computing Services Newsletter*, May/June 1984, 6; Neil James, 'Changes to central computing facilities', *University of Otago Computing Centre Newsletter*, March/April 1985, 3–5; 'History', *University of Otago Computing Services Centre Newsletter*, July/August 1985; Neil James, 'The year in retrospect', *University of Otago Computing Services Centre Newsletter*, November/December 1985, 3–5
35. Farah Dwyer, 'Hardware for sale', *University of Otago Computing Centre Newsletter*, January/February 1985, 14.
36. James, 'Year in retrospect'.
37. Marjan Lousberg, 'CAL at Otago', *University of Otago Computing Services Centre Newsletter*, May 1991, 3.
38. Donald Ellis, 'The CAL labs', *University of Otago Computing Services Centre Newsletter*, April 1990, 4; Dick Martin, 'Macintosh – CAL labs', *University of Otago Computing Services Centre Newsletter*, May 1991, 4.
39. Neil James, 'Director's comment – managing scarce resources', *University of Otago Computing Services Centre Newsletter*, April 1990, 3–4.
40. James, 'Year in retrospect'; Computing Services Centre Annual Report, 1987, Records of Registry and Central Administration, AG-180-7/15, HC.
41. Neil James, 'Director's comment – funding and networking', *University of Otago Computing Services Centre Newsletter*, June 1990, 3; Neil James, 'Electronic communications at the University of Otago', *Campus LAN*, February 1996, 6–7; Noeline Alcorn, *Ko Te Tangata: A history of the University of Waikato: The first fifty years* (Wellington: Steele Roberts, 2014), 153–55.
42. 'Otago with world leaders in computer networking technology', *UON*, October 1990, 7.
43. Neil James, 'The second Gutenburg revolution', *University of Otago Computing Services Centre Newsletter*, September 1991, 3–6. The first Gutenburg revolution resulted from new access to knowledge through the printing press.
44. 'Computing resource room offers equal opportunities', *UON*, May 1993, 2; Lala Frazer, 'Computing resource rooms', *Campus LAN*, December 1993, 7–8; Neil James, 'Planning for information technology in the university', *Campus LAN*, February 1994, 1.
45. 'Otago leads the way', *Campus LAN*, February 1995, 4.
46. Neil James, 'Director's comment – rationalisation of services', *University of Otago Computing Services Centre Newsletter*, July 1991, 2.
47. 'Upgrading the network', *UON*, March 1995, 1; Ian Greig, 'The new computer network', *Campus LAN*, September 1995, 6–8; 'Major university computer network completed', *UON*, August/September 1997, 1; 'Electronic network completed', *UON*, March 1998, 6.
48. 'Director of information services sees two dimensional role', *UON*, February 1995, 3.
49. Neil James, 'CSC becomes ITS', *Campus LAN*, February 1996, 1.
50. 'Greater scope for IT specialist', *OB*, 15 July 2005, 5.
51. 'New IT director takes information gathering trip to US', *OB*, 15 July 2005, 5.
52. 'Cellular network trials wireless computing', *OB*, 16 May 2003, 9; 'Otago wireless and proud', *OB*, 23 February 2007, 1.
53. 'Fifty years of Information Technology Services at the University of Otago', Otago Bulletin Board, 23 August 2016: www.otago.ac.nz/otagobulletin/news/otago619732.html

54. 'New position will help chart the future of IT at Otago', *UON*, May 1999, 5.
55. 'Future state network project', Information Technology Services: www.otago.ac.nz/its/services/network/otago081472.html; Vaughan Elder, 'Overdue, $6m over budget', *ODT*, 23 January 2017: www.odt.co.nz/news/campus/university-of-otago/overdue-6m-over-budget
56. 'New on-line teaching and learning support software looks the goods', *UON*, December 2000, 10; 'Fifty years of Information Technology Services'.
57. 'New appointment will enhance the university's web presence', *UON*, March 1999, 4; 'Web services': www.otago.ac.nz/webservices/index.html
58. 'University joins prestigious few on iTunes U', *OB*, 13 June 2008, 1.
59. 'Otago's sociable new social media adviser', Otago Bulletin Board, 13 April 2015: www.otago.ac.nz/otagobulletin/people/otago090263.html
60. Health Service Annual Report, 1947, Faculty of Medicine, Dean's Department records, MS–4326/141, HC; *UOAR*, 1961; Charles Hercus & Gordon Bell, *The Otago Medical School under the First Three Deans* (Edinburgh: Livingstone, 1964), 259–61.
61. Health Service Annual Report, 1947, Faculty of Medicine, Dean's Department records, MS–4326/141, HC.
62. Health Service Annual Report, 1980, Records of Registry and Central Administration, AG-180-7/14, HC.
63. Health Service Annual Report, 1951, Records of Registry and Central Administration, AG-180-7/04, HC.
64. Self-review, University of Otago Review of Student Health Services, 2010, 6.
65. Student Health Service Annual Report, 1975, Records of Registry and Central Administration, AG-180-7/13, HC.
66. Barbara Brookes, *A History of New Zealand Women* (Wellington: Bridget Williams Books, 2016), 330.
67. Health Service Annual Report, 1965, Student Health Service, Director's papers, MS–1280/003, HC. In an article in *Critic* the following year, Strang wrote that it was suggested that the student health service should prescribe the pill when requested, but its medical officers were 'under no direction from anyone as to how and what they prescribe to meet the medical needs of any situation'. He did not state clearly whether or not they might use that discretion to prescribe for the unmarried, hinting that it had become a possibility. See D. Strang, 'Responsibility and sex', *Critic*, 4 August 1966, 4.
68. Rosemarie Smith to author, 10 April 2017.
69. Health Service Annual Report, 1947, Faculty of Medicine, Dean's Department records, MS–4326/141, HC; Health Service Annual Report, 1948, Student Health Service, Director's papers, MS–1280/004, HC.
70. Health Service Annual Report, 1965, Student Health Service, Director's papers, MS–1280/003, HC.
71. Greg Hughson, 'A brief history of chaplaincy at the university and the polytechnic', in Self-review, University of Otago Review of Ecumenical and Catholic Chaplaincy, 2009, 4–7.
72. Report of counselling in Otago University for 1968, Records of Registry and Central Administration, AG-180-7/09, HC.
73. Counselling Service Annual Report, 1976 and 1978, Student Services Annual Report, 1989, Records of Registry and Central Administration, AG-180-7/13 and 7/14, AG-758/085, HC.
74. 'Retirements: Mr Lewis Lowery', *UON*, December 1993, 13. On increasing stress related to employment, see Counselling Service Annual Report, 1980, Records of Registry and Central Administration, AG-180-7/14, HC.
75. Counselling Service Annual Report, 1976, Records of Registry and Central Administration, AG-180-7/13, HC.
76. Counselling Service Annual Report, 1986 and 1987, Records of Registry and Central Administration, AG-758/085, HC.
77. Health Service Annual Report, 1986, Records of Registry and Central Administration, AG-758/085, HC.
78. 'Learning centre proposal resurfaces', *UON*, October 1993, 9. On Crooks' assistance with the Counselling Service courses, see Counselling Service Annual Report, 1981, Records of Registry and Central Administration, AG-180-7/14, HC.
79. 'Excellent response to workshops', *UON*, May 2000, 3.
80. 'Student Learning Development', Higher Education Development Centre: www.otago.ac.nz/hedc/students/index.html
81. 'Equal opportunity officer', *UON*, February 1988, 12; 'Equal opportunity officer', *UON*, May 1988, 6; J.M. Child, *Equal Employment Opportunities, University of Otago* (Dunedin: University of Otago, 1988).
82. 'Deafness is no barrier', *UON*, February 1994, 18.
83. Mark Wright, 'Whatever happened to … Disability Information and Support?', *UOM*, no. 31, 2012, 50–51; 'Vale, Donna-Rose McKay', Otago Bulletin Board, 16 December 2013: www.otago.ac.nz/otagobulletin/news/otago061345.html
84. 'Disabled students', *UON*, May 1982, 12.
85. 'Disabled action and support group – would you help?', *UON*, August 1988, 11; 'Disabled students' support and action group', *UON*, September 1990, 5; Student Services Annual Report, 1990, Records of Registry and Central Administration, AG-758/085, HC.
86. 'Disabilities research officer appointed', *UON*, September 1990, 5; 'The column', *UON*, April 1991, 18.
87. Wright, 'Disability Information and Support'.
88. 'Maori liaison officer', *UON*, May 1988, 3.
89. Khyla Russell interview; 'Our woman in the registry', *Mea Maori: Otago University Maori Centre Newsletter*, November 1989, 6.
90. *Mea Maori*, November 1989, 1; New Zealand Universities Review Committee, *New Zealand Universities: Partners in national development* (Wellington: New Zealand Vice-Chancellors Committee, 1987), 68–72.
91. *Mea Maori*, November 1989, 1–2; Self-review, University of Otago Review of Te Huka Matauraka-Maori Centre, 2006, 4.
92. Pearl Matahiki interview.

93. 'Mahi Tauira – students work', *Mea Maori*, November 1989, 4; 'Tofa soifua Linda and Mua: A korero with Mua', *Mea Maori*, November 1989, 16.
94. Miria Thorn, 'Maori Centre', *Nga Rongo Korero: University of Otago Maori Centre Newsletter*, June 1991, 7.
95. Pearl Matahiki interview; Self-review, University of Otago Review of Te Huka Matauraka-Maori Centre, 2006, 4–7.
96. David Thomson, 'Maori student numbers on the rise', *UON*, September 1994, 9.
97. Self-review, University of Otago Review of Te Huka Matauraka-Maori Centre, 2006, 4.
98. Pearl Matahiki interview; Self-review, University of Otago Review of Te Huka Matauraka-Maori Centre, 2006, 5–7; 'Kaitakawaenga Māori appointed to support Māori students', *OB*, 14 November 2003, 9; 'Powhiri – at Otakou marae', *OB*, 24 February 2006, 24; Rose Harrison, 'Māori pre-graduation', *OB*, 10 August 2007, 4.
99. Ian Dougherty, 'Māori centre celebrates', *UOM*, no. 40, March 2015, 23.
100. Interviews with Tofilau Nina Kirifi-Alai and David Richardson; Self-review, University of Otago Review of Pacific Islands Centre, 2006, 1.
101. Tofilau Nina Kirifi-Alai interview; Self-review, University of Otago Review of Pacific Islands Centre, 2006, 1; 'History of the Pacific Islands Centre', Pacific Islands Centre: www.otago.ac.nz/pacific/pacificatotago/otago022925.html; 'Pacific Island centre opens', *OB*, 11 July 2003, 8; 'Honour for Pacific Island centre manager', *OB*, 20 April 2007, 4.
102. Tofilau Nina Kirifi-Alai interview; Self-review, University of Otago Review of Pacific Islands Centre, 2006, 1; 'History of the Pacific Islands Centre'; 'Pacific voices symposium III', *OB*, 6 October 2006, 2; 'Pacific Island centre moves', *OB*, 6 October 2006, 7.
103. Tofilau Nina Kirifi-Alai interview; 'History of the Pacific Islands Centre'; 'On campus experience', *OB*, 18 May 2007, 7.
104. Tofilau Nina Kirifi-Alai interview; 'Helping Pacific pupils on the path to university', *OB*, 27 June 2008, 1.
105. 'Pacific focus', *UOM*, no. 41, 2015, 30–31.

12: TEACHING

1. Angus Ross, 'The university and the community: The University of Otago from within, since 1930', 12, script for Faculty of Arts Open Lectures – centennial series, 1969, MS-0835, HC.
2. Arts and Music Faculty Annual Report, 1948, Records of Registry and Central Administration, AG-180-7/03, HC.
3. J.H. Murdoch, 'Teaching reminiscences', 19–25, New Zealand Council for Educational Research: Educational reminiscences, 88-005–10, Alexander Turnbull Library.
4. Muriel May, *Freshly Remembered: Half a century of school* (Christchurch: Whitcombe & Tombs, 1975), 75, 77.
5. Hugh Parton, *The University of New Zealand* (Auckland: Auckland University Press/University Grants Committee, 1979), 21–22.
6. 'Passing events', *OUR*, May 1898, 8–10.
7. 'Summary for Europe', *ODT*, 15 March 1898, 2.
8. Parton, *University of New Zealand*, 60–64.
9. D.W. Carmalt Jones, *Annals of the University of Otago Medical School 1875–1939* (Wellington: Reed, 1945), 112.
10. Parton, *University of New Zealand*, 60–64, 207–8; W.P. Morrell, *The University of Otago: A centennial history* (Dunedin: University of Otago Press, 1969), 190–91.
11. Sam Elworthy, *Ritual Song of Defiance: A social history of students at the University of Otago* (Dunedin: Otago University Students' Association, 1990), 123–24.
12. 'C.I.A. continuous internal assessment: Our greatest bungle?', *1977 Handbook: The student's viewpoint*, 15.
13. 'Academia', *OUSA Orientation Handbook*, 1975, 31–33.
14. OUSA President Annual Report, 1981, OUSA records, MS–4227/296, HC.
15. 'Otago Institute', *ES*, 14 May 1884, 1; Rosi Crane, '"A dangerous visionary"? The lectures of the evolutionist T.J. Parker', *Journal of New Zealand Studies*, no. 15, 2013, 36–49.
16. Jim Sullivan, 'Jack, Robert', from DNZB: https://teara.govt.nz/en/biographies/4j1/jack-robert. For just two examples of the many and varied instances of the university's use of media to reach the community, see 'University radio', *UON*, November 1982, 4; 'University makes impact on iTunes U', *OB*, 11 July 2008, 3.
17. Meredith Atkinson, 'Labour and learning: A new alliance', *ES*, 13 May 1915, 4.
18. Roy Shuker, *Educating the workers? A history of the Workers' Education Association in New Zealand* (Palmerston North: Dunmore Press, 1984); James Dakin, 'Looking back', in John Benseman, Brian Findsen & Miriama Scott (eds), *The Fourth Sector: Adult and community education in Aotearoa/New Zealand* (Palmerston North: Dunmore Press, 1996), 21–37.
19. 'Workers' Educational Association', *ES*, 9 March 1916, 6.
20. 'Workers' Educational Association', *Southland Times*, 1 June 1915, 7.
21. 'Workers' Educational Association', *Southland Times*, 25 March 1916, 7.
22. Dakin, 'Looking back'.
23. 'Workers' Educational Association', *ODT*, 11 March 1930, 2; Tim Beaglehole, 'Beaglehole, John Cawte', from DNZB: www.teara.govt.nz/en/biographies/5b16/beaglehole-john-cawte
24. Workers' Educational Association Annual Report, 1937, Records of Registry and Central Administration, AG-180-7/02, HC; Dakin, 'Looking back'.
25. Workers' Educational Association Annual Report, 1943, Records of Registry and Central Administration, AG-180-7/02, HC.
26. *UOAR*, 1948; Dakin, 'Looking back'.
27. 'Workers' Educational Association', *ODT*, 11 March 1930, 2; Regional Council of Adult Education Annual Report, 1949, Records of Registry and Central Administration, AG-180-7/03, HC.
28. Dakin, 'Looking back'; *UOC*, 1965, xlix-xlx.
29. Dorothy Page, *Anatomy of a Medical School: A history of*

medicine at the University of Otago 1875–2000 (Dunedin: Otago University Press, 2008), 29–30.
30. J.B. Mackie, 'Dunedin days – some reminiscences', *Geological Society of New Zealand Newsletter*, no. 60, 1983, 12–15.
31. Arts and Science Faculty Annual Report, 1940, Records of Registry and Central Administration, AG-180-7/02, HC.
32. 'Educational technology', *UON*, May 1975, 1–3.
33. John Howells interview.
34. 'AVLC activity covers wide range', *UON*, April 1977, 1–2.
35. 'Learning and teaching programme under way', *UON*, June 1976, 10.
36. 'Staff training coming?', *UON*, April 1975, 1–2; 'HERAC begins to forge ahead', *UON*, August 1977, 1–2; 'HERAC/AVLC', *UON*, April 1979, 4.
37. 'HEDC activity', *UON*, October 1983, 11–12.
38. 'Staff rush to improve teaching skills', *UON*, June 1987, 5.
39. *UOC*, 1996, 305. A certificate qualification was added in 1999: see *UOC*, 1999, 101.
40. 'Resources to enhance learning and teaching', 2002, Committee for the Advancement of Learning and Teaching papers, DVC Academic Executive Assistant records, r.6880, box 4, HC.
41. *UOC*, 1988, 120–121; 'HEDC on top of the mountain', *UON*, November/December 1995, 4.
42. Self-review, University of Otago Review of Higher Education Development Centre, 2010, 1, 5.
43. 'Extension role', *UON*, July 1975, 14; 'Colour slide lectures', *UON*, September 1974, 9.
44. J.M.R. Owens, *Campus Beyond the Walls: The first 25 years of Massey University's extramural programme* (Palmerston North: Dunmore Press, 1985).
45. *UOAR*, 1984; 'Significant events from the past year', *UON*, February 1985, 1–2.
46. Fiona Stuart, 'Reflections on distance teaching and learning by Otago staff', in Kwok-Wing Lai, Sarah Stein, Penny Field & Keryn Pratt (eds), *Our World in Your Place: 30 years of distance learning and teaching at the University of Otago* (Dunedin: Distance Learning Office, University of Otago, 2016), 20–39.
47. 'New venture', *UON*, October 1985, 3.
48. Elizabeth Purdie, 'Distance learning at Otago: A history from 1984 to 2000', in Lai, Stein, Field & Pratt, *Our World in Your Place*, 2–6.
49. Stuart, 'Reflections on distance teaching and learning'.
50. Penny Field, 'Educating New Zealand dietitians at a distance: The Otago experience', in Lai, Stein, Field & Pratt, *Our World in Your Place*, 63–73; Sarah Stein, 'Distance learning at the University of Otago from 2000 to the present: The story continues', in Lai, Stein, Field & Pratt, *Our World in Your Place*, 7–10.
51. Rob Griffiths, '30 years of occupational and aviation medicine', in Lai, Stein, Field & Pratt, *Our World in Your Place*, 74–88.
52. Brian O'Rourke interview; University Extension Annual Report, 1986, Records of Registry and Central Administration, AG-180-7/15, HC.
53. Brian O'Rourke interview.
54. Brian Findsen and Jennie Harré Hindmarsh, 'Adult and community education in the universities', in Benseman, Findsen & Scott, *Fourth Sector*, 193–209.
55. University Extension Annual Report, 1984, Division of Academic Services Annual Report, 1992, Records of Registry and Central Administration, AG-180-7/15 and AG-758/085, HC.
56. 'Review of University Extension, University of Otago: Report to the Vice-Chancellor from the Review Panel, 10 May 1994', University Council papers, OUSA records, MS–4242/448, HC.
57. 'A theory of devolution', *UON*, September 1995, 7.
58. John Gibb, 'Extension to close', *ODT*, 14 June 1995, 1.
59. Purdie, 'Distance learning at Otago'.
60. Stein, 'Distance learning at the University of Otago'.
61. Austin Gee, Robert G. Patman & Chris Rudd, 'Debating New Zealand's foreign relations: The role and impact of the University of Otago Foreign Policy School 1966–1976', *Kōtuitui: New Zealand Journal of Social Sciences*, vol. 12, 2017, 256–76.
62. Brian O'Rourke interview; 'About U3A', University of the Third Age Dunedin: https://u3adunedin.org.nz/?About%20U3A
63. 'Recent academic developments offer flexibility and variety', *Otago Graduate*, 1991, 14; Derek Holton, 'On papers and semesters', *UON*, June 1996, 4; *UOC*, 1991–1992.
64. 'Senate', *UON*, March 1992, 4–5.
65. 'Semesters: The good, the bad and the unknown', *UON*, December 1993, 5; 'To semesterise papers, or not to semesterise papers …', *UON*, September 1994, 4.
66. Holton, 'Papers and semesters'.
67. Arts and Music Faculty Annual Report, 1971 and 1972, Records of Registry and Central Administration, AG-180-7/11, HC; Self-review, University of Otago Review of Summer School, 2007, 2.
68. Final Report of the Summer School Working Party, 2000, Vice-Chancellor's Office records, MS–4394/0941, HC.
69. Merv Smith interview; Self-review, University of Otago Review of Summer School, 2007, 3–5.
70. 'Summer school attracts growing student numbers', *OB*, 27 February 2004, 8.
71. *Summer School Prospectus*, 2001–2010; 'Debut for Arabic language at summer school', *OB*, 28 January 2005, 7; John Gibb, 'Summer school boosts Dunedin's economy', *ODT*, 28 December 2012: www.odt.co.nz/news/dunedin/summer-school-boosts-dunedins-economy; John Gibb, 'Summer school numbers rise', *ODT*, 22 January 2013: www.odt.co.nz/news/dunedin/summer-school-numbers-rise; Self-review, University of Otago Review of Summer School, 2007, 12–13.
72. Self-review, University of Otago Review of Summer School, 2007, 5, 10.
73. Report of University of Otago Review of Summer School, 2007, 5–6.
74. Report of University of Otago Review of Summer School and Continuing Education, 2013, 3.
75. Graeme Fogelberg interview; *University Foundation Studies Prospectus*, 1997.

76. *UOC*, 1998–2009.
77. Report of University of Otago Review of Language Centre and Foundation Year, 2013, 8–9.
78. University of Otago Foundation Studies Ltd, Director's notes to accompany annual financial statements, 1997, Vice-Chancellor's Office records, MS–4394/119, HC; University of Otago Foundation Year, Academic Summary, 1998, Vice-Chancellor's Office records, MS–4394/325, HC; 'Programme blooming', *UON*, March 2000, 5.
79. 'Foundation studies to be offered in Auckland', *UON*, November/December 1998, 4; University of Otago Foundation Studies Ltd, Director's notes to accompany annual financial statements, 1997, Vice-Chancellor's Office records, MS–4394/119, HC; *UOAR*, 1998, 13; 'University at the plaza', *UOM*, no. 32, 2012, 36.
80. Ian Dougherty, *Continuing Education of Quality: A 50th anniversary history of Otago Polytechnic 1966–2016 and of its predecessors from 1870* (Dunedin: Otago Polytechnic, 2016), 64.
81. Self-review, University of Otago Review of Foundation Studies, 2005, 7; University of Otago Foundation Studies Ltd, Director's notes to accompany annual financial statements, 1997, Vice-Chancellor's Office records, MS–4394/119, HC; Report of University of Otago Review of Language Centre and Foundation Year, 2013, 11, 44.
82. Report of University of Otago Review of Language Centre and Foundation Year, 2013, 12–16; *UOAR*, 2015, 27, 67.
83. Report of University of Otago Review of Otago Language Centre and Foundation Year, 2013, 19.
84. *UOAR*, 2010, 28.
85. *UOAR*, 2001, 54; 2002, 75; 'Our history', Te Tapuae o Rēhua: www.tetapuae.co.nz/about-us/our-history/
86. *UOAR*, 2009, 31; 2012, 49; 2014, 63.
87. Memo from DVC (Academic) to heads of academic departments, 11 February 2002; Committee for the Advancement of Learning and Teaching minutes, 28 February 2002 and 20 August 2003; all in Committee for the Advancement of Learning and Teaching papers, DVC Academic Executive Assistant records, r.6880, box 4, HC; 'Otago's inaugural teaching excellence awards', *OB*, 13 August 2004, 4.
88. 'Three Christchurch staff honoured for teaching excellence', *OB*, 27 February 2004, 9; 'Inaugural Dunedin School of Medicine teaching awards', *OB*, 5 November 2004, 10.
89. Steven Sutton, report to OUSA executive, 1 July to 1 September 2002, OUSA records, MS–4219/003, HC.
90. John Gibb, 'Award surprises lecturer', *ODT*, 9 November 2002, 2.
91. 'Supervision awards', *OB*, 12 December 2003, 9; Gregory Whyte, 'Teaching awards', *Critic*, 13 September 2010: www.critic.co.nz/news/article/576/teaching-awards; 'Top teachers recognised by Otago students', *OB*, 29 October 2010, 3.
92. John Lewis, 'Uni teaching underrated, lecturer says', *ODT*, 10 July 2013: www.odt.co.nz/news/dunedin/uni-teaching-underrated-lecturer-says; Vaughan Elder, 'Union backs criticism', *ODT*, 11 July 2013: www.odt.co.nz/news/dunedin/union-backs-criticism
93. Vaughan Elder, 'Research not priority over education', *ODT*, 25 March 2017: www.odt.co.nz/news/campus/university-of-otago/research-not-priority-over-education
94. 'Recognition for outstanding teachers', Otago Bulletin Board, 2 March 2015: www.otago.ac.nz/otagobulletin/news/otago087842.html
95. Rebekah White, 'Jacinta Ruru: "Māori had their own legal system and continue to have their own legal system"', *Mana*, 17 March 2017: www.mana.co.nz/news/jacinta-ruru.html; Dale Husband, 'Jacinta Ruru: Our legal system is still too deaf to the Māori voice', E-Tangata, 4 September 2016: http://e-tangata.co.nz/news/our-legal-system-is-deaf-to-the-maori-voice

13: BUILDINGS

1. Ben Schrader, *The Big Smoke: New Zealand cities 1840–1920* (Wellington: Bridget Williams Books, 2016), 107–10.
2. 'The post office building', *ODT*, 16 November 1867, 5.
3. *UOAR*, 1871.
4. G.E. Thompson, *A History of the University of Otago (1869–1919)* (Dunedin: Wilkie, 1919), 85–88.
5. 'Provincial council', *ES*, 13 May 1874, 3.
6. *ES*, 7 August 1874, 2.
7. *UOAR*, 1876, 1878 and 1879.
8. 'Historic heritage', Sustainability @ Otago: www.otago.ac.nz/sustainability/campus-environment/historic-heritage.html
9. 'Beautiful universities around the world', *Telegraph*, 16 August 2012: www.telegraph.co.uk/expat/education-and-family/beautiful-universities-around-the-world/; '15 of the world's most beautiful universities revealed', *Huffington Post*, 11 July 2013: www.huffingtonpost.co.uk/2013/07/11/worlds-most-beautiful-universities_n_3578402.html
10. Eric Dunlop, *The Story of the Dunedin Botanic Garden: New Zealand's first* (Dunedin: Friends of the Dunedin Botanic Garden, 2002), 33–34.
11. 'Diverting the Leith', *ODT*, 11 September 1897, 2; Thompson, *University of Otago*, 89–91; 'Historic heritage'.
12. *UOAR*, 1897, 1899, 1905 and 1906.
13. 'Leith flood protection scheme: Flood history', Otago Regional Council: www.orc.govt.nz/Publications-and-Reports/Flood-protection-and-drainage-schemes-/LeithFloodProtectionScheme/Flood-history/
14. 'Floods in the city', *ODT*, 23 April 1923, 8; 'Dental School in danger', *ODT*, 24 April 1923, 8; 'The Dental School', *ODT*, 26 April 1923, 10.
15. 'After the storm', *ODT*, 21 March 1929, 8.
16. 'University's most photographed view transformed', Otago Bulletin Board, 4 December 2014: www.otago.ac.nz/otagobulletin/news/otago083718.html
17. Chris Morris, '"Surf's up!" as Leith seethes', *ODT*, 26 May 2010: www.odt.co.nz/news/dunedin/surfs-leith-seethes

18. Anne Marchant, 'Bury, Maxwell', from DNZB: www.teara.govt.nz/en/biographies/2b52/bury-maxwell
19. 'The University', *ODT*, 15 August 1877, 2.
20. Report of the Royal Commission on the University of New Zealand, *AJHR*, 1879, H-01; W.P. Morrell, *The University of Otago: A centennial history* (Dunedin: University of Otago Press, 1969), 49–50.
21. 'University of Otago', *ES*, 10 July 1877, 2.
22. Report of the Royal Commission on the University of New Zealand, *AJHR*, 1879, H-01; Thompson, *University of Otago*, 94–98; 'Celebrated Clocktower Building almost 100 years old', *UON*, February 1979, 1–2.
23. *UOAR*, 1884.
24. *From Bury to Blair: Architects' conceptions of the University of Otago* (Dunedin: University of Otago, 1994), 8.
25. Richard Norris interview.
26. Rick Sibson, 'Musings from a stone building', *UON*, June 1995, 9–10.
27. *UOAR*, 1911 and 1913.
28. 'The Hon. Richard Oliver', *ODT*, 17 January 1911, 10; *Bury to Blair*, 6–7.
29. 'Celebrated Clocktower Building almost 100 years old'; *Bury to Blair*, 7.
30. *UOAR*, 1962.
31. Sibson, 'Musings from a stone building'.
32. 'Seismic strengthening at the University of Otago', Seismic programme: www.otago.ac.nz/seismicprogramme/index.html
33. Vaughan Elder, 'Earthquake-risk aquarium to be demolished', *ODT*, 18 July 2012: www.odt.co.nz/news/dunedin/earthquake-risk-aquarium-be-demolished
34. 'The Dental School', *ODT*, 27 April 1908, supplement, 4; *UOAR*, 1907, 1908.
35. *Bury to Blair*, 10; 'Staff Club', *UON*, October 1979, 2–3.
36. School of Mines Annual Report, *AJHR*, 1909, E-07.
37. Greg Bowron, 'Anscombe, Edmund', from DNZB: www.teara.govt.nz/en/biographies/4a17/anscombe-edmund; 'New school of mines', *ES*, 19 August 1909, 4.
38. Gregor Macaulay, 'Otago figures richly grotesque', *OB*, 8 October 2004, 2; Karen Hogg, 'Whatever happened to ... the architect's folly?', *UOM*, no. 43, 2016, 54–55.
39. '0900 examination results service', *UON*, November 1994, 4; Loulou Callister-Baker, 'Getting around the orthodoxy', *Critic*, 13 May 2013, 20–23. An 0900 phone service became the replacement source of early exam results until computer notification took over.
40. *UOAR*, 1911.
41. 'Home science building', *ES*, 26 April 1920, 6.
42. *School of Home Science History, 1911–1961* (Dunedin: University of Otago, School of Home Science, 1962), 17–19; 'News from the School of Home Science', *Journal of the Association of Home Science Alumnae of New Zealand*, 1969, 106.
43. 'CAPS building', *UON*, December 1994, 10–11; 'University of Otago Home Science block', Heritage New Zealand: www.heritage.org.nz/the-list/details/2226
44. *Options for Future Campus Development*, Campus Master Plan, 2010, 85–89: www.otago.ac.nz/administration/campusmasterplan/
45. 'Officers' Training Corps: Drill hall at the Otago University', *ES*, 2 October 1919, 2; Ministry of Culture and Heritage, 'Hospital ships', New Zealand History, 2015: https://nzhistory.govt.nz/war/merchant-marine/hospital-ships
46. 'Maheno and Marama Hall', *ODT*, 19 April 1923, 5; Dorothy Page, *Anatomy of a Medical School: A history of medicine at the University of Otago 1875–2000* (Dunedin: Otago University Press, 2008), 72–73.
47. 'Maheno and Marama Hall', *ODT*, 19 April 1923, 5; 'Marama Hall', *UON*, October 1994, 10.
48. Page, *Anatomy of a Medical School*, 74–75.
49. 'The Otago Medical School. Proposed extensions: An appeal to the citizens. Wanted, £7500', *ODT*, 5 March 1914, 8.
50. D.W. Carmalt Jones, *Annals of the University of Otago Medical School 1875–1939* (Wellington: Reed, 1945), 152–53; Charles Hercus & Gordon Bell, *The Otago Medical School under the First Three Deans* (Edinburgh: Livingstone, 1964), 46. On Dawson, see Donald Gordon, 'Dawson, William', in Jane Thomson (ed.), *Southern People: A dictionary of Otago Southland biography* (Dunedin: Longacre Press/Dunedin City Council, 1998), 122–23.
51. Page, *Anatomy of a Medical School*, 76–77; Carmalt Jones, *Annals*, 179–80.
52. 'The Medical School: New building opened', *ODT*, 3 February 1927, 7.
53. Rosemarie Patterson, *A Bob Both Ways: Celebrating 100 years of Naylor Love* (Dunedin: Advertising & Art, 2010), 71–72.
54. Page, *Anatomy of a Medical School*, 184–86.
55. *The Dunedin Hospital Ward Block with its Medical School Facilities* (Dunedin: Otago Hospital Board, 1980); Page, *Anatomy of a Medical School*, 187; 'About buildings', *UON*, July 1974, 10–11.
56. David Skegg, 'Partnership crucial to our hospital's future', *ODT*, 21 March 2017: www.odt.co.nz/opinion/partnership-crucial-our-hospitals-future
57. Carmalt Jones, *Annals*, 179.
58. 'New dental school', *ODT*, 12 June 1926, 8.
59. 'Dental school', Heritage New Zealand: www.heritage.org.nz/the-list/details/7618; 'Dental school', *UON*, November 1994, 10–11.
60. Dental Faculty Annual Report, 1980 and 1983, Records of Registry and Central Administration, AG-180-7/14 and 7/15, HC.
61. Timothy Brown, 'Work to start on $200m varsity projects', *ODT*, 7 May 2015: www.odt.co.nz/news/dunedin/work-start–200m-varsity-projects; 'Dental school project progresses at pace', Faculty of Dentistry, 9 June 2016: www.otago.ac.nz/dentistry/about/news/otago614131.html
62. 'Significant events from the past year', *UON*, February 1985, 1–2; 'New building adds to "auspicious time" for Dunedin study', Otago Bulletin Board, 23 February 2017: www.otago.ac.nz/otagobulletin/news/otago636521.html
63. Carolyn Burns, 'One hundred and twenty-five years of zoology', speech notes, 2002, 3; Science Faculty

Annual Report, 1963, Records of Registry and Central Administration, AG-180-7/08, HC.

64. *UOAR*, 1962; 'New habitat for the Botany Department', *UON*, March 1994, 4.
65. Burns, 'One hundred and twenty-five years of Zoology'; *UOAR*, 2003, 22.
66. Kim Dungey, 'Behind the façade', *ODT*, 7 June 2014: www.odt.co.nz/lifestyle/home-garden/behind-facade; 'Te Pā opens', *UOM*, no. 39, 2014, 38–39.
67. I am grateful to architectural history experts David Murray and Michael Findlay, who helped me identify candidates for the oldest building, and DCC archivist Chris Scott, who checked the historic rates records for confirmation.
68. Chris Scott to author, 5 September 2014; birth notices, *ODT*, 16 October 1862, 4 and 18 January 1864, 4; Arthur Calcutt burial record, Southern Cemetery, Dunedin City Council cemeteries search: www.dunedin.govt.nz/facilities/cemeteries/cemeteries_search?recordid=93156&type=Burial; 'An old colonist', *ES*, 27 May 1895, 3.
69. Peter Holland, Hugh Kidd & Richard Welch (eds), *From Mellor to Hocken: Fifty years of geography at the University of Otago* (Dunedin: Department of Geography, University of Otago, 1995), 1, 5, 37.
70. F.G. Soper, 'University of Otago: Ten years as vice-chancellor 1954 to 1963', Frederick Soper papers, 90–161, Box 2, HC.
71. Sam Elworthy, *Ritual Song of Defiance: A social history of students at the University of Otago* (Dunedin: Otago University Students' Association, 1990), 86.
72. Works and Services Department, 'History of University of Otago development', 1980, in Campus development background reports, OUSA archives, MS-4227/202, HC.
73. 'History of University of Otago development'.
74. *UOAR*, 1964.
75. Morrell, *University of Otago*, 231.
76. 'History of University of Otago development'; Dorothy Page interview with Robin Williams; *UOAR*, 1968, 1970, 1974, 1976.
77. *UOAR*, 1980.
78. John Patrick interview.
79. Campus master plan: www.otago.ac.nz/administration/campusmasterplan/index.html
80. David Skegg, 'A vision for the future', *ODT*, 17 May 2010: www.otago.ac.nz/news/news/otago008355.html
81. Allison Rudd, 'Ailing post-1960s buildings on university's demolition list', *ODT*, 9 June 2010: www.odt.co.nz/news/dunedin/ailing-post-1960s-buildings-universitys-demolition-list
82. Jock McEldowney interview; *Bury to Blair*, 20.
83. 'University extensions: Building for science unit', *ES*, 7 July 1964, 1; 'University block may span Leith', *ODT*, 8 July 1964, 3; 'Working in new science building', *ODT*, 2 September 1965, 5; Brian Cox interview.
84. Mason & Wales, 'Design report: Proposed Arts Building, phase 1 for the University of Otago', Angus Ross papers, MS-1050/014, HC.
85. *UOAR*, 1979; Stuart Strachan, 'The Hocken Collections 1910 to 2007', in Stuart Strachan & Linda Tyler (eds), *Kā Taoka Hākena: Treasures from the Hocken Collections* (Dunedin: Otago University Press, 2007), 21–26; 'New building for Hocken library', *UON*, April 1996, 8; *UOAR*, 2006, 13; 'Cultures mingle at Te Tumu opening', *OB*, 24 February 2006, 1, 4.
86. 'New lecture block colourful – but controversial', *ODT*, 28 February 1974, 1.
87. Ted McCoy, *A Southern Architecture: The work of Ted McCoy* (Dunedin: Otago University Press, 2007), 125.
88. Facebook comment by Nigel Stanger, in response to links to blog post: Ali Clarke, 'Lost in lecture theatres', University of Otago 1869–2019 – writing a history, 17 February 2014: https://otago150years.wordpress.com/2014/02/17/lost-in-lecture-theatres/. This post attracted numerous responses from people who had been confused by the building.
89. Arthur Campbell interview.
90. *UOAR*, 1968; 'New chemistry building now in full use', *ES*, 16 March 1971, 16.
91. Allingham & Harrison, 'Design report: University of Otago biochemistry block', 1966, Department of Biochemistry records, MS-2260/012, HC.
92. *UOAR*, 1972; *Bury to Blair*, 21.
93. 'New "front door" to university', *ES*, 3 October 1972, 1; *UOAR*, 1970.
94. 'University science building approved', *ODT*, 27 February 1974, 1; *ES*, 18 December 1974, 6; *UOAR*, 1977; 'New habitat for the Botany Department', *UON*, March 1994, 4; Geoff Baylis, letter to the editor, *UON*, May 1994, 19. For a sketch of the Science III building as originally designed, see *ODT*, 23 August 1972, 1.
95. *UOAR*, 1975.
96. *UOAR*, 1979.
97. *UOAR*, 1985 and 1986.
98. 'Castle Theatre – up and running', *UON*, April 1988, 1–2; *UOAR*, 1991, 7.
99. McCoy, *Southern Architecture*, 162–65.
100. *UOAR*, 1987.
101. *UOAR*, 1986; Commerce Faculty Annual Report, 1985 and 1986, Records of Registry and Central Administration, AG-180-7/15, HC.
102. *UOAR*, 1990.
103. John Balaslou (ed.), *John Blair: Architect* (Auckland: New Zealand Architectural Publications Trust, 2010), 113.
104. John Gibb, 'Complaints of leaks and noise', *ODT*, 4 March 1993, 1; Glenda Price, 'Student slips on wet atrium tiles, breaks jaw', *ODT*, 17 July 1996, 5; Wilma McCorkindale, 'Raindrops stop falling on their heads', *Dunedin Star Midweek*, 16 April 1997, 24; Tom McKinlay, 'Problems with atrium', *ODT*, 1 April 2004, 5; Tom McKinlay, 'Commerce building cops $100,000 damage', *ODT*, 10 February 2005, 4.
105. David Loughrey, 'Hazardous building costs varsity', *ODT*, 1 September 2015: www.odt.co.nz/news/dunedin/hazardous-building-costs-varsity
106. David Loughrey, '$120k safety fix for commerce

building', *ODT*, 3 March 2016: www.odt.co.nz/news/dunedin/120k-safety-fix-commerce-building
107. 'What's happening', Otago Business School building redevelopment: https://blogs.otago.ac.nz/bsredevelopment/whats-happening/; 'Staff choose café coffee in Business redevelopment', Otago Bulletin Board, 25 May 2017: www.otago.ac.nz/otagobulletin/news/otago651593.html; 'Otago Business School building redevelopment opens', Otago Bulletin Board, 7 December 2017: www.otago.ac.nz/otagobulletin/news/otago670571.html
108. Geoffrey White interview.
109. 'Psychology building wins award', *UON*, February 1991, 4.
110. Geoffrey White interview; 'History', *Psychology Handbook*, 2014, 4–5.
111. *Bury to Blair*, 24; 'New student health services building plans unveiled', *UON*, April–May 1995, 7; Frank Campbell, 'Executive development complex', *UON*, December 1993, 18; Graeme Fogelberg interview.
112. *Bury to Blair*, 24.
113. 'Marine studies centre formally announced', *UON*, September 1996, 1; 'Marine studies centre opened at Portobello', *ODT*, 17 December 1998, 4; Vaughan Elder, 'Aquarium to be demolished', *ODT*, 21 March 2016: www.odt.co.nz/news/dunedin/aquarium-be-demolished; 'Demolition finished at Portobello – work starting', Otago Bulletin Board, 14 October 2016: www.otago.ac.nz/otagobulletin/news/otago624195.html; 'Priority development plan', University of Otago Property Services: www.otago.ac.nz/propertyservices/about/#PDP
114. David Eggleton, 'Scarfies', *Architecture New Zealand*, September/October 2000, 22–32; 'Construction of new lecture theatre complex to start in 1999', *UON*, November–December 1998, 12; *UOAR*, 1999, 13.
115. *UOAR*, 1999, 13; Patterson, *Bob Both Ways*, 237–38.
116. *UOAR*, 1998, 13; 'St David Street building takes two architects' awards', *UON*, July 1999, 6; 'St David 2 building redevelopment about to start', Otago Bulletin Board, 2 November 2017: www.otago.ac.nz/otagobulletin/news/otago667285.html
117. 'Otago's new visitors' centre in full swing', Otago Bulletin Board, 24 February 2014: www.otago.ac.nz/otagobulletin/news/otago065628.html
118. 'Street diversion', *UON*, October 1975, 11–12; Diagram of Blake-Kelly plan, Campus development background reports, OUSA archives, MS–4227/202, HC.
119. 'A new bridge over the Leith', *UON*, April 1991, 2; *UOAR*, 2003, 21–22; 2004, 17; interviews with Jan Flood and Graeme Fogelberg; 'Anger over university bridge', *Dunedin Star Midweek*, 26 November 1997, 1; 'OUSA group starts petition', *ODT*, 24 May 1999, 4; 'Students back opposition to bridge', *ODT*, 29 April 2004, 5; Victoria Bartle, 'Troubled bridge over calm waters', *New Zealand Heritage*, no. 90, 2003, 6.
120. Graeme Fogelberg interview; 'Information services complex takes shape', *UON*, August 1996, 1.
121. *UOAR*, 2001, 13.
122. 'Work to begin demolishing balconies on university Arts Building', Otago Bulletin Board, 3 December 2015: www.otago.ac.nz/otagobulletin/news/otago364601.html
123. Kevin Brown, 'Other days – other ways', *UON*, October 1986, 16; 'Works and services', *UON*, March 1974, 5; 'News in brief', *UON*, August 1974, 5.
124. 'Works workings', *UON*, November 1976, 5.
125. 'New building adds to "auspicious time" for Dunedin Study', Otago Bulletin Board, 23 February 2017: www.otago.ac.nz/otagobulletin/news/otago636521.html
126. University of Otago Property Services: www.otago.ac.nz/propertyservices/index.html
127. 'More detail on university operations group changes', Otago Bulletin Board, 27 March 2017: www.otago.ac.nz/otagobulletin/news/otago639654.html

14: OTAGO'S PLACE IN THE WORLD

1. 'Behind the new TV ad campaign', *OB*, 8 August 2008, 4.
2. Others in Chile and Argentina are further south; Universidad Nacional de Tierra del Fuego is the most southerly.
3. 'Otago staff return from relief work in Samoa', *OB*, 13 November 2009, 1.
4. 'Otago University forges links with PI partners', *OB*, 4 April 2003, 5; 'PI/Otago links strengthened', *OB*, 16 July 2004, 8.
5. 'Samoan delegations', *OB*, 6 October 2006, 4; 'Samoan sojourn strengthens bonds', *OB*, 30 November 2007, 10; 'Apia home for Otago', *OB*, 22 January 2010, 3.
6. 'Samoa trip builds relationships', Otago Bulletin Board, 4 July 2016: www.otago.ac.nz/otagobulletin/news/otago616486.html
7. *University of Otago Pacific Strategic Framework 2013–2020* (Dunedin: University of Otago, 2013).
8. 'Otago welcomes first Director Pacific Development', Otago Bulletin Board, 20 November 2013: www.otago.ac.nz/otagobulletin/people/otago059401.html
9. 'Pacific focus', *UOM*, no. 41, 2015, 30–31.
10. *University of Otago: Development of the Māori Strategic Framework* (Dunedin: University of Otago, c. 2007), 3.
11. 'In the spirit of partnership', *UON*, August 1996, 4.
12. *Treaty of Waitangi Review of the University of Otago* (Dunedin: University of Otago, 1998), 1, 3, 11–12.
13. *Treaty of Waitangi Review*, 21, 28.
14. *UOAR*, 2000, 52; 'University and Ngai Tahu re-sign MoU', *OB*, 30 November 2007, 3; Sam Stevens, 'Going forward', *UOM*, no. 37, 2014, 9–11.
15. *UOAR*, 2001, 11, 66.
16. 'Vigorous discussion over research consultation with Māori', *OB*, 19 September 2003, 2; 'Māori research facilitator appointed', *OB*, 24 March 2006, 4.
17. *Development of the Māori Strategic Framework*.
18. 'Office of Māori Development established', *OB*, 11 July 2008, 3.
19. Stevens, 'Going forward'.
20. *Treaty of Waitangi Review*, 11.
21. 'University of Otago signs MoU with Ngāti Toa', *OB*, 16 May 2008, 7.

22. Stevens, 'Going forward'.
23. 'Milestone Māori medical graduation inspires staff', Otago Bulletin Board: 13 December 2016: www.otago.ac.nz/otagobulletin/news/otago629407.html
24. 'Maori name for University', *UON*, February 1990, 1.
25. 'Civic concern', *UON*, November 1981, 4–5.
26. 'University generates $630 million in economic benefits', *UON*, July 1998, 5.
27. 'Billion dollar impact', *OB*, 20 May 2005, 4.
28. Margot Taylor, 'City's $1 billion industry', *ODT*, 10 August 2016: www.odt.co.nz/news/dunedin/citys-1-billion-industry
29. 'A cat, a flat, and the legend of "Mr Tui"', Dunedin Flat Names Project, 12 January 2010: https://dunedinflatnames.co.nz/2010/01/12/a-cat-a-flat-and-the-legend-of-mr-tui/
30. 'The Rob Roy Dairy – a Dunedin ice cream tradition', Alumni and Friends, University of Otago: https://uoalumni.otago.ac.nz/content/rob-roy-dairy-%E2%80%93-dunedin-ice-cream-tradition; 'Dry summer comes with silver lining for some', *ODT*, 19 March 2015: www.odt.co.nz/news/dunedin/dry-summer-comes-silver-lining-some
31. Peter Chin interview.
32. Ibid. The Fortune Theatre did close suddenly in 2018, though there are moves to replace it with some other form of professional theatre in Dunedin.
33. All previous recipients are listed on the University of Otago website: www.otago.ac.nz/otagofellows/index.html
34. Lawrence Jones (ed.), *Nurse to the Imagination: 50 years of the Robert Burns Fellowship* (Dunedin: Otago University Press, 2008), 7–11.
35. Alan Horsman interview.
36. Jones, *Nurse to the Imagination*, 7–11.
37. Charles Brasch, 'Notes', *Landfall*, vol. 13, 1959, 3.
38. Alan Horsman interview; Jones, *Nurse to the Imagination*, 7–11.
39. 'Fellowship set up in perpetuity', *ES*, 28 July 1965, 12; 'The articles governing the Frances Hodgkins Fellowship', 1964, Records of Registry and Central Administration, AG-180-31/0950, HC; Virginia Were, 'There's an artist in the house', *Art News*, vol. 22, no. 3, 2002, 48–50.
40. 'Articles governing the Frances Hodgkins Fellowship'; Were, 'Artist in the house'.
41. Linda Herrick, 'My mate Mike Illingworth', *New Zealand Herald*, 20 January 2002: www.nzherald.co.nz/lifestyle/news/article.cfm?c_id=6&objectid=787063; Megan Dunn, 'Bewilderment: An over-the-shoulder view of Michael Illingworth', *Off the Wall*, no. 2, 2013: http://arts.tepapa.govt.nz/off-the-wall/5505/bewilderment; Aaron Lister & Damian Skinner, *A Tourist in Paradise Lost: The art of Michael Illingworth* (Wellington: City Gallery, 2001), 16.
42. Ian Dougherty, *Continuing Education of Quality: A history of Otago Polytechnic and its predecessors 1870–2006* (Dunedin: Otago Polytechnic, 2006), 7, 14.
43. Rebecca Fox, 'Fellowship leaves imprint', *ODT*, 3 November 2016: www.odt.co.nz/entertainment/arts/fellowship-leaves-imprint
44. Cameron Drawbridge (ed.), *Tanya Ashken: Jeweller, silversmith, sculptor* (Wellington: C. Drawbridge, 2016), 5.
45. Anthony Ritchie, 'Fellows remembered: The Mozart Fellowship reunion', *Canzona*, vol. 28, no. 49, 2007, 98–101.
46. John Drummond, 'Opera in Allen Hall', in Lisa Warrington & Alison Finigan (eds), *Allen Hall: 100 years 100+ voices* (Dunedin: Department of Music, Theatre Studies Programme, University of Otago, 2014), 88–96 (the performance was in Marama Hall); Ritchie, 'Fellows remembered'.
47. Arts and Music Faculty Annual Report, 1976, Records of Registry and Central Administration, AG-180-7/13, HC.
48. '2014 Mozart Fellow's taste in music', Otago Bulletin Board, 26 November 2014: www.otago.ac.nz/otagobulletin/people/otago083188.html; 'Imagination and senses stimulated at concert', Otago Bulletin Board, 5 August 2015: www.otago.ac.nz/otagobulletin/people/otago118279.html
49. 'Student's vision inspires dance fellowship', *OB*, 23 April 2004, 1, 3.
50. Lyne Pringle, 'Upwards jeté: A brief overview of community dance and dance in the community', *DANZ Quarterly*, no. 34, 2014, 46–47.
51. 'Dance and disability – the rhythm of life', *OB*, 7 October 2005, 4; 'First Caroline Plummer Dance Fellowship awarded', *OB*, 3 December 2004, 3.
52. Pringle, 'Upwards jeté'.
53. David Keen, *In a Class of its Own: A Dunedin College of Education anniversary history* (Dunedin: Dunedin College of Education, 2001), 205–06.
54. '2007 Children's Writer in Residence announced', *OB*, 26 January 2007, 4; 'Children's Writer in Residence', *OB*, 12 June 2009, 6.
55. Rebecca Fox, 'Fellowship leaves imprint', *ODT*, 3 November 2016: www.odt.co.nz/entertainment/arts/fellowship-leaves-imprint
56. 'Remembering Hone Tuwhare', *OB*, 25 January 2008, 3.
57. Jones, *Nurse to the Imagination*, 104–05.
58. 'Fellowship funds', *UON*, August 1979, 2. In 1986 the university decided to withhold the Frances Hodgkins Fellowship for a year to build up its capital, but donations from the Queen Elizabeth II Arts Council and M.W. James Trust meant it could be offered for a shorter term of six months. See 'Fellowship retained', *UON*, February 1987, 2.
59. Jean McGill & Linda Rodda, *Catalogue of Pictures in the Hocken Library* (Dunedin: Otago University Library, 1948); Linda Tyler, 'Paintings and drawings', in Stuart Strachan & Linda Tyler (eds), *Kā Taoka Hākena: Treasures from the Hocken Collections* (Dunedin: Otago University Press, 2007), 159–60.
60. Stuart Strachan, 'The Hocken Collections 1910 to 2007', in Strachan & Tyler, *Kā Taoka Hākena*, 23–24; Tyler, 'Paintings and drawings'; Sarah Quigley, 'Brasch, Charles Orwell', from DNZB: www.teara.govt.nz/en/biographies/5b40/brasch-charles-orwell; Peter Entwisle, 'Kennedy, Rodney Eric', from DNZB: www.teara.govt.

nz/en/biographies/5k7/kennedy-rodney-eric; Rosemary Entwisle, 'Rodney Kennedy: Hocken Library benefactor', in *The Kennedy Gift: Rodney Kennedy (1909–89) and his gift to the Hocken Library* (Dunedin: Hocken Library, University of Otago, 1990), 21–22; Linda Tyler, 'A matter of taste: Charles Brasch as art collector', in Donald Kerr (ed.), *Enduring Legacy: Charles Brasch, patron, poet and collector* (Dunedin: Otago University Press, 2003), 49–56.

61. Tony Harland, Toni Tidswell, David Everett, Leigh Hale & Neil Pickering, 'Neoliberalism and the academic as critic and conscience of society', *Teaching in Higher Education*, vol. 15, 2010, 85–96. On the origins of the 'critic and conscience' ideal in the act, see Barbara Grant, 'The history of "critic and conscience of society"': www.youtube.com/watch?v=Riza19tIxGc
62. 'The Prime Minister's Science Prize 2014': www.pmscienceprizes.org.nz/previous-winners/2014-science/
63. Simon Nathan, 'Arsenic at Waiuta', Signposts: A blog about the Encylopedia of New Zealand, 25 July 2013: http://blog.teara.govt.nz/2013/07/25/arsenic-at-waiuta/; Simon Nathan to author, 7 April 2017; Sarah-Jane O'Connor, 'Mine clean-up to cost $3m', Stuff, 25 February 2015: www.stuff.co.nz/environment/66644317/mine-cleanup-to-cost-3m
64. Education Amendment, 1989, Part 14, Section 162 (incorporating amendments to 2017).
65. 'Research awards': www.otago.ac.nz/research/awards/index.html
66. 'University of Otago honours Chemistry reseach leader', Otago Bulletin Board, 23 July 2015: www.otago.ac.nz/news/news/otago116217.html; 'University of Otago honours research leader', Department of Anatomy, 22 July 2016: www.otago.ac.nz/anatomy/news/otago617849.html; 'Leading Otago neuroscientist awarded Distinguished Research Medal', Dunedin School of Medicine, 30 September 2011: www.otago.ac.nz/dsm/news/archive/otago025093.html; Ian Dougherty, 'The accidental parasitologist', *UOM*, no. 36, 2013, 6–8.
67. Eloise Gibson, 'Rogue code', *New Zealand Listener*, 11 March 2017, 14–22.
68. 'Longitudinal studies: A national taonga', He Kitenga, 14 May 2013: www.otago.ac.nz/healthsciences/news/media/hekitenga/otago045632.html
69. Neil Pearce, *Adverse Reactions: The fenoterol story* (Auckland: Auckland University Press, 2007). See chapter 10 for further discussion.
70. 'Parry Guilford to receive Otago's highest honour', Otago Bulletin Board, 3 October 2017: www.otago.ac.nz/otagobulletin/news/otago665199.html
71. 'Sapere aude: A query', *UON*, July 1994, 18; John Gibb, 'Use knowledge wisely, graduates advised', *ODT*, 18 May 2015: www.odt.co.nz/news/dunedin/use-knowledge-wisely-graduates-advised

Select bibliography

UNPUBLISHED SOURCES

Interviews

INTERVIEWED BY ALISON CLARKE

Sadie Andrews, January 2014
John Barsby, February 2014
Douglas Booth, August 2014
John Broughton, January 2014
Beverley Burrell, November 2015
Arthur Campbell, July 2013
Nancy and Melville Carr, July 2013
Peter Chin, February 2015
Ian Chirnside, April 2014
Ewan Coleman, September 2015
Sunny Collings, September 2015
Roger Collins, September 2013
Annabel Cooper, February 2014
Brian Cox, July 2013
Bill Dawson, November 2014
Ashley Day, June 2014
Elaine Donaldson, May 2013
John Drummond, October 2014
Fred Fastier, May 2013
Peter Fenton, March 2014
Jan Flood, October 2016
Jim Flynn, July 2013
Graeme Fogelberg, April 2014
Alan Geare, January 2014
Colin Geary, February 2014
Alyth Grant, May 2014
Tim Gray, May 2013
Stephen Hall-Jones, September 2014
Jocelyn Harris, October 2013
Harlene Hayne, October 2016
Mark Henaghan, May 2014
Peter Holland, June 2013
Grant Hopkins, March 2014
Alan Horsman, May 2013
John Howells, February 2014
Peter Innes, July 2013
John Jillett, January 2014
Warwick Johnson, October 2013
Basil Jones, June 2013
Donna Jones, August 2014
Peter Joyce, December 2015
Shirley Kelly, October 2014
Nina Kirifi-Alai, August 2014
Raechel Laing, October 2014
Rob Lawson, February 2014
Helen Leach, March 2014
Margaret Loutit, May 2013
Jock McEldowney, May 2013
Honor McKellar, October 2014
David McKenzie, July 2013
Lyall McLean, June 2013
Jim Mann, August 2014
Alan Mark, August 2013
Pearl Matahiki, November 2014
Peter Matheson, September 2013
Janet Mitchell, November 2014
Mere Montgomery, July 2014
Alan Musgrave, September 2013
Gavin Munro, September 2013
James Ng, February 2015
Richard Norris, May 2014
Thomas O'Donnell, April 2014
Brian O'Rourke, December 2013
Dorothy Page, October 2013
Gordon Parry, June 2013
Gordon Parsonson, June 2013
John Patrick, June 2014
George Petersen, October 2013
Toroa Pohatu, May 2015
Michael Reilly, February 2014
Bridget Rennie, August 2014
David Richardson, July 2014
Glenys Roome, September 2013
Khyla Russell, December 2014
David Skegg, January 2014
Mervyn Smith, August 2013
Peter Stupples, February 2014
Rex Thomson, May 2014
Colin Townsend, November 2014
Ann Trotter, August 2013
Eric Walton, March 2014
Don Warrington, May 2014
Lisa Warrington, February 2014
Geoffrey White, February 2014
Mike Wilson, March 2014
Hank Wolfe, October 2013
Ann Wylie, June 2013

INTERVIEWED BY DOROTHY PAGE

John Adams, August 2006
Don Beaven, March 2004
John Borrie, May 2001
Geoffrey Brinkman, 2002
John Campbell, April 2004
Alan Clarke, November 2003

Chris Heath, December 2004
Barbara Heslop, July 2001
John Heslop, February 2002
Linda Holloway, July 2006
Andrew Hornblow, August 2002
John Hunter, November 2001
David Jones, August 2006
Peter Joyce, June 2006
Donald Malcolm, February 2001
John Nacey, July 2006
James and Marion Robinson, July 2001
Peter Schwartz, December 2004
David Stewart, June 2006
Bill Trotter, July 2001
Robin Williams, August 2008
Group interview with Graham Mortimer and George Petersen, May 2006
Group interview with John Campbell, Chris Heath, David Skegg and David Stewart, February 2001

Alexander Turnbull Library, Wellington

Murdoch, J.H. 'Teaching reminiscences'. New Zealand Council for Educational Research: Educational reminiscences, 88-005-10

Archives New Zealand, Wellington

Department of Education records:
Students from Overseas Attending New Zealand Universities, Remission of Fees, R18178076
University of Otago Reserves and Endowments file, R7243084
University Grants Committee. Statistics files, R12485703 and R12485704

Hocken Collections Uare Taoka o Hākena, University of Otago Library

Bacon, Donald. Papers, MS-2523
Bahr, Margaret. Stan Hughes interviews, MS-1675
Blackie, Agnes. Papers, ARC-0329
Fisher, Allan. Papers, MS-4304
Harris, Jocelyn. Papers, various
Mason, Elizabeth. Papers, Misc-MS-1400
Neilson, John. Papers, MS-2842
New Zealand Institute of Medical Laboratory Science. Records, MS-3620
Otago University Students' Association. Records, ARC-0130
Park, James. Papers, MS-0233
Petersen, George. Papers, r.6975
Ross, Angus. Papers, various
Smithells, Philip. Papers, ARC-0494
Soper, Frederick. Papers, 90-161
University of Otago records:
Department of Biochemistry, ARC-0218
Department of Botany, ARC-0776
Department of Marine Science, ARC-0748
Department of University Extension, various
Development and Alumni Relations Office, John Mackie interview, MS-4126
Division of Commerce, ARC-0753
Faculty of Consumer and Applied Sciences, various
Faculty of Medicine, Dean's Department, ARC-0193
Medical Library Historical Collection, ARC-0187
Registry and Central Administration, ARC-0018
Student Health Service, MS-1280
Vice-Chancellor's Office, ARC-0792
Wesley Residential Hall, Methodist Central Mission (Dunedin). Records, SER-04698
Williamson, Alexander. Papers, Misc-MS-0454

University of Otago Corporate Records Office

Quality Advancement Unit. Records of University of Otago reviews

Theses and unpublished essays

Butcher, Andrew Pieter. 'No place like home: The experiences of South-East Asian international university students in New Zealand and their re-entry into their countries of origin'. PhD thesis, Massey University, 2002.
Cook, Morgan. '"If I cannot get some more help, I cannot change it": Student culture and change at University College, Dunedin 1969–2007'. BA (Hons) dissertation, University of Otago, 2010.
Cousins, Kimberly. 'Evaluation of Campus Watch: A community-based initiative to reduce alcohol-related harm and social disorder in a university setting'. PhD thesis, University of Otago, 2012.
Donnelly, Gina. 'Women and children first and last'. BA (Hons) dissertation, University of Otago, 1994.
Dooley, Sharon. 'Ivory tower idyll: Students at the University of Otago in the depression, 1929–1936'. BA (Hons) dissertation, University of Otago, 1983.
Evans, Tecwyn. 'The University of Otago capping sextet 1903–1993'. MusB (Hons) research project, University of Otago, 1993.
Jackson, Peter Anthony. 'The mind of a nation: A philosophical and historical critique of psychology in New Zealand'. PhD thesis, Massey University, 1998.
Maclaurin, Emmet. 'Otago University student interest in growing environmental problems between 1968 and 1984'. History 353 essay, University of Otago, 2014.
Nash, Mary. 'People, policies and practice: Social work education in Aotearoa/New Zealand from 1949–1995'. PhD thesis, Massey University, 1998.
Pohatu, Godfrey. 'The university, Maori studies and Treaty praxis'. PhD thesis, University of Otago, 1999.

Other unpublished items supplied to author

Burns, Carolyn. 'One hundred and twenty-five years of zoology'. Speech, Department of Zoology 125th anniversary, 2002.

Cole, David. 'Both ends of the knife'.

Heslop, Barbara. Various papers.

Howard, Neil. 'Life at university – fifties style'.

Matthews, Kyle. Speech, OUSA 125th anniversary, 2015.

Reilly, Michael. 'A history of Maori, Pacific and Indigenous Studies at Otago University, 1969–2008: A personal view'.

Richardson, David. 'Creating cultural change – Campus Watch: A most fortunate experiment', paper for Campus and Student Security Conference, 2014.

Turner, Harold. Address at opening of Turner Wing, Arana Hall, 4 June 1994. Courtesy of Bill Dawson.

'Wellington School of Medicine: Comments, historical data and abstracts up to 1991'. Unpublished compilation. Courtesy of University of Otago, Wellington.

University of Otago Annual Reports

1870: published in *Otago Daily Times*, 20 July 1870.

1871 to 1877: published in *Otago Provincial Council Votes and Proceedings*.

1877 to 1938: published in *Appendix to the Journals of the House of Representatives*.

1939 to 1960: unpublished (except for accounts and/or brief references in national summary in *Appendix to the Journals of the House of Representatives*); unpublished versions in University of Otago, Records of Registry and Central Administration, ARC-0018, Hocken Collections.

1961 to 1989: published in *Appendix to the Journals of the House of Representatives*.

1990 onwards: published by University of Otago.

PERIODICALS

Appendix to the Journals of the House of Representatives
Campus LAN
Critic
Dominican: Magazine of Dominican Hall
Evening Star
Falus
Mea Maori: Otago University Maori Centre Newsletter
New Zealand Dental Journal
New Zealand Medical Journal
New Zealand Society of Accountants Year Book
Otago Bulletin
Otago Daily Times
Otago Graduate
Otago Humanities Review
Otago University Review
Otago Witness
OUSA Orientation Handbook
School of Mines and Metallurgy Bulletin
Science Record
Shadows: The New Zealand Journal of Medical Radiation Therapy
University of New Zealand Calendar
University of Otago Calendar
University of Otago Computing Services Newsletter
University of Otago Magazine
University of Otago Newsletter
University of Otago Students' Handbook

BOOKS AND JOURNAL ARTICLES

Adams, Lucy S. *Thomas Dagger Adams: Professor of Classics at the University of Otago*. Wellington: A.H. & A.W. Reed, 1954.

Alcorn, Noeline. *Ko te Tangata: A history of the University of Waikato, the first fifty years*. Wellington: Steele Roberts, 2014.

—— 'Teacher education policy in New Zealand since 1970'. *Waikato Journal of Education*, vol. 18, no. 1, 2015, 37–48.

Anderson, R.D. *Education and Opportunity in Victorian Scotland: Schools and universities*. Oxford: Clarendon, 1983.

Angus, John. *A History of the Otago Hospital Board and its Predecessors*. Dunedin: Otago Hospital Board, 1984.

Barber, L.H. & R.J. Towers. *Wellington Hospital 1847–1976*. Wellington: Wellington Hospital Board, 1976.

Barretta-Herman, Angeline. 'Development of social work in New Zealand: 1969–1988'. *Social Work Review*, vol. 5, no. 4, 1993, 4–8, vol. 5, no. 5, 30–35, vol. 6, no. 3, 1994, 12–18.

Barrowman, Rachel. *Victoria University of Wellington 1899–1999: A history*. Wellington: Victoria University Press, 1999.

Barsby, John. 'Classics at Otago 3: The Manton period (1949–65)'. *Australasian Society for Classical Studies Proceedings*, vol. 32, 2011, 5.

Batham, E.J. 'History of the Portobello Marine Biological Station'. *Australian Journal of Science*, vol. 19, 1956, 87–91.

Beaglehole, J.C. *The University of New Zealand: An historical study*. Wellington: New Zealand Council for Educational Research, 1937.

Belgrave, Michael. *From Empire's Servant to Global Citizen: A history of Massey University*. Auckland: Massey University Press, 2016.

Bennett, Francis. *A Canterbury Tale: The autobiography of Dr Francis Bennett*. Wellington: Oxford University Press, 1980.

Bennett, Neville. *Asian Students in New Zealand*. Wellington: Institute of Policy Studies, Victoria University of Wellington, 1998.

Benseman, John, Brian Findsen & Miriama Scott, eds. *The Fourth Sector: Adult and community education in*

Aotearoa/New Zealand. Palmerston North: Dunmore Press, 1996.

Berry, Christine. *The Zealand Student Christian Movement, 1896–1996: A centennial history*. Christchurch: Student Christian Movement of Aotearoa, 1998.

Blyth, Conrad. 'Early academic economics in New Zealand (notes on its history from the 1870s to the 1950s)'. *University of Auckland Department of Economics Working Papers Series*, no. 266, 2008.

Borrie, J.F. 'Radiography training in New Zealand: An historical survey'. *Radiography*, vol. 40, 1974, 2–8.

Breward, Ian. *Grace and Truth: A history of Theological Hall, Knox College, Dunedin 1876–1975*. Dunedin: Theological Education Committee, Presbyterian Church of New Zealand, 1975.

Brickell, Chris. 'Those "other sociologists": Social analysis before sociology'. *New Zealand Sociology*, vol. 22, no. 1, 2007, 4–27.

Brickell, Chris, Martin Tolich & Bonnie Scarth. 'Sociology before sociology at Otago University'. *New Zealand Sociology*, vol. 29, no. 4, 2014, 27–44.

Brookes, Barbara. 'Academic motherhood' [in press].

Brookes, Barbara, Charlotte Macdonald & Margaret Tennant, eds. *Women In History 2*. Wellington: Bridget Williams Books, 1992.

Brookes, Barbara & Dorothy Page, eds. *Communities of Women: Historical perspectives*. Dunedin: Otago University Press, 2002.

Brooking, T.W.H. *A History of Dentistry in New Zealand*. Dunedin: New Zealand Dental Association, 1980.

Brown, Harvey. *Pickerill: Pioneer in plastic surgery, dental education and dental research*. Dunedin: Otago University Press, 2007.

Brunton, Warwick. *The Medicine of the Future: A history of the Department of Preventive and Social Medicine, University of Otago 1886–2011*. Dunedin: Department of Preventive & Social Medicine, 2011.

Burgess, Marie E. *Nursing in New Zealand Society*. Auckland: Longman Paul, 1984.

Carmalt Jones, D.W. *Annals of the University of Otago Medical School 1875–1939*. Wellington: Reed, 1945.

Carpenter, Helen. *An Improved System of Nursing Education for New Zealand*. Wellington: Department of Health, 1971.

Chambers, Ron. *Justice and Jellybeans: From Ulster policeman to Otago University proctor*. Dunedin: Missing Stocks Press, 2006.

The Christchurch Clinical School of Medicine: After ten years. Christchurch: Christchurch Clinical School of Medicine, 1982.

Christie, Ronald V. *Report on the Medical School*. Dunedin: University of Otago, 1968.

Clarke, Alison. *A Living Tradition: A centennial history of Knox College, Dunedin 1909–2009*. Dunedin: Knox College, 2009.

Coleman, Karen. 'Relocating radiation therapy: The true story'. *Shadows: The New Zealand Journal of Medical Radiation Therapy*, vol. 45, no. 3, 2002, 12–14.

Collins, Jenny. 'Beyond the domestic sphere? A home science education at the University of New Zealand, 1911–1936'. *Journal of Educational Administration and History*, vol. 41, no. 2, 2009, 115–30.

—— 'Glorified housekeepers or pioneering professionals? The professional lives of home science graduates from the University of New Zealand'. *History of Education Review*, vol. 37, no. 2, 2008, 40–51.

The Colombo Plan at 50: A New Zealand perspective. Wellington: New Zealand Official Development Assistance, Ministry of Foreign Affairs & Trade, 2001.

Coombes, Reg. *Pharmacy in New Zealand: Aspects and reminiscences*. Auckland: Ray Richards for the Pharmaceutical Society of New Zealand, 1981.

Cowan, T.K. *Commerce at Otago 1912–1987: A personal perspective*. Abridged edn. Dunedin: University of Otago, 1988.

Crane, Rosi. '"A dangerous visionary"? The lectures of the evolutionist T.J. Parker'. *Journal of New Zealand Studies*, vol. 15, 2013, 36–49.

—— 'A "strange fauna": T.J. Parker (1850–1897) and the creation of zoological knowledge in Otago'. *New Zealand Journal of History*, vol. 49, no. 2 (2015), 60–80.

Crawford, Ron. *History of Tertiary Education Reforms in New Zealand*. Research note 2016/1. Wellington: New Zealand Productivity Commission, 2016.

Crooks, Dion. *A History: New Zealand Dietetic Association (Inc) and dietetics in New Zealand*. Wellington: New Zealand Dietetic Association, 1993.

Coughtrey, Millen. *The Graduation Address, on the Occasion of the Conferring, for the First Time in New Zealand, of the Degrees of LL.D and M.B. of the New Zealand University*. Dunedin: Otago Daily Times, 1887.

—— *The Introductory Address in the Faculty of Medicine of Otago University*. Dunedin: Mackay, Risk, Munro & Co, 1875.

Culture of Change: Beginnings at the University of Otago. Dunedin: Departments of English and History, University of Otago, 2006.

Cullen, Michael. *Lawfully Occupied: The centennial history of the Otago District Law Society*. Dunedin: Otago District Law Society, 1979.

Cumming, Ian & Alan Cumming. *History of State Education in New Zealand 1840–1975*. Wellington: Pitman, 1978.

Dacker, Bill. *Te Mamae me te Aroha, The Pain and the Love: A history of Kai Tahu Whanui in Otago, 1844–1994*. Dunedin: University of Otago/Dunedin City Council, 1994.

Devonport, Bernadette F. 'An introduction to the interaction between the universities and the Institute of Chartered Accountants of New Zealand, 1910 to the present day'. *Pacific Accounting Review*, vol. 21, no. 2, 2009, 150–69.

Dougherty, Ian. *Bricklayers and Mortarboards: A history of New Zealand polytechnics and institutes of technology*. Palmerston North: Dunmore Press, 1999.

—— *Central Institute of Technology 1960–2001: A brief history*. Upper Hutt: Central Institute of Technology, 2001.

—— *Continuing Education of Quality: A history of Otago Polytechnic and its predecessors 1870–2006*. Dunedin: Otago Polytechnic, 2006.

The Education of Medical Undergraduates in New Zealand: Report of the review committee set up by the Medical Council of New Zealand, Wellington: Medical Council of New Zealand, 1988.

Elworthy, Sam. *Ritual Song of Defiance: A social history of students at the University of Otago*. Dunedin: Otago University Students' Association, 1990.

Farry, Patrick, John Adams, Lucie Walters, Paul Worley & Susan Dovey. 'Development of the Rural Immersion Programme for 5th-year medical students at the University of Otago'. *New Zealand Medical Journal*, vol. 123, no. 1323, 2010, 16–23.

Fastier, F.N. *Pharmacy Teaching at Otago University: How it began*. Dunedin: Amidine Publications, 1992.

—— *Recollections of an Old Scarfie*. Dunedin: Amidine Publications, 2004.

Finigan, Alison, ed. *Partnerships for Excellence: Celebrating 10 years of the Leading Thinkers initiative*. Dunedin: Development & Alumni Relations Office, University of Otago, 2014.

Fitzgerald, Tanya. 'An absent presence: Women professors at the University of New Zealand 1911–1961'. *Journal of Educational Administration and History*, vol. 39, no. 3, 2007, 239–53.

—— 'Academic housework? Women professors at the University of New Zealand 1911–1961'. *New Zealand Journal of Education Studies*, vol. 42, nos 1 and 2, 115–28.

Franks, Peter. *The Reluctant Unionists – From Ivory Tower to the Real World: A history of the New Zealand University Technicians Union, 1971–1991*. Wellington: Association of University Staff of New Zealand, 1993.

From Bury to Blair: Architects' conceptions of the University of Otago. Dunedin: University of Otago, 1994.

Gardiner, John. *Student Digs Known as the Bach*. Auckland: J. Gardiner, 1996.

Gardner, W.J. *Colonial Cap and Gown: Studies in the mid-Victorian universities of Australasia*. Christchurch: University of Canterbury, 1979.

Gardner, W.J., E.T. Beardsley & T.E. Carter, *A History of the University of Canterbury 1873–1973*. Christchurch: University of Canterbury, 1973.

Gathercole, Peter. 'Otago 1958–1968'. *Archaeology in New Zealand*, vol. 43, nos 3 & 4, 2000, 206–19, 283–96.

Gauld, Robin. *Revolving Doors: New Zealand's health reforms – the continuing saga*. 2nd edn. Wellington: Health Services Research Centre & Institute of Policy Studies, Victoria University of Wellington, 2009.

Grant, Susannah. *Vision for the Future: A centennial history of St Margaret's College, Dunedin 1911–2011*. Dunedin: St Margaret's College, 2010.

Grayeff, Felix. *Migrant Scholar: An autobiography*. Universitätsbibliothek Freiburg i. Br., 1986.

Griffiths, George. *Otago University at Cricket: Its history, records and statistics*. Dunedin: Otago Heritage Books, 1978.

Hargreaves, Ray. *Selwyn College's First Century: A history and list of residents 1893–1992*. Dunedin: Centennial Committee, Selwyn College Board of Governors, 1993.

Hercus, Charles & Gordon Bell, *The Otago Medical School Under the First Three Deans*. Edinburgh: Livingstone, 1964.

Heydon, Susan & Stephen Duffull. *Pharmacy at Otago: The first 50 years: The school, the profession and the people*. Dunedin: New Zealand's National School of Pharmacy, University of Otago, 2013.

History of the New Zealand Federation of University Women. Dunedin: New Zealand Federation of University Women, Otago Branch, 1954.

The History of Te Tumu. Dunedin: Te Tumu, School of Maori, Pacific & Indigenous Studies, 2006.

Hocken, A.G. *Geology at Otago: The first 100 years*. Wellington: Geological Society of New Zealand, 2003.

Holland, Peter, Hugh Kidd & Richard Welch, eds. *From Mellor to Hocken: Fifty years of geography at the University of Otago*. Dunedin: Department of Geography, University of Otago, 1995.

Hughes, Beryl. 'Nursing education: The collapse of the Diploma of Nursing at the University of Otago, 1925-1926'. *New Zealand Journal of History*, vol. 12, no. 1, 1978, 17–33.

Jamieson, Hugh, ed. *The Development of Medical Physics and Biomedical Engineering in New Zealand Hospitals 1945–1995*. 2nd edn. Dannevirke: H. Jamieson, 1995,

Jennings, M.A. *Aunt Pearl's Story*. Suva: M. Jennings, 1981.

Johnston, Carol Morton & Harry Morton. *Dunedin Teachers College: The first hundred years*. Dunedin: Dunedin Teachers College, 1976.

Jones, Lawrence. 'New Zealand studies at Otago'. *Kite: Newsletter of the New Zealand Literature Association*, no. 2, 1992, 4–5.

——, ed. *Nurse to the Imagination: 50 years of the Robert Burns Fellowship*. Dunedin: Otago University Press, 2008.

Joyce, Peter, Gary Nicholls, Kim Thomas & Tim Wilkinson, eds. *The Christchurch Experience: 40 years of research and teaching*. Christchurch: University of Otago, Christchurch, 2015.

Keen, David. *In a Class of its Own: A Dunedin College of Education anniversary history*. Dunedin: Dunedin College of Education, 2001.

King, J.E., ed. *A Biographical Dictionary of Australia and New Zealand Economists*. Cheltenham: Edward Elgar Publishing, 2007.

Lai, Kwok-Wing, Sarah Stein, Penny Field & Keryn Pratt, eds. *Our World in Your Place: 30 years of distance learning and teaching at the University of Otago*. Dunedin: Distance Learning Office, University of Otago, 2016.

Lambie, Mary. *My Story: Memoirs of a New Zealand nurse*. Christchurch: N.M. Peryer Ltd, 1956.

Macaulay, G.A. *A Triumph of Improvisation: The Stuart Residence Halls Council, Stuart House, Arana Hall, Carrington Hall 1941–1991*. Dunedin: Stuart Residence Halls Council, 1991.

McCarthy, Mary Augustine. *Star in the South: The centennial history of the New Zealand Dominican Sisters*. Dunedin: St Dominic's Priory, 1970.

McCoy, Ted. *A Southern Architecture: The work of Ted McCoy*. Dunedin: Otago University Press, 2007.

Mackie, John. *Captain Jack, Surveyor and Engineer: The autobiography of John Mackie*. Wellington: New Zealand Institute of Surveyors, 2007.

—— 'Dunedin days – some reminiscences'. *Geological Society of New Zealand newsletter*, no. 60, 1983, 12–15.

—— 'Further reminiscences with a geological flavour'. *Geological Society of New Zealand newsletter*, no. 61, 1983, 51–53.

—— 'Dunedin days – further reminiscences'. *Geological Society of New Zealand newsletter*, no. 64, 1984, 30–33.

McLean, Lyall. *A History of Economics and the Development of Commerce Degrees at the University of Otago 1871–2009*. Dunedin: L. McLean, 2011.

Matich, Maurice. *From Beacon Point: My journey, my story*. Wellington: Phantom House, 2013.

May, Muriel. *Freshly Remembered: Half a century of school*. Christchurch: Whitcombe & Tombs, 1975.

Mayer, Wolf. 'William Noel Benson (1885–1957): Insights into the life and work of an eminent geologist'. *Earth Sciences History*, vol. 32, no. 1, 2013, 55–85.

Mikaere, Buddy. *Te Maiharoa and the Promised Land*. Auckland: Reed, 1988.

Mitchell, F.W., ed. *Looking Ahead in New Zealand Education*. Wellington: Reed, 1971.

Montgomery, Mere. *Otago University Maori Club 1972 to 1975*. Dunedin: M. Montgomery, 1993.

Moore, Christopher, George Rolleston, John Riminton & Andrew Hornblow. *A Vision Realised: The Christchurch School of Medicine, University of Otago 1972–1997*. Christchurch: Christchurch School of Medicine, 1998.

Morrell, W.P. *The University of Otago: A centennial history*. Dunedin: University of Otago Press, 1969.

Nathan, Judith & Simon Nathan. *My Dearest Georgie: Transcriptions of 24 letters from James Hector to his wife Georgiana*. Wellington: Geoscience Society of New Zealand, 2015.

Nolan, Melanie. 'Putting the state in its place: The domestic education debate in New Zealand'. *History of Education*, vol. 30, no. 1, 2001, 13–33.

Norris, Peter. *Southernmost Seminary: The story of Holy Cross College, Mosgiel (1900–97)*. Dunedin: Holy Cross Seminary, 1999.

North, K.A.K. *Report on Medical Education in New Zealand and the need for a third medical school*. Wellington: Victoria University of Wellington, 1970.

Nye, Edwin R., ed. *Medical Research in Otago 1922–1997: As portrayed by 75 years of the Proceedings of the University of Otago Medical School*. Dunedin: Otago Medical School Research Society, 1998.

Openshaw, Roger, Greg Lee & Howard Lee. *Challenging the Myths: Rethinking New Zealand's educational history*. Palmerston North: Dunmore Press, 1993.

The Otago University Jubilee 1869–1919: Ceremonies and celebrations. Dunedin: Evening Star, 1920.

Otago University Review (Special Number): A history of the Otago University during its minority. Dunedin: OUSA, 1893.

Otago University Rugby Football Club 1886–1969. Dunedin: Light Blues Association, 1969.

Pack, Angela R.C. 'Women in New Zealand dentistry, 1880–1980'. *New Zealand Dental Journal*, vol. 77, 1981, 19–25.

Page, Dorothy. *Anatomy of a Medical School: A history of medicine at the University of Otago 1875–2000*. Dunedin: Otago University Press, 2008.

Parry, Gordon. *The Otago School of Mines 1879–1979: An historical sketch*. Dunedin: Otago School of Mines, University of Otago, 1979.

Parsonson, G.S. *A Brief History of the Otago School of Mines 1871–1971*. Dunedin: University of Otago, 1971.

Parton, Hugh. *The University of New Zealand*. Auckland: Auckland University Press/University Grants Committee, 1979.

Peake, Barrie M. 'The last 25 years of chemistry in Otago and Southland'. *Chemistry in New Zealand*, vol. 75, no. 3, 2011, 141–46.

Pearce, Neil. *Adverse Reactions: The fenoterol story*. Auckland: Auckland University Press, 2007.

Performance-Based Research Fund, Evaluating Research Excellence – the 2012 Assessment: Final Report. Wellington: Tertiary Education Commission, 2013.

Probert, John C. & Christopher H. Atkinson. 'New Zealand: one small country's history of radiation oncology'. *International Journal of Radiation Oncology, Biology, Physics*, vol. 36, 1996, 481–86.

Rae, Simon. *Challenge and Change: An account of theological education and ministry training at Knox College, Dunedin, 1976–2010*. Dunedin: Knox Centre for Ministry & Leadership, Presbyterian Church of Aotearoa New Zealand, 2011.

Report of the Commission on Education in New Zealand. Wellington: Government Printer, 1962.

Report of the Committee on New Zealand Universities, December 1959. Wellington: Government Printer, 1960.

Roll of the Graduates of the University of Otago. Dunedin: University of Otago, 1989.

Ryan, James, Keith Sutton & Malcolm Baigent. *Australasian Radiology: A history*. Sydney: McGraw-Hill, 1996.

Salmon, E. Beatrice. *A Profession in Transition: Issues in nursing in New Zealand over two decades, 1961–1981*. Wellington: C.L. Bailey Nursing Education Trust, 1982.

Salmond, Clare. *The First 25 Years of the Department of Public Health (Formerly, Department of Community Health) at the Wellington School of Medicine and Health Sciences*. Wellington: Wellington School of Medicine & Health Sciences, 2004.

A Salute to the Captain: Celebrating the 100th birthday of Emeritus Professor J.B. Mackie, 3 September 2010. Dunedin: Development & Alumni Relations Office, University of Otago, 2010.

Satur, Julie & Barbara Dewson. 'A history of the dental and oral health therapy profession in Australia and New Zealand'. *Australian and New Zealand Journal of Dental and Oral Health Therapy*, vol. 1, no. 1, 2012, 13–16.

Scholefield, G.H., ed. *A Dictionary of New Zealand Biography*. Wellington: Department of Internal Affairs, 1940.

School of Home Science History, 1911–1961. Dunedin: University of Otago, School of Home Science, 1962.

Schwarz, Viola Angelika. *Walter Edwin Griesbach (1888–1968): Life and work*. Trans. John S. Dawson. Dunedin: J.S. Dawson, 2002.

Shaw, Louise. *In Our Hands: 100 years of the School of Physiotherapy in Otago 1913–2013*. Dunedin: University of Otago School of Physiotherapy, 2013.

—— *Making a Difference: A history of the Auckland College of Education 1881–2004*. Auckland: Auckland University Press, 2006.

Shuker, Roy. *Educating the Workers? A history of the Workers' Education Association in New Zealand*. Palmerston North: Dunmore Press, 1984.

Sinclair, Keith. *A History of the University of Auckland 1883–1983*. Auckland: Auckland University Press, 1983.

Sinclair, R.A., ed. *The Commerce Review*. Dunedin: Otago Commerce Students' Association, 1969.

Smillie, John. 'Law at Otago: 1873–1998'. *Otago Law Review*, vol. 9, no. 2, 1998, 187–94.

Social Work Education in New Zealand Universities: A report. Palmerston North: University Grants Committee, 1981.

Soper, Eileen L. *The Leaves Turn*. Dunedin: John McIndoe, 1973.

Soper, F.G. 'Chemistry in New Zealand'. *Chemistry in New Zealand*, vol. 39, 1975, 97–101.

Stepping Up: A celebration of six decades of history at Aquinas College. Dunedin: Development & Alumni Relations Office, University of Otago, 2011.

Stockwell, R.F. *The Origins of the Dental Profession in New Zealand*. Dunedin: New Zealand Dental Association, 1977.

Stothart, Robert A. *The Development of Physical Education in New Zealand*. Auckland: Heinemann, 1974.

Strachan, Stuart & Linda Tyler, eds. *Kā Taoka Hākena: Treasures from the Hocken Collections*. Dunedin: Otago University Press, 2007.

Strack, Mick, ed. *Survey Marks: A 2013 celebration, 50 years of the School of Surveying at Otago University, 125 years of the New Zealand Institute of Surveyors*. Dunedin: School of Surveying, University of Otago & New Zealand Institute of Surveyors, 2013.

Strong, A.G. *History of the Development of University Education in Home Science in New Zealand 1911–1936*. Dunedin: University of Otago, 1937.

Tansley, Rebecca. *Studholme: A century of life and learning*. Dunedin: University of Otago, 2015.

Tarling, Nicholas. *International Students in New Zealand: The making of policy since 1950*. Auckland: New Zealand Asian Institute, University of Auckland, 2004.

—— *Professionals and Unionists: A history of the Association of University Staff 1923–98*. Wellington: Association of University Staff, 2000.

Taylor, Leah. *Dunedin School of Massage: The first ten years of physiotherapy training in New Zealand*. Dunedin: L. Taylor, 1988.

Thompson, G.E. *A History of the University of Otago (1869–1919)*. Dunedin: Wilkie, 1919.

Thomson, Arthur S. *The Story of New Zealand: Past and present – savage and civilized*. London: John Murray, 1859.

Thomson, George M. & Thomas Anderton. *History of the Portobello Marine Fish-hatchery and Biological Station*. Wellington: Dominion of New Zealand Board of Science and Art, 1921.

Thomson, Jane, ed. *Southern People: A dictionary of Otago Southland biography*. Dunedin: Longacre Press, 1998.

Thomson, Rex. *School of Physical Education 50th Reunion 1948–1998*. Dunedin: School of Physical Education, 1998.

The Time Keepers. *Tower Turmoil: Characters and controversies at the University of Otago*. Dunedin: Department of History, University of Otago, 2005.

Treaty of Waitangi Review of the University of Otago. Dunedin: University of Otago, 1998.

Trow, Donald G. & Stephen A. Zeff. *Accounting Education and the Profession in New Zealand: Profiles of the pioneering academics and the early university accounting departments 1900–1970*. Wellington: New Zealand Institute of Chartered Accountants, 2010.

Turner, H.W. *Halls of Residence*. Wellington: New Zealand Council for Educational Research, 1953.

University of Otago: Development of the Māori Strategic Framework. Dunedin: University of Otago, c. 2007.

Waite, Greg, Jocelyn Harris & Heather Murray, eds. *World and Stage: Essays for Colin Gibson*. Dunedin: Department of English, University of Otago, 1998.

Ward, Sheila, Hilary Hunt & Quentin Furlong. *Otago University Staff Families Association 1948–2008*. Dunedin: Otago University Staff Families Association, 2008.

Warrington, Lisa and Alison Finigan, eds. *Allen Hall: 100 years, 100+ voices*. Dunedin: Department of Music, Theatre Studies Programme, University of Otago, 2014.

Whiting, Rosalind H. & Christine Wright. 'Explaining gender inequity in the New Zealand accounting profession'. *British Accounting Review*, vol. 22, 2001, 191–222.

Wilkie, Yvonne. *Weaving Vision, Heritage and Hope: 150 years of the Presbyterian Synod of Otago and Southland 1866 to 2016*. Dunedin: Synod of Otago and Southland, Presbyterian Church of Aotearoa New Zealand, 2016.

Wilson, David. 'The student revolt against paternalism: Student protest and the mixed flatting controversy at the University of Otago'. *Flinders Journal of History and Politics*, vol. 22, 2002, 141–62.

ONLINE

Blain Biographical Directory of Anglican Clergy in the South Pacific: http://anglicanhistory.org/nz/blain_directory/

Heritage New Zealand: www.heritage.org.nz/the-list

Otago Bulletin Board: www.otago.ac.nz/otagobulletin/index.html

Papers Past: https://paperspast.natlib.govt.nz/

Register (Fasti) of New Zealand Presbyterian Ministers, Deaconesses & Missionaries 1840 to 2015, Archives Research Centre, Presbyterian Church of Aotearoa New Zealand: www.presbyterian.org.nz/archives/page143.htm

Reserve Bank of New Zealand inflation calculator: www.rbnz.govt.nz/monetary-policy/inflation-calculator

Te Ara – the Encyclopedia of New Zealand (incorporating the Dictionary of New Zealand Biography): https://teara.govt.nz/en

Williams, Susannah. 'The Jewish doctors in New Zealand 1933–1945': www.holocaustcentre.org.nz/remember/refuge-in-nz/jewish-doctors

Index

Page numbers in **bold** refer to illustrations.